MUSES OF ONE MIND

Muses of One Mind

THE LITERARY ANALYSIS OF EXPERIENCE AND ITS CONTINUITY

Wesley Trimpi

PRINCETON UNIVERSITY PRESS

PRINCETON, NEW JERSEY

Published by Princeton University Press, 41 William Street, Princeton, New Jersey 08540
In the United Kingdom: Princeton University Press, Guildford, Surrey

Library of Congress Cataloging in Publication Data will be found
on the last printed page of this book

ISBN 0-691-06568-3

Publication of this book has been aided by a grant from the Bollingen Foundation.

This book has been composed in Linotron Aldus

Clothbound editions of Princeton University Press books are printed on acid-free
paper, and binding materials are chosen for strength and durability

Paperbacks, although satisfactory for personal collections, are not
usually suitable for library rebinding.

Printed in the United States of America by Princeton University Press,
Princeton, New Jersey

For Helen

CONTENTS

Part Three. The Quality of Fiction: The Rhetorical Transmission of Literary Theory

PREFACE

HESIOD BEGINS his *Theogony* by giving an account of how he became a poet. One day near Mount Helicon, he says, the Muses, who first declared to him that they could not only feign things which seemed to be true but could also speak the truth, taught him to compose his songs. They 'breathed' into him a voice which had the divine power to tell of things to come as well as of what had passed and told him that he must praise the blessed life of the gods, but, most of all, he must sing about the Muses themselves. To sing about them properly, however, is to articulate their own 'discourse,' and, since he regards what they say as the poet's principal subject, Hesiod defines the nature of poetry in terms of the combined offices which they perform.

He describes the nine Muses at their birth as being "of one mind" (κούρας ὁμόφρονας, *Theog.* 60) in their freedom from care and their desire to express themselves in song. This 'single-mindedness' unites them, as in a harmonious chorus (39), and enables them to perform those offices which are pleasing to the mind of Zeus (37, 51). As the daughters of Zeus and Memory, together they recollect, preserve, and celebrate the integrated activities and the cumulative wisdom of the gods. They offer to us as human beings, furthermore, the possibility of sharing in the contents of this wisdom to the extent that we realize our capacity to understand and describe our experience. In this sense, the Muses, together, provide the psyche with the sources of its coherence and express this coherence as mutually dependent principles of order. These principles, in turn, later give direction to the various disciplines which define and exercise the speculative, the prudential, and the productive activities of the consciousness.

Hesiod emphasizes the coordination of these three kinds of activity in his account of the offices of the Muses. They give joy to the mind of Zeus by "telling of things that are and that shall be and that were aforetime with consenting voice (φωνῇ ὁμηρεῦσαι, 39)," and by celebrating the birth of the gods, the excellence of their lord, and the race of men. In addition to this speculative gift of knowledge, they offer the prudential grounds of justice in singing the laws (νόμους, 66) and the ways (ἤθεα, 66) of the immortals to whom the father of heaven had "distributed fairly . . . their portions and declared their privileges." Calliope, especially, must see to it that earthly princes at their birth be nourished by heaven with gracious speech so that they may settle "causes with true judgements" and with judicious self-assurance. Such wisdom is necessary to princes "because when the people are being misguided in their assembly, they set right the matter again with ease, persuading them with gentle words." For, when a prince "passes through a gathering, they greet him as a god with gentle reverence, and he is conspicuous amongst the assembled: such is the holy gift of the Muses to men."

To these philosophical and rhetorical responsibilities—of transmitting knowledge and of persuading men to equitable decisions and action respectively—is added the obligation of expressing the *performance* of these offices with graceful elegance. The insistence upon formal beauty reechoes through these lines of the *Theogony* (36–103) in such phrases as "sweet sound," "lily-like voice," "lovely voice," "sweet voice," "lovely sound," "sweet dew upon his tongue," "gracious words," "gentle words." Such artistic excellence is prerequisite to the singers' and harpers' ability to recompose the troubled spirit by recounting the heroic achievements of men and the blessed life of the gods. The 'discourse' of the Muses, then, might be considered the product of a single purpose insofar as they collectively express and realize these potentialities of the human intelligence as a whole rather than as fragmented into the more exclusively didactic or formal intentions of particular artistic doctrines.

The most complete linguistic expression of the 'discourse' of the Muses I shall call 'literary discourse' and use Hesiod's description of their offices as a point of departure in accounting historically for the terms in which the value of literature has been questioned and defended. The principal topics which recur in discussions of its value are the primary materials of the history of literary theory. Since the earliest theoretical discussions began by treating the nature and purpose of literature in relation to those of other disciplines, the language of these discussions drew upon those disciplines for terms in which to define the literary analysis of experience. Whenever the analytical intentions which these borrowed terms originally expressed have been neglected or lost, the conception of literature and, as a result, the expectations of what it can and ought to be have become seriously restricted. Such restricted conceptions of literature, in turn, strongly affect how compositions are actually written. That is, an inadequate understanding of the original and potential resources of literary discourse has led to the impoverishment of literature itself.

Such restricted conceptions have occurred most commonly when either the speculative, the prudential, or the productive activity, reflected in Hesiod's account of the Muses, has been emphasized at the expense of one or both of the other two. I shall call the purposes of these activities the cognitive, the judicative, and the formal intentions of literature in order to indicate their participation in the three major disciplines which, Plutarch says, gain their end through discourse of reason: philosophy, rhetoric, and mathematics (*Mor.* 744D). To the extent that literature shares the intentions of these disciplines, the literary analysis of experience draws upon their procedures of analysis. In order to describe the latent presence of philosophical, rhetorical, and mathematical procedures in literary composition, and thereby to show the impoverishment that may be caused by any literary theory which fails to recognize their respective contributions, I have included some technical discussion of their functions. Despite the fact that this technical discussion requires some awkward repetition if the reader is to keep the terms clearly in mind, I have seen no way of omitting it. It has been such omissions in the past which have led theorists to overlook the functions which these latent procedures have always performed in the composition of literary works. Despite the cumbersome intricacy of the technical vocabulary, however, I hope the reader may recognize the fact that the three principal objectives of literary discourse correspond to Plato's three principal components of the highest good: the true, the justly measured, and the beautiful (*Philebus* 65BE).

At its best, literary theory articulates the ways to achieve and maintain the delicate balance between the cognitive, the judicative, and the formal intentions of literature. This balance is not a static suspension secured by fixed components of equal weight but a fluid corrective process which can only approximate, moment by moment, a hypothetically perfect adjustment. This constant resistance to imbalance in literary discourse, and to the consequently impoverished conceptions of literature, can never be 'resolved' or expressed as a 'solution' which can be said to constitute a 'theory' in the modern sense of the word. In responding to the contingent emergencies of the situation to be understood and represented, this adjustive process is analogous to the responses of style in search of decorum, of the emotions in search of the 'mean,' and of the judgment in search of equity. The right balance resembles decorum, the 'mean,' and equity insofar as they, too, are all expressions of continuous requalification rather than the application of the fixed criteria of literary 'rules,' moral sanctions, and legal statutes. When a literary theory fails to recognize and resist any tendencies toward imbalance, it will gradually reduce literature to its cognitive 'philosophical' intention, or to its exhortatory 'rhetorical' intention, or to its purely formal 'mathematical' intention. Any such reduction commonly distorts or excludes some part of experience and, thereby, prevents the full potentialities of the literary work from being realized. Too exclusive a preoccupation with the definition and transmission of knowledge leads to an abstract didacticism. Too exclusive a preoccupation with the means of persuasion leads to the exploitation of language for the sake of display or of psychagogic manipulation. Too exclusive a preoccupation with the structural principles leads to one type or another of 'formalism.'

Supporters of various types of formalism today might ask why literary theory need take into consideration at all the objectives and materials of philosophy and rhetoric once the requirements of a beautiful composition have been satisfied. Any such question ignores the fact that literature, in its representation of human experience, reveals in its characters and in their thoughts and actions varying degrees of cognition and judgment. Without philosophical inquiry, there would be no attempt to know the truth. Without rhetorical inquiry, there would be no analysis of a particular set of circumstances, no judgment made of those circumstances, no appropriate action moved, and no persuasion of an audience to accept that judgment and action as equitable according to due measure.

On the other hand, both those who see literature primarily as a philosophical instrument for acquiring and transmitting knowledge and those who see it primarily as a rhetorical instrument of persuasion for the sake of either expediency or ideological propaganda are equally shortsighted. They have, in the first place, already narrowed the disciplines of philosophy and rhetoric themselves by regarding the objective of the first as the acquisition of information and that of the second as utility or proselytism. They have, in the second place, narrowed the conception of literature by identifying it with either of these objectives. Those concerned chiefly with knowledge will judge a literary work on the basis of whether what it says about its subject is *true* or *false*. Those concerned chiefly with persuasion will judge the work on its degree of affectiveness and, then, judge that affectiveness itself on the basis of whether what the work urges its audience to believe about its subject is *right* or *wrong* according to utilitarian criteria. That is to say, both the cognitive and the exhortative intentions—and this would be true even if they had not been restricted—surrender the judgment of a literary work to the pragmatic demands of the immediate circumstances. In such a surrender, each of these intentions must remain separate from the other and, because neither can explore its potential relationship with the other, each must remain incomplete. Neither has accepted that immunity which the literary analysis of experience, through its third function, provides: a 'license' to fictionalize analogous to the license granted to the *archai* of geometrical demonstration, which permits the assumption both of the existence of events independent of history and of the principles of their formal coherence.

In sum, to be complete, a theory of literature must integrate and fulfill the kinds of obligations analogous to those briefly indicated in Hesiod's description of the Muses. Their freedom from the restraint of cares permits them to express themselves in songs which are 'made' to combine—like Plato's concept of the good—the true, the just, and the beautiful. Like the permanent coherence of geometrical discourse, beauty of form must, among other things, secure for the literary representation of experience a freedom from historical change in order to preserve the relation between the philosophical contemplation of truth and the rhetorical argument for equitable response and action. However much the terms which describe the required balance of these objectives may vary from period to period, the critical efforts to achieve and maintain the balance over the centuries may be said to have established a continuity of literary theory.

In trying to describe the principles underlying this continuity, I have used the word 'theory' in its older Greek sense of 'viewing' or 'observing' something as a whole in order to understand it. This meaning of inclusive 'observation' or 'contemplation' is different from the modern connotations of a 'theory' as an idea to be tested, a body of doctrine to be believed, or a program to be instituted. In this modern sense, a person may favor one or more theories which oppose other competing theories, and insofar as he defends one as preferable or puts several together in a different combination or develops a new one himself, he may be called a 'theorist.' Arguments in favor of one theory or another then tend to be separated from their original contexts, to restrict their attention to methodology and dogma, and, finally, to become the special subject matter of the theorists themselves. Once a theory has become in its own right the subject of academic dispute, it has lost its empirical intention denoted by the word *theoria*.

Since I can offer no 'doctrine of literature,' I can make no claim to being a 'literary theorist' in this modern sense. Rather, I have tried to describe—no matter how critical terminologies have varied with shifting historical contexts—what has remained consistent in the inquiries into the nature of literature. Such inquiries have shared with a number of other arts and sciences the persistent attempt to achieve and integrate the general objectives of understanding, judgment, and formal coherence. These objectives are often expressed as conceptual principles of order, as just estimations of particular instances, and as self-contained systems of internal consistency. In literature itself, the philosophical intention *to know* and *to present* the essential nature of things has usually contributed the conceptual knowledge of general principles. The rhetorical intention *to judge* a particular set of circumstances and *to persuade* others to act upon its evaluation of these circumstances has usually discriminated relevant from irrelevant empirical data. One might say, then, that even within the objectives of literary discourse philosophical and rhetorical forms of inquiry have had to maintain the balance between the conventional methodologies of conceptualism and empiricism. How closely analogous this balance in literature has been to that in other arts and, even physical, sciences can be seen by comparing Philip Sidney with Francis Bacon.

However much the types of materials which Sidney deals with may differ from those treated by Bacon, the readjustment of general principles to the sources of sensation to be accounted for remains relatively constant from one discipline to another. The negotiation between the poet's conception of experience, for instance, and its ethical raw materials, as described by Sidney, is strikingly similar to the negotiation between the natural philosopher's conception of experience and his data as described by Bacon. Bacon seeks a 'middle course (*ratio media*)' between the rationalistic spider and the empirical ant, and finds that the bee "gathers its material from the flowers of the garden and of the field, but transforms and digests it by a power of its own." The bee goes about the true business of the scientist and represents "a closer and purer league between these two faculties, the experimental and the rational." The *ratio media* in Bacon's material holds a position analogous to that of poetry in Sidney's: the balance between philosophical precept and historical example. This balance, which Bacon wishes for scientific and Sidney for literary analysis, is an activity, rather than a possession, of the mind. If we add the 'formal' function necessary to preserve this activity, the relation of the conceptual, the empirical, and the formal procedures to one another will correspond to the relation between the intentions of philosophy, rhetoric, and mathematics.

Just as in the preceding comparison of one discipline with another, so also within any single discipline: there are certain constant objectives and habits of mind to be observed below the shifting vocabulary from period to period. It is only by recognizing how these underlying intentions are, in fact, persistent attempts to resist different forms of imbalance that the variations of terminology, responding to the historical process and being recorded by literary interpreters, become intelligible. The literary historian must especially notice two types of change which threaten the accuracy of philological interpretation.

The first type of change occurs when new terms arise which perform functions that earlier terms, having become too imprecise or restricted, no longer fulfill. This happens when a given term in the discipline itself—say philosophy—from which a word has been borrowed for the discussion of literature, becomes narrowed. To the extent that the original term no longer describes the objectives or procedures of philosophy, which the literary analysis of experience, nevertheless, continues to share, and literary theory tries to describe, a new term, often from an entirely different context, must be substituted for it or combined with it. Let me give an example which has important implications for the history of the arts.

By the first century A.D., the meaning of two of the four Aristotelian explanations or 'causes'—the 'formal' cause and the 'final' cause—of why things come to be as they are had become sufficiently narrowed to require an additional 'exemplary' cause to supplement them. In the process of restricting all causation to the efficient cause (with the material cause understood), Seneca testifies that a fifth, Platonic, cause had by then become associated with the four Peripatetic causes. He illustrates all five of these causes by using the example of an artist's making a statue. First, with respect to the first four, or Aristotelian, principles, Seneca says that the first, or material, cause is the bronze from which the statue is cast. The second, or efficient, cause is the artist who must shape the bronze. The third, or formal, cause is the shape which the artist impresses on the bronze. And the fourth, or final, cause is the purpose for which the statue is made (*Ep.* 65.5–6). To these four he adds the fifth Platonic cause, the exemplary, and places it between Aristotle's formal and final causes: "the material is the bronze, the agent is the artist, the make-up is the form which is adapted to the material, the model is the pattern (*exemplar*) imitated by the agent, the end in view is the purpose in the maker's mind" (8). What is suggestive is the fact that the *need* for the additional exemplary cause can be accounted for in part by the *restriction* of the formal and final causes as Seneca defines them.

With respect to the formal cause, Seneca asks, "Do you maintain that form is a cause? This is only what the artist stamps upon his work" (*hanc inponit artifex operi*, 13): form is but a shape impressed upon the work (*inpressa facies*, 5). 'Form,' here, has been reduced to the external lineaments of shapes and surfaces. Similarly restricted, the final cause is what "attracted the artist (*quod invitavit artificem*) . . . when he made the statue" (6): it could have been money, fame, or religious zeal. It is simply "that which leads him to undertake to create something" (*propter quod ad faciendum aliquid accedit*, 14). The power, previously implicit in the biological connotations of these 'causes,' as Aristotle describes them, to inform a process and to account for the realization or completion of any given organism or product is seriously diminished in Seneca's metaphor. It is precisely such restrictions in the meaning of formal and final causation that the Platonic cause might supplement. The fifth cause is an exemplary model (*exemplar, quam [sc. causam] ipse idean vocat*, 7): the connotations of *idean* reinforce the restricted function of the original formal cause (εἶδος), while the connotations of *exemplar*, holding up a pattern of complete realization to be pursued, reinforce that of the final cause (τέλος). One can here distinguish between a requirement for a meaning's remaining constant and terminology constantly depleting itself only to be rebuilt out of whatever material it has at hand for the purpose which it is immediately required to fulfill. The inadequacy of the reconstructed terminology itself to recover fully the original meaning will lead, in turn, to the need for further supplementation.

The second type of change which the philologist must take into account resembles, in its effects, the one just described. To keep pace with the inevitable fluctuations of the historical process, it becomes necessary to distinguish separate meanings within a single more general concept that is no longer sufficiently definitive in its reference. A concept, X, that is, may have to be differentiated into various kinds or degrees of X—into X_1 and X_2 and X_3—or into a modification of its former meaning and an entirely new concept—X_1 and Y, Y_1 and Z, and so forth. The philological danger lies in not keeping up with the stages of differentiation, with the result that one may identify X with X_1, or even with Y, or may mistake the later more restricted for the earlier more general meaning or vice versa. Just such a danger arises from the later differentiation and specialization of the integrated activities of the Muses which Hesiod has described.

In his discussion of the Muses, Plutarch has his brother, Lamprias, account for their number in a way which reveals the later fragmentation of Hesiod's conception of their function as well as the original division of all discourse into three types of disciplines.

In my opinion the ancients, observing that all branches of knowledge and crafts that attain their end by the use of words (διὰ λόγου) belong to one of three kinds, namely the philosophical, the rhetorical, or the mathematical (τῷ φιλοσόφῳ καὶ τῷ ῥητορικῷ καὶ τῷ μαθηματικῷ), considered them to be the gracious gifts of three goddesses, whom they named Muses. Later, in Hesiod's days in fact, by which time these faculties were being more clearly seen, they began to distinguish different parts and forms; they then observed that each faculty in its turn contained three different things. The mathematical genus includes music, arithmetic, and geometry, the philosophical comprises logic, ethics, and natural science, while in the rhetorical it is said that the original laudatory kind was joined first by the deliberative, and finally by the forensic.

Although Plutarch goes on to say that the Muses do have a unified body of knowledge in common to express and transmit, he does not suggest with Hesiod that the varied offices of the poet embody the collective activities of the Muses themselves. For Hesiod, the Muses exist as various aspects of one another, one implying all the others, and they enable the poet to transmit a general cultural and artistic inheritance. For Plutarch, their office has been differentiated clearly into nine various disciplines, and poetry has been restricted to the category of music, itself now under the protection of one of three Muses subordinated to mathematical discourse. It would be a serious error to identify Plutarch's didactic and formalistic conception of poetry with that implied by Hesiod's introduction to the *Theogony* on the assumption that the Muses represented the same poetic activities in both writers.

While Plutarch assumes that his brother's explanation of the original number of the Muses is unusual, the differentiation of rational discourse into philosophical, rhetorical, and mathematical disciplines, which frequently competed with one another, is traditional. Such rivalry encouraged the separation and antagonism between the cognitive, judicative, and formal intentions of literature. As these intentions became identified or contrasted with one competing activity or another, technical discussions of those disciplines whose functions poetry had originally coordinated gradually led to more restricted conceptions of literary discourse itself. It is the purpose of this study to describe the nature of these restrictions placed upon the literary analysis of experience and of the ever-recurring efforts to overcome them.[1]

---

[1] The quotations in this Preface have been taken in the order of their appearance from the following editions: *Hesiod*, trans. H. G. Evelyn-White, Loeb Classical Library [= LCL] (London, 1970); *Novum Organum* 1.95, in *The Works of Francis Bacon*, ed. J. Spedding, R. L. Ellis, and D. D. Heath, 14 vols. (London, 1858–1874), 4:1:93; *Seneca ad Lucilium Epistulae Morales*, trans. R. M. Gummere, LCL, 3 vols. (London, 1961); "Table-talk" 9.14, in *Plutarch's Moralia* (744CF), trans. F. H. Sandbach, LCL, 15 vols. (London, 1961), 9:271–75. In adapting my title for this book from Hesiod's phrase κούρας ὁμόφρονας— which M. L. West explains as meaning simply " 'of like disposition,' as might be expected of children born together of the same parents" (*Hesiod Theogony* [Oxford, 1966], p. 176)—I want to emphasize two things. First, this shared 'disposition,' with its desire for song and its immunity from care, is a necessary condition of artistic freedom from obligations which might otherwise restrict the activities of the Muses. And, second, these activities, for which the condition of being 'of one mind' is necessary, express here the three intentions which, I shall argue, it has always been the purpose of literature to combine.

Acknowledgments

I AM INDEBTED to the American Council of Learned Societies for a grant in 1963–1964 during which time I began my research on Parts One and Three of this study and to the National Endowment for the Humanities for a grant in 1977 to write Part Two. I wish to acknowledge my gratitude to the late Father Edwin Quain, whose interest and support, as editor, led to the publication of earlier versions of Parts One and Three in *Traditio* in 1971 and 1974 respectively, and to Professor Morton Bloomfield for his first suggesting *Traditio* to me as well as for his continuing encouragement over the years. Since in the original version of Part One the terms of analysis were incomplete, I have redefined them here, and, in the process, I hope to have restated the argument with greater precision. In Part Three I have frequently revised passages both in general conception and in particular details. Of the many personal debts to students and friends, I would like to mention especially those to Professors Kathy Eden, William Race, and Steven Shankman for their careful criticism of the text; to the late Professors T.B.L. Webster and E. L. Bundy for valuable specific advice at various periods of my research; and to Professor Eric Voegelin for often sharing his extensive knowledge and analytic insight with me in conversation over the past few years.

Part One

Literary Discourse and the Ancient Hypothesis of Fiction

IN HIS ETYMOLOGICAL reflections in the *Cratylus* (406A), Plato suggests that "the Muses and music in general are named, apparently, from μῶσθαι, searching, and philosophy." The word μῶσθαι (from μῶμαι), meaning 'to strive after,' 'to long for,' or 'to desire eagerly,' shares with 'philosophy' (φιλοσοφία) the conception of 'loving' and with 'searching' (ζήτησις) the conception of 'inquiry.' As in Hesiod's account of the Muses, these conceptions express again the unifying tension, in both the mind and the emotions, toward an equilibrium of cognition (with respect to wisdom) and action (with respect to judging wisdom desirable and to striving for it). The nature of this tension is in part expressed in these words by the connotation of a covetous 'yearning' for understanding, and this intense desire suggests the motivating power of beauty itself. Like Hesiod, Plato implies that the very name 'Muses' defines as their essential 'virtue' their power to integrate the true, the just, and the beautiful.[1]

I shall argue in Part One that literature, as the most complete expression of the Muses, participates in their excellence precisely by virtue of its power to draw upon and integrate the energies of the cognitive, judicative, and formal disciplines. Cicero gives eloquent testimony of this interrelationship in an influential passage in his *De oratore* (3.57–61). He is criticizing Socrates for having narrowed the contemporary conception of philosophy, a discipline which had originally included "the whole study and practice of the liberal sciences (*omnis rerum optimarum cognitio atque in eis exercitatio*)." By his efforts, Socrates "separated the science of wise thinking from that of elegant speaking, though in reality they are closely linked together." From him, therefore, "has sprung the undoubtedly absurd and unprofitable and reprehensible severance between the tongue and the brain, leading to our having one set of professors to teach us to think and another to teach us to speak." The separation of rhetorical from philosophical disciplines was, for Cic-

---

[1] *Plato: Cratylus, Parmenides, Greater Hippias, Lesser Hippias*, trans. H. N. Fowler, LCL (London, 1970). This etymology of the word 'Muses' has persisted: see, for example, Clement of Alexandria, *Against the Pagans* 31; Cassiodorus, *Institutiones* 2.5, quoting Clement; Isidore, *Etymologiae* 3.15.1, perhaps quoting Cassiodorus. In his "Coronation Oration," Petrarch takes two lines from Virgil (*Georg.* 3.291–92) as his 'text,' *sed me Parnasi deserta per ardua dulcis / raptat amor*, and glosses the last three words very much in the spirit of Plato: "The phrase 'dulcis raptat amor' suggests the ardent eagerness of a studious mind—and we should note the force of 'amor' in itself, of 'dulcis amor,' and of 'amor' having the power to urge one upward. This difficulty and this eagerness are closely related, and are dependent each upon the other: for he who undertakes to climb the 'ardua deserta Parnasi' must indeed long intensely for that which he seeks to attain; and he who loves to climb is doubtless the better prepared thereby to attain through study that in which his mind delights. For study without longing and without great mental pleasure and delight cannot attain the desired results" (trans. E. H. Wilkins, *Studies in the Life and Works of Petrarch* [Cambridge, 1955], p. 301).

ero, explicitly opposed to the early *paideia* and to the literature which transmitted its intentions. In the old days, he says,

The same system of instruction (*doctrina*) seems to have imparted education both in right conduct and in good speech; nor were the professors in two separate groups, but the same masters gave instruction both in ethics and in rhetoric, for instance the great Phoenix in Homer, who says that he was assigned to the young Achilles by his father Peleus to accompany him to the wars in order to make him "an orator and man of action too."[2]

It is Homer's protagonists, his fiction, and, by extension, *poesis* itself, which, in the literary representation of experience, have achieved the formal means to establish and express the proper relation between the cognitive and judicative activities of the mind.

[2] Cicero, *De Oratore*, trans. E. W. Sutton and H. Rackham, LCL, 2 vols. (London, 1959). All subsequent citations will be to this edition. Though he does not mention Cicero in his "To Plato: In Defence of Oratory," Aelius Aristides comments (387) that "the ancients also joined these faculties together and did not discriminate between them. Homer said that Phoenix had been sent by Peleus to Achilles 'to be a speaker of words and doer of deeds,' since the same man knew what ought to be said and what ought to be done" (*Aristides*, Orat. 2.384–93, trans. C. A. Behr, LCL [London, 1973]). Aristides then goes on to associate the intentions of the Homeric speakers with the activities which Hesiod attributes to the Muses in the *Theogony* (80–90). There, Hesiod "speaks not only almost in the same way, but also says precisely the same things as Homer," maintaining "that the title of wise and the ability to speak well are attributes of the same man. . . . Rightly does Hesiod expound, and justly he requites the Muses, from whom he got his ability to speak about these matters" (391). If "to speak well" combines formal excellence with judicious advice (here, persuasion to action) and both are joined with cognition (here, wisdom), then, what the Muses teach Hesiod closely resembles "literary discourse" as described in the Preface. Both Cicero and Aristides are referring to *Il*.ix.443.

1. 'Literary Discourse': Muses
of One Mind

THE HISTORIAN of literary theory is concerned specifically with understanding why people began to discuss literary works in the terms
that they did. The nature and the sources of their initial terminology
reveal much about the premises upon which they formulated and defended an 'art' of literature. The premises of the emergence of such an
art were, to a great extent, to determine the problems of its survival.

The earliest discussions of any complexity about literature survive
from a relatively late period[1] and in a terminology which had been
already developed for the treatment of other arts and disciplines. The
adoption of terms from geometry, music, medicine, politics, ethics, dialectic, rhetoric, and the plastic arts by those who first discussed the
purposes and deficiencies of literature suggests how a literary theory
may have been forming in a borrowed vocabulary prior to the recorded
documents as well as the ways in which later theorists would perceive,
define, and defend their critical principles. The terms themselves would
have already predetermined to some extent the most significant theoretical problems as well as the methods by which practical criticism was
to try to meet them.[2]

The word 'literature' itself is too general to use today in talking about
the origins of literary theory. There would be disagreement, for instance,
whether a Platonic dialogue were literature. If one claims that the *Phaedrus* is, then what of the *Laws*? What of an oration by Demosthenes or
Cicero, Lucretius' *De rerum natura*, or St. Paul's *Epistles*? How are
Lucan's *Pharsalia*, St. Augustine's *Confessions*, or Boethius' *Consolation of Philosophy* to be categorized? For more effective classification, I

---

[1] Aristotle observes that even in rhetoric the study of language and style had only
recently made much progress (*Rhet.* 3.1, 1403b36–38). *Aristotle's Rhetoric and Poetics*,
trans. W. Rhys Roberts and I. Bywater (New York, 1954), p. 165. All references to the
Rhetoric will be to this edition unless otherwise assigned.

[2] For a subtle survey of terminology and method, see Richard McKeon, "The Philosophical Bases of Art and Criticism," in *Critics and Criticism*, ed. R. S. Crane (Chicago,
1952), pp. 463–545.

shall use the term 'discourse' to refer, in the most general sense, to anything written or spoken about subjects traditionally associated with any of Plutarch's three main categories of the arts and sciences. I shall then qualify the term by making two distinctions which derive from the earliest controversies over language and its proper use. The first distinction concerns the respective purposes and subjects of the three categories, and the second the manner in which these categories treat their respective subjects.

With regard to *purpose and subject*, the purely formal disciplines of mathematical discourse actually have no content beyond the assertion of their own existence and of the coherent relation between their parts or propositions; they have no purpose beyond lucid self-consistency. By virtue of providing principles of order analogous to those of geometry for philosophy and rhetoric as well as for literature, they establish the formal conditions which enable the literary analysis of experience to integrate the materials and intentions of philosophical and rhetorical discourse. The nature of these conditions and how they permit literature to combine formal with cognitive and judicative procedures of inquiry may best, therefore, be treated in Chapter 2 on "The Hypothesis of Literary Discourse." The purpose and subject of philosophical and rhetorical discourse, on the other hand, may be briefly summarized and distinguished here. Philosophy has as its heuristic purpose the investigation and description of men and the world they live in. Its subjects are divided into logic (mental and verbal activities), ethics (moral choice and action), and physics (the natural sciences). Rhetoric has as its judicative purpose persuasion and action. When it treats the subjects of communal importance in political assemblies it is called *deliberative*; when it treats the subjects of public or private legal controversies in the forum or courtroom, it is called *forensic*; when it treats the topics of praise or dispraise of men, places, things, or actions, it is called *epideictic* or *encomiastic*.

With respect to the *manner of treatment*, both philosophy and rhetoric—and, as we shall see in Chapter 2, to a lesser extent mathematics—may treat their respective materials in two ways which may ultimately be related to a Platonic distinction in ethics. We may call the first way 'specialized discourse,' a language developed to treat a specific, and usually technical, subject. The second way may be called 'unspecialized' or 'general discourse': it is a language developed to deal with problems that concern men *qua* human beings rather than men as specialists in given disciplines. In the *Protagoras* (318B–23B) Socrates points out that when special advice is required, one goes to those few individual experts who can give it, such as to the architect for advice on building, but when political advice is required, it makes no difference what specific art the adviser practices, since all men are expected to participate as citizens in the government. Plato then illustrates the distinction by the myth of Prometheus, who, seeing men so ill-endowed after their creation, gave them the technical arts to supply their needs. These were insufficient, however, to enable them to form communities to protect themselves, so Zeus had a sense of ethical prudence and justice distributed, not to specific individuals, as in the other arts, but to all men. Out of such simple origins grow the conflicting criteria which for centuries are to make the moral justification of the arts, particularly the fine arts, so difficult to establish. The artist who makes things is judged *as artist* in relation to the quality of his product, i.e. a good knife maker is one who makes a good knife, but when he is considered *as a human being*, he is judged not by the quality of his product but by the quality of his actions, which reveal his ethical condition as 'actor.' The goodness lies not in the product but in the agent. The persistence of these terms has tended to perpetuate a belief in the amorality of all the arts. An early attempt to resolve the conflict may be apparent, though very dimly, in the initial motivations to formulate a literary theory.[3]

This distinction between specialized and unspecialized or general discourse can be applied to the subject matters and activities of both philosophy and rhetoric. In rhetorical discourse *generality* usually referred to the extent of applicability to particular instances, not to the degree of abstraction, and encouraged a liberation from the tyranny of particular events and from a technical methodology. In philosophical discourse, however, the 'general' question tended to lose its reference to particular instances and depart to abstraction; it was criticized for its lack of applicability to the majority of human problems, for its abstruseness. Liberalization in philosophical discourse, then, was the reverse of liberalization in rhetorical discourse. To escape from an academic abstruseness (its peculiar conservatism), philosophy had to try to root its general questions in particular applications. Rhetorical discourse, on the other hand, in order to liberalize itself, had to locate its particular, circumstantial issue in a broader context, to see, for instance, the ethical implications in any legal action or deliberative decision. Justice is concerned not just with 'Did he kill the tyrant?' but with 'Is it a good thing to kill a tyrant?' Without the more general questions, law is reduced to in-

---

[3] These distinctions were given their most influential formulation by Aristotle (*E.N.* 6.4–5) and were adapted from him by St. Thomas Aquinas (*S.T.*, I, II qu. 21 ar. 2 and qu. 57 ar. 3 and 5), from whom I have borrowed the example of the knife. For a perceptively detailed account of their origin, development, and extension into the controversy over the contemplative and active life, see Werner Jaeger, *Aristotle*, trans. R. Robinson (Oxford, 1948), pp. 426–61.

Intentions and Terminologies Forming an Incipient Theory of 'Literary Discourse' as It Emerges Out of the Cultural Tradition of the *paideia* in Early Antiquity

Philosophical Discourse		*Rhetorical Discourse*	
Specialized	*Unspecialized*	*Unspecialized*	*Specialized*
1. *Physics*: abstract speculation about nature.	1. *Physics*: natural history; the application of such empirical knowledge to practical disciplines like medicine and agriculture.	1. *Forensic*: specific legal problems seen in the broad context of ethical issues; justice; the true revelation of events.	1. *Forensic*: manuals of eristic disputation; equivocation; intricacies of procedure and *status*; verbal traps; victory as opposed to justice as an end.
2. *Ethics*: dialectical pursuit of abstruse questions in isolation from practical concerns; systems of dogma.	2. *Ethics*: prudence in political and private matters; the proper end of disciplines, their place in education; the analysis of ethical propositions through moral dialectic and their exemplification in particular circumstances.	2. *Epideictic*: a broadening of themes and their implications; inventiveness; truth of judgment.	2. *Epideictic*: rigorous application of rhetorical *topoi* from manuals; academic exercises on trivial subjects; verbal ingenuity and paradox for their own sake.
3. *Logic*: eristic disputation; the assimilation of all formal principles to those of mathematics; the imposition of such formal principles and schemata upon all interpretations of reality.	3. *Logic*: principles of order as expressed in *all* rational disciplines—speculative, prudential, and productive.	3. *Deliberative*: major public issues debated at large in political assembly.	3. *Deliberative*: private counsel, written in letters or given 'in chamber'; epideictic cultivation of diplomatic communication and formal refinements of protocol.

genious equivocation for the sake of expediency—to which its form of conservatism is always tending. Both philosophy and rhetoric in their most liberal forms, then, tend toward the middle and toward one another in order to achieve the proper balance between the general issue and the particular instance. These distinctions may be seen more easily in the accompanying diagram where some of the heuristic and judicative activities are briefly indicated.

It is difficult to say at what point a fourth category of discourse, which for lack of a better term I shall call 'literary discourse' (in the sense of fiction, *poesis*), began to be distinguished from the disciplines of philosophical, rhetorical, and mathematical discourse. That is, at what point did literary discourse began *to be written about as distinct*, to be enunciated by a body of statement which might constitute a 'theory of literature' in the sense that Aristotle's *Poetics* is distinct from his *Rhetoric*. If such a theory of literary discourse is to form, it will probably begin by consolidating various attitudes and vocabularies already present in suspension. Like a kind of incipient solar system, forming among others with whose gravitational forces it must compete, it must draw in its future components toward some center of gravity, a center sufficiently stable to resist the pull of the strongest systems of discourse already formed. In the beginning that center was probably the literature itself, which invited description and analysis in the way that Aristotle describes a body of specific plays. In response to its competing forces, such a theory of literature would tend first to distinguish itself especially from philosophy and rhetoric and exclude what was most conservative in these established categories of discourse, what was most peculiar to each of their respective subject matters.[4] It would appropriate from both of them, on the other hand, what lies in the least stable suspension at the liberal borders where they most nearly approximate one another. It is here that a theory of literary discourse might be conceived and discussed in terms already in existence.

A further conjecture may be added. One reason for the formulation of a theory about literary discourse was the recognition of the tendency for philosophy and rhetoric to revert constantly to their respective specialized forms of discourse. The balanced relation between a general concept, in law or ethics, and the circumstantial and emotional intricacies of particular experiences and events was constantly threatened. Such a

---

[4] This is even partially reflected in the subsequent history of the two principal definitions of poetry, metrical composition and imitation (*mimesis*). The first states its relation to the prose composition of oratory and the second, in being concerned with the object and representation of certain types of knowledge, to philosophy.

loss would threaten not only intellectual but emotional order, since our emotional responses to events are disposed as they are to such a high degree by our conceptions of the general issues involved. That such a balance might find a more stable existence in literature than in the uneasy combination of two activities whose intentions were often opposed is suggested, at least, by the enduring influence of the Homeric epics upon the cultural traditions of the *paideia*. A theory of literary discourse might well develop to define and preserve this inheritance before becoming specialized itself in technical manuals of poetics.[5]

Such a development gains plausibility, as it were, after the fact. From the time of the controversies over discourse in the earliest documents, the analysis of literature has had to cope with the instabilities inherited with its borrowed, composite terminology in two principal regards. First, it has had to resist recurrent efforts to reduce literature either to philosophical discourse by a didactic concern with factual or with doctrinal truth alone, or to rhetorical discourse by a preoccupation solely with the manipulation of language for its exhortatory, emotional effects upon the audience, or to mathematical discourse by an exclusive concern with formal coherence. Attempts continue, that is, to reduce literature either to a lucid conceptual content, or to pragmatically persuasive expression, or to an aesthetically beautiful construction. Second, and correlatively, literary theory has had to protect the formal unity of artistic composition against the particular principles of order imposed by specialized disciplines. The ideal of a perfect combination of knowledge and eloquence, as Cicero later restated it from the best of his Greek sources, insisted upon the awareness of any particular event in relation to its broadest context of implications (*De orat.* 3.120–21). This awareness expresses itself formally as a unity not only in the artistic work but in all orders of experience, from the simplest to the most complicated. Cicero concludes his *De oratore* and *Orator* with what amounts to a mystical experience of universal harmony, and he describes it in terms of rhythm

---

[5] For descriptions of a culture which would be congenial to such a development, see Hans von Arnim, *Leben und Werke des Dio von Prusa* (Berlin, 1898), pp. 1–114; Werner Jaeger, *Paideia: The Ideals of Greek Culture*, trans. G. Highet, 3 vols. (New York, 1944); H. I. Marrou, *Histoire de l'éducation dans l'antiquité* (Paris, 1960). The cultural ideal itself, even when most nearly approximated, was instable. A. D. Leeman comments that "the boundary between philosophy and oratory, where Cicero lodges his *orator perfectus*, is a no man's land." He cites Cicero's letter to Atticus (9.4) in which the orator lists eight "theses," which, dealing with political matters, were applicable to his own circumstances. By debating them as exercises he both profits and relieves his melancholy. *Orationis Ratio, The Stylistic Theories and Practice of the Roman Orators, Historians and Philosophers* (Amsterdam, 1963), 1:123–24. This application of general themes to particular, personal events, thesis to hypothesis, reflects the desire, characteristic of literary discourse, to repossess the no man's land.

in prose. Rhythm is the great weapon against disparateness, as are all forms of composition (*cum* + *ponere*)—that by which men have power to hold things together. While these had always been the ideals of any form of unspecialized discourse, specialized discourse led in the other direction: toward discreteness, disparateness, and the isolation of particulars. It narrowed its aim to immediate achievements; it developed techniques. It tended to subvert the whole in the interest of particular parts, and threatened the formally unified composition with gradual fragmentation. The most specialized form of forensic rhetoric, eristic debate, for instance, resembled the eristic disputation about abstruse questions of the most specialized form of philosophy. Both tended to break up experience into discrete units of fragmentary *quaestiones* and to impose that structure upon less specialized forms of discourse. Such an imposition was made easier by the fact that in the development of human disciplines as a whole, unspecialized discourse has naturally tended toward specialization, generalization toward specific methodology, theory toward technique. It is the conservative impulse toward the consolidation of gains and the immediate taking of profits. In the history of literary theory it may be observed, almost with the authority of a natural law, that the literary procedures of specialized discourse will impose their structures on those of unspecialized discourse whenever no countermeasures are taken. It has been the activity of practical criticism to take such countermeasures.

A. Plato and Isocrates

Plato, Isocrates, and Aristotle all frequently criticized the use of overspecialized discourse in philosophy and rhetoric. For Plato, his predecessors had narrowed philosophy to speculative questions about the physical universe which could never be answered and which could, ultimately, have no bearing upon human happiness. Similarly, he criticized those who wrote manuals of legal rhetoric which offered techniques for debate but were not concerned with the potentialities of language to define and teach the qualities of justice. His ideal of philosophical discourse was a form of dialectic, described in the *Republic*, which could free itself from the technical terms, with their imposed conclusions, of specialized disciplines. For him this meant a language stripped as much as possible of reference to material appearances in order to grasp conceptual relations with the strict swiftness of mathematics. His ideal of rhetorical discourse, as outlined in the *Phaedrus*, was a language which gained its persuasiveness from the breadth of knowledge and regard for truth that the speaker revealed. Taken literally, this description shares much with the Isocratean ideals of political oratory and with Aristotle's analysis of those qualities which make language persuasive in his *Rhetoric*. It is ironic that in addition to some of his philosophical principles, the cultural circumstances in which Plato found himself forced him to resist the sophists with greater specialization in philosophical discourse and to leave the defense of the liberal borders of both disciplines to others.

The professional sophists of Plato's day freely crossed the borderline between philosophy and rhetoric in the subject matter they treated. In practice they generally taught either techniques of a fairly practical nature or transmitted a body of assumptions and commonplaces about the physical universe or human behavior, which had come down to them through the Greek *paideia* in forms similar to those given them by Homer and Hesiod. The sophist and the rhapsode both offered a popular morality which was conservative and which generally protected its society from insecurity and reform. It was precisely this cultural security that Socrates challenged, and, finding it rooted firmly in the literature itself, he was forced to question the value of literature in education. Plato criticized the rhetorician and the poet for claiming to have specific knowledge about the things they spoke of, when, in reality, they were simply repeating other people's opinions. His attack takes the same form in the *Gorgias* as in the *Ion*: neither rhetoric nor poetry has a specific body of knowledge to teach. They are not bad because they should do something other than teach, but because they teach badly. They fail even in the simplest kind of teaching, the giving of factual information. Had Homer possessed a body of professional knowledge, he might have found employment and a release from his blind wanderings. It was probably this criticism of the general culture as much as the abstruseness of Socratic dialectic which led Aristophanes to burlesque Socrates in his 'thinking-shop' (*phrontisterion*) and led Isocrates to criticize the isolation of the Platonic Academy. Whatever the causes, Plato became associated with the specialized discourse of philosophy in the controversies over language in the fourth century. The degree to which his philosophic criticism of the mimetic arts contributed to this association can best be treated in Chapter 2.

The importance of Isocrates' *Helen* lies less in its prescriptions for epideictic oratory than in its defense and implied description of unspecialized discourse. Like Plato (*Phaedrus*, 229C), Isocrates objected up to the end of his life (*Panath.*, 1) to a preoccupation with mythological fictions, but to this form of idleness he added a number of other activities which he considered too narrow for a man seriously concerned with human experience. Some, he says (*Helen*, 1–5), delight in being able to discuss "an absurd and self-contradictory subject" (ὑπόθεσιν ἄτοπον καὶ παράδοξον),[6] while others grow old in asserting that it is impossible to say what is false or to speak on both sides of the same question. Still others (like Plato) maintain that courage and wisdom and justice are identical, while others "waste their time in captious disputations" that are entirely useless. Such novelties of invention have not just arisen with recent rhetoricians but go back to the older sophists, such as Protagoras and Gorgias, Zeno and Melissus. These men showed "that it is easy to contrive false statements on any subject" proposed, but instead of such verbal quibbles they should have pursued the truth in order "to instruct their pupils in the practical affairs of our government, . . . bearing in mind that likely conjecture about useful things is far preferable to exact knowledge of the useless, and that to be a little superior in important things is of greater worth than to be pre-eminent in petty things that are without value for living." Such men beguile their students for money with such "eristic disputations," for the young are "inclined toward what is extraordinary and astounding" (6–7). They teach them to lie in that they encourage them to praise what is not praiseworthy in order to show their ingenuity in paradox. What sensible man would praise misfortune? Such topics are chosen out of weakness and in order to avoid competition. Furthermore, they are easy to deal with, for there are only a few ways to treat them, while "discourses that are of general import" call upon "a variety of forms and occasions . . . whose opportune use is hard to learn, and their composition is more difficult." No one who has chosen to praise bumblebees or salt is at a loss for words, but those who speak of what is good or noble "have all fallen far short of the possibilities which these subjects offer." Whatever a speaker may chance to say on a trifling topic can be original, but on important subjects few find what has not previously been said (8–13). This is the reason why Isocrates chooses Helen to praise, and praises Gorgias for having also chosen such a famous and challenging subject. But Gorgias has made a single, and all-important, error: although he intended to write an encomium of Helen, "he has actually spoken a defence of her conduct." Now, a defense draws upon different topics and actions than an encomium does, and Isocrates will try to praise the woman in a way that no one else had done (14–15).

This introduction to the *Helen* is one of several Isocratean passages

---

[6] *Isocrates*, trans. G. Norlin and L. van Hook, LCL, 3 vols. (London, 1928–1945). All references to Isocrates will be to this edition. Paradoxical encomia continued to be practiced and criticized. In addition to Lucian's satires, see the interesting example in *The Life of Apollonius* (4.30) by Philostratus.

of great importance in the development of literary theory. Specialized discourse of both a philosophical and rhetorical nature is rejected in the interest of a language which can deal with subjects which draw upon the broadest experience. There is a pragmatic concern for usefulness as opposed to speculation, for the active life of politics as opposed to the contemplative life of the Academy, and for the public good as opposed to individual accomplishment. These concerns may not lead to the most exceptional human attainments, but they provided a set of intellectual attitudes within which a theory of literature could develop and, more important, be protected from rival disciplines as much as possible. Isocrates was, ultimately, to pass on the literary culture of the *paideia* to Cicero, and rhetoric, conceived in its most liberal, i.e. philosophical, form, was to transmit the most vital principles of literary theory.

Two further things about this passage may be mentioned at this point. The first is the juxtaposition of a "likely conjecture" against an "exact knowledge." Isocrates' preference for a "likely conjecture" may well be an allusion to Plato's criticism and an early assertion of the value of a concept of *probability* in examining anything subject to change. Aristotle will defend the mimetic arts against Plato in a similar way: by giving a philosophical justification of probability. The second thing to be observed is Isocrates' explicit awareness of the imposition of one form of organization upon another. In making an encomium Gorgias has slipped into the topics and material of a defense. The principles of order in forensic debate in which a defense would be made are more specialized than those of the encomium, and the future tendency for rhetoric to impose the forms of its more conservative type upon the more liberal branches of oratory is already suggested here.[7]

Isocrates' unfinished discourse, *Against the Sophists*, applies the same criticism of specialization to education in general. Professors, devoting themselves to disputation, claim to teach their students what they can do in life to become happy and prosperous; in other words, they claim to know the future, when it is quite clear that they themselves cannot do much with the present (1–8). Likewise, the rhetorician who teaches political discourse often claims to make students, who have neither talent nor experience, into good orators as simply as he could teach the letters

---

[7] This imposition is later revealed in Hermagoras' development of his system of *status*, which, perhaps as was characteristic of the Hellenistic period generally, led to an almost exclusive concern with forensic oratory. The victory of his system over Aristotle's is a clear example of the more specialized form of an art overcoming the less. Cicero's ultimate liberalization of rhetoric was effected by a return to Aristotelian and Isocratean traditions. See F. Solmsen, "The Aristotelian Tradition in Ancient Rhetoric," *AJP* 62 (1941):180, 189–90. For Hermagoras see D. Matthes, "Hermagoras von Temnos 1904–55," *Lustrum* 3 (1958):58–214.

of the alphabet to them. This is a fallacious analogy because it compares "an art with hard and fast rules to a creative process." Letters always remain the same, while oratory is good only if it is appropriate to the occasion in its propriety of style and originality of treatment. Formal training can only make men more skillful who are already gifted. A knowledge of the materials of a discourse is not difficult to acquire, but to show how to choose and organize those which are pertinent to the occasion and express them in appropriate language is the power of only the most excellent teacher (9–18). The early writers of forensic manuals taught students how to pick out the weakest terms of their opponents in order to discredit them, and made no effort to educate them in any other way. Isocrates himself denies that just living can be taught, for there is no art for reforming the soul, but the proper instruction in political discourse can still contribute to the formation of a good character (19–21).

Besides the rhetorical specialization of the early manuals, Isocrates objects in this brief treatise to the philosopher who specializes in the science of virtue. There is no art by which to make people good. What the rhetorical education can provide in its stead, he describes most clearly in his *Antidosis*. It is the practical skill to draw inferences from circumstance and to gain sufficient confidence in an inferred probability to advise and act upon it. There is "no system of knowledge [that] can possibly cover these occasions, since in all cases they elude our science." Yet those who "are able to discern the consequences which for the most part grow out of them, will most often meet these occasions in the right way" (*Antidosis*, 184).[8] Since there is no science men can possess by which they can know what to do and say, those men are wise who are able by their "powers of conjecture to arrive generally at the best course" (271). Though no art "can implant honesty and justice in depraved natures" and those who try grow weary in their vain pretensions, a man can become better if he desires to speak well. To speak well is to speak in a just and important cause for the common good; to select and follow personally the most illustrious human examples of the courses of recommended action; and to establish the most honorable character he can among his fellow citizens, for "the argument which is made by a man's life is of more weight than that which is furnished by words" (274–78). As for skills like disputation and geometry, such studies are ex-

---

[8] See Norlin's note: "The distinction usually drawn, in Plato for instance, between δόξα and ἐπιστήμη, the one 'opinion,' the other 'knowledge,' is not exactly that made by Isocrates. δόξα is here, not irresponsible opinion, but a working theory based on practical experience—judgement or insight in dealing with the uncertain contingencies of any human situation which presents itself. In this realm, he holds, there can be no exact science."

cellent preliminary training for the mind but are "of no benefit to us after we have mastered them." They are "a gymnastic of the mind and a preparation for philosophy"; they increase our aptitude for mastering more important subjects. Young men should not, however, spend too much time with such "barren subtleties" nor "be stranded on the speculations of the ancient sophists" who argue about the number of elements in the universe. Such curiosities are "jugglers' tricks," and men who wish "to do some good in the world must banish utterly from their interests all vain speculations and all activities which have no bearing on our lives" (261–69).

Isocrates often repeats these ideas, and, although Plato himself constantly criticizes many similar types of specialization, Isocrates as rhetorician seems to be shadowboxing with the Academy throughout his works. What Plato ultimately desires is a dialectical discourse which may attain certainty by demonstration, while Isocrates defends a discourse that can persuade by probability. Plato seeks to escape, by means of dialectic, from a linguistic dependence upon the illusory association of sense impressions; Isocrates seeks a way to exist in, and to infer a conjectural order from, the psychological circumstances which constitute his awareness of events. As H. I. Marrou points out, the contrast in their intentions is similar to the distinction Pascal makes in the seventeenth century between the *esprit de géométrie* and the *esprit de finesse*.[9] When the mathematical mind tries to operate intuitively or the intuitive mind mathematically, their respective principles of order are confused in ways analogous to the disorder which results from the imposition of either philosophical or rhetorical discourse upon the other's subject matter. Both the philosopher and the mathematician, however, will tend to be more conservative and exclusive than the rhetorician and

---

[9] Marrou, *Histoire de l'éducation*, pp. 134–36. For Pascal, the *esprit de finesse* is a 'feeling' (*sentiment*), a 'sense' of a situation, based on experience. In anticipating his distinction, Isocrates shares something with Aristotle's view that ethical departures from the 'mean' must finally be judged by an act of individual perception (αἴσθησις) rather than by a fixed principle (*E.N.* 2.9.8). For general accounts of Isocrates' cultural and intellectual development see Jaeger, *Paideia*, 3:46–155 and Marrou, pp. 121–36. For his subsequent influence, see Marrou, passim, and H. M. Hubbell, *The Influence of Isocrates on Cicero, Dionysius and Aristides* (New Haven, 1913). Von Arnim describes the persistence of sophistic ideals—despite Plato's and Aristotle's attempt to break with them—even within the 'philosophical' schools, *Leben und Werke*, pp. 63–67. G. M. A. Grube, *The Greek and Roman Critics* (Toronto, 1965), comments very generally with regard to poetry on how "the two approaches, the philosophical and the rhetorical, continue side by side through the fourth century," how Isocrates combined them in his concept of general education (pp. 37–40), how Aristotle "may be said to have brought them together in the *Rhetoric*" (p. 102), and on how Cicero later defends general culture "in an age of over-specialization" (pp. 171–75). Grube's conclusion that "neither Plato nor Aristotle even attempt to define the nature of poetry" (p. 102) is perplexing in view of the subjects he discusses in relation to them.

the master of *finesse*. For, whereas one who attempts to persuade on the basis of probability will never decline to use a certainty in his favor, one who demonstrates a certainty cannot often admit an argument from probability.

B. Plato and Aristotle

As philosophy became associated with specialized learning, the liberal borders of philosophy and rhetoric, where each most nearly shared the intention of the other, fell under the protection of Isocrates and the continuing rhetorical culture. Despite Plato's own defense and practice of liberal forms of both rhetorical and philosophical discourse, dialectic remains for him primarily a method for defining essences. All other arts, he claims, have as their specific objects the opinions of men, or things that grow or are put together; even mathematical studies are rooted in their own premises (which are, in turn, rooted in phenomena), and cannot reach a knowledge of first principles. Only dialectic is free to discuss things as they exist prior to, and separable from, their appearances (*Rep.* 533BC). By grasping what is not subject to variation in their nature, it may escape the limitations of probability. Aristotle, on the other hand, substitutes a system of syllogistic logic for Plato's diaeretic dialectic. He develops the resources of reasoning and definition necessary for the establishment of propositions and for the analysis of proofs capable of defending them and, thereby, arrives at a more flexible method for gathering and organizing any body of knowledge however subject to the world of becoming it may be. As a result of its greater flexibility, he is able to adapt his method to rhetoric and the other arts of discourse.[10]

[10] Broadly speaking, Aristotle differentiates Platonic dialectic, which includes both inductive analysis and deductive demonstration, into (1) demonstrative reasoning from true premises, (2) dialectical reasoning (both inductive and deductive) from generally accepted opinions, and (3) eristic reasoning from opinions seemingly held in common (*Top.* 1.1, *Post. An.* 1.1, *Pr. An.* 1.1). Dialectical, as opposed to demonstrative, reasoning involves a process of interrogation with a real or imaginary opponent (77a33–34); it assumes premises which are either affirmative or negative (72a9–11) but which are always open to objection (76b25–26). F. Solmsen, *Die Entwicklung der Aristotelischen Logik und Rhetorik* (Berlin, 1929), p. 86, remarks: "Wie die Form des Sokratesdialoges und die paradigmatische Sokratesgestalt das ästhetische Korrelat der platonischen εἶδος-Konzeption sind, so sind die Pragmatien als λόγοι καθόλου das Korrelat zum aristotelischen καθόλου-Begriff und die Entwicklung vom Dialog zur Pragmatie läuft der vom εἶδος zum καθόλου bis in Einzelheiten hinein parallel." With respect to the *Poetics* Solmsen later observes: "I should not hesitate to say that the whole body of thought contained in chs. VII–IX has originated in the application of the Platonic εἶδος to the phenomenon of poetry . . . ," "The Origins and Methods of Aristotle's Poetics," *CQ* 29 (1935):198.

Within the boundaries of rhetoric itself, Aristotle offered an alternate system of discourse to that of Isocrates. Insofar as he attempted to make rhetoric into an art as logically coherent and teachable as his system of dialectic, he liberalized rhetoric by drawing it back toward philosophy away from more specialized and exclusively rhetorical techniques. As a result, whatever the similarities and differences between the two competing rhetorical systems,[11] one seems always to overhear Aristotle in conversation, not with Isocrates, but with Plato. The more the discipline of rhetoric approximates the discipline of philosophy, the more attention must be given to keeping them distinct and to defending rhetoric as a legitimate activity. Plato, having established the terms in which the validity of rhetorical and literary discourse had been questioned, determined the grounds on which Aristotle had to defend them.

When Ion tries to defend the sophistic view of poetry as a means of transferring useful knowledge (*Ion*, 536ff.), Socrates points out that in fact Ion has no specific knowledge, and hence cannot be said to practice art, since "each separate art . . . has had assigned to it by the deity the power of knowing a particular occupation" (537C).[12] Plato's assumptions are those of specialized discourse: poetry is to be judged by the accuracy of its content (538E), and the rhapsode has shown he has no claim to such accuracy. The same method of attack is directed against the sophists (*Protagoras*, 312E) and the rhetoricians (*Gorgias*, 459–60). Rhetoricians and sophists are identical (*Gorgias*, 520), and poets may be considered sophists in disguise (*Protagoras*, 316D). Aristotle's defense of the arts of discourse has one principal answer to all these assumptions: dialectic, rhetoric, and poetry (as implied in *Poetics* 25.1–7, 17–18) *should* have no specific subject matter. They are 'universal,' and are responsible to no particular science. Almost as a response to Socrates' complaint to Gorgias that rhetoric is not an art because it cannot offer any account of its own methods, of its own nature, or of any cause of its effects (*Gorgias*, 465A), Aristotle states that, on the contrary, rhetoric is "the faculty of observing in any given case the available means of persuasion"

---

[11] Isocrates, frankly distrusting any system developed to handle all occasions, had nothing comparable to Aristotle's proofs to offer to the orator. Though he probably confined the appeal to the emotions of the audience principally to the proem and epilogue, he would have appreciated Aristotle's great emphasis upon their manipulation, and he did insist with Aristotle upon the importance of the speaker's reputed character. Also, he would have applauded Aristotle's intention to supply a method for political oratory which the earlier manuals had slighted in the interest of forensic debate (see *Rhet.* 1354b22ff.; cf. 1418a21–36).

[12] Trans. L. Cooper in *The Collected Dialogues of Plato*, ed. E. Hamilton and H. Cairns (New York, 1963), p. 223. Not only does Ion lack the knowledge of a specialized content but a knowledge of the *art* of moving souls—psychagogia—itself as Plato describes it in the *Phaedrus* 269E–70A, 70E–72B.

and "this is not a function of any other art." Each other art can "instruct or persuade about its own particular subject matter" (*Rhet.*, 1355b26–36), while "neither rhetoric nor dialectic is the scientific study of any one separate subject: both are faculties for providing arguments" (1356a32–35).[13] Now, there are two types of 'lines of argument,' or topics: the general lines which belong properly to rhetoric and dialectic, and the special lines which "apply only to particular groups or classes of things." When this distinction is neglected, "people fail to notice that the more correctly they handle their particular subject the further they are getting away from pure rhetoric or dialectic." The proper general topic, such as 'the more or less,' will serve as a basis for either discipline, and, having no special subject matter, "will not increase our understanding of any particular class of things." The better one establishes the special topics, however, the nearer he comes to setting up a particular "science to which the principles thus discovered belong" (*Rhet.*, 1358a3–35; cf. 1359b9–19). Aristotle's distinctions are helpful in both describing specialized and unspecialized discourse and in revealing their importance in his argument with Plato.

The second general issue on which Aristotle responds specifically to Plato in his own terms has equal importance for the history of literary discourse, and that is the issue of probability. Plato's distrust of information gained both from the senses and from 'opinion' persists throughout his work. Neither of these sources of knowledge is capable of more than an approximation of truth; the verisimilar can never demonstrate more than probability, and the energetic mind must never permit the emotions to acquiesce in the probable. Even in the passages in the *Phaedrus*, which in so many ways offer an outline for Aristotle's art of rhetoric, whose 'demonstrations' are to be based as firmly as possible on those of dialectic (*Rhet.* 1355a3–19), Plato retains his vigilance. The student of rhetoric should be someone already in possession of the truth (*Phaedrus*, 260D); only opportunists, such as Tisias and Gorgias, thought that "probability deserves more respect than truth" (267A), and in a similar manner he criticizes other writers of forensic manuals. Subsequently, in an ironic fashion similar to Lucian's praise of rhetorical charlatans (*Professor of Public Speaking*), he praises the swiftest method of advancement: the young orator need not concern himself with ethical

---

[13] See von Arnim, pp. 67–70. F. Solmsen, "The Aristotelian Tradition . . . ," pp. 39–41, describes how Aristotle makes the *topoi* into 'forms' of argument rather than specific bodies of material. These forms are more abstract and general (καθόλου) than any achieved by previous rhetorical systems. For Cicero, as well, "they are not connected with any definite subject matter, and yet they are applicable to every subject" (p. 173). For the continued use of *topoi* in medieval sermons, see H. Caplan, *CP* 28 (1933):73–96, repr. with other important essays in *Of Eloquence* (Ithaca, 1970).

truth, nor with learning who are good and just men. In court nobody cares "for the truth about these matters, but only about what is plausible" and "probable." "Even actual facts ought sometimes not be stated, if they don't tally with probability; they should be replaced by what is probable, whether in prosecution or defense; whatever you say, you simply must pursue this probability they talk of, and can say good-by to the truth forever." The probable, furthermore, is only "that which commends itself to the multitude" (272D–73B). Although the multitude has confidence in probability because it is based on "a likeness to truth," in reality, such "likenesses can always be best discovered by one who knows the truth." And a man wise enough to know the truth will speak primarily not to sway his fellowmen but to please the gods (273D–74A). The listeners must be reminded of the truth, which has previously been "written in the soul," by "those lessons on justice and honor and goodness that are expounded . . . for the sake of instruction" (277E–78B). This attitude toward persuasion leaves little room for a concept of probability.[14]

In Aristotle, who constructs his rhetorical system upon a strict analogy with his logical system, the enthymeme, or rhetorical syllogism, reaches a probable conclusion from probable premises in the same way as the logical syllogism reaches a certain conclusion from certain premises in the demonstrative sciences. The man skilled in one will be skilled in the other since "the true and the approximately true are apprehended by the same faculty" and "the man who makes a good guess at truth is likely to make a good guess at probabilities" (*Rhet.*, 1355a8–18). Now most often the orator tries to persuade his audience to take one of several alternative actions, and, since all "actions have a contingent character," the premises of enthymemes will "be only usually true." Things which

---

[14] *Plato's Phaedrus*, trans. R. Hackforth in *The Collected Dialogues of Plato*. Socrates particularly insists on a knowledge of what is good and evil (260C). The rhetorician, therefore, must cultivate philosophy, since rhetoric, as an art which leads the soul by means of words (261A), requires a knowledge to do this (262B) which is achieved through "division" (263B) and an ordering of material (264BC) achieved through dialectic (265Dff.). To acquire the art of rhetoric, for which Pericles went to Anaxagoras (270A), it is necessary to be able to analyze the soul (270B) if one is to proceed scientifically (τέχνη), not merely by practice (τριβῇ) and routine (ἐμπειρίᾳ): "Since the function of oratory is in fact to influence men's souls, the intending orator must know what types of soul there are" (271D, 277BC). Such knowledge constitutes the *art* of rhetoric and in itself does not refer explicitly to the content of speeches (270E–71A). F. Solmsen, "Aristotle and Cicero on the Orator's Playing upon the Feelings," *CP* 33 (1938):402–4, discusses Plato's conception of "types of soul" (εἴδη ψυχῆς) as fixed, while Aristotle seems to see them as varying in accordance with the psychological states which the orator can bring about in his audience. For some early background for the relation of knowledge to art in the Augustan period, particularly with respect to Horace, see my article "Horace's 'Ut Pictura Poesis': The Argument for Stylistic Decorum," *Traditio* 34 (1978):58–64.

usually happen, however, which do not belong "to the class of the 'contingent' or 'variable,' " cannot be considered probabilities (1357a23–38). Of the four kinds of alleged fact upon which enthymemes can be based, the first, probability or "what is, or is supposed to be, usually true," can always be challenged by raising an instance to the contrary. But such an objection is frequently spurious in that it does not show that a premise is not probable but that it is not inevitable. The defendant is not to refute an accusation by proving "the charge is not *bound* to be true: he must do so by showing that it is not *likely* to be true." This likelihood will be more convincing the more "the thing in question *both* happens *oftener* as we represent it *and* happens more *as* we represent it" (1402b13–1403a2). Aristotle here analyzes and defends the "likely conjecture" which Isocrates could only justify by invoking the vaguely pragmatic authority of general experience. Futhermore, Aristotle's defense of the independence of rhetoric from a specific science and from the necessity of stating an inevitable or certain truth is fundamental to his defense of the mimetic arts, which Plato criticized principally for their confinement to verisimilitude. In the *Rhetoric* Aristotle argues against Plato for the philosophical validity of the verisimilar, which, we shall see, he develops in his theory of *mimesis* in the *Poetics* (*Rhet.*, 1371a30–71b12; cf. *Poet.*, 1448b5–19).[15]

C. Lucian: *The Double Indictment*

I should like to conclude these tentative considerations about the origins of literary discourse with the treatment of a dialogue by Lucian written nearly five hundred years after Aristotle's *Rhetoric*. Although Lucian lived in a world which had changed completely, not once but

---

[15] These generalizations with regard to discourse are consistent with Aristotle's intellectual development. Jaeger describes how in the early *Protrepticus* Aristotle accepted Plato's view of ethics and politics as theoretical sciences "proceeding *more geometrico*" and then later abandoned the ideal of mathematical exactness in his *Ethics* and *Politics* (*Aristotle*, pp. 82–88). With regard to the more specialized form of philosophical discourse (i.e. the more general definition), Jaeger says "Aristotle here [cf. *E.N.* II. 7, 1107a29] replies that the more general ethical propositions are the more empty and ineffective they are" (p. 85). The movement toward greater particular application in ethics corresponds to one toward unspecialized philosophical discourse. In his later period, this movement is reflected in his researches where "the individual is now almost an end in itself" (p. 328). Despite this, Jaeger stresses that he avoided the fragmentary Hellenistic antiquarianism, because, perhaps as a result of his Platonic inheritance, his method consisted of "applying the principle of form to the details of reality, the idea of the uniformity of nature" (p. 328). His aim was "all along to make the Idea capable of producing knowledge of appearances" (p. 381). He lived "not in the Ideal world but in the tension between Idea and experience" (p. 399).

many times, since the fourth century, if one considers the issues and the principles in accordance with which those issues are discussed, it is the continuity in the tradition of critical commentary which appears most significant. The social and political conditions of the second century A.D., which are reflected in a writer of the Second Sophistic such as Aelius Aristides, have little in common with those of the early sophists. Yet the culture satirized throughout Lucian's works is in many ways a composite of the worst characteristics pointed out from the time of Aristophanes.

The Double Indictment is particularly illuminating because, first, it is a theoretical defense of a new literary genre—the satirical dialogue—and, second, it is a criticism of conservative tendencies in the two rival disciplines of philosophy and rhetoric. It is, in other words, a kind of recapitulation in miniature of the process I have suggested for the emergence of literary theory itself. The dialogue opens with Zeus satirizing the commonplace that the gods live happily, free from care. One of his many harassments is his obligation to arbitrate in human litigations, and at the moment he has fallen behind in them. He, therefore, sends his daughter, Justice, with Hermes to set up a court to hear those cases "entered by professions or pursuits or sciences against men" (13).[16] Among those to be argued are "Intemperance *v.* the Academy *in re* Polemo: kidnapping"; "Stoa *v.* Pleasure: alienation of affections—because Pleasure coaxed away her lover, Dionysius"; "Painting *v.* Pyrrho: breach of contract," and "Oratory *v.* the Syrian [Lucian]: neglect. Dialogue [Dialectic] *v.* the same: maltreatment." When it comes to Lucian's trial, Oratory is the first to speak against him (26ff.). Oratory found Lucian as a boy wandering in Ionia, trained him, and finally married him. She then accompanied him on lucrative lecture tours through Asia and Greece, Italy and Gaul. Once rich, he leaves her "for that bearded man in the mantle, Dialogue, who is said to be the son of Philosophy" (28). As a result, Oratory complains, "he has curtailed the freedom and the range of my speeches and has confined himself to brief, disjointed questions." Instead of speaking in a powerful voice, "he fits together and spells out short paragraphs" for which his audience, instead of applause, can but manage a smile or a sigh. In his self-defense Lucian admits the facts of his education and marriage, but he justifies his desertion on the grounds that Oratory became corrupt, soliciting lovers wherever they went, so that he was forced to divorce her. Furthermore, it was time that a man already forty years old should leave the strenuous

---

[16] *Lucian*, trans. A. M. Harmon, LCL, 8 vols. (London, 1921) 3:109. For a similar defense of his attempt to combine philosophy with comedy, see *To One Who Said "You're a Prometheus in Words,"* 6:417–27.

active life and go to the Academy or Lyceum "to walk about with . . . Dialogue," conversing "quietly without feeling any need of praise and applause" (32). The judgment is decided in Lucian's favor.

Dialogue next makes his accusation (33ff.). He would prefer not to make "a long speech, but to discuss the matter a little at a time," as is his practice. He will speak in the customary way of the courts, however, even though he is "completely uninformed and inexperienced in such matters." This allusion to the Socratic *Apology* is the first of several to Plato's works, which reveal clearly the context of Lucian's defense. "I was formerly dignified," continues Dialogue, "and pondered upon the gods and nature and the cycle of the universe, treading the air high up above the clouds where 'great Zeus in heaven driving his winged car' sweeps on." Lucian (in his satires) has dragged him down from "heaven's back" and broken his wings.[17] He has removed the tragic mask and made Dialogue speak satirically in the manner of the comic poets, "mocking all that is holy and scoffing at all that is right." Dialogue, furthermore, has been turned into a mixed form of prose and verse, and, made up of different elements, looks like a centaur. Lucian's defense is important, and in it one can hear the ancient criticisms made by Isocrates in his *Against the Sophists*. When I began to use Dialogue, Lucian says, "he was still dour . . . and had been reduced to a skeleton through continual questions." He seemed "awe-inspiring" but in no way "agreeable to the public," so I made him walk "on the ground like a human being," clean himself up, and smile. Then "I paired him with Comedy" to attract those listeners "who formerly feared his prickles and avoided . . . him as if he were a sea-urchin."

I know, however, what hurts him most. It is that I do not sit and quibble with him about those obscure, subtle themes of his, like "whether the soul is immortal," and "when God made the world, how many pints of pure, changeless substance he poured into the vessel in which he concocted the universe," and "whether rhetoric is the false counterpart of a subdivision of political science, the fourth form of parasitic occupation." Somehow he delights in dissecting such problems, just as people like to scratch where it itches. Reflection is sweet to him, and he sets great store by himself if they say that not everyone can grasp his penetrating speculations about "ideas."

He "demands those wings of his and gazes on high without seeing what lies at his feet." Lucian again wins the judgment.

The fact that Lucian is trying to define a particular kind of satiric dialogue is not as significant as the fact that he must distinguish and

---

[17] The editor notes that these are allusions to Aristophanes' *The Clouds* (l. 225) and to Plato's *Phaedrus*, 246E and 247B.

defend it, as a form of literary discourse, from both rhetoric and philosophy. Although he criticizes the imitators of Plato's dialogues and the epideictic speeches of the rhetorical sophists, he, nevertheless, implies what can be utilized from both. In turning the instrument of dialectic sharply against the popular image of the most specialized form of philosophy, he, nonetheless, is retaining the philosophical, or at least ethical, justification which literary satire had always claimed. By the same token, once rhetoric could be freed from the restricted cult of form and professionalism of the Second Sophistic and more general human concerns could deepen the emotional responses of listeners to their immediate circumstances, rhetoric could engage them emotionally more effectively than philosophical precept. These were, in other words, the most liberal objectives of both philosophy and rhetoric in the fourth century B.C. With respect to subject matter and style, Lucian conceives of literary discourse in a terminology explicitly borrowed from its two strongest original competitors and excludes the conservative characteristics which have remained peculiar to them.

2. The Hypothesis of Literary Discourse

THE VALIDITY of the following discussion of fiction (*poesis*) does not depend upon the historical existence of the conditions just described as potentially congenial to the formulation of a theory of literary discourse. Yet the subsequent appearance of certain terminologies renders the prior existence of the conditions increasingly probable. It now becomes possible, for instance, to substitute relatively technical terms, found in the early writers themselves, for the more cumbersome phrases I have previously used to distinguish types of discourse. The terms 'thesis' and 'hypothesis,' for example, and the corresponding Latin terminology generated by them, *positio* and *causa, quaestio indefinita* or *generalis* and *quaestio definita* or *specialis*, and the rhetorical exercises of the *suasoria* and the *controversia* all reflect, it will be seen, to a greater or lesser degree their origins in philosophical, rhetorical, and mathematical discourse. Both theses and hypotheses, furthermore, have their more specialized and less specialized forms, and these, in turn, bring into the Latin tradition a critical vocabulary upon which a literary theory continues to be developed in order to cope with problems latent in the terms themselves. Since, as in the very beginning, this vocabulary is still primarily borrowed from other disciplines, one must select those uses with care which are most pertinent to literature. To do this it is first necessary to clarify the terms 'thesis' and 'hypothesis' in the disciplines of philosophy and rhetoric.

For both disciplines the word 'thesis' means a 'stand' or 'position' and is translated *positio*; 'hypothesis,' whose Latin form is *suppositio* (*sub + ponere*), means a 'placing under,' and, by extension, 'what one has placed under,' or a 'subtending.' Philosophy, however, begins its investigation with a thesis (or problem) which is 'given' to be verified (or resolved), while rhetoric begins its investigation with a hypothesis or specific set of circumstances or case (*causa*) which is 'given' to be judged. Philosophical inquiry analyzes its given thesis into its *under*lying hypothetical *archai* (be they premises, elements, or causes) which, once discovered and redisposed in division and synthesis, will verify the original thesis which may then be regarded as a demonstrated conclusion. Rhetorical inquiry, on the other hand, analyzes its given hypothesis into theses (be they general propositions, questions, or definitions) which, once revealed, may be used to interpret the original, insufficiently differentiated, circumstances in order that we may judge them. In sum, philosophy seeks to verify its given thesis by analyzing it into the hypothetical components or premises which may subsequently succeed in demonstrating it. Rhetoric seeks to judge its given hypothesis by analyzing its circumstances into theses in terms of which judgment, and subsequently an 'action,' becomes possible. Except for the inversion of the terminology—in that philosophical analysis begins with a thesis while rhetorical analysis begins with a hypothesis—their general procedures of inquiry and demonstration are similar. Whether we begin with the given philosophical thesis or with the given rhetorical hypothesis, we return to it in the end through a process of analysis and synthesis.[1]

In his *Adversus geometras* (1–6) Sextus Empiricus distinguishes the use of 'hypothesis' in literature from its use in rhetoric and in the physical and mathematical sciences toward the end of the second century A.D. Sextus introduces his attack upon geometers by observing that they were habitually forced to defend their conclusions by seeking refuge in hypotheses. Before attacking such a method, he differentiates three of the principal meanings of the word.

In one sense it means the *peripeteia* (or "argument" or "plot") of a drama, as we say that there is a tragic or a comic "hypothesis," and certain "hypotheses" of Dicaearchus of the stories of Euripides and Sophocles, meaning by "hypothesis" nothing else than the *peripeteia* of the drama. And "hypothesis" is used with another signification in rhetoric, as investigation of particulars, in which sense the sophists are wont to say often in their discourses, "One must posit the hypothesis" (οἱ σοφισταὶ πολλάκις εἰώθασιν ἐν ταῖς διατριβαῖς λέγειν "θετέον ὑπόθεσιν"). Moreover, in a third application we term the starting-point of proofs (ἀρχὴν ἀποδείξεων) "hypothesis," it being the postulating something for the purpose of proving something.

---

[1] Although designating the initial circumstances which appear 'on the surface' so to speak, rhetorical hypotheses may, nevertheless, be said to *under*lie something else in two senses. First, since (in order to be understood and judged) the hypothesis is ultimately to be considered a species of the genus thesis, the *sub* will, in the end, carry the meaning of having been placed under a more inclusive heading (or headings) and of sharing characteristics, indicated by that heading, with other species. Second, the given initial situation may be said to *support*, like a foundation, the legal investigation itself in that it is the reason (*arche*) for pursuing all subsequent inquiry into the events.

This third use of 'hypothesis' we would loosely call 'scientific' today. Sextus gives as examples of it three hypotheses from medicine used by Asclepiades to demonstrate the initial condition which produces fever, the first of which examples Galen also refers to as a 'hypothesis' (*Nat. Fac.* 80). Despite the cognitive intention of disciplines which are, like medicine, related to 'physics,' Sextus is stressing here the 'formal' procedures of demonstration, which for our purposes I have included under 'mathematical' discourse. Indeed, Sextus continues by saying that this third meaning is "the 'hypothesis' which the Geometers adopt when they wish to prove anything geometrically (γεωμετρικῶς ἀποδεῖξαι)." Such a hypothesis corresponds to Aristotle's definition of a 'beginning' (ἀρχή) as "the point from which a thing (πρᾶγμα) is first comprehensible . . . *e.g.* the hypotheses of demonstrations (ἀποδείξεων αἱ ὑποθέσεις)."[2]

Sextus distinguishes here, then, the hypothesizing functions in literary discourse of the dramatists, in rhetorical (and perhaps philosophical) discourse of the sophists, and in 'arithmetical' discourse of the geometers. The third function of "postulating something for the purpose of proving something" else—a beginning, as Aristotle says, "from which a thing is first comprehensible"—is the most comprehensive and, in a sense, includes the others. In positing both the existence of something and the principles of order by which that thing achieves coherence and becomes intelligible, the hypothesis of geometry remains latent in, and may thus coordinate, the hypotheses of the other discursive disciplines. For drama, composition 'begins' with the *given* sequence of events to be interpreted; for rhetoric, investigation 'begins' with the particular *given* circumstances to be judged; and for philosophy, inquiry 'begins'

---

[2] *Sextus Empiricus*, trans. R. G. Bury, LCL, 4 vols. (Cambridge, 1933–1949), 4:245–47; Aristotle, *Metaphysics*, 1013a16–18, LCL, 2 vols. (London, 1968). Of Plutarch's three original categories of discourse, Sextus mentions only the mathematical and the rhetorical explicitly; the philosophical appears to have dropped out. Yet, as exemplifications of rhetoric, the 'diatribes' of the sophists suggest the inclusion of philosophical materials along with the "investigation of particulars" by the rhetoricians proper. If the word "sophist" does not refer to both moral philosophers and rhetoricians, Sextus may be including the philosophical use of hypothesis among the "number of different senses" which he refers to in the same passage but does not discuss. One of the most useful discussions of the hypothesizing functions of all mental processes, particularly of reflection (διανοεῖσθαι), is that by J. Klein, *Greek Mathematical Thought and the Origin Of Algebra*, trans. E. Brann (Cambridge, Mass., 1968), pp. 69–79 (hereafter cited as *Greek Mathematical Thought*). Klein reminds us that "we must not overlook the fact that the procedure by 'hypothesis' stressed by Plato is *not* a specifically 'scientific' method but is that original attitude of human reflection prior to all science which is revealed directly in speech as it exhibits and judges things" (p. 73), a statement which might serve as an epigraph for Part One of this study.

with the particular *given* problem to be understood. Literature, that is, utilizes postulated beginnings and principles of coherence, most clearly illustrated by geometry, as consistently as rhetoric and philosophy. In each case, the self-consistency of mathematical demonstration lends, like a common denominator, its structural stability and coherence to rhetorical, philosophical, and literary arguments. Insofar as such demonstration may serve as a common denominator, it may formally coordinate the judicative intention of rhetoric and the cognitive intention of philosophy, along with their subject matters, with the 'poetic' intention of literature. To make the ligatures of this coordination clear, I wish to show in this chapter what the mathematical function of hypothesis has in common with the hypotheses of rhetoric, philosophy, and *poesis* respectively.

In the first of the following four subsections, I need describe the relation between the hypotheses of geometry and of rhetoric only briefly, since I shall treat the formal structure of rhetorical argumentation in detail in Part Three of this study. The second subsection takes up the formal hypothesizing function of geometrical analysis in relation to the cognitive hypothesis of moral dialectic. The third subsection shows what the geometrical hypothesis, which posits certain conditions for the construction of a proof, shares with the literary hypothesis of the dramatic outline, which posits certain characters and events for the construction of a plot. The fourth subsection of this chapter illustrates how mimetic probability makes this form of representation palpable and persuasive. Since mathematics emerges here as the coordinator of the three categories of disciplines mentioned by Plutarch of which it is one, its function may be mentioned first from now on in referring to the formal, cognitive, and judicative objectives latent in the poetic analysis of experience.

A. The Rhetorical Hypothesis

In the quotation just cited, Sextus defines the scientific or geometrical hypothesis as "the starting point of proofs (ἀρχὴν ἀποδείξεων)" which postulates something for the sake of proving something else. As I suggested there, he may be recalling Aristotle's definition of a beginning as the point from which a thing first becomes comprehensible of which the hypotheses of demonstration might be regarded as examples. When Quintilian comments upon what geometry contributes to rhetoric and to its circumstantial materials of the rhetorical hypothesis, it is precisely this demonstrative function of formal dialectic which he emphasizes.

A knowledge of geometry, Quintilian says, is obviously necessary in legal disputes over boundaries and measurements,

But geometry and oratory are related in a yet more important way than this. In the first place logical development (*ordo*) is one of the necessities of geometry. And is it not equally a necessity for oratory? Geometry arrives at its conclusions from definite premises (*ex prioribus*), and by arguing from what is certain proves what was previously uncertain. Is not this just what we do in speaking? Again are not the problems of geometry almost entirely solved by the syllogistic method, a fact which makes the majority assert that geometry bears a closer resemblance to logic (*dialecticae*) than to rhetoric? But even the orator will sometimes, though rarely, prove his point by formal logic. For, if necessary, he will use the syllogism, and he will certainly make use of the enthymeme which is a rhetorical form of syllogism. Further the most absolute form of proof is that which is generally known as linear demonstration (γραμμικαὶ ἀποδείξεις). And what is the aim of oratory if not proof? Again oratory sometimes detects falsehoods closely resembling the truth by the use of geometrical methods. (1.10.37–39)[3]

In addition to its contribution of formal coherence to argumentation, geometry rises "to the consideration of the system of the universe (*ad rationem usque mundi*): for by its calculations it demonstrates the fixed and ordained courses of the stars" (1.10.46), and thereby we learn that nothing happens without order and a cause (*inordinatum atque fortuitum*). Geometrical reasoning, then, helps to order the disparate events, both human and divine, of the rhetorical hypothesis into a coherent interpretation.

When the hypothetical method of scientific demonstration, which postulates something for the purpose of proving something else, is brought to bear upon the miscellaneous materials in the rhetorical hypothesis of

---

[3] *Institutio Oratoria*, trans. H. E. Butler, LCL, 4 vols. (London, 1953). In commenting on Plato's *Laws* (690A), W. Jaeger points out that the word 'axiom' itself originally meant a " 'claim to own' in the juristic sense" and only toward the end of Plato's life acquired the meaning of "an assumption which cannot be proved but does not need proof, and which is used as a point of departure in a scientific train of reasoning." It is interesting that the axiom, which, like the formal intention of fiction, is both an assertion of existence and a principle of order, should, as Jaeger goes on to say, retain its earlier connotation: "So we must take the mathematical meaning of 'axiom' here, because Plato is discussing the general principles on which politics is based. That does not exclude the first sense, 'claim to possess.' For 'axiom' in the mathematical sense too is a claim or a demand, which is self-explanatory: that is, the original legal sense is still alive in the word," *Paideia*, 3:235. A. Michel explicitly emphasizes the assertion of existence in the narrative structure of rhetorical hypotheses: "Ainsi, rien n'est plus lié à la dialectique qu'un récit. Mais d'autre part, comme il décrit des faits particuliers, comme il insiste surtout sur leur existence, il se déroule dans la conjecture et dans l' 'hypothèse,' " *Rhétorique et philosophie chez Cicéron, essai sur les fondaments philosophiques de l'art de persuader* (Paris, 1960), p. 230.

a given case, a fictional supposition may often be the most convenient 'starting point of proofs.' Quintilian, in fact, speaks of *argumenta* drawn from fictional suppositions (καθ' ὑπόθεσιν) in the same way as a scientist might speak of his assumptions or a dramatist of the *argumenta* of his plots: "when I speak of fictitious arguments I mean the proposition of something (*proponere aliquid*) which, if true, would either solve a problem (*quaestionem*) or contribute to its solution" (5.10.95–96). The solution of a 'question'—philosophical or rhetorical or both—by means of a fiction, 'posited' like the *archai* of a geometrical proof, suggests the ways in which the formal, cognitive, and judicative hypotheses combine their energies in the literary hypothesis of fiction. The fictional *argumentum* can realize potentialities for analyzing human experience not present in the three principal categories of discourse, taken individually, which it utilizes.

The use of 'hypothesis' in a literary context is not restricted to summary or outline, but has gradually come to refer to fiction itself or rather to the historically important type of fictional narrative, the verisimilar. Sextus himself states this elsewhere when he says "fiction (πλάσμα) is the narrating things (πραγμάτων) which are not real events but are similar to real events (ὁμοίως δὲ τοῖς γενομένοις) in the telling, such as the hypothetical situations in comedies and mimes (ὡς αἱ κωμικαὶ ὑποθέσεις καὶ οἱ μῖμοι)."[4] Such supposed situations are 'hypothetical' in that they are 'posited' and, on the basis of verisimilitude, are accepted temporarily as saying something about what is real. Similarly, Quintilian says (4.2.53) that the narration of the 'facts' in a legal case may depart from the truth provided that they are given a verisimilar "air of credibility, as is done in comedy and farce (*ductus rei credibilis, qualis in comoediis etiam et in mimis*)." If the account of events has sufficient coherence and the judge accepts the first part as true, he will anticipate and accept the later part whether it be true or not.[5] In fact, since it is as hard "to make the

----

[4] "Against the Grammarians," 263, *Sextus*, 4:149. Sextus is repeating here the Hellenistic distinction between the historical narrative of true events (ἱστορία), the narration of things like truth (πλάσματα), and the legend which has no relation to truth at all (μῦθος). Plutarch divides mimes into *hypotheseis* with prolonged action and much stage equipment and *paignia* or farces which apparently were briefer, simpler, and more licentious (*Mor.* 712E). For the earlier literary uses of 'hypothesis,' see Appendix A.

[5] Compare *De inv.* 1.19 and 1.33. The reverse is also true since in the *narratio* we should "present the outcome in such a way that the facts that have preceded can also be known, although we have not spoken of them" (*Rhetorica ad Herennium*, 1.14, trans. H. Caplan, LCL [London, 1964]). The narration, furthermore, must be handled with equal care when it is true as when it is fictitious (1.16). For Cicero, as well as Quintilian, *narratio est rerum explicatio et quaedam quasi sedes ac fundamentum constituendae fidei* (*De part. orat.* 31). He makes interesting distinctions between geometrical and philosophical demonstration in accordance with which the rhetorical and poetic argument might more closely resemble the former (*Tusc.* 5.18; cf. *De off.* 3.33).

judge believe what we say when it is true as it will when it is fictitious"
(4.2.34), either a *ficta narratio* may be used for exciting emotion (4.2.19)
or the 'historical' order of events may be altered for purposes of coherence
and effect (4.2.83). The principal requirements are that the fiction chosen
must not violate the known (given) facts nor, whatever its digressions,
a rigorous self-consistency (4.2.89–96). As we shall see, Aristotle recognizes similar requirements in his *Rhetoric* (3.16) and *Poetics*.[6]

Rhetoric, then, may draw upon the deductive power of the geometrical
hypothesis in order to give a persuasive interpretation of the disparate
contents of a particular case. Since these contents include, as Quintilian
says in reporting the views of Apollodorus, "a combination of persons,
circumstances of place and time, motives, means, incidents, acts, instruments, speeches, the letter and the spirit of the law," we should
"understand a *cause* in the sense of the Greek *hypothesis*" (3.5.17–18).
In order to establish premises for a 'deductive' demonstration amid such
random products of 'inductive' observation, the orator may make use
of fictional suppositions (καθ᾽ ὑπόθεσιν) to provide *archai* or points of
departure for constructing his arguments. Such fictional premises must,
equally, be presupposed before the outlined *argumenta* of dramatic hypotheses can become finished works of literature which are both fictitious
and require principles for ordering an indeterminate number of particular
events and details according to probability or necessity.

In Latin the initial situation or rhetorical hypothesis is called the
'definite question' (*quaestio definita*). The orator must first interpret the
initial situation by analyzing it into 'indefinite questions' (*quaestiones
indefinitae*) or theses, and then, in order to make a case for a given
interpretation, he must synthesize the results of the analysis into a
persuasively coherent argument for presentation in court. In Part Three
I shall discuss the rhetorical functions of hypothesis and thesis in detail
as well as their formal contribution to persuasive argumentation which
Quintilian has compared to the contribution of geometry. Here I wish
only to show how these functions reflect the competing rhetorical and
philosophical intentions which, as I pointed out in the preceding chapter,
were present in the origins of literary discourse itself. The rhetorical
balance of formal, cognitive, and judicative obligations analogous to that
of literature suggests how literary theory might be able to survive, almost
parasitically, in the more specialized discipline of oratory.

[6] In addition to passages cited in Part Three and the bibliography given in Appendix A,
pp. 371–81, on the use of the historical and fictional example, see Aristotle's *Rhet.* 1.2,
2.20; *Prob.* 18.3; *Rhet. ad Alex.* 1428a25–26, 29a25–27, 38b1–5, 39a1–12; *Rhet. ad Her.*
4.2–6, 62ff. and Caplan's notes; Cicero, *Top.* 44f.; *De inv.* 1.49, 2.118; *De part. orat.*
40; Quintilian 5.11.1–35, 12.4.1–2. For the rhetorical distortions of history for emotional
effect, see *Brut.* 42–43.

In Quintilian's concise treatment of the terms (3.5.5–18), definite questions, which the Greeks call "hypotheses (ὑποθέσεις)" and the Romans call "causes (*causae*)," involve facts, persons, times, and similar circumstances (*sunt ex complexu rerum, personarum, temporum, ceterorumque*).[7] These questions not only belong to the province of rhetorical discourse but are associated primarily with the most specialized, the forensic, type rather than with the less specialized, the deliberative, type of rhetoric. Indefinite questions, on the other hand, which the Greeks call "theses" and the Romans call "propositions," may be argued on either side (*in utramque partem*) without any reference to specific persons or circumstances. Since they concern either general civic obligations (*quaestiones universales civiles*) or philosophical issues (*philosopho convenientes*), they arise primarily within the context of philosophical discourse. Cicero, he says, distinguishes two kinds of theses, one concerned with knowledge (*scientia*), such as "Is the world governed by providence?" and one concerned with choosing a course of action (*actio*), such as "Should we enter politics?" The cognitive thesis tends to be more specialized and abstract than the practical thesis which holds, therefore, a 'liberal' position in philosophy comparable to the deliberative, rather than forensic, debate in rhetoric. The practical thesis shares, that is, the ethical, even political, concerns of deliberative oratory.

Quintilian, in fact, posits a third alternative falling between the practical thesis of philosophy and the suasorial theme of rhetoric which holds that middle ground most congenial to the formation and preservation of a theory of literature. Indefinite questions, he says, "which have no connexion with particular persons are generally given a specific reference." The question " 'Ought we to take a share in the government of our country?' is abstract" (*simplex* = ἁπλόος). But if we ask whether we should do this while a tyrant is in power, we add a specific reference which tacitly implies both a definite person (*subest velet latens persona*) and a tacit "admission of time and quality" (*subestque et temporis et qualitatis tacita vis*). The location of a general issue in "time and quality"—that is, in circumstances which define when and what kind of thing has happened—resembles the construction of a fiction: the thesis is particularized in hypothesis but not so far as to become either a given

---

[7] As a commentary on this passage, see J. Cousin, *Études sur Quintilien* (Paris, 1936), 1:173–75. The most conservative form of rhetoric, the *quaestio definita*, represented the principle of individualization as well as history. Cf. Minturno, paraphrasing Aristotle: "Onda il Poeta a guisa di Filosofo riduce la cosa al genere, ed alla natura universale; l'Istorico, sicome l'Oratore, quando tratta le cause, al particolare descende," *L'Arte Poetica* (1563, repr. in Naples, 1725), p. 39.

specific case or a true historical account.[8] One can also reverse the direction. By moving from disparate particulars back toward a thesis, it is possible to reveal a meaning in the context of specific events, a way of 'making something of them,' which has not previously been apparent.[9] There are some, Quintilian continues, who regard questions "which have reference to persons and particular cases" as theses: "for instance, if Orestes be accused, we shall have a *cause*: whereas if it is put as a question, namely 'Was Orestes rightly acquitted?' it will be a *thesis*"

[8] Adrianus Turnebus comments on Quintilian's description of this "middle ground" (quoted from *M. Fabii Quintiliani de Institutione Oratoria . . . per Petrum Burmannum*, Ludg. Bat., 1720, p. 232): "Medium quoddam genus inter *thesin & hypothesin* ponere videtur, nulla singulari definitaque persona conclusum, ad aliquid tamen referri, id est latentis temporis vel personae angustiis contineri, ut, *an resp. administranda in tyrannide.*" The fact that Aphthonius includes this 'middle genus' in the casuistic exercise of his *progymnasmata* called "the proposal of a law" (discussed in Part Three of this study) emphasizes its importance for both legal and literary fictions. The use of fictions in law is treated by Hans Vaihinger, *The Philosophy of 'As If,'* trans. C. K. Ogden (London, 1924), pp. 33–35; L. L. Fuller, *Legal Fictions* (Stanford, 1967), which has an extensive bibliography on Vaihinger's discussion (pp. 94–96); O. Barfield, "Poetic Diction and Legal Fiction," *Essays Presented to Charles Williams* (London, 1947), pp. 106–27; and E. Kantorowicz, "The Sovereignty of the Artist: a Note on Legal Maxims and Renaissance Theories of Art," *Selected Studies* (New York, 1965), pp. 352–65. Kantorowicz comments that "fiction was rather something artfully 'created' by the art of the jurist; it was an achievement to his credit because fiction made manifest certain legal consequences, which had been hidden before or which by nature did not exist. For by fiction the jurist could create (so to speak, from nothing) a legal person, a *persona ficta*—a corporation, for example—and endow it with a truth and a life of its own; or he could interpret an existing body, such as the *corpus mysticum* of the Church, in the sense of a fictitious person, and gain a heuristic element by means of which he might arrive at new insights into administration, property rights, and other conditions" (p. 355). So Sidney, arguing the right of the poet to use fictional names to give "a conceite of an actuall truth," asks in *An Apology for Poetry*: "And doth the Lawyer lye then, when vnder the names of *Iohn a stile* and *Iohn a noakes* hee puts his case? But that is easily answered. Theyr naming of men is but to make theyr picture the more liuely, and not to builde any historie; paynting men, they cannot leaue men namelesse. We see we cannot play at Chesse but wee must giue names to our Chesse-men; and yet, mee thinks, hee were a very partiall Champion of truth that would say we lyed for giuing a peece of wood the reuerend title of a Bishop" (*Elizabethan Critical Essays*, ed. G. G. Smith [Oxford, 1904], 1:185–86). It is interesting that in the next century Sidney's argument for fictional names and his specific legal examples are used by John Wallis, in his *A Treatise of Algebra* (London, 1685), to explain François Viète's reference to algebraic letters for indefinite magnitudes as *species* and attributes this term to Viète's background in civil law (J. Klein, *Greek Mathematical Thought*, p. 321, n. 10). W. Jaeger, however, points out that such geometrical terms as 'axiom' were originally understood in a juristic sense of making a claim of ownership. See above, Chap. 2, nn. 3, 9, 38; Chap. 14, n. 12, and Appendix A, n. 10. This discussion of hypothetical names is relevant to ὀνόματα ἐπιτιθεμένη of Aristotle's *Poetics*: see pp. 50–55 of this chapter.

[9] Turnebus observes how these two movements can function together: "*Theses*, ut docuit Fabius, pleraeque ad deliberativum pertinent genus, & adjectis modo personis, suasoriae fiunt, nam deliberationis initium ducitur *ab hypothesi*, sed postea revocatur *ad thesin*: atque ita interdum de toto genere disceptamus, cum tamen causa pendeat ab *hypothesi*" (*Quintiliani de Institutione Oratoria . . . per Burmannum*, p. 232).

(3.5.11). One might rephrase the example: if we simply ask how it can be proved that Hamlet killed Claudius, we can expect a dramatized trial or detective story, but if we ask whether he is justified in killing Claudius, we include more of the materials of the completed play.[10]

The orator may move into this middle ground, then, from either direction—from the unlimited applicability of the generic thesis or from the delimited specification of the individual case. If, on the other hand, he moves outward from the middle in either of these directions toward its respective extreme, he will no longer be able to perceive a principle of order in the random details of a particular case clearly enough to render them comprehensible. It may be for this reason that Quintilian rephrases his observations which were cited previously. One may also, he says, call indefinite questions (*infinitae*) general (*generales*) and definite questions (*finitae*) special (*speciales*). But if one does so, he must, nevertheless, remember that "in every special question the general question is implicit, since the *genus* is logically prior to the *species* (*in omni autem speciali utique inest generalis, ut quae si prior*)." This intrusion of general considerations is most likely to occur when qualitative issues enter the case. As we shall see in the third part of this study, "The Quality of Fiction," it is when 'quality' enters the case that fictional suppositions become most useful in eliciting and controlling the feelings of the audience.[11]

---

[10] See G. Reichel, *Quaestiones Progymnasmaticae* (Lipsiae, 1909), p. 62: "Cuius περιστάσεως partes sunt sex, quibus adiectis θέσις in ὑπόθεσιν mutatur vel, ut planius dicam, quaestio infinita fit causa finita. Hermagora quoque teste sine circumstantia 'ulla omnino controversia non potest esse,' nam circumstantia est, 'quod hypothesin, id est controversiam efficiat.' " Reichel is quoting St. Augustine, *De Rhetorica* in *Rhetores Latini Minores*, ed. C. Halm (Lipsiae, 1863), p. 141. For a helpful account of the early development of theses and hypotheses, particularly as a background for later rhetorical practice, see Reichel, pp. 10–11, 27, 97–107; D. Matthes, *Lustrum* 3 (1958); and S. F. Bonner, *Roman Declamation* (Berkeley, 1949), pp. 1–26. Matthes points out that even in Hermagoras a thesis often presupposes some circumstantial controversy and vice versa. A thesis about matricide in general is not totally lacking in *personae*: "ihr liegt vielmehr ebenso wie der ὑπόθεσις ein πρόσωπον zugrunde, jedoch im Gegensatz zu dieser, bei der es sich um ein πρόσωπον ἰδίαν ποιότητα ἔχον (ὡρισμένον) handelt, ein πρόσωπον κοινὴν ποιότητα ἔχον (ἀόριστον). Danach kann man sagen, dass der Hauptunterschied zwischen θέσις und ὑπόθεσις in dem κοινῶς bzw. ἰδίως ζητεῖν zu suchen ist," p. 126. Matthes adds that "In diesem Sinne unterscheidet schon Aristoteles das καθόλου und das καθ' ἕκαστον (κατὰ μέρος) ζητεῖν, ohne dass bei ihm in diesem Zusammenhange schon die Bezeichnungen θέσις und ὑπόθεσις gebraucht wären" (p. 126, n. 1). One of the examples of καθόλου he cites from the *Poetics* (1451b6).

[11] Quintilian says (5.10.95–99) "that arguments are drawn not merely from admitted facts, but from fictitious suppositions, which the Greeks style καθ' ὑπόθεσιν" and that such "suppositions are also exceedingly useful when we are concerned with the quality of an act (*verum eadem fictio valet et ad qualitates*)." Quality introduces a generic consideration into a particular case and fictional hypotheses are useful where quality is concerned: the implication is that fiction may be a good means of investigating the generic

B. The Hypotheses of Geometry and Moral Dialectic

In the beginning of his attack upon geometry (*Adv. geom.*, 1–17), Sextus sets apart the rhetorical and dramatic usages of 'hypothesis' in order to concentrate upon those hypotheses behind which the geometers take refuge. These are suppositions which are temporarily assented to without a necessary belief in their 'truth' for the purpose of reaching or demonstrating a further conclusion. His criticism of geometrical suppositions bears upon the history of literary theory because it offers a simple and adulterated form of the Platonic distrust of verisimilitude and of the probability of fictional premises to anybody wishing to attack the arts. For Sextus, a supposition is either true or false. If it is true, let us state it as a conclusion and not "postulate it as though it were not true." If, on the other hand, it "is false, no help will emerge from the hypothesis," because from such "rotten foundations" no principles of inquiry can emerge. Conclusions, furthermore, are not made reliable by the logical consistency with which they proceed if their original premises are undemonstrated. Sextus has no patience with probability.[12] And similarly with regard to fiction, he states that grammarians who explain verisimilar or legendary narratives in poems to students really have no profession "since there exists no art which deals with things false and unreal" (*Adv. gram.*, 265). Despite Plato's insistence in the *Sophist* that linguistic arts can indeed deal with 'the false,' his criticism of poets, rhetoricians, and professional explicators of literature (*Prot.* 339ff.) for lacking a definable subject matter echoes clearly across the centuries. It is not surprising that a skeptical philosopher would restate the charge that the sophistic tradition had no specific body of knowledge to teach, but the similarity of the charge to that against geometry, a technical discipline, has importance for fiction.

---

implication of any particular situation. For Hermagoras' analysis of 'quality,' see D. Matthes, *Lustrum* 3 (1958):147–64. Kantorowicz describes how the civil law 'imitates' the natural law as the artist imitates nature for medieval jurists. "The art of the legislator, however, though determined by the general natural law, has to 'adinvent' the *particulare* of the positive law ('Ius positivum . . . est per industriam hominum adinventum')—that is, the particular application of the general law of nature to a limited space and a limited time— yet in such a fashion that the *particulare* still reflected the *generale* of the law of nature" (Kantorowicz, "Sovereignty of the Artist," pp. 355–56). The invention of the *particulare* was often of a fiction. See Appendix A.

[12] In "Against the Rhetoricians" (60–71), Sextus attacks the aim of persuasion by defining "credible" in three senses: belief in something true, in something like truth (verisimilar), and in something both true and false. The second sense (the probable) is a belief in what is false but which we are deceived into believing in; its validity is no greater than simple error, and it is more dangerous than error. For further attacks on the probable, see "Against the Logicians," 1.166–89, and "Outlines of Pyrrhonism," 1.226–31.

Among the objects treated by the arts those treated by geometry, such as straight lines, circles, and relations of angles, and solid objects generated by these forms, Plato says, possess a beauty and give a pleasure which is "pure (καθαρός)." By "pure" Plato means those forms (and the pleasure derived from them) "the want of which is unfelt and pain-less, whereas the satisfaction furnished by them is felt by the senses, pleasant, and unmixed with pain" (*Philebus* 51BC).[13] Consequently, those productive arts will be most excellent and give the purest pleasure which depend most securely upon accurate measurement, such as house-building (56B). Even here one must evaluate less highly "the arts of reckoning and measuring as they are used in building and in trade when compared with philosophical geometry and elaborate computations (φι-λοσοφίαν γεωμετρίας τε καὶ λογισμῶν καταμελετωμένων)" (56E–57A). In such a comparison the latter work, done by the 'scientific' geometer, is "immeasurably superior in accuracy and truth about measures and numbers" to the former work, done by the merely "arithmetical and metrical" artist (57CD). The description of beauty in terms of meas-urement and proportion and of its relation to the good later in the dialogue passes into the Christian traditions, where geometric principles, in accordance with which God has made and adorned the universe, become the foundation of aesthetics.

In the *Republic* Plato describes the most profitable studies as those able to "draw the soul away from the world of becoming to the world of being" (521D),[14] and these most often are concerned with calculation and the nature of number. They must, however, direct "the soul up-ward," compelling it "to discourse about pure numbers," not those "attached to visible and tangible bodies" (525D). Accordingly, the proper study of geometry must go beyond its practical applications in construc-tion and surveying and pursue "the knowledge of that which always is, . . . of the eternally existent," drawing "the soul to truth" (527AB). Similarly, the astronomer's objective should be not the observation of the actual physical bodies, but the contemplation of their forms of mo-tion. The visible patterns of stars may aid us in the study of permanent movements but only in the way that "diagrams drawn with special care and elaboration by Daedalus or some other craftsman or painter" can. "For anyone acquainted with geometry who saw such designs would admit the beauty of the workmanship," but he would not expect to find there any permanent mathematical truths (529DE). Therefore, since

---

[13] *Philebus*, trans. H. N. Fowler, LCL (Cambridge, 1952).

[14] *The Republic*, trans. P. Shorey, LCL, 2 vols. (Cambridge, 1946). This translation is used in the text unless otherwise indicated. For the development of Plato's hypothetical method, see R. Robinson, *Plato's Earlier Dialectic* (Ithaca, 1941), esp. pp. 97–191.

sensory data, derived either from physical objects themselves or from diagrams, can never do more than approximate the permanent world of ideas, Plato places dialectic, which functions independently of sense impressions, above even the mathematical arts. Geometry is only a "dreaming about being," for it cannot leave the assumptions it employs nor give any account of them. And where the starting point (ἀρχή) is unknown, the argument and its conclusions can never yield a true knowledge or science. Dialectic is the only process of inquiry that, "doing away with hypotheses (ὑποθέσεις)," founded on sensory data, can advance to first principles and find confirmation there (533CD).

Plato distinguishes these 'scientific' hypotheses, which must find their beginnings in sensory experience and be asserted arbitrarily as self-evident, from a type of hypothesis dialectic itself can use. The distinction emerges in his important description of the categories of knowledge in the sixth book of the *Republic* (509D–511E). He first divides apprehensible entities into the visible and the intelligible and then subdivides each of these categories into two. These four categories are conceived as a hierarchy of entities, based upon the degrees of clarity and certainty with which they can be perceived, which begins with the lower half of the visible objects and culminates in the upper half of intelligible objects. The lowest category is composed of 'images,' the objects of conjecture, such as reflections upon water; the second consists of actual objects, animate and inanimate, which have the power to cast such reflections and which form the material of belief or opinion: these two classes constitute visible entities. The third and fourth categories contain intelligible entities. The third has the same relation to the second as the second to the first; that is, it treats as its images those objects of the second class which, in turn, cast their images to form the objects of the lowest class. The third category, containing the objects of the demonstrative sciences, is under the control of the understanding. The fourth category consists of first principles, the objects of reason, which, independent of sensory data, works solely with ideas. It is in order to clarify the difference between the third and fourth categories that Plato distinguishes the types of hypothesis used in a scientific discipline like geometry from the type used in dialectic.

As examples of the third category of entities, which are objects of the understanding, he suggests those postulates which geometers take as self-evident assumptions (ὑποθέσεις). Without offering any demonstration of these, they pursue "the inquiry from this point on consistently," and make use of visual diagrams, even though they are not concerned with the figures themselves but with what they represent: "The very things which they mould and draw, which have shadows and images of themselves in water, these things they treat in their turn as only images, but what they really seek is to get sight of those realities which can be seen only by the mind" (510CE). The mind, then, can attain this category of the 'understanding' by employing hypotheses, but it cannot proceed "to a first principle because of its inability to extricate itself from and rise above its assumptions" and because "it uses as images or likenesses the very objects that are themselves copied and adumbrated by the class below them" (511A). The fourth class of entities, however, is

That which the reason itself lays hold of by the power of dialectics, treating its assumptions not as absolute beginnings but literally as hypotheses, underpinnings, footings, and springboards so to speak, to enable it to rise to that which requires no assumption and is the starting-point of all, and after attaining to that again taking hold of the first dependencies from it, so to proceed downward to the conclusion, making no use whatever of any object of sense but only of pure ideas moving on through ideas to ideas and ending with ideas. (511BC)

Dialectic is, therefore, more accurate than the "arts and sciences whose assumptions are arbitrary starting-points," since these arts contemplate intelligible truths but depend still upon the evidence of the senses. This third category of entities, the geometer's realm of the understanding, is "something intermediate between opinion and reason" (511D).[15]

Although in his early explanation of dialectical demonstration Plato drew upon the analogy of the hypothetical demonstrations of geometry (*Meno*, 86E–87B), here the differences are very clear. Dialectic pursues first principles and alone knows how to discover them. The scientific arts of geometry, astronomy, and calculation, still rooted in sensation, know only how to hunt for knowledge in the shadows of experience, to use Plato's metaphor (*Euthydemus*, 290BC), and must yield their prey— even those truths they discover beyond their diagrams—"to the dialecticians to use properly,"[16] as huntsmen give their game to cooks. All such arts, as Socrates warns again in the *Phaedo* (92D), which base their

[15] Jaeger comments that because mathematical arts "abstract the truth from sensible objects and try to see the essence of the mathematical objects . . . with the eyes of the mind, they are very close to the highest philosophical methods of reaching knowledge. But on the other hand they are tied to the world of sense and the stage of knowledge which is appropriate to it (i.e. opinion) in two ways: (1) they start with hypotheses built around sensible figures, although their theorems do not really concern the visual images at all; (2) they do not attempt, in principle, to rise above these hypotheses which are taken as true ('adopted'), and because they follow them out logically right to the last possible deduction, they are forced to treat them as principles (ἀρχαί) at the same time" (*Paideia*, 2:289–90). On the functions of hypothesis with respect to the categories of the Divided Line, see J. Klein, *Greek Mathematical Thought*, pp. 69–79.

[16] *Euthydemus*, trans. W.R.M. Lamb, LCL (London, 1924).

demonstration on mere probability, threaten the certainty of dialectic. As those of poetic fictions, their constructs lie in the 'middle area' between the realms of the intelligible and the sensible. For Plato, this area is a "space" which receives images, a principle of location (*Tim.* 51D–52C) which it is necessary to postulate before reflections of the eternal principles can be perceived, however dimly, in the sensory world. This location entertains a fluidity of forms, apprehended as "in a dream" of space and time where a corporeal world exists that can only be described, according to John Burnet, in mythological language. Like the inadequate dialectician confined to this location, the geometer also, Plato says (533C), can only dream of being; and, later, Neoplatonists, like Proclus, felt that Euclid dealt with a realm between the intelligible and sensory worlds, ominous and shadowy, apprehended by the imagination.[17] For our purposes it is by means of a common analogy with these 'intermediate' constructs of geometry[18] that we can see the relation of fictional *argumenta* to dialectical demonstration. That is, it will be seen that the analogies between the formal hypothesis of geometry and, on the one hand, the dramatic hypothesis and, on the other, the cognitive hypothesis elucidate the relation of literature to philosophy.

One need not wait for the Neoplatonists to associate this world of the geometers with the dreamlike world of the imagination. Aristotle himself carefully explains the relation between images and diagrams (*De mem.* 1).

It is impossible even to think without an image. The same process occurs in thinking as in drawing a diagram; for in this case although we make no use of the fact that the magnitude of a triangle is a finite quantity, yet we draw it as having a finite magnitude. In the same way the man who is thinking, though he may not be thinking of a finite magnitude, still puts a finite magnitude before his eyes, though he does not think of it as such. And even if its nature is that

---

[17] John Burnet, *Greek Philosophy: Thales to Plato* (London, 1924), p. 344. For the historical development of the idea of spatial 'location' in the memorial and imaginative faculties, see Francis A. Yates, *The Art of Memory* (Chicago, 1966). For the many variations of the idea of the imagination as an intermediary between the sensible and intelligible worlds, see M. W. Bundy, *The Theory of Imagination in Classical and Mediaeval Thought*, Univ. of Ill. Sts. in Lang. and Lit. 12 (Urbana, 1927), esp. pp. 45, 96f., 117ff., 148–50, 158–59, 170–71, and Edgar De Bruyne, *Études d'esthétique médiévale* (Brugge, 1946), esp. 2, Chap. 5: "*L'esthétique des Victorins.*" For geometry as a discipline of this intermediate location and its relation to the imagination in Proclus, see Chap. 8, pp. 203–10 of this study. For St. Augustine, as well, both the 'suppositions' of literary fictions and of geometrical diagrams belong to the province of the imagination (see Chap. 2, n. 46).

[18] On the disagreement between Plato and Aristotle concerning the independent existence of such intermediate constructs, see W. D. Ross, *Aristotle's Metaphysics* (Oxford, 1958), 1:166–68. For a general summary of the problem, see Ross' *Aristotle* (London, 1966), pp. 157–59.

of a magnitude, but an unlimited one, he still puts before him a finite magnitude, but thinks of it as a magnitude without limit.[19]

The whole internal world of the imagination is viewed of necessity as one of arbitrarily imposed delimitations of space, which recalls Plato's *Timaeus* (51–52) and looks forward to the development of the art of memory in which images are assigned to geometrically conceived areas. The process of giving imaginary magnitudes to things we think about is certainly prerequisite to imagining a sequence of actions in time.[20] In the *Poetics* (chap. 7) temporal magnitude is compared to the spatial magnitude of animate creatures; the duration of dramatic action is a function of the memory ("such as can be easily remembered as a whole") as the magnitude of a beautiful creature is a function of vision. Time is to space as memory is to visual image.[21]

The crucial implication is that images and diagrams are necessary to thought. In the simplest sense, lines in a diagram are fictions: a one-inch line does not literally represent a length of one inch but any length the draftsman designates. For Plato, the necessity of such diagrams is one of the great weaknesses of geometry, for, like the mimetic arts, the figure must utilize actual objects, even though the geometer's intention is to describe the relationships of which the objects themselves in the diagrams are imitations. In contrast to Plato, Aristotle defends the validity of the hypothetical diagrams and their dependence on appearance and probability, in a way similar to that by which he defends fiction in

[19] Translated by J. H. Randall in his *Aristotle* (New York, 1965), p. 96. Aristotle gives a similar argument in *De anima* 3.7; 431b2–20. Ross comments that "Aristotle seems here to be setting himself against Plato's view, expressed in the Divided Line . . . ," *Aristotle*, p. 148.

[20] Of Aristotle's admiration for Homer's powers of visualization, G. F. Else comments that "the poet's abstract conception, the σύστασις τοῦ μύθου, is translated into words" by the imagination. *Aristotle's Poetics: The Argument* (Cambridge, 1963), p. 502. In objecting to the interpretation of Aristotle's view of poetry as a representational 'copy' of life, R. S. Crane stresses the psychological nature of the object itself which is imitated: "The object imitated is internal and hence strictly 'poetic' in the sense that it exists only as the intelligible and moving pattern of incidents, states of feeling, or images which the poet has constructed in the sequence of his words by analogy with some pattern of human experience such as men have either known or believed possible or at least thought of as something that ought to be," *The Language of Criticism and the Structure of Poetry* (Toronto, 1953), p. 56. As stated here, however, such a psychological 'internalizing' of the objects of imitation suggests a later context of ideas in the developments traced by E. Panofsky, *Idea*, trans. J. Peake (Columbia, S.C., 1968) or M. W. Bundy, *The Theory of Imagination in Classical and Mediaeval Thought*.

[21] Else observes that "in Aristotle's theory of vision the size of the thing seen and the time required to see it *are* interconnected. Magnitude, motion, and time are strictly correlative: *Phys.* 4.11.219a10; ibid. 12.220b15; 6.2.233a10. . . . Hence there is an 'imperceptible time' corresponding to the imperceptible magnitude" (p. 285, n. 10). See Chap. 2, n. 17 above. The 'organic' comparison is Plato's (*Phaedrus* 264C).

the *Poetics*, in the *Prior Analytics* (1.41; 49b33–50a4). He points out that there is no absurdity in the schematized diagrams of syllogisms, for "we do not base our argument upon the reality of a particular example; we are doing the same as the geometrician who says that such-and-such a one-foot line or straight line or line without breadth exists when it does not, yet does not use his illustrations in the sense that he argues from them."[22] That is, we "use the setting out of terms (ἐκτίθεσθαι) as one uses sense-perception," not as necessary conditions of demonstration, like premises, but as illustrations. It is not necessary that the illustrative example be true in itself for it to utilize our sensory experience and signify an order within it. In the *Posterior Analytics* (1.10; 76b24–77a4) Aristotle states that a hypothesis (ὑπόθεσις) cannot be that which is "in itself necessarily true and must be thought to be so." On the contrary,

Hypotheses consist of assumptions from which the conclusion follows in virtue of their being what they are. Thus the geometrician's hypotheses are not false, as some have maintained, saying that one should not make use of falsehood, and that the geometrician is guilty of falsehood in asserting that the line which he has drawn is a foot long, or straight, when it is not; the geometrician does not infer anything from the existence of the particular line which he himself has mentioned, but only from the facts which his diagrams illustrate. (76b37–77a3)[23]

The critics of geometric diagrams mentioned here are probably the Platonists referred to with respect to geometry in the fourteenth book of the *Metaphysics* (1089a20-26) in which Aristotle criticizes Plato's theory of Ideas. The connection between the justification of the hypothesis in the arts and sciences, which Plato felt it the ultimate duty of dialectic to destroy,[24] and that of a fiction based on probability may be further clarified by considering how the process of geometrical analysis is reflected in dialectic itself.

How the geometrical hypothesis, regarded as a coordinating analogy, may reveal something of the relation between fiction and dialectic, and by extension between fiction and philosophical discourse, is suggested by studies in Greek mathematical and logical terminologies.[25] In the

---

[22] *Prior Analytics*, trans. H. Tredennick, LCL (Cambridge, 1938). It is precisely these 'non-existent' hypothetical concepts that Sextus attacks.

[23] *Posterior Analytics*, trans. H. Tredennick, LCL (Cambridge, 1960). Cicero offers an early defense of fiction as an illustrative example in his *De officiis* (3.39) which is analogous to this justification of geometric diagrams. See pp. 278-79 of this study.

[24] John Burnet defends this extreme rendering of ἀναιροῦσα τὰς ὑποθέσεις (pp. 228–30).

[25] Particularly useful are the studies of F. M. Cornford, H. D. P. Lee, B. Einarson, and R. Robinson referred to in the following notes. I have found Cornford's essay, "Math-

beginning of his consideration of Plato's dialectical ascent through the four categories of entities, F. M. Cornford remarks that "mathematics serves as the easiest bridge from the sense world to the intelligible, and should precede the study of moral Ideas" (p. 38). Mathematics, nevertheless, can rise no higher than the third category of intelligibility, the world of generalization and understanding. From this point it reasons downward deductively to its conclusion from premises assumed to be self-evident. Plato distrusted both the fragmentary variety and the indemonstrability of such hypotheses. Had he dealt with geometry, he probably would have found it necessary to consolidate the various hypotheses by moving upward to more and more inclusive ones, perhaps even to a single one, so that a complete science could be explained by subsequent deduction. He describes such an upward movement explicitly, however, only in his account of dialectic in distinguishing it from the mathematical disciplines (511B). "In mathematical proof," Cornford explains, "the mind 'travels' down through an argument limited by the premises assumed, 'as if the mind could not mount above its hypotheses.' . . . Dialectic includes an opposite movement of thought, upwards, 'treating its hypotheses not as principles but literally as hypotheses, positions laid down, like steps which discourse can mount upon and take off from [ἀλλὰ τῷ ὄντι ὑποθέσεις, οἶον ἐπιβάσεις τε καὶ ὁρμάς], in order that, advancing all the way to that which rests on no hypothesis—to the principle of the whole—it may apprehend that' " (pp. 42–43).[26] Yet it is curious, Cornford observes, that Proclus later seems to have associated Plato's dialectical ascent with geometrical procedures, an apparent paradox since the deductive mathematical proof lacks an upward movement. As an answer he suggests that Plato, in formulating his description of dialectic, might have been already drawing upon a process of reasoning available to him and later used by Aristotle in the analysis of a mathematical diagram.

Cornford summarizes Aristotle's uses of *diagramma*: (1) the given figure in which divisions exist potentially (before the straight line is divided and its parts assembled to form the figure); (2) the figure completed "by making the divisions actual and thus exhibiting the proof in

---

ematics and Dialectic in the *Republic* VI–VII," *Mind* 41 (1932):37–52, 173–90, the most valuable. Whether or not one accepts his central thesis explaining Proclus' comments on Platonic dialectic, which Robinson does not (*Mind* 45, pp. 464–73), the implications for fiction in the material he discusses remain forceful. Page references to his essay are given in my text.

[26] Cornford explains the metaphor as that of climbing a stair. "The primary and common meaning of ὁρμή is 'impulse' or 'effort' or 'impetus.' It is nearer to 'spring' than to 'springboard,' " p. 42, n. 2. For various interpretations of this 'upward' movement, see Robinson, *Plato's Earlier Dialectic*, pp. 162–91.

a picture, so that one has only to look at it to see the reason (prior truth) actually displayed in the construction itself"; (3) and "the proof whose 'elements' are so made obvious to inspection" (p. 45).[27] As in Plato's description of dialectical ascent and descent, in Aristotle both an upward (analytic) and a downward (synthetic) movement may be illustrated by the construction of a geometrical diagram, according to Cornford:

> Themistius [commenting on *Anal. Post.* 1.12] defines analysis as "assuming a true conclusion and then discovering the premises by which it is inferred." Where the problem is a construction, the geometer may start by contemplating a picture of the conclusion desired. In the *Meno* instance, he would draw the given rectangle and a triangle inscribed in the given circle, and then consider what properties his rectangle must have. Those properties are "elements" in the solution. Thus he takes the construction to pieces. The opposite process is *synthesis*, "putting together" this element and others in the proper deductive order. So Aristotle says that one may "analyse a diagram and not be able to put it together again" [*Soph. Elen.* 175a27]. Each step in the demonstration is a component "contained in" the complete *diagramma* (diagram, construction, proof). (pp. 45–46)

The entire process begins to resemble the construction of a dramatic plot.

To make this resemblance between plot and diagram clearer, I shall summarize the description of analysis and synthesis by the Euclidean commentator, Pappus, quoted by Cornford (pp. 46–48).

> Analysis is the procedure which starts from the desired conclusion, taken as agreed, through *the succession of sequent steps* (διὰ τῶν ἑξῆς ἀκολούθων—steps that in Analysis are traversed upwards, from each proposition to a prior proposition implied in it) to something agreed upon in Synthesis (some proposition previously proved and now admitted). For in Analysis we suppose (ὑποθέμενοι) the desired result to be already accomplished, and look for that (prior proposition) from which it results, and then again for the prior proposition leading to *that*, until, by tracing our steps backwards in this way, we meet with something already known or holding the rank of a first principle.

Synthesis reverses the process: " 'we take as already done the last step reached in the Analysis' " and follow the logical order down to the desired result. Analysis may be either theoretical (to prove a theorem) or problematical (to solve a problem of construction). In *theoretical*

---

[27] Cornford offers an illustration of going through these steps after which the geometer will "frame his demonstration in full discursive form—a deduction starting from the hypothesis, 'Let there be a triangle ABC' (*Eucl.* 1.32)," p. 45. The reader will find further useful commentary on the procedures of mathematical analysis and synthesis (to be treated next in this chapter) in J. Klein's *Greek Mathematical Thought*, pp. 163–68, 320–21, 345–47, and nn. 217–18, 235–37.

analysis, we assume the conclusion as existent and true; then through
steps, taken as true and hypothetically existing (" 'these assumptions
of existence are as yet unproved hypotheses awaiting confirmation in
the Synthesis' "), advance upwards till we come to something " 'admitted to be implied, as a necessary premiss or "element," in the conclusion we started from.' " The synthetic demonstration will then trav-
erse the same sequence of steps downward. In *problematical* analysis,

We assume the (construction) propounded as if it were known; and next advance
(upwards) through the sequent steps, taken as true, as far as something admitted
(a construction, possible or impossible, admitted to be a necessary element in
the desired construction). Then if (1) the admitted thing is possible and obtain-
able—"given," as the mathematicians say—the construction propounded will
be possible too, and once more the demonstration will correspond, in the reverse
order, to the Analysis; but if (2) we come upon something admitted that is
impossible, the problem also will be impossible.

In summary, Cornford writes that "the *problem* was something to be
done; its solution was the fruit of action (πράττειν) which brought out
into actual existence the elementary constructions divined by intuition
as latent in the given figure, and exhibited them in a completed diagram"
(pp. 48–49).

The revelation of the elementary construction, existing, latent, in a
given figure and its exhibition in a completed diagram offers an analogy
for the formal construction of a literary fiction. The writer senses the
possibility of an order, existing, latent, in the experience which he contemplates. By an intuitive act he selects those essential characters and
events, as the elements of his dramatic hypothesis or plot outline, necessary to demonstrate, subsequently in the written play, the order which
he originally sensed. While the plot outline corresponds to the elementary construction which the geometer intuits in the figure that he contemplates, the finished tragedy corresponds to the completed diagram.
The demonstration that the audience may acquiesce in the catastrophe
as probable or necessary corresponds to the demonstration that the observer may accept with confidence the integrity of the fully presented
geometrical proof.

The formal process in each case consists in analysis and synthesis.
The geometer's potentially intelligible figures contain within them the
(latent) principles or *archai* which will be able to explain them, as the
writer's potentially intelligible experience contains within it the (latent)
principles or *archai* which will be able to account for it. In analysis, the
mathematician works 'backwards' or 'upwards' to the necessary premises
(the hypothetical *archai* of his elementary construction) without which

his demonstration could not begin or proceed consistently. The writer, likewise, analyzes his experience by working 'backwards' or 'upwards' to the necessary premises of the dramatic hypothesis—that is, to the essential minimum of characters and events without which the action could not begin and evolve as he wishes it to do. (Such hypothetical outlines can subsequently be used again.) Once these initial premises are given and accepted in each case, the synthesis corresponds to the 'downward' or 'forward' deductive demonstration of how both types of 'action' work out. The working out and construction of the geometrical diagram is analogous to the final plotting and composition of the literary fiction.

The analogy so far between geometrical and literary analysis has emphasized the formal or demonstrative intentions of both disciplines. By turning now to the further analogy between geometry and moral dialectic and by regarding geometry as a common denominator between the formal procedures of dialectic and literature, we have a context in which to observe the heuristic intentions shared by the moral and the literary analyses of experience.

Cornford points out that for mathematics the intuition used in the "upward spring of thought is one of the meanings of *noesis*" and that the deductive descent of synthesis corresponds to one of the meanings of *dianoia* (p. 48). Recalling Plato's comparison of the reasoning by geometers to a dream (533B), he comments that

Their intellectual understanding of a coherent, but isolated, piece of deductive reasoning is *dianoia*; they will not "come to have *nous*" or genuine knowledge until they have gone up to intuitive apprehension of the indemonstrable principle of their whole science. . . . So long as bits of the structure are allowed to depend on questionable hypotheses, there will be an atmosphere of dimness and uncertainty in the state of mind. (pp. 50–51)

In the *Poetics* Aristotle defines *dianoia* or 'thought' as the third component in the composition of a tragedy and says that it consists in spoken arguments for or against a proposition. The fragmentary nature of *dianoia* is reflected in his caution against thinking of a drama as a string of "speeches expressive of character and well-turned expressions (λέξεις) and arguments (διανοίας)." However coherent in themselves, isolated speeches cannot be stitched together to make a unified play (1450a28–37). The unity lies, rather, in the plot, in the first principle or *arche* of tragedy by virtue of which the action becomes comprehensible. Plato (*Phaedrus* 268CE) and Isocrates (*Against the Sophists*, 16–17) make similar observations. The first principles of geometry, although grasped by *noesis*, remain rooted in the sensory realm and therefore fail to achieve any ultimate unity.

The first principles of moral dialectic, on the other hand, however analogous its analytical procedures may be to those of mathematics, is not prevented by the nature of its hypotheses from reaching a 'unified' conception of the ethical *problema* as a whole, of possible responses to it, and of their consequences. The heuristic analysis and synthesis of philosophy, that is, may reach and define a more inclusively significant truth about human experience than can be accounted for by the deductive premises of formal mathematical demonstration. In the same way, insofar as the dramatic plot, as a first principle, can render the total action comprehensible, literature achieves a unity and inclusiveness which assimilates and surpasses a purely formal self-consistency.

Benedict Einarson describes how the Socratic debate, as practiced in the moral dialectic of the Academy, "set up a statement, such as 'pleasure is good,' called θέσις or πρόβλημα, which was attacked by one party, the questioner, and defended by the respondent. . . . It is clear that the questioner would have to discover his arguments by a method exactly parallel to that of analysis in geometry: he would have to take the conclusion he wished to establish and work back from it until he reached a group of premises he felt sure would be acceptable to his interlocutor" (p. 37).[28] The object of moral dialectic is the definition of the Good, and the dialectician seeks such a definition, according to Cornford, by fighting his way through all the *elenchi* in his discourse. His objective here is not, as in mathematics, an assumption of existence, "but an inadequate tentative definition, *suggested* by the respondent, submitted to criticism by the questioner in the *elenchus*, and either amended or abandoned altogether. . . . Such suggestions are mere stepping-stones which are kicked away in the ascent to the correct definition" (pp. 181–82). A hypothesis is suggested about a definition by intuition; the questioner then 'deduces' with his *elenchus* until some consequence is arrived at which for some *other* reason is unacceptable. The respondent then suggests another definition, and the process continues through *elenchi* "by

[28] "On Certain Mathematical Terms in Aristotle's Logic," *AJP* 57 (1936):33–54, 151–72. Page references to this essay are given in my text. Einarson comments that the words θέσις and πρόβλημα were synonymous with the phrase τὸ ἐξ ἀρχῆς (p. 40). That the phrase was used for "begging the question" suggests "that Aristotle considered the conclusion as a starting point" (p. 39): "The 'begging' of the ἐξ ἀρχῆς is then originally the assumption (by use of the appropriate verb in the imperative) of the actual construction the problem is to establish, or of a construction only possible if the former is valid" (pp. 49–50). The procedure is that of analysis in general: "having the conclusion in mind, we determine what premises are necessary for its establishment" (p. 54). See Robinson, *Plato's Earlier Dialectic*, on Plato's elenchus (pp. 7–20) and its relation to the 'upward' movement of his hypothetical method (pp. 179–88).

using hypotheses as 'positions laid down for discourse to mount upon and take off from' in a series of leaps, each of which 'abolishes' the previous stepping-stone" (p. 183).

H. D. P. Lee, following Cornford, discusses other movements of moral dialectic that are parallel to mathematical analysis.[29] In pursuing a definition, "the dialectician must first, by seeing unity in a manifold, reach the genus (συναγωγή); and then by a process of division (διαίρεσις) define the species under consideration" (p. 119). The upward, intuitive movement attempts to reach a hypothesis about a generic quality; the downward movement (διάνοια) demonstrates whether or not this generic quality inheres in particular groups of individuals to distinguish them as species. Lee goes on to argue that Aristotle's method of arriving at first principles is adopted from the geometrical procedure of Socratic dialectic, and that both systems follow the general lines of mathematics (p. 123). Plato's distinction of the two movements, νόησις vs. διάνοια, corresponds to Aristotle's distinction of νοῦς vs. ἐπιστήμη (p. 120), but the important thing for our purposes is that Aristotle associates the intuitive νοῦς with a process of induction (ἐπαγωγή) which can reach first principles by means of universals (καθόλου) in both physics and ethics.[30] But whereas in physics, one instance may be sufficient to demonstrate a principle, in ethics many instances, drawn from experience, are necessary. It is by "repeated moral judgements we reach the ἀρχαί of ethics" (pp. 121–22).

It is for the purpose of reaching and demonstrating first principles that Aristotle developed the syllogism as a scientific method. Einarson says that "the analogy of this [method] with mathematical 'analysis' is clear: we have the reasoning, especially the conclusion, given: the problem is to find the syllogism which produced it. In this case Aristotle is using ἀνάλυσις of passing from the conclusion to the principle from which it is deduced, and thus connecting the conclusion with its source, and not primarily of the process whereby the reasoning is retraced" (p. 39). The purpose of this method is not to discover new facts; it is to find understandable *archai*, that is, hypotheses or causes, why the fact, with which we started, is as it is, why it follows from these premises as a conclusion. J. H. Randall comments that what is discovered is "not new facts, but the connection, the demonstration, the proof and expla-

[29] "Geometrical Method and Aristotle's Account of First Principles," *CQ* 29 (1935):113–24. Page references to this essay are given in my text.

[30] For the relation between the Platonic hypotheses in the *Republic* and the Aristotelian *archai*, see F. Solmsen, *Die Entwicklung der aristotelischen Logik und Rhetorik*, pp. 92–107.

nation.''[31] The *archai*, in explaining the 'reasons why,' will offer "a formalized science like Euclidean geometry" (p. 41). Aristotle selects hypotheses advanced by his predecessors, revises them, and then confronts the consequences directly derived from them with the facts. They are then perceived as the principles in the consequences of which we are able to see the meaning of factual situations. The mind sees them not "in isolation from the facts they explain," but "it 'sees' their truth in the subject matter" itself (p. 44). Of the three terms of a syllogism "the middle, *to meson*, is the 'reason why,' *to dioti*, the connecting link, between the conclusion and the premises," and science seeks, in supplying such links, "to trace such an intelligible structure between things" (p. 48).[32]

One can restate this syllogistic process in terms which offer an analogy with that of literary composition.[33] (*a*) By the time one actually begins to write, he would ordinarily have more or less in mind the essential facts (incidents or situations) capable of containing and generating the

---

[31] *Aristotle*, p. 40. Randall's third chapter, "Science as Right Talking: The Analysis of Discourse," esp. pp. 40–51, contains interesting implications for fiction.

[32] Ross describes how the 'middle term' becomes the essential cause in a syllogistic definition and how any one of the four causes "may function as the middle term whereby the existence of that whose cause it is is proved," *Aristotle*, p. 51. On causes, see also pp. 71–73. Earlier in my paragraph presently being annotated, Einarson compares syllogistic demonstration to mathematical ἀνάλυσις (*analysis, resolutio*). Analysis is the resolution of anything complex into its elements, according to the Oxford Dictionary, and in logic its specific function is to find out causes by their effects. There is an interesting use of the word, which may bear some of these technical implications, as well as those from grammar, in Spenser's account of the structure of the *Faerie Queene*. "Because the beginning of the whole worke seemeth abrupte and as depending upon other antecedents," it is necessary to explain that "an historiographer discourseth of affayres orderly as they were donne, accounting as well the times as the actions; but a poet thrusteth into the middest, even where it most concerneth him, and there recoursing to the thinges forepaste, and divining of things to come, maketh a pleasing analysis of all," *The Complete Poetical Works of Edmund Spenser*, ed. R. E. N. Dodge (Cambridge, Mass., 1908), p. 137. In order to 'resolve' the narration better, i.e. to reveal causes by recounting effects, the poet abandons the chronological order; he can thus reveal through analysis these "other antecedents" (i.e. 'premises' or 'causes' of the action when taken up) more clearly than the chronological order of the historian might be able to do. See the following note.

[33] Randall extends his analysis to drama: "In real life, in history, we can hardly discern *why* things have to be as they are: there are far too many complicated and chance or accidental factors. The universal that is implicit there does not stand out clearly. But in tragedy the poet can improve on nature, and show the inevitable dependence of destiny on character. He can make plain not the mere bare event, the 'fact that,' *to hoti*, but also the 'reason why,' *to dioti*: he can disclose how it had to be the way it was" (p. 290). W. K. Wimsatt and C. Brooks observe that "the terms *beginning, middle*, and *end* emphasize a specially close cohesion of causes" and resemble the syllogistic terms *major, minor*, and *middle*. They say, further, that, if one thinks in terms of enthymeme, "a counterpart of the syllogism in the realm of probability," the "events in a drama would yield not one but several middle terms, so that we should have the kind of chain of suspended syllogisms known as Aristotelian sorites" (*Literary Criticism*, [New York, 1967], pp. 30–32).

completed action. This initial sketch or skeletal plot may serve as the premise or hypothesis in which the conclusion as well as the beginning is 'given.' We are told that given circumstances led to given consequences for given (unspecified) persons. (b) The immediate question is *why*, and the 'middle' hypothetical premise or premises are 'discovered,' which reveal why things happened as they happened. The interconnections of the actions emerge as causes, revealed as 'qualities' and as feelings or motivations: 'an intelligible structure between things' is gradually traced. (c) At this point we have established both the initial premises of the skeletal outline (concerning *what* things happened) and the 'middle' premises of motive and choice (concerning *why* things happened as they did). We now arrive at the 'conclusion' but not the conclusion simply asserted in the outline of the initial hypothesis. Our conclusion now is that of a 'demonstration' that events happened as they might or ought to have happened, the demonstration that, granting our first premise, our 'middle' or explanatory premises are indeed as they ought to be. We can accept them and acquiesce in them, seeing that, in looking again from the catastrophe back over the action, they appear probable or necessary.[34] We approach here a concept of fiction as a consistent hypothetical construction in the sense that Aristotle can say that statements, however contrived, may be accepted as correct with respect to their hypotheses. In fact, a fiction may be regarded as such a statement forced to suit a hypothesis (*Meta.* 13.7, 1082b2–4, 32–33).[35]

[34] In his edition of the *Poetics* (Oxford, 1968), D. W. Lucas cites Dryden's dedication to *The Rival Ladies* (1664): "When the whole plot is laid open, the spectators may rest satisfied that every cause was powerful enough to produce the effect it had . . . till they [i.e. cause and effect] all reached the conclusion necessary" (p. 298).

[35] Lucian, *Hermotimus* (73–75), uses skeptical terms, often resembling those of Plato (*Rep.* 533C) and Sextus, to describe how "philosophers grant the premises (ἀρχάς) of the various systems and then believe everything that follows, supposing that the consistency you find, false though it is, is a proof of its essential truth." As illustrations of the power of consistency Lucian uses arithmetic—if someone claims twice five is seven "he will clearly go on to say that four times five is certainly fourteen, and so on"—and geometry: "in the beginning it presents certain monstrous postulates and demands that we consent to them though they cannot exist—for instance points without parts, lines without breadth, and so on—and on these rotten foundations it erects its structure and claims to demonstrate truths, in spite of the fact that it starts from a false beginning." The most detailed illustration, however, is drawn from poetic fictions. Suppose a poet "were to say that there was once a man with three heads and six hands, and suppose that you facilely accepted this without asking if it were possible, just believing, he would at once follow it up by filling in the details appropriately. . . . Who would disbelieve these details now—details which are consistent with the first outline? . . . Once you admit the premises the rest comes flooding in . . . and disbelief is difficult. . . . You go forward led by the consistency of what came after, not considering that things may be consistent and false" (trans. K. Kilburn, LCL, 6:397–99). Once again a passage from Lucian illustrates the continuity of the earlier terminology: in this case the explicit analogy between philosophical, mathematical, and fictional premises, on the one hand, and the psychological power of consistency in arguing from such premises, on the other.

C. The Dramatic Hypothesis: Aristotle's *Poetics*

The usage of 'hypothesis' for dramatic plot reflects the original meanings of its corresponding verbal forms as directly as its more specialized applications in mathematics, rhetoric, and philosophy. In his discussion of the term, John Burnet speaks of the early significations of the verb ὑποτίθεσθαι: "firstly that of setting before oneself or others a task to be done, and secondly that of setting before oneself or others a subject to be treated, in a speech, for instance, or a drama."[36] Although Aristotle does not use the noun 'hypothesis' in the *Poetics*, he uses its verbal forms to describe how a subject should be set out and treated in a drama. The phraseology carries associations of the usages pertinent to the other types of discourse which I have been discussing in Part One.

In the seventeenth chapter of the *Poetics* Aristotle describes the construction of both a drama and an epic. "The argument of the play," he writes, ". . . should be first drafted in general terms (ἐκτίθεσθαι καθόλου), then expanded with episodes,"[37] and he gives as an example the 'general outline' of *Iphigenia*.

[36] Burnet, *Greek Philosophy*, p. 162. Burnet continues: "This usage is as old as Homer, and by a natural extension the verb is freely used in Ionic of suggesting a course of action. That way of speaking accounts for Euclid's use of the word 'given,' and also of perfect imperatives like 'let there be given' (δεδόσθω). The original idea is that of a piece of work given out to be done, and the proposition accordingly ends up with a statement that it has been done." Burnet suggests that the material for ὑπόθεσις in Liddell and Scott might be rearranged to "be read in the order iii., iv., i.2, ii.2, ii.1" (p. 163). Robinson's general discussion of the root meanings of the word is helpful (*Plato's Earlier Dialectic*, pp. 97–117). He stresses the provisional nature of τίθημι itself, 'to posit,' and says ὑποτίθεμαι, 'to posit as a preliminary,' is the specialized variation nearest to the root verb (p. 100). He emphasizes that the 'positing' is generally with a view to future action and that the noun in Plato derives its meaning from its verbal form (pp. 102–3). The sense of 'something suggested' (ὑποτίθεσθαι τινι) to be discussed has a bearing upon the response of an audience, since Aristotle is very careful to describe it (*Post. an.*, 76b25–30) as something agreed upon temporarily, and hence it is "*relatively to the learner*, an hypothesis" (Lee, p. 116). Robinson observes that the word "often applied to the answerer's thesis" (*Plato's Earlier Dialectic*, p. 115). Cornford discusses this meaning in relation to mathematics (pp. 39–40) and quotes Sir Thomas Heath's definition: "the determination of the conditions or limits of the possibility of a solution of a problem." He notes that for Aristotle even a coin, as an agreed measure, may be "hypothetical" (p. 40, n. 2). The word λῆμμα has a variety of meanings closely approximating those of ὑπόθεσις. For its mathematical meanings, see Einarson, pp. 47, n. 63, 51–53, and for others Liddell and Scott. In *A Latin Dictionary* Lewis and Short give for *lemma* (λῆμμα): a subject for consideration or explication, theme, matter, subject, contents; a title of an epigram indicating a subject or the epigram itself; a story; an assumption of a syllogism (i.e. *sub falsa lemmatis specie latens*, A. Gellius, 9.16.7). These parallel sets of meanings testify not only to the repeated pattern of associations reflected in each word but perhaps beyond them to intellectual habits of ancient culture congenial to the emergence of the idea of fiction in the ways I have been describing.

[37] *Aristotle's Poetics: The Argument*, G. Else (Cambridge, Mass., 1963), p. 503. All

A certain girl has been sacrificed but spirited away from her sacrificers without their seeing how; she has been installed in another country, in which it is the custom to sacrifice all foreigners to the goddess, and has been invested with this priesthood. Some time later the priestess' brother happens to arrive (the fact that the god ordered him to go there [for what reason, is outside the "general"], and for what purpose, is outside the plot); and having arrived and been captured, is at the point of being sacrificed when he recognizes ⟨his sister⟩, [either the way Euripides made him do it or the way Polyidus did, saying as a man naturally might, "So, not only my sister but I too was destined to be sacrificed!"] and from that comes his salvation. After this, and not until then, one may assign the various names and expand with episodes (μετὰ ταῦτα δὲ ἤδη ὑποθέντα τὰ ὀνόματα ἐπεισοδιοῦν).

The 'outline' is a perfect example of a 'hypothesis,' and this is reflected in the verbal forms ἐκτίθεσθαι and ὑποθέντα which are related to the same root verb (τίθημι) as ὑπόθεσις. One is given the bare incidents without specific agents like the elements of a geometrical problem; names and motives, to be brought out in composition, are excluded for the moment.[38] The way for the poet, Else comments, is to "get a view of the general or 'universal' structure of his own plot" (p. 505) and to avoid having inappropriate episodes endanger the καθόλου "is to 'lay out' the story in abstract form, *without the names*" (which might tempt the poet into irrelevant narrative detail and speeches). "Everything that could or would happen only to the particular persons Iphigenia and Orestes is excluded by hypothesis and may only be brought in later, in the form of 'episodes' " (p. 506).[39] It is clear that the reasons *why* Orestes

references will be to Else's translation and commentary, unless otherwise assigned, and will be included in the text.

[38] Einarson's remarks upon the resemblance between the language of the *Prior Analytics* and mathematics are particularly relevant to this passage from the *Poetics*. With reference to 31a18ff. he says: "The first sentence here corresponds to Euclid's enunciation of the thing to be proved. The proof begins, as often in Euclid, with the third person imperative ἔστωσαν and the assigning of letters to the elements under discussion. For Aristotle's ἐπεὶ οὖν there are many parallels in Euclid, where it introduces the proof proper after the ἔκθεσις or assignment of the general elements of the enunciation to particular elements, diagrams with letters of the alphabet" (pp. 171–72). The word ἔκθεσις means that which is set out in a figure in geometry and in the setting out of a syllogism, "the most common meaning of the group of words ἔκθεσις, ἐκτίθεσθαι, and ἐκκεῖσθαι being that of taking numbers out of their context in the number scale and setting them out as terms in a progression or ἀναλογία" (p. 162). Taking numbers out of scale in order to establish a separate progression resembles the removal of events from the historical continuum and recombining them to suit a dramatic 'hypothesis.' The setting out of general elements of enunciation prior to the proof corresponds to drafting the argument of the play in a general, hypothetical outline—ἐκτίθεσθαι καθόλου to use Aristotle's phrase from the *Poetics*. The assigning of letters to the diagram suggests the addition of names. Sextus uses the term ἔκθεσις for setting forth matters of legend (μῦθος) and fiction (*Adv. Gram.* 263f.).

[39] After the description of the dramatic plot, virtually paraphrased later by Minturno among others (*De Poeta* [Venetiis, 1559], pp. 128–29), Aristotle gives an even more

comes to Tauris lie outside the general plot. Yet the reasons are very important to the finished construction. His landing in Tauris by accident must not be *left* as an (improbable) possibility; it must be *made* plausible by the reasonable account Orestes gives his sister in the form of a narrated episode. This feeling for 'connectedness' and for logical unity is strong enough to lead Athena to recapitulate his motivations at the end of the play.

The word ὑποθέντα, from ὑποτίθημι, carries the meaning of a 'placing under,' and, indeed, Bywater translates the phrase "after the proper names have been fixed as a basis for the story" and comments that "the proper names are required to . . . impart to it an appearance of reality."[40] The suggestion here is of a further and further 'hypothesization' or particularization in circumstance. Names are placed 'under' the hypothesis of bare events and become part of a more detailed hypothesis. After the names, the episodes are filled in, offering causes and establishing consistency with sequential connections, and as a result the action is 'hypothesized' still further.[41] The premises of a given action are followed by the premises of a given set of characters and, in turn, by given episodes which offer the reasons why, the *archai* of any intellectual investigation.

---

extreme summary of the *Odyssey*: "This is the core; the rest is episodes." In treating destructive arguments, his comments on hypothesis would not be out of place in the *Poetics*: "Now it is clear that he who makes the hypothesis makes the problem universal, though it is posited in a particular form; for he demands that the maker of a particular admission should make a universal admission, since he demands that, if an attribute belongs in a particular case, it belongs in like manner to all" (*Topica*, 3.6; 120a2–5, trans. E. S. Forster, LCL, [Cambridge, 1960]).

[40] *Aristotle on the Art of Poetry* (Oxford, 1909), pp. 51, 246. S. H. Butcher translates the sentence: "After this, the names being once given, it remains to fill in the episodes," *Aristotle's Theory of Poetry and Fine Art*, ed. J. Gassner (New York, 1951), p. 63. In discussing the relation of art to nature in Aristotle, T. B. L. Webster translates a passage on the growth of embryos from *On the Generation of Animals* (743b20–25) which applies well to the construction of a plot: " 'everything is defined first by outlines, and later takes on colours, hardness, and softness, just as if nature, who constructs it, were a painter. For painters first draw the lines and then cover the painted animals with colours,' " (*Art and Literature in Fourth-Century Athens* [London, 1956], p. 54).

[41] Webster relates Aristotle's biological conception of species to his assertion of the universality of poetry: "The theory is a direct answer to Plato; poetry is not an imitation of an imitation of a reality but creates a new reality, which is itself a union of individual and universal. I believe that Aristotle here views a play in rather the same way as he views Socrates or a particular house. Socrates is the universal, man (the species), realised and individualised by this matter. The particular house is the universal, house, realised and individualised by these bricks and mortar. The *Iphigenia in Tauris* is similarly a universal story realised and individualised by these episodes, verses, and names" (*Art and Literature*, pp. 55–56). That episodes may 'fill in' intermediate causes and thus articulate the universal was mentioned by Renaissance critics: for Bartolomeo Maranta the episode "does nothing else but extend and augment the plot and the universal by telling how what is summarized in the universal has come about" (quoted in B. Weinberg, *A History of Literary Criticism in the Italian Renaissance* [Chicago, 1961], p. 472).

The completed drama ultimately 'demonstrates' that the actions outlined can indeed be seen to happen with probability or necessity in accord with the middle terms of causation 'discovered' by the dramatist.[42]

The process of which Chapter 17 is an exemplification is described more theoretically and related to the central distinctions of the *Poetics* in Chapter 9. I shall quote the first fifteen lines.

From what has been said it is clear too that the poet's job is not to tell what has happened but the kind of things that *can* happen, i.e., the kind of events that are possible according to probability or necessity. For the difference between the historian and the poet is not in their presenting accounts that are versified or not versified, since it would be possible for Herodotus' work to be put into verses and it would be no less a kind of history with verse than it is without verses; rather the difference is this: the one tells what has happened, the other the kind of things that can happen. And in fact that is why the writing of poetry is a more philosophical activity, and one to be taken more seriously, than the writing of history; for poetry tells us rather the universals, history the particulars. "Universal" means what kinds of thing a certain kind of person will say or do in accordance with probability or necessity, which is what poetic composition aims at, tacking on names afterward (ὀνόματα ἐπιτιθεμένη); while "particular" is what Alcibiades did or had done to him. Now in the case of comedy this has become clear; for they construct the plot with the use of probabilities, then (and not until then) assign whatever names occur to them (συστήσαντες γὰρ τὸν μῦθον διὰ τῶν εἰκότων, οὕτω τὰ τυχόντα ὀνόματα ὑποτιθέασι), rather than composing their work about a particular individual as the "iambic" poets do.

It is probable that no passage in literary theory has encouraged more persistently the distinction between history, philosophy, and poetry. The distinction reinforces, by reiterating, the terms of the conjectural origins of literary theory discussed in Chapter 1. As Minturno was to

---

[42] Such an interpretation is borne out by a later use of ὑποτίθημι. Polybius criticizes the 'tragical' (i.e. rhetorical) histories of Phylarchus for their fictional additions which, he implies, would even be out of place in drama, since they aim more at sensationalism than plausibility: "Phylarchus simply narrates most of such catastrophes and does not even suggest their causes or the nature of these causes (περιπετειῶν, οὐχ ὑποτιθεὶς αἰτίαν καὶ τρόπον τοῖς γινομένοις), without which it is impossible in any case to feel either legitimate pity or proper anger" (*The Histories*, 2.56.13, trans. W. R. Paton, LCL, 6 vols. [London, 1922]). The cause or way something happened should be literally 'hypothesized' in order to move the emotions properly. Furthermore, it is insufficient to bring in exaggerated tales to explain why the causes are tragic (7.7.1–2, 6). B. L. Ullman (*TAPA* 73 [1942]:25–53, esp. 41) and F. W. Walbank (*A Historical Commentary on Polybius* [Oxford, 1957], 1:259–70) discuss Polybius' criticism of the 'tragical' school of history and the scholarship on the subject. In the Renaissance Antonio Riccoboni implies with Polybius that universality is revealed by means of articulated causation: "Poetry treats universal things; that is, it considers single facts universally or as they might have come about through many causes and in many ways" (Weinberg, *History of Literary Criticism*, p. 607).

say in the Renaissance, history and rhetoric both represent the principle of individualization as opposed to that of generalization represented by philosophy. Once a coherent structure of cause and effect, analogous to geometrical demonstration, has given its materials their form, literature holds in balance the objectives of all three categories of discourse mentioned by Plutarch. The equilibrium that it maintains expresses the experience of the total human personality, abstracted neither to formal self-consistency, to cognitive precept, nor to particular expediency.[43]

Of the phrase ὀνόματα ἐπιτιθεμένη Else comments that "the assignment of names to the characters is neither in accordance with the universalizing aim of poetry nor at variance with it, but simply *subsequent*" (p. 308). Both in this phrase and in the reference to adding names a few lines later, he emphasizes the arbitrariness of their selection: "The 'hypothesis' is what one tacks on after the fact, on top of the basic principles" (p. 309, n. 25). Bywater, on the other hand, again sees a 'subtending,' glossing ὑποτιθέασι as " 'lay down as a foundation,' so that the story may look like one founded on fact" (p. 191). Although it seems contradictory to refer to a foundation as 'subsequent' to a construction, a relation between the two interpretations emerges in Aristotle's discussion of the logical fallacy peculiar to fiction in Chapter 24 (pp. 622–23). Epic more than tragedy may employ wonderful episodes which are 'irrational.'

But Homer more than anyone else has taught the other poets also how to tell untruths in the right way. This is a matter of false reasoning. Namely people think that if a certain thing (B) exists or happens when another thing (A) exists or has happened, then if the second thing (B) is true, the first (A) must be true or be happening also (but it is untrue); hence they feel, if the first item is untrue but something else must necessarily be true or happen if it *is* true, ⟨that they⟩ must add it (A); for because we know that the later thing is true our mind reasons falsely that the first one is true also.

[43] For the early meanings of ἱστορία, see Pierre Louis, "Le mot ΊΣΤΟΡΙΑ chez Aristote," *Rev. de Philol.* 29 (1955):39–44. With regard to its usage in the *Poetics* Louis observes that "Il est d'ailleurs assez probable que ce sens de récit d'événement passé n'est qu'un sens dérivé. L'historien, avant d'être un narrateur de récits véridiques, est nécessairement un enquêteur qui cherche à s'informer" (p. 41). The primary emphasis is upon the empirical observation of particular events: history, "c'est la connaissance des faits particuliers à partir desquels s'élabore la science" (p. 44). The ἵστωρ, from οἶδα, "est celui qui sait pour avoir vu" (p. 43); the etymology continues in the Middle Ages (see H. de Lubac, *Exégèse Médiévale* [Paris, 1959], part 1, pp. 425ff.). For the early blurring of the distinction between history and poetry, particularly through the influence of tragedy and of Isocratean rhetoric, see B. L. Ullman, "History and Tragedy," *TAPA* 73 (1942):25–53. F. W. Walbank questions whether the Aristotelian distinction itself was representative of Greek historiographical attitudes at any time, "History and Tragedy," *Historia* 9 (1960):216–34.

Aristotle himself gives an example of this fallacy in his *De sophisticis elenchis* (167b1ff.): "if it rains, the ground is wet: the ground is wet: therefore it rains."[44] The point is that in terms of credibility, it is precisely the 'subsequent,' or in this case the consequent (B) which does lay a foundation of belief in what preceded (A), even if A is indeed false. In plot-construction, further particularization must always be subsequent to the initial premises of action. The added 'hypothesis' of names is "tacked . . . on top of basic principles," but at the same time in rooting the action deeper and deeper in circumstance the poet gives it a basis in experience which makes the initial premises more intelligible and persuasive. The process has analogies with the 'discovery' of the middle terms of *archai* in the syllogistic relation between philosophical assumptions—and their reflection in rhetorical enthymemes—as discussed in the preceding section.

This explanation of how the epic poet renders 'untruth' plausible introduces the clearest defense of the 'probable impossibility,' which Else stresses in his commentary should be resorted to only if 'irrational' incidents must be admitted as a last recourse (pp. 623–31). "One should," he translates (p. 623), "on the one hand choose impossibilities that are (made) plausible in preference to possibilities that are (left) implausible," and such impossibilities should be excluded from the plot proper and confined to episodes. A narrative becomes plausible by gaining causal connections.[45] That these connections should be fictional when others

---

[44] Translated by Butcher, *Aristotle's Theory of Poetry*, p. 172, n. 1, who explains the false inference as being based on the assumptions "that because a given thing is the necessary consequent of a given antecedent, the consequent necessarily implies the antecedent. Antecedent and consequent are wrongly assumed to be reciprocally convertible." Compare Lucian's statement in Chap. 2, n. 35 above, particularly "You go forward led by the consistency of what came after, not considering that things may be consistent and false." It is significant that Aristotle says that such "Reciprocation is more usual in mathematical problems, because mathematics never assumes an accident but only definitions." In such a case, "Let A be a real fact, whose reality implies that of certain other facts, e.g., B. which I know to be real; then from the latter I will prove the existence of A" (*Post. an.*, 78a7–12).

[45] One of the earliest extant discussions of comedy, the *Tractatus Coislinianus*, draws heavily upon this Aristotelian terminology. According to Grube's summary (*Greek and Roman Critics*, pp. 141–42, 144–49), laughter is provoked by verbal wit or by situation. Of the nine types of situations, three seem to be an intentional subversion of tragic coherence: (3) impossibility (ἐκ τοῦ ἀδυνάτου), (4) reaching a possible end through illogical means (ἐκ τοῦ δυνατοῦ καὶ ἀνακολούθου), and (9) lack of logical sequence (ὅταν ἀσυνάρτητος ὁ λόγος ᾖ καὶ μηδεμίαν ἀκολουθίαν ἔχει). L. Cooper sees these as conscious distortions of the structure of tragedy for purposes of humor (*An Aristotelian Theory of Comedy* [New York, 1922], pp. 45–47, 187, 191, 194, 217, 244–49, 257–59). More important, however, may be the influence of Hellenistic categories of narrative and of the gradual association of tragedy with history (ἱστορία) and of comedy with fictions (πλάσματα). As

are lacking, Aristotle illustrates, in dealing with rhetorical persuasion, by drawing his example from drama. Narrative, he says (*Rhetoric*, 1417a16–17b6), must depict (the speaker's) character, and to this end must reveal moral purpose, which the 'mathematical discourses' (i.e. technical treatises) do not do, since they represent no one as pursuing an end. For persuasive consistency, "Where any detail may appear incredible, then add the cause of it; of this Sophocles provides an example in the *Antigone*, where Antigone says she had cared more for her brother than for husband or children, since if the latter perished they might be replaced, 'But since my father and mother in their graves / Lie dead, no brother can be born to me.' " Again, descriptive details which reveal the emotions depict character persuasively, since "the audience take the truth of what they know as so much evidence for the truth of what they do not," of which Homer offers many examples. This persuasion by inference strongly resembles the fallacy described in the *Poetics*.

It is the causation, which is made explicit by the plot and completes the 'demonstration' from hypothetical premises on the basis of probability or necessity, that distinguishes poetry from history. How precisely this distinction survives in the history of literary theory can be heard in Sidney's adaptation of the ninth chapter of the *Poetics*, when, objecting to the historian, he says that "manie times he must tell euents whereof he can yeelde no cause: or, if hee doe, it must be poeticall."[46] Aristotle

---

credibility is sought more in the historical or the true, comedy might be associated more with the unreal or fabulous (μῦθος) and, perhaps, participate in the greater license with regard to logical coherence.

[46] *An Apology for Poetry*, *Eliz. Crit. Ess.*, 1:168–69; also Minturno, *De Poeta* (Venetiis, 1559), p. 119, who cites Virgil's *Musa mihi causas memora* (*Aen.* 1.8). Sidney's use of the English word derived from the Latin form of 'hypothesis' in relation to causation is most suggestive: "The Historian, wanting the precept, is so tyed, not to what shoulde bee but to what is, to the particuler truth of things and not to the general reason of things, that hys example draweth no necessary consequence, and therefore a lesse fruitfull doctrine. Nowe dooth the peerelesse Poet performe both: for whatsoeuer the Philosopher sayth shoulde be doone, hee giueth a perfect picture of it in some one, by whom hee presupposeth it was doone. So as hee coupleth the general notion with the particuler example" (p. 164). The poet completes his "picture" of an action (that is, offers motivations) by means of a 'presupposition' that it was done by a certain kind of person. As Lucian had done earlier, St. Augustine in his seventh epistle associates imaginary presuppositions in epic and drama with those in geometry. He divides the images of the fantasy according to their origin either in the senses, the imagination, or the reason. By means of those images in the imagination "for the sake of illustration in discourse, we ourselves suppose things which have no existence . . . ; or when we call up . . . a lively conception of the things described while we read history, or hear, or compose, or refuse to believe fabulous narrations." This happens when picturing "the appearance of Aeneas, or of Medea with her team of winged dragons, or of Chremes, or Parmeno. . . . Moreover, we often say, when carrying on a discussion, 'Suppose that three worlds, such as the one which we inhabit, were placed one above another'; or, 'Suppose the earth to be enclosed within a four-sided figure,' and

chooses history to distinguish from poetry because it, too, narrates the actions of men. Fact, or what actually happened, is the natural rival of fiction, and more than this, in a Platonic context history seems to have an ontological priority. History presents the world of appearances; drama represents, in imitation, this same world, but the play produced is further removed from the intelligible permanence of ideal forms than even apparent facts. It is not about the ontological priority of subject matters, however, that Aristotle argues, for poetry does treat historical as well as fictional material (*Poetics*, 1451b29–33). He points out instead that fiction must make coherent what history is often forced to relate as discrete and disconnected events wherever they have happened and for whatever reason. Fiction must be logical, while history may be alogical.[47] Thus the words 'universal' and 'philosophical' have the connotation of 'completion' in the sense that a conception is 'complete' when it expresses the nature of a thing, or the significance of an action, as a whole.

This conceptual completeness, *logically* articulated by the relation of the particular to the universal, coincides with the structural completeness, *formally* articulated by the relation of the part to the whole. Both the logical (cognitive/judicative) principles of order and the formal (struc-

---

so on: for all such things we picture to ourselves, and imagine according to the mood and direction of our thoughts." The third class of images, those originating in the reason, embody forth concepts of number and measure, found partly in the nature of things and partly in sciences such as geometry and music. *Works of St. Augustine*, ed. P. Schaff, *Nicene and Post-Nicene Fathers* (New York, 1892), 1:225. See Bundy, *Theory of Imagination*, pp. 153–72.

[47] History is a record of random effects (from man's point of view as distinct from God's, which includes a knowledge of causes), and its literary procedures, as in a chronicle, reflect a random progression. Insofar as an historian 'interprets' the effects (events), he is 'constructing,' not 'recording,' but his construction is never *certain, final,* or *true.* It must be constantly revised in accordance with new data about events: in this sense its allegiance is always to the events, not to any given construct of events. Its progressions are undelimited and random insofar as they are subservient to subsequent effects occurring or being discovered by chance. (When his memory fails, Thucydides admits he constructs speeches which are plausibly demanded by various occasions [1.21–22]. Such speeches would be subject to revision, however, if more details were learned about the occasions.) This is also the procedure of the fantasy, in which sense impressions are the events, the equivalent of effects; they are reflected in the fantasy, recorded, and later 'interpreted' to give a construct of the stimuli by other faculties. Fiction is distinct from fantasy in the same way that it is distinct from history. In fiction there is no randomness; causes are 'discovered' (given) for effects: it is always 'true.' In the Renaissance Dionigi Atanagi writes: "The order of poetry is certain, connected, and linked, since because of the inter-relationship of its actions it makes one out of many, one toward which it directs all the others as servants and domestics serve a mistress. . . . The order of history is for the most part uncertain, disjointed, and fortuitous, since its actions are not similar and linked but separate and diverse; neither does one depend from another nor do they relate to a single end" (Weinberg, *History of Literary Criticism*, p. 458).

tural) principles of order work together by virtue of the fact that each participates in what Else calls "the grand law of poetry" (p. 282): that everything must be presented as happening according to probability or necessity, both of which embody a relation of cause to effect. Aristotle states the cognitive / judicative principles of order in Chapter 9 by the logical relation of the specific (καθ' ἕκαστον) to the generic (καθόλου); in Chapters 17–18, 23–24 he states the formal principle of order in similar terms, the part (κατὰ μέρος = by episodes, each, taken severally, treated as ἕκαστον) in its structural relation to the whole (ὅλην / καθόλου).[48] The specific is *logically* related to the generic as effect to cause insofar as we may understand the nature of something as a 'species' by virtue of our recognizing its genus. The part is *formally* related to the whole as effect to cause insofar as we may perceive and construct an order of parts by recognizing how each is subordinated to the whole. The cognitive / judicative relation of individual to universal, that is, is articulated in the finished narrative by the structural relation of the particular incident to the total action. Almost in answer to Plato, ethical significance and formal structure, through their mutual dependence upon the relation of cause and effect, become reflections of one another in the mimetic probability of a work of art.[49]

[48] Aristotle uses the terms καθ' ἕκαστον/καθόλου interchangeably with κατὰ μέρος/καθόλου in his *Rhetoric* (1.2.15–16, 1357a35–57b2): "A Probability is a thing that usually happens; not, however, as some definitions would suggest, anything whatever that usually happens, but only if it belongs to the class of the 'contingent' or 'variable.' It bears the same relation to that in respect of which it is probable as the universal bears to the particular (ὡς τὸ καθόλου πρὸς τὸ κατὰ μέρος). Of Signs, one kind bears the same relation to the statement it supports as the particular (καθ' ἕκαστον) bears to the universal (πρὸς τὸ καθόλου), the other the same as the universal (καθόλου) bears to the particular (πρὸς τὸ κατὰ μέρος)." See, as well, 'Problemata' 18.3, quot. Appendix A, n. 15.

[49] D. W. Lucas comments on the 'universal' in 1451b8 (*Poetics* [Oxford, 1968]): "When the universal regularities are revealed, events are intelligible: τίμιον τὸ καθόλου ὅτι δηλοῖ τὴν αἰτίαν (*An. Post.* 88a5), 'the universal is precious because it reveals the cause.' " The necessity for seeing 'parts' only in relation to 'wholes,' even in the most minute subjects of research, pervades Aristotle's works. It is as true of biology in *On the Parts of Animals* (whose introduction is translated by Jaeger, *Aristotle*, pp. 338–39) as of metaphysics, which, he says, "is based on physics according to Aristotle in the first place because it is nothing but the conceptually necessary completion of the experimentally revealed system of moving nature" (p. 380). So fiction might be said to be the conceptually necessary completion of observed historical events. In an article on "The Function of the Myth in Plato's Philosophy," *JHI* 10 (1949):463–81, L. Edelstein suggests that Plato regarded his 'ethical' myths of the afterlife in a similar way: that is, that they could be used to complete an argument (v. *Rep.* 614A) and in this way become "an addition to rational knowledge" (p. 473). Analogous to the unity of composition stressed by Plato (*Phaedrus* 264–68) is the Aristotelian change from an organization of an oration by 'parts' to one of 'functions' operating throughout the whole speech to insure affectivity (see Solmsen, "The Aristotelian Tradition . . . , " pp. 37f.). For Aristotle's use of letters and syllables to illustrate the formal relation of parts to wholes, see *Metaphysics* 7.17; 104b11–33.

D. Mimetic Probability

Plato's criticism of mimetic representation falls chiefly under three headings. (1) Poetry does not imitate the Forms but their images in the world of appearance, and hence the poem is an imitation of an imitation. (2) Poetry is immoral in that (*a*) it applies to gods and heroes the mediocrity, the vices, and the passions of human nature and (*b*) when it imitates men, it permits bad men to become happy. (3) Poetry does not engage the rational part of the soul but agitates the lower passions which produce pleasure or pain. Aristotle's response to Plato's first criticism is that when one deals in a literary work with the probable possibility, he gains a universality (τὸ καθόλου), the philosophical counterpart of the Forms, since, according to Atkins' interpretation, the poet constructs out of the confusion of "everyday existence an intelligible picture, free from unreason, in which are revealed the permanent possibilities of human nature."[50] Aristotle answers Plato's second objection simply by saying that tragedy imitates a serious action without stipulating legendary or divine figures as necessary and by substituting the doctrine of *catharsis* for that of 'poetic justice.' As for Plato's third objection, although Aristotle believed with Plato that the emotions were perturbations of the soul, he thought that the passions, if properly controlled, could be necessary and irreplaceable aids to the will. While Plato regarded the effect of certain music and dance, of hymns, and of his philosophical myths upon the feelings as beneficial, Aristotle defended the affective influence of the mimetic arts in general.[51]

In accounting for the origins of poetry (*Poetics*, 1448b4–24), Aristotle describes the intellectual pleasure derived from works of imitation by

---

[50] J. W. H. Atkins, *Literary Criticism in Antiquity*, 2 vols. (London, 1952), 1:80.

[51] This brief summary is based on A. Rostagni, *La Poetica di Aristotele* (Torino, 1927), pp. xxxv–xli. Edelstein argues that Plato regarded the emotional effects of myths about the afterlife as good because "the ethical myth speaks to man's passions; it rouses and confirms hopes; it enhances courage and allays fears" ("Function of the Myth," p. 474). Such a "myth, shaped in accordance with reason, brings to the realm of the passions the light of the intellect; it instigates man to act with hope and confidence toward the goal which reason has set before him" (p. 477). See P. Friedländer, *Plato*, tr. H. Meyerhoff (New York, 1958), 1:171–210. For the powers of the fantasy in Plato's later work, see Bundy, pp. 46–58. In his *Rhetoric* Aristotle raised the categories of ἦθος and πάθος to the level of that of "rhetorical arguments" in delineating these three as the three types of proof. Later, perhaps under the influence of Hermagoras' scholastic distinctions of *status*, *ethos* and *pathos* were relegated to the proem and the epilogue of the speech. Cicero restricted them in the same way in his early work, but in his mature treatises he reinstated them (in the *officia* of *delectare* and *permovere*) in much the same way as he did the 'thesis.' There is, I believe, a relation between the two reinstatements. On these subjects see the articles of Solmsen cited previously and my more detailed discussion of rhetoric in Part Three.

all men, not merely by philosophers (p. 124). The reason he gives is based on the acquisition of knowledge through inference, and he repeats this philosophical justification of mimesis several times in the *Rhetoric*. "Again, since learning and wondering are pleasant, it follows that such things as acts of imitation must be pleasant—for instance, painting, sculpture, poetry—and every product of skillful imitation: this latter, even if the object imitated is not itself pleasant; for it is not the object itself which here gives delight; the spectator draws inferences ('That is a so-and-so') and thus learns something fresh" (*Rhetoric*, 1371b4–10).[52] For Plato, such learning would have little more authority than opinion; with regard to knowledge, the problem of mimesis lay very much in its object of imitation. This is apparent in his strangely haunting reply to a group of imagined tragic poets (σπουδαίων . . . ποιητῶν) who have asked permission to perform their tragedies in his state (*Laws*, 817B).

Respected visitors, we are ourselves authors of a tragedy, and that the finest and best we know how to make. In fact, our whole polity has been constructed as a dramatization (μίμησις) of a noble and perfect life; that is what *we* hold to be in truth the most real of tragedies. Thus you are poets, and we also are poets in the same style, rival artists and rival actors, and that in the finest of all dramas, one which indeed can be produced only by a code of true law—or at least that is our faith.[53]

Part, at least, of his "tragedy," his "dramatization of a noble and perfect life," is the *Republic* itself, in which he comes, at one point, as near as he ever does to justifying mimetic probability.

Socrates says that he has sketched in the *Republic* a pattern (παρά-δειγμα) of "the character of the perfectly just man, supposing him to exist," but in no sense has he intended "to demonstrate the possibility of the realization" of such a pattern in any particular man. His description will suffer no more from this lack of demonstration than the portrait by a painter "who, after portraying a pattern of the ideally beautiful man and omitting no touch required for the perfection of the picture, should not be able to prove that it is actually possible for such a man to exist." Yet, even in the absence of such proof, "if we can discover how a state might be constituted most nearly answering to our description, you must say that we have discovered that possibility of realization." The imitation in language of the best state, in other words, may reveal "how most probably and in what respect these things would be most nearly realized" (472B–73A). There is a concession here, as in *Rep.* 592B, to the moral value of a probable approximation, but the

[52] This passage along with *Rhetoric* 1410b5–35 and 1412a17–25 are discussed in Chap. 8 with respect to 'proportional metaphors.' See pp. 173–75 of this study.

[53] *Laws*, trans. A. E. Taylor in *The Collected Dialogues of Plato*. See pp. 273–75 of this study.

object of imitation remains a conceptual model. The clarity of our perception of it, resulting from its very independence from historical circumstances, makes the model more 'real' in the sense that intelligibility and existence are functions of one another.[54] Plato's descriptive definition of the hypothetical state resembles the demonstration (or solution) of a philosophical thesis (or problem), a conclusion from premises discovered by various dialectical analyses. As at the end of the *Phaedrus*, such dialectic is 'serious' discourse and can be said to rival tragedy in the *Laws* (816D–17D) in an ironical sense, because, among literary genres, tragedy has claimed more prestige than more ephemeral entertainments (παίγνια).

In contrast, the literary, as opposed to the dialectical, hypothesis may be illustrated by Isocrates' introduction to his autobiographical *Antidosis* (1–12), in which he, too, wishes to dramatize the noble life of a just man. To do this, he chooses a mimetic fiction explicitly because it can combine the formal, cognitive, and judicative intentions of literature. Since he is writing something to be read, rather than to be delivered as a forensic or encomiastic speech, Isocrates says it is necessary to explain in a preface why he has chosen a form so "novel and different in character." He explains how, recently, when he was brought to trial, he discovered enemies that he had not been previously aware of, and as a result he considered how to vindicate his character to critics and to posterity. He decided, he says, to compose a defense which would be "a true image of my thought and of my whole life (εἰκὼν τῆς ἐμῆς διανοίας καὶ τῶν ἄλλων τῶν ἐμοὶ βεβιωμένων)." In order to cover all the points without arousing the displeasure of his readers, he continues, he will "adopt the fiction of a trial (ὑποθείμην ἀγῶνα) . . . [in which] a sycophant had brought an indictment . . . while I, for my part, cast my speech in the form of a defence in court (ἐμαυτὸν δ' ἐν ἀπολογίας σχήματι τοὺς λόγους ποιούμενον)."

Such a defense is not easy to write, Isocrates continues, because it must combine both rhetorical and philosophical material in a coherent structure.

While some things in my discourse are appropriate to be spoken in a courtroom, others are out of place amid such controversies, being frank discussions about philosophy and expositions of its power. There is in it, also, matter which it would be well for young men to hear before they set out to gain knowledge

---

[54] Jaeger notes that in *Rep.* 511D "the basis of the comparison between the four stages described by Plato is the difference in *clearness* (σαφήνεια, sometimes ἀσάφεια) which they represent. Σαφήνεια means not only intelligibility but reality: cf. 510a9: ἀληθείᾳ." *Paideia*, 2:417, n. 61. Although Aristotle regards the exemplary model as a legitimate subject of tragedy, he discusses it as one of several ways to justify departures from factual truth (*Poet.* 25.6).

and an education; and there is much, besides, of what I have written in the past, inserted in the present discussion, not without reason nor without fitness, but with due appropriateness to the subject in hand. Now to view as a whole so great an extent of subject matter, to harmonize and bring together (συναρμόσαι καὶ συναγαγεῖν) so many diverse varieties of discourse, to connect smoothly what follows with what goes before, and to make all parts consonant one with another, was by no means an easy undertaking.

Such "a mixed discourse, composed with an eye to all these subjects (ὑποθέσεις)," is particularly in need of a formal principle of order. The word 'hypothesis' is used not only in the rhetorical sense of matter set out for judgment, but it carries some of the connotations of its verbal form used previously in this chapter (ὑποθείμην ἀγῶνα). Aristotle uses such verbal forms in the *Poetics* for hypothesizing, first the outline of essential events, and then the more particular details of plotting. Isocrates has cast around for a form and ended up by choosing to 'imitate' his own trial, which he had just been through. He will let a 'fiction' of the trial, of the *quaestio definita*, be not only a foundation underlying what he wishes to present in his defense but also a starting point from which he can develop a lucid presentation of the *archai* or reasons why he should be vindicated.[55] The fiction, furthermore, will offer a form in which to express an image (εἰκών) of his thought (διανοίας), not just the thought itself as a thesis in the narrow sense of a debated opinion, but a harmonized, smoothly connected whole in which the parts find unity—an image of his life whose 'wholeness' emerges in the realization of the reasons why he acted as he did.[56]

[55] Without reference to this passage, Jaeger comments generally on Isocrates' method: "This method of laying down a supreme principle or aim of action he calls a *hypothesis*, a 'laying of foundations'—because all further arguments must rest upon it. In several other passages in his speeches we can observe this effort to find a generally accepted hypothesis: it is an essential element in his political thought, and is to be explained by the influence of Plato's intellectual method. Ultimately, it is a procedure borrowed from mathematics" (*Paideia*, 3:93). Jaeger calls attention (3:310, n. 56) to *Nic.* 13, which reads as follows: "for it is through this training that you can soonest become such a man as we have assumed (ὑπεθέμεθα) that one must be who is to perform properly the duties of a king, and to govern the state as he should."

[56] I shall treat the importance of Aristotle's discussion of equity for the concept of 'wholeness' in Part Three. Suffice it to say here that where it is impossible for legal statutes "to be complete owing to the endless possible cases" which can arise, "equity bids us be merciful to the weakness of human nature; to think less about the laws than about the man who framed them, and less about what he said than about what he meant; not to consider the actions of the accused so much as his intentions; nor this or that detail so much as the whole story; to ask not what a man is now but what he has always or usually been" (*Rhet.* 1.13; 1374a27–32, 1374b11–16). What a man "has always or usually been" is near the "universal" which poetry aims to reveal: "What kinds of thing a certain kind of person will say or do in accordance with probability or necessity" (*Poet.* 1451b9–10). When Polybius criticizes Phylarchus for omitting causes (οὐχ ὑποτιθεὶς αἰτίαν καὶ τρό-πον) without which there can be neither "legitimate pity or proper anger" aroused (2.56.13),

Without the Aristotelian reevaluation of the emotions it would have been difficult to escape Plato's ethical objections to the mimetic representation of motive and action. A fiction, under the controlled circumstances of a play or of an account such as that of Isocrates, might now examine the emotional responses of 'ordinary' people hypothetically in a particular context and present them coherently to the audience. Presented with an imitation stripped of the accidents of the historical world, in which they can understand the *probable* possibility, the members of the audience can respond to the imitation in a way that they could not respond to the *historical* possibility of what actually did or could happen to them in their individual lives. To say, with Plato, that the literary and visual arts should primarily depict the exemplary model is to justify these arts too exclusively on the cognitive grounds of philosophy. Or, in a similar way, to try, with later moralists, to make a fictional narrative pass for, and express the austere judgments of, history on the basis of the fact that its characters happened to be historical, is to justify poetry too exclusively on the judicative grounds of rhetoric. It is neither a conceptual model, in accordance with which *every* man ought to act, nor simply a more accurate recapitulation of events which appear to have happened, that Isocrates wishes to portray here. It is a totally coordinated 'image of thought and life,' a total character whose inner coherence, now lost in fragments too far below the surface of historical incident to be seen, must be 'remade' by means of a fiction in order to be apprehended.[57]

he continues by stressing that what "properly" causes emotions is important, because the interpretation of the motive is important in a defense. Such considerations are matters of equity for "in every such case the final criterion of good and evil lies not in what is done, but in the different reason and different purposes of the doer (ἐν ταῖς αἰτίαις καὶ προαιρέσεσι τῶν πραττόντων καὶ ταῖς τούτων διαφοραῖς)." In both the hypothetical causation and the determination of equity the word αἰτία is used. Perhaps the logical extreme of the influence of the rhetorical concern with equity is reflected in Plutarch's defense of poetry where probable consistency in events has been replaced by consistent morality in 'thought': in reading any literature, he says, "it is useful also to seek after the cause (αἰτίαν) of each thing that is said," in order to see if it is morally acceptable as a model of conduct. "How to Study Poetry" (28AB), *Plutarch's Moralia*, trans. F. C. Babbitt, LCL, 15 vols. (London, 1960), 1:147.

[57] Such an apprehension, intended to vindicate Isocrates in the eyes of his audience, is consistent with Else's interpretation of 'catharsis' (pp. 224–32, 423–50). Butcher (*Aristotle's Theory of Poetry*, p. 245) and others cite Plato's *Sophist* (229E–230E) to illustrate the medical use of the term, but the passage has further implications for this study. Plato is describing the cathartic effect of the elenchus upon the respondent who is 'purified' of his pretense to knowledge by experiencing the shame of refutation. Once purified he can begin to learn properly. The emotional acquiescence, brought about by the hypothetical method of moral dialectic, corresponds to the emotional acceptance of the synthesis of 'given' events, brought about by observing the 'elenchic' and consistent selection of means within the fictional hypothesis.

3. The Literary Thesis

IF A WORK OF LITERATURE can be said to express a 'thesis,' as well as a hypothesis, it must be in the sense of a general meaning or significance which permits the members of the audience to understand their experience of the work as a whole in relation to the individually varied experiences of their own lives. Such a thesis might, by serving as a moral principle of order for the work itself, increase their awareness of alternative, more finely adjusted, responses to the circumstances of the past or the present than had previously seemed possible.

In order to identify a thesis of this kind, we might begin by establishing its relation to the hypothesis of essential events. Would these events 'underlie' the literary thesis, like a scientific 'beginning' (*arche*) of geometrical demonstration, by postulating the existence of a situation (problem) to be explained and then establishing consistent principles of analysis? Would the events 'underlie' the thesis like hypothetical premises capable of verifying it by philosophical definitions? Or would they 'underlie' it as the individual circumstances of the rhetorical 'definite question' might be organized under, and judged in accordance with, the generic issue of the 'indefinite question'? Whatever its relation to the literary hypothesis of essential events, the literary thesis should not be identified with the coordinating theorem to be mathematically demonstrated nor with the dialectical thesis to be philosophically verified nor with the generic thesis to be rhetorically developed. It must, instead, like the literary hypothesis, draw upon and combine the respective functions of the 'thesis' as they exist in all three of the main categories of discourse I have been discussing. It is in the interest of describing this combination of functions that Aristotle distinguishes the universal of poetic imitation from the thesis of rhetoric and, by implication, from the thesis of Platonic dialectic.

When Plato describes the best form of discourse at the end of the *Phaedrus*, he strongly prefers the didactic effectiveness of oral dialectic to the less flexible formal perfections of written composition. He concludes by telling Phaedrus that if Lysias, the speech writer, or Homer, the poet, or Solon, the composer of laws, "can defend his statements when challenged, and can demonstrate the inferiority of his writings [to his spoken defense of the truth of what he says] . . . , he ought not to be designated by a name drawn from those writings, but by one that indicates his serious pursuit (ἀλλ' ἐφ' οἷς ἐσπούδακεν ἐκείνων) . . . [that is] 'lover of wisdom' (φιλόσοφον)." On the other hand, Plato continues, "one who has nothing to show of more value than the literary works on whose phrases he spends hours, twisting them this way and that, pasting them together and pulling them apart, will rightly . . . be called a poet or speech writer or law writer" (278CE). The dialectical defense of "statements when challenged" suggests that for Plato the questioning and verification of theses, rather than the making of poetic compositions, deserve to be called serious and to receive the attention of the philosopher.

In the *Poetics* Aristotle borrows Plato's terms 'serious' and 'philosophical' but shifts their application in two ways. First, and more generally, they no longer apply to what, in poetic composition, would be analogous to the rhetorical amplification of a thesis but rather to the distinguishing power of poetry to bring out the significance for the audience of the actions represented on the stage. In Chapter 6 Aristotle restricts the function most resembling that of a thesis to 'thought' or argumentation (διάνοια) by means of which the characters "try to prove some argument or else state a general view" in their dialogue (p. 238). Later, he distinguishes further: the composing of such speeches belongs to the political (i.e. ethical) art or to rhetoric. Ethics provides terms of analysis to those speeches which deliberate about moral choice, and rhetoric gives form to those "speeches in which the persons try to prove that something is so or not so, or express some general view" (p. 263).[1] However important the 'theses' debated in these speeches, their content can neither be identified with the universal nor account for why the universal makes poetry 'more philosophical' (φιλοσοφώτερον) or 'more serious' (σπουδαιότερον) than history. Any identification of the universal of poetry with either the thesis of philosophy or of rhetoric, in an attempt to justify literature on moral grounds, would reduce the purpose of the literary work to its cognitive or to its judicative intentions.[2] We must try to describe here the nature of a literary thesis which,

[1] For this difficult passage (1450b4–12), see Else's commentary, esp. pp. 270–71, and compare the translations of Butcher and Bywater. The main point is that what Aristotle says of 'thought' resembles closely his definition of a 'thesis' (*Top.* 104b19ff.) as well as the later embodiment of a thesis in the literary exercise of the *suasoria*. Such declamations, in turn, greatly influenced all types of set speeches, such as the Elizabethan soliloquy: "To be or not to be, that is the question" (i.e. the matter to be considered *generally*, not the decision *specifically* about the speaker's committing suicide at that moment).

[2] In the Renaissance, for instance, the *universalis* of Aristotle continued to be glossed as the *quaestio indefinita* of Cicero. See *Aristotelis de Poetica Liber . . . per Theodorum*

by retaining the philosophical seriousness of Aristotle's universal, avoids such a reduction.[3]

The conception of a literary thesis in the broader ethical sense of Aristotle's universal must draw, like the literary hypothesis, upon the three categories of discourse but with a slightly different emphasis. While the literary hypothesis reflects more clearly the debt to geometry incurred by Plato up to and including the *Republic*, the nature and function of the literary thesis reflect more clearly the procedures of moral dialectic in the *Phaedrus* (265D–66D, 273DE, 277B) and in the later dialogues. Aristotle's analysis of arriving at first principles in the *Posterior Analytics* (2.19), or moral choice in the *Nicomachean Ethics* (3.3), and of discovering the middle terms of the syllogism appear as well to reflect Plato's later method. While Aristotle compares both deliberation of moral choice and syllogistic argumentation to geometrical analysis, their primary function is to select among ethical alternatives, to verify definitions, or to reveal structures of causation rather than to posit formal assumptions of existence, axiomatic principles of a science, or the arbitrary points of departure for self-consistent demonstration. The cognitive intention to discover and define generic principles of causation (hypotheses) in the philosophical problem (thesis to be explained) corresponds, in this regard, to the judicative intentions to discover and define generic principles of adjudication (theses) in the rhetorical problem (hypothesis to be judged). Once allowances are made for the inversion of these terminologies, what Quintilian says of rhetoric holds as well for moral dialectic: "the *genus* is logically prior to the *species*," especially when 'qualities' enter into consideration (3.5.9–10).

Moral Ideas, Cornford says, with reference to the *Timaeus* (30C), are genera "which can be conceived as containing, potentially latent within

---

Goulstonum [bound with *Aristotelis de Poetica Liber ex versione Theodori Goulstoni*] (Cantbrigiae, 1696), p. 26: "Poësis Philosophiae similior, quàm historia. Siquidem Poëtae Fabula, Universales ac Indefinitas captet." In comedies theses were 'proposed' for illustration in plays to serve a didactic purpose: "Sunt in singulis Comoediis certae quaedam theses de hominum diversis moribus, ingeniis, & officiis propositae, quae multum faciunt ad vitam sapienter & civiliter instituendam" (*P. Terentii Afri Poetae Lepidissimi Comoediae* [Parisiis, 1552], p. 675).

[3] In this broader sense of a universal, the 'thesis' connotes the generic within the specific, not isolated in abstraction but immanent in a given particular situation. This 'fictional' combination of (assumed) circumstantial existence and definitive significance is suggested by the way Aristotle distinguishes these technical terms: "A thesis which assumes one or the other part of a proposition, *i.e.*, that something does, or does not exist, is a *hypothesis*; a thesis which does not do this is a definition. A definition is a kind of thesis (or laying-down), because the arithmetician lays it down that to be a unit is to be quantitatively indivisible; but it is not a hypothesis, because to define the nature of a unit is not the same as to assert its existence" (72a19–25). "Thesis" retains something of the generic quality as definition and something of the asserted existence of initial premises of action (plot outline) as hypothesis (see Chap. 2, n. 39).

them, the species." In attempting to grasp these Ideas one ascends by hypothetically assumed generic qualities in an "act of divining by intuition the unity pervading a manifold 'gathered together' (συναγωγή). This unity becomes the 'genus' that must stand at the head of the table. The downward process is 'Division,' discerning 'differences' within this unity and arranging them in proper logical sequence" (p. 49). These movements in obtaining dialectical definitions, Cornford says, correspond to the movements of the geometer's articulation of his proof in diagrammatic constructions. The dialectician's contemplation of the genus proposed for division becomes analogous to the geometer's contemplation of the potential elementary constructions intuited in his given figure. In the subsequent division

The final definition of the species sets out in explicit form (λόγος) the elements (differences) contained in the essence defined, as the geometer's completed diagram exhibits the elements in the demonstration. Each, in reaching his results, eliminates, step by step, irrelevant elements: the dialectician, as he selects each *differentia*, rejects its alternative; the geometer retains only the elements that will figure in his demonstration and rejects others that occur to him but are found not to lead to his conclusion. (p. 50)

Moral dialectic pursues definitions, and definitions express generic qualities. Its hypotheses, which are temporarily assumed generic qualities, are tried out by being traced downward through *elenchi* to the initially disparate material to be described. If they do not 'explain' it, new ones are sought. The final definition reveals an acceptable generic quality, which, once demonstrated as actually existing within, and as ordering, particulars (by virtue of which these particulars can now be called species), is a conclusion formally analogous to the geometer's completed diagram. How these moral qualities, no longer genera temporarily assumed but definitions formally demonstrated, resolve the dialectical problem of essence resembles the way in which universals resolve the problem of characterization in the action of a play. The exclusion of irrelevant elements in the construction of a diagram corresponds, as well, to the exclusion of irrelevant episodes in a dramatic composition.

Both the logical terms of genus and species in Aristotle and the ontological terms of classes and 'species' in Plato establish the priority of the generic questions to be argued in law and the generic definition of 'idea' to be analyzed in ethics. The priority of generic questions and definitions suggest by analogy the function of the universal in the construction of a play, but in themselves they do not establish the nature and priority of the literary thesis in relation to the literary hypothesis. One must ask more specifically what is prior to the hypothetical starting points of a rhetorical, dialectical, or a literary 'demonstration.' The central Aristotelian answer to such a question is the conclusion for the demonstration of which the hypothesis, thesis, or plot outline are selected in the first place.

The dramatist might be said to start with a partial understanding of the events he wishes to treat, as well as a partial perception of his conclusion. Such partial insights are beginnings comparable to those of the dialectician which lead to his "divining by intuition the unity pervading a manifold" (συναγωγή). Like the dialectician, the writer perceives by intuition a unity of essential events capable, when assumed as premises in outline, of yielding the conclusion in accordance with probability or necessity. The dramatic hypothesis, that is, corresponds, formally, to the elementary constructions intuited in the figure which the geometer contemplates and, cognitively, to the generic definitions intuited in the ethical problem which the dialectician considers. To be successful, the dramatic hypothesis must contain *in potentia* the ethical as well as formal principles of development which can determine the far more numerous particular actions of the completed play. The demonstration of how these principles are actually implicit in these actions reveals the psychological and ethical causation in accordance with which the writer can state his thesis about why events concluded as they did. One way to describe the priority of such a thesis to the dramatic hypothesis is to consider it in relation to the Aristotelian principle that actuality is prior to potentiality (*Meta.* 9.8–9).[4]

If the dramatic hypothesis contains latent within it all the potential action of the completed play, the actualization of those events in episode and dialogue in accord with probability or necessity may be said to express the literary thesis of the author. In Aristotelian terms (*Meta.* 9.8.11), this actualization is not only a process itself but its purpose is *to be* an activity or the product of an activity:

The activity (τὸ ἔργον) is the end (τέλος), and the actuality (ἐνέργεια) is the activity; hence the term "actuality" is derived from "activity," and tends to have the meaning of "complete reality" (ἐντελέχειαν).

It is precisely in order to represent this completeness of reality that *poesis* brings out, by means of the universal, the significance of the actions it portrays more seriously and philosophically than history does. The reason for this is that actualization in a productive art like poetry

---

[4] For the priority of genus to species, see *Categories* 13, esp. 15a5. On potentiality and actuality, see Ross, *Aristotle*, pp. 176ff. Later (p. 285), he observes that character corresponds to potentiality, plot to actuality: the play is then potentiality-in-actualization, i.e. character-in-action. Actualization and plot are 'prior' to potentiality and character.

is the activity of thought itself (αἴτιον δὲ ὅτι νόησις ἡ ἐνέργεια, 1051a31). Aristotle illustrates the act of 'realizing' this thought in a formal structure by comparing the movement from potentiality to actuality to proceeding from the initial insight about geometrical relations to the finished construction of a diagram (9.9.4–5).

> Geometrical constructions, too, are discovered by an actualization, because it is by dividing that we discover them. If the division were already done, they would be obvious; but as it is the division is only there potentially. Why is the sum of the interior angles of a triangle equal to two right angles? Because the angles about one point in a straight line are equal to two right angles. If the line parallel to the side had been already drawn, the answer would have been obvious at sight. . . . Thus it is evident that the potential constructions are discovered by being actualized. The reason for this is that the actualization is an act of thinking. Thus potentiality comes from actuality (and therefore it is by constructive action [ποιοῦντες] that we acquire knowledge).

The relation of hypothesis to thesis in literature may, similarly, be described as that of potentiality (δύναμις) to actuality (ἐνέργεια). In something made, like a poem, "the actuality resides in the thing produced; e.g. the act of building in the thing built, the act of weaving in the thing woven, and so on; and in general the motion resides in the thing moved" (*Meta.* 9.8.13). Here the priority of thesis to hypothesis is more complete than that of generic to specific questions or ethical qualities in rhetoric or moral dialectic. The major step has been made from propositional instruments of classification and definition to the poem itself as a part, and an expression, of reality.[5]

The literary hypothesis, then, may be said to contain *in potentia* the literary thesis. Aristotle suggests how the articulation of the thesis in the process of composition might integrate the mathematical, philosophical, and rhetorical analyses of experience in the following description of moral choice. The description might apply either to the writer's conception of the narrative action as a whole or to the deliberations which he attributes to his individual characters. Deliberation concerns the arts more than the sciences, for the arts, "though subject to rules that generally hold good, are uncertain in their issue." Those who deliberate, furthermore, are concerned, not with ends, but with means, and, as examples, Aristotle chooses three types of people who may represent, broadly speaking, the productive, speculative, and practical

---

[5] *Aristotle: The Metaphysics*, trans. H. Tredennick, LCL, 2 vols. (London, 1968). In the *Nicomachean Ethics*, Aristotle comments that "we exist in activity, since we exist by living and doing," so "one who has made something exists actively. . . . This is in fact a fundamental principle of nature: what a thing is potentially, that its work reveals in actuality" (9.7.4, 1168a7–10, trans. H. Rackham, LCL [London, 1956]).

disciplines: the doctor (as producer of health), the statesman (as ethical philosopher), and the orator (as adjudicator). All three

Take some end for granted, and consider how and by what means it can be achieved. If they find that there are several means of achieving it, they proceed to consider which of these will attain it most easily and best. If there is only one means by which it can be accomplished, they ask how it is to be accomplished by that means, and by what means that means can itself be achieved, until they reach the first link in the chain of causes, which is the last in the order of discovery. (For when deliberating one seems in the procedure described to be pursuing an investigation or analysis that resembles the analysis of a figure in geometry—indeed it appears that though not all investigation is deliberation, for example, mathematical investigation is not, yet all deliberation is investigation—and the last step in the analysis seems to be the first step in the execution of the design.) Then, if they have come up against an impossibility, they abandon the project—for instance, if it requires money and money cannot be procured; but if on the other hand it proves to be something possible, they begin to act. By possible, I mean able to be performed by our agency—things we do through the agency of our friends counting in a sense as done by ourselves, since the origin of their action is in us.

The choices of means are seen as links of causation. When one is proposed which is, for some (other) reason, impossible, it is rejected and another is chosen. If it proves to be possible, the action may continue.[6]

In its more vital sense of an activity, the literary thesis illuminates the process of the consciousness' being actualized in deliberations and

[6] *Nicomachean Ethics* 3.3.11–13, 1112b15–29. First principles in ethics and in mathematics, furthermore, are compared to one another in *E.N.* 7.8.4, while passages in the *Eudemian Ethics* are also suggestive for the fictional analysis and presentation of ethical deliberation. One never deliberates about the final end in the practical or productive sciences but simply regards the end as "a starting-point or assumption (ἀρχὴ καὶ ὑπόθεσις), like the postulates (ὑποθέσεις) in the theoretical sciences" (2.10.22–23). If good health is to be produced, it will be necessary "for such and such a thing to be provided—just as in mathematics, if the angles of a triangle are together equal to two right angles, such and such a consequence necessarily follows. Therefore the End is the starting-point of the process of thought, but the conclusion of the process of thought is the starting-point of action" (2.11.5–6). Since the end is assumed, it is by his choice of means that we judge a man's character—"that is, not by what he does but what he does it for" (2.11.9). Nevertheless—and this is where *poesis* as an imitation of what men do (rather than of their characters) becomes so important as an instrument of ethical analysis—"because it is not easy to see the quality (ὁποία) of a man's purpose we are forced to judge his character from his actions" (2.11.12 cf. *Mag. mor.* 1.19.3). The *Magna moralia* makes a further distinction: whereas in ethics the explanation of an action is the "final cause" for which the action is performed, in mathematics the explanation is the "formal cause," i.e. the definition of *principia*, which "informs" the consequent steps of the demonstration (1.17.8–11; cf. 1.10–11). In the *Posterior Analytics*, Aristotle defines the most complete explanation of *why* a man has acted in a certain way as the ultimate (final) cause, and when we know this, our knowledge of his action is said to be the best or most "universal" knowledge (1.24, 85b28–86a4).

choices like those described previously. There the formal intention is again illustrated by geometrical analysis, the heuristic intention by the discovery and definition of means to a given end, and the judicative intention by the decision to act upon the means which has been discovered and defined. All three types of intention should express themselves simultaneously for the audience of a skillfully composed literary work so that no one intention becomes conspicuous. The thesis is not an extractable precept—however often it is abstracted to precept—but rather a principle of order revealed in the ethical consistency of human actions. It expresses the significance of the causation which leads from premises to conclusion in accordance with necessity or probability. Like the conclusion in syllogistic reasoning, this significance is assumed to exist, however inarticulately, from the beginning. Like the 'middle terms,' the increasingly particularized 'reasons why' in the process of plotting become themselves more and more detailed hypothetical premises which must abide by, and thus illustrate, the principles of order. Ultimately, the author's thesis brings the audience 'back' to the catastrophe (now demonstrated like the syllogistic conclusion) which had been originally assumed and then included as one of the essential elements in the dramatic hypothesis.

The literary thesis includes the intention of the rhetorical as well as of the dialectical thesis. The increasingly detailed articulation in speeches and episodes of the 'reasons why' things have happened as they have shares, simultaneously, in the gradual return to the full set of circumstances of the case to be judged, first by the author and then by the audience. These circumstances of the *quaestio definita*, the initial controversy to be adjudicated, may now, after being analyzed into their latent 'indefinite questions,' be interpreted in relation to one another. The more definitively the rhetorician, with the help of his generic questions, hypothesizes the 'reasons why,' the more he can demonstrate and persuade the jury to accept his judgment of the events. The psychagogic effect of his argument upon the jury resembles the dramatist's power to convince the audience of his thesis, namely, that its members may, with good conscience, acquiesce emotionally in the catastrophe of the play.

Both the judicative and the cognitive principles of order participate in, and are integrated by, the formal principle of demonstration, which not only postulates the existence both of the particular controversy to be judged and of the knowledge necessary to judge it, but also establishes a structure sufficiently coherent to make that judgment lucid and persuasive. The process by which the consciousness maintains the balance of these three activities gradually reveals the thesis as the end or *telos* of the literary analysis of experience. It is the motive for all composition whose purpose is to represent as complete an understanding as possible of a portion of reality. The thesis is, therefore, prior to the hypothesizing functions of the three categories of discourse and, therefore, to the literary hypothesis which coordinates them. Once posited, these functions become the instruments of comprehension and construction whereby the thesis may be expressed as a work of art.[7]

[7] Since the doctor is included among others who deliberate about the means to an end in Aristotle's analysis quoted above in the text, a brief Hippocratian passage on medicine seems a salutary comment on the art of producing a literary work: "For so I think the whole art has been set forth, by observing some part of the final end in each of the many particulars, and then combining all into a single whole. So one must pay attention to generalities in incidents [i.e. recurrences experienced in particular cases?], with help and quietness rather than with professions and the excuses that accompany ill-success" (*Precepts* 2, *Hippocrates*, trans. W. H. S. Jones, LCL, 4 vols. [London, 1923–1931]).

4. Summary and Conclusion

of Part One

THE TERMINOLOGY BORROWED from the disciplines of mathematics, philosophy, and rhetoric enabled a theory of literature not only to formulate and defend its own objectives, but to combine and stabilize the antithetical intentions of philosophical and rhetorical discourse. Philosophy and rhetoric each had their specialized (conservative) and unspecialized (liberal) forms. For philosophy, the liberal form was a discipline such as ethics which sought to define the qualities of individual choice and action by an analysis of particular 'means' to given intermediate and final ends. The definitions of moral dialectic were intended to elucidate specific situations by practical application rather than to construct abstract systems out of specialized terminologies. While the liberal concerns of ethics could not lose sight of the particular situations, the liberal form of rhetoric had to keep clearly in view the generic significance, the more inclusive questions of justice and equity, implicit in any specific case. The more generically significant the question in a rhetorical controversy, the more it resembled the specifically applicable definition of moral dialectic. The more the liberal forms of rhetorical and philosophical discourse approached each other, the more they participated in the aims of literary discourse, which could draw upon both their energies to alleviate the conservative persistence of their ancient antagonism.

This participation is schematically clear in the first three components of Aristotle's analysis of tragedy: plot (μῦθος), character (ἦθος), and 'thought' (διάνοια). The definitions of ethics and the generic questions of rhetoric are permitted to complement one another by virtue of the fictional structure of events. Characters are "those indications by virtue of which we say that the persons performing the action have certain moral qualities, and 'thought' the passages in which by means of speech they try to prove some argument or else state a general view" (1450a6–8). Aristotle proceeds to assign 'thought,' so similar to the rhetorical thesis, specifically to the art of politics or rhetoric (1450b5–6). Both the

'character' of ethics and the 'thought' of rhetoric virtually become functions of one another in the final actualization of the plot in words and
actions. It seems clear, on the surface at least, that the liberal objectives
of philosophy and those of rhetoric have resolved their differences in
the simplest constituent elements of *poesis*. Yet philosophy, however
pragmatic the situations are which ethics treats, concerns truth in the
ontological sense of true and false, while rhetoric, however theoretical
the issues are which its theses raise, concerns truth in the *judicial* sense
of right and wrong. It is not yet clear, that is, how literary discourse
combines these disparate purposes and arrives at a more significant analysis of human experience than either discipline could do by itself. To
make this clearer, we must relate again their intentions to the formal
intention of mathematical discourse by reviewing their three respective
forms of analysis and synthesis. These forms are best differentiated in
terms of their use of 'hypothesis' and 'thesis.'

Both rhetoric and moral dialectic share the formal principle of demonstration, which is analogous to that employed in the construction of
mathematical diagrams, with literary composition itself. This formal
principle, functioning as a common denominator, permits the plot to
assimilate the analysis of both rhetorical questions of equity and of
philosophical definitions of moral qualities—which are implicit in such
questions—into its structure. In fact, it is just such a formal principle
which joins and holds the rhetorical and philosophical subject matters
together in the delicate balance of literary decorum. As a self-sufficient
principle of coordination, it enables them to survive by preventing their
slipping back into their respective specialized disciplines. The formal
principle of demonstration may, furthermore, preserve the emotions
defined by a work of literature when the rhetorical and philosophical
issues, which originally elicited these emotions, have lost their meaning
or importance. The technical excellence of diction, syntax, and rhythm,
for instance, may so precisely qualify the feelings appropriate to such
issues that the experience continues to be recoverable in later periods.

In the formal analysis of mathematics, the hypothesis is an assumption
made about the existence of something for the sake of proving some
other thing and in Aristotle's *Metaphysics* (5.1.2) represents the point
from which (ὅθεν) that other thing becomes intelligible. It is a necessary
condition or instrument in the demonstration of something known or
to be known without itself being concerned with *what* is known. It
assumes the existence of something to be learned, be it in the form of
a problem to be solved, a thesis to be verified, or a judgment to be
reached, and asserts (without proving it) a first step in the solution, the
verification, or the decision. The first step implies an order of subsequent

steps, and ultimately this order generates the conditions by which we recognize that a conclusion can be or has been reached.[1] This deductive procedure, characteristic of geometrical demonstration, establishes the purely formal relations in a discursive sequence of propositions. The demonstrative hypothesis, therefore, posits the conditions under which philosophical, rhetorical, and literary discourse express their form. It cannot, however, lead to a conclusion, or thesis, about experience in the way that philosophical or rhetorical hypotheses do, because it *has no* subject matter. It can be said to have a thesis only in the form of a conviction that its results can be repeatedly confirmed. Such a thesis becomes a purely formal principle which, as in other types of 'formalism,' exhausts its verification in its own coherence and its 'subject matter' in the very act of achieving self-consistency.

In the cognitive analysis of philosophy, one begins with a given thesis (or problem) *to be understood* and analyzes it into one or more hypotheses on the basis of which he, in returning (through division and synthesis) to the initial thesis (or problem), can verify (or resolve) it. In the judicative analysis of rhetoric, the hypothesis consists of a given set of particular circumstances *to be judged* in order that a particular *action* may be taken. The hypothesis is analyzed into theses which contain *in potentia* the criteria which, when applied to the given circumstances, can clarify and evaluate the initial situation.

All three hypothesizing functions are present, potentially, in the literary hypothesis (or dramatic outline) and contribute principles of order to the composition of the completed work. The mathematical hypotheses, or *archai*, might be said to be present by virtue of their positing the existence of the minimum of agents and events, as yet unspecified, necessary to generate the total action. The mathematical hypotheses might be said, in addition, to offer a 'poetic license' or 'license to fictionalize' in the sense that the geometrical *archai* permit one to proceed in the problem of construction. And, finally, they might be regarded as contributing the logical conditions by which the plot could develop according to probability or necessity.

The philosophical and rhetorical hypotheses, on the other hand, are concerned with questions of content. The philosophical hypotheses might be said to be potentially present in the literary *argumentum* (or outline) as latent definitions capable of articulating the moral qualities to be

---

[1] Lee, acknowledging that "each science assumes the existence of the genus of which it is its business to prove the essential attributes," observes that Euclid's postulates correspond to Aristotle's hypotheses: Euclid must "*assume* the possibility of constructing a certain minimum of figures, from which it would be possible to *prove* the possibility of constructing the rest" (p. 115). So also "according to Aristotle the geometer must assume the existence of points and lines (76b5)" (p. 115, n. 1).

brought out in subsequent delineations of character. Since ethical definitions are concerned with truth and falsehood, however, they will estimate actions primarily in accord with general prohibitions ("Thou shalt or shalt not . . . ") or with legal statutes which prescribe explicit penalties or rewards for explicit acts. They will deal more, that is, with the question of whether a given action is truly of such and such a nature or not (and therefore worthy of such and such a reward or penalty) rather than with whether the action is right or wrong, in the sense of justified or unjustified, in the particular circumstances of the plot. The question of justification can only be raised and resolved with reference to a definite case (*quaestio definita*). The rhetorical hypothesis might be said to be potentially present in the given agents and incidents of the dramatic outline insofar as they are capable of generating, through increasing qualification, a specific controversy which the audience must judge according to equity rather than to the letter of the law.

The principles of order derived from these hypothesizing functions operate simultaneously in the experience of a literary work. For the purposes of clarification, however, we may differentiate their respective activities in relation to the stages plausibly passed through in the construction of a fiction. A writer might start with the undifferentiated raw material of experience: he wishes, say, to write a novel about his or someone else's experiences during the war. By a process of inductive analysis and selection, he forms those essential events, real or imaginary, into a literary hypothesis which might be capable both of yielding the completed narrative and of demonstrating a 'thesis' that these experiences could be interpreted in a certain way. Once he had conceived the basic direction of the plot, he could begin the actual composition in the form of a deductive synthesis which articulates, by an increasing division of the principal actions into speech and episode, the reasons why the events took place as they did. If the audience accepts these reasons as just, it will acquiesce in the catastrophe. The various stages of composition, in whatever sequence they actually occur, draw upon the cooperative agency of rhetorical, philosophical, and mathematical analysis for their order and significance.

The writer draws upon rhetorical analysis as soon as he has selected for interpretation the (as yet unexplained) circumstances of his story which resemble the *quaestio definita* of the rhetorical hypothesis. Once selected, these circumstances may then be analyzed into the generic questions or theses, serving as premises on the basis of which the given case could be argued with a logical precision indebted to geometrical demonstration. Before we penalize or reward a person for killing a tyrant, that is, we must consider the general issue of whether it is just to kill a tyrant in the first place. Such a general issue, however, immediately involves definitive questions of moral dialectic such as 'what is justice?' and the rhetorical thesis becomes, temporarily, one or more theses of philosophy. Each philosophical thesis is then analyzed into its own hypotheses—by a process which again resembles that of geometry—on the basis of whose premises a thesis about the nature of justice could be defended. Once verified in the synthesis of moral dialectic, the philosophical thesis about justice becomes acceptable as a definition of justice. The rhetorician, in turn, by using this definition to answer the general question of whether it is just to kill a tyrant, transmutes the philosopher's thesis into his own once again. Having selected the most useful topics latent in this thesis, he can then return to the original circumstances and with the aid of these topics try to persuade the jury that the definite question should be decided in such and such a way. This persuasion of the jury corresponds to the writer's persuasion of his audience that it may accept his interpretation of his experiences as reliable and just.

I have 'pulled' these processes of rhetorical and philosophical analysis out like an old-fashioned telescope to show the coexistence and interdependent functions of their respective forms of thesis and hypothesis. The final theses which permit the rhetorician to argue persuasively have already been through, and sophisticated by, a philosophical analysis, however rudimentary, of moral dialectic. More inclusive still, the literary thesis has already absorbed the results of both philosophical and rhetorical analysis by virtue of the potentiality which literature shares with these disciplines to realize, in their own materials, some of the formal organization of mathematical products. The process of analyzing the (as yet 'unarticulated') geometrical figure and then of synthesizing it in a complete diagram is analogous to the process of analyzing the (as yet undifferentiated) literary materials into the plot outline and then of synthesizing them in the actual composition of the work. The literary synthesis achieved by a division of the outlined events into greater and greater diversity of speeches and episodes corresponds to the geometrical synthesis achieved by a division of elementary constructions into lines and planes. While the materials of geometrical construction are points, lines, and surfaces, those of poetic construction are words, thoughts, and actions—the materials, that is, of philosophy and rhetoric (see pp. 42–45 of this study).

We may conclude by illustrating the process of fictional construction with the example from antiquity already mentioned in Chapter 2. We observe or hear of a tragic incident: a son has killed his mother. We ask how this could have come about. After working back through an analysis of various alternatives, we postulate a general outline of events (or borrow one already postulated) which might have led to such an outcome. This outline is the literary hypothesis. Now ready to begin the actual composition, we work forward from the outline by 'dividing' it into more and more characters, speeches, and incidents, synthesizing them all by filling in names and episodes. If we do not have to violate necessity or probability, our explanation will offer a persuasive 'thesis' about why such tragic events could have happened in the ways we have revealed.[2]

To be persuasive, our account of the Orestean events must ultimately share in the logical consistency of mathematics. But, since drama imitates the actions of human agents, consistency alone will be insufficient. Moral questions, whose analysis is the subject of dialectic, will have to reveal the ethical significance of actions through a series of deliberations and choices whose interrelation Aristotle compares to geometrical analysis. The logical structure will make the ethical events plausible through self-consistency; moral dialectic will give that consistency a human significance in its pursuit of the definition of the Good.[3] If left to themselves, however, since questions of consistency and truth do not involve action (cf. De an. 431b10–12), both principles of order would culminate in general propositions. The dramatist, therefore, must grasp in the initial outline of events a rhetorical principle as well which can bring out for dramatization a specific controversy, a *quaestio definita*, to be judged first by the poet and then by the audience.

Both the dramatist and the orator, furthermore, persuade their re-

[2] In describing the extent of mathematical presuppositions in attitudes toward certainty, probability, and the arts, T. B. L. Webster observes that "mathematical proof has universal validity; it is what the Greeks call 'necessary' (anankaion)." Such a "necessity" was often invoked to control the arguments from probability: "Thus the mathematical arguments provide a framework within which the general truths established by observation or otherwise can be related to each other" (*Greek Art and Literature 700–530 B.C.* [London, 1959], pp. 95–96).

[3] In distinguishing Plato's hypothetical method in the *Republic* from that in the *Meno* and *Phaedo*, Robinson argues that the method used to achieve the highest category on the Divided Line "has gone back to being practically the Socratic elenchus" (*Plato's Earlier Dialectic*, p. 184). He later criticizes the method for avoiding an infinite regress only by means of the assumption (unacceptable today even in geometry) that a premise could be examined dialectically without assuming other premises: "What seemed to Plato the gradual forging of a hypothesis to which there were no objections turns out . . . to be merely the gradual forging of a consistent set of beliefs; and it therefore does not escape the stricture passed in the *Cratylus*, that consistency is no guarantee of truth" (p. 190). It is interesting that the exclusion of other premises was precisely what the fictional hypothesis (once again in agreement with Euclidean geometry) enabled the poet to do. Literary discourse might avoid the danger of infinite regress by its very power to delimit its philosophical premises with stipulated circumstances, analogous to the rhetorical hypothesis, in a fictional plot (cf. Sextus, *Pyrr.* 1.168). The desire to justify a type of discourse which could avoid this danger may have influenced the development of literary theory after Plato.

spective listeners to regard such and such a particular action as just or unjust by removing the discussion to the most generic questions involved in the controversy. Quintilian uses the plot of the play in question as an example: "There are some who hold that even those questions which have reference to persons and particular cases may at times be called *theses*, provided only they are put slightly differently: for instance, if Orestes be accused, we shall have a *cause*: whereas if it is put as question, namely 'Was Orestes rightly acquitted?' it will be a *thesis*" (3.5.11). Such a thesis claims a temporary freedom from its immediate implication in circumstantial details in order that the orator may step back and 'make something of' the facts as a whole. This freedom permits rhetoric to contribute its share to the universalizing function of the literary thesis. Permanently free of historical circumstances, the fictional imitation presents an individual situation in which the assertion of existence, the conditions of formal coherence, and the deliberations of moral choice may be rhetorically analyzed for the judgment of the audience.

Part Two

Knowledge and Representation: The Philosophical Premises of Literary Decorum

In Part One of this study I tried to describe how the literary analysis of experience participates in the intentions and discursive procedures of the three main categories of discourse: mathematics, philosophy, and rhetoric. Disciplines associated with these three categories originally provided terms in which those who questioned and defended the value of literature could formulate and transmit a body of observations which could gradually develop into a literary theory. Perhaps the principal obligation of such a theory was to preserve a balance among the functions appropriate to these disciplines as expressed, however tacitly, in the terms themselves. For it is evident that a writer might emphasize his formal, his heuristic, or his judicative intelligence at the expense of one or both of the other two only at the risk of impoverishing his work by failing to draw fully on all the potential resources of his art.

In Part One I described the ways in which the formal principle of order in a work of literature might combine, as a common denominator, philosophical and rhetorical materials and integrate their energies in fulfilling the potentialities of literary discourse. In Parts Two and Three respectively I shall try to describe how the competing disciplines of philosophy and rhetoric contributed their terms of analysis, and thereby their characteristic vulnerabilities, to literary theory. While an over-emphasis upon formal structure has resulted historically in aestheticism, too great a preoccupation with either philosophy or rhetoric, especially when isolated from one another, has resulted in purely utilitarian expectations of literature. The aesthetic theory of the formalist and the didactic theory of the pragmatist suffer from complementary deformations: each slights the artistic expression of that portion of experience which the other emphasizes.

When philosophy and rhetoric revert to their original antagonism toward one another, their influence upon literary discourse tends to become conservative. The philosophical influence becomes conservative in its attempt to reduce literary expression to ever more simplified and inclusive propositions about facts, doctrines, or methods. Such propositions tend to be expressed in more and more rigidly schematic allegories or in symbols which are invariable and arbitrarily transferable from one literary context to another. It will be seen that the more generic the symbol, the more drained of qualitative particularity it may tend to become, and, consequently, the more the work itself, which embodies it, may revert toward the quantitative formalism of geometrical demonstration. As we shall see, such conservative influences on literature culminate in the Neoplatonic reconstruction of ancient literary theory and become the sources of modern Symbolism.

The rhetorical influence becomes conservative, on the other hand, in its insistence upon an ever more detailed verisimilitude in presenting the circumstances of individual cases. The greater the psychological conviction that a narrative account bears a one-to-one relation to the facts it represents, the more the representation of any given situation achieves the illusion of mimetic probability. Under the conservative influence of rhetoric, therefore, literary theory has tended to evaluate fictional representations on the basis of their measurable approximations to historical fact. Such approximations to fact might be compared 'quantitatively' to one another in terms of degrees of verisimilar proportions analogous to the relations expressed in mathematical propositions. As in the case of philosophy, the conservative influence of rhetoric has tended to make literary representation seek the logical and psychological security of formal precision.

In Part Two I shall discuss the nature of literary decorum by emphasizing its relation to the philosophical acquisition of knowledge rather than to either the geometrical assumption of form or to the rhetorical manipulation of style.[1] It will be seen that the nature of the objects we experience determines, to a great extent, the kind and accuracy of the knowledge we can have of them. The kind of knowledge we arrive at, in turn, will determine the type and degree of stylistic detail—as well as influence its formal arrangement—by which we may properly represent that knowledge. The style of the representation, in its turn, makes specific psychagogic claims upon the responses of the audience which must be appropriate to the nature of the object if decorum is to be achieved. The achievement of decorum, in this sense, may be said to begin, then, as a cognitive activity. We must estimate the intelligibility of an object and learn what we can about it before we interpret or evaluate it. Only then can we properly persuade the members of an audience to accept our judgment, to acquiesce, in other words, in the emotional response which the style of our representation of the object demands from them.

The term 'decorum,' in its most general sense, refers to the criteria

---

[1] In emphasizing the relation of decorum to philosophical discourse in Part Two and the relation of rhetorical to literary argumentation in Part Three, I have given a minimum of attention in this study to what we usually think of as 'style' (*elocutio*). The reader may remedy this neglect by consulting many thorough studies, beginning with E. Norden's *Die Antike Kunstprosa* (1898), on the ancient treatment of diction, figures, and periodic structure. There are, however, certain problems and texts concerning 'style' which are pertinent to the issues treated in Part Two. I have discussed some of these texts briefly in Chapter 7, but many, which I had previously gathered together in two articles, cannot economically be cited again. When appropriate, therefore, I shall refer the reader to the articles themselves: "The Meaning of Horace's Ut Pictura Poesis," JWCI 36 (1973):1–34 (hereafter cited as MHP) and "Horace's 'Ut Pictura Poesis': The Argument for Stylistic Decorum," *Traditio* 34 (1978):29–73 (hereafter cited as HASD).

to be observed in judging those things in our experience whose excellence lends itself more appropriately to qualitative than to quantitative measurement. The Greek distinction between these two types of measurement, formulated most clearly by Plato (*Statesman* 283D–84E) and Aristotle (*E.N.* 2.6), applies to all the arts and sciences, and decorum, therefore, designates the principles of both ethical and aesthetic judgment.[2] When taken more narrowly with respect to a given art, such as literature, decorum refers to the realization and balance of those intentions which are characteristic of that particular art. Like the cognitive negotiation in the acquisition of knowledge described below, however, decorum itself cannot be expressed as a fixed ratio of components or produced by a fixed series of steps. It is not to be weighed out, once and for all, in specific ingredients either to be combined together at once or to be added in sequence as in a chemical experiment. It is, rather, a continuing process, an avoidance moment by moment of an imbalance among the energies contributed, in the case of literature, by all three categories of discourse which I have been describing. Having emphasized the formal contribution in Part One, I shall now examine the cognitive, before proceeding in Part Three to the judicative, contributions to the literary analysis of experience.

[2] For a more detailed discussion and application of the two types of measurement, see Chap. 8, pp. 171–73 and esp. Chap. 10, pp. 266–75.

5. The Cognitive Conditions of Literary Representation

Both rhetoric and dialectic, according to Aristotle (*Rhet.* 1.1–4), are 'faculties' trained to provide arguments rather than 'sciences,' such as geometry or physics, developed to investigate, organize, and transmit specific bodies of knowledge. Rhetoric deals primarily with subjects involving practical questions of legal and political ethics, while dialectic treats all practical and theoretical problems involved in what we loosely call the philosophical or scientific disciplines. Not only does dialectic deal with a broader range of questions than rhetoric, but philosophy, in its widest sense, employs, in addition to dialectic, other methods of reasoning when these methods are appropriate to the material under consideration. Because of this greater breadth of both topics and methods, we must discriminate more precisely the ways in which philosophical discourse is related to literature beyond the simple philosophical content of literary works. Any such discrimination, however, which might restrict the types of problems to be taken up or of the theses to be verified, prohibit any questions from being asked about them, or curtail any methods of analysis to be used in answering the questions would defeat the very purpose of philosophy itself: the investigation and explanation of all existent things (cf. *Meta.* 4.3.6–8). Literature, furthermore, is as much concerned with representing any given interpretation of reality as philosophy is with verifying its truth. We must not seek, therefore, to relate philosophy to literature by limiting philosophical problems, questions, or methods but by relating the knowledge which they produce to its artistic expression: to relate, that is, knowledge to representation.

While rhetoric seeks the means of persuading an audience to accept and act upon a given judgment, philosophy seeks a knowledge of existent things and of existence itself. In an important distinction for literary representation, Aristotle maintains that we acquire knowledge by proceeding from what is more apprehensible to the senses but less intelligible with respect to its own nature to what is more intelligible with respect to its own nature but less apprehensible to the senses. We begin, that is, inductively from the composite objects of our experience. Although these objects are more immediately apprehensible to our perceptions, and therefore are more intelligible to us (ἡμῖν), they are, nevertheless, implicated in the processes of sensation and are, therefore, less knowable in themselves (ἁπλῶς, ὅλως). Philosophical analysis consists in our using these things which are immediately clearer to us to progress ('upward' or 'inward') to those things, such as causes, origins, elemental components, or scientific principles (*Meta.* 5.11.5), which are logically or ontologically prior and hence more intelligible in the absolute sense (*Meta.* 7.4.2–3). Once grasped, these principles may be used as starting points (ἀρχαί) for a deductive synthesis. Such a synthesis, by returning ('downward' or 'outward') to the composite object of our experience (the *problema* or *thesis* which we initially set out to explain or defend), can 'demonstrate' that these prior elements and causes do indeed constitute and account for the object's being what it is. In this process of analysis and synthesis our understanding of the object becomes most *complete*— rather than becoming most perceptually or demonstratively *accurate*— a completeness derived from neither kind of intelligibility in isolation from the other but from a negotiation between the two. Where this negotiation takes place, the inherent intelligibility of first principles clarifies our apprehension of those things perceived by the senses. The apprehensibility of sensory objects, in turn, embodies and expresses the luminosity of the intellective principles in the order, intensity, and clarity of our perceptions. In this reciprocation we experience the greatest degree of consciousness, and it is the knowledge derived from this experience which the literary and visual arts strive to represent.[1]

The logical terminology of this distinction between the two types of intelligibility, however, can easily give us a misleading account of how we acquire knowledge. The additional formulation of a 'point' of most refined negotiation or of fullest reciprocation between *them* also remains rooted in the verbal context of inductive and deductive dialectic. It is,

---

[1] Without undertaking a review of the various derivations and meanings suggested for the word νοῦς or 'intelligence,' I would like to suggest that one of its functions, and perhaps its most complete function, is the apprehension of that knowledge derived from our experience of this 'negotiation' or 'reciprocation.' For an analysis compatible with this meaning of the word, see J. H. Lesher, "The Meaning of NOYΣ in the Posterior Analytics," *Phronesis* 18 (1973):44–68. Because of the complexity of the philosophical problem, however, I have avoided this, or any other, usage of the words 'nous' and 'noetic' whenever possible. In seeking alternative descriptive terms, I have used the unsatifactory words 'intuitive,' 'intuitively,' and 'intuition,' but only in accordance with Lesher's valuable precaution: "If to intuit something is simply to have an insight or realize the truth of some proposition then certainly νοῦς will be intuitive knowledge and νόησις will be an act of intuition. If however we mean by 'intuition' a faculty which acquires knowledge about the world in an *a priori* or non-empirical manner, then it will be inappropriate to think of the Aristotelian νοῦς as intuition" (p. 64).

therefore, important to remember that such a point does not simply refer to another logical form of beginning, to a third kind of logical *arche* located somewhere in between the formulations of our first intellective principles and the perceptions of our first 'aesthetic' principles. Such a point refers, rather, to *the* beginning, the *arche* of consciousness itself, whose origins are similarly undemonstrable. The intelligible cause and the perceptible effect of dialectic are both subsidiary instruments in the analysis of our conscious experience and, hence, derive from, and are subsequent to, it. These instruments can, in an absolute sense, no more 'place' our consciousness of reality in time than a measuring rod can 'locate' the unit which calibrates it in space. Despite their subsidiary status, however, the intelligible cause and the perceptible effect as terms of traditional philosophical inquiry have so often been used to define what the consciousness becomes aware of that they may help us to explain certain historical problems in the way we speak about our representation of experience.

The 'point' of greatest reciprocation, which philosophical analysis and synthesis endeavor to reveal, may be considered a hypothetically perfect adjustment between the intuitive intellection of first principles and the equally intuitive perception of sensory impressions. Like the 'mean' of ethics, 'equity' of law, and 'decorum' of the literary and visual arts, this adjustment is qualitatively absolute in the sense that we can—except perhaps in moments of rare illumination—only approximate it, to a greater or less degree, in our conscious experience. Ordinarily, our most approximate adjustment would take place when a deductive synthesis could confirm the results of an inductive analysis and thus permit us to comprehend most completely the composite object initially presented to our senses. Difficulties, however, may arise which would prevent either a very precise adjustment or any adjustment at all. We simply may not be able to arrive at intellective first principles from our immediate experience, or, having postulated or 'leapt to' these first principles, we may not be able to negotiate the distance from them back to what may be empirically apprehended. The middle ground between the 'intellective' and the 'aesthetic' poles of cognition, even if not impassable, may, nevertheless, appear forbidding or may hide its terrain in mysterious labyrinths of intermediate causation. In this case, the would-be literary traveler may abandon the discursive probability of public discourse for the visionary certainty of private illumination. In such an event, no matter how persistently either or both of the extremes may be sought intuitively, if they cannot be discursively related to one another, less articulate forms of knowledge will result, which will, in turn, encourage less articulate ways of representing what is known. It is necessary, therefore, to clarify further the nature of these extremes, which constitute the intuitive *archai* of our reasoning, in order to relate the problems of philosophical inquiry more closely to those of artistic representation.

The most universal things, Aristotle says in describing the subject of his *Metaphysics* (*Meta.* 1.2; 6.1), are "perhaps the hardest for man to grasp, because they are furthest removed from the senses," and the most exact (ἀκριβέσταται) sciences will be those most concerned with discovering universal principles.[2] These are speculative sciences which investigate the causes appropriate to physics, mathematics, and 'theology,' for these causes are both the most desirable kind of instrumental knowledge (perhaps because of their inclusiveness) and the most intelligible with respect to their own nature. Whereas physics deals with mutable things and some kinds of mathematics deal with objects not separable from matter, the primary science of 'metaphysics' alone studies what is immutable *and* separable from matter—studies, that is, Being as such and the attributes which belong to it *qua* Being. 'Metaphysics' also seeks to state "for what end each action is to be done" with respect to "the Good in each particular case" and, more generally, with respect to "the highest Good in the whole of nature," since the Good, insofar as it is an end, is a cause (*Meta.* 1.2.4–8; 6.1.8–12). For these reasons, the acquisition of such a science might, mistakenly, be considered "beyond human power," while, on the contrary, it is actually the most divine and precious form of human knowledge in view of the fact that it either concerns divine matters or is the peculiar possession of God. Its acquisition, furthermore, must result in a transformation of our point of view. For our inquiry, which begins in "wondering that things should be as they are, *e.g.* with regard to marionettes, or the solstices, or the incommensurability of the diagonal of a square," must end with the contrary and better view appropriate to men who have come to understand such things (*Meta.* 1.2.12–16).[3]

---

[2] It is important for the reader to bear in mind from the beginning that there are two kinds of cognitive exactness (ἀκρίβεια) which correspond to the two types of intelligibility to be discussed in this study in detail. The first kind is characteristic of our knowledge of objects which are more immediately apprehensible to the senses; the second of our knowledge of things more intelligible in themselves. 'Metaphysics' and the mathematical sciences strive primarily for the second kind of exactness (cf. *Meta.* 13.3.6), while the more empirical arts and sciences must strive primarily for an accuracy of sensory detail (ἡμῖν) and then for principles which, once arrived at, may be considered in themselves (ἁπλῶς) as accurate points of departure for future inquiry. For a good account of ἀκρίβεια as it occurs in *Post. An.* 2.19, discussed in this study, see Lesher, "Meaning of ΝΟΥΣ," pp. 62–64.

[3] On the knowledge and representation of the divine, see H. A. Wolfson, "The Knowability and Describability of God in Plato and Aristotle," *HSCP* 56–57 (1947):233–49. For the later period, see Wolfson, "Albinus and Plotinus on Divine Attributes," *Harv. Theol.*

How these universal principles of the speculative sciences are reached, while touched on in the first chapter of the *Metaphysics*, forms the subject of the last chapter of the *Posterior Analytics*. We can proceed, Aristotle says, to these principles from our initial empirical inquiry into why things should be as they are because of the very nature of our sensory perceptions. Our perceptions are not simply the bare sensory data which an electrical apparatus might pick up and record on a graph. On the contrary, they already have a potentiality for order by virtue of the fact that "the act of perception involves the universal." What we perceive in a thing is what it shares with other things.[4] Such perceptions give rise to memory, and repeated memories give rise to experience.

The memories, though numerically many, constitute a single experience (ἐμπειρία). And experience, that is the universal when established (ἠρεμήσαντος = 'come to rest') as a whole in the soul—the One that corresponds to the Many, the unity that is identically present in them all—provides the starting-point of art and science: art in the world of process and science in the world of facts. Thus these faculties . . . arise from sense-perception, just as, when a retreat has occurred in battle, if one man halts so does another, and then another, until the original position is restored. The soul is so constituted that it is capable of the same sort of process. . . . As soon as one individual percept has 'come to a halt' (στάντος) in the soul, this is the first beginning of the presence there of a universal (because although it is the particular that we perceive, the act of perception involves the universal, *e.g.*, 'man,' not 'a man, Callias'). Then other 'halts' (ἵσταται) occur among these ⟨proximate⟩ universals, until the indivisible genera or ⟨ultimate⟩ universals are established.[5]

Rev. 45 (1952):115–30; E. R. Dodds' comments on "The Unknown God in Neoplatonism," *Proclus: The Elements of Theology* (Oxford, 1963), Appendix I; and the article by G. B. Ladner cited in Chap. 8, n. 5. For general studies, see W. Jaeger, *The Theology of the Early Greek Philosophers* (Oxford, 1967); B. Snell, *The Discovery of the Mind* (Cambridge, Mass., 1953), esp. Chaps. 2 and 7; and E. Voegelin, *The World of the Polis*, vol. 2 of *Order and History* (Baton Rouge, 1957).

[4] An observation made by Sir David Ross: the transition "from sense to reason" is "made possible by the fact that perception itself has an element of the universal; we perceive a particular thing, it is true, but what we perceive in it is characters which it shares with other things" (*Aristotle* [London, 1966], p. 55).

[5] *Posterior Analytics* 2.19, 100a5–b2. For the relation between arriving at first principles and arriving at universals, see Lesher, "Meaning of ΝΟΥΣ," pp. 60–62. For Plato's account of recollection (ἀνάμνησις), see *Phaedrus* 249C. For Aristotle, induction performs many of the functions of Platonic recollection (*Pr. An.* 2.21) and the single experience, made up of many memories, establishes itself by literally "coming to rest" (ἠρεμήσαντος, 100a6) in the soul. The close association of "knowing (ἐπίσταμαι)" with "taking a stand (ἐφίσταμαι)" is common to both Plato (*Crat.* 437AB) and Aristotle (*Phys.* 247b10–17). It also accounts, as we shall see in Part Three, for the concept of στάσις in the establishment of the *status* or question at issue in a legal controversy. If the experience were that of a literary work, single memories of seeing or reading it on different occasions might, equally, coalesce to establish a starting point (ἀρχή) for understanding the work and, subsequently, for formulating an art of literature itself. In similar terms, J. V. Cunningham describes

It is because general concepts (τὸ καθόλου) are built up inductively from sensory perception (αἴσθησις), Aristotle continues, that we are able to reach, first, intermediate, then, primary principles by means of intuition. Since these 'intellectively' intuited first principles of science originally arise from our 'aesthetically' intuited first principles of perception and subsequently become the necessary premises of deductive demonstration, the senses, though incapable by themselves of arriving at scientific knowledge, are the ultimate source of it (*Post. an.* 2.19; cf. 1.18, 1.31).[6]

Since, for Aristotle, a universal may be a synthesis of remembered instances coming together and holding steady as a single experience and, at the same time, may provide the starting point for the arts and disciplines dealing with the realm of process (100a8–9), it is important to recall his analysis of memory. If, when we remember, we perceive something like an impression (τύπος) or a picture (γραφή), how is it, he asks, that this perception of something present in the mind can become a memory of something no longer present there? Such remembrance almost implies "that one can also see and hear what is not present."

But surely in a sense this can and does occur. Just as the picture painted on the panel is at once a picture (ζῷον) and a portrait (εἰκών), and though one and the same, is both, yet the essence of the two is not the same, and it is possible to think of it both as a picture and as a portrait, so in the same way we must regard the mental picture within us (τὸ ἐν ἡμῖν φάντασμα) both as an object of contemplation in itself (καθ' αὐτό) and as a mental picture of something else. In so far as we consider it in itself, it is an object of contemplation or a mental picture, but in so far as we consider it in relation to something else, *e.g.*, as a likeness, it is also an aid to memory. . . . Memorizing preserves the memory of something by constant reminding. This is nothing but the repeated contemplation of an object as a likeness, and not independently.[7]

---

how, after reading a work a number of times, our experience of it "grows steady" and seems "to come together" to express its unity. Since a composition may be repeatedly experienced, it gains a stability, a permanence, by virtue of the fact that its principles of order can be continually rediscovered. It becomes "a potentiality of experience waiting to be realized" (*Tradition and Poetic Structure* [Denver, 1960], p. 22–24).

[6] The Hippocratian procedures of research resemble Aristotle's analysis and, indeed, anticipate Bacon's epistemological recommendations. One must not rest with plausible theories but attend "to experience combined with reason," for a "theory is a composite memory of things apprehended with sense-perception. For the sense-perception, coming first in experience and conveying to the intellect the things subjected to it, is clearly imaged, and the intellect, receiving these things many times, noting the occasion, the time and the manner, stores them up in itself and remembers" (*Precepts 1–2, Hippocrates*, trans. W. H. S. Jones, LCL, 4 vols. [London, 1923–1931]).

[7] *On Memory and Recollection* 1; 450b12–51a14, included, along with *De Insomniis*, in *Aristotle: On the Soul, Parva Naturalia, On Breath*, trans. W. S. Hett, LCL (London, 1964). For Aristotelian psychology generally, see J. I. Beare, *Greek Theories of Elementary Cognition from Alcmaeon to Aristotle* (Oxford, 1906), esp. pp. 290–336, R. Sorabji,

The "repeated contemplation of an object as a likeness (τὸ θεωρεῖν πολλάκις ὡς εἰκόνα)," which gives rise to memory here, is the first stage of the process leading to the "repeated memories (μνήμης πολλάκις . . . γιγνομένης)" of the same object or event, which give rise to experience in the *Posterior Analytics* (2.19; 100a4–5). We should be able, that is, to gather the many repeated impressions in the memory into a single experience. Having grasped the universal premises by virtue of which that experience has become significant, we might, then, subsequently reason 'outward' from these premises to render analogous objects or events more intelligible. The original perceptions and the premises intuited from them, however, are often very imprecise.

Continuing with his pictorial analogy, Aristotle observes that we cannot always be sure that the impression which apparently earlier (real) sensations have left in the soul is indeed derived from them until we reflect and remember that we have heard or seen this particular 'something' before. This occurs "whenever we first think of it as itself, and then change and think of it as referring to something else." In the case of lunatics, the opposite occurs, for they speak of "their mental pictures as if they had actually taken place, and as if they actually remembered them." This happens because the lunatic "regards as a likeness what is not a likeness" (*De mem.* 451a7–12).

It is especially easy to mistake a mental picture for a mental portrait or to assume that something which had never taken place had really occurred when the imagination is disturbed. Aristotle distinguishes the imagination (φαντασία) from sensation (αἴσθησις), opinion (δόξα), knowledge (ἐπιστήμη), and intelligence (νοῦς), and from any combination of these in his *De anima* (3.3). Being simply a "movement produced by sensation actively operating," imagination does not primarily perform a judgmental function. It differs, therefore, from opinion in its effect upon us in that when we have an opinion that something is frightening or desirable we immediately feel fear or love, but when we look into our imagination, "we are like spectators looking at something dreadful or encouraging in a picture" (*De an.* 427b22–5). As long as our judging faculties reassure us that what our imagination shows us is not real and therefore no more threatening than what we see in the picture, we may contemplate its images, as they linger in the mind, with emotional detachment. When our judgment, however, becomes "temporarily clouded over by emotion, or disease, or sleep," we are no longer prevented from responding to these same images as if they were the truth-bearing impressions which they resemble (*De mem.* 429a7–8).

Aristotle On Memory (Providence, 1972), and, specifically on the imagination, M.-D. Philippe, "Φαντασία in the Philosophy of Aristotle," *The Thomist* 35 (1971):1–42.

In the *De insomniis* Aristotle observes further how easily we are deceived about our impressions when we are in emotional states. Even from faint resemblances, the coward in his fear thinks that he sees his enemy, the lover in his passion his beloved: in each case, the higher the degree of excitement, the weaker the resemblance necessary to stimulate the imagination. Men, too, "in fever sometimes think that they see animals on the walls from the slight resemblance of marks in a pattern." So closely does the degree of illusion occasionally correspond to the degree of emotion that "those who are not very ill are aware that the impression is false, but if the malady is more severe, they move themselves in accordance with what they think they see" (*De insomn.* 460b1–16). In these pathological states, the judgment, which had been necessary to keep the phantasm from being regarded as a likeness, is suspended. Such an event corresponds to Aristotle's earlier example of the loss of emotional detachment on the part of the spectator who begins to identify himself with the characters portrayed. Similarly, as we shall see, a sophist such as Plato describes might try to make his listeners take his fantastic images, presented to their inner eye by verbal accounts of heightened emotional power, as eicastically true.[8]

Aristotle's observations on psychology illustrate the recurring hazards in arriving inductively at universal principles from perceptual principles—particularly in ethical matters, which admit of great variation. His terms clarify my earlier distinctions about the consciousness. While divine things such as the heavenly bodies of the physical cosmos are objects whose nature may, to some extent, be accessible to 'aesthetic' intuition, a knowledge of their ultimate causes, to say nothing of Being as such, rests uneasily upon the *archai* of sensory perceptions alone (cf. *Post. an.* 1.31). The 'distance' is too great with respect to both the remoteness of these bodies from the senses and to the scale of increasing ontological disparity between the visible cosmos and the divine sources, of its ultimate explanation. The more distant and diverse these sources, the greater the difficulty of our glimpsing them and bringing them to bear on that medial 'point' of negotiation at which we become most aware, within our natural limitations, of their elucidating presence in the things around us. The greater this difficulty, the greater the tendency to transform or 'hypostatize' either the 'abstract' universal or the equally 'abstract' particular into that ultimate form of knowledge which, in reality, exists only in their mutual reciprocation. When either type of logical instrument replaces this form of knowledge as the object of phil-

[8] Passages related to these on the psychagogic powers of the fantasy: Plato, *Rep.* 476C, *Phil.* 38E–40E: Plutarch, *Mor.* 759C; Longinus, 15; Quintilian, 6.2.25–35; St. Augustine, *De trin.* 11.4.

osophical insight, the problems of representing our experience of those things which can be only imperfectly known become increasingly difficult.

Such transformations are particularly dangerous for literary theory. The universal, which Aristotle says poetry has the power to reveal, is always in danger of becoming an independent object of knowledge, and hence of representation.[9] The danger arises because the first terms of logical dichotomies—such as prior vs. posterior or universal vs. particular—have a tendency to claim not only an instrumental but an ontological superiority over the second. When the first terms classify things which are further removed from immediate experience and more difficult to grasp, they appear to be 'better' or 'more existent' than the second terms rather than simply more generically efficient in including a greater number of individual instances. This efficiency can lead to our confusing them with, and even preferring them to, the existent things *for whose sake* we sought them as premises of demonstration in the first place.[10] When, for instance, Aristotle is occasionally misquoted from the Renaissance on as saying that poetry imitates the universal, while history imitates the particular, his observations might easily be used to support a didactic theory of poetry. For if poetry aimed simply to 'imitate' recurrent patterns of behavior and to express these patterns in general ethical formulations about human nature, poems might easily become simply repositories of moral precepts. What Aristotle is actually saying is that poetry imitates men and their actions in a way *different* from that of history. The fact that poetry is not confined to presenting actual occurrences with historical accuracy, and thereby becomes more 'serious' and 'philosophical,' is a methodological condition of poetic forms of representation. It is by means of the universal—which is precious because it reveals causation (*Post. an.* 88a5)—that motivations may be analyzed more precisely and the poem may evaluate human experience more completely. Because of this essential 'property' of poetry, the poet can persuasively reveal the significance of his story for an audience more

---

[9] So Aristotle himself complains that "present-day thinkers tend to regard universals as substance, because genera are universal, and they hold that these are more truly principles and substances because they approach the question theoretically" (*Meta.* 12.1.2, 1069a27–29).

[10] A simple example may be useful. To illustrate the analysis of composite wholes into their elements, Plato uses the analysis of syntax into words, words into syllables, and syllables into letters (*Crat.* 424B–25B; cf. *Statesman* 277E–78D). The elementary letters are logically prior to the finished composition (cf. Aristotle, *Categories* 12; *Meta.* 7.17.8–12) and more universal, since out of them many particular compositions may be made. Yet, as students of literature, we would not regard the letters themselves as more excellent or more existent than the finished work: the alphabet exists for the sake of *Hamlet*, not *Hamlet* for the sake of the alphabet.

fully than the historian can. The universal itself, however, could never be legitimately hypostatized as the 'object' to be imitated, for it is not an 'object' at all. It is merely a logical instrument more appropriate to poetry than to history.

If, on the other hand, the particular were to become an independent object of knowledge, and hence of representation, it would be as abstract a conception as the universal. Stripped by definition of all universal qualities, it would remain a purely hypothetical *datum* which could not even be experienced, since what we experience of things is what they share with other things. Were a literary theory to suggest how one might represent such unique particulars as objects, it could only recommend trying to isolate independent impressions of them in images which, however sharply imagined individually, could have little or no connection with each other or with human experience as a whole.[11]

With these preliminary observations on the philosophical analysis of experience, we may turn more directly to the problem of representation. To what extent does the nature of the object of knowledge determine the degree of accuracy of our inquiry into it? How do the qualitative nature of the object and the accuracy of our inquiry affect its artistic representation? Although I shall be primarily concerned with literature, I hope that the illustrative analogies drawn from discussions of the visual arts will bear, to some extent, upon related problems in painting and sculpture.

[11] The isolation of such particulars was one of the central objectives of the Imagist movement in twentieth-century poetry. Wallace Stevens implies the limitation of such a theory in his poem "The Course of a Particular," where he traces the 'progress' of sensory impressions to pure abstraction.

6. The Ancient Dilemma of Knowledge and Representation

In order to describe the extent to which epistemological considerations bear upon the attainment of stylistic decorum, I shall try to clarify some of the important relations between knowledge and representation by recalling an ancient dilemma. As an illustration of the antitheses of the dilemma, I shall borrow an anecdote about how a Greek and an Egyptian disagreed over the proper way to represent the gods. The reader should regard the anecdote, not as a literal analogue or model of either the philosophical or artistic problems involved, but as a kind of parable which draws various issues into a coherent association with one another. This parabolic 'freedom from history' is especially appropriate to antitheses whose expression changes from period to period but whose essential points of contradiction remain relatively constant (see pp. 103–104 of this chapter).

A. The Horns of the Dilemma

The ancient dilemma of knowledge and representation arises originally because there are not only different kinds of knowledge to which the mind has different degrees of access, but also because there are two different ways of evaluating knowledge itself. It is helpful to formulate the dilemma as a distinction between the excellence of the object to be represented and the accuracy with which the mind may know the object. This distinction, in turn, is made up of two premises and it subsequently becomes an antithesis. Aristotle states the first premise, when he distinguishes the two different ways of evaluating knowledge, in the opening sentence of his treatise *On the Soul*:

We regard all knowledge as beautiful (καλῶν) and valuable (τιμίων), but one kind more so than another, either in virtue of its accuracy (κατ' ἀκρίβειαν), or because it relates to higher (βελτιόνων) and more wonderful (θαυμασιωτέρων) things.

On both these counts it is reasonable to regard the inquiry concerning the soul as of the first importance.[1]

The first premise, then, states that the value of knowledge may be measured in two ways: first, with respect to the importance of its object, and second, with respect to the completeness or accuracy of its information about its object. The first way considers *what* is known, the second *how* it is known. The second premise of the distinction between excellence of object and accuracy of knowledge states simply that these two ways of evaluating knowledge are inversely proportionate to one another. That is, the more excellent the object, the less apprehensible and hence the less exactly it may be represented. On the other hand, the more accurately the object may be known and represented, the less removed and hence the less exceptional it is apt to be. The two premises of the distinction may be stated as a completed antithesis and the opposing terms established. Greater nobility or excellence of objects (though less exactly known and representable) is one term of the antithesis; greater accuracy of knowledge and representation (though of less exceptional objects) is the other.

One of the most beautiful formulations of the antithesis occurs in Aristotle's treatise *On the Parts of Animals.*

Of the works of Nature there are, we hold, two kinds: those which are brought into being and perish, and those which are free from these processes throughout all ages. The latter are of the highest worth and are divine, but our opportunities for the study of them are somewhat scanty, since there is but little evidence available to our senses to enable us to consider them and all the things that we long to know about. We have better means of information, however, concerning the things that perish, that is to say, plants and animals, because we live among them; and anyone who will but take enough trouble can learn much concerning every one of their kinds. Yet each of the two groups has its attractiveness. For although our grasp of the eternal things is but slight, nevertheless the joy which it brings is, by reason of their excellence and worth, greater than that of knowing all things that are here below; just as the joy of a fleeting and partial glimpse of those whom we love is greater than that of an accurate view (δι' ἀκριβείας ἰδεῖν) of other things, no matter how numerous or how great they are. But

---

[1] *Aristotle: On the Soul* 1.1, 402a1–5, trans. W. S. Hett, LCL (London, 1964). See P. Merlan's interesting remarks on ἀκρίβεια in *From Platonism to Neoplatonism* (The Hague, 1968), pp. 144–47, 151–52. He cites P. Siwek's translation of the term by *inquisitio subtilior* (*Aristotelis De anima libri tres*, 1943–46), which, along with other observations of Merlan, is relevant for its stylistic usages discussed later (see Chap. 7, pp. 139–43). See also Lesher's remarks on ἀκίβεια, "Meaning of ΝΟΥΣ," pp. 62–64. Aristotle repeats the opening observation of the *De anima* as an example of a useful distinction in his *Topica* (8.1, 157a8–10), and in the *Metaphysics* he repeats half the definition: "each science is reckoned higher or lower in accordance with the proper object of its study" (11.7.9, 1064b5–6).

inasmuch as it is possible for us to obtain more and better information about things here on the earth, our knowledge of them has the advantage over the other; and moreover, because they are nearer to us and more akin to our Nature, they are able to make up some of their leeway as against the philosophy which contemplates the things that are divine.

Even the animals least attractive to the senses, Aristotle continues, can give to the natural philosopher who studies their nature the greatest pleasure. So, too, if the mere likenesses which painters and sculptors make of these lesser things please us, so much more will the contemplation of their natural causes. In all natural things, small as well as large, there is something of the marvelous; gods, as Heracleitus says, may even be found in the kitchen.[2]

The antithesis between excellence of the object to be known and accuracy with respect to knowledge of the object, furthermore, often determined how what is known should be represented in the literary and visual arts. An example occurs in Plato's *Critias*. In his projected trilogy, the *Timaeus*, the *Critias*, and the *Hermocrates*, Plato designates the subject matter to be treated by each speaker. Timaeus will treat the origins and physical nature of the universe; Critias will treat men and their relations with one another. The *Critias* opens with Timaeus' expressing relief at being able to relinquish the discussion to Critias, who immediately asks for an even greater indulgence on the part of the audience than Timaeus had requested (*Critias*, 107A). For, since all listeners are in a state of inexperience and ignorance about such elevated matters as the gods, the speaker can take greater liberties than he can about subjects so familiar to everyone that each might question his account of things. All accounts that we give of things, he says,

Must be, of course, of the nature of imitations (μίμησις) and representations (ἀπεικασία); and if we look at the portraiture of divine and of human bodies as executed by painters, in respect of the ease or difficulty with which they succeed in imitating their subjects in the opinion of onlookers, we shall notice in the first place that as regards the earth and mountains and rivers and woods and the whole of heaven, with the things that exist and move therein, we are content if a man is able to represent them with even a small degree of likeness; and further, that, inasmuch as we have no exact (ἀκριβές) knowledge about such objects, we do not examine closely or criticize the paintings, but tolerate, in such cases, an inexact and deceptive sketch (σκιαγραφία). On the other hand, whenever a painter tries to render a likeness of our own bodies, we quickly perceive what is defective because of our constant familiar acquaintance with them, and become severe critics of him who fails to bring out to the full all the points of similarity. And precisely the same thing happens, as we should notice,

---

[2] *Aristotle: Parts of Animals* 1.5, 644b23–45a23, trans. A. L. Peck, LCL (London, 1968).

in the case of discourses: in respect of what is celestial and divine we are satisfied if the account possesses even a small degree of likelihood, but we examine with precision (ἀκριβῶς) what is mortal and human. (*Critias* 107BD)[3]

A skiagraphic sketch refers to a likeness roughly outlined in shadows and shading probably meant to be seen at a distance. When used as a metaphor for certain kinds of literary representation, the term refers to a lack of exact refinement and verisimilitude, corresponding in the plastic arts to a lack of accurate modulations of color, of meticulousness of line, and of exactitude of proportion. The shadowed sketch or rough outline as an illustration of a verbal account of something whose nature does not permit detailed precision was also applied as a metaphor directly to style alone.

In his *Rhetoric* (3.12) Aristotle uses the same skiagraphic analogy as Plato does to refer to the style of spoken oratory proper to large public assemblies, outdoors in the noise, dust, and sun, where accurate refinements of rhetorical artifice, characteristic of written compositions to be read at leisure in comfortable surroundings, would simply be lost. Despite their apparent lack of artistic polish, however, such deliberative speeches addressed to large gatherings treated matters of the greatest importance to the democratic state (1.1.10). They required the most emotionally forceful delivery on the part of the orator to persuade their miscellaneous audience to a single course of action. Not only did the situation demand a dramatic and uncluttered simplicity of presentation, but the very fact that such speeches dealt with the future prevented their outline of events from being overly specific. The informal abruptness and repetition of such a style, Aristotle points out, is also characteristic of certain dramatic effects of Homer's style. Since the epics were composed to be recited orally rather than read at leisure, it is not surprising that they might also cultivate the histrionic force of agonistic debate. Both the deliberative and epic styles might understandably, that is, avoid

---

[3] *Plato: Timaeus, Critias, Cleitophon, Menexenus, Epistles*, trans. R. G. Bury, LCL (London, 1966). Timaeus himself had said much the same thing: "Wherefore, Socrates, if in our treatment of a great host of matters regarding the Gods and the generation of the Universe we prove unable to give accounts that are always in all respects self-consistent and perfectly exact, be not thou surprised; rather we should be content if we can furnish accounts that are inferior to none in likelihood, remembering that both I who speak and you who judge are but human creatures, so that it becomes us to accept the likely account of these and forbear to search beyond it" (*Tim.* 29CD). In a satirical vignette of a literary dabbler who, after composing paradoxical encomia, wishes to write one of Zeus, Philostratus has Apollonius of Tyana make the young man admit that one can write better panegyrics about what one knows than about what one does not know. The sage then ironically suggests the young man's father as a more suitable subject than Zeus, but the youth, falling into the trap, confesses that he fears disgracing his father by not doing justice to his excellence (*Life of Apollonius* 4.30).

those meticulous rhetorical *schemata* and similes worked out with perfect verisimilitude proper to written epideictic speeches and, by extension, poems. The antithesis, here, between importance of subject and refined exactness of rhetoric is clearly of the same nature as that between excellence and accuracy of stylistic representation with respect to the arts.

When Horace defines the obligations of the critic in his epistle to the Pisos, he cautions the critic to be tolerant of occasional imperfections in a work on the scale of Homer's whose elevated subject so often achieves its appropriate stylistic excellence. Total accuracy in verisimilar detail is not to be demanded. Introducing the ancient skiagraphic analogy with the phrase *ut pictura poesis*, Horace compares poetry with painting (*A.P.* 361–65):

A poem is like a picture: one strikes you more, the nearer you stand; another, the farther away. One prefers the shade; the other will wish to be seen in the full light of day and does not fear the critical insight of the judge. The one pleased but once; the other, though called for many times, will always please.

The picture seen from a distance, in the open sun, is comparable to the elevated works of Homer. The stylistic excellences appropriate to epic should not be made to fear a critic looking with a sharp eye for inaccuracies in the refined detail characteristic of paintings made for close inspection and of poems written for leisurely perusal.[4] It is just such a critic that, in the Platonic dialogue, Critias fears when he is about to describe familiar things whose depiction must be more meticulous—in the etymological sense of fearful of criticism (*meticulosus*)—because his errors in verisimilitude will be apparent to all. In his comic portrait of Euripides in the *Frogs*, Aristophanes anticipates this observation (959–60)—which Horace himself applies to comedy (*Ep.* 2.1.168–70)—and in his *Olympic Discourse*, Dio Chrysostom has the sculptor Pheidias echo it (*Orat.* 12.79).

Similarly, in his treatise *On the Sublime* (35–36) Longinus associates the emotional effect that Homer produces to that produced by the view, not this time of a skiagraphic painting, but of a colossal statue. The distance necessary to take the colossus in at a glance will conceal those refinements of verisimilitude which would be apparent to closer scrutiny. As Critias associates Timaeus' subject, properly treated in an adumbrated sketch, with mountains, rivers, and woods, as well as with celestial movements, Longinus associates the effects of the Homeric style, not

---

[4] *Ars poetica* 361–65, trans. H. R. Fairclough, (with modifications), in *Horace: Satires, Epistles, and Ars Poetica*, LCL (London, 1936). I have argued in detail for this interpretation of these lines in the articles on Horace designated MHP and HASD in Part Two: Introduction, n. 1.

only with the colossus, but with the wonderful in nature: the Nile, the ocean, and the eruptions of Etna. In contrast to the astounding, though faulty, colossus is the smaller, verisimilarly perfect statue of Polycleitus, which lacks the grandeur of nature but possesses the exactitude of art. Since man is "by nature . . . a being gifted with speech," his literature will owe its most excellent effects to nature (*ingenium*) and thereby evoke some of the natural wonder aroused by the colossus, while statues will owe their "likeness to man" to an accurate artistic meticulousness. These distinctions correspond to the two ways Aristotle said (*De an.* 1.1) the beauty of knowledge might be evaluated—either in virtue of the fact that it relates to higher and more wonderful things, or in virtue of its accuracy. With respect to the artistic representation of things known, the first way seems to correspond to the excellence of nature, the second to that of art, and the Aristotelian terms for 'wonderful' and 'accurate' are identical to those of Longinus.[5]

These, then, are the terms of the dilemma expressed in the completed antithesis: a subject matter of greater importance which can be less perfectly known and represented, on the one hand, and a less significant subject matter which can be more accurately known and represented on the other. Innocent enough on the surface, the antithesis conceals, nevertheless, rather formidable consequences.

If one accepts the antithesis as valid, he has two choices. Either (1) he may assume the incompatibility of its two opposing terms—the excellence of an object as opposed to the accuracy of an inquiry into it—and pursue these terms separately; or (2) he may attempt to relate one to the other in order to relax the tension between them. The first choice accepts (and exploits) their separateness; the second recognizes the advantage of arriving at more exact methods of treating more excellent subjects. For the literary analysis of experience, I regard the first choice as conservative and pessimistic; the second, as liberal and optimistic.

To take the first choice: if one pursues each term separately, the nobler object of knowledge—such as the gods, the cosmic order, or other primary causes contemplated at a distance—must be approached by means of *a priori* assumptions or through some form of divination. One may either *believe* in its existence and character or not believe in them. The representation of familiar objects and processes, on the contrary, undistracted by first or final causes, may concentrate upon the strictest accuracy. One will have, in other words, if he keeps the terms separate, a mystical vision on the one hand and a natural empiricism on the other. The only communication between these two extremes will be through

---

[5] *Longinus On the Sublime*, ed. and trans. W. R. Roberts (London, 1935).

symbols whose external forms, however familiar and meticulously rendered in themselves, will express little or nothing of the nature of the things they signify. In the event of such symbolism, the accurately rendered natural object must 'stand in place of' rather than 'depict' the more important object of contemplation.

If one, however, takes the second choice and wishes to relate one term of the antithesis to the other and to mitigate the dichotomy between them, such a symbol must be regarded as a sigh of despair. The first term—concerned with the quality of the object—will require a commensurate second term—concerned with the quality of inquiry. The relation between these terms can no longer be expressed by an arbitrarily stipulated symbolic equivalence. The relationship must, on the contrary, be made comprehensible through some rational principle, method, or art by which it can be transmitted and verified by the experience of different people in different periods. Any such 'artistic' principle of analysis will seek to lessen, by measuring, the separation and mutual exclusiveness of the terms of our antithesis.

These two choices with respect to the dilemma are perfectly illustrated by an argument between Apollonius, a Greek, and Thespesion, an Egyptian, over the question of how a god should be represented in sculpture. The scene is depicted by Flavius Philostratus in his *Life of Apollonius of Tyana* (6.19). In response to the Greek's criticism that the gods of Egypt are ignobly represented by the shapes of animals, the Egyptian asks sarcastically how Pheidias could presume to portray Zeus in a form more appropriate to his excellence when Pheidias had never even seen him. The Greek responds that while ordinary imitation (μίμησις) can create only what it has seen, the imagination (φαντασία) can create what it has not seen, for it will 'presuppose' (ὑποθήσεται) what it has not seen with reference to existing things.[6] Fear, furthermore, often drives imitation off, but not imagination, for it progresses without dismay to the end it has proposed.[7] To be sure, the Greek continues, "your animals

---

[6] Μίμησις μὲν γὰρ δημιουργήσει, ὃ εἶδεν, φαντασία δὲ καὶ ὃ μὴ εἶδεν, ὑποθήσεται γὰρ αὐτὸ πρὸς τὴν ἀναφορὰν τοῦ ὄντος. *Philostratus: The Life of Apollonius of Tyana*, trans. F. C. Conybeare, LCL, 2 vols. (London, 1969), 2.78–79. My interpretation of this sentence, differing considerably from the translator's, coincides with that of E. Birmelin, "Die kunsttheoretischen Gedanken in Philosotrats Apollonios," *Philologus* 88 [N.F. 42] (1933):149–80, 392–414, specifically 396–97. Birmelin stresses the fact that when Philostratus criticizes imitation, he is criticizing a conception of mimesis which has changed from Aristotle's conception of it to one of simple verisimilar reproduction (399–401). The recognition of the need to invoke another term, 'imagination,' once the meaning of the term 'imitation' had itself become restricted, is an excellent example of the second type of change, mentioned in the Preface to this study, which the philologist must take into account.

[7] Καὶ μίμησιν μὲν πολλάκις ἐκκρούσει ἔκπληξις, φαντασίαν δὲ οὐδέν, χωρεῖ γὰρ ἀνέκπληκτος πρὸς ὃ αὐτὴ ὑπέθετο. Birmelin explains this curious observation satisfactorily in

and your birds may be esteemed and of much price as likenesses (εἰκόνων), but the gods will be very much lowered in their dignity." On
the contrary, replies the Egyptian, we show our wisdom by our modest
reverence for the gods by fashioning "their forms as symbols (ξυμβολικά) of a profound inner meaning, so as to enhance their solemnity
and august character." Clearly, the Egyptian represents our first choice:
that of keeping the terms of the antithesis separate. A verisimilarly
accurate representation of a familiar form of an animal, functioning as
an arbitrary symbol, may 'stand in place of' or contain within it, but
never express the character of, an inscrutably distant divinity. The Greek,
on the contrary, wishes to bring the two terms closer together by having
his representation of the god be an imaginative conception which expresses at least some of the divine superiority in its visual form.

With respect to the power of language to represent the most excellent
qualities of divine and human natures, the Greek's argument may be
illustrated by the very purpose of the Longinian treatise *On the Sublime*
(1–2). Caecilius, against whom Longinus is writing, had maintained that
the achievement of the most excellent effects of style, necessary for the
most complete control of an audience's emotions, was a natural gift and,
therefore, beyond the capacity of art. Longinus responds that since Nature herself was organized in accordance with a certain system (μέθοδος)
of laws, a system both reflected in the natural gift of human discourse
and apprehensible to the reason, art might, by empirically analyzing the
emotional effects of stylistic excellence, arrive at a knowledge of their
causes and eventually be able to reproduce them.[8] Any such development

terms of Aristotelian psychology. According to the *De anima* (427b21–25), when we judge
something to be threatening, we are frightened by it, but when we (only) imagine (that)
such a threatening thing (could exist), we are like spectators looking at something dreadful
in a picture (without fearing it). She compares this passage to that in *Poetics* (1448b9ff.)
where Aristotle explains that even painful things when seen in a picture give pleasure,
because through such an imitation (in its original broader meaning) we can learn something
new (397, 401–2). A second (albeit perhaps less plausible) explanation, however, becomes
possible if one takes the word for 'drives off,' ἐκκρούσει, in its sense of 'hisses off the
stage' (Lat. *explodere*): "fear [of criticism] often hisses [used figuratively for 'drives']
imitation off [the stage], but not imagination, for imagination progresses without dismay
to the end proposed." Fear of being so criticized suggests that 'meticulousness' which
Critias shows arising in one about to imitate familiar things where the slightest discrepancy
with the model will be apparent to all. The verbal forms of ὑποτίθημι in the passage—
ὑποθήσεται and ὑπέθετο—both connote the laying down of a fictional presupposition, in
the sense that Sidney uses the term 'presupposeth' (see esp. Chap. 2, nn. 20 and 46 but
also nn. 8, 36, 38, and 42). LSJ testify to Philostratus' use of the verb in this sense by
citing *Heroicus* 4.4: ὡς ὑποτιθέμενον = (Homer) "as a composer of fiction."

[8] So Quintilian (9.4.120): "It is possible to have an inadequate understanding of what
it is precisely that makes for severity or charm, but yet to produce the required effect
better by taking nature for our guide in place of art: none the less there will always be
some principle of art underlying the promptings of nature (*sed naturae ipsi ars inerit*)."
One purpose of Aristotle's inductive method in the *Posterior Analytics* (2.19) was certainly
the discovery of such principles of art.

of a 'method' for describing and controlling what had been previously regarded as too complex or remote to be accurately analyzed and possessed depends on a type of inquiry commensurate in its accuracy and certainty with the complexity of the object it investigates. Any such inquiry, in seeking to penetrate the *terra adhuc incognita* of 'nature' by 'art' in order to understand, represent, and utilize her territory, reflects our continuing effort to find empirical or logical consolation in the face of uncertainty about what we experience. Such an endeavor had always been one of the primary objectives of Greek philosophy and most often characterizes what we regard as typically 'classical' in neoclassical recoveries.[9]

In opposition to the neoclassical attitudes toward knowledge and representation in the arts, the Egyptian's argument is articulated with increasing conviction and detail by the Christian and Neoplatonic mystical traditions. In the late fifth century, for instance, the Pseudo-Dionysius recognizes the two forms of representation defended by Apollonius and Thespesion respectively: the Greek form proceeds by means of holy images made to resemble the significant qualities of their objects; the Egyptian form proceeds by means of images whose incongruity with their objects is carried to the point of paradox and absurdity. Favoring the Egyptian's position, Dionysius explains his preference by referring to the animal symbolization of the Evangelists and of certain divine attributes in biblical imagery. The astounding discrepancy, he points out, between the symbol and what it stands in place of indicates the untraversable distance between the human and the divine. To strive for a greater commensurateness would be to suggest divine attributes which cannot be known, for, as St. Thomas says, citing Dionysius, "what He [God] is *not* is clearer to us than what He is. Therefore similitudes drawn from things farthest away from God form within us a truer estimate that God is above whatsoever we may say or think of Him."[10]

From this it should be apparent that the dilemma posed by the arguments of Apollonius and Thespesion over artistic decorum anticipates and characterizes the antagonism, becoming increasingly pronounced during the first five centuries A.D., between mimetic and symbolic procedures of representation. Moreover, in considering the philosophical premises of decorum, the reader should keep in mind that the more

---

[9] Plato and Aristotle discuss this 'classical' endeavor, which sums up much of what might be called the Greek intellectual enterprise, in various places. See, for example, *Rep.* 504DE, 511E; *Phaedrus* 265D–66C, 273DE, 277B; *Phil.* 57A–59C; *E.N.* 6.4–7.

[10] *S.T.* I. Q. 1, a 9, r. 3. St. Thomas is drawing on the *De cael. hier.* I.1–II.4 in his defense of the use of metaphor in Holy Scripture. His arguments derive as well from St. Augustine (cf. *De doct. christ.* 2.4). For an earlier and very detailed analysis of Egyptian hieroglyphic symbolization by a Christian contemporary of Philostratus, Clement of Alexandria, see Chap. 8, n. 22, of this study.

excellent, inclusive, complex, permanent, or simply desirable object of knowledge will change from period to period. As the object changes, so will its location in the *natura* of the physical order or in the *ingenium* of the psychic order, so will the kind of inquiry necessary to approach the object, and so, additionally, will the difficulties to be overcome in the object's representation. But the consequences of the dilemma posed by our antithesis and of the artistic efforts to overcome them remain relatively constant, albeit in ever-varying combinations, to the present day. We can gain further insight into the persistence of these consequences by returning to examine Plato's analysis of the dilemma itself in the *Sophist* and then by relating the terms of his analysis in greater detail to Aristotle's two types of intelligibility.

B. Plato's *Sophist*

In the *Sophist* Plato proposes and utilizes a dialectical method of inquiry capable of attaining an accuracy more commensurate with the excellence, complexity, or intelligibility (absolutely speaking) of its object than that offered by contemporary sophists. The dialogue sets out to define the general concept of a sophist by accurately distinguishing his activity from that of a philosopher. In order to do this, it becomes necessary to contrast their attitudes toward the existence, the knowledge, and the representation of objects. In sketching the most important distinctions that Plato makes for the representational resources of language, I shall indicate how they foreshadow those expressed by Philostratus in the debate he posed between the Egyptian and the Greek.

In the course of hunting the sophist down with ever finer nets of specification, Plato's protagonist, the Eleatic Stranger, anticipates a response that his quarry might make to charges of venality and malicious deception. Those people, the sophist might protest, who claim that the things he says are not true and yet who, at the same time, also claim that these untrue things have sufficient existence to be used as evidence against him are ignoring the principle that what is false can have no reality. For them to assert that "what is not" *is* is to contradict themselves. The sophist, that is, could use in his own defense and with his own interpretation Parmenides' frequently repeated admonition "never shall this be proved—that things that are not are, but do thou, in thy inquiry, hold back thy thought from this way." If falsity can have no existence, there can be no such thing as a falsifier: if a sophist is a falsifier, he cannot be real; if he is real, he cannot be a falsifier; yet it is admitted that he is real, so, therefore, what he says cannot be false.

This eristic argument leads ultimately to the equal validity of all opinion, and in such relativism the sophist may easily hide.

To forestall this defense, the Eleatic Stranger, himself a student of Parmenides, is forced to establish (against this use of his master's admonition) the real existence of 'what is not' by pointing out that this phrase does not mean something contrary to what exists but only something that is different (258B).[11] This distinction permits the comprehension of degrees of existence and of truth lying between complete Being and complete non-Being, between the completely true and the completely false. Parmenides' conception of reality, on the other hand, as a single unity, coherent and all-inclusive, untouched by process or Becoming, has no place for such intermediate gradations. Without these we cannot discriminate, nor our language specify, relative amounts of truth and falsity, and without such estimation no type of inquiry can be judged more accurate, nor any type of object more excellent, than another. The Eleatic Stranger, in insisting upon that very inquiry which the Eleatic Parmenides had forbidden, describes the Greek intellectual enterprise in its most 'classical' form.

Since the Stranger describes the sophist as an image maker (εἰδωλο-ποιόν), he foresees the sophist's relegation of the image (εἴδωλον) to the status of other types of falsity which have no existence (239D). By arguing for the epistemological necessity of degrees of existence, he can defend the capacity of the verisimilar image itself to express intermediate degrees of truth (cf. *Crat.* 432C–34A; *States.* 284AB; *Phil.* 12E–18D, 40C–41B). It is this justification of the image—and, by implication, of the mimetic arts—which relates the problems of knowledge in Plato's dialogue to the representational problems discussed by Philostratus. The immeasurable gulf between a mutually exclusive (changeless) truth and (varying) appearance, an area where no discrimination is possible, shelters the sophist from rational pursuit and corresponds to that untraversable distance between the divine and the human which the Egyptian claims can only be overcome by animal symbols. The Stranger, on the other hand, recognizes the fact that reality cannot be reduced to either the invariable principles of Being or to phenomena in the process of Becoming; it must include them both (249CD). If, in experiencing real-

---

[11] All quotations from the *Sophist* are taken from F. M. Cornford's translation (with commentary) in *Plato's Theory of Knowledge* (London, 1935) as it is reprinted, with minor revisions, in *The Collected Dialogues of Plato*, ed. E. Hamilton and H. Cairns (New York, 1961). The reader should consult, as well, the introduction, translation, and notes of A. E. Taylor, especially on such difficult problems as the identification of the gods and the Titans in the parable discussed in this study, in *Plato: The Sophist & The Statesman* (New York, 1961). See, in addition, J. Klein, *Greek Mathematical Thought*, pp. 82–99 and *Plato's Trilogy* (Chicago, 1977), pp. 7–74.

ity, we in fact experience both, how are they to be related and how is the experience of their relation to be known and represented? The answer is that the realm of phenomenal change cannot be known 'directly' but must be approached through a dialectical analysis of the generically and specifically interrelated Forms or concepts expressed in the meanings of nouns and verbs. These 'names' and 'actions,' in turn, combine in statements which we can recognize as relatively true or false descriptions of what we experience. Our dialectical power to grasp and apply these formal principles, however shadowy they remain, to perceptual phenomena corresponds to the imaginative power of Homer and Pheidias to intuit and represent, however skiagraphically, the excellence of Zeus in the materials of their respective arts.

In order to challenge the sophistic identification of the Parmenidean term 'what is not' with nonexistence, the philosophic Stranger shows the great difficulties of any such definition by describing the differences of opinion over 'what is.' He first surveys the contradictory definitions of reality by the fifth-century Ionian and Eleatic philosophers (242B–45E) and then recasts those who hold opinions about what is real into two general groups: the 'materialists' and the 'idealists.' He compares the quarrel between them to the battle between the gigantic Titans and the gods. The giants try "to drag everything down to earth out of heaven and the unseen . . . and strenuously affirm that real existence belongs only to that which can be handled. . . . They define reality as the same thing as body." In opposition,

Their adversaries are very wary in defending their position somewhere in the heights of the unseen, maintaining with all their force that true reality consists in certain intelligible and bodiless forms. In the clash of argument they shatter and pulverize those bodies which their opponents wield, and what those others allege to be true reality they call, not real being, but a sort of moving process of becoming. On this issue an interminable battle is always going on between the two camps. (246AC)

Both extremes are wrong, and the Stranger, arguing against each in turn, tries to mitigate their mutual exclusiveness (246E–49D). The irreconcilability of its protagonists makes this quarrel analogous, again, to the debate described by Philostratus. The parallel does not lie in the identification of the Egyptian or the Greek with either the 'materialist' or the 'idealist.' Rather, the sophist would accept with Thespesion the irreconcilable separation of the human from the divine as a necessary condition, while the Eleatic Stranger would endeavor with Apollonius to diminish it.

Of particular importance with respect to Philostratus are the arguments which the Stranger offers against both the Titans and the gods. In each case, he argues against the mutual exclusiveness of their positions and, by bringing them into relation with one another, he tries to reduce the distance between the intelligible and sensory realms. With greater reciprocity between the two realms, greater dialectical articulateness becomes possible. The intellective *archai*, as explanatory principles, become more able to elucidate the aesthetic *archai* where they bear upon one another in our consciousness of the phenomenal world. The sophist, like the Egyptian, would keep the realms separate; the Stranger, like the Greek, would relate them to one another insofar as the limitations of human nature permit. While their exclusive separation leads to more 'conservative' forms, their reciprocal correlation leads to more 'liberal' forms of artistic representation. How is this correlation to be accomplished?

The giants at their most intransigent do not admit the existence of anything that they cannot see and touch (247C). In a hypothetical cross-examination, the Stranger raises the possibility that if the more tolerant among them could be brought to admit the existence of a soul or justice or wisdom, all of which are invisible, they would then have to accept the fact that a small part, at least, of reality is bodiless. If they accepted the fact that not only corporeal but (some) incorporeal things were "real," they might be brought to agree that the common reality of these things lay in their "power (δύναμις) either to affect anything else or to be affected, in however small a degree, by the most insignificant agent, though it be only once" (247E). In his commentary, F. M. Cornford points out that the Platonic *dynamis* "can be defined as the property or quality which reveals the nature of a thing." It is the *dynamis* which "makes it possible to give each thing a name conforming to its peculiar constitution, and places things in separate groups." It is "at once a principle of knowledge and a principle of diversity." The reasonable materialist, then, must surrender tangibility as the identifying mark of the real and substitute the power of acting and being acted upon, which would apply to "justice" as well as to coldness or smallness. He is thus brought some way "towards the full admission that . . . Justice itself, is real—a unique object of thought that can be known without any use of the bodily senses."[12] Through the recognition of the *dynamis* of a

---

[12] *Plato's Theory of Knowledge*, pp. 233–38. Cornford points out that "the term *dynamis* stands for the characteristic property of bodies, their exterior and sensible aspect, which makes it possible to determine and specify them. Thanks to the *dynamis*, the mysterious 'nature' (*physis*), the substantial 'form' (*eidos*) or primordial element, makes itself known, and does so by its action. This explains why it was possible, especially at a later date, to pass from the known to the unknown, from the appearance to the reality, and how easy

concept as well as of an object, that is, he is brought part way up into that middle area between the realm of intelligible first principles and the realm of perceptual phenomena which these principles can elucidate.

Similarly, while the most conservative gods admit neither motion nor process in the changeless Eleatic world of Being, the Stranger imagines the possibility that the more tolerant gods might be made to grant that the soul can know and that Being can be known. With this granted, if in addition these gods would admit that knowing is a form of action and being known a form of being acted upon and, at the same time, that their reality can be known and thereby be acted upon, that reality could not be changeless but must be as susceptible to *dynamis* as the reality of the giants. In fact, if it were changeless, there would be no room for life or the soul or understanding in the perfectly existent. The more reasonable gods, that is, are presented as being brought to admit that the realm of changeless Forms must share reality with the realm of process and Becoming. They have been led down into the middle region in order that experience and intellection can take place. They bring the unvarying Forms to life in the motion of the psychic processes to which these Forms give order. Neither the Pythagorean Becoming nor the Eleatic Being can be intelligible in isolation. The sum of things must include both "all that is unchangeable and all that is in change" (249D) if it is to be known and represented.

The myth of the Titans and gods as Plato presents it illustrates the division so fatal to the making of verisimilar objects, such as the image, and to any quest for a method of inquiry capable of a more precise account than arbitrary symbols might give of more excellent things. When the strife between giant and god becomes most intense—when, that is, the 'materialist' and 'idealist' become most intractably conservative—the sophist may gain his greatest safety in the shadowy illusions that he casts. The philosopher, on the other hand, no more to be identified with the 'idealist' than the sophist with the 'materialist,' heals the division between them by means of dialectic. Dialectic reveals how a genus is properly divided into species and species are recollected into a genus, as well as how a more inclusive characteristic, such as *sameness* or *difference*, may pervade many wholes and, while remaining unified in itself, still permit these wholes to exist separately. The knowledge (ἐπι-στήμη) of how these "blending" (ξύμμιξις, 252B) and "combining" (ἐπικοινωνίας, 252D) processes take place is offered by the arts. In the arts of discourse, some terms of predication can combine with others in definition and some cannot just as certain letters can combine to make

---

it was to identify the 'nature' (*physis*) with the *dynamis*" (p. 235). Cornford cites Hippocrates, *De nat. hom.* 5 and Plato, *Protag.* 349B.

up syllables while others cannot (253AD). Similarly, one general concept, such as difference, may 'partake' of another, such as existence, without becoming it, and at the same time each may participate in myriads of other concepts with respect to which each general concept both *is* and *is not* (254B–59B). To deny this power to combine is to defy the "philosophical Muse," for the separation of "everything from everything else means a complete abolition of all discourse, for any discourse we can have owes its existence to the weaving together of forms (τῶν εἰδῶν συμπλοκήν)," and "to rob us of discourse would be to rob us of philosophy" (259D–60A). "What is not" in the sense of "the different" is a form itself and, partaking of existence, can confer a form of existence upon "false" verbal images if, indeed, it can be shown to "blend" with truth in discourse. The Stranger argues that it can by showing that, like letters, words placed together make grammatical sense only "by weaving together" nouns and verbs whose resulting propositions will be false if they assert something different from what actually is (260A–63B). If one doubts the power of discourse to 'implicate' the true in this kind of falsity, he will have no justification for claiming that this opinion is more fallacious than that; without relative degrees of rightness or wrongness, each one will appear as true as any other. No judgment, then, will be able to arrive at the significance of anything that we experience at that point of maximum negotiation described in Chapter 5. The changeless realm of (true) Being and the fluctuating realm of (false) Becoming will each remain separate and unrelated to the other. Whoever wishes to grasp and express their relation in the obscurity where the sophist takes refuge between them must fall back upon the arbitrarily stipulated symbol which, according to Philostratus' Egyptian, alone can express the solemnity of the gods.[13]

Plato observes two distinctions about the nature of perception and cognition in the *Sophist*. The first distinction, as we shall see, is primarily ontological, emphasizing the qualitative relation of the viewer to the object, whereas the second is psychological, emphasizing the quantitative or spatial relation between them. In the course of the dialogue, the Stranger, using all the resources of the philosophic Muse to bring the realms of Being and Becoming into negotiation with one another, and thereby to expose the sophist, is forced to define the type of image maker the sophist most resembles. In so doing, he introduces his famous psychological distinction between eicastic and fantastic kinds of images (235D–36C) by first discussing the ontological distinction between mimetic

---

[13] In place of Thespesion's arbitrary symbols Plato describes dialectic as the most excellent method of inquiry and representation. See Chap. 6, n. 26 and the Platonic passages cited there.

imitations and reality itself. The sophist has appeared to claim a knowledge of all things, human and divine, about which he can teach the art of controversy. To show that this universal knowledge can be only apparent, the Stranger offers an analogy: "Suppose a man professed to know, not how to speak or dispute about everything, but how to produce all things in actual fact by a single form of skill" (233D). The fact that the skill selected is mimesis itself (τὸ μιμητικόν) reemphasizes the close connection between knowledge and its representation which is the theme of the dialogue. A draftsman can deceive young people into believing his images are really the things imitated if he shows his drawings to them at a distance (πόρρωθεν), for, as Aristotle points out, "the inexperienced are like those who view things from a distance."[14] Similar to the art of drawing, there is an art of discourse which can deceive young listeners who are still far removed (πόρρω) from reality "by means of words that cheat (γοητεύειν) the ear, exhibiting images of all things in a shadow play of discourse (εἴδωλα λεγόμενα)." When, as the listeners grow older, they come "into closer touch (ἐγγύθεν) with realities" and see them clearly (ἐναργῶς), "what seemed important (μεγάλα) will now appear trifling (σμικρά) and what seemed easy, difficult, and all the illusions (φαντάσματα) created in discourse" will vanish in the face of the actual problems of life (234BD). Degrees of importance are figuratively referred to as degrees of magnitude which, combined with degrees of distance and of clarity, permit the continuation of the metaphor to be developed in optical terms.

The sophist, in claiming unlimited knowledge, is now shown to be a kind of wizard (γόης), and imitator of realities (μιμητὴς ὢν τῶν ὄντων), who belongs to the class of illusionists (θαυματοποιῶν). This general category, however, where he still can elude detection, must be subdivided into two kinds of imitation if he is to be caught: the making of likenesses (εἰκαστική) and the making of semblances (φανταστική) which only appear to be likenesses under certain conditions. The eicastic image is an accurate "copy that conforms to the proportions of the original in all three dimensions (παραδείγματος συμμετρίας τις ἐν μήκει καὶ πλάτει καὶ βάθει) and giving moreover the proper color (χρώματα) to every part" (cf. Laws 667D–69E). The fantastic image, on the other hand, corresponds to works of painting or sculpture of exceptional size in which the true proportions of symmetrical figures could not be reproduced without distortion: "the upper parts would look too small, and the lower

[14] De Soph. Elench. 1, 164b27, in Aristotle: On Sophistical Refutations, On Coming-to-be and Passing-away, On the Cosmos, trans. E. S. Forster and D. J. Furley, LCL (London, 1965).

too large, because we see the one at a distance (πόρρωθεν), the other close at hand (ἐγγύθεν)." This type of image

Appears to be a likeness of a well-made figure because it is not seen from a satisfactory point of view (ἱκανῶς ὁρᾶν), but to a spectator with eyes that could fully take in so large an object [it] would not be even like the original it professes to resemble. (236B)

The illusionistic foreshortening compensates for the optical distortions caused by the unequal distance between the eye and the different parts of the body depicted in the painting or sculpture. Rather than being caused by the spectator's being too far away from the figure, however, the distortions here are actually caused by his standing too near to take it in as a whole. Were he to step back far enough to see it completely, the compensations for the distortion would become distortions themselves, and, once they could be eliminated, the figure would acquire greater eicastic verisimilitude. In the case of such foreshortening, remoteness and proximity are neither good or bad in themselves. The proper degree of distance of the spectator from the object, relative to its size and shape, determines the verisimilitude of the image.

These two distinctions—between realities and imitations and between eicastic and fantastic types of imitation—are both stated in terms of practical optics. In the first, however, obscurity results more from the ontological status of the object than from its remoteness: to see the object more clearly one must change the *kind* of thing it is. Greater proximity, for instance, can never make mimetic representations, which are by nature indistinct, less obscure however much it can help to reveal that they *are* obscure and therefore to be distrusted. This inherent 'darkness' will be equally present in such 'excellent' objects as the heavens whose nature not only makes them impossible to approach but, being divine themselves, are perhaps comprehensible only to God (*Meta.* 1.2.9–14; cf. *De caelo* 2.3, 286a3–8). In both instances, the beneficial or harmful effects of obscurity will vary with the object and with the uses it is put to. The representation of an object which is indeterminate, unpredictable, or simply indistinct by nature I shall continue to call 'skiagraphic.' It emphasizes the 'ontological' relation of the object to the viewer rather than the 'psychological' relation dependent on the optical conditions of visual perspective. The early metaphorical uses of the term seem to express the degree of intelligibility of things considered with respect to their own nature (ἁπλῶς) rather than the degree of their intelligibility with respect to our perceptions of them (ἡμῖν).

While the first distinction between realities and imitations is ontological, the second between eicastic and fantastic imitations or images is primarily psychological. Any departure from a specific degree of distance, either toward or away from the object, causes distortion in the perception of the viewer. To see the object more clearly either he must change his point of observation or the artist must compensate for the visual errors by the art of perspective. The artistic representation which accomplishes such corrections I shall call 'skenographic'—a term applied by Aristotle to stage scenery—which seeks to secure the viewer's psychological 'participation' by establishing his precise spatial relation to the object within geometrically *quantitative* planes of Euclidean optics.[15]

Related, perhaps, to these two types of representation are two corresponding types of obscurity appropriate to the sophist and to the philosopher respectively. While the sophist conceals himself in the illusions cast by his fantastic images, the philosopher, who observes the world from his position in the light above, will appear, in Milton's phrase, "dark with excessive bright" and almost as hard to discern as a god (216C).

> The Sophist takes refuge in the darkness of not-being, where he is at home and has the knack of feeling his way, and it is the darkness of the place that makes him so hard to perceive. . . . Whereas the philosopher, whose thoughts constantly dwell upon the nature of reality, is difficult to see because his region is so bright, for the eye of the vulgar soul cannot endure to keep its gaze fixed on the divine. (254AB)

The imagery here suggests the broader philosophical context of the episode of the cave in the *Republic* (514–21C). The sophistic manipulator of illusions becomes the adroit competitor in the underground skirmish with shadows (520C). Not only does the competitor have the knack for feeling his way, but his eyes are sharp in the half-light which he prefers to the brilliance above: "How keen is the vision of the little soul, how quick it is to discern the things that interest it, a proof that it is not a poor vision which it has, but one forcibly enlisted in the service of evil, so that the sharper its sight the more mischief it accomplishes" (519A; cf. *Theaet.* 172C–77B, *Laws* 689CD). By contrast, the philosopher, descending from divine contemplation in the true sunlight to the miserable dimness below, may well appear "ridiculous, if, while still blinking through the gloom, and before he has become sufficiently accustomed to the environing darkness, he is compelled in courtrooms or elsewhere to contend about the shadows of justice or the images (ἀγαλμάτων) that

---

[15] See my article on "The Early Metaphorical Uses of ΣΚΙΑΓΡΑΦΙΑ and ΣΚΗΝΟΓΡΑΦΙΑ," *Traditio* 34 (1978):403–13. Both 'skiagraphic' and 'skenographic' images, in their extreme (i.e. conservative) forms, approach the enigmatic symbol.

cast the shadows" (517D). The sensible observer, therefore, must remember

That there are two distinct disturbances of the eyes arising from two causes, according as the shift is from light to darkness or from darkness to light, and, believing that the same thing happens to the soul too, whenever he saw a soul perturbed and unable to discern something, he would not laugh unthinkingly, but would observe whether coming from a brighter life its vision was obscured by the unfamiliar darkness, or whether the passage from the deeper dark of ignorance into a more luminous world and the greater brightness had dazzled its vision. (518AB)

The light of the nocturnal day (νυχτερινῆς τινὸς ἡμέρας) and the contrasting brilliance of true sunlight (521C) account, then, for two corresponding types of darkness. The man descending again to the "puppet theatre" (514B) must 'evaluate' impressions which become 'skenographic' insofar that they now challenge his estimating faculty with conflicting perceptions of shapes against a background of relative refinements of highlight and shading (516CE). The man emerging from the cave, on the other hand, since he looks up toward things silhouetted against a background of brilliant light, can grasp all that he sees only in 'skiagraphic' outline.

Our sophist, then, would feel secure in the shadowy courtroom of Plato's subterranean theater. His soul will resemble that described in the *Phaedo* (81BD) which has always preferred the refuge of bodily sensations and feared what is "shadowy and invisible to the eyes but is intelligible and tangible to philosophy." The 'distant' darkness which causes this "fear of the invisible and of the other world" arises from the incomprehensibility of the most excellent things and will lead the timid soul to desire again the 'closer' darkness of the phenomenal world (cf. 79AE, 82E–83E). As we shall see later, such distinctions suggest a philosophical context for discriminating among literary styles on the basis of decorum. The elevated subject matter of epic, for instance, will require a style comparable to the less visually articulated skiagraphic representation of Horace's more distant picture to be seen in full light (*Ars poet.* 361–65). The more familiar subjects of ordinary life will require a style comparable to the more meticulously accurate lines and modulated colors of his picture to be examined close at hand which 'loves' the *obscurum* for its own protection. Whatever their differences, philosophical and literary discourse both try to grasp their object at that 'distance' of greatest lucidity and to express its significance with an exactness appropriate to its nature. At such a distance, the object, and hence its representation, will suffer least from either type of obscurity.[16]

C. Aristotle: The Two Forms of Intelligibility

Since the Muses are present on Olympus and know all things, while we hear and know nothing but rumor, Homer asks them to add to what is known to men something of what can only be known to the gods (*Il.* 2.484–86). By telling us of things beyond our powers of perception, the Muses increase human knowledge by enabling us to communicate, through their mediation, with the remoteness of the divine. It is in the spirit of such mediation that Plato insists in the *Sophist* not only upon the metaphorical negotiation between heaven and earth but upon the real negotiation between various activities of the human soul.

Plato describes the reconciliation between the giants and the gods as a parable for the integration of the changing forms of Becoming with the changeless form of Being. Such an integration offers a paradigm for all the processes of reality as well as of the dialectical description of them as a blending and combining of *genera* and *species*. All the arts preserve a knowledge of these processes in ways analogous to that in which the arts of discourse disclose what terms of predication can combine with others to establish definitions and what letters can combine with others to make up syllables (253AD). Were one to cease weaving these conceptual forms together, he would be deprived of the Muses (ἀμούσου, 259E) and, thus deprived of discourse, be deprived of philosophy itself (ἀφιλοσόφου, 259E). Plato's insight that the divinely conceived Forms of Being and the humanly perceived forms of Becoming must be reconciled by a discursively articulated negotiation between them is, in itself, an attempt to resolve the ancient dilemma of knowledge and representation. Aristotle reformulates this attempt in psychological terms which are more easily adaptable to the analysis of individual sciences and, hence, to formulating the philosophical premises of literary decorum. His brief comment in *On Sophistical Refutations* summarizes much of what Plato analyzes in the *Sophist*: "the man, then, who views general

---

[16] Quotations from the *Phaedo* are from *Plato: Euthyphro, Apology, Crito, Phaedo, Phaedrus*, trans. F. N. Fowler, LCL (London, 1966). I have discussed the relevance of these Platonic texts for the decorum of literary styles with references to Horace's analogy between painting and poetry in HASD, pp. 47–49 (see Part Two: Introduction, n. 1). Relevant, in turn, to Plato's texts is the preceding summary of the comparison between Aeschylus and Euripides (HASD, pp. 44–46). In the later phrasing of Dio Chrysostom (52.15), Aeschylus possesses an abrupt simplicity (τὸ αὔθαδες καὶ ἁπλοῦν), while Euripides a shrewd precision (τὸ ἀκριβές καὶ δριμύ).

principles in the light of the particular case is a dialectician, while he who only apparently does this is a sophist" (11, 171b7–8).

Were Aristotle to use Plato's metaphor, he might be said to differentiate, logically and epistemologically, the knowledge appropriate to the realm of the gods from that appropriate to the realm of the giants by distinguishing between two types of intelligibility.[17] Things may be known, he says, either with respect to their own nature—that is, absolutely (ἁπλῶς)—on the one hand, or with respect to our own perceptions—that is, relative to us (ἡμῖν)—on the other. The kinds of things known absolutely are first principles in the form of constituent elements or causes which, being indemonstrable (since they cannot be derived discursively by deduction from prior principles), must be grasped intuitively. The kinds of things known relative to us are first principles in the form of sensory impressions or perceptions which, being likewise discursively indemonstrable, must likewise be grasped by intuition. There are, then two different kinds of intuition: things known ἁπλῶς are reached by an intellective intuition; those known ἡμῖν by an aesthetic intuition.[18] Although the ways in which these two types of intuition reach their respective first principles (archai) are diametrically opposed, they have one thing in common: neither depends upon discursive reason.

Intuited first principles alone, however, be they intellective or aes-

[17] W. Jaeger's comment that Aristotle did not live "in the Ideal world but in the tension between Idea and experience" (Aristotle, p. 399), might equally apply to Plato with respect to his parable of the Titans and the gods. E. Voegelin frequently speaks of this tension, and one passage is particularly applicable here: "The tension between the experience of the flow of 'things' and the experience of a direction in the soul toward the divine 'All-Wise,' as well as the tension between the symbols expressing these experiences, will remain from now on, in varying degrees of consciousness, a dominant type of Hellenic speculation on order into the late work of Plato and into Aristotle. The tension did not break. Neither did the erotic orientation of the soul toward the sophon grow into an eschatological desire to escape the world; nor did the passionate participation in the flux and strife of 'things' degenerate into a romantic surrender to the flux of history or to eternal recurrence. The emotional balance between the two possibilities was precarious, and in the generation of sophists after Heraclitus the strain began to show; lesser figures would break under it, but the great thinkers maintained the balance," The World of the Polis, vol. 2 of Order and History (Baton Rouge, 1957), p. 236. For quite a different point of view, and one strikingly nearer to that of the Neoplatonists, compare the Ps. Aristotelian On the Cosmos 1: "It was not possible by means of the body to reach the heavenly region or to leave the earth and explore that heavenly place, in the manner once attempted by the foolish Aloadae [i.e. Giants]: so the soul, by means of philosophy, taking the mind (νοῦν) as its guide, has crossed the frontier, and made the journey out of its own land by a path that does not tire the traveller" (391a8–12).

[18] For Plato's early discrimination of the objects of intellection and perception in the light of his doctrines of the Forms and Recollection, see Cornford's brief summary of the Phaedo 65D–79A in Plato and Parmenides, repr. in The Library of Liberal Arts (New York, n.d.), pp. 74–76. For a later discussion of Aristotle's two types of intelligibility, which implies their function in the inductive method as described in Post. An. 2.19, see Sextus Empiricus, Adv. log. 1.217–26.

thetic, can never produce knowledge nor establish sciences without there being, in addition, discursive demonstrations that these principles do, indeed, account for how a thing came to be as it is or to act as it does. Thus intuited first principles and discursive reasoning must be combined for the fullest understanding of the experiences to be analyzed by any art or discipline. Aristotle is particularly clear about this combination in his definition of "wisdom." A man is said to be wise who possesses wisdom in all that he does rather than in any particular accomplishments. Such wisdom may be said to be the most 'accurate' (ἀκριβεστάτη), and hence the most excellent, form of knowledge. For the wise man "must not only know the conclusions that follow from his first principles, but also have a true conception of those principles themselves." Wisdom, that is, "must be a combination of Intelligence (νοῦς) and Scientific Knowledge (ἐπιστήμη): it must be a consummated knowledge of the most exalted objects" (E.N. 6.7.2–3; 1141a17–20). It is through such wisdom, I should say, that the ancient quest for a method of inquiry commensurate in its accuracy with the excellence of its objects appears to attain its goal. If its attainment demands a knowledge of first principles and of the conclusions which follow from them, the intuitive procedures of intelligence (νοῦς) and the demonstrative procedures of scientific knowledge (ἐπιστήμη) must complement one another. Their cooperation will of necessity involve first principles of both types of intelligibility, as well as their discursive relation to one another, in a single process of cognition.[19] Such wisdom is not unlike the final understanding, the 'literary thesis' itself, which the Muse, in revealing the first principles of divine causation (Aen. 1.8), enables Virgil to 'demonstrate' in the subsequent argument of his poem.

In order to see the consistency with which Aristotle distinguishes first principles on the basis of these two forms of intelligibility, it is helpful to summarize his division of the objects of knowledge and the intellectual faculties appropriate to each. While he divides what can be known, with respect to things themselves, into physical, practical, and logical objects, he divides philosophical inquiry, with respect to the human faculties which acquire and use what is known, into theoretical, practical, and productive arts and sciences. Certain kinds of objects require certain kinds of disciplines, and the completeness of any body of knowledge will

[19] For a brief statement of this reciprocation which constitutes wisdom, see Mag. mor. 1.34.14. J. H. Randall, Aristotle (New York, 1960), pp. 40–51, esp. p. 46, gives a clear summary of the meaning of wisdom with respect to first principles and discursive reasoning with interesting implications for literary structure. See, however, Lesher's qualification of Randall's conclusion, "Meaning of ΝΟΥΣ," p. 59. Most important is E. Voegelin, "Reason: The Classic Experience," Southern Review 10 (1974):237–64, repr. in Anamnesis (Notre Dame, 1978), pp. 89–115.

depend both upon the kind of object involved and upon the accuracy of inquiry which its nature permits. The theoretical sciences include physics, mathematics, and metaphysics; their objective is the truth about things contemplated for their own sake. The practical sciences include ethics and politics and seek the truth about action with respect to the choice of means and ends. The productive sciences aim at the true description of how things are made.

The most exact sciences, such as mathematics and metaphysics whose subject matter is invariable, may begin their discursive demonstrations from intellective principles of logical priority (*archai*) which are better known in themselves (ἁπλῶς). The physical sciences, which are less exact because their subject matter is variable, more frequently must start their analysis with aesthetic principles derived from sensory impressions which are better known to our own perceptions (ἡμῖν). The ethical sciences whose subject, human behavior, is perhaps the most variable of all, are even less exact than physics. In order to qualify as science, in the broad sense of that term, they must most often reach their universal principles—from which demonstration can then begin—entirely from aesthetic intuition better known, again, with respect to ourselves (ἡμῖν).[20]

Aristotle's most comprehensive distinction between the two types of intelligibility occurs in his treatment of logic insofar as logic may be called the instrument (*organon*) for the acquisition and transmission of all kinds of scientific knowledge. Its subject matter is the demonstrative and dialectical processes of reasoning and definition necessary for the establishment of propositions and for the analysis of proofs capable of defending them. The knowledge expressed by these processes is said to be unqualified, or absolute (ἁπλῶς, 71b16), when an event cannot be otherwise than as it is known and when its cause is certain. Absolute knowledge can be obtained by syllogistic demonstration—leaving inductive procedures aside for the moment—from premises which are true, primary (indemonstrable), causative, prior (in so much as they are causative), and better known than their conclusions. In addition we must remember that

There are two senses in which things are prior and more knowable. That which is prior in nature (τῇ φύσει) is not the same as that which is prior in relation to us (πρὸς ἡμᾶς), and that which is ⟨naturally⟩ more knowable is not the same as that which is more knowable by us. By "prior" or "more knowable" in relation to us I mean that which is nearer to our perception (ἐγγύτερον τῆς αἰσθήσεως), and by "prior" or "more knowable" in the absolute sense (ἁπλῶς) I mean that which is further (πορρώτερον) from it. The most universal concepts

---

[20] See D. Ross, *Aristotle*, pp. 188–89.

(τὰ καθόλου μάλιστα) are furthest from our perception, and particulars (τὰ καθ' ἕκαστα) are nearest to it; and these are opposite to one another. (*Post an.* 1.2; 71b34–72a6; cf. *Meta.* 7.4.2–3)

This broad, logical discrimination between kinds of intelligibility recurs in the treatment of the more specialized mathematical, physical, and ethical subject matters.

With respect to mathematics, in explaining how to test the firmness of a definition in his *Topics*, Aristotle uses an illustration from geometry. The quality of a definition will be in proportion to the priority and intelligibility of its terms. But in judging its quality we must remember again that a definition may be

Composed either of terms which are less intelligible absolutely (ἁπλῶς) or of terms which are less intelligible to us (ἡμῖν); for both meanings are possible. Thus absolutely the prior is more intelligible than the posterior; for example, a point is more intelligible than a line, a line than a plane, and a plane than a solid, just as also a unit is more intelligible than a number, since it is prior to and the starting-point (ἀρχή) of all number. Similarly a letter is more intelligible than a syllable. To us, however, the converse sometimes happens; for a solid falls most under our perception, and a plane more than a line, and a line more than a point. For most people recognize such things as solids and planes before they recognize lines and points; for the former can be grasped by an ordinary understanding, the latter only by one which is accurate and superior. (*Top.* 6.4; 141b4–15)

Although it is more scientific (ἐπιστημονικώτερον, 141b16) to begin with (prior) terms which are absolutely intelligible, nevertheless, for those who are incapable of acquiring knowledge in this way, it is necessary to begin with (posterior) terms which are intelligible to them. Though the latter is the weaker method, definitions which draw their terms "neither from what is more intelligible absolutely (ἐκ τῶν ἁπλῶς γνωριμωτέρων) nor from what is more intelligible to us (ἐκ τῶν ἡμῖν)" are the weakest of all (142a13–15).[21]

In the same spirit, Aristotle begins his *Physics* (1.1) by stating that we come to understand physical nature through gaining an insight into principles (ἀρχαί), causes (αἴτια), or elements (στοιχεῖα). But unlike the formulations of mathematical definitions, we must start with the composite objects of our experience.

Now the path (ὁδός) of investigation must lie from what is more immediately cognizable and clear to us (ἡμῖν), to what is clearer and more intimately cog-

---

[21] *Aristotle: Topica*, trans. E. S. Forster, printed with *Posterior Analytics*, trans. H. Tredennick, LCL (London, 1966). In the *Metaphysics* Aristotle again distinguishes those things which are prior in knowledge with respect to 'formula' (κατὰ τὸν λόγον) from those prior with respect to perception (κατὰ τὴν αἴσθησιν). "Universals are prior in formula, but particulars in perception" (5.11.5, 1018b32–34).

nizable in its own nature (τῇ φύσει); for it is not the same thing to be directly accessible to our cognition (ἡμῖν) and to be intrinsically intelligible (ἁπλῶς). Hence, in advancing to that which is intrinsically more luminous and by its nature accessible to deeper knowledge, we must needs start from what is more immediately within our cognition, though in its own nature less fully accessible to understanding. (Ph. 184a17–22)

The metaphor of a 'distance' to first principles in the Posterior Analytics changes here in the Physics to one of a visual clarity. Aristotle proceeds to distinguish the composite 'whole' object which immediately and clearly confronts our senses from its constituent parts, which, being hidden and obscure to us, must be revealed through analysis.

Now the things most obvious and immediately cognizable by us are concrete and particular, rather than abstract and general; whereas elements and principles are only accessible to us afterwards, as derived from the concrete data when we have analysed them. So we must advance from the concrete whole (καθόλου) to the several constituents (τὰ καθ' ἕκαστα) which it embraces; for it is the concrete whole (τὸ ὅλον) that is the more readily cognizable by the senses. And by calling the concrete a "whole" I mean that it embraces in a simple complex (καθόλου) a diversity of constituent elements, factors, or properties. (Ph. 184a23–27)

This 'concrete whole' forms a composite unity which can only be understood through its analysis into individual elements and their subsequent synthesis back into the original composition. The relation of the 'given' whole to its constituent elements is that of a noun to its specifying definition.

The relation of names to definitions will throw some light on this point; for the name gives an unanalyzed indication of the thing ("circle," for instance), but the definition analyses out some characteristic property or properties. A variant of the same thing may be noted in children, who begin by calling every man "father" and every woman "mother," till they learn to sever out the special relation to which the terms properly apply. (Ph. 184b10–15)

The noun 'father' comes by degrees to designate a particular man by specifying the relation between parent and child.[22]

When Aristotle distinguishes the two types of intelligibility with respect to ethical choice of means and ends in the Nicomachean Ethics,

[22] Aristotle: The Physics 1.1, trans. P. H. Wicksteed and F. M. Cornford, LCL, 2 vols. (London, 1957). See also 1.5, 189a3–8: "To this extent, then, they [previous thinkers] agree and differ, and do worse or better one than the other; some . . . , beginning with what is more accessible to intelligence (κατὰ τὸν λόγον) and others with what is more accessible to sense (κατὰ τὴν αἴσθησιν); for the general (τὸ καθόλου) is approached by the intelligence and the particular (τὸ καθ' ἕκαστον) by the senses, since the mind (λόγος) grasps the universal principle and the senses the partial application (κατὰ μέρος)." The concept of generality (τὸ καθόλου) is used in the logical sense here, while in Chap. 1 it refers simply to the given composite whole to be analyzed into its constituent elements. The introductory comments by the editors are particularly helpful as are their notes.

he relies even more upon the psychological means of arriving at first principles which he describes in the *Posterior Analytics* (2.19). We must not overlook, he says again, the distinction

Between arguments that start from first principles and those that lead to first principles. It was a good practice of Plato to raise this question, and to enquire whether the right procedure (ὁδός) was to start from or to lead up to the first principles, as in a race-course one may run from the judges to the far end of the track or reversely. Now no doubt it is proper to start from the known. But "the known" has two meanings—"what is known to us (ἡμῖν)," which is one thing, and "what is knowable in itself (ἁπλῶς)," which is another. Perhaps then for us at all events it is proper to start from what is known to us. (*E.N.* 1095a31–95b4)

One reason for starting primarily with principles apprehensible to us rather than those knowable in themselves is that conceptions of moral excellence, justice, and the good involve such differences of opinion that no certain premises can be assumed. Many go so far as to claim such conceptions are merely conventions and have no existence in the nature of things. In such a situation, we are thrown back to a great extent upon our own experience and, proceeding from its repeated instances collected in the memory, must arrive at universal principles of judgment by intuitive induction.[23]

It is useful to recall at this point Aristotle's explanation of the inductive method quoted above in Chapter 5. In the *Posterior Analytics* (2.19) he writes that although memories are multiple, they may constitute a single experience. This experience, in relation to them, is a universal which comes to rest as "a whole in the soul," as "the One that corresponds to the Many, the unity that is identically present" in each individual memory. The first perception that comes to rest in the soul is the beginning of the universal's formulation by virtue of the fact that the act of perception itself grasps the generic form of "man" before it recognizes this or that individual man. So, in the metaphor of the *Physics*, children apply a familiar name indiscriminately to all members of a genus before recognizing that the noun specifies only particular individuals within the genus. The universals produced in this way by this 'generic' capacity of the senses themselves form the intellective principles (*archai*) of the arts and sciences.

If ethics is to become a "science" in the way just described by the *Posterior Analytics*, universal (first) principles of action must be reached

---

[23] *Aristotle: The Nicomachean Ethics*, trans. H. Rackham, LCL (London, 1956).

through individual achievements of a 'habit' of virtue. Aristotle defines virtue as "a settled disposition (ἕξις) of the mind determining the choice of actions and emotions, consisting essentially in the observance of the mean relative to us . . . as the prudent man (ὁ φρόνιμος) would determine it" (E.N.2.6.15; 1106b36–07a2). In explaining the significance of "relative to us," he says that all things may be divided "either with respect to the thing itself (κατ' αὐτὸ τὸ πρᾶγμα) or relatively to us (πρὸς ἡμᾶς) (E.N. 1106a28). By respect to the thing itself, he means a quantitative measurement such as that which can produce equal portions of a line by dividing it at the midpoint equidistant from either end; such equality of length will be "one and the same for everybody." By relative to us, he means a qualitative measurement "which is neither too much nor too little" with respect to the individual situation and so cannot be "one and the same for everybody." Virtue, like all arts and sciences, achieves its excellence by accommodating itself to this second, or qualitative, form of measurement which tries to approximate the mean (2.6.4–10). While the knowledge, then, of things measured with respect to themselves—like equal quantities—owes more to what is intelligible absolutely (ἁπλῶς), such as equality itself, the knowledge of things measured relative to each situation, like virtue, owes more to what is intelligible with respect to ourselves (ἡμῖν). Insofar as there is a method in the *Nicomachean Ethics* for learning how to achieve the mean in our actions, it must resemble that of arriving at the first principles of all the arts and sciences in the *Posterior Analytics*. In each text we must attain our objectives inductively from what is prior with regard to our own perceptions.[24]

If (particular) virtuous actions are the final expression of such (universal) ethical principles as can be realized through adhering to the mean, how is the mean itself to be determined? Aristotle says that it is to be determined in accordance with the judgment of the prudent man. While speculative wisdom (σοφία) is chiefly concerned with the grasping and demonstration of ultimate ends, such as happiness or the Good (cf. *Meta.* 1.1.17–2.8), prudence or practical wisdom (φρόνησις) is chiefly con-

---

[24] For Plato's view of quantitative and qualitative measurement, see *States.* 283D–85B, esp. 284AC where the existence of the qualitative mean is made a condition of the existence of the arts in a manner explicitly analogous to making the existence of 'not-being' a condition for all discourse in the *Sophist*. All linguistic comparison is based on qualitative measure (*Crat.* 432C–34A); and for Aristotle the senses themselves have the power to judge because they perceive things in relation to an inherent mean (*De an.* 2.11, 424a), while in ethics—which seeks, as all the arts and sciences, a mean (μέσον) relative, not to the thing, but to us (E.N. 2.6.8)—right approximation to the mean in particular circumstances depends upon perception (E.N. 2.9.8). From Lesher's discussion of νοῦς in Aristotle's ethics, one might conclude that it is precisely the νοῦς, in its broadest role, which apprehends the mean ("Meaning of ΝΟΥΣ," pp. 66–68).

cerned with intermediate ends and the means by which they can be attained. Wisdom combines, as first principles, precise definitions with discursive demonstration to establish scientific knowledge of all things human *and* divine (*E.N.* 6.7.5); prudence deliberates about the affairs of men (6.7.6). Prudence draws its most general principles from the universal experience of men who deliberate about individual decisions, but it also requires a "knowledge of particular facts even more than knowledge of general principles" (6.7.7). It must, that is, arrive at its general principles by calculating, on the basis of observation, which human actions will, as means, lead to desirable ends. Since both general principles and particular circumstances are involved, when Aristotle indicates the relation of prudence to Intelligence (νοῦς) by the word ἀν-τίκειται (1142a25), the word should not be taken so much in the sense of "opposite to" as of "corresponding to, though with a difference."[25] For the prudent man must grasp by a kind of practical intuition those among the various kinds (*genera*) of means which might lead to an ultimate end such as happiness. Then, through testing out one 'generic' means after the other by "dividing" it, imaginatively, into its possible 'specific' consequences, and thereby becoming able to reject most of the alternatives, he can finally choose the means most likely to attain the end.[26] Since the first principles of prudence are so conjectural and its materials so variable, it is capable of far less precision than wisdom whose *archai* are more intelligible with respect to their own nature.

[25] I am following D. J. Allan's suggestion of this reading of ἀντίκειται. He comments that "there is, after all, a correspondence between the intuition of the particular by the φρόνιμος [prudent man], and that of the indemonstrable first premisses of the sciences; in the one case in order to start the discursive reasoning, in the other to bring it to an end" ("The Practical Syllogism," *Autour d'Aristote* [Louvain, 1955], p. 329). This is plausible, because in the passage as a whole (6.8.9, 1142a25–30), Aristotle compares our perception of the ultimate particular thing (to be done) to our perception that the ultimate figure in mathematics is a triangle; and in 6.11.4, νοῦς not only seizes primary definitions of demonstration but "in practical inferences it apprehends the ultimate and contingent fact . . . ; hence we must have perception (αἴσθησιν) of particulars, and this immediate perception is Intelligence (νοῦς)." Intelligence, then, "is both a beginning and an end, for these things are both the starting-point and the subject matter of demonstration" (1143b10–11).

[26] For the procedures of moral dialectic in the Academy, see Chap. 2, pp. 44–49, Chap. 3, pp. 64–72. On p. 66 I argued that Aristotle seems to be drawing on Platonic dialectic in order to adapt his own inductive method to ethical deliberation. Plato pursues intuitively a possible generic definition by (tentatively) "collecting (συναγωγή)" individual concepts or types (Forms) together on the grounds that one or more of them might contain the distinctive characteristics—the generic Form—capable of yielding the definition of the concept under inquiry. He then tests what he suspects to be the most generic Form—that capable of yielding the desired definition—by "dividing (διαίρεσις)" it into its different kinds of specific Forms until that kind most resembling the original concept to be defined emerges. See *Phaedrus* 265D, 266B, 273DE, 277BC; *Statesman* 262BE, 287C; *Republic* 537C; and, for a helpful summary, Cornford, *Plato's Theory of Knowledge*, pp. 184–87, on dialectic in the *Sophist*.

These functions of the two types of intelligibility in logic, geometry, physics, and ethics account for the varying degrees of accuracy to be expected from the different arts and sciences. In the first two books of his *Nicomachean Ethics*, Aristotle excuses himself three times for not striving for greater precision than the nature of his subject permits. At *E.N.* 1.3.1 he notes that "the same exactness (τὸ ἀκριβές) must not be expected in all departments of philosophy alike, any more than in all the products of the arts and crafts." Subjects such as Justice and the Good involve such differences of opinion, such general and uncertain premises, that the reader must be content with but a "broad outline of the truth" and with conclusions which are only valid for the most part. For, he says, "it is the mark of an educated mind to expect that amount of exactness in each kind which the nature of the particular subject admits." And, therefore, it is "equally unreasonable to accept merely probable conclusions from a mathematician and to demand strict demonstrations from an orator" (1.3.1–4; 1094b12–27). Later (*E.N.* 1.7.17–19), he repeats his intention of "making a rough sketch (ὑποτυπῶσαι)" an "outline (περιγραφή)" to be gradually filled in (ἀναγράψαι), since one must not look for equal exactitude in all disciplines but for that "appropriate to the particular line of inquiry (μεθόδῳ)." A carpenter and a geometrician both seek after a right angle, for instance, but in different ways: "the former is content with that approximation to it which satisfies the purpose of his work; the latter, being a student of truth, looks for its essence or essential attributes" (1098a21-32). The orator with his verbal compositions and the craftsman with his plastic constructions are both contrasted with the mathematician with respect to exact demonstration. The practical discipline of ethics and the productive arts of rhetoric and carpentry cannot compete with the theoretical science of geometry. The distinction is so important for Aristotle that he returns to it when he introduces his principal definition of virtue.

The whole theory of conduct is bound to be an outline only and not an exact system, in accordance with the rule we laid down at the beginning, that philosophical theories must only be required to correspond to their subject matter; and matters of conduct and expediency have nothing fixed or invariable about them. (2.2.3)

If this is true of the general theory of ethics, he continues, even less precision is to be expected in dealing with "particular cases of conduct" where "the agents themselves have to consider what is suited to the circumstances on each occasion" (2.2.4).[27]

---

[27] Aristotle's comments on why depiction of character and moral purpose are foreign to mathematical treatises (*Rhet.* 3.16) are not only pertinent to ethics, as here, but to equity in law: for the passages, see Chap. 10, n. 28. Indeed, mathematical accuracy is not

The ancient dilemma of knowledge and representation becomes particularly critical in the less exact arts and sciences which are dependent for their first principles upon our knowledge of things better known with respect to our perceptions than with respect to themselves. Such arts and sciences include most of the humanistic and literary disciplines in which the achievement of the mean in ethics or decorum in literature is a continuing tentative adjustment of qualities that can never be fixed in exact quantitative ratios. The ancient dilemma itself reflects an essential handicap in our pursuit of wisdom: the difficulty in finding a method of inquiry commensurate in its accuracy with the excellence of its object is analogous to the difficulty in finding a method of demonstration commensurate in its certainty with the excellence of the first principles from which it derives its conclusions. In the humanistic disciplines, especially, the more important the subject, the less exact the method of inquiry into it, as well as the representation of it, is apt to be.

Those concerned with the literary expression of humanistic principles have tended to be somewhat ambivalent about these consequences of the ancient dilemma. If they have acquiesced in a certain artistic imprecision in treating major ethical or political issues, on the one hand, they have, nevertheless, regretted, on the other, the restrictions imposed upon artistic technique by the important, though inexact, nature of the subject. Isocrates, for instance, in opposing these restrictions, developed his highly refined style precisely in order that it be worthy of the most important matters of state, but, at the same time, he insisted that a general conception of important things, however imprecisely apprehended, is superior to precise knowledge of trivial matters. He criticizes the sophistic rhetoricians for trying to prove verbal quibbles rather than training their students in the practical affairs of government by reminding them that "likely conjecture about useful things is far preferable to exact (ἀκριβῶς) knowledge of the useless, and that to be a little superior in important things is of greater worth than to be pre-eminent in petty

---

always to be sought even in lectures, for one must carefully seek that degree of exactitude which is appropriate to the subject and the audience (*Meta.* 2.3.1–4). As in the *Philebus* (56A–7E), and in his treatment of educational disciplines in *Rep.* VII, Plato often discriminates between the degrees of exactness characteristic of various arts and sciences. Perhaps preceding both philosophers and influencing their use of medical or gymnastic analogies to describe the ethical mean (see Chap. 10, pp. 266–69), Hippocrates and/or his followers also observe the impossibility of arriving at precise criteria or norms for health with respect to exercise and diet. Like equity in law, individual constitutions and foods are too various for physicians to put down in writing rigidly exact rules (*Regimen* 2 and 67). Some measure is necessary, but "no measure, neither number nor weight, by reference to which knowledge can be made exact, can be found except bodily feeling" (*Ancient Medicine* 9.15–18 in *Hippocrates*, trans. W. H. S. Jones, LCL, 4 vols. [London, 1923–1931]).

things that are without value for living" (*Helen* 4–5). Centuries later, St. Thomas expresses the same conviction in his commentary on the opening sentence of Aristotle's treatise *On the Soul* with which we began this chapter.

Now there is this difference between sciences, that some excel in certainty and yet are concerned with inferior objects, while others with higher and better objects are nevertheless less certain. All the same, that science is the better which is about better and nobler things; . . . we have a greater desire for even a little knowledge of noble and exalted things—even for a conjectural and probable sort of knowledge—than for a great and certain knowledge of inferior things. For the former is noble in itself and essentially, but the latter only through its quality or mode.

Since, as Isocrates was fond of repeating, there can be no exact science for teaching men how to be just, the Good must be sketched first in a rough outline, a *circumscriptio* which, in his commentary on the *Ethics* (1.7), Thomas says must be drawn figuratively (*figuraliter*) in similitudes (*secundum quamdam similitudinariam et extrinsecam quodammodo descriptionem*). This ancient division between the qualitative and quantitative sciences is summarized epigrammatically by Richard of Bury: "Tully does not appeal to Euclid, nor does Euclid rely upon Tully."[28]

[28] *The Love of Books: The Philobiblon of Richard de Bury*, trans. E. C. Thomas (London, 1925), p.14; *Sancti Thomae Aquinatis In Decem Libros Ethicorum Aristotelis ad Nicomachum Expositio*, ed. R. M. Spiazzi (Torino, 1964), p. 35; *Aristotle's De Anima . . . and the Commentary of St. Thomas Aquinas*, ed. K. Foster and S. Humphries (London, 1951), pp. 45–46. The articles of Question 1 in the *Summa Theologica* are pertinent to the ancient assumption that the more honorable the object of a science, the more honorable the science (cf. Aristotle, *Rhet.* 1.7.19–20; *Meta.* 11.7.9). Plato insists that—given our human limitations—he can give only a probable account of the most excellent things (*Tim.* 29CD), and Cicero later claims to offer only an adumbration of the best orator that, although an exact delineation is not possible, may nevertheless suggest those qualities which he ought to have (*Orator* 19, 43, 100f.). In his commentary on *Ethics* 1.7, St. Thomas refers to the sketch, which offers an external outline of *bonum finale hominis, quod est felicitas*, as a *notificatio* of a thing by means of its own special attributes. For this reason, one speaks 'figuratively' first, and then fills in later what *fuit prius figuraliter determinatum (In Decem Libros Ethicorum)*. In commenting on *E.N.* 1.3, Thomas distinguishes the subject matter of ethics (from that of the speculative sciences) by saying again that its truth must be shown figuratively, *idest verisimiliter; et hoc est procedere ex propriis principiis huius scientiae*. For moral science is concerned with voluntary arts, and the will is moved not only by the good but by the apparent good, the appearances of which are deceptive because the *materia moralis est varia et difformis*. What appears in certain circumstances to be right appears in others to be wrong, and *in hoc multiplex error contingit (In Decem Libros Ethicorum*, pp. 9–10). The question of quality, then, becomes a 'ground' of negotiation between first principles and their reflection in disparate phenomena. See Chap. 10, n. 28. The connection between the 'prefiguring' of biblical exegesis and the presentation *figuraliter* in an outline to be later completed or brought to perfection will be treated briefly in Chap. 14 of this study. For the ability of a fictional *paradeigma* (μῦθος) to achieve a knowledge and representation of the most serious matters, see Appendix A.

A figurative adumbration, then, will seem at first to be appropriate to the representation of nobler and more exalted things about which our knowledge is slight, while our greater certainty about inferior things permits more precise delineation. Yet the boldly simplified skiagraphic style cannot provide in itself a solution to the dilemma of knowledge and representation. It can become as fixed and lifeless as the more exactly verisimilar or the more arbitrarily symbolic styles between which, ideally, it should achieve a balanced decorum. Such rigidity becomes a hazard as soon as we forget that the principle of decorum itself is the expression of a process governed by the philosophical premises illustrated by Plato's Titans and gods in combination with Aristotle's two forms of intelligibility. The Titans, as materialists, would restrict our knowledge to the things more knowable with respect to our perceptions (ἡμῖν); the gods, as idealists, to things more knowable in themselves (ἁπλῶς). Our comprehension of reality, however, derives from neither kind of intelligibility in isolation from the other but from the reciprocation between the two permitted by a discursive articulation of their interrelationship. The Titans and the gods, that is, must relax their intransigence if the mind is to understand its experience and the arts are to represent that understanding. As expressed in the ancient dilemma of knowledge and representation, the Greek Apollonius, like Longinus, strives for their negotiation, while the Egyptian Thespesion, like the pseudo-Dionysius, despairs of its possibility. For the first, decorum might be achieved, however incompletely, in mimetic forms; for the second, only in symbols.

Although the two kinds of intelligibility can influence how we *approach* an object of knowledge, we can *know* it in our experience only at the point of reciprocity between them where its significance becomes lucid. The extent to which we can know the object at this point will vary according to its nature, and, according to its nature, the decorum, with which our experience of it at this point is represented, will admit of varying degrees of exactitude. The appropriate degree of exactitude must be adjusted, not to the intellective or aesthetic *archai* of our method of inquiry but to the essential nature of the object itself. The essential nature of the heavens and their significance, for example, will permit less perceptually, though more mathematically, precise detail than those of our garden. Here the choice of detail and its degree of exactness is relatively obvious. When Pheidias, however, models his statue of Zeus on Homer's description, he must choose among widely varying alternatives. He does not, like Philostratus' Egyptian, try to represent the god by a symbol whose verisimilarly exact external form has only an arbitrarily stipulated relation to what it signifies. In this case, the abstract significance and its empirically precise embodiment remain separate, and the experience of the divine presence remains unarticulated save for the ritual of tradition. Homer and Pheidias, on the other hand, experience a divinely 'given' order in the cosmos and represent it by a human form, because, of living things, men participate most in rationality. The experience of the divine is portrayed, that is, at a point of greater reciprocation, however simplified in verisimilar detail it must necessarily be as a result of human limitations and the nature of the subject. To gain this reciprocation, some of the intelligibility proper to the nature of the god (the comprehensiveness of his significance) and some of the intelligibility proper to our perception (the verisimilar exactness of his form) must be sacrificed. The argument between mimesis and symbolism, that is, once both forms of representation have been freed from their logical, ontological, and theological commitments, must be adjudicated before the ancient tribunal of artistic decorum itself.

7. COGNITION AND DECORUM

THE DISTINCTION between the two types of intelligibility helps to define the method of inquiry commensurate in its accuracy with the excellence of its objects and, hence, bears upon the ancient dilemma of knowledge and representation. With respect to knowledge, the greatest possible accuracy appropriate to the nature of the object will be gained at that point where principles of intellection (better known in themselves) and principles of perception (better known to us) may be brought into a discursive relation with one another. With respect to representation, a style will achieve its greatest possible decorum when it elicits from the audience that amount and kind of emotion appropriate to the importance of the subject *as experienced* at that point of greatest lucidity. The discursive relation between the intellective and perceptual principles of order, necessary to both knowledge and representation, will be destroyed if either kind of principle is lost. This loss may occur whenever the two kinds of principle are reduced to one either (1) through the sacrifice of one kind in the interest of the other or (2) through their identification with one another. Having dealt with some of the epistemological consequences of such a loss, we must turn to its consequences for stylistic decorum. Any treatment of decorum must first of all take up the psychagogic problem of how to persuade a certain kind of audience on a certain kind of occasion under certain kinds of conditions. We must first consider what psychagogic effects, if any, the two types of intelligibility in themselves may have upon styles of representation.

A. Intelligibility and Psychagogia

At first glance, any affective connection between the way in which something may best be known, either in itself (ἁπλῶς) or relative to us (ἡμῖν), and a certain kind or intensity of emotion appears to be slight. Nevertheless, certain associations of this kind seem to lie hidden in assumptions about the nature of decorum in early discussions of style. One of the most famous passages in Aristotle's *Metaphysics* may help to bring them to light.

It is through wonder that men now begin and originally began to philosophize; wondering in the first place at obvious perplexities, and then by gradual progression raising questions about the greater matters too, e.g. about the changes of the moon and of the sun, about the stars and about the origin of the universe. Now he who wonders and is perplexed feels that he is ignorant (thus the myth-lover is in a sense a philosopher, since myths are composed of wonders); therefore if it was to escape ignorance that men studied philosophy, it is obvious that they pursued science for the sake of knowledge, and not for any practical utility (1.2.9–10).[1]

Myths possess a philosophical energy inasmuch as they are able to lead the listener through simple astonishment to sophisticated inquiry. But the most important thing for us is the fact that wonder is progressive: it starts with perplexities which are literally close at hand (τὰ πρόχειρα, 982b13), and therefore obvious to our perceptions, and then proceeds gradually (κατὰ μικρόν, 982b14) to be concerned with such greater and more distant matters as the heavenly bodies and even the origins of the cosmos itself. That is, wonder, in both philosophy and literature, begins with things knowable relative to us (ἡμῖν) and progresses to things knowable with respect to their own nature (ἁπλῶς), from the familiar, ordinary, and predictable to the foreign, uncommon, and unexpected. That kind of wonder which incites us to metaphysical speculation, Aristotle implies, must be the most powerful of all because no "other form of knowledge is more precious than this; for what is most divine is most precious" (1.2.13). A scale of things causing increasing wonder is clearly suggested here, and, by implication, a scale of emotional intensity corresponding to degrees of astonishment aroused by their revelation.

Things which must be known by the first principles of their own nature, furthermore, cannot be accounted for; while they may be recognized as causes for subsequent effects, their own causes are undemonstrable. Since they themselves, therefore, amount to effects without causes, they are traditional sources of wonder. The psychagogic effect of things known ἁπλῶς, or a priori, that is, will tend to resemble the effect of those things which are unfamiliar, distinctive, or exalted precisely because we do not know how 'to arrive at them' by prior principles which might explain how they came to be as they are. Having assumed them as premises of an argument, we proceed deductively from them. Conversely, arguments proceeding from perceptual beginnings relative

---

[1] For a later restatement of the educative power of wonder and myth, see Strabo, 1.2.8–9. Plato, as well as Aristotle (see also *Rhet.* 1.11, 1371a30–35), emphasizes the fact that all inquiry begins with wonder (*Theaet.* 155D). In the same spirit, Plutarch remarks that the inquirer who demands a reasonable explanation (τὸ εὔλογον) for each and every thing will end by destroying wonder in all things and, thereby, philosophy itself, since philosophy begins with our being puzzled by what we cannot explain (*Mor.* 680D).

to the familiar things close at hand (ἡμῖν) will, in their collection of discrete particulars, tend to relax our emotional expectations. In fact, the effects of these two procedures correspond to the early division of types of style into those making a psychagogic appeal (to the ear), most suitable for emotional persuasion, and those concerned with the meticulous scrutiny (by the eye) of things and events, most suitable for scientific investigation. If there is such an association between the ways in which things are known and their emotional effect upon us, it should hold, as well, for the artistic means of evoking the feelings appropriate to our experience of the subject being represented.[2] We may best discover these artistic means by differentiating further the most pertinent meanings of ἁπλῶς.

In their edition of Aristotle's *Rhetoric*, E. M. Cope and J. E. Sandys distinguish four meanings of ἁπλῶς among the numerous usages cited by Bonitz in his *Index Aristotelicus*. First, the primary meaning closest to its derivation, the editors say, appears to be *simply, purely, without mixture*, as opposed to composite; elements, for instance, in their uncombined state are called ἁπλᾶ σώματα. When this meaning of the word is "applied in a moral sense to human character, it denotes 'simplicity' (of composition), 'singleness' of heart and purpose, as opposed to 'duplicity.' " The second, and commonest, signification, however, is that of "*simpliciter et sine exceptione* 'generally' or 'universally,' as opposed to καθ' ἕκαστον, 'specifically,' 'particularly,' 'individually.' . . . Hence it signifies 'altogether,' 'absolutely,' *omnino*." The third meaning of ἁπλῶς is "absolutely" or "in itself" (= καθ' αὑτόν), the meaning we have been distinguishing from "the relative" (πρός τι) and "relatively to us" (ἡμῖν). The fourth meaning distinguished by the editors is that occurring at *Meta.* 1.5.16, 987a21, which refers to a subject's having been treated too simply, "too carelessly, without taking sufficient pains with it, with insufficient *elaboration*; '*negligenter*.' " The first and fourth of these meanings bear directly on the relation between stylistic decorum and the knowledge of both the subject and the audience addressed.[3]

---

[2] For the causes of wonder and its emotional effect in tragedy from antiquity through the Renaissance, see J. V. Cunningham, *Woe or Wonder* (Denver, 1951), Chap. 4: "Wonder." Many passages cited and elucidated by Cunningham illustrate the later transmission of the philosophical premises of decorum outlined in Part Two of this study. For the continuing efforts in the seventeenth and eighteenth centuries to achieve the stylistic effects of wonder, especially in the epic, see S. I. Shankman, *Pope's Iliad: Homer in the Age of Passion* (Princeton, 1983). For the greater emotional concentration achieved through the suspension of inductive procedures—normally necessary to arrive at the causes or *archai*—in the deductive presentation of the fictional 'argument' of events, see pp. 299–301 of this study. Our unemotional response to familiar things and events is mentioned by Sextus Empiricus among others (*Pyrr.* 1.141–44).

[3] *The Rhetoric of Aristotle*, ed. with commentary by E. M. Cope and J. E. Sandys, 3 vols. (Cambridge, 1877), 1:30–31, 42.

Plato makes these relations strikingly clear in the *Phaedrus* (277BC).

A man must know the truth about all the particular things of which he speaks or writes, and must be able to define everything separately; then when he has defined them, he must know how to divide them by classes until further division is impossible; and in the same way he must understand the nature of the soul, must find out the class of speech adapted to each nature, and must arrange and adorn his discourse accordingly, offering to the complex soul elaborate and harmonius discourses, and simple talks to the simple soul. Until he has attained to all this, he will not be able to speak by the method of art, so far as speech can be controlled by method, either for purposes of instruction or of persuasion.

In this passage, which epitomizes so much of what Aristotle subsequently analyzes in his *Rhetoric*, Plato already suggests the connection between the first and fourth meanings of ἁπλῶς. It is decorous to address those characterized by simplicity of heart (ψυχῇ . . . ἁπλῇ) with a style simple (λόγους . . . ἁπλοῦς) in order and refinement, while for a sophisticated (ποικίλη) audience elaborate (ποικίλους) and thoroughly harmonious (παναρμονίους) styles are appropriate.[4] The simpler style would be insufficiently elaborated, that is, for a highly sophisticated listener, for a detailed scientific investigation, or for the intricate analysis of evidence in a complicated legal case. Yet it would be appropriate to the audience, the occasion, and the topics of deliberative oratory for several reasons.

The deliberative orator must address his psychagogic powers to some hypothetical 'common' member of his large and miscellaneous audience. In his *Rhetoric* Aristotle calls such a member ἁπλοῦς (1.2.13) and char-

---

[4] *Phaedrus*, trans. H. N. Fowler, LCL (London, 1966). As the Neoplatonists were later to do, Plato prefers simplicity in both soul and style. With respect to rhetoric, for instance, Socrates tries ironically to outdo Lysias' praise of the nonlover by being more sophisticatedly "ingenious" (ποικιλώτερον, *Phaedrus* 236B). And, more important, in a passage which must be kept in mind throughout the rest of Part Two, Plato associates mimesis itself in several ways with the complex soul: " 'And does not the fretful part of us present many and varied (ποικίλην) occasions for imitation, while the intelligent and temperate disposition, always remaining approximately the same, is neither easy to imitate nor to be understood when imitated, especially by a nondescript mob assembled in the theatre? For the representation imitates a type that is alien to them.' " The mimetic poet, therefore, will be "devoted to the fretful and complicated type (ποικίλον) of character because it is easy to imitate" (*Rep.* 604E–5A; cf. 404E). The phrase "always remaining approximately the same" (αὐτὸ αὑτῷ) has the value of ἁπλόος in the antithesis of ἁπλόος - ποικίλος. Later, this terminology runs consistently throughout the literary essays of Dionysius of Halicarnassus. In his *Isaeus*, Dionysius describes Lysias as a straightforward (ἁπλοῦς) man (3), whose style has the simplicity (ἁπλότητα) of old-fashioned painting (4). In contrast, Isaeus has more technical skill and pays more attention to detail (ἀκριβεστέρα) and to varied (ποικίλοις) figures and developments (3). Not hiding his art, Isaeus amplifies his proofs with detail (ἀκριβῶς), while Lysias, confining himself to a general outline (ἁπλῶς), appears naturalistic, spontaneous, and candid (16). As a stylistic term, ἁπλῶς is synonymous with "uncomplicatedly" (ἀπεριέργως, *Demosth.* 9) and "plainly" (ἀφελῶς, *Demosth.* 9, *Lys.* 8). For Plutarch, τὸ ἁπλοῦν means insufficient elaboration which cannot move an audience, while τὸ ποικίλον (= variety) stirs the emotions by astonishing its listeners (*Mor.* 25D).

acterizes him as one "who cannot take in at a glance (συνορᾶν) a complicated argument, or follow a long chain of reasoning" (1.2.12). Cope glosses ἁπλοῦς as "a simple, uncultivated person" and says the word is used in the first sense distinguished above. Its meaning, he continues, "is opposed here rather to the 'complications' of an advanced stage of civilization and refinement, than to duplicity of character, and expresses 'an elementary state of cultivation.' " He cites as similar a use of the word in the *Politics* (2.5, 1268b39) to describe the rude, primitive laws of uncivilized (βαρβαρικούς) people. This usage suggests, in addition to Cope's first sense, his fourth sense of the word to denote insufficient elaboration or archaic simplicity.[5] In a general way, then, the Platonic and Aristotelian uses of ἁπλόος to characterize both a kind of person and a kind of style are analogous. In philosophy, the soul most receptive to the most important revelations of dialectic will be unsophisticated and responsive to the simplest statement of the truth. In rhetoric, the 'common' auditor of a deliberative oration on the most important communal issues will be equally unsophisticated and equally responsive to the simplest elaborations of style. Whereas for Plato, however, the 'simpler' soul should be as undistracted as possible by emotion, for Aristotle, the 'simpler' members of the audience will be those whose passions can be most easily manipulated. Later, he describes the stylistic devices most appropriate to the agonistic conditions of oral delivery necessary to persuade such an audience.

In the third book of his *Rhetoric*, Aristotle sharply separates certain stylistic qualities of spoken oratory and Homeric recitation from those of written compositions meant to be read or listened to with close attention for their artistic refinements (*Rhet.* 3.12). He then subdivides the oral or public style into a deliberative (δημηγορική) and a forensic (δικανική) category and immediately further subdivides the forensic into its less and more exact manifestations.

The deliberative style is exactly like a rough sketch (σκιαγραφία), for the greater the crowd, the further off is the point of view (πορρωτέρω ἡ θέα); wherefore in both too much refinement (τὰ ἀκριβῆ) is a superfluity and even a disadvantage (περίεργα καὶ χείρω). But the forensic style is more finished (ἀκριβεστέρα), and more so before a single judge, because there is least opportunity of employing rhetorical devices, since the mind more readily takes in at a glance (εὐσύνοπτον) what belongs to the subject and what is foreign to it; there is no discussion, so the judgement is clear. This is why the same orators do not excel in all these styles; where action [i.e. histrionic delivery] is most effective, there the style

---

[5] For the term ἁπλῶς being used for the inadequate flexibility of written law in general, as in *Rhet.* 1.13.14, see my discussion of equity in Part Three, pp. 266–75. Isocrates uses the term, as we shall see, in its pejorative sense of 'inartistic,' 'commonplace,' or 'negligent.'

is least finished (ἥκιστα ἀκρίβεια ἔνι), and this is a case which voice, especially a loud one, is needed. The epideictic style (ἐπιδεικτική) is especially suited to written compositions, for its function is reading; and next to it comes the forensic style (3.12.5–6; 1414a7–18).[6]

The deliberative style of oratory and the skiagraphic style of painting are both executed in simple outline without elaboration; each, that is, would correspond generally to the first but most specifically to the fourth meaning of ἁπλῶς listed previously. Heard or seen from a distance, a highly finished style, on the other hand, would be superfluous and even a disadvantage. Neither the ear nor the eye would, physically, be able to perceive much of its detail or subtlety, and what little might appear would be more likely to distract than to involve the audience emotionally. Such artfulness, however, begins to be effective in the public type of forensic debate and more effective still in the smaller (private) trials. These three gradations of artifice refer to styles of *spoken* oratory, while contrasted with all three, the *written* (epideictic) style, forming a fourth gradation, demands the highest finish of all.

Since deliberative oratory deals with matters of general importance to the whole community, Aristotle assumes its greater nobility (1.1.10) as well as its greater difficulty—in that it deals with the future and cannot be mastered simply by the diligent application of forensic rules (3.17.10). These common interests involve the most widely accepted ultimate ends, the recoverable first principles of prudential wisdom better known with respect to themselves (ἁπλῶς), which may render intelligible alternative solutions to practical problems at hand. The emotions will be more easily aroused by these communal problems than they will be by the intricacies of a private forensic trial which is confined to the interests of a few individuals and to the empirical interpretation of evidence. Since the deliberative style may count on an audience already emotionally engaged in the issues, it will not need the intricate argument and finished detail necessary to beguile a judge whose personal welfare is not involved in his decision. The roughhewn presentation in a large assembly may blur with impunity the sharp lines between what is and is not precisely pertinent to the issue in the interests of psychagogic control. Closer up, before a few and then a single judge, these lines will

---

[6] *Aristotle: The "Art" of Rhetoric*, trans. J. H. Freese, LCL (London, 1975). In contrast to the inexperienced (ἁπλόος) member of the large miscellaneous audience who cannot take a complicated argument "in at a glance" (συνορᾶν, 1.2.12), it is the single judge, who, less swayed by emotional involvement, can take "in at a glance" (εὐσύνοπτον) precisely what is pertinent to the case and what is not. The inexperienced listeners, as Aristotle says in another context, "are like those who view things from a distance" (*De soph. elench.* 1, trans. E. S. Forester, LCL [London, 1965]), and would then appropriately be addressed in a skiagraphic style.

be 'seen' more and more clearly so that a heightened emotional style cannot cover them over, and subtler tricks which attempt to conceal them in its stead must be that much more accurately disguised.[7] These stylistic distinctions clearly reflect the ancient dilemma of knowledge and representation: the roughly articulated style of the assembly is appropriate to the most important topics for the community, while the style of precise argumentation or epideictic exactness is required to treat the less important subjects of the courtroom or auditorium. Aristotle concludes his distinctions between the oral and written styles by reasserting the qualities necessary for all persuasive language which make up his doctrine of decorum, the appropriate relation of style to its subject and its audience. To these qualities we must now turn.

Appropriateness (τὸ πρέπον) in language is established "by the expression of emotion and character, and by proportion to the subject matter" (3.7.1). Of these three variables "style is proportionate to the subject matter when neither weighty matters are treated offhand, nor trifling matters with dignity, and no embellishment is attached to an ordinary word" (3.7.2). Similarly, the expression of emotion will be appropriate when the language reflects in its tone and intensity the quality and significance of the subject in accordance with which the speaker desires to move his listeners. Lastly, style will reflect the speaker's character appropriately when the words chosen are in keeping with the 'disposition' (ἕξις) which he wishes to represent himself as possessing to this or that particular audience. It is best not to make these types of decorum correspond at any time too exactly with one another, lest the speech seem obviously contrived and the listeners become suspicious. With suitably varying degrees of each in due season (εὐκαίρως, 3.7.8), the artfulness may be disguised and thereby become effective.

Aristotle's analysis of the three variable components of decorum reflects a relation analogous to that between knowledge and representation. To achieve the best style, the speaker must aim at a method of representation appropriately commensurate, in the force and control of its authority to move the audience, with the significance of its topic and

[7] Since deliberative oratory deals with future events which are contingent rather than with past events which are "necessary" (*Rhet.* 3.17.5), it can offer but a general sketch of policy in which the audience, nevertheless, has a strong personal stake. Despite his broadly outlined argument, the orator may easily draw upon the emotional excitement of his listeners to influence them, since, as Aristotle makes clear in his psychological treatises, the imagination of people who are passionate (or feverish) is particularly vulnerable. For the more exact learning necessary to plead before a single judge, see HASD, nn. 8 and 21. Cicero reflects Aristotle's distinction in terms of the rivalry between rhetoric and philosophy by juxtaposing popular oratory (which the learned lack) against the refinements of sound learning (which fluent speakers lack) in the preface to his *Orator* (11–13).

what is said about it. He describes the artistic means of producing the expression judged to be in keeping with the situation as the proportionate combination of unusual forms of speech, which provide distinctiveness, and of ordinary forms of speech, which provide clarity. Since common usage will presumably be the possession of everybody, the orator or poet, as artist, will concern himself primarily with the kind and frequency of those departures from ordinary usage necessary to arouse the admiration proper to the dignity of the subject. The terms in which these departures are discussed are the same in the *Poetics* and in the *Rhetoric*.[8]

In poetry the perfection of style is to be clear (σαφῆ) without being mean (ταπεινήν). The clearest style, however, uses only current (κυρίων) words and runs the risk, therefore, of being undistinguished. For diction to become more 'dignified' (σεμνή) it must depart from ordinary language (τὸ ἰδιωτικόν) and, to do this, it must use an unfamiliar vocabulary (τοῖς ξενικοῖς), such as strange, metaphorical, or lengthened words. While a style that is simply clear risks being flat, one made up only of unusual words will be enigmatic or outlandish (βαρβαρισμός). A balance, therefore, between familiar words to insure perspicuousness (σαφήνειαν) and unfamiliar words to render the style distinctive (σεμνή) is required (*Poet.* 22.1–7).

In the *Rhetoric* (3.2.1ff.) Aristotle discusses the style of prose in the identical terms of clarity without meanness and distinctiveness without exaggeration with respect to the dignity of the subject. While words in their ordinary forms will be clear, departures from common usage will make the style more commanding. Because men admire what is remote (τῶν ἀπόντων, 3.2.3) and because what arouses admiration (τὸ θαυμαστόν, 3.2.3) is pleasing, the speaker, if he is to catch the attention of his audience, must give his familiar speech (διάλεκτον) a "foreign air"

---

[8] In the eyes of Dionysius of Halicarnassus, Demosthenes seems to have best achieved the kind of balance which Aristotle proposed. His *Demosthenes*, as we have it, opens with descriptions of the distinctive style, represented by Thucydides, and the familiar style, represented by Lysias. The relation between them is that of the highest to the lowest note on the musical scale: the highest note excites tension, the lowest relaxes it (2). Demosthenes achieves a balance between these extremes as they appear in various qualities of style (8), particularly between the Thucydidean obscurity and the Lysian familiarity (10). He represents, that is, the proper Aristotelian proportion of distinctiveness to simplicity, and this mixture is appropriate for the varying education of a mixed audience (15, 34). Later, Demosthenes is portrayed as combining the austere style, characteristic of political oratory, with the elegant style characteristic of written speeches: since austerity is appropriate for dignity of subject and elegance for precise refinement, he has achieved a style commensurate in its accuracy with the excellence of his subject (36, 38, 44–45). Dionysius offers perhaps the best adaptation of Aristotle's distinctions in *Rhetoric* 3.12 to Augustan society (44–45). On the difference between austerity in oral composition and the labored gravity of the written artificial style, see *Thucydides* 24. In this treatise Dionysius again asserts that artifice and scholastic subtlety are out of place in oral confrontations (49–51).

(ξένην, 3.2.3). Since such an effect, however, is more appropriate to poetry—because its subject matter is more remote from ordinary life than that of prose—he must use unfamiliar diction with restraint lest it become conspicuous. It is for this reason that "those who practice this artifice must conceal it and avoid the appearance of speaking artificially instead of naturally; for that which is natural persuades, but the artificial does not" (3.2.4). In sum, "if a speaker manages well, there will be something 'foreign' about his speech, while possibly the art may not be detected, and his meaning will be clear. And this, as we have said, is the chief merit of rhetorical language" (3.2.7).[9]

Aristotle's balanced mean (τὸ μέτριον, 3.3.3) between clarity (without meanness) and distinctiveness (without extravagance) constitutes a criterion of decorum capable of articulating degrees and kinds of feeling appropriate to the subject, the audience, and the occasion. The foreign air of the remote, which arouses the strong emotions of wonder, however, will be less dependent on unusually distinctive diction in oral than in written composition. In deliberative oratory it will arise from vivid, forceful metaphor, an uncommonly dramatic rhythm of asyndetic syntax and abrupt transitions of delivery. These effects will heighten the agonistic tension over the outcome of events incapable of being treated with the precision appropriate to things which may be scrutinized close at hand. Since such oratory deals with decisions about the future, it deals with events and their causes which are not intelligible with respect to ourselves (ἡμῖν). They are intelligible, so to speak, only with respect to their own nature (ἁπλῶς) which will be revealed only in the course of time when they, rather than we, are ready. Since it is the nature of such events to concern all the men of the community in their role, not as members of special professions, but as human beings, such oratory takes place under the conditions characteristic of large assemblies. These conditions, in turn, render a skiagraphic style appropriate, which in written or epideictic compositions would appear insufficiently elaborated (ἁπλῶς).

---

[9] Epistemologically speaking, it is metaphor which expresses the interdependence of knowledge and representation in terms of a balanced mean between foreign and familiar diction (Rhet. 3.10.2–3)—and much the same thing applies to mimesis itself (Rhet. 1.11): for the pertinent passages, see pp. 173–75 and Chap. 8, n. 12. In similar terms Aristotle suggests that the balance between familiar language (τὸ σύνηθες) and the technical—and hence esoteric—precision (τὸ ἀκριβές) of mathematics be appropriate to the audience and to the subject (Meta. 2.3). With respect to clarity, the danger of too much accuracy resembles that of too much 'distinctiveness.' The emotional effects of the familiar and the unusual or distinctive are interestingly commented on by the author of the Rhetorica ad Herennium (3.35–37) with respect to memory and in general by Sextus Empiricus in the Outlines of Pyrrhonism 1.141–44. For Longinus, the psychagogic demands of 'distinctiveness' may become excessive and affected when they claim more emotion than the importance of the subject deserves (3.5, 30.1–2). And Seneca cautions against the extremes of both the distinctive and the familiar (Ep. 100.5, 114.13–14).

The broadly etched psychagogic style, then, is appropriate to the subject, the audience, and the occasion (with its accompanying conditions), all of which share, in one way or another, the quality of simplicity (ἁπλότης). As stated earlier, the discrepancy between the importance of the subject and the lack of artistic refinement congenial to it reflects once more the ancient dilemma concerning the kind of thing that is known and the method appropriate to its representation.

In whatever discipline the dilemma occurs, however, the corresponding quest for a method of knowledge and representation commensurate in its accuracy with the excellence of its subject is also likely to arise. It is just such a quest that leads Isocrates to develop the Platonic distinctions in the passage quoted previously from the *Phaedrus* (277BC) in a different direction from Aristotle. He wishes to bring the most accurate capabilities of art at *our disposal* to bear upon those issues *at whose disposal* we have most often found ourselves. To do this he appears to make the assumption that those who will decide upon such political issues will be likely to possess a soul which is sophisticated (ποικίλος) rather than simple (ἁπλόος) in Plato's sense. The style, then, appropriate to moving them must be varied and elaborate (ποικίλος). Whereas Aristotle considers the less premeditated, agonistic style appropriate to the subjects treated by deliberative oratory, Isocrates regards the written, epideictic style as appropriate for matters of state (*Paneg.* 4–5). He regards the informal, less elaborate style, on the other hand, as appropriate to the subjects treated in the practical, spontaneous, and hence artless, debates of ordinary trials.

There are some who carp at discourses which are beyond the powers of ordinary men and have been elaborated with extreme care (λίαν ἀπηκριβωμένοις), and who have gone so far astray that they judge the most ambitious oratory by the standard of the pleas made in the petty actions of the courts; as if both kinds should be alike and should not be distinguished, the one by plainness of style (ἀσφαλῶς), the other by display (ἐπιδεικτικῶς); or as if they themselves saw clearly the happy mean, while the man who knows how to speak elegantly (ἀκριβῶς) could not speak simply and plainly (ἁπλῶς) if he chose. (*Paneg.* 11)[10]

The unelaborated style now appears mainly appropriate to the less important issues of private trials while the highly finished compositions

[10] In his *Oration to Philip* (25–29), Isocrates, while recognizing the psychagogic power of oral composition, defends, by asking indulgence for, his written address in terms which resemble Aristotle's and uses ἁπλῶς again for the simple (minimally adequate) style appropriate to the simple statement of the facts (28). He repeats some of his distinctions in his *Letter to Dionysius* (2–3). In a similar spirit, Plutarch later (*Mor.* 25D) praises the poem which has a variety of unexpected events (and hence is ποικίλος) for its emotional power (ἔκπληξις), while the poem which is insufficiently elaborated is flat, since sameness (τὸ ἁπλοῦν) is unemotional (ἀπαθές) and inartistic (ἄμουσον).

are worthy of affairs of state. The ideal of written has replaced that of oral composition, and the way is set for the development of the three Roman *genera dicendi*, of which the most moving style, the *genus grande*, will now require the greatest exactitude in the handling of rhythm, syntax, and ornament.

Conforming to the Aristotelian qualities of clarity and distinctiveness are two original intentions (*officia*) of language with their two corresponding 'characters' (*genera*) of style. The first is that of demonstrative argument which strives for clarity and subtlety in handling the 'facts' (πϱάγματα) within the given limits of the case; proper to it is the plainer style (ἰσχνός; *genus humile, tenue, subtile, argutum*). The second intention is that of affective expression which strives for delightful or forceful persuasion in drawing on all the topics of *pathos* and *ethos*, as well as on the relevant circumstances, whether they concern the stated facts of the case or not; proper to it is the more distinctive, pathetic or vehement style (ἁδϱός; *genus grande*). According to G. L. Hendrickson, the vehement style, aiming at emotional force capable of 'leading the soul' (ψυχαγωγία), "was further differentiated into two forms, the one of stylistic finish and elaboration (*cultus*), the other of vehemence and passion (*vis*)." While vehemence remained the chief characteristic of the *genus grande*, finish came to be associated with the middle style or *genus floridum* by the Roman rhetoricians. Demosthenes came to exemplify the quality of *vis*, Isocrates of *cultus*.[11]

As distinctiveness seems to have divided its affective powers between *vis* and *cultus*, the other complementary Aristotelian virtue of clarity appears to have taken two forms as well: the *claritas* of the *genus grande* and the *subtilitas* of the *genus tenue*. Compatible with *vis* and the psychagogic intentions of deliberative oratory, the *claritas* of the *genus grande* retains something of the simple and broadly sketched outlines of skiagraphic representation. Compatible with the artificial elaborations of *cultus*, and the scholastic intentions of meticulous scientific investigation, the *subtilitas* of the *genus tenue* consists of accurate distinctions and intricate connections. *Vis* and *claritas* remain *simplex* (ἁπλόος); *cultus* and *subtilitas* remain *varius* (ποικίλος). *Cultus* and *subtilitas*, the products of diligent precision (ἀϰϱίβεια), remain antithetical to the *intensity* of the affective style insofar as they relax the listener's emotions

[11] G. L. Hendrickson, "The Origin and Meaning of the Ancient Characters of Style," *AJP* 26 (1905):290. See also Hendrickson's "The Peripatetic Mean of Style and the Three Stylistic Characters," *AJP* 25 (1904):125–46. More recently, F. Quadlbauer has brought together a particularly helpful survey of the early Greek and Latin terminology in "Die genera dicendi bis Plinius d.J.," *Wiener Studien* 71 (1958):55–111 and has continued it in "Die antike Theorie der Genera Dicendi im lateinischen Mittelalter," *Akad. D. Wissens. zu Wien Sitzungsberichte* 241.2 (Wien, 1962):3–292.

by distracting him in mid-course with articulated detail. The same qualities remain antithetical to the *clarity* of the affective style insofar as
they distract the listener from a sense of the total argument by focusing
his attention on individual logical steps or on expedient digressions. The
encroaching ideal of ἀκρίβεια whether in the guise of the *genus floridum*
or *genus tenue*, upon the forum and the lesser courts, so apparent in
the schools of declamation and later in both the Second Sophistic and
the archaistic Attic Revival, became the central concern for Cicero in his
Brutus and *Orator* (cf. Quintilian, 5.14.27–32).

Corresponding to the three Roman *officia* of the orator—to inform
or teach (*docere*), to delight (*delectare*), to move (*movere*)—the *genus
medium* was concerned with delighting or conciliating, while the *genus
tenue* and *genus grande* were responsible for instructing or proving and
moving respectively (*Orat.* 69, *Brut.* 185, *De orat.* 2.115, Quint. 12.10.59).
Since, however, a greater variety of subjects and occasions may delight
us than may teach or move us, *dilectare* appears to have been a more
flexible *officium* than *docere* and *movere*. Similarly, its corresponding
stylistic quality of *suavitas* seems more inclusive than *subtilitas* (*acu-
men*) and *gravitas* (*fulmen*) and, in fact, Cicero calls the middle style a
polished combination of arguments developed with breadth and subtlety
(*latae eruditaeque disputationes*) and of all kinds of figures both of
thought and diction (*verborum . . . lumina omnia, multa etiam senten-
tiarum*).

It is commonly the philosophic schools which produce such orators: and unless
he be brought face to face with the more robust speaker, the orator whom I am
describing will find approval on his own merits. It is, as a matter of fact, a
brilliant (*insigne*) and florid (*florens*), highly coloured (*pictum*) and polished
(*expolitum*) style in which all the charms of language and thought are inter-
twined. The sophists are the source from which all this has flowed into the
forum, but scorned by the simple (*subtilibus*) and rejected by the grand (*gra-
vibus*), it found a resting-place in the middle class (*mediocritate*) of which I am
speaking. (*Orat.* 95–96)

The main characteristic of the *genus medium* is its delicate precision, a
cultivated charm which owes its life to the ἀκρίβεια of sophistic *dili-
gentia*. While it can share a disputatious subtlety with the *genus tenue*
and a verbal luxuriance with the *genus grande*, because it lacks the lucid
economy of the first and the agonistic force of the second, it is nominally
distinguished from both. Yet, up to a point, while the plainer and the
more commanding styles are both closely associated with specific kinds
of subjects, intentions, and audiences, the 'cultivated' attributes of the
middle style may fluctuate in the service of each (cf. *Orat.* 100).

In the eyes of most ancient critics, Isocrates and his followers were wrong in seeking an adequate form of representation primarily in epideictic display. The artistic sophistication of such written compositions lacked the psychagogic power appropriate to the communal significance of political issues. In fact, in calling attention to themselves and thereby relaxing the emotional expectations of the audience, the refinements of *cultus* could threaten to obscure the very principle of stylistic decorum that Isocrates set out to articulate: a style which could most accurately invoke and maintain the emotion most appropriate to the most important situations.[12] The precision of epideictic art could put a certain limited range of emotions within our power by giving us a knowledge of how to control them. But it could not replace the tension, generated by the *agon* itself, between causal principles—which could be known only in themselves and revealed to us only through the process of time—and the challenging circumstances immediately confronting us. The emotions solicited by the meticulous ideal of *cultus* were restricted in a way similar to those encouraged by that of *subtilitas*: wonder they could both command but a wonder confined to an astonishment at our technical ability to know and control those things especially which are prior and more intelligible with respect to our own perceptions. The forces lying beyond our knowledge and power, and therefore prior and better known with respect to themselves, drew upon emotions of a different kind. And between these emotions, associated with causes to be revealed, and those in the closer ranges of our experience an adjustment of decorum could be made corresponding to the discursive adjustment between the intellective and the aesthetic poles of intelligibility. But in associating the agonistic style, whose emotional force was motivated by things less under our control, with the random banalities of familiar litigation, Isocrates psychagogically reduced the two poles to one. The refinements of the epideictic style, which he had hoped might arouse the stronger feelings, in the end achieved, as did litigious subtlety, the emotional detachment of artistic ingenuity. With an emotional disengagement from all agonistic involvement, a balanced relation between the two kinds of emotion disappears. And with its disappearance, the concept of decorum as a

---

[12] Dionysius of Halicarnassus comments repeatedly upon the characteristics of Isocrates' style which make it more suitable for reading and private recitations than for the forum. In *Isocrates* he describes his style as loosely knit, diffuse, ceremonious, ornate (ποικίλην), and over-elaborate (περιεργοτέραν). It aims at polish, not simplicity (ἀφελῶς), and therefore cannot take the stress of the courts, where intensity of feeling is demanded (2, 20). Striving always for a musical effect, his rhythms are labored; his figures are crude, frigid, and farfetched; his periodic structure long-winded and padded (2). These characteristics are always out of place in deliberative or forensic oratory (12) and cannot avoid leading to monotony (13). See as well *Demosthenes* 18.

process of continuous readjustment becomes a concept of decorum as fixed configurations of stylistic *schemata*.[13]

B. 'Longinus' on the Most Excellent Style

Aristotle describes decorum as a balanced proportion between two qualities of language. The first is an 'extraordinary' or 'foreign' syntax and diction necessary to provide a distinctiveness capable of arousing emotional excitement or wonder. The second is a current and familiar syntax and diction capable of providing the clarity necessary for ready aural comprehension. Such a proportion may avoid both the undue meanness of ordinary speech, appropriate to everyday matters, and the undue elevation of striking expressions appropriate to the dignity of the most important issues. Since the greater the dignity of the subject the greater the emotional response demanded by it, Aristotle's discussion of decorum gives a psychagogic extension to the ancient dilemma of knowledge and representation. As the most complete knowledge depends on finding a method of inquiry commensurate in its exactness with the excellence of its subject, the most decorous representation depends on achieving a clarity commensurate with the dignity of what it represents.

According to Aristotle's distinction between the styles appropriate for oral and written composition, deliberative oratory, in treating important communal issues before a large miscellaneous assembly, would demand a strikingly affective distinctiveness and a histrionic delivery. Yet, at the same time, these qualities would be ineffective without the clarity necessary for immediate comprehension by an audience largely unsophisticated and untrained in the topics debated. Since, however, the deliberative style has little opportunity for artistic elaboration, it must gain

---

[13] In the earliest surviving Roman treatise, for instance, distinctiveness (*dignitas*) has clearly become a matter of embellishment (*exornatio*) by means of a varied disposition of figures (*Rhet. ad Her.* 4.18ff.). My articles on Horace cited in the first note to Part Two contain many references in ancient criticism to striving too laboriously for artistic precision (ἀκρίβεια) to the exclusion of other stylistic virtues. Further citations may be mentioned here. The author of the *Rhet. ad Alex.* uses ἀκριβῆ (= petty) antithetically to μεγάλα (= noble) in describing both character and style (22, 1434b30). Much later Philostratus echoes the tradition by saying that it was precisely because Aristides' "natural talent was not in line with extempore eloquence" that "he strove after extreme accuracy" (582) and "the elaborate cogitation of a theme" (585): "the desire not to produce anything except after long cogitation keeps the mind too busy and robs it of alertness" (585). In the same spirit, Eunapius contrasts Libanius' precise erudition with Homer's lack of "pains about every single foot of his verses" and Pheidias' disregard for the exploitation of any given detail— in the interest, in each case, of the total effect, which is as hard to define as the grace which captivates us in beautiful bodies (497). *Philostratus and Eunapius: The Lives of the Sophists*, trans. W. C. Wright, LCL (London, 1968).

its clarity from a broadly etched, skiagraphic outline of the reasons why a given position should be taken on an issue rather than from a logically clear and precise argument. Similarly, with respect to syntax and diction, clarity must come from boldly juxtaposed assertions and dramatically asyndetic repetition rather than from elegant figures smoothly cemented by intricate rhythms and syntactical connections. Given the inexact nature of general ethical principles and the uncertainty of their application, only a style of the most intense psychagogic power might sufficiently unify the varying opinions and emotional anxieties of the community to enable it to make relatively unanimous decisions on important problems. While Aristotle found such 'decorous' energy in the abrupt and repetitive, histrionic simplicity of agonistic debate, which also characterized for him certain stylistic effects of Homer's treatment of celebrated and remote events, Isocrates developed the sophistic ideals of written composition. Psychagogic power was henceforth to be sought in the written elaboration of language under the control of artists at leisure to work out beforehand much of the stylistic subtlety to appear later in their presentations.

As the written tradition became more and more dominant, it fell more and more under scholastic analysis and refinement. Neoclassical recoveries and pedagogical requirements led to ever subtler forms of stylistic imitation and erudition. The psychagogic energy of the oral tradition of agonistic debate, on the other hand, came to be regarded increasingly as the means of persuading a predominately illiterate or uneducated, as opposed to simply a miscellaneous, audience. Long before, and certainly long after, Longinus wrote his 'epistle' on the most excellent style, what remained of the original intentions of deliberative oratory had become and were to remain sociological rather than political in the way that Aristotle had conceived of them. With the oral style confined to the special therapeutic needs of practical situations and the written styles confined increasingly to various forms of epideictic display, conventions of literary decorum suffered more and more from formalism and preciosity. It is in reaction against this preciosity, especially in rhetoric, that Longinus seeks to recover the Aristotelian emphasis upon the politically responsible use of the agonistic style. Yet Longinus was also the beneficiary of centuries of sophistic analysis of style, and he could not abandon its technical contributions. As a result, he represents a striking coordination of the Aristotelian and Isocratean attitudes toward political rhetoric. His reconsideration of the value of Isocratean figures in the light of, and in relation to, Aristotle's psychological insight into the emotional resources of oral composition remains one of the most successful neoclassical resolutions of the ancient dilemma, a resolution not so completely achieved again, perhaps, until Dr. Johnson recaptures, for English literature at least, so much of its essential spirit.[14]

In his treatise περὶ ὕψους, Longinus arrives at his synthesis of the Aristotelian and Isocratean traditions under the influence of Middle Stoicism as transmitted by Panaetius and Posidonius. According to these later Stoics, human nature (φύσις) is conceived of as a part, extension, or expression of a universal or cosmic Nature (φύσις). This cosmic Nature owes its order and coherent operation to rational principles which exist, by analogy, in human beings as reason (λόγος). Insofar as men act in accord with their reason, they may be said to follow, or to act in accordance with, Nature (κατὰ φύσιν). Because they participate in the rational principles of the cosmos, they can perceive the 'laws' of its operation, and these laws may be said to constitute a way or 'method' by which Nature 'realizes' or 'expresses' itself. Men, by extension, because of their reason (λόγος, ratio) are able to 'express' themselves in discourse (λόγος, oratio). As Nature may be said to possess an 'art' of expression in the comprehensibility of its laws, men may be said to possess a corresponding 'art' in their power to express conceptions arising from their given natural ability or ingenium. The human dichotomy of 'genius' and 'art,' natura or ingenium and ars, forms an analogy with the divine dichotomy of Nature (φύσις) and its power or art (δύναμις, μέθοδος, τέχνη) to express its 'order' (κόσμος). To relate ars to ingenium in the attainment of a style commensurate with the greatest human conceptions, and thus to redefine the antithesis of the ancient dilemma, Longinus draws upon the analogous commensurateness in the divine cosmos itself.

As a point of departure, Longinus sets out to correct certain errors in the treatment of the most excellent style by the rhetorician Caecilius, an Augustan contemporary of Dionysius of Halicarnassus. Two things, Longinus says, are necessary in any systematic treatise: the one is the statement of the subject and "the other, which although second in order ranks higher in importance, is an indication of the methods (μεθόδων)

---

[14] As the oral, or deliberative, style of oratory became more associated with political or religious issues addressed to largely uneducated assemblies, the genres of written composition sought to appeal to ever smaller and more discriminating, often private, audiences. The corresponding rivalry between the older oral conventions of Homeric composition and the more refined conventions of written poems is outlined in the articles cited in the preceding note (see esp. HASD, p. 46, n. 21). It is their mutual attempt to regain, or at least to recognize, some of the stylistic breadth and power of oral composition—while sacrificing as few technical refinements of written composition as possible—that Horace and Longinus most resemble one another in their attitudes toward decorum. In their own period and in their own way, both critics see in the rigorous simplicity of Homer's style, as well as in his range of subject matter, a healthy corrective to the preciosities of both Alexandrian poetic conventions and of the renewed extravagances of sophistic display.

by which we may attain our end." Now Caecilius gives many examples of the nature of the sublime (τὸ ὑψηλόν), but the means (δι' ὅτου τρόπου) by which we are to raise "our own capacities (φύσεις) to a certain pitch of elevation he has, strangely enough, omitted as unnecessary" (1.1). To judge by his silence, Caecilius appears to acquiesce in the mutually exclusive roles of *ars* and *ingenium*—to have renounced, that is, the ancient quest for an *art* capable of helping to secure the most excellent effects which the best of our natural gifts may occasionally seize.[15]

As if Longinus himself assumed such a renunciation on the part of Caecilius, he immediately raises the first, and central, question of his treatise (2.1): "whether there is such a thing as an art (τέχνη) of the sublime" at all. There are those—and he implies Caecilius is among them—who hold that such excellence is innate (γεννᾶται) and cannot be taught by any art. The product of such natural powers, furthermore, like other works of Nature (τὰ φυσικὰ ἔργα), may even be weakened by being brought under artistic rules (τεχνολογίαις). Longinus responds that Nature itself does not like to act at random (εἰκαῖον) without a principle of order (ἀμέθοδον) in what it produces. For, while Nature may serve as the underlying pattern and force of generation to be followed, art (μέθοδος), by defining quantities and indicating occasions, can establish practical habits of production which do not wander from the way. In order to achieve excellent expression, natural ability needs the guidance and restraint of knowledge. Good fortune in one's innate gifts, which is in the hands of Nature, must, according to Demosthenes, be accompanied by prudent advice, which is in the hands of art, if these are not to be wasted, and the same thing holds true for all literary discourse. Most important, it is only by art that we can completely understand the fact that certain literary excellences are dependent on natural ability alone (2.1–3).[16] Longinus returns to this fundamental relation between *ars* and *ingenium*, so similar to that expressed by Horace (*A.P.* 295–301, 366–90, 408–11), at the end of his discussion of Homer. His direct reference to the opening of his treatise at this point (36.4) indicates, first, that the failure to recognize this relation constitutes

---

[15] *Longinus On the Sublime*, trans. W. R. Roberts (Cambridge, 1935). All citations will be from this translation unless otherwise assigned. The reader should consult the excellent introduction, as well as the translation of individual passages in the commentary, by D. A. Russell in his *'Longinus' On the Sublime* (Oxford, 1964).

[16] This strong defense of art and its relation to nature reach back, of course, through Aristotle to Plato (*Phaedrus* 269D–72B, *Laws* 888C–90D). For Horace's echo of this Platonic tradition in the *Ars poetica*, esp. 295–97, see HASD:72, n. 53. In his second oration, "To Plato: In Defense of Oratory," Aristides sums up the arguments first on behalf of nature and then on behalf of art in terms which anticipate the controversies over decorum in the eighteenth century.

the broadest weakness of Caecilius' approach to the problem and, second, that the chapters on the criticism of Homer, far from being a digression, best illustrate the central concern of the treatise: the place of art in the achievement of the highest excellences which is usually attributed to the gift of Nature.

The four chapters on criticism (33–36) arise, quite naturally, in response to Caecilius' 'Attic' preference for the correctness of Lysias to the occasional 'Asiatic' exuberance of Plato (32.8). As in the beginning of Chapter 2, this opinion of Caecilius raises a general question: should we prefer a poem or a speech which achieves either greater or more numerous excellences (33.1; cf. Horace, *Ars poet.* 351) at the cost of some attendant faults or a work of moderate quality which is wholly free of error? Longinus freely admits that the highest achievements will not be free of flaws; while pettiness (μικρότητος, 33.2) often accompanies complete accuracy (τὸ ἐν παντὶ ἀκριβές, 33.2), in what is sublime there will be some errors which ought to be condoned. Since greater enterprises incur greater risks, the critic must be tolerant. I myself, he says, have "noted not a few errors on the part of Homer and other writers of the greatest distinction, and the slips they have made afford me anything but pleasure." Yet "I do not term them wilful errors, but rather oversights of a random and casual kind, due to neglect and introduced with all the heedlessness of genius" (33.4). These passages draw upon sources very similar to those used by Horace in the *Ars poetica* (347–60). There are faults, Horace writes, which we willingly pardon, for "when the beauties in a poem are more in number, I shall not take offense at a few blots (*maculis*, 352) which a careless (*incuria*, 352) hand has let drop, or human frailty (*humana . . . natura*, 353) has failed to avert." The poet, on the other hand, who often makes the same errors, makes us smile even when he surprises us with a good line. "Yet I also feel aggrieved (*indignor*, 359), whenever good Homer 'nods,' but when a work is long, a drowsy mood may well creep over it." Like Longinus, Horace emphasizes the unintentional nature of the flaws in Homer *as well as* his regret that they must be there at all.[17]

---

[17] These similarities have often been noted, but Longinus' impatience with even Homer's negligence here—as indeed with anyone who, aiming at elevation to avoid seeming flat, becomes tumid and then offers the excuse that " 'failure in a great attempt is at least a noble error' " (3.3)—has been insufficiently stressed. C. O. Brink, for instance, in pointing out this parallel between Horace (*A.P.* 352) and Longinus (33.4), begins his citation of the latter passage just after Longinus' crucial words "and the slips . . . afford me anything but pleasure (ἥκιστα τοῖς πταίσμασιν ἀρεσκόμενος)." Brink then goes on to claim that the parallel is inexact, since Longinus "regards risks as a *necessary* concomitant of greatness" (33.2), while Horace is unwilling "to share romantic admiration of 'necessary faults.' " Later, when he does cite the crucial words as a gloss on Horace's *indignor* (359), Brink makes no qualification of his earlier remarks on Longinus' romantic admiration of

Beginning with Homer and Apollonius Rhodius, Longinus then gives a series of illustrative comparisons between writers who aim at higher excellence but are less exact and those who achieve great accuracy and *cultus* (τῷ γλαφυρῷ, 33.5) in smaller subjects. These comparisons lead him back, in Chapter 34, to the Attic/Asian controversy in which he contrasts the orator Hyperides, who achieves, along with subtlety and refinement (cf. Cic. *Orat.* 110), an Isocratean mixture of types of excellence, with Demosthenes, who is excellent in fewer rhetorical styles but who excels Hyperides in elevation. This comparison, in turn, leads the discussion, in Chapter 35, back to the specific disagreement with Caecilius over Lysias and Plato (32.8), which originally introduced these chapters (33–36).

What consideration, Longinus opens his thirty-fifth chapter by asking, has led writers who are equal to the gods to feel superior to a thoroughly consistent accuracy (ἀκριβείας)? Among others, he answers, is the realization that Nature has brought men into life and the vast universe as into a great assembly (πανήγυριν), to be spectators of the contests and of the most dedicated contestants for honor. To this purpose it has implanted in our soul a love for what is more divine than we and for what our inventiveness is ready to seek even beyond the boundaries of space. For this reason, by natural inclination (φυσικῶς) we do not admire (οὐ . . . θαυμάζομεν) small streams, however clear (διαυγῆ) and useful (χρήσιμα), but the great rivers like the Nile, Danube, Rhine, and even more, the ocean.

Nor are we so much amazed at this little flame that we kindle ourselves, because it keeps its light clear, as at the fires of heaven, though often obscured; nor do we think it more wonderful than the craters of Etna, whose emissions bring up rocks and whole hills out of the depths, and sometimes pour forth rivers of the earth-born, spontaneous fire. (35.4)

In all such matters we say "the useful and necessary are easily available to man; the unusual (τὸ παράδοξον) always excites our wonder (θαυμαστόν)." Throughout this chapter Longinus contrasts the emotional force of wonder about things known, however obscurely, with respect to their own nature with the affective power of our clearer knowledge about things not more divine than ourselves.[18]

Whereas the wonders of Nature are often astounding but not useful, the highest excellence in literature combines utility (χρείας) and profit

---

necessary faults. With respect to this admiration the two notes remain separate from each other and neither cites Longinus' criticism of the excuse for tumidity given in 3.3. *Horace on Poetry: The 'Ars Poetica'* (Cambridge, 1971), pp. 363, 367.

[18] The translations quoted in this paragraph are by D. A. Russell, *'Longinus' On the Sublime*, p. 167.

(ὠφελείας) with grandeur (τὸ μέγεθος, 36.1). Though far from faultless, authors such as Homer, Demosthenes, and Plato, whose excellence makes them nearly divine, redeem their occasional lapses by a single stroke. The judgment of posterity (cf. 7.4, 14.1–3), therefore, has always awarded the victory to these authors over those who lay claim to a meticulous accuracy (36.1–2). The comparison with sculpture by which Longinus immediately clarifies and concludes his discussion of these writers holds a place parallel to the analogy between poetry and painting by which Horace illustrates his advice to the critic (A.P. 361–65). While Longinus seems to leave the plastic arts locked in the antithesis of the ancient dilemma, he suggests a resolution of the antithesis for literature based upon the Stoic analogy of the Law (λόγος, ratio) of Nature and reason with its power of expression (ratio and oratio) in men.

In reply, however, to the writer who maintains that the faulty Colossus is not superior to the Spearman of Polycleitus, it is obvious to remark among many other things that in art the utmost exactitude (ἀκριβέστατον) is admired, grandeur in the works of nature; and that it is by nature that man is a being gifted with speech. In statues likeness (τὸ ὅμοιον) to man is the quality required; in discourse we demand, as I said, that which transcends the human. Nevertheless— and the counsel about to be given reverts to the beginning of our memoir— since freedom from failings is for the most part the successful result of art, and excellence (though it may be unevenly sustained) the result of sublimity, the employment of art is in every way a fitting aid to nature; for it is the conjunction of the two which tends to ensure perfection. (36.3–4)[19]

Sculpture appealing to the eye demands the exactitude of art, while discourse, the expression of the human embodiment of the cosmic logos, in describing things to the ear which are beyond our human capacity to perceive and represent in detail, need have less fear of the critic's exacting eye for verisimilitude. In the terms of the Critias (107) the style of Homer, Demosthenes, and Plato may decorously share, in varying degrees, the less articulated simplicity of Timaeus' skiagraphic sketch. Caecilius, on the other hand, were we to place him in Philostratus'

---

[19] Strabo compares his Geography to a colossus: "Now just as in judging of the merits of colossal statues we do not examine each individual part with minute care, but rather consider the general effect and endeavour to see if the statue as a whole is pleasing, so should this book of mine be judged. For it, too, is a colossal work, in that it deals with the facts about large things only, and wholes, except as some petty thing may stir the interest of the studious or the practical man" (The Geography of Strabo 1.1.23, trans. H. L. Jones and J.R.S. Sterrett, LCL, 8 vols. [London, 1917]). Philostratus continues to use the asymmetrical, yet impressive, colossus to illustrate characteristics of style in quoting Herodes' criticism of Hadrian the Phoenician: " 'these [speeches] might well be great fragments of a colossus.' Thus while he tried to correct his disjointed and ill-constructed style as a fault of youth, he applauded the grandeur both of his words and his ideas" (The Lives of the Sophists 586).

discussion of sculpture—whose terms we shall see Dio Chrysostom extending to literature—might well deny, like the Egyptian Thespesion, the power of art to express, however gropingly, the significance of Nature's greatest human or cosmic achievements. Art and nature would then remain antithetical. *Ars* would be responsible for an accurate verisimilitude, established in relation to our own perceptions (ἡμῖν), and *ingenium* for the good fortune (εὐτυχία, 2.3) of intellective insight into principles more clearly and immediately known with respect to themselves (ἁπλῶς). If art and natural talent must function separately, the artist has no choice but to work now as an empiricist, now as a visionary. In each case, his work is in danger of becoming an enigma, and he a diviner.

Longinus is strongly predisposed to the deliberative style and to the competitive conditions of agonistic debate as Aristotle describes them in his *Rhetoric* (3.12). Life is a competition for honors in an immense contest whose place of assembly shares its boundaries with the universe itself. Writers and speakers compete with one another by emulating the great works of the past; even more, they are in actual combat with the ancient authors they imitate and must face the ordeal (ἀγώνισμα, 14.2) of their judgment as if they were to come back to life (cf. 13, 14.1–3, 7.4). There is nothing scholastic, retiring, or 'shaded' in his views of style or imitation; he does not wish to please a coterie of declaimers but to be of use to "public men" (πολιτικοῖς, 1.2). These intentions and the emotions appropriate to them are clearly those of deliberative oratory. Yet the fact that the 'trial' by earlier writers is to take place before either a judicial or theatrical audience (δικαστήριον καὶ θέατρον, 14.2) suggests that the Isocratean epideictic ideal of written composition, after steadily consolidating its virtues of ἀκρίβεια over the centuries, takes its place beside the agonistic ideal of *psychagogia*. In fact, the artistic control of figures, as illustrated in Chapter 16, becomes for Longinus one of the principal means (τρόπος, μέθοδος, τέχνη) for attaining that excellence sufficiently moving to carry an audience 'outside of itself' (ἔκστασις, 1.4).[20]

[20] Russell acknowledges the place of Aristotle's distinction between written and oral composition (*Rhet.* 3.12) in the development of oratory which leads up to Longinus' conception of the most excellent style (p. xxxiii). I would like to stress even more the 'agonistic' qualities of both such a conception and of the competitive emulation necessary to realize it. As developed further in this study, Longinus seems to regard these qualities as capable of freeing public oratory from stylistic mannerisms of the private coterie, or school, of declamation. (For Horace's analogous resistance to scholastic preciosity, see the articles cited in the first note of Part Two). For Plato, the judge of a legal trial held a position comparable to the audience in a poetic competition (*Theaet.* 173C). Longinus continues to stress the 'agonistic' nature of this association (14.2), which is all the more apt to be forgotten as the assembly (πανήγυριν) in which both types of contest take place

Both Aristotelian and Isocratean criteria are brought together in Chapter 17. As if by nature (φύσει, 17.1), "figures bring support to the sublime, and on their part derive support in turn from it in a wonderful degree (θαυμαστῶς, 17.1)." They must be handled cautiously, however, because if they become conspicuous, the speaker will be suspected of setting a trap. In this event, the judge, particularly if he, like Aristotle's single judge, makes the principle decision in the case, will resent such childish attempts to deceive him and will resist all persuasion. Figures are best, then, when hidden, and they may be hidden well beneath an elevated and passionate style, which can cover over the art (τέχνη, 17.2) controlling them. How is the figure actually to be concealed? By the light of sublimity itself (τῷ φωτὶ αὐτῷ, 17.2).

For just as all dim lights are extinguished in the blaze of the sun, so do the artifices of rhetoric fade from view when bathed in the pervading splendour of sublimity. Something like this happens also in the art of painting. For although light and shade, as depicted in colours, lie side by side upon the same surface, light nevertheless meets the vision first, and not only stands out, but also seems far nearer. So also with the manifestations of passion and the sublime in literature. They lie nearer to our minds through a sort of natural kinship and through their own radiance, and always strike our attention before the figures, whose art they throw into the shade and as it were keep in concealment. (17.2–3)

The lesser lights (τἀμυδρὰ φέγγη) of rhetorical devices (σοφίσματα) will be 'shaded out' by the pervasive brilliance (φῶς, ἥλιος) of sublimity in the same way as the light (φέγγος) from a small flame of our own making must later yield its powers to astonish us to the luminosity of the heavens (35.4).

Longinus' psychological explanation of the importance (16) and decorous restraint (17) of figures draws again upon the Stoic relation between the cosmic and the human *logos*. As the lighter areas in a picture, seeming nearer, catch the eye before the darker ones, the most passionate and excellent effects of style "lie nearer to our minds through a sort of natural kinship (συγγένειαν, 17.3)." We become aware of their radiance before we do of the lesser brilliance of artistic *schemata*. This radiance 'brings to light' in the consciousness those emotions appropriate to things more accessible to *ingenium* (ἁπλῶς), and this illumination, in turn, qualifies and is qualified by the emotions appropriate to things more amenable to *ars* (ἡμῖν). These two kinds of feeling qualify one another,

---

increasingly resembles a theater of epideictic display. In fact, Dionysius of Halicarnassus associates a πανήγυρις with a school (σχολή) in opposition to a political or judicial convocation (*Dem.* 44). It is only through their being 'concealed' by the renewed agonistic vitality that the Isocratean figures can regain their effectiveness.

that is, in the same way as the two types of intelligibility. Decorum becomes the process of maintaining the balance between kinds of affective expression appropriate to the balance maintained between types of elucidation. In achieving decorum, the most excellent style must avoid both undue elevation in the depiction of the gods and undue meticulousness in the depiction of men. Overly contrived attempts at elevation such as produce tumidity (3) or crescendos of amplification (11–12) result in the same triviality as an overly diligent striving for labored 'scholastic' conceptions (3.4), pedantic humor (4.4), ostentatious figures of speech (16–17), preciously refined rhythms which, becoming predictable, grow monotonous (41), and the amassing of excessive descriptive detail (43). The stylistic devices which produce agonistic effects (18–20, 22–23, 28), on the other hand, are able to reestablish decorum by their power to conceal these excessively artificial attempts which, if left conspicuous, would arouse suspicion and thereby become ineffective.

Longinus gives a practical example of how to avoid too much and too heterogeneous detail which leads to triviality in description. He quotes an account by Theopompus of a procession of a Persian king bearing gifts to Egypt. Along with the vast caravan of precious goods and trappings are individually described the ordinary beasts of burden with food supplies, common utensils, and weapons. So numerous were these *impedimenta* that " 'those who were approaching from a distance took them to be hills, and eminences confronting them' " (43.2). Longinus complains that, by including "bags and condiments and sacks," the historian "conveys the impression of a confectioner's shop," so much do these mundane details, given out of context (παρὰ καιρόν, 43.3), offend the reader. He might better "have described the scene in broad outline (ὡς ὁλοσχερῶς, 43.4) just as he says that hills blocked their way, and with regard to the preparations generally have spoken of 'waggons and camels and the multitude of beasts of burden carrying everything that ministers to the luxury and enjoyment of the table.' " Longinus then gives two other examples of descriptive phrasing which might sum up the magnificence of the caravan without falling into such manneristic particularity. Theopompus has destroyed his effect by a skenographic realism which might better have been reduced to a skiagraphic outline as it might appear from a distance (note πόρρωθεν, 43.2). In his rephrasing of the historian's assiduous particularity, Longinus anticipates the neoclassical pursuit of simplicity in the generalization of a minimum of detail.[21]

[21] For the relevance of this passage to later critical distinctions, see my discussion of 'skiagraphia' in *Traditio* (1978):412, n. 12 and S. Elledge, "The Background and Development in English Criticism of the Theories of Generality and Particularity," *PMLA* 62

While Aristotle observed certain similarities between the psychagogically elevated styles of Homeric epic and skiagraphic painting, Longinus compares Homer himself to a colossal statue. The dimensions of
Eris in the *Iliad* (4.440–43), he says, whose head reaches to heaven while
her feet remain on earth, might equally be taken as the measure of the
poet (9.4). The comparison is fitting perhaps for two reasons. First,
Longinus, in praising Homer's descriptions both of the gods and of men,
recognizes the poet's insight into the necessary relationship between the
human and the divine—much as Plato insisted upon the philosophical
negotiation between the Titans and the gods in the *Sophist*. Second, Eris
is the goddess of strife both in the sense of war and, as Hesiod is careful
to distinguish (*Works and Days* 11–26), in the sense of profitable competition. It is good for men, he says, that craftsman be angry with
craftsman and singer be jealous of singer (φθονέει καὶ ἀοιδὸς ἀοιδῷ,
26). As we have seen, Longinus in a similar spirit attributes the highest
literary achievements to just such agonistic rivalry (7.4, 13, 14.1–3).

Longinus' only reservation about Homer's general sense of decorum
(τὸ πρέπον, 9.7) is that, in telling of the feuds and passions of the gods,
he seems "to have made, as far as lay within his power, gods of the men
concerned in the Siege of Troy, and men of the gods," for the gods begin
to seem immortal for their miseries rather than for their divine nature.
In the context which I have been trying to establish, the indecorum lies
precisely in the danger of losing the necessary polarity between the
human and the divine. If the distance between men and the gods is
narrowed almost to the point of identifying them, the distinction between
the two poles, and hence any negotiation between them, becomes increasingly difficult, if not impossible. Much superior to the descriptions
of the gods in battle, Longinus continues, are those which "represent
the divine nature as it really is—pure (ἄκρατον) and great and undefiled"
(9.8). Ἄκρατος (= simple, unmixed, absolute) here carries many of the
connotations of ἁπλόος.

Longinus concludes Chapter 9 of his treatise with his famous comparison of the *Odyssey* with the *Iliad* (9.11–15). He considers the *Odyssey* an inferior product of Homer's old age, when people are fond of
fabulous tales. While the *Iliad* is full of action (δραματικόν, 9.13) and
contention (ἐναγώνιον, 9.13), with its "quick-wheeling (ἀγχίστροφον,

(March 1947):147–82, esp. 160–61. Strabo, too, uses ὁλοσχερῶς for maps roughly outlined,
associating it with ἁπλῶς, in contrast to maps which measure lands exactly (γεωμετρικῶς).
With respect to a country's size and shape, it is sufficient to state its length and breadth
and its general form. The greater the territory one sections, furthermore, the rougher the
map of each section may be (2.1.30). These observations are based on a distinction between
geometrical and geographical methods of measurement, the former clearly being more
ἀκριβής, the latter more ἁπλοῦς (2.1.40).

9.13)'' style characteristic of political controversy (πολιτικόν, 9.13), the *Odyssey* turns in its mythological (μυθικόν, 9.14) material away from the stress of practical (πρακτικοῦ, 9.14) problems. The adjectives describing the *Iliad* closely resemble those used by Aristotle to describe the histrionic style of agonistic debate in a large political assembly, while the detached relaxation in imaginary adventure suggests the unhurried enjoyment of epideictic refinement. The reason he has made this comparison, Longinus continues, is to show, first, that even the greatest writers are apt in old age to fall into the implausible fantasies; and, second, that they are equally apt to turn from subjects which arouse great passion to the delineation of character. "For such are the details which Homer gives, with an eye to characterization, of life in the home of Odysseus; they form as it were a comedy of manners (κωμῳδία . . . ἠθολογουμένη, 9.15)." The subject and style of the *Iliad* evoke for Longinus the stronger emotions appropriate to extraordinary things which are better known in themselves (ἁπλῶς)—and hence more wonderful and less amenable to the calmer feelings appropriate to detailed representation. Those of the *Odyssey* evoke familiar things which are better known with respect to our own perceptions (ἡμῖν) and hence more amenable to exact imitation.

Longinus sees in the *Odyssey*, then, a paradoxical combination of familiar facts with implausible fantasy—a combination which might easily characterize a work too much confined to a verisimilar imitation of things most perceptible to us (ἡμῖν). What falls before our eyes can be readily known and represented, but what falls just outside our range of vision is immediately, by definition, unknowable and hence fabulous, if not, as with Plato's intransigent Titan, unreal. Whatever the justice of Longinus' judgment in this instance, his observations suggest that in juxtaposing the fabulous, remote, or esoteric against the realistic, even trivial, details of everyday life, Homer resolves the antithesis of the ancient dilemma less well in the *Odyssey* than in the *Iliad*. More in accord with Thespesion than Apollonius, familiar things capable of verifiably accurate representation are allowed to take their place side by side with the miraculous which cannot be accounted for at all. Despite their adjacent proximity, however, there can be little discursive exchange between ordinary things intelligible to us and fabulous things only knowable in themselves. As in the obscure regions of the undelimited, where Plato's Eleatic Stranger pursues the sophist, there are no logical steps by which to move from the more to the less known.

In a related context, Caecilius maintains that if natural ability (*ingenium*)—being under the control of chance—failed to achieve the most excellent style, art (*ars*)—being under our own control—could contribute little or nothing to its achievement. *Ingenium* alone is responsible for representing the essential significance of the most excellent subject with appropriate distinctiveness, while *ars*, confined to technical achievements of verisimilitude, cannot hope to express the nature of such excellence. Caecilius' firm antithesis between art and nature, that is, conforms to certain presuppositions of Thespesion about symbolic representation, while Longinus, in striving to express some of that essential significance in the external form of the work of art, has more in common with Apollonius. Some of the difficulties in representing the most excellent things with decorum are interestingly discussed by Dio Chrysostom at the end of the first century A.D.

C. Dio Chrysostom: 'On Man's First Conception of God'

Dio's encomiastic "Olympic Discourse," delivered at Olympia in 97 A.D., explicitly discusses the problems of knowing and representing the most excellent things in the literary and visual arts. His discussion offers a practical illustration of the ancient dilemma in terms easily related to the philosophical distinctions described in the preceding chapters. He extends these distinctions, furthermore, to the debate between the arts which culminates in the comparison or *paragone* between the respective virtues of the eye and the ear. The *paragone*, in turn, leads us back to the relative degrees of precision to be expected in the knowledge offered by various disciplines and to the appropriate exactness of the artistic representation of what is known. Dio sketches in broad outlines, that is, certain philosophical premises of stylistic decorum which underlie the treatment of experience in antiquity and continue to recur in subsequent periods of neoclassical revival.

Dio chooses to eulogize Pheidias' statue of Zeus as a topic suitable for the occasion. Having pointed out that the sculptor has taken Homer's description of the god as his model, Dio begins a philosophical consideration of how men form their conception (δόξαν) of the deity (26). Such a conception comes from two sources, one innate and one acquired. With respect to the first source, every creature gifted with reason has an innate (ἔμφυτος, 27) and inevitable (ἀναγκαία, 27) idea of the deity, arising naturally without human interference, which clearly reveals the god's close kinship (ξυγγένειαν, 27) with human beings. In previous ages, men did not live "dispersed far away from the divine being or beyond his borders apart by themselves," but growing up in his company, they received understanding from him. Living beneath the divine heavenly bodies and surrounded by the natural beauties of the earth, they took delight in designating the objects they perceived by symbols (σύμβολα, 28), "thus easily acquiring memories and concepts of innumerable things" (28). Although informed about the cosmos by their senses, human beings owed their superiority over the other animals primarily to their ability to reason and reflect about the divinity.[22]

In the language of late Stoicism, similar to that in the thirty-fifth chapter of Longinus' treatise, Dio says (33ff.) that the universe itself was like a mystic shrine into which men were initiated as if into a priesthood. How could they not but wonder at the marvels of nature and at the leader of the cosmic choir who directed the heavens and earth in their dance as a skillful pilot his ship? How could their senses (αἴσθησιν, 34) tell them nothing of such visible gods as the sun, or their intuition have no suspicion (ὑποψίαν, 34) about the invisible ruler of the universe? The divine intelligence as revealed throughout the natural order ought to be itself a sufficient answer to any Epicurean banishment of the gods "out of their own state and kingdom, clean out of this ordered universe to alien regions, even as unfortunate human beings are banished to sundry uninhabited isles" (37). These descriptions of how the gods reveal their divine nature anticipate some of the ways in which the men of late antiquity were to conceive of and respond to the ancient dilemma.[23]

Our rational nature, then, is the first of two main sources for our conceptions of the divine. The second source, of which Dio distinguishes four subdivisions, is not innate but externally acquired from tradition: conceptions derived from poetic narrations, from legislative prescriptions, from visual representations and from philosophical analysis which "by means of reason interprets and proclaims the divine nature, most truly, perhaps, and most perfectly" (47). Since his subject is Pheidias, Dio begins his encomium by enumerating six kinds of visual representations. The first two are pictorial, the last four sculptural (44). The first kind of pictorial image is done "by means of a rough sketch (σκιαγραφίᾳ), very indistinct (ἀσθενεῖ) and deceptive (ἀπατηλῇ) to the eye." The second is done "by the blending of colours and by line-drawing, which produces a result which we can almost say is the most accurate (τὸ

---

[22] All references to Dio will be to *Dio Chrysostom*, trans. J. W. Cohoon, LCL, 5 vols. (London, 1961). On Dio, see M. Valgimigli, "La critica omerica presso Dione Crisostomo" in *Studi di storia e di critica dedicati a Pio Carlo Falletti* (Bologna, 1915), pp. 1–45, and esp. P. Hagen, *Quaestiones Dioneae* (Kiliae, 1887), who cites numerous classical parallels for the passages and themes with which I am most concerned in this section.

[23] Some of the Stoic terminology which Dio and Longinus share is brought out by Russell in his notes to *On the Sublime*, Chap. 35. The close similarity of their language and attitudes suggests, along with other evidence, the probability that Longinus belongs to the first century A.D., a probability which Russell accepts (pp. xxii–xxx). Knowing the visible gods through the senses and the invisible gods through an intuitive surmise reflects the Aristotelian distinction between the two types of intelligibility.

ἀκριβέστατον) of all." Plato had observed (*Critias* 107C) that "inasmuch as we have no exact knowledge (οὐδὲν εἰδότες ἀκριβές)" of such divine objects as the heavens, we "tolerate, in such cases, an inexact and deceptive sketch (σκιαγραφίᾳ δὲ ἀσαφεῖ καὶ ἀπατηλῷ)." Dio, using ἀσθενής (= poor, insignificant, without strength or intensity) for Plato's ἀσαφής (= visually indistinct, uncertain), seems to emphasize, rather, the artistic limitations of a primitive technique as distinguished from more accurate and sophisticated pictorial styles. The skiagraphic sketch, originally considered a necessary compromise in depicting divine qualities which could not be portrayed in detail because of *their* very nature, now appears to Dio as a compromise necessary for an artist incapable, because of *his* inability, of making visually accurate representations. Yet the decorum of the skiagraphic style in representing what is clear only to the gods themselves (ἁπλῶς)—and hence obscure to us (ἡμῖν)—continues to be recognized as a means of suggesting an archaic dignity, an unfamiliar distinctiveness, right up to the present day. It seems to be primarily this problem of the appropriate exactness in representing what cannot be seen by the eye—raised first here with respect to painting—which leads Dio to contrast the more rigorous demands for verisimilitude of Pheidian sculpture with the greater freedom of Homeric language.[24]

Neither painters nor sculptors were "satisfied to display their cleverness and skill on commonplace subjects, but by exhibiting all sorts of likenesses (εἰκόνας, 45) and representations (διαθέσεις, 45) of gods" filled their patrons "with an ample and varied conception of the divine." Although they followed the earlier image-making (εἰδωλοποιίαν, 45) of the poets, who appealed only to the ear, they interpreted divine attributes for the eye alone of their "more numerous and less cultivated spectators" (46). With these introductory observations, Dio proceeds to ask Pheidias himself whether the human form he chose was actually "appropriate to a god" and "worthy of the divine nature" (52). Previously, each person, having no clear knowledge (οὐδὲν σαφὲς εἰδότες) of Zeus, formed his own idea of the god in his dreams, but Pheidias has now presented, by the power of his art, such a brilliant demonstration (λαμπρὸν ἀποδείξας) that no one can hold a different one (53). In his reply, the sculptor recognizes his responsibility to explain why his conception should be accepted as a "true likeness . . . in no way falling short of the best portrayal of the divinity that is within the capacity of

[24] Plato speaks of the contrast between the simple outline and the more sophisticated blending of colors in the *Statesman* (277C). Like Dio, Philostratus contrasts the skiagraphic sketch to a more richly colored painting—the 'color' in this case being compared to versatility of wit (*The Lives of the Sophists* 592). For a discussion of changes in the metaphorical uses of 'skiagraphia,' see *Traditio* (1978):403–13.

human beings to make" (55). He first says that he took his conception of Zeus from Homer because poets can make men accept any idea, while sculptors are bound to a verisimilar standard of comparison of their works with their models and with other works (cf. Longinus, 36.3). Such a standard could not be applied to the representation of heavenly appearances, however marvelous they are in themselves, for the imitation of distant crescents and orbs is simple (ἁπλῆ, 58) and no challenge to the artist's skill (ἄτεχνος, 58). The divine purposes behind these appearances, as indeed all forms of intelligence, are forever hidden and, therefore, beyond the power of the artist to represent, "for all men are utterly incapable of observing such attributes with their eyes or of learning of them by inquiry" (59). But, Pheidias says, since men recognize that their own form contains a mind and its purposes, he has, like Homer, attributed to Zeus a human body, for lack of a better illustration (παράδειγμα) of a being capable of supreme rationality. By such a shape he has been able "to indicate that which is invisible and unportrayable by means of something portrayable and visible, using the function of a symbol (συμβόλου δυνάμει) . . . better than certain barbarians, who are said to represent the divine by animals"—thus using symbols as points of departure "which are trivial (σμικράς) and absurd (ἀτόπους)" (59). Although the human form functions here as a symbol, it is not arbitrary as in the animal symbolization of the gods for which Apollonius will criticize the Egyptians. The symbol here, on the contrary, expresses, however incompletely, in its physical form some of the superior attributes of the deity.[25]

[25] The word 'symbol' (σύμβολον) has a wide spectrum of meanings, and its literary uses may refer to anything from simple words or language—as opposed to the things they refer to (De soph. elench. 1, 165a6–10)—to the cryptic image, discussed in the next chapter, whose hidden significance must be 'deciphered.' For the word's etymology and range of usages, see P. Crome's useful appendix to his Symbol und Unzulänglichkeit der Sprache (München, 1970), pp. 201–11. The reader may enter the scholarship on the 'literary symbol' through works such as Crome's as well as studies cited in their notes and bibliographies. See, for instance, J. A. Coulter, The Literary Microcosm (Leiden, 1976); J. Pépin, Mythe et allégorie (Paris, 1958); F. Buffière, Les mythes d'Homère et la pensée Grecque (Paris, 1956) and Héraclite: allégories d'Homère (Paris, 1962); G. R. Hocke, Manierismus in der Literatur (Hamburg, 1959); E. H. Gombrich, "Icones Symbolicae," in Symbolic Images (London, 1972); G. B. Ladner, "Medieval and Modern Understanding of Symbolism: A Comparison," Speculum 54, 2 (1979):223–56. Dio's justification of the human form as a proper representation of the divine is similar to that which St. Augustine has preserved by Varro (City of God 7.5). In her article on Philostratus, cited previously (Chap. 6, n. 6), E. Birmelin mentions Varro and remarks that Dio appears to be adapting a Posidonian conception of the symbol to the visual arts: "Das poseidonische Symbol unterscheidet sich von dem ägyptischen Tiersymbol, das blosses Sinnbild ist, dadurch, dass es Ausdrucksform für das Wesen des Gottes und somit geeignet ist, eine Kunstauffassung zu tragen, wie sie Aristoteles geschaffen hat. So dürfen wir uns night wundern, dass wir hier bie Dio die aristotelische μίμησις-Theorie wiederfinden" (pp. 413–14, n. 98). As in the case of Philostratus, she continues, Dio is not drawing on a theory of divine inspiration

Furthermore, Pheidias continues, none would claim that no images of the gods should be exhibited and that men should only contemplate the heavens from a great distance (μακρόθεν, 60). For men have a great desire to honor the deity from close at hand (ἐγγύθεν, 60) with sacrifices and garlands, and, if they had no statues, they would choose less appropriate trees and rocks to worship (60–61). Yet, in comparison with Homer's representations, all artistic portraits of the gods must appear inadequate.

For an extravagant [δαψιλές = possessing abundant resources] thing is poetry and in every respect resourceful and a law unto itself, and by the assistance of the tongue and a multitude of words is able all by itself to express all the devisings of the heart, and whatever conception it may arrive at concerning any shape or action or emotion or magnitude, it can never be at a loss, since the voice of a Messenger can disclose with perfect clearness (ἐναργῶς) each and all these things. (64)

While Homer could exploit this freedom of language, the sculptor is bound to his materials and dependent on his assistants. While poets may include all shapes and movements, actions and speeches, in varying temporal relations, sculptors are committed to a single model and pose whose image, embracing "the whole of the god's nature (φύσιν, 70) and power (δύναμιν, 70)," they sometimes must keep in mind over many years (65–71).[26]

The *paragone* between Pheidias and Homer derives many of its distinctions from the ancient rivalry between the eye and the ear.

Indeed, the popular saying that the eyes are more trustworthy than the ears is perhaps true, yet they are much harder to convince and demand much greater clearness (ἐναργείας); for while the eye agrees exactly with what it sees, it is not impossible to excite and cheat the ear by filling it with representations under the spell (γεγοητευμένα) of metre and sound. (71)

---

or madness but on a mimetic theory which attempts to arrive at a form which can best express the *nature* of God: "μίμησις ist die künstlerische Interpretation von Gott, Welt, und Leben."

[26] Dio mentions the ability and the freedom of the 'messenger' (*nuntius*) to report any or all events which happen in connection with the ancient rivalry between the eye and the ear discussed in this study. Homer, he says (67), can take advantage of such freedom because, as Aristotle recommends for stylistic decorum, he combines the familiar with the exotic in diction and content (cf. Strabo, 1.2.7). While the eyes are more trustworthy than the ears (cf. Herodotus, 1.8; Aristotle, 437a4–17; Seneca, *Ep.* 6.5), they are 'critics' harder to convince than the ears—as Plato's Critias had implied (*Critias* 107D). Horace's recommendation of the *nuntius* in treating what is too incredible for the eyes to believe when represented on stage (*A.P.* 179–88) is central to all subsequent discussions of dramatic appeals to the eye vs. those to the ear. See E. Burke, *A Philosophical Enquiry into the Origin of Our Ideas of the Sublime and the Beautiful* 2.3–4, who, citing Horace, gives preference to appeals to the ear.

While a poet may increase numbers and magnitudes at will, as Homer does in his description of Eris, a sculptor is bound to respect specific dimensions if he hopes, insofar as it is possible for men, to conceive and represent the divine and inexplicable nature of the god (72–74). Pheidias has represented the god's sovereignty by the strength and grandeur of the statue, his fatherhood by its gentleness, his justice by its majesty (σεμνότης, 77), his assurance of "kinship between gods and men . . . by the mere similarity in shape (τὸ τῆς μορφῆς ὅμοιον, 77)"—already expressed (55–57) in making the human form a symbol (σύμβολον, 77) of the divine—his benevolence by its goodness, and his benefactions by its simplicity (ἁπλότης, 77) and magnificence (μεγαλοφροσύνη, 77). While these attributes can be represented without words, the god who sends lightning and other heavenly signs as portents of strife and who weighs men's fates in a balance, this unseen god cannot be represented in such activities. Only Homer may portray Zeus, crowned with clouds, shaking the earth and Olympus in the imagination of his listeners (cf. Strabo, 8.3.30), for Pheidias must submit his work, "close at hand (ἐγγύθεν, 79) and in full view (σαφῆ, 79)," to the severe scrutiny of his observers' eyes.

The effect of Homeric language upon the ear, then, is skiagraphic in the earlier sense that Critias applied the term to Timaeus' description of those parts of the cosmos whose nature was too indistinct to testify against the accuracy of his account. Insofar as Dio conceives of the effectiveness of sculpture, even in the portrayal of divine attributes, as more narrowly dependent on eicastic representation than is poetry, he sees the plastic arts as more confined to those things most effectively known relative to ourselves. Insofar, however, as he has Pheidias borrow a description from Homer more commensurate in its dignity with the object it portrays than the animal forms of the Egyptians can be, he reasserts, with Plato, the power of language to establish intermediate stages between the sensible and the intelligible worlds. He anticipates, that is, the Greek optimism of Apollonius, in contrast to the Egyptian pessimism of Thespesion, about the power of the arts to express a relation between an intellective intuition of first principles and an aesthetic intuition of perceptual experience. Dio says that Pheidias illuminates our experience of the god by his exhibiting (ἀποδείξας) the rationality of the divine artist in choosing a human form for him (53). The connotations of 'demonstrative proof' of the word ἀποδείχνυμι itself emphasizes the fact that discursive reason, in descending from first principles of intellection to order those of our immediate perception, brings about, in large part, the reciprocation between these two types of intuition.

In his eleventh, or "Trojan," discourse, Dio has an Egyptian priest strongly criticize the liberties which Homer has taken with the historical events of the Trojan war as well as the fictions which the Greek poets generally have told in order to delight their audience. The priest, Dio reports, claims to have complete knowledge of the war whose history the poets have distorted because the Greeks both give them "full licence to tell any untruth they wish" and then proceed to "trust them in everything they say and even quote them at times as witnesses in matters of dispute" (42). The Egyptians, by contrast, have made it "illegal to say anything in verse" and, indeed, "have no poetry at all, since they know this is but the charm (φάρμακον, 42) with which pleasure lures the ear." For, whoever looks for truth has no more need of verse, which deceives, than he who is thirsty has need of wine, which intoxicates (11.42–43). The priest sees literature here as being either (fictionally) false or (factually) true, between which poles there is no middle ground such as the probable. Since poetry is clearly fictional, it deceives and, therefore, should be rejected. If fable and fact are 'mixed' in a single work, as Homer has mixed the miraculous with the verisimilar in the *Odyssey* according to Longinus, they remain arbitrarily juxtaposed and essentially unrelatable. Since fiction, furthermore, brings no reliable (factual) knowledge to the reader, the nature of what it represents is (scientifically) unknowable. The juxtaposition of the fictitious with the true, therefore, shares something with the symbolic representation of the gods recommended by the Egyptian Thespesion. The symbol expresses the significance of what is unknowable by an arbitrarily stipulated, though accurately depicted, animal form. There is no 'reasonable road' from what is empirically evident relative to us in the representation of the form to those principles of causation, intelligible and undemonstrable in themselves, which might elucidate our experience of the divine.

I bring up this traditional controversy between history and fiction, which I shall treat later in more detail, only to show at this point certain of its relations to the antithesis of the ancient dilemma developed in Part Two. Empirical events, however evident to us, will remain as obscure as the causes necessary to interpret them until the significance of such causes can be understood. The 'principles' or *archai* with which any interpretation begins must often be assumed and expressed as 'fictional' premises, since, as Sidney says, the historian often "must tell euents whereof he can yeelde no cause: or, if hee doe, it must be poeticall." The more mythologically fabulous the alleged causation, the greater the discrepancy between causes—whose nature, being assumed, can only (eventually) be known in respect to themselves (ἁπλῶς)—and the events which we perceive before us as effects (ἡμῖν). Such a discrepancy resembles that between Thespesion's divine principles of cosmic order and the 'verisimilarly' rendered animal, as opposed to the 'typically' rendered human, symbol.[27] Dio's Egyptian priest's willing separation of poetry from history and Thespesion's willing separation of the intellective and aesthetic premises of knowledge become for Sidney the separation of cause from effect. The more unreconcilable the fabulous and the historical in literary theory, furthermore, the more poetry will suffer from an obscurantism analogous to that which shelters Plato's sophist in the twilight battlefield between the intransigent gods and Titans. Thespesion accepts and even defends this obscurantism, for to him the more arbitrary the relation of a symbol's form to its significance, the deeper the symbolic respect shown for the dignity of the gods. And so to this day it has appeared to some that the more arbitrary the relation between the 'external form' of the sensory image and what that form is supposed to signify, the more psychologically forceful the literary expression seems to be.

Literature, however, is not the representation, however accurate, of either things known relative to us or of things known 'absolutely' with respect to their own nature, but of things as they are revealed by both types of intelligibility in relation to one another. What is revealed solely by one type of intelligence in isolation from the other remains an abstraction, a potential material of the consciousness awaiting realization, as the unanalyzed 'name' awaits definition (*Physics* 1.1) and the mere picture awaits recognition (*De mem.* 1). What remains in such isolation becomes enigmatic. The obscurity in representing the subjective perception arises, like that of an 'anamorphosic' painting, from the need for an ever more intricately contrived perspective which requires some kind of 'special knowledge' to be understood. The obscurity in representing the *a priori* principle arises from the need for an ever more generalized 'skiagraphic simplification' until it becomes an outline so inclusive that it contains anything and nothing. The avoidance of both these types of obscurity has been the principal concern of stylistic decorum, especially since Aristotle's formulation of decorum as a balance between clarity without meanness and distinction without extravagance.

In summary, then, several observations might be made as a conclusion to this chapter. The decorum of the skiagraphic style appropriate to the agonistic intensity of deliberative oratory may be threatened, to use Aristotle's terminology, by either an excessively familiar clarity or by

---

[27] The importance of 'typical' (from τύπος) in representation is brought out in Plato's *Cratylus* (432E): words and statements need not be, arithmetically speaking, exact accounts, "so long as the intrinsic quality of the thing (τύπος ἐνῇ τοῦ πράγματος) named is retained." Earlier, such a quality is called "the essence (ἡ οὐσία)" of the thing (393D). *Plato: Cratylus, Parmenides, Greater Hippias, Lesser Hippias,* trans. H. N. Fowler, LCL (London, 1970).

an excessively foreign distinctiveness. Excessive familiarity might introduce into the skiagraphic representation a more exact verisimilitude and completeness of detail than would be appropriate to its subject matter and occasion—and so run the risk of falling into a manneristic particularity which could impede its psychagogic momentum. Excessive foreignness, on the other hand, might easily turn the representation of what was remote from our knowledge—either because of its distance (in time or space) or its excellence—into a purely formal, overly simplified, even stereotyped, image or elevated phrase. However abstruse such figurative expressions, they might, nevertheless, exert an emotional power over the audience quite unsupported by the quality of the speaker's analysis of the situation. Such expressions would draw their power in part from the enigmatic suggestiveness of wonder characteristic of the arbitrariness of symbols.

The decorum of the epideictic style—a style which Isocrates seems to hope might overcome the Aristotelian antithesis between a refined precision (ἀκρίβεια) of written composition and an emotional intensity (ψυχαγωγία) of oral spontaneity—may be threatened in two ways which are inversely parallel to those threatening the skiagraphic style. An excessively familiar clarity, which forces the oral agonistic style into indecorous detail, forces the written epideictic style into indecorous banality and platitude. An excessively foreign distinctiveness, on the other hand, which forces the oral style into abstract stereotypes, forces the written style into technical intricacies which, in calling special attention to themselves, become equally abstract and often must be appreciated from some special esoteric perspective. The extreme forms of both skiagraphic and epideictic distinctiveness, that is, however antithetical to one another their types of abstraction, will both end in enigma. The representation of things primarily knowable with respect to their own nature (ἁπλῶς) is in danger of being reduced to the ineffable symbol, that of things primarily knowable with respect to our perceptions (ἡμῖν), to the ineffable impression. If we are to understand the significance of either at their respective extremes, we shall require special, esoteric information. Those who believe that they have such information and regard it as their private possession, like a gnostic 'key' to the artistic work, have tended to treat the arts themselves as if they were forms of secular religion. This 'gnostic aestheticism,' which has increasingly dominated literary theory from the Enlightenment to the present, has perhaps its principal source, as we shall see, in the Neoplatonic reconstruction, of classical assumptions about knowledge and representation, classical assumptions which are still clearly expressed by Longinus and Dio Chrysostom in the first century A.D.

8. The Neoplatonic Reconstruction
of Literary Theory

ONE MAY SPEAK more precisely about the consequences of Neoplatonism for literary theory than about a specific Neoplatonic recovery, transmission, or revision of ancient critical principles. Plotinus was not directly concerned with literature, and his general aesthetic assumptions, derived from his metaphysical and psychological doctrines, emerge primarily in his comments on the visual arts. Proclus has left us the most extensive Neoplatonic treatment of poetry—perhaps the most historically important defense of *poesis* in late antiquity—as a by-product of his pedagogical intention to demonstrate the exegetical coherence of Platonic texts. Yet Plotinus offers us a reconstruction of reality from whose philosophical presuppositions Proclus later works out an interpretation of literature which anticipates much of the analysis of the literary and visual arts from the early Middle Ages to the present. In this chapter I want to point out those Neoplatonic assumptions about the knowledge and representations of experience which have, perhaps, contributed most to the subsequent development of literary theory and to the problems of its transmission.

Speaking within the broadest context of this study, I would say that Neoplatonic thinkers, in coping with the ancient rivalry between rhetoric and philosophy, tended to subordinate, rather than relate, rhetoric to philosophy. They tended to regard rhetoric as that pragmatic part of philosophy itself which gave public expression to its doctrines and urged its audience to accept them. This assimilation of rhetorical by philosophical inquiry, however, should not be construed as a 'reconciliation' of the antithetical intentions of these disciplines such as that undertaken by Aristotle or Cicero. Both these men saw the cognitive function of philosophy and the judicative function of rhetoric as independent, though complementary, activities. The cognitive discrimination between true and false and the judicative discrimination between right and wrong were individual acts whose integrity must be maintained if a relationship between them was to exist. I argued in Part One that literature itself might best integrate these individual activities with one another—thus resolving the antithesis between them—without sacrificing either.

The line, of course, between subordination and integration is thin and at best, perhaps, a matter of emphasis. When rhetoric, under Stoic or Neoplatonic influences among others, assumes the cognitive responsibility of proclaiming given beliefs to be true, and therefore to be accepted, as opposed to discovering and analyzing the arguments for and against their acceptance, it can easily become ancillary to some form of ideology. Under the color of coordinating and promoting given doctrines or policies (*de propaganda fide*), that is, rhetoric may claim a degree of certainty inappropriate for an art of probability. This claim to true belief might be seen both as a salutary reintegration of the two disciplines and as an ennobling of rhetoric through its association with philosophy. I have just expressed doubts about the nature of the reintegration. With regard to nobility, if rhetoric is to gain prestige by advocating philosophical doctrines, it must sacrifice its traditional character as an art, like dialectic, which has no special body of scientific knowledge or of doctrine to transmit. It inquires into how to persuade, not what to teach. It seeks to convince an audience that taking action upon such and such a judgment of an individual situation is right or wrong (on a given occasion), not that such and such an opinion is (always) true or false. Once this intention and the methods of argumentation appropriate to it are set aside, what there remains of rhetoric to 'ennoble' is primarily its technical elaboration of style. In this way, nearly all rhetorical activities become reduced to elocution, and this formalism, as we shall see, is characteristic of the Neoplatonic influence on the arts as a whole. In order to show the effects of this formalism upon the proper balance between the mathematical, cognitive, and judicative intentions of literary theory, I shall turn now to Plotinus and Proclus.[1]

---

[1] G. L. Kustas describes how Neoplatonic attitudes toward discourse might be seen historically as "reintegrating" rhetoric with philosophy and consequently as "ennobling" rhetoric through its claim to promote doctrinal truth in his valuable *Studies in Byzantine Rhetoric* (Thessalonica, 1973). Despite the fact that he appears to regard this form of reintegration (actually more a form of identification) and the transcendence of rhetoric over its classical confinement to the realm of probability as salutary, his study offers most detailed evidence for the historical developments I want to suggest. He shows how "with Proclus the philosophical presuppositions which in Hermogenes have sometimes to be read between the lines became more explicit. Proclus in effect joins rhetoric and metaphysics and in so doing ennobles rhetorical values, supplying them with a religious base" (p. 144; cf. passim pp. 11–62, 118–19, 144–53, 175–79, 185–86). Although he is interested in different issues, Kustas' evidence reveals indirectly the strong Neoplatonic encouragement of formalism in the arts of discourse as well as the rhetorical transmission of this influence through the Middle Ages to the Renaissance.

A. Plotinus

I must restrict myself here to describing briefly those distinctions or doctrines of Plotinus' philosophical system which seem most clearly to bear upon the subsequent developments of literary theory. Such a restriction must of necessity do an injustice to Plotinus as a thinker and to the importance of his influence, however indirect, upon literature as a topic.[2] His influence, particularly as it is reflected in later Neoplatonists, has often been less than beneficial and exemplifies, I believe, certain kinds of imbalance which have always threatened the literary analysis of experience. The effects of imbalance have become especially apparent in the encroaching forms of aestheticism, and of the pragmatic theories reacting against them, over the past several hundred years. These effects, in turn, have become harder and harder to perceive today because they often express themselves in the very methodologies, both within and outside the Academy, which, instead of analyzing the deficiencies, have simply led to the further impoverishment of literary studies. I hope the reader may become more aware of how we have spent this Neoplatonic inheritance when he reconsiders it in the light of the problems raised in Part Two of this study. For the sake of simplicity, I shall organize my discussion of Plotinus under the following headings:

1. Similarity and Identity
2. Knowledge: Purity and Extension
3. Representation: Discourse and Vision
4. Decorum: Quality, Praxis, and Power

1. Similarity and Identity. The relationship of objects more appropriately known to us (ἡμῖν) to those more appropriately known in themselves (ἁπλῶς) is an ever-recurrent theme in Platonic speculation. In the *Parmenides* (132A–33A) Socrates suggests that the objects of our im-

---

[2] To correct this injustice to Plotinus as a thinker, the reader has enormous resources at his disposal. Each year brings out important new studies of Neoplatonism, and I give below only a few works which, with their bibliographies, may serve as a way into the subject. Perhaps most generally helpful is *The Cambridge History of Later Greek and Early Medieval Philosophy*, ed. A. H. Armstrong (Cambridge, 1967; hereafter cited as CHLGP); also, E. Bréhier, *The Philosophy of Plotinus* (Chicago, 1958), W. Theiler, *Die Vorbereitung des Neuplatonismus* (Berlin, 1964), and, more recently for the later Neoplatonic tradition, S. Gersh, *From Iamblichus to Eriugena* (Leiden, 1978). Standard editions, translations, and investigations of the sources of Plotinus are included in these studies. The broad interest in Neoplatonism is further testified to by international conferences whose papers have been subsequently published in such collections as *Néoplatonisme* (Paris, 1971), *Plotino e il neoplatonismo in oriente e in occidente* (Roma, 1974), and *The Significance of Neoplatonism* (Norfolk, 1976).

mediate experience participate in the ideas (παραδείγματα, 132D) as likenesses (ὁμοιώματα, 132D) by assimilating (εἰκασθῆναι, 132D) themselves to the ideas. But if this is the case, Parmenides objects, "can that idea avoid being like the thing which resembles it, in so far as the thing has been made to resemble it; or is there any possibility that the like be unlike its like?" (132D). If we grant the fact that the idea must resemble what participates in it, we must recognize the consequences of the further fact that whenever two things become like each other by virtue of participating in something common to both, what is common to them both must always emerge as the (new) absolute idea. Consequently, "it is impossible that anything be like the idea, or the idea like anything; for if they are alike, some further idea, in addition to the first, will always appear, and if that is like anything, still another, and a new idea will always be arising, if the idea is like that which partakes of it" (132E). It is, therefore, Parmenides concludes (133A), "not by likeness that other things partake of ideas." Although Plato discusses this problem in ontological terms, any conception of 'likeness' will have a bearing on the two types of intelligibility and on the artistic representation of what their combined functions reveal.

Perhaps as an answer to Parmenides, Plotinus distinguishes two types of likeness (ὁμοίωσις) in an essay on the nature of virtue (*Enn.* 1.2) which introduces a number of topics pertinent to our discussion.[3] Plotinus says (*Enn.* 1.2.1), citing the *Theaetetus* 176AB, that if the soul wishes to elude moral evils, it must escape from its worldly existence which they inhabit. To escape this existence we must become like God (θεῷ . . . ὁμοιωθῆναι, 1.2.1.4) through acquiring virtue and thereby, presumably, becoming like the intelligible principle by imitating or participating in the virtues it possesses. But because the intelligible principle does not possess those civic virtues of practical wisdom which involve proportion and order achieved through discursive reason (τὸ λογιζόμενον, 1.2.1.17), men must acquire their ethical virtues by assimilating themselves to archetypical virtues of an entirely different kind. It is,

---

[3] As Armstrong notes, E. Bréhier suggests this connection between *Parmenides* 132Dff. and Plotinus' distinction between types of likeness—*Plotin: Ennéades*, 7 vols. (Paris, 1924–1938), 1:50. In the later Neoplatonic tradition, however, the connection is clearly articulated. In commenting on the *Parmenides* 132D–33A, Proclus observes that Socrates would have been able to say that there are two types of likeness, which he describes in the manner of Plotinus, and thus would have been able to resolve the dilemma of participation (see *Proclus le philosophe: commentaire sur le Parmenide*, trans. A.E.D. Chaignet, 3 vols. [Frankfurt am Main, 1962], 2:70ff.). Plotinus' ἐπισημηνάμενοι ὡς ἡ ὁμοίωσις διττή and the passage following seem to be echoed by Proclus' τὸ ὅμοιον εἶναι διττόν and the subsequent lines (see *Procli Philosophi Platonici Opera Inedita Pars Tertia* [Hildesheim, 1961], col. 912). E. R. Dodds discusses Proclus' concern with the dilemma in his commentary on Proposition 5 in *Proclus: The Elements of Theology* (Oxford, 1963), p. 191.

therefore, necessary to consider in what way we may be made like these divine archetypes which are themselves not civic virtues in the ordinary sense but which, when imitated by us, express themselves in our imitations of them *as* civic virtues. We can avoid the infinite regression, Plotinus might say, which Parmenides pointed out in the doctrine of participation through similarity by recognizing the lack of similarity between the intelligible archetypes and the virtues which we nevertheless achieve through 'imitating' them.

To explain how two essentially dissimilar things can become more like one another—how men, that is, can be made to resemble God—Plotinus makes his important distinction.

We should note that there are two kinds of likeness; one requires that there should be something the same in the things which are alike; this applies to things which derive their likeness equally from the same principle. But in the case of two things of which one is like the other, but the other is primary, not reciprocally related to the thing in its likeness and not said to be like it, likeness must be understood in a different sense; we must not require the same form in both, but rather a different one, since likeness has come about in this different way. (1.2.2)[4]

The first kind of likeness is that appropriate to civic virtues which "set us in order and make us better by giving limit and measure to our desires, and putting measure into all our experience." Insofar as these civic virtues can measure out and impose form on the soul, "they are made like the measure There and have a trace in them of the Best There." Yet form and proportion, though enabling us to move away from an "altogether unmeasured" matter toward the Good, can never enable us to be *like* the Good, because the Good itself, being above all form, is formless. We can become like the Good only by making ourselves receptive to its powers which may be regarded as virtues in the sense that they enable us to become virtuous as a result of our responding to them. These divine powers are called 'purifications' (καθάρσεις, 1.2.3.9), and, by receiving their influence, we can become like them only in the second

---

[4] I have used two English translations of Plotinus throughout this chapter: unless otherwise assigned, citations of *Enneads* 1–3 will be from *Plotinus*, trans. A. H. Armstrong, LCL, 6 vols. (London, 1966–) and citation of *Enneads* 4–6 will be from *Plotinus: The Enneads*, trans. S. Mackenna, revised by B. S. Page with a foreword by E. R. Dodds and an introduction by P. Henry, S.J. (London, 1962). I have consulted as well the translation of selected essays by E. O'Brien, S.J., in *The Essential Plotinus* (New York, 1964) and by E. R. Dodds, *Select Passages Illustrating Neoplatonism* (London, 1923), as well as the translations in French by E. Bréhier (cited in the preceding note); in German by R. Harder (*Plotin*, 5 vols. [Leipzig, 1930–1937]); and in Italian by V. Cilento (*Plotino: Enneadi*, 4 vols. [Bari, 1947–1949]).

sense of likeness which is not reciprocal. We become like God through purification, but God in no way becomes like us.[5]

I would like to illustrate these two types of likeness by examples from geometry similar to those later used by Nicholas of Cusa. The first type resembles a comparison between the same *kind* of figure—say, two triangles, A_1 and A_2, which are similar to one another on the basis of a commonly shared triangularity A. Once their common denominator is established, that denominator cannot increase or decrease. Triangle A_1, that is, cannot be more or less similar to triangle A_2 on the basis of more or less triangularity but on the basis of *other* shared characteristics. The persuasiveness of the comparison lies in our acceptance of the common denominator as plausible grounds for our inferring similarity between as many other characteristics as possible and thus for our perceiving something new about the figures. The second type of likeness, on the other hand, resembles a comparison between two *different kinds* of figure, A and B. An equilateral polygon A, for instance, has nothing essentially in common with a circle B, although it approaches circularity as the number of its sides increases and approaches infinity. Three differences between the two types of likeness may be noted. First, the criterion of triangularity, though invariable, permits a number of kinds of reciprocal similarities to appear between the triangles, while the equilateral polygon, though varying in its degree of similarity to a circle, permits only one kind of approximation to circularity. Second, whereas the similarity between triangles A_1 and A_2 is reciprocal, that between polygon A and circle B is not. An equilateral polygon, that is, may increasingly resemble a circle without violating the definitive conditions of its being an equilateral polygon; a circle, on the other hand, violates the conditions of its circularity with its first step toward becoming a

[5] The two types of likeness bear dramatically upon the Christian debates over the propriety of images. See G. B. Ladner, "The Concept of the Image in the Greek Fathers and the Byzantine Iconoclastic Controversy," *Dumbarton Oaks Papers* 7 (1953):1–34, esp. p. 13 where Ladner comments on a quotation from the Pseudo-Dionysius (*De div. nom.* 9.6): " 'Things of the same order can have reciprocal similarity . . . but in the case of cause and effect He shall not admit mutual reciprocity.' In other words, we must try to become similar to God, but God will never be similar to us." See R. A. Markus, " 'Imago' and 'Similitudo' in Augustine," *Revue des études augustiniennes* 10 (1964):125–43. One of Plotinus' criticisms of the Gnostics bears upon the nonreciprocality of the second type of likeness: "by giving names to a multitude of intelligible realities they think they will appear to have discovered the exact truth, though by this very multiplicity they bring the intelligible nature into the likeness of the sense-world, the inferior world, when one ought there in the intelligible to aim at the smallest possible number" (2.9.6). (See A. C. Lloyd's remarks on how the temptation to hypostatize intermediate realities increased after Plotinus' death, CHLGP, pp. 281–82). When Plotinus discusses the prudential virtues appropriate to the first type of likeness, his terms are indebted to Aristotelian ethics (cf. 1.3.6.7–14).

polygon of any kind. Finally, while triangle A_1 cannot carry its resemblance to triangle A_2 beyond the various kinds of similarity permitted by their shared triangularity, the polygon carries its similarity to a circle to the point of becoming identical with it.

The distinction between similarity and identity is as important for theology as (we shall gradually see) it is for literature. In referring to Platonic passages in his essay on the virtues, Plotinus makes certain important, though inconspicuous, changes. At *Theaetetus* 176B, Plato said that "we ought to try to escape from earth to the dwelling of the gods as quickly as we can; and to escape is to become like God, so far as this is possible (φυγὴ δὲ ὁμοίωσις θεῷ κατὰ τὸ δυνατόν)" for men to do.[6] Each time Plotinus cites this passage (1.2.1 and 3), he omits the qualifying phrase "so far as this is possible." The omission is probably not accidental. For, after describing in section 5 how the good man can bring his irrational impulses under the control of reason by imitating the actions of a sage, he begins section 6 with the following qualification.

Our concern, though, is not to be out of sin, but to be god. If, then, there is still any element of involuntary impulse of this sort, a man in this state will be a god or spirit who is double, or rather who has with him someone else who possesses a different kind of virtue: if there is nothing, he will be simply god, and one of those gods who follow the First.

Plotinus has changed Plato's "to become like God (ὁμοίωσις θεῷ," cited in the first section of his essay as θεῷ . . . ὁμοιωθῆναι, into "to be god (θεὸν εἶναι)" in his sixth section. In shifting from imitating the wise man to imitating God, the similarity of the first type of likeness has become the identity of the second.

To explain the doctrine of the assimilation to God in the *Theaetetus*, Plotinus draws on the doctrine of purification in the *Phaedo* (66A–69D) and, perhaps, in the *Phaedrus* (252C–53C) as well, where both doctrines seem to be combined. With respect to assimilation in the *Phaedrus* (253AC), Plato makes it clear that men may be led "to the likeness of the god whom they honor (εἰς ὁμοιότητα αὑτοῖς τῷ θεῷ, ὃν ἂν τιμῶσι, 253B)" only in "so far as it is possible for a man to have part in God (καθ' ὅσον δυνατὸν θεοῦ ἀνθρώπῳ μετασχεῖν, 253A)." Equally, in view of our human limitations, complete purification in the *Phaedo* is a condition only attainable with death (66DE). In the beginning of his fifth section, however, Plotinus implies that it is the "amount of purification (ἐπὶ πόσον κάθαρσις)" attainable in life which can indicate "what we are made like and with what god we are identified (οὕτω γὰρ καὶ ἡ

---

[6] *Plato: Theaetetus, Sophist*, trans. H. N. Fowler, LCL (London, 1967).

ὁμοίωσις τίνι φανερὰ καὶ ἡ ταυτότης τίνι θεῷ).''[7] Here again, in contrast to Plato, Plotinus thinks in terms of an identity with God rather than in terms of a degree of resemblance to him which must necessarily be in keeping with our human deficiencies. Similarity (ὁμοίωσις) to a kind of being (i.e. a god), that is, appears here to presuppose an identity (ταυτότης) with a particular god.

Plotinus concludes his essay by summarizing the distinctions just discussed. The good man as a possessor of the practical virtues of prudence will act according to them as circumstances require.

But when he reaches higher principles and different measures he will act according to these. For instance, he will not make self-control consist in that former observance of measure and limit, but will altogether separate himself, as far as possible, from his lower nature and will not live the life of the good man which civic virtue requires. He will leave that behind, and choose another, the life of the gods: for it is to them, not to good men, that we are to be made like. Likeness to good men is the likeness of two pictures of the same subject to each other; but likeness to the gods is likeness to the model (πρὸς παράδειγμα), a being of a different kind to ourselves. (1.2.7)

We may now turn to the important implications which Plotinus' distinction between the two types of likeness has for a theory of literary decorum.

These implications become clear when we contrast the Platonic and Aristotelian assumptions about measurement and proportion in the arts and sciences with those expressed previously by Plotinus. One of the most representative postulates of earlier Greek thought is that ''excess and deficiency are measureable not only in relative terms but also in respect of attainment of a norm or due measure'' (*Statesman* 284B). As expressed here by Plato, the postulate depends upon the distinction between two types of measurement, that ''concerned with the relative greatness of smallness of objects'' and that ''concerned with their size in relation to the fixed norm to which they must approximate if they

---

[7] On the Plotinian attainment of divinity in this life, see A. H. Armstrong, CHLGP, p. 230. In the course of the dramatic shift from the Platonic to the Plotinian formulation of the ''assimilation to God,'' an intermediate position is expressed by the Middle Platonists. J. Dillon, *The Middle Platonists 80 B.C. to A.D. 220* (Cornell, 1977), pp. 122–23, translates Eudorus of Alexandria who is commenting on the Pythagorian aim of assimilation to God: ''Plato defined this more clearly by adding: 'according as is possible (*kata to dynaton*),' and it is only possible by wisdom (*phronêsis*).'' Dillon points out that ''for Plato, '*kata to dynaton*' meant 'as far as possible (for a mere mortal)'; Eudorus takes it to mean rather 'according to that part of us which is capable of this,' that is to say, the intellect.'' Eudorus makes the limit of our assimilation depend on our individual intelligence, not on our humanity. Dillon later describes how Albinus held a similar view (p. 299). For the importance of Albinus generally, see Dillon's entire discussion (pp. 267–306) and R. E. Witt, *Albinus and the History of Middle Platonism* (Amsterdam, 1971).

are to exist at all" (283D). All the arts owe the goodness (ἀγαθά, 284B) and beauty (καλά) of their products to the second, τὸ μέτρον, which seeks to establish "due occasion, due time, due performance (τὸ μέτριον καὶ τὸ πρέπον καὶ τὸν καιρόν), and all such standards as have removed their abode from the extremes (ἐσχάτων) and are now settled about the mean (τὸ μέσον, 284E)." The relation between quantitative and qualitative measurement enters into the conception and formulation of nearly all the physical and moral sciences. Those who confuse the quantitative criteria of number, length, depth, breadth, or thickness in relation to their opposites with the qualitative criteria of "due measure" make a serious mistake (284E–85A).[8] The resemblance of this mistake to that of confusing the two types of likeness and the consequences of both mistakes for literary decorum may be illustrated by a passage in the *Cratylus* (431D–32E).

As the Stranger did in the *Sophist*, Socrates explains to Cratylus that falsehood exists, that statements may be more or less correct, and that the degree of their correctness is ascertainable. Cratylus objects by responding that if letters in a word—and, by extension, words in a sentence—are transposed, "it is not true that the name is written, but written incorrectly; it is not written at all, but immediately becomes a different word" (432A). Socrates then points out that Cratylus has confused qualitative with quantitative measurement.

It may be that what you say would be true of those things which must necessarily consist of a certain number or cease to exist at all, as ten, for instance, or any number you like, if you add or subtract anything is immediately another number; but this is not the kind of correctness which applies to quality or to images in general; on the contrary, the image must not by any means reproduce all the qualities of that which it imitates, if it is to be an image. See if I am not right. Would there be two things, Cratylus and the image of Cratylus, if some god should not merely imitate your colour and form, as painters do, but should also make all the inner parts like yours, should reproduce the same flexibility and warmth, should put into them motion, life, and intellect, such as exist in you, and in short, should place beside you a duplicate of all your qualities? Would there be in such an event Cratylus and an image of Cratylus, or two Cratyluses? (432AC)

There would be, of course, two Cratyluses, and the image along with its grounds of similarity to its model would vanish in identity. Images and statements, therefore, do not cease to be images and statements just because they are not identical to the original models they imitate. They

---

[8] *Plato's Statesman*, trans. J. B. Skemp as repr. with minor corrections in *The Collected Dialogues of Plato*, ed. E. Hamilton and H. Cairns (New York, 1961).

will remain more or less recognizably correct imitations "so long as the intrinsic quality of the thing named is retained" (432E).[9]

The intrinsic quality corresponds to the features of the person, in Plotinus' first type of likeness, who sits for two portraits which resemble each other more or less as each resembles him. Similarity is necessary for all qualitatively measured criteria and hence for all forms of artistic 'appropriateness.' Thus insofar as Plotinus relies on the second type of likeness to avoid the consequences of similarity which Parmenides had pointed out, his metaphysical system will be uncongenial to the requirements of literary decorum. The second nonreciprocal likeness to an archetype—leading to identity—will seek instead exactly equivalent quantities whose measurement is ascertainable by the mathematical arts. As will later become apparent, what Plotinus brings out in his essay on the virtues are the logical and theological grounds for the separation of symbolic from metaphorical and mimetic literary procedures.[10]

In his *De generatione et corruptione*, Aristotle anticipates the relevance of Plotinus' essay for literary theory in a helpful distinction: "But 'analogy (τὸ κατ' ἀναλογίαν),' while it signifies similarity (τὸ ὅμοιον) in quality (ἐν ποιῷ), signifies equality (τὸ ἴσον) in quantity (ἐν ποσῷ)."[11]

---

[9] See Chap. 7, n. 27, of this study. The importance of 'similarity' for the inductive method of arriving at universal principles, for hypothetical reasoning, for the assignment of definitions, and for establishing generic terms of metaphorical comparisons is well brought out by Aristotle in the *Topica* (1.18, 108b7–32) and in the '*Problemata*' (18.3). See B. Snell, *The Discovery of the Mind*, Chap. 9: "From Myth to Logic: The Role of the Comparison," esp. pp. 207–8, 221, for interesting observations which bear upon Part Two of this study.

[10] The central importance of Plotinus' distinction between the two types of likeness for the Neoplatonic differentiation of mimetic from symbolic procedures of representation will appear most clearly in my later discussion of Proclus (see Chap. 8, n. 50). Plotinus' first likeness appropriate to "civic virtues" will correspond to Proclus' images which treat ethical and political experience mimetically (εἰκονικῶς); his second likeness, appropriate for man's assimilation to God, to Proclus' images which treat the divine symbolically (συμβολικῶς). Proclus regards the mimetic image as instructing (παιδευτικός), the symbolic image as inspiring (ἐνθεαστικός). (J. A. Coulter discusses these distinctions of Proclus— particularly with respect to *In Plat. Tim. Comm.* 1.30.11–18 and *In Plat. Rem Pub. Comm.* 76.17–86.23—without reference to Plotinus in his *The Literary Microcosm*, pp. 40–56; cf. p. 81. See also O. Casel, *De philosophorum Graecorum silentio mystico* [Giessen, 1919], pp. 149ff. and P. Crome, *Symbol und Unzulänglichkeit*, pp. 190–91). One important result of these Neoplatonic distinctions between types of representation is that the didactic type becomes the polar antithesis of the mystical type. If one wishes to avoid the didactic, then, he must turn away from the public world of ethical community to the private world of visionary communion. The antithesis anticipates the isolation of the 'aesthetic' experience from practical concerns of ordinary life in the eighteenth through twentieth centuries; it coordinates various influences on the identification of 'aestheticism' with theosophy; and it contributes to the conversion of the arts into forms of secular religion.

[11] *On Coming-to-be and Passing-away* 2.6, 333a30–31, trans. E. S. Forester, LCL (London, 1965). Aristotle offers an interesting restatement of these distinctions in the *Physics* (7.4), where he wishes to describe relative velocities of recovery from illness. "The term 'equal' cannot be used of a *quale*: in that category what corresponds to equality in

In proportional comparisons qualities are similar (or dissimilar) to qualities, magnitudes are equal (or unequal) to magnitudes. The qualitative nature of language and images, which Socrates explains to Cratylus, appears clearly in Aristotle's observations on the 'proportional' metaphor (ἡ κατ' ἀναλογίαν μεταφορά). "Metaphors must be drawn . . . from things that are related to the original thing, and yet not obviously so related—just as in philosophy also an acute mind will perceive resemblances (τὸ ὅμοιον) even in things far apart" (*Rhet.* 3.11.5; 1412a11–13). Perceiving resemblances offers us new insights which are most easily transmitted through words.

Now strange words simply puzzle us; ordinary words convey only what we know already; it is from metaphor that we can best get hold of something fresh. When the poet calls old age "a withered stalk," he conveys a new idea, a new fact, to us by means of the general notion of "lost bloom," which is common to both things. (3.10.2; 1410b12–15)

With respect to knowledge and representation metaphor represents a qualitative 'mean,' which Aristotle defines as decorum (τὸ πρέπον), between a language which is overly familiar and one which is not familiar enough.
    What is true for metaphor and similes, is true for mimesis in general.

Again, since learning and wondering are pleasant, it follows that such things as acts of imitation must be pleasant—for instance, painting, sculpture, poetry—and every product of skilful imitation; this latter, even if the object imitated is not itself pleasant; for it is not the object itself which here gives delight; the spectator draws inferences ("That is a so-and-so") and thus learns something fresh. Dramatic turns of fortune and hairbreadth escapes from perils are pleasant, because we feel all such things are wonderful. (1.11.23–24; 1371b5–12)

Aristotle repeats these observations with respect to the εἰκών in the fourth chapter of the *Poetics* and with respect to παράδειγμα (*exemplum*) in the '*Problemata*' (18.3), and later Strabo will echo them in defending myth (1.2.8). They describe the cognitive resources upon which decorum must draw to resist an imbalance among the mathematical, philosophical,

---

the category of quantity is *likeness* (ὁμοιότης). Let us take 'equal velocity,' then, to mean 'making *the same* change in the same time' " (249b1–4). The principal discussion of these terms is in *Categories* 6: "Of nothing, moreover, save quantities can we affirm these two terms [equal and unequal]. For we never say this disposition (διάθεσις) is 'equal' to that or 'unequal.' We say it is 'like' (ὁμοία) or 'unlike.' One quality—whiteness, for instance—is never compared with another in terms or on the grounds of equality. Such things are termed 'like' and 'unlike.' Thus our calling something 'equal,' 'unequal,' is the mark, above all marks, of quantity" (6a32–36). Plutarch (*Mor.* 720AB) associates equality with matter and likeness with form in the creation of the cosmos, and, as an analogy to the creation suggests Euclid's construction of a (third) figure 'equal' to a first figure and 'similar' to a second figure (*Elements* 6.25).

and rhetorical intentions of literary discourse. These observations all apply to the first (reciprocal) likeness which Plotinus wishes ultimately to sacrifice for the second (nonreciprocal) likeness. We may see more clearly why the symbol became the literary expression of this second likeness and what that meant for the transmission of literary theory by examining further characteristics of Plotinian doctrine.[12]

2. *Knowledge: Purity and Extension.* Up to this point I have emphasized the cognitive and psychagogic conditions of grasping things better known with respect to their own nature (ἁπλῶς) and things better known with respect to us (ἡμῖν). These psychological conditions relevant to the two types of intelligibility may also be differentiated in accordance with the ontological disparity between 'the simple' (τὸ ἁπλοῦν) and 'the composite' (τὸ σύνθετον) in the Neoplatonic description of reality. 'The composite' will, generally speaking, correspond to that object better known with respect to ourselves, 'the simple' to that better known with respect to its own nature.

Plotinus distinguishes between two extreme kinds of simplicity (ἁπλότης). The simplicity of things at the highest extreme consists in the unified integration and concentration of their powers to function as originative causes and activities. The simplicity of things at the lowest extreme, on the contrary, results from the dissipation of these powers, since in passing into and through composite beings, they expend their potency in reaching the very limit of creation (6.7.13). To paraphrase

---

[12] Plotinus' distinction between the two kinds of likeness helps to demonstrate that there is a difference of kind rather than simply of degree between metaphor and symbol among the Neoplatonists. Apparently assuming more a difference of degree—that of enigmaticness—than of kind, Coulter, on the contrary, maintains in a discussion of simile, metaphor, and symbol that metaphor, in Aristotle's sense of "proportional metaphor" (cf. *Rhet.* 3.4.1–4, 3.11.1; *Poet.* 21.6), brings out hidden correspondences and so is closer to the symbol than to the simile (pp. 68–72). Like the "seeming irrationality" of symbols, "metaphors are, in their form at least, irrational. To say that a man *is* a lion makes no 'sense' at all." Like a riddle, the metaphor "must obviously mean something other than what it says (unlike a simile which says that A is only *like* B)." These statements are misleading, particularly with respect to metaphors which are "proportional (κατ' ἀναλογίαν)," because the "analogy" involved here (and in *Poet.* 21.6)—like that of Plotinus' first (reciprocal) kind of likeness—is clearly a Platonic and an Aristotelian "logical ratio" rather than a Neoplatonic "sympathetic affinity" (see Chap. 8, nn. 32 and 52). Aristotle, furthermore, associates the structural form of such metaphors explicitly with that of similes (*Rhet.* 3.4.1–4, 3.11.4). And although metaphors may provide riddles and vice versa, we are to draw our metaphorical comparison from things whose kinship is familiar so that their relation to one another can be easily perceived (*Rhet.* 3.2.12). If it is to be 'realized,' the metaphor must, through its context, make clear the common denominator between the terms being compared—which should be reciprocal (3.4.4)—whereas the symbol is not obliged to do this. Although without reference to Plotinus' two kinds of likeness, Crome, nevertheless, distinguishes at length between his use of metaphors and his use of symbols (*Symbol und Unzulänglichkeit*, pp. 90–122).

E. R. Dodds, who comments on this passage in the *Enneads*, the term "simple" (ἁπλόος) may refer either to a thing's organic unity or to its incapacity to differentiate itself further. The higher a thing stands in the scale of Being, the more simple it is in the sense of its organic unity, but the less simple it is in the sense of its greater potentiality for differentiation. In the first sense complete simplicity is found only in the One; in the second, only in Matter.[13] While the higher a thing ascends in the scale of Being, the simpler its composition becomes, the lower a thing descends in the scale, the simpler its resources become either to divide or to unify itself. The unity of the One, that is, 'contains' within it an infinite power to divide itself into many; the number two has already lost 'half' of this power. Potentiality for differentiation exhausts itself with each step of its descent into multiplicity until matter is ultimately reached and all division ends.

Both the One—the absolute principle of unity—and matter—the absolute principle of disparity—are ἁπλᾶ. Both are principles of indetermination; incorporeal and ineffable, they have neither form, relation, nor, strictly speaking, existence. For the One, as the first substantial category, or hypostasis, of reality is prior to, and 'above,' the second hypostasis made up of Intelligence, Being, and Form. And, since all Form and Being are determinations or delimitations, the One, which has no limits, can be identified with neither (cf. 6.7.38). Matter, equally to avoid determination, must be without even a corporeal degree of Being, since to be a body is to participate in dimensions which confer limitations of form. Whatever negative characteristics they have in common, these ontological extremes are antithetical to one another and embrace the carefully discriminated and coordinated energies of the intermediate composite reality between them (τὸ μεταξύ).

If today one were to illustrate these extremes diagrammatically, it would be best to conceive of them as 'inner' and 'outer' rather than as 'higher' and 'lower.' The One, or first hypostasis, is best conceived as the common center of a series of expanding spheres, the outermost of which is unembodied matter. Insofar as we can speak of a 'chain of Being,' it would correspond to a radius commencing with the first sphere— that is, with the second hypostasis of Being and the Forms—and extending to the sphere just before that of absolute matter—the privation of all Form. The essential paradox of the Plotinian system is that the One at the center, while it shares nothing of their nature, is both the

[13] Dodds' original statement is as follows: "The term 'simple' (haploûs) may describe either absence of internal differentiation, or organic unity. The higher a thing stands in the scale of Being, the less simple it is in the former sense, the more simple in the latter. Complete simplicity in the first meaning of the word is found only in Matter; in the second, only in the One," *Select Passages Illustrating Neoplatonism* (London, 1923), p. 45, n. 1.

original cause and ultimate end of every activity in the other spheres. This paradox of how the One may be the center of, and yet include, its own spheres—of how, that is, it may be immanent in, and yet transcend, them—becomes less obscure if we consider the One as the ultimate symbol of power as well as of unity.

The power of the One consists in its ability to differentiate itself (outward) into the manifold forms, objects, and actions—even beyond these into matter itself—of the universe. This differentiation of power, which Plotinus calls a "procession" or a "moving outward" (πρόοδος), is accompanied by a contrary impulse called a "turning around" or "return" (ἐπιστροφή). This turning around, this pulling back into the center of those forces which had been released, constitutes the restoration of both the universal whole and the preservation of the individual part. Dodds comments that "the value which Reality necessarily lost in the process of expansion or unfolding is restored to it again by the voluntary act of Return, without thereby annihilating the individuality which the expansive process is perpetually creating."[14] As the force moves outward from the One, which can never be depleted, it may be thought of as 'taking on' or 'being converted into' various conditions or activities which are proper to the things which 'utilize' or 'participate in' it. The One, extending its potency throughout the universe, becomes immanent in every existent thing in decreasing degrees until it reaches 'pure' matter which can absorb none of its effects. By virtue of the unity and purity (incompositeness) of this potency, all existent things are parts of a single whole. When the energy reconcentrates itself in its return to the One, these parts, while retaining their individuality as things, transcend their limitations as things by 'assimilating' themselves to the whole. The same source of energy which extends to them the power to participate in its effects, draws them back to itself through their 'voluntary' acts of purification.

While the extended power of the One expresses itself in the second hypostasis of the Intelligence as the formal, existential, and intellectual principles, in the third hypostasis of the Soul it expresses itself as the principle of animation. The spectrum of animate beings reaches from the cosmic existence of the planets, which borders on the realm of the Intelligence, to the corporeal beings, which border on the realm of unembodied matter. If the categories of reality are conceived as spheres which share the One as a common center, each further sphere participates in the manifestations of the primal force expressed within the spheres which

---

[14] "Tradition and Personal Achievement in the Philosophy of Plotinus," *Jour. of Rom. Stud.* 50 (1960):3–4. Dodds' brief essay is one of the most helpful introductions to Plotinian thought.

it encloses. Things within the spectrum of the Soul, that is, will partic-ipate in the unity and order of the first two hypostases. The further out the sphere is from the center, the more composite and the less organically unified the objects are which it contains. In the realm of animate beings like human souls which deal with material bodies, the range of reality which the consciousness may experience at different times is enormous. Dodds distinguishes this spectrum of the soul (ψυχή) from what we (ἡμεῖς) are conscious of at any given moment. For Plotinus, he says,

The Psyche is, as Plato put it (*Tim.* 90 a), like a tree growing upside down, whose roots are in Heaven, but whose branches extend downwards into a physical body; its experience ranges through the entire gamut of Being, from the negative darkness of Matter to the divine darkness of the One. Man's personality is a continuum: there is not one part which is natural, another which is divine and comes from outside, like Aristotle's νοῦς θύραθεν; there is no sharp line between Psyche and Nous. But the ego-consciousness never covers the whole of this continuum: it fluctuates like a spotlight, embracing now a higher and now a lower sector; and as it fluctuates it creates an apparent, but not a real, break between the part of the continuum which is within the circle of consciousness and the part which is outside it. In ordinary life there fall below it the functions of the physiological life-principle which directly controls the body: not only are processes like breathing and digestion outside of conscious control and, normally, of conscious awareness, but Plotinus recognizes (anticipating Leibniz) that there are sensations which do not reach consciousness unless we specially direct at-tention to them (4, 4, 8; 5. 1, 12), and also (anticipating Freud) that there are desires which "remain in the appetitive part and are unknown to us" (4, 8, 8, 9). The same is true of the permanent dispositions which result from past experiences or mental acts.[15]

The Plotinian term ἡμεῖς for our immediate consciousness of things (in contrast to τὸ ἁπλοῦν for the absolute simplicity of matter or of the One) gives a stronger ontological emphasis to Aristotle's more epistemological term ἡμῖν for things apprehended more clearly with respect to ourselves (in contrast to ἁπλῶς for things better known with respect to their own nature).

With respect to knowledge, the Plotinian 'we' (ἡμεῖς) may be thought of as the understanding (διάνοια) which 'negotiates' between intelligible and sensible experiences.

We are not the Intellectual-Principle; we represent it in virtue of that highest reasoning faculty which draws upon it. Again; we perceive by means of the

---

[15] Ibid., p. 5. Dodds' phrase "from the negative darkness of Matter to the divine darkness of the One" suggests the Neoplatonic continuation of the distinction between the two types of darkness discussed above in relation to the *Sophist*. The extension of this dis-tinction to style, suggested in connection with Plato and treated in detail in the articles on Horace cited in n. 1 of Part Two, is specifically reflected, as we shall see, in Proclus.

perceptive faculty and are not, ourselves, the percipients: may we then say the same of the understanding (the principle of reasoning and discursive thought)? No: our reasoning is our own; we ourselves think the thoughts that occupy the understanding—for this is actually the We—but the operation of the Intellectual-Principle enters from above us as that of the sensitive faculty from below; the We is the Soul at its highest, the mid-point between two powers, between the sensitive principle, inferior to us, and the intellectual principle superior. We think of the perceptive act as integral to ourselves because our sense-perception is uninterrupted; we hesitate as to the Intellectual-Principle both because we are not always occupied with it and because it exists apart, not a principle inclining to us but one to which we incline when we choose to look upwards. The sensitive principle is our scout (αἴσθησις δὲ ἡμῖν ἄγγελος); the Intellectual-Principle our King. (5.3.3)

The Plotinian dianoetic understanding corresponds to the dialectic which Plato describes as being able to unite the idealist gods with the materialist Titans. But whereas for Plato the attainment and preservation of this union is the objective of philosophical discourse in the *Sophist*, for Plotinus it is only a stage in the return to the One, a stage to be completed as soon as possible.[16]

To move 'beyond' our immediate consciousness to the absolute purity (ἁπλότης) of the One, it seems necessary, according to Plotinus, to move back 'through,' as it were, and 'out the inner border' of our consciousness toward the center. We seem to pass, that is, 'back through' our awareness of ourselves (ἡμᾶς) and leave that awareness behind with the impurities which we acquired in our procession outward from the One. To make this passage we must first focus our conscious attention upon what is present in the soul as a residue of the first two hypostases. To reveal and articulate this presence, we may utilize a Platonic form of dialectic which seeks to be as 'purified' as possible of the propositional procedures of discursive demonstration. Such a dialectic must end by contemplating that unity which it has discerned, and, in doing this, "it leaves what is called logical activity (λογικὴν πραγματείαν), about propositions and syllogisms, to another art, as it might leave knowing how to write"

---

[16] See A. H. Armstrong's discussion of this passage (5.3.3), CHLGP, pp. 225–26. Elsewhere Armstrong summarizes the paradox of this return: "Beyond the Platonic-Aristotelian Intellect-Intelligible, the world of real being which is Νοῦς and νοητά, lies the One or Good beyond being, which is neither intelligent nor intelligible. When we have completed our understanding of reality, we have to leave it all behind in order to find what turns out to be the only thing we want, the source of all values and the goal of all desire, which alone makes it worth the effort to attain to Νοῦς on the way, as it is the only reason why Νοῦς is there at all" ("Elements in the Thought of Plotinus at Variance with Classical Intellectualism," *JHS* 93 [1973]:13). Dodds comments, however, that, with the exception of the passages from the *Enneads* he cites in relation to Proposition 121, the conception of an intelligence higher than Νοῦς is largely post-Plotinian (*Elements of Theology*, p. 266).

syllogisms, to another art, as it might leave knowing how to write" (1.3.4). Since dialectic deals with real beings rather than with statements about them, "whatever is submitted to it it perceives by directing intuition, as sense-perception (αἴσθησις) also does, but it hands over petty precisions of speech (ἀκριβολογεῖσθαι) to another discipline which finds satisfaction in them" (1.3.5). As the chief instrument of philosophy, the more restrictively intuitive dialectic becomes, the more it will tend to subordinate the conceptual functions of definition and discursive analysis to the direct apprehension of purer states of being, states which become progressively less expressible in language.[17]

The hypostatic categories of reality, proceeding from the inexhaustible resource of the One, 'expand' outward into forms of being which have to exist—and which we can only know—in space and time. Paradoxically, while this procession expands 'outwardly' in space and time, with respect to degrees of reality each member of the procession is ontologically shrinking 'inwardly' in its power to differentiate itself. In existential terms, that is, the many produced by procession do not become more than the One but, like smaller and smaller fractions of a unit, can only become less. While the One differentiates—and sends forth—its portion of energy, it nevertheless continues to inform these portions and to contain them as parts of itself. In this sense, the procession from the One is simply an articulation of the potential divisibility already present within its unity. The energy proceeds outward as if it were a light beam which was projecting that potential multiplicity through a lens at its very source onto a series of spherical concave screens at various distances from the center. We may be said to perceive these multiple reflections on the inner surfaces of these hypostatic spheres much as we might on the inner walls of Plato's cave. The further out the spheres, the deeper the walls of the cavern (cf. 4.8.1, 3).

The paradox that the One is contained by its participants in their formal differentiation and, at the same time, contains its participants in

---

[17] As Bréhier comments, "Quite different [from that of Plato, Aristotle, and the Stoics] is the Plotinian conception of the relation of the individual to the universal being. It is no longer a rational unity which he is seeking but a mystical unification in which individual consciousness is to disappear" (*The Philosophy of Plotinus*, p. 110). Earlier, he cites Eucken's observation that for Plotinus knowledge "as immediate union with things is transformed into an obscure emotion, a vital feeling without form, an intangible *Stimmung*. Intellectualism has destroyed itself through its own exaggeration" (*The Philosophy of Plotinus*, p. 103). Bréhier responds by defending Plotinian dialectic (citing *Enn*. 1.3.4) as "a natural science which bears upon realities" as distinct from logic which is a "practical technique which deals only with the propositions and rules of reasoning" (p. 104). Yet, one might reply, if dialectic is a science describing nature, nature may come to be conceived as that which is describable by dialectic. And, indeed, Bréhier later astutely discriminates Plotinian from Platonic dialectic on just these grounds (pp. 141–42).

its 'field' of energies gives all forms of procession a positive and negative value. Their positive value lies in their bringing new beings into existence which, as reflections of the higher orders of reality, can render these orders more apprehensible to us. Their negative value lies in the fact that these beings are, at the same time, only obscure imitations of these orders and can only regain their clarity and potency through reconcentrating their energies by returning back toward their original sources. Conceived diagrammatically, as Plotinus might render them, two radii from the common center of the spheres will meet any given sphere at two points on its inner surface (cf. 6.8.18, 6.9.8). An arc drawn between these two points, proportionate to the angle between the radii where they originate, will constitute the differentiated 'extension' upon that sphere of the undivided unity of the center. The arc of extension, that is, constitutes the composite reflection, existing in space and time, of the timeless, dimensionless purity of its source. To recover that purity, the arc must reassimilate itself to the point by, first, drawing back toward it and, then, by both diminishing its sequential length and by increasing its concentrated force as it returns toward the One. This pattern of procession and return occurs repeatedly in Plotinus' account of knowledge and its representation.

When the Soul, growing restless in its contemplation of eternity, turns away and moves outward, differentiating itself in manifold experiences, it produces time which is an image, as Plato says (*Tim.* 37D), of eternity. By squandering itself in division, the Soul proceeds to ever weaker extension and creates our world of sense in imitation of the intelligible world. What was unified there becomes dispersed here, what was a simultaneous whole there becomes a continuous succession here. What was ever complete there comes into being, here, part by part. For the Soul must imitate what is already whole and unbounded "by intending to be always making an increase in its being" in time, for this is how its being can come to resemble eternal Being, which is infinite (3.7.11; cf. 1.5.7). Time comes into existence in the Soul when, by the motion involved in the act of contemplating itself, the Soul becomes a plurality (6.2.6).

What is true of the movement of time in the Soul is also true of the movement of reason in the mind. While we grasp the simple and unified objects of knowledge by acts of immediate intuition, we grasp composite objects, which have become differentiated in time and space, part by part in the cumulative and sequential steps of discursive reasoning. The reasoning faculty "is not a unity but a thing of parts; it brings the bodily nature into the inquiry, borrowing its principles from the corporeal: thus it thinks of the Essential Existence as corporeal and as a thing of parts; it baulks at the unity because it does not start from the appropriate principles." This happens because of the nature of reality.

On the one hand there is the unstable, exposed to all sorts of change, distributed in place, not so much Being as Becoming: on the other, there is that which exists eternally, not divided, subject to no change of state, neither coming into being nor falling from it, set in no region or place or support, emerging from nowhere, entering into nothing, fast within itself. In dealing with that lower order we would reason from its own nature and the characteristics it exhibits; thus, on a plausible foundation, we achieve plausible results by a plausible system of deduction: similarly, in dealing with the Intellectual, the only way is to grasp the nature of the essence concerned and so lay the sure foundations of the argument, not forgetfully straying over into that other order but basing our treatment on what is essential to the Nature with which we deal. (6.5.2)

In sum: "reason unravelling gives process; Intellectual-Principle has unbroken knowledge and has, moreover, an Act unattended by knowing, a vision by another approach" (6.7.35).

Discursive reason, then, which must take things up successively part by part in order to express itself, can make no progress in the intelligible realm of the absolutely simple (ἐν δὲ πάντῃ ἁπλῷ) where only intuitive contact is possible (5.3.17). Even the universe itself was not fashioned according to a rational design of consequences deduced from premises (5.8.7, 3.2.14), since the creating Intellect would not conceive of reality as being the result of a logical process as we might do (1.8.2). Nor, within the universe, does Nature, now, work out her intricate generations by discursive reasoning (3.8.3). Beyond these animate and intelligible realms, the principle of the One is completely inaccessible to knowledge itself. For "in knowing, soul or mind abandons its unity; it cannot remain a simplex: knowing is taking account of things; that accounting is multiple; the mind thus plunging into number and multiplicity departs from unity" (6.9.4). Because of the nature of knowledge and reason, whoever attempts to know or predicate the Good only destroys its unity (3.8.11). Even the term 'oneness' should not be applied to the ultimate simplicity (ἁπλότητος), since any quality falsifies what cannot be qualified beyond the negation of plurality (5.5.6). Plotinus states this negation by borrowing the Pythagorean pun on the name Apollo (α = not, πολλῶν = of many), and implies that this attribute may be best expressed by silence.[18] If one associates Apollo not only with music, medicine, and prophecy but with the literary arts as well, the pun anticipates some of the consequences which the Plotinian

---

[18] In a different context, Plato comments that the Thessalians called Apollo "the simple one" ('Ἁπλοῦν) to bring out his simplicity (τὸ ἁπλοῦν) which they identified with the truth (τὸ ἀληθές) of his revelations (*Crat.* 405C).

epistemology subsequently had for literary theory. In the representation of that knowledge which reason has gathered sequentially and retains, for the most part, only under discrete topics, the arts of discourse can but lead our conception of reality into further fragmentation.

3. Representation: Discourse and Vision. In Plotinus' thought the fragmentation of reality which results from the discursive acquisition of knowledge is further intensified when that knowledge is represented in words.

As the spoken word is an imitation of that in the soul, so the word in the soul is an imitation of that in something else: as the uttered word, then, is broken up into parts as compared with that in the soul, so is that in the soul as compared with that before it [in the Intellect], which it interprets. (1.2.3)

What is true of spoken words will be even more true, it may be inferred, of written words which are their further image and reflection.[19] It is in this context of thought that we must understand Plotinus' few passages which bear directly upon the understanding of fictional narrative and upon the ancient dilemma of knowledge and representation.

The rational principle as "the product and expression of Intellect," he says, "coming after Intellect and no longer belonging to it, but being in something else, is said to lie in the garden of Zeus, lying there at the time when it is said that Aphrodite came into existence in the realm of being" (3.5.9.20). During this treatment of the Platonic myth of Eros (*Symp.* 203B), Plotinus comments upon how the limitations of the narrative presentation of reality as a process must be overcome by careful interpretation of the story.

But myths, if they are really going to be myths, must separate in time the things of which they tell, and set apart from each other many realities which are together, but distinct in rank or powers, at points where rational discussions, also, make generations of things ungenerated, and themselves, too, separate things which are together; the myths, when they have taught us as well as they can, allow the man who has understood them to put together again that which they have separated. (3.5.9.24–29)

The narrative of myth takes the essential purity of an as yet incomposite reality and 'extends' it in space, time, and incident. If the myths are

[19] So mental conceptions, which, so long as they remain undivided within, will elude our memory, must be 'broken up' and extended into language which, in turn, further extends them into images which reflect these conceptions back, as in a mirror, so that they may be recollected (4.3.30). The process resembles the 'projection' of geometrical ideas outward into images on the 'screen' of the imagination as Proclus describes it in this chapter in his commentary on Euclid.

well constructed (it is implied), after teaching us what they can in their extended form, they will then "allow the man who has understood them to put together (συναιρεῖν) again that which they have separated" (3.5.9.28). This putting together of disparate narrative materials corresponds to the reconcentration of any process extended in space and time back into its purer unity. In the geometrical analogy, it corresponds to the bringing of the ends of the arc on the inner surface of the sphere back along the radial lines toward the center until the ends meet at their central point of origin.[20]

In this way, everything that is multiple seeks self-concentration in order to have a perception of itself as a whole (συναισθάνεσθαι αὐτοῦ, 5.6.5).[21] This perception of degrees of unity is, at the same time, a perception of degrees of existence, since a thing can be said to exist in proportion to its inner coherence; let that coherence fall into fragments, and the thing ceases to be (6.9.1). Likewise, a well-recounted myth for Plotinus has the power and the responsibility, when properly interpreted, to reconcentrate the meaning of its incidents into a single symbolic expression. Increasingly with later writers, such symbols come to express the integration of sympathetic forces gathered once again—with the return of events which had suffered extension in narrative representation—into unity.

Were Plotinus to deal directly with literature, he would clearly prefer symbolic to mimetic literary procedures. The symbol offers us an instanteous visualization of a reality too unified to be grasped by discursive reason or to be represented by ordinary language.

The wise of Egypt—whether in precise knowledge or by a prompting of nature—indicated the truth where, in their effort towards philosophical statement, they

---

[20] Crome translates the passage just quoted (p. 99) and later comments: "Die Mythen als Erzählungen, die aus verschiedenen einzelnen Momenten zusammengesetzt sind, zeigen das Ursprüngliche zerlegt in seine zeitliche Vereinzelung" (p. 122). For other good observations on the same passage, see J. Pépin, Mythe et allégorie (Paris, 1958), p. 191. Among the many psychological analogues for this hermeneutic reduction of narrative incident is Plotinus' account of the soul's forgetting its earthly, and hence sequential, memories in its flight from multiplicity: "It seeks to escape the unbounded (τὸ ἄπειρον) by drawing all to unity, for only thus is it free from entanglement, light-footed, self-conducted. Thus it is that even in this world the soul which has the desire of the other is putting away, amid its actual life, all that is foreign to that order. While it is in the heavenly regions it puts away more again. Little of what it gathered here is taken with it to the Intellectual Realm" (4.3.32). Mackenna's phrase for the soul in flight—"light-footed, self-conducted (ἐλαφρὰ καὶ δι' αὑτῆς)"—shows the curious grace which, despite stylistic idiosyncrasies, frequently brings his translation to life.

[21] In his commentary on the Enneads, Bréhier observes that 'synaesthesia' bears the connotation of the Stoic 'sympatheia' (vol. 5, p. 116, n. 2), and A. Graeser discusses some cases in which these terms approximate one another, Plotinus and the Stoics (Leiden, 1972), pp. 126–37.

left aside the writing-forms that take in the detail of words and sentences—those characters that represent sounds and convey the propositions of reasoning—and drew pictures instead, engraving in the temple-inscriptions a separate image for every separate item: thus they exhibited the absence of discursiveness in the Intellectual Realm. For each manifestation of knowledge and wisdom is a distinct image, an object in itself, an immediate unity, not an aggregate of discursive reasoning and detailed willing. Later from this wisdom in unity there appears, in another form of being, an image, already less compact, which announces the original in terms of discourse and unravels the causes by which things are such that the wonder rises how a generated world can be so excellent. (5.8.6)

This passage lays down in the barest possible terms the presuppositions of all subsequent symbolist theories of the literary and the visual arts. But the terms themselves, which have often been used independently of their context to support various aesthetic attitudes, are not as important to recognize as the nature of the philosophical system which gave, and still gives, to them their essential meaning. If one accepts the validity of an aesthetic attitude expressed in such terms, that is, he is obliged to accept or qualify the presuppositions which produced them.[22]

The hieroglyphic symbol enables the 'reader' to grasp intuitively and simultaneously the relation of sequential experiences to one another and to the intelligible Forms of the second hypostasis. Expressed as auton-

---

[22] Clement of Alexandria's earlier schematization of mimetic and symbolic kinds of Egyptian hieroglyphs is interesting to compare to Plotinus' description just quoted. J. Pépin outlines Clement's distinctions in *Mythe et allégorie*, pp. 265–75 and breaks them down as follows (p. 269):

(1) Écriture *épistolographique*
(2) — *hiératique*
(3) — *hiéroglyphique* { (a) *cyriologique* { (α) *par simple imitation*
                      { (b) *symbolique* { (β) *tropique ou métaphorique*
                                         { (γ) *allégorico-énigmatique*

He then quotes J. Vergote's translation of the central passage (5.4) in Clement's *Stromata*: "Ceux qui parmi les Égyptiens reçoivent de l'instruction apprennent d'abord le genre d'écriture égyptienne qu'on appelle 'épistolographique' (ἐπιστολογραφικὴ [μέθοδος]); en second lieu, le genre hiératique (ἱερατική), dont se servent les hiérogrammates; enfin et en dernier lieu, le genre hiéroglyphique (ἱερογλυφική) qui, en partie, exprime les choses au propre (κυριολογική) au moyen des lettres primaires (πρῶτα στοιχεῖα), et qui, en partie, est pictographique (συμβολική). Dans la méthode pictographique, une espèce exprime les choses au propre par imitation (κατὰ μίμησιν), une autre espèce écrit pour ainsi dire d'une façon métaphorique (τροπικῶς), tandis qu'une troisième espèce est franchement allégorisante au moyen de certaines énigmes (ἀλληγορεῖται κατά τινας αἰνιγμούς). . . ." This passage continues by giving examples. Pépin then goes on to point out the similar, but less complete, schematization in Porphyry's *Life of Pythagoras*. For the literature on the symbolic significance of hieroglyphs, see Pépin, p. 269, n. 15, and O. Stählin, *Clemens Alexandrinus: Stromata Buch I–VI* (Berlin, 1960), 2:533–34 (n. to p. 339). Both scholars emphasize the importance of J. Vergote, "Clément d'Alexandrie et l'écriture égyptienne. Essai d'interprétation de *Stromates* V, 4, 20–21," *Le Muséon* 52 (1939):199–221.

omous unities without discursive extension in time and space, these symbols share the principles of beauty which Plotinus set against the traditional canons of visual decorum. Most people, he says, think that beauty, which exists in music and combinations of words as well as in things seen, consists in a "good proportion (συμμετρία) of the parts to each other and to the whole, with the addition of good colour." On this theory nothing single (μόνον) or simple (ἁπλοῦν) could be beautiful, because there would be no parts to bring into harmony, or, if there were parts, beauty would not lie in them but in the whole composition. But we know that in things seen or heard, in "beautiful ways of life or laws or studies or branches in knowledge," and in the virtues of the soul beauty cannot consist of balanced proportion and number. It cannot be measured (1.6.1). Beauty, rather, is that which is perceived when the soul recognizes in our world a likeness or trace of the intelligible reality and returns, in its delight, to itself and remembers what it still possesses within itself of the One and the Forms. Things in this world are beautiful by participating in form, which must be understood more in the onto-logical than in the visual sense. "The beautiful body comes into being by sharing in a formative power which comes from the divine forms" (1.6.2). For, as in Plotinus' second type of likeness, "the soul's becoming something good and beautiful is its being made like to God" (1.6.6).[23]

The perception of beauty is brought about by an experience of pu-rification, of stripping off what we have accumulated in our excursion into extension, in order "not to be left without a share in the best of visions," for he "who fails to attain it has failed utterly" (1.6.7). To become worthy of it, we must cut away what is morally excessive, straighten what is crooked, and clarify what is dark, as the sculptor clears away the excess surfaces of stone to reveal the beautiful face within.

If you have become this, and see it, and are at home with yourself in purity, with nothing hindering you from becoming in this way one, with no inward mixture of anything else, but wholly yourself, nothing but true light, not meas-ured by dimensions, or bounded by shape into littleness, or expanded to size by unboundedness, but everywhere unmeasured, because greater than all measure and superior to all quantity; when you see that you have become this, then you have become sight; you can trust yourself then; you have already ascended and

---

[23] For general treatments of Plotinus' aesthetic attitudes, see E. de Keyser, La signifi-cation de l'art dans les Ennéades de Plotin (Louvain, 1955); F. Bourbon de Petrella, Il Problema dell'Arte e della bellezza in Plotino (Florence, 1956); and A. Grabar, "Plotin et les origines de l'esthétique médiévale," Cahiers archéologiques (Paris, 1946):15–34, which is discussed in detail in the conclusion to this chapter. For a survey of Plotinus' metaphorical comparisons, see R. Ferwerda, La signification des images et des métaphores dans la pensée de Plotin (Groningen, 1965).

need no one to show you; concentrate your gaze and see. This alone is the eye that sees the great beauty. (1.6.9)[24]

Beauty, then, lies not in the symmetry of shape, color, or size but in the animating light of intellection (1.6.5), as a painting which brings less well-proportioned features to life surpasses a portrait of a face perfectly symmetrical but without animation (6.7.22).

In fact, the greatest beauty, like the One, is indeterminate.

When therefore we name beauty, all such shape must be dismissed; nothing visible is to be conceived, or at once we descend from beauty to what but bears the name in virtue of some faint participation. This formless Form is beautiful as Form, beautiful in proportion as we strip away all shape, even that given in thought to mark difference, as for instance the difference between Justice and Sophrosyny, beautiful in their difference.

The "Nature best and most to be loved may be found there only where there is no least touch of Form." When something is given form and presented to the mind, we ask "what Beyond imposed that shape."

Shape and idea and measure will always be beautiful, but the Authentic Beauty, or rather the Beyond-Beauty, cannot be under measure and therefore cannot have admitted shape or be Idea: the primal Beauty, The First, must be without Form; the beauty of that higher realm must be, simply, the Nature of the Intellectual Good.

Since shape is conferred by what has no shape, the primary nature of beauty is formless (6.7.33).

These statements of Plotinus are, of course, perfectly consistent with his analysis of experience provided that we remember that he thinks of beauty primarily as an ontological and ethical rather than an aesthetic expression of reality. The presuppositions that the most complete realization of form is to be without form, that all form has, in a sense, the potentiality to be formless, and that this formlessness is a desirable and necessary condition of absolute purity appear paradoxical chiefly when they are applied to the arts. However much Plotinus himself might have restricted such an application, its consequences for literature and the visual arts have been increasingly momentous since the seventeenth

[24] Bréhier comments on the implications of a conception of contemplation which involves an ascent to a region where nothing is really distinguishable: "According to a comparison suggested by Plotinus, the sensible is to the intelligible as the face is to the expression. In the sensible face there are symmetrical parts and calculable dimensions. The expression can be neither subdivided nor measured. But if every definite object constitutes an obstacle, the very logic of the system forbids anyone to envisage, in contemplation, anything but the act of contemplating which is itself its own object; and that is in fact exactly the inference Plotinus draws." *The Philosophy of Plotinus*, trans. J. Thomas (Chicago, 1958), p. 5.

century. The primary consequence has been, paradoxically, an ever increasing emphasis upon the formal, at the expense of the cognitive and judicative, intentions of literary theory.

The apparent paradox lies in the fact that a doctrine which regards the supreme reality as formless and our experience of it as purified of all formal expectations should have been from the beginning so congenial to the development of various kinds of formalism in the arts. We must look for the reasons for this congeniality in other Plotinian doctrines. First, the Intellectual-Principle of the second hypostasis includes, and virtually identifies, existence and the Platonic Forms (6.9.1). Beings exist and acquire their essences, that is, by virtue of their participation in the formal principles of Intelligence (5.5.5). Second, each further extension outward from the One is a reflection of the formal organization of the preceding stage in the procession toward pure matter. Matter alone has no further power to cast a reflection; it can only remain passively receptive of the images cast upon it. Although the differentiating energies proceeding from the One through the orders of Intelligence and animation become increasingly composite and less pure, their power to cast successive reflections upon the more diffuse states of existence derives from, and manifests itself as, form. The composite, existent thing is what it is because of the generating vitality of its informing principles of unity, intellection, and arrangement. This great emphasis upon form as the manifestation of being in the realm of becoming easily turns into an emphasis upon the formal principles in those artistic theories which had always regarded the arts as imposing form upon a recalcitrant material (cf. 1.6.3, 3.3.6, 5.8.1).[25]

A third and most important reason for the Neoplatonic encouragement of formalism lies, perhaps, in the concept of purification. As one strips away the material components of composite things, he returns, form by purer form, to the source of all form, the purity—undelimited itself by

[25] A. H. Armstrong comments that it is true for Plotinus that "the forms in matter are ghostly and sterile, not truly real but only the remotest reflections of the true realities in the world of Intellect. . . . But Plotinus is so concerned to stress the absolute unreality of matter that he makes it very clear that everything observable in the material universe, including its spatiality and corporeality—everything, that is, except its necessary imperfection—is form, not matter, and all activity in it is the activity of soul; and form and soul as such are good," *CHLGP*, pp. 230–31. In addition, Bréhier's distinctions between the Aristotelian and Plotinian conception of form are most helpful. Whereas for Aristotle form combines with matter to make a single concrete thing, for Plotinus form, "allowing itself to be seduced by the image of itself offered to it by matter, unites with this image in withdrawing itself from the ground of its own reality." Matter itself has too little existence and is too indeterminable to unite with form, which passes over it "like a reflection without leaving any traces." With matter remaining spectral beneath it, form alone, as the agent of the soul, offers an apprehensible consistency to the sensible world (*The Philosophy of Plotinus*, pp. 174–75).

any form—of the One. This process of reversion and reconcentration eliminates gradually all that is not formal—all, that is, which would normally concern the cognitive and judicative intentions of the literary analysis of experience. As we shall see, the contemplative activity of *gnosis* completely predominates over the ethical concerns of *praxis*. But *gnosis* in no sense is to be confused with the heuristic activity of philosophical discourse which has all knowledge as its object. The objective of *gnosis* is to learn and teach others how to turn away from the objects of knowledge, especially from those objects whose nature must be grasped by discursive reasoning. The ultimate objective of *gnosis* is a condition of catharsis rather than of cognition. Although this ultimate purity admits no formal predication, its very formlessness is formalistic in that it expresses a negation of all specific content. Purity is the only form, that is, sufficiently undetermined to express a reality whose power to determine itself is infinite. Any formal or existential delimitation would, of necessity, have already impaired this power to differentiate itself into composite things.[26]

This conception of 'negative form' is, to be sure, an ontological rather than an artistic principle. When extended to the arts, however, it could offer a metaphysical justification of nonobjective representation in painting and of nondiscursive methods of composition in literature. From the eighteenth century on, for instance, literary symbols have been increasingly associated with the expression of 'purity'—the *pureté* of French poetic theory—which could be achieved through the elimination of denotative reference and of the coherent structure of logical propositions. The stylistic attempts to obscure or conceal completely the external comprehensibility of the object through enigmatic juxtaposition in order to release and represent an inner, intuited source of informing energy have been particularly prevalent in twentieth-century aesthetic attitudes. The fact that this intuited formal energy, real or imaginary, has often been regarded as a spontaneous artistic force working autonomously within, and often in spite of, the passive artist has precedent, as well, in the Plotinian analysis of productive activity.

Everything that is produced either by nature or by art is made by some form of wisdom.

[26] For a discussion of Neoplatonic purification, see H. E. Barnes, "Katharsis in the *Enneads* of Plotinus," *TAPA* 73 (1942):358–82. It is only through our purification that true knowledge of the highest realities can be grasped, just as living gold could come to know itself only when its impurities were stripped away (4.7.10). The differences of Plotinian from Socratic and Stoic conceptions of self-knowledge, as stated by Bréhier, clearly reflect this emphasis on *gnosis* over *praxis* (*The Philosophy of Plotinus*, pp. 107–108). See pp. 238–39 of this study.

No doubt the wisdom of the artist may be the guide of the work; it is sufficient explanation of the wisdom exhibited in the arts; but the artist himself goes back, after all, to that wisdom in Nature which is embodied in himself; and this is not a wisdom built up of theorems but one totality, not a wisdom consisting of manifold detail co-ordinated into a unity but rather a unity working out into detail.

If we trace the source of this wisdom back through the artist, Nature, and the Soul, we shall find that it derives ultimately from the Intellectual Principle in the second hypostasis of existence and the Intelligible Forms. The wisdom of the divine Beings of that sphere does not consist of scientific propositions but is immediately self-evident as an existent thing (5.8.5). So in the higher orders of the cosmic Soul, where wisdom is eternal and integral, there is no place for reasoning or calculation. Although the products of the Soul are various, there is no reason to assume that the psychic powers which produce them are diverse. "On the contrary, the more varied the product, the more certain the unchanging identity of the producer" (4.4.11). Just because the lower orders of the Soul, which manifest themselves as Nature, produce a multiplicity of forms, one should not think that production occurs through deliberative reasoning. Reasoning is an act of seeking and learning, but the Soul knows and does not seek or run into perplexities in its creation (4.4.12). Nature herself, unlike the geometer, contemplates her forms directly into existence without the need of intermediary instruments, diagrams, or deductive demonstration (3.8.3–4).

We are not to think that the Soul acts upon the object by conformity to any external judgement; there is no pause for willing or planning: any such procedure would not be an act of sheer nature, but one of applied art: but art is of later origin than soul; it is an imitator, producing dim and feeble copies—toys, things of no great worth—and it is dependent upon all sorts of mechanism by which alone its images can be produced.[27]

---

[27] The original of this passage (ἡ [ψυχῆς] δὲ ποιεῖ οὐκ ἐπακτῷ γνώμῃ, οὐδὲ βουλὴν ἢ σκέψιν ἀναμείνασα· οὕτω γὰρ ἂν οὐ κατὰ φύσιν, ἀλλὰ κατ' ἐπακτὸν τέχνην ἂν ποιοῖ. Τέχνη γὰρ ὑστέρα αὐτῆς, καὶ μιμεῖται ἀμυδρὰ καὶ ἀσθενῆ ποιοῦσα μιμήματα, παίγνια ἄττα καὶ οὐ πολλοῦ ἄξια, μηχαναῖς πολλαῖς εἰς εἰδώλων φύσιν προσχρωμένη, 4.3.10, 14–19) seems to be indebted to Plato's Laws 889B–90D and especially to echo 889CD: "As a later product of these [nature and chance or their products], art comes later; and it, being mortal itself and of mortal birth, begets later playthings which share but little in truth, being images of a sort akin to the arts themselves—images such as painting begets, and music, and the arts which accompany these" (τέχνην δὲ ὕστερον ἐκ τούτων ὑστέραν γενομένην, αὐτὴν θνητὴν ἐκ θνητῶν, ὕστερα γεγεννηκέναι παιδιάς τινας ἀληθείας οὐ σφόδρα μετεχούσας, ἀλλὰ εἴδωλ' ἄττα ξυγγενῆ ἑαυτῶν, οἷ' ἡ γραφικὴ γεννᾷ καὶ μουσικὴ καὶ ὅσαι ταύταις εἰσὶ συνέριθοι τέχναι). R. G. Bury—whose Plato: The Laws, LCL, 2 vols. (London, 1968) I have just cited—notes that those whom Plato is criticizing here for belittling the arts and "convention" (νόμος) are Archelaus and his followers. The matter is worth comment because, when it comes to the arts, Plotinus takes an anti-Platonic position in

Only in the more extended stages of the Soul, as manifested in our present life, must art contend with the parts of a whole whose previous unity required no art to maintain it (4.3.10).

Reasoning begins with the descent of the soul into the body. "It is the act of the Soul fallen into perplexity, distracted with cares, diminished in strength: the need of deliberation goes with the less self-sufficing intelligence; craftsmen faced by a difficulty stop to consider; where there is no problem, their art works on by its own forthright power." This forthright, almost unconscious, power of art, Plotinus implies, is a reflection of that activity of the higher souls which "flows uninterruptedly from the Intellectual-Principle." This activity there employs no words and deliberates over none of the doubts and difficulties which plague us here. It falls into place by sheer force of its nature, without compulsion or conformity; having no need of speech, it knows and is known by sight alone (4.3.18).

Plotinus seems to conceive of art as another form of radiating energy which is more immediately effective in the higher orders, less effective as it reaches the more fragmentary extensions of our lives. Within our lives, it is implied, art realizes its greatest potentiality when it reflects, even imitates, the autonomous spontaneity of these orders which are free from unrest and the need of rational control. The stone of the statue becomes beautiful in the artist's hand "in virtue of the Form or Idea introduced by the art."

This form is not in the material; it is in the designer before ever it enters the stone; and the artificer holds it not by his equipment of eyes and hands but by his participation in his art. The beauty, therefore, exists in a far higher state in the art; for it does not come over integrally into the work; that original beauty is not transferred; what comes over is a derivative and a minor: and even that shows itself upon the statue not integrally and with entire realization of intention but only in so far as it has subdued the resistance of the material. (5.8.1)

The beauty of the art itself precedes the artist's conception of a beautiful work and enters into the statue, not in accordance with the artist's intention (οἷον ἐβούλετο) but with how much the stone will yield to art (ὅσον εἶξεν ὁ λίθος τῇ τέχνῃ).

---

the philosophical controversy which offers a context for the literary debate of nature (*ingenium*) vs. art (*ars*). (For the relation of Plato's passage to Horace's defense of *misera ars* over vatic inspiration in *A.P.* 295–97, see HASD, p. 72, n. 53.) The fact that the chief representative of Neoplatonism takes a position antithetical to Plato's (and Longinus') on such inclusive issues as those of the value of reason, its function in the arts, and art itself is important for the history of literary theory. Plotinus here anticipates again Proclus' preference for 'entheastic' over 'paideutic' representation (see Chap. 8, n. 10), and this preference is founded in part on a deterministic view of nature and artistic activity.

Art, then, creating in the image of its own nature and content, and working by the Idea or Reason-Principle of the beautiful object it is to produce, must itself be beautiful in a far higher and purer degree since it is the seat and source of that beauty, indwelling in the art, which must naturally be more complete than any comeliness of the external. In the degree in which the beauty is diffused by entering into matter, it is so much the weaker than that concentrated in unity; everything that reaches outwards is the less for it, strength less strong, heat less hot, every power less potent, and so beauty less beautiful.

These passages clearly imply the artist's passivity. The less conscious interference he offers, the less derived and diffused the beauty will be in the object. Discursive reason is to concern itself only with technical problems, and these problems are, at best, but impoverishing distractions.[28]

The fact that "the art exhibited in the material work derives from an art yet higher" is in complete agreement with Plotinus' metaphysical system. It is only in accord with this system that he immediately goes on to make the influential qualification which has been cited out of context as a direct answer to Plato's criticism of imitation.

Still the arts are not to be slighted on the ground that they create by imitation of natural objects; for, to begin with, these natural objects are themselves imitations; then, we must recognize that they [the arts] give no bare reproduction of the thing seen but go back to the Reason-Principles from which Nature itself derives, and, furthermore, that much of their work is all their own; they are holders of beauty and add where nature is lacking. Thus Pheidias wrought the Zeus upon no model among things of sense but by apprehending what form Zeus must take if he chose to become manifest to sight. (5.8.1)[29]

This concession to imitation is little more than a link in a metaphysical system where even matter can be said to be "gripped by the Forms of the Intellectual Realm" and "held by the Ideas of the elements" (5.8.7).

[28] These passages on art reflect Plotinus' more general attitude toward the consciousness itself, which becomes more effective the less we are aware of it. "Conscious awareness, in fact, is likely to enfeeble the very activities of which there is consciousness; only when they are alone are they pure and more genuinely active and living" (1.4.10). He gives the example of the reader who "is not necessarily aware that he is reading, least of all when he is really concentrating." See Armstrong's article in *JHS* 93 (1973):13–22 cited in this chapter, n. 16, esp. pp. 14–17.

[29] In contrast, Philostratus had said that the imagination of Pheidias might grasp the form of Zeus by 'presupposing' what it had not seen with reference to existing things (see Chap. 6, pp. 103–104, and n. 6). Such an assumption reflects an earlier Greek view. W. Jaeger, commenting on the theology of the Milesian naturalists, remarks that Zeus "does not belong to the realm of things that meet the senses; and beyond that realm we cannot go. Even if we recognize that eyes and ears do not reach very far, and that imagination travels immeasurable distances beyond the bounds of direct perception, the ὄντα that imagination finds will always be of the same sort as the things that present themselves to the senses, or at least very similar." *The Theology of the Early Greek Philosophers* (Oxford, 1967), p. 19. On the concept of "really existent things (τὰ ὄντα)," see Jaeger, ibid., p. 197, n. 2.

In the first place, the concession occurs as a final and sole qualification in an argument which had come to the point of virtually denying any beauty to mimetic works of art. To quote the concession out of context is to see it in a more positive light than Plotinus would have himself. Imitative arts like painting, sculpture, and pantomime were, for him, sensory imitations of movements, forms, and symmetries of our world which discursive reason alone, with all its indirection, might relate to a more unified reality through habit (ἕξις) and observation (5.9.11). Secondly, there is really no way for the artist to make the higher reality inform, and manifest itself in, the works he produces except by drawing it down, as it were, by some form of sympathetic magic. But art, we must remember, is neither a form of magic nor of mysticism nor of religion. It originates in the capacity of the human mind itself to understand and represent its experience. That experience may, of course, include the magical, the mystical, or the religious, but the art which represents these is a function of the intuitive and discursive resources of the human understanding. When the artist rejects Plotinus' first reciprocating (mimetic) form of likeness for his second nonreciprocating (symbolic) form, he is in danger of abandoning his conscious control over his medium and of becoming the passive transmitter of the powers he invokes. The consequences for decorum are greater in the literary than in the visual arts.[30]

4. *Decorum: Quality, Praxis, and Power.* We may conclude these remarks on Plotinus by considering what place a concept of literary decorum might hold in his metaphysical system. To do this, it will be useful to recall Aristotle's general division of comparative relation into arithmetical and geometrical types of proportion. He calls the second type, which is more adaptable to the analysis of qualities, analogical

[30] It is worth mentioning that Plotinus' attitudes toward art, albeit that he seems to have developed them to conform with his metaphysical system, often correspond to theses popularly debated on both sides of the question by the rhetoricians of the preceding centuries. In his speech "To Plato: In Defence of Oratory," for instance, Aristides first argues the thesis that artistic excellence is entirely due to nature, not at all to art, and that, therefore, Plato could not attack rhetoric effectively by simply saying that it was not an art. Subsequently, Aristides argues the opposite position—that rhetoric is, indeed, an art and that art is most valuable. The ingenious, and probably ironic, arguments in behalf of untaught natural genius whose inspiration can only be corrupted by art anticipate Plotinus' disparagement of the imitative arts as capable only of producing trifles (4.3.10). 'Artistic' beauty, says Aristides, comes not from clever art but from divine inspiration (88), and quite a few details of his argument would probably have been congenial to the Neoplatonists (esp. in 48–127). (A. Sheppard makes a similar observation with respect to Aristides and Proclus in her study [pp. 131–32] discussed below in n. 36.) In fact, the entire debate foreshadows, in its terms and issues, the arguments in the eighteenth century over reason vs. experience, education vs. creativity, civic sophistication vs. primitive innocence, all of which are related to the antithesis of art vs. nature.

proportion and then observes further, in a passage quoted earlier, that while arguments by analogy (κατ' ἀναλογίαν) signify similarity (ὅμοιον) in quality (ποιῷ), they signify equality (ἴσον) in quantity (ποσῷ). In proportional correspondences qualities are (more or less) similar to qualities, magnitudes equal (or unequal) to magnitudes.[31] In discussing the distributions of Providence, Plotinus is careful to describe the "correspondences" between degrees of existence throughout the universe in terms of analogical rather than arithmetical proportions. With respect to the two types of analogy itself, however, despite his lack of enthusiasm for Plato's mathematical descriptions of existence, Plotinus expresses the relations between the parts of the universe and the whole more in quantitative ratios of equality than in qualitative degrees of similarity. This practice is consistent with his preference for the second (nonreciprocal) likeness, appropriate to symbolism, over the first (reciprocal) likeness, appropriate to mimesis.

For Aristotle (1412a5–12), the proportional metaphor (ἡ κατ' ἀναλογίαν μεταφορά) expresses similarity (τὸ ὅμοιον), and such similarities, as Socrates points out to Cratylus (431D–32E), are appropriate to images and discourse which concern quality. All the qualitative arts, in fact, seek to attain "due measure" by establishing their standard of measurement in relation to the mean rather than to the extremes relevant to the quantitative greatness and smallness of their objects (Statesman, 283D–84E). Plotinus, on the other hand, describes the corresponding progressions of reality by analogies expressing quantities of power in relation to quantities of magnitude. The cosmos, even when stripped of its material nature, should appear like

An intelligible sphere embracing the form imposed upon the universe, [consisting of] souls in their order which without bodies give magnitude and advance to dimension according to the intelligible pattern, so that what has come into being may become equal, to the extent of its power, by its magnitude to the partlessness of its archetype: for greatness in the intelligible world is in power, here below in bulk.

Even when embodied, the Soul of the universe possesses "that amount of power with which it made the nature of body, not beautiful in itself, to share in beauty as far as it was possible for it to be beautified" (2.9.17). The infinite quantity of force in the One turns into relative quantities of magnitude in the manifold world according to proportional (κατ' ἀναλογίαν), as opposed to simple arithmetical, distribution.

[31] See pp. 173–75 of this study. Plutarch echoes the terms of Aristotle's subdivision in the various connections he draws in Quaest. conviv. 8.2.4 (Mor. 720AB).

Providence, then, which in its descent from above reaches from the beginning to the end, is not equal (ἴση) as in a numerical distribution (κατ᾽ ἀριθμόν) but differs in different places according to a law of correspondence (κατ᾽ ἀναλογίαν), just as in a single living creature, which is dependent on its principle down to its last and lowest part, each part having its own, the better part having the better part of the activity, and that which is at the lower limit still active in its own way and undergoing the experiences which are proper to it as regards its own nature and its co-ordination with anything else. (3.3.5)[32]

Such correspondences hold all things together: "the worse is related to the worse as the better is to the better, for instance, as eye is to eye, so is foot to foot, the one to the other; or, if you like, as virtue is to justice, so is vice to injustice" (3.3.6).

For the gathering together of all things into one is the principle, in which all are together and all make a whole. And individual things proceed from this principle while it remains within; they come from it as from a single root which remains static in itself, but they flower out into a divided multiplicity, each one bearing an image (εἴδωλον) of that higher reality, but when they reach this lower world one comes to be in one place and one in another, and some are

---

[32] This passage, and more especially the following quotation from 3.3.6 as Bréhier and Armstrong note, seem to allude to *Tim.* 31C–32C. When Plotinus distinguishes his "law of correspondences" from arithmetic proportion, however, he is not simply invoking the geometric proportion of mathematics, but also a distinction between two types of equality distinguished by Plato and Aristotle in the distribution of justice and political power. In the *Laws* (757BC), Plato says the first type, proceeding by arithmetical proportion, would simply distribute portions equally to each person, while the second, proceeding by geometrical proportion, would dispense more to the greater and more worthy and less to the lesser and less worthy. "Giving due measure to each according to nature," the second type, the way of Zeus, "assigns in proportion what is fitting (τὸ πρέπον) to each" (cf. 744C and *Gorgias* 465BC, 508AB). In the *Nicomachean Ethics* (5.2.12–13, 5.3.6–17, 5.4.2–3; 8.7.3) Aristotle distinguishes (communal) distribution of justice from (private) correction by justice, the first dispensed according to geometric proportion, the second according to arithmetic proportion. Here, as in the *Politics* (3.5.8, 5.1.6–7), the distribution of equal portions to each person is contrasted with distribution according to worth (κατ᾽ ἀξίαν) of each to the community. In describing the distributions of 'powers' by Providence, Plotinus seems to be drawing most heavily on these political uses of analogy or upon a conflation, perhaps, of the political (*Laws* 757BC) and the cosmic (*Tim.* 31C–32C) uses such as appears in Plutarch's "Convivial Question" (8.2) cited in the preceding note: "What Plato meant by saying that God is always doing geometry." Proclus, in his *In Platonis Timaeum Commentaria* (ed. E. Diehl, 3 vols. [Amsterdam, 1965], 2.18.20–2.20.9, and trans. A. J. Festugière, *Proclus: Commentaire sur le Timée*, 5 vols. [Paris, 1967], 2.41–43), carefully distinguishes between arithmetic, geometric, and harmonic proportions and says that each type comes into existence by departing from equality. Unlike Plotinus' emphasis upon analogical correspondences, Proclus later describes the relation between the stages of descent of divine power from gradation to gradation as arithmetical (κατ᾽ ἀριθμόν, *In Plat. Rem. Pub. Comm.* 1.113.26), which may indicate an increasing tendency toward quantification in Neoplatonic thought. When Proclus speaks of analogical correspondences, on the other hand, they are tightly linked to a logic of genus and species: see *Elements of Theology*, Prop. 108 and p. 277 of Dodds' commentary.

close to the root and others advance farther and split up to the point of becoming, so to speak, branches and twigs and fruits and leaves. (3.3.7)

The quantitative nature of Plotinian analogy lies not, of course, in the 'geometric' form of its proportions but in the fact that they express relations between quantities of force and causation. Magnitudes relate to one another proportionally to their distance from the One, to their diversification of unity, to their temporal extension of simultaneity, and to their differentiated realization of pure potentiality. No matter how vividly sensory Plotinus' descriptions of related things appear to be, the relations as logical ratios remain spectral and disembodied.

The unity of the One manifests itself not as extension but as power. Coherence lies not in mass but in force.

We must therefore take the Unity as infinite not in measureless extension or numerable quantity but in fathomless depths of power. (6.9.6)

As this power becomes 'quantified' in extended magnitudes, its substantial energies are dissipated as qualities reflected in composite things.

In the intelligible world all qualities, as we call them, must be assumed to be activities (ἐνεργείας), taking their qualitativeness from the way we think about them, because each and every one of them is an individual characteristic, that is, they mark off the substances in relation to each other and have their own individual character in relation to themselves.

Heat, for instance, is an activity rather than a quality of fire, but when it is isolated in something else, it is "no longer a shape of substance but only a trace (ἴχνος), a shadow (σκιάν), an image (εἰκόνα), abandoning its substance, of which it was an activity (ἐνέργεια), to be a quality (ποιότητα)." Only that which has fallen away (ἐκπεσόν) from being a form and an activity to being an incidental attribute can be regarded as pure quality (2.6.3). If we concern ourselves too much with such qualities in our investigation of substantial reality, we will become lost in random distraction (2.6.2).

As in extended magnitudes the principle of unity is power, so in things appropriately judged in accordance with qualities the principle of unity is a 'quantity' of formal energy derived from substantial activity. Both principles of unity are quantitative standards of degrees of force rather than qualitative standards of degrees of resemblance. If qualities are only residual reflections of dissipated activities, they can offer no reliable common property for establishing similarity. The appropriate arts can no longer measure their objects by the fluid balance of the 'mean,' as Plato and Aristotle describe it, but only by the fixed quantities established in relation to the extremes. For power, which is calibrated on a single scale of more and less, expresses in its extended proportional magnitudes the only relation of the parts to the whole: power becomes, in a word, the principle of decorum itself.

The term 'decorum' (τὸ πρέπον), which occurs most frequently, perhaps, in Plotinus' discussion of Providence (πρόνοια), has for him primarily an ontological, rather than an artistic, meaning.

For there is fitness (τὸ πρέπον) and beauty in the whole only if each individual is stationed where he ought to be—the one who utters evil sounds in darkness and Tartarus: for there to make these sounds is beautiful; and this whole is beautiful, not if each is Linus but if each by contributing his own sound helps towards the perfection of a single melody, himself, too, sounding the note of life, but a lesser, worse, and more incomplete life; just as in a pan-pipe there is not one note only but a note which is weaker and duller contributes to the melody of the whole pan-pipe, because the melody is divided into parts which are not equal, and all the notes of the pipe are unequal, but the melody is complete, made up of all. (3.2.17)

Parts which are unequal, unnatural, or unharmonious in themselves may well be beautifully disposed according to the nature of the whole.

To explain the necessary existence of partial evils to ensure the good of the whole, Plotinus elaborates a comparison between the maker of the cosmos and the maker of a play and then abandons it for the musical analogy introduced previously. The formal principle, deriving from the complete and single Intellect, manifests itself in our composite world not as a whole but in parts which are often antithetical to one another and in conflict. Yet, despite their conflict, these parts ultimately form one structure as "the plot of the play is one though it contains in itself many battles." Most significant, perhaps, is Plotinus' reason for finding the comparison based on literary decorum inadequate.

Of course, the play brings the conflicting elements into a kind of harmonious concordance, by composing the complete story of the persons in conflict; but in the universe the battle of conflicting elements springs from a single rational principle; so that it would be better for one to compare it to the melody (ἁρμονία) which results from conflicting sounds, and one will then enquire why there are the conflicting sounds in the rational proportions [of musical scales].

As Isocrates attempted to present a totally coordinated image of his thought and life in the *Antidosis*, the dramatist, here, might resolve the tensions in his 'plot' by "composing the complete story of the persons in conflict." But such a resolution would inadequately represent the cosmic harmony precisely because it would not preserve the tensions between the parts in conflict. These tensions are necessary because the whole "should be one pattern made out of opposites (ἐξ ἐναντίων), since it is opposition of this kind which gives it its structure" and existence.

Since it [the whole] is rational pattern it has distinctions in itself, and the extreme distinction is opposition (ἐναντίωσις); so that if in general it makes one thing different from another, it will also make them different in the extreme, and not different in a lesser degree; so by making one thing different from another in the highest degree it will necessarily make the opposites (τὰ ἐναντία), and will be complete if it makes itself not only into different things but into opposite things. (3.2.16)

The entire conception of a harmony of opposites leads naturally to an emphasis upon the juxtaposition of quantitative extremes relative to one another rather than to an emphasis upon 'due measure.'

The more differentiated nature becomes, the more opposed its individual parts become to one another and the more the interests of particular men come into conflict. There will be, nevertheless, as in the play mentioned previously, a place in the cosmic drama for men fit (πρέπων) for either good or evil roles.

Each place is fitted to their characters, so as to be in tune with the rational principle of the universe, since each individual is fitted in, according to justice, in the parts of the universe designed to receive him; just as each string is set in its own proper place according to the rational proportion which governs the sounding of notes, of whatever quality its power of producing a note is. (3.2.17)[33]

The abandonment of the literary for the musical analogy again suggests a conception of decorum as an exactly measurable proportion—a measurement, that is, based upon relative extremes. In fact, the conception of decorum as the relation of discordant fragments to one another in their procession from, and return to, the unity of the One has severed most of its connections with the Aristotelian mean (μεσότης) in ethics and with the psychagogic control in artistic representation.

Plotinus recognizes the power of literature to sway the mind (4.4.31) as well as the (somewhat questionable) value of art generally to force us to give serious attention to our way of life (2.3.18). Yet these artistic effects have traditionally concerned prudential action (πρᾶξις) rather than contemplation (γνῶσις), the qualitative disposition of emotion rather than the purification of all emotional commitments. For Plotinus, on

[33] The concept of suitability (τὸ πρέπον) in the extended dramatic and musical metaphors in this section (3.2.17) is clearly related to both Plato's cosmic (*Tim.* 31C–32C) and Aristotle's judicial or legislative (*E.N.* 5.2–4, *Pol.* 5.1.6–7) discussions of nonarithmetical distribution. Plotinus is speaking both of the cosmic justice in placing men of unequal moral worth in different locations and, in thus granting them honors unequally, of the establishment of universal harmony. His whole discussion of decorum in these passages (3.2.14–17) seems to reflect Cicero's *De officiis* 1.96–98.

the other hand, such action and feeling become shadowy substitutes for contemplation and reasoning for men who are too weak to grasp the vision of simpler realities. Longing to grasp this vision, they are carried into action for the same reason that, in the arts, they want to make objects in order to see them.

Everywhere we shall find that making and action are either a weakening or a consequence of contemplation; a weakening, if the doer or maker had nothing in view beyond the thing done, a consequence if he had another prior object of contemplation better than what he made. For who, if he is able to contemplate what is truly real will deliberately go after its image? (3.8.4)

Everything, in fact, which draws us away from 'reality' and entangles us in worldly cares is a kind of bewitchment.

What we look to, draws us magically. Only the self-intent go free of magic. Hence every action has magic as its source, and the entire life of the practical man is a bewitchment: we move to that only which has wrought a fascination upon us. . . . For what conceivably turns a man to the external? He is drawn, drawn by the arts not of magicians but of the natural order which administers the deceiving draught and links this to that, not in local contact but in the fellowship of the philtre. (4.4.43)

"Contemplation alone stands untouched by magic," while marriage and children (the baits of desire) along with the activities motivated by gain, political power, and security—as well as by the necessities resulting from natural insufficiencies—all of these subscribe to "the cajoling force of nature." Actions done with the recollection that the good lies elsewhere, to be sure, elude bewitchment, but those who, forgetting this, pursue lesser goods are victims of magical attractions toward unreality.

The sorcery of Nature is at work in this; to pursue the non-good as a good, drawn in unreasoning impulse by its specious appearance: it is to be led un-knowing down paths unchosen; and what can we call that but magic? Alone in immunity from magic is he who, though drawn by the alien parts of his total being, withholds his assent to their standards of worth, recognizing the good only where his authentic self sees and knows it, neither drawn nor pursuing, but tranquilly possessing and so never charmed away. (4.4.44)

All the ordinary world of practical experience, of human life and action, which contains the primary subject matter of literature and the visual arts, falls under the sorcerer's control. Insofar as the artist deals with this world, he is a magician, and the 'charm' of decorum, insofar as it reflects 'due measure' in the traditional sense, can only impede—by helping us to adjust to our intermediate, composite environment (τὸ μεταξύ)—the purification of our enchantment.

In conclusion, I can only reiterate the fact that I have tried here to isolate those presuppositions and doctrines of Plotinus which can be shown to have subsequently influenced literary theory. Such an isolation can do little justice to his metaphysical system as a whole and is, in addition, unfair in that the arts were not really his concern. Most of all it fails to give any idea of the consistent intensity, the resilient dignity, and the pervasive optimism of his total conception. His love for a world which he is persuaded we must all leave as soon as possible appears again and again as a haunting paradox. In the midst of his discussion of worldly sorceries, he can say with resignation that "under duress of human nature, and in the spirit of adaptation to the needs of existence . . . it certainly seems reasonable to fit oneself into life rather than to withdraw from it" (4.4.44). In its appreciation of the physical universe, his criticism of the Gnostics (2.9), when taken in the context of his intellectual commitments, is one of the most moving affirmations of life in late antiquity.[34] But, despite this emotional complexity, we have paid dearly for the pathos that we feel within the system. We can see something of the nature of this price by turning to Proclus, who builds upon Plotinian assumptions in formulating his interpretation of literature.

B. Proclus

Perhaps the most striking contribution which Proclus makes to the Neoplatonic tradition is his recasting of its eclectic materials into a coherent system of axiomatic propositions. While his exegetical commentaries and his *Platonic Theology* retain a looser, even digressive, structure, he constructs his *Elements of Theology* with the deductive strictness of Euclid's *Elements of Geometry*. He adds to the logical exposition of ontological realities, already latent in the Plotinian correspondences of force and magnitude, a precision akin to that of geometrical demonstration. If the weakness of the Neoplatonic system lies, as E. R. Dodds observes, in the "assumption that the structure of the cosmos exactly

---

[34] E. R. Dodds concludes his famous article, "The *Parmenides* of Plato and the Origin of the Neoplatonic 'One,' " *CQ* 22 (1928):129–42, with the following observations: "If anyone doubts that Plotinus was a man of genius, let him study the efforts of Plotinus' nearest predecessors and followers. Let him soak for a while in the theosophical maunderings of Philo and the Hermetists, in the venomous fanaticism of Tertullian, in the teatable transcendentalism of Plutarch, in the cultured commonplaces of Maximus, in the amiable pieties of Porphyry, in the really unspeakable spiritualistic drivellings of the *de Mysteriis*—let him do that, and if ever he gets his head above water again, he will see Plotinus in his true historical perspective as the one man who still knew how to think clearly in an age which was beginning to forget what thinking meant."

reproduces the structure of Greek logic,"[35] the delineations of such a universe will express themselves more readily and clearly in terms of quantitative proportions than of qualitative similarities. For Proclus, the logic of geometry could offer a paradigm against which to measure the coherence of all discursive disciplines, even of an art like poetry whose subject matter is human experience rather than mathematical relationship. Once all discursive reasoning, that is, has been reduced to geometrical reasoning, all other forms of cognitive and judicative, to say nothing of poetic, argumentation could either accommodate themselves to that of mathematics or appear to proceed on other than discursive principles. Two consequences of this reduction appear in Proclus' discussion of poetry.

First, the Neoplatonists describe their knowledge of both ontological and psychological realities in terms of logical proportions between unity and extension. The cognitive function of literary analysis, therefore, whose intention is to express this knowledge of the whole, will conform more easily to the Neoplatonic paradigm of mathematical propositions than the judicative function, whose intention is to judge individual situations which are parts of the whole. Proclus will discuss literature, that is, in terms of 'levels' of cognition whose objects are related to one another in terms of powers and magnitudes. Consequently, his defense of Homer, as a literary theory, reduces literature almost entirely to its formal and philosophical intentions—which become in the Neoplatonic system nearly identified with one another. Second, those experiences which must be analyzed discursively by methods of argumentation other than those conforming most to mathematical propositions become, along with their appropriate types of representation, less worthy of poetic treatment than those experiences whose analysis does conform to the geometrical paradigm. Since Proclus discusses the subjects and methods both of geometry and of poetry in terms analogous to those in the Platonic metaphor of the Divided Line, his treatment of the imagination in the *Commentary on the First Book of Euclid's Elements* throws valuable light on his treatment of mimetic and symbolic representation in

---

[35] *Proclus: The Elements of Theology*, trans. E. R. Dodds (Oxford, 1963), p. xxv. Dodds continues: "All rationalist systems are to some extent exposed to criticism on these lines; but in Proclus ontology becomes so manifestly the projected shadow of logic as to present what is almost a *reductio ad absurdum* of rationalism. In form a metaphysic of Being, the *Elements* embodies what is in substance a doctrine of categories: the cause is but a reflection of the 'because,' and the Aristotelian apparatus of genus, species and differentia is transformed into an objectively conceived hierarchy of entities or forces." Perhaps with such Plotinian observations in mind as "from one single Soul many and different souls proceed, as higher and lower species proceed from a single genus" (4.8.3, quoted from Bréhier's *The Philosophy of Plotinus*, p. 68), Dodds later remarks that so much in Proclus "is but the hardening into an explicit law of what is implicit in Plotinus" (pp. 269–70).

his *Commentary on the Republic*. Before showing the close relation of poetry to geometry, and thereby the strong Neoplatonic contribution to literary formalism, I shall review Plato's metaphor, already described in Chapter 2, so that the reader may have it freshly in mind.[36]

Plato represents the degree of intelligibility among apprehensible entities by gradations on a perpendicular line. He divides this scale by a horizontal line which separates intelligible entities (νοητόν) above the line from visible entities (ὁρατόν) below it. He then subdivides each of these divisions into two. The resulting four categories correspond to a hierarchy of entities, based upon the degree of clarity and certainty with which they can be known. This scale begins with the lower subdivision of the visible objects and rises to the higher subdivision of intelligible objects. The lowest category is composed of images (εἰκόνες), the objects of conjecture (εἰκασία), such as shadows (σκιάς) and reflections (φαντάσματα) on water and "on surfaces of dense, smooth and bright texture." The second consists of actual objects, animate and inanimate, which have the power to cast such reflections and which form the material of belief (πίστις) or opinion (δόξα). These two categories include all visible entities. The third and fourth categories contain intelligible entities. The third has the same relation to the second as the second to the first; that is, it casts as its images those objects of the second category

---

[36] Proclus' categorization of the generic 'kinds' of poetry, like so much of Plato's discussion of imitation, accommodates itself readily to the four levels of the Divided Line (*In Plat. Rem Pub. Comm.* 1.191.26–29): "It is in this way, then, that Plato has thought good also to divide up the kinds of poetry (γένη τῆς ποιητικῆς): one as being superior to scientific knowledge (ἐπιστήμης), the second as having such knowledge (ἐπιστημονικόν), the third as having responsible opinion (ὀρθοδοξαστικόν), and the fourth as being inferior to responsible opinion (τῆς ὀρθῆς δόξης ἀπολειπόμενον)." This accommodation of types of poetry to the categories of the Divided Line accounts more easily for the ultimate origins of Proclus' second, or "didactic," kind of poetry and for the fact that he makes his original three kinds of poetry into four than the more speculative alternatives suggested by one recent commentator (A. D. R. Sheppard, *Studies on the 5th and 6th Essays of Proclus' Commentary on the Republic*, Hypomnemata 61 [Göttingen, 1980]). The problem arises because of Proclus' elastic concept of the *nous*. As Sheppard says, he uses it "to cover both νοῦς and διάνοια" (p. 99), but he also associates it with the highest activity of the mind, which he describes as a reflection of the "one in the soul" or the summit of the soul or the *nous* itself (ἡ ἀκρότης τῆς ψυχῆς or τοῦ νοῦ, pp. 97–98). In either case, the lower part of the *nous* (*lato sensu*) is left to deal with the scientific activities of ἐπιστήμη. Proclus associates this lower part with "didactic" or "scientific" poetry in Homer, which treats the knowledge of things in accordance with understanding and prudence (ἐπιστήμονα τῶν ὄντων καὶ κατὰ νοῦν καὶ φρόνησιν ἐνεργοῦσαν, 1.186.23–24), and this knowledge corresponds exactly to that of Plato's second category of the Divided Line appropriate to διάνοια. The separation of this second type of poetry from the first, with regard to subject matter, corresponds, then, to the division of Plato's two categories above the Line from one another. The discrimination of mimetic representation into eicastic and fantastic imitation corresponds even more clearly to the division between Plato's two categories below the Line. It is not so much a matter here of variations in terminology describing the faculties of the soul as it is of similarities between what those faculties are to treat.

which, in turn, cast their images to form the objects of the lowest category. The third category, which includes the objects of mathematics and deductive reasoning, is under the control of the understanding (διά-νοια). The fourth category consists of first principles, the objects of reason (νοῦς), which, independent of the sensory images still necessary for dianoetic demonstration, works dialectically with ideas alone. The four faculties "participate in clearness (σαφηνείας) and precision in the same degree as their objects partake of truth (ἀληθείας) and reality" (511E). If we apply Plato's metaphor to Aristotle's two types of intelligibility, objects below the line will be prior and clearer with respect to our perception of them (ἡμῖν), however illusory they may be; objects above the line will be prior and clearer with respect to themselves (ἁπλῶς), however difficult to perceive. For Proclus, geometry is the discipline which can best negotiate discursively between the two realms.

1. *The Commentary on Euclid's* Elements. Proclus opens his prologue to his commentary on Euclid by stating that "mathematical being necessarily belongs neither among the first nor among the last and least simple of the kinds of being, but occupies the middle ground (μέσην χώραν) between partless realities—simple (ἁπλῶν), incomposite, and indivisible—and divisible things characterized by every variety (ποικίλαις) of composition and differentiation."

The unchangeable, stable, and incontrovertible character of the propositions about it shows that it is superior to the kinds of things that move about in matter. But the discursiveness (διεξοδικόν) of [mathematical] procedure, its dealing with its subjects as extended, and its setting up of different prior principles for different objects—these give to mathematical being a rank below that indivisible nature that is completely grounded in itself. (p. 3)[37]

Proclus proceeds to designate the highest, the intermediate, and the lowest types of being as objects of knowledge proper to particular faculties in terms analogous to those of Plato's divided line (*Rep.* 511BE). As at first in his discussion of poetry, he represents the lowest type as including objects appropriate to the two Platonic categories below the line. To the highest, indivisible realities he assigns intellect, which discerns the intelligible with simplicity, immediacy, and purity. To the lowest, divisible things perceived by the senses he assigns opinion, which discerns truth

---

[37] *Proclus: A Commentary on the First Book of Euclid's Elements*, trans. G. R. Morrow (Princeton, 1970). All references will be to this translation and will be included in the text. The Greek words are cited from *In Primum Euclidis Elementorum Librum Commentarii*, ed. G. Freidlein (Leipzig, 1873). Although inferior as a discipline to theology, geometry offers us the best preparation for grasping the truth about the gods (Morrow, pp. 18–19).

obscurely. To the intermediate beings, such as the forms studied by mathematics, he assigns understanding (διάνοιαν). While second in rank to intellect, understanding is more perfect, more exact (ἀκριβε-στέρα), and purer (καθαρωτέρα) than opinion,

For it traverses (διεξοδεύει) and unfolds (ἀναπλοῖ) the measureless content of Nous by making articulate its concentrated intellectual insight, and then gathers together again the things it has distinguished and refers them back to Nous. (p. 3)

Mathematical objects, "and in general all the objects of the understanding," are, nevertheless, "only images (εἰκόνες), imitating in their divided fashion the indivisible and in their multiform fashion (πολυειδῶς) the uniform patterns (μονοειδῆ παραδείγματα) of being." They have not risen above the particularity, compositeness, and "the reality that belongs to likenesses (εἰκόσιν)." Nor have they "escaped from the soul's varied (ποικίλας) and discursive (διεξοδικάς) ways of thinking" appropriate to "the intermediate status (μεσότης) of mathematical genera and species" occupying the ground between things (τὸ μεταξύ) as yet undifferentiated and things already dispersed in the world of matter (p. 4). Since Proclus is commenting on a mathematical treatise, it is natural that mathematical objects should be those objects of the understanding principally in question. Yet throughout his discussion he implies, I feel, that mathematics is perhaps the art most capable of being a model for all the arts to follow in their negotiation between the poles of the ancient dilemma of knowledge and representation.[38]

In the "ordered cosmos of its ideas (διάκοσμον τῶν λόγων)," the science of geometry is "coextensive with all existing things, applies its reasoning to them all, and includes all their kinds in itself." In its highest ranges of vision it glimpses "the special properties of the divine orders and the powers of the intellectual forms" and reflects them for us in images (εἰκόνων) and figures (σχήματα) appropriate to the gods.

In the middle regions of knowledge it unfolds and develops the ideas (λόγους) that are in the understanding; it investigates their variety (ποικιλίαν), exhibiting

---

[38] These and the remaining passages of Proclus' Euclidean commentary discussed in relation to the representational arts might be profitably examined in the light of the Neoplatonic tendencies to equate the soul with 'Platonic mathematicals.' Too far-reaching to be summarized here, these tendencies are pointed out by J. Dillon, *The Middle Platonists 80 B.C. to A.D. 220* (Cornell, 1977), esp. pp. 48, 110–12, 263, 350, 409, and P. Merlan analyzes them in detail in *From Platonism to Neoplatonism* (The Hague, 1968). See esp. Chaps. 1 and 2, and later, pp. 83, 107–8 (where Merlan discusses Proclus' first prologue to his Euclidean commentary), 145–46, and 221–31. The reader should see, as well, the context of E. R. Dodds' remark that "with Speusippus we are already well started on the road to Neoplatonism" (p. 140) in his article on the *Parmenides* and the Neoplatonic One cited in n. 34 of this chapter.

their modes of existence and their properties, their similarities and differences; and the forms of figures shaped from them in imagination it comprehends within fixed boundaries and refers back to the essential being of the ideas. (p. 50)

In its lowest ranges of observation, geometry examines the "species of elementary perceptible bodies" and their natural powers in orders to explain "how their causes are contained in advance in its own ideas." If we regard the entire 'cosmic' structure of this science as a whole, then, we shall see that

It contains likenesses (εἰκόνας) of all intelligible kinds (νοητῶν) and paradigms (παραδείγματα) of sensible ones (αἰσθητῶν); but the forms of the understanding constitute its essence, and through this middle region (διὰ μέσων) it ranges upwards and downwards to everything that is or comes to be. (p. 50)

Nor does geometry simply describe this scale of being but offers "pictures of all the virtues (τῶν ἀρετῶν τὰς εἰκόνας)—intellectual, moral, and physical—and presents in due order all the forms of political constitution, showing from its own nature the variety of the revolutions they undergo" (p. 50). Such pictures express the figures of coherence which illuminate the universe and have their psychological extension in the images of the imagination.

Although every figure (σχῆμα) may be said to result from change produced in things "that are struck, or divided, or decreased, or added to, or altered in form or affected" in various other ways, this account, Proclus observes, is imprecise. Figures may be produced by art, as in sculpture, or by nature, as in either sublunary shapes or in the heavenly bodies—bodies which reflect in their motions the figures of super-celestial realities which exist unseen beyond them. The "ineffable figures of the gods" themselves, in turn, order these intelligible figures and impose unifying boundaries upon the descending cosmic hierarchy. Figure, thus, "begins above with the gods themselves and extends down to the lowest orders of beings, exhibiting even in them its derivation from the first of causes." We cannot say, therefore, "that figures in the sense world are produced by additions or subtractions or alterations."

For such incomplete processes could not contain the original and primary cause of their products. . . . Rather we shall posit that the causes mentioned are subservient to others in the process of generation and affirm that the end is defined for them by other and precedent causes. (pp. 109–12)

Prior, then, to the forms of sensory objects are the intelligible figures of divine ideas. Although we are moved by senses, we actually project, by means of the imagination, ideas within us which are "images of things other than themselves."

While the Nous has its own contents as its objects of knowledge which neither come from outside itself nor take on shape or figure, and while sensory perception has objects which are external to itself and constantly take on different forms, the imagination, "occupying the central position in the scale of knowing, is moved by itself to put forth what it knows." But because the imagination is inside the body, "when it draws its objects out of the undivided center of its life, it expresses them in the medium of division, extension, and figure."

For this reason everything that it thinks is a picture or a shape of its thought. It thinks the circle as extended, and although this circle is free of external matter, it possesses an intelligible matter provided by the imagination itself. This is why there is more than one circle in the imagination, as there is more than one circle in the sense world; for with extension there appear also differences in size and number among circles and triangles. (p. 42)

The circle in the understanding, however, is "one and simple (ἁπλοῦς) and unextended, and magnitude itself is without magnitude there, and figure without shape. . . . But the circle in imagination is divisible, formed, extended—not one only, but one and many, and not a form only, but a form in instances—whereas the circle in sensible things is inferior in precision, infected with straightness, and falls short of the purity of immaterial circles" (p. 43).

For the understanding contains the ideas but, being unable to see them when they are wrapped up, unfolds and exposes them and presents them to the imagination sitting in the vestibule; and in imagination, or with its aid, it explicates its knowledge of them, happy in their separation from sensible things and finding in the matter of imagination (φανταστὴν ὕλην) a medium apt for receiving its forms. Thus thinking in geometry occurs with the aid of the imagination. Its syntheses and divisions of the figures are imaginary; and its knowing, though on the way to understanding being, still does not reach it, since the understanding is looking at things outside itself. . . . But if it should ever be able to roll up its extensions and figures and view their plurality as a unity without figure, then in turning back to itself it would obtain a superior vision of the partless, unextended, and essential geometrical ideas that constitute its equipment. This achievement would itself be the perfect culmination of geometrical inquiry, truly a gift of Hermes, leading geometry out of Calypso's arms, so to speak, to more perfect intellectual insight and emancipating it from the pictures projected in imagination. (pp. 44-45)

Proclus evokes, here, the Neoplatonic allegorization of Odysseus' return to Ithaca as the turning around and return of the soul to the 'homeland' of the One. It is geometry itself which is to negotiate this hazardous journey from the images projected diagrammatically upon the 'screen' of the imagination back to their indivisible source in the Nous.[39]

As the ideas, which we project as images of things other than themselves, unfold within us, we understand through them "sensible things of which they are paradigms and intelligible and divine things of which they are likenesses." They reveal "the forms of the gods and the uniform (ἐνοειδῆ) boundaries of the universe by which the gods, without command, bring all things back to themselves and enclose them." The gods, who comprehend all shapes, have the power to generate them in things; Nature, to generate them in appearances; and the soul, only to 'generate' them in thought.

Therefore just as nature stands creatively above the visible figures, so the soul, exercising her capacity to know, projects on the imagination, as on a mirror, the ideas of the figures; and the imagination, receiving in pictorial form these impressions of the ideas within the soul, by their means affords the soul an opportunity to turn inward from the pictures and attend to herself.

It is as if "a man looking at himself in a mirror and marvelling at the power of nature and at his own appearance should wish to look upon himself directly and possess such a power as would enable him to become at the same time the seer and the object seen."

In the same way, when the soul is looking outside herself at the imagination, seeing the figures depicted there and being struck by their beauty and orderedness, she is admiring her own ideas from which they are derived; and though she adores their beauty, she dismisses it as something reflected and seeks her own beauty. She wants to penetrate within herself to see the circle and the triangle there, all things without parts and all in one another, to become one with what she sees and enfold their plurality, to behold the secret and ineffable figures in the inaccessible places and shrines of the gods, to uncover the unadorned divine beauty and see the circle more partless than any center, the triangle without extension, and every other object of knowledge that has regained unity. (pp. 112–13)

These striking passages articulate, in terms of mathematical figures and images, the progression of the unified symbol into the discontinuous intervals of narrative events and the subsequent reconcentration of those events back into symbol previously described by Plotinus.[40]

---

[39] Porphyry treats the allegory of Odysseus in *The Cave of the Nymphs*, ed. L. Westerink et al., in *Arethusa Monographs* 1 (Buffalo, 1969). Compare Plotinus: "We shall put out to sea, as Odysseus did, from the witch Circe or Calypso—as the poet says (I think with a hidden meaning)—and was not content to stay though he had delights of the eyes and lived among much beauty of sense" (1.6.8).

[40] J. Klein's observations on the development of mathematical symbols often have suggestive implications for the development of literary symbolism after the Renaissance, *Greek*

One of the most ingenious illustrations of these mathematical figures is Proclus' description of angles.

The angle is a symbol (σύμβολον) and a likeness (εἰκόνα), we say, of the coherence that obtains in the realm of divine things—of the orderliness that leads diverse things to unity, divided things to the indivisible, and plurality to conjunction and communion. For the angle functions as a bond between the several lines and planes, focussing magnitude upon the unextendedness of points and holding together every figure that is constructed by means of it. Hence the Oracles call these angular conjunctions (γωνιακὰς συμβολάς) the "bonds" of the figures, because of their resemblance to the constraining unities and couplings in the divine world by which things separated are joined to one another.

Circular lines which are ever bending back upon themselves are images of Nous and intelligible forms. A right angle is an "image of perfection, undeviating energy, intelligent limit and boundary," while obtuse and acute angles are "likenesses of indefinite change, irrelevant progression, differentiation, partition, and unlimitedness (τὸ ἄπειρον) in general" (pp. 104–7).

It is because of the "boundlessness" (ἀοριστία) of the imagination itself that geometry may employ a finite line hypothetically (ἐξ ὑποθέσεως) as a 'figure' for an infinite line required for a diagrammatic demonstration. The infinite can exist in the imagination but cannot be known by it, since in order to know infinity the imagination would have to give it form and limit which would render it finite. The infinite, then, must remain an "uncertain" object, and, in fact, the imagination "calls infinite all that it abandons, as immeasurable and incomprehensible to thought."

Just as sight recognizes darkness by the experience of not seeing, so imagination recognizes the infinite by not understanding it. It produces it indeed, because it has an indivisible power of proceeding without end, and it knows that the infinite exists because it does not know it. (pp. 222–23)[41]

These passages exemplify the quantifying function of the imagination as it expresses dimensionless 'figures' in geometrical extensions of point,

Mathematical Thought, pp. 122–23, 175, 192; on Proclus and the Cartesian development of the *mathesis universalis*, pp. 181–85; and on the relation of geometrical symbolization to the imagination, esp. with respect to Proclus and Descartes, pp. 200–211. See n. 54 of this chapter. See, as well, A. Charles, "L'imagination, miroir de l'âme selon Proclus," in *Le Néoplatonisme*, Colloques Internationaux du Centre National de la Recherche Scientifique (Paris, 1971), pp. 241–51. With respect to its importance for his view of the imagination, the author stresses Proclus' categorization of the types of sensation (pp. 243–44)—which also reflects Plato's division of the Divided Line—in his commentary on the *Timaeus* (*In Tim.* 2.83.16–84; Festugière, 3.118–19).

[41] For Proclus' comments on infinity in relation to Plotinus' observations on matter, see Chap. 8, n. 65.

line, and surface. Aristotle has commented, to be sure, that the mind must visualize indefinite quantities as definite (hypothetical) diagrammatic images if we are to conceptualize them (*De mem.* 1; *Meta.* 13.3.8, 14.2.9–10). But the Neoplatonic construction of reality places an ontological emphasis upon quantities of force becoming quantities of magnitude which, when articulated in materials of the imagination, goes beyond Aristotle in laying the formalistic foundations of aestheticism.

Proclus borrows Aristotelian terms (cf. *Meta.* 13.3.10–12) for the general principles of beauty which he says are preeminently expressed by the mathematical sciences: order (τάξις), symmetry (συμμετρία), and definiteness (τὸ ὡρισμένον). He gives to these general principles, however, a strong logical emphasis and defines each in Neoplatonic concepts of 'cosmic' processions in both geometrical theorems and ontological realities. Geometry achieves order in its procedures by deriving more complex theorems (ποικιλωτέρων) from more primary and simpler ones (ἀπλουστέρων), for "later propositions are always dependent on their predecessors." Symmetry appears in the interrelation of demonstrations with one another and in their common reference back to the intelligible reality; for "the measure common to all parts of the science is Nous, from which it gets its principles and to which it directs the minds of its students." Definiteness results from the permanent certainty of ideas (ἀκινήτοις λόγοις), for, unlike the objects of perception or opinion, the objects of geometry "always present themselves as the same, made definite by intelligible forms." The fact that these logical formulations should characterize mathematics is not as significant as the fact that they should locate the principal sources of the beautiful in the axiomatic priorities of the Proclean construction (pp. 22–23).[42]

Proclus follows Plotinus in separating the apprehension of intelligible realities, whether these are mathematical objects or simply sources of beauty, from the civic satisfaction of human needs. The vision that results from grasping the principle conducive to the beauty of body and soul as well as of mathematical objects relieves, not our ordinary necessities, but "the hindrances that the senses present to our knowing the whole of things."

Just as we judge the usefulness or uselessness of the cathartic virtues in general by looking not to the needs of living (βιωτικὰς χρείας), but rather to the life of contemplation, so we must refer the purpose of mathematics to intellectual insight and the consummation of wisdom.

---

[42] For Proclus' correspondingly strong emphasis upon the mathematical nature of analogy, see his commentary on *Timaeus* 31C–32C (Festugière, 3.41–42), and the discussion of analogy by S. Gersh, ΚΙΝΗΣΙΣ ΑΚΙΝΗΤΟΣ: *A Study of Spiritual Motion in the Philosophy of Proclus* (Leiden, 1973), pp. 83–90.

However much we first may have concerned ourselves with practical things "akin to perception" rather than with things "apprehended by Nous," we ought now to turn to what can "release the soul from the world of generation and remind it of being." In fact, the whole life of our soul is "so constituted by nature as to move from the imperfect (ἀτελοῦς) towards the perfect" (pp. 23–25). This identification of the ultimate principles of order with a purity primarily attainable through excluding scientific and prudential considerations from the experience of beauty anticipates the forms of aestheticism, articulated clearly by Kant, which have dominated the literary arts since the eighteenth century.

2. *The Commentary on Plato's* Republic. Proclus' careful description of the precise psychological maneuvers of the imagination within the geometrical quest and 'portrayal' of reality in his commentary on Euclid coincides in important ways with his account of the function of poetic images in his commentary on Plato's *Republic*.[43] That he assigns a formal and cognitive nature to this function owes much to his 'quantifying' conception of the imagination as an extension of mathematical proportions and explains, in part, the Neoplatonic preference for symbolic over mimetic images. In his commentary on the *Republic*, which contains the most detailed defense of poetry in late antiquity, Proclus tries to reconcile Plato's apparent admiration for Homer, as revealed in frequent citations, with his ultimate banishment of the poet from the polis. Proclus resolves this contradiction by analyzing Homer's poetic intentions and practice in accordance with philosophical presuppositions about reality derived from Plotinus and other Neoplatonists. Probably no other defense of literature has analyzed the procedures of literary representation in terms so directly derived from a philosophical system. Probably in no other defense have the problems of knowledge and representation been so inextricably bound together.

In defending Homer against Plato's criticisms of poetry, Proclus uses terms analogous to those of the Divided Line, but first, again regarding the objects appropriate to the two categories below the line as a single type, he applies this division to three kinds of life in the soul (τριττὰς ἐν ψυχῇ . . . ζωάς, 1.177.14–15). The higher two correspond to Plato's noetic and dianoetic divisions above the line, while the third combines the categories of belief and conjecture below the line into a single unit. The highest life, for Proclus, is led in a contemplative union with the

---

[43] The following passages in the commentary on the *Republic*, most of which are discussed in this chapter, are particularly interesting to compare with Proclus' observations on Euclid: 1.111.15–114.29; 1.177.24–179.32; 1.180–92; 2.107.15–109.2.

gods, through whose care the soul is awakened to what within itself is assimilable to the One. The second type of life, in its lesser dignity and power, is but an image of the first. In it, however, the soul, now thrown back upon its own scientific resources and activities, may still unfold the multiple interrelations of things, observe their deviations, coordinate the mind with its observations of them, and reproduce this image of the intellective life by rendering a coherent order of first principles. This dianoetic reproduction represents the life of practical reason, as well as the mathematical and scientific disciplines, which Proclus later identifies with the prudential concerns of the epic heroes. The third type of life, that below the line, is caught up in the fluctuating forces of the phenomenal world and compelled to rely on imaginative impressions (φαντασίαις) and random sensations (αἰσθήσεσιν ἀλόγοις, 1.178.3–6). It is in this life that the mimetic arts produce their imitations of all natural objects.[44]

Proclus then proceeds to divide the functions and 'kinds' of poetry, which resemble those of geometry previously discussed, in accordance with the three lives which he has just described (1.178.7–179.32). Corresponding to the highest life is the conception of poetry as a divinely inspired madness (μανία), which raises the human mind out of itself into the domain of the eternal causes and, at the same time, draws the celestial powers down into the soul of the poet. It may bridge, in this way, the distance between men and the gods, and in their union the poet, cognizant of the divine order, may communicate its symmetry to even the lowest psychic activities by the technical handling of rhythm and meter. As prophecy seeks to express the truths and erotic furor to possess beauty, so the first kind of poetry tries to embody the divine proportions (συμμετρίαν θείαν) of the One. The function of the second kind of poetry corresponds to the rational and prudential activities of the soul, and, considering the essence of things, describes the virtues or deficiencies of what is said and done.[45] It advocates intelligent moderation, the cultivation of prudence (φρόνησις), and the recollection (ἀνάμνησις) of the cyclical states of the soul and of its relation to the celestial order in these revolutions. In contrast to the noetic and dianoetic, the

[44] The references included in the text are to *Proclus Diadochus in Platonis Rem Publicam Commentarii*, ed. G. Kroll, 2 vols. (Lipsiae, 1899). My paraphrases and translations in English are adapted from *Proclus: Commentaire sur la République*, trans. A. J. Festugière, 3 vols. (Paris, 1970). Proclus' types of life correspond in their rough outlines to the classical division of the three lives and its extension to Aristotle's discrimination of three faculties of the mind, the theoretical or speculative, the prudential or pragmatic, and the productive or artistic.

[45] Plotinus' first type of likeness would seem to be more appropriate to the prudential activities of Proclus' second kind of poem, his second type of likeness to Proclus' first kind of poem.

third kind of poetry, representing the visible world below the divided line, is a mixture of opinions (δόξαις) and of impressions (φαντασίαις). It is composed entirely by means of imitation (μιμητική), whether it intends simply to copy the object or to give an illusory semblance of it. Such poetry amplifies the smallest passions, manipulates the emotional dispositions of its listeners with its changing harmonies and variegated (ποικίλος) rhythms, and represents the nature of its objects not as they are but as they appear to the ordinary person (τοῖς πολλοῖς). It is like a kind of deceptive sketch (σκιαγραφία) rather than like an exact account (γνῶσις ἀκριβής) of its actual subject. Its purpose is the leading of the soul (ψυχαγωγίαν) by playing upon the audience's expectations of joy and sorrow.[46] This kind of poetry is divided into the art of copying (τὸ εἰκαστικόν), which tries to represent the imitated object correctly (πρὸς τὴν ὀρθότητα), and the art of producing a semblance (τὸ φανταστικόν), which reduces an imitation (μίμησιν) to a mere impression (φαινομένην).

In segregating mimetic images below the line and then subdividing them into *eicastic* and *phantastic* kinds of images, Proclus quotes directly from the *Sophist* (235D–36A). Once the distinction is established, he exemplifies eicastic imitation by a passage from the *Laws* (667C–68C). The context of this passage contains, perhaps, Plato's most positive appreciation of verisimilar representation. He is speaking of the phonic contributions (μουσική, 673A) to choral performances and emphasizes the fact that their perfection lies in the correctness (ὀρθότης) of their imitation of the beautiful (τοῦ καλοῦ μιμήματα) rather than in the incidental pleasure which accompanies them (668AB). In order to illustrate fantastic imitation, on the other hand, Proclus cites Plato's discussion in the *Republic* of *all* mimetic representations as being at the third remove from truth (597E–98B). The fantastic is inferior to the eicastic image chiefly because it is concerned only to beguile an unsuspecting audience with its illusions. Here Proclus borrows the general ontological distinction between imitations and reality, for which Plato used a skiagraphic analogy, to discriminate the more from the less illusionistic kind of imitation. One effect of the fantastic image's being identified with the lowest category on the Divided Line may have been its subsequent association with the nonexistent object.[47]

[46] Here again, as in the style of deliberative oratory, psychagogic power is associated with the skiagraphic outline, an association anticipated in Aristotelian psychology.

[47] Despite the fact that even the lowest objects have some reality, in the Renaissance the fantastic image tended sometimes to be associated with the representation of things which have no existence at all. See E. Panofsky, *Idea*, trans. J. S. Peake (Columbia, S.C., 1968), p. 215; for the disagreement between Mazzone and Tasso over the existential status of the objects of poetic imitation, see Tasso's *Discorsi del Poema Eroico*, Lib. 2, in *Torquato Tasso: Prose* (Milano, 1959), esp. pp. 524–33.

Proclus' analysis illustrates the developments I have been tracing. He categorizes the art of poetry with respect to the ontological nature of the types of subjects, and the kinds of knowledge we can have of them, in terms analogous to Plato's diagrammatic division between intelligible and visible objects. All forms of poetry which represent objects corresponding to those below the line are mimetic with respect to the existential status of their subjects, and mimesis, as distinct from noetic and dianoetic images of objects corresponding to those above the line, is compared to a skiagraphia. He then establishes a fourth category by subdividing all skiagraphic representation into eicastic and fantastic types of imitation in accordance with the skenographic distinction in the *Sophist*. Eicastic imitation corresponds, then, to Plato's third category of belief, fantastic to his fourth of conjecture. Ontological and psychological criteria are here completely interwoven in accordance with the general discrepancy, already emphasized by Proclus, between the nature of the gods and the ways in which men subjectively perceive them (1.111.16–27). Each god remains one and the same in his simplicity (ἁπλοῦν) without attempting to deceive anyone, but he appears in various forms (ποικίλον) to his human spectators who must ascertain the divine properties according to their own capacities. While the god remains uniform, human beings "participate" in his nature either according to their intellect (νοῦς), which grasps things directly in their totality, or to their rational soul (ψυχὴ νοερά), which arrives at things discursively, or to their imagination (φαντασία), which perceives things figuratively, or to their sensation (αἴσθησις), which knows things only as impressions. Thus the divine nature is uniform in itself but multiform with respect to our varying methods of cognition. The highest form of poetry will be that which can represent the most excellent object in its unity with the least interference of the subjective limitations of human inquiry.[48]

Later, Proclus applies his epistemological and poetic categories to Homer (1.192.5–196.2). When Homer is possessed by the divine inspiration of the muses and reveals such unified mystical conceptions (τὰ μυστικὰ . . . νοήματα) about the gods, he speaks as a poet of the first category. When he writes in detail about the life of the soul, the natural elements, and political duties, he composes discursively in accordance with the second category of knowledge (κατὰ τὴν ἐπιστήμην). When he describes people and their actions in stylistic terms appropriate to them, he follows

[48] On the descent of divine power through a stratification of the gods, see Proclus' *Elements of Theology*, Props. 124–25, 128–29, 140 and Dodds' comments on p. 260—with his conclusion: "that Homer's Olympians, the most vividly conceived anthropomorphic beings in all literature, should have ended their career on the dusty shelves of this museum of metaphysical abstractions is one of time's strangest ironies."

the third category of eicastic imitation. When he concerns himself with how things appear to ordinary people and not with what they actually are (ἀλήθειαν τοῦ ὄντος), he achieves but the fourth category of the fantastic poet. For, when the sun is said to sink in the sea, the poet cannot even be said to be 'imitating' its actual motions but rather to be showing how they appear because of the distance (διὰ τὴν ἀπόστασιν). When, however, he represents his heroes fighting, deliberating, or speaking according to the various types (εἴδη) and habits of human beings, he offers an eicastic representation. When, furthermore, he reveals the constitution of the soul, the difference between the phantom image and soul which makes use of the image, and the order of elements in the universe, he composes a "learned poetry" (ἐπιστήμονα τῆς ποιητικῆς). And, finally, when he discusses the monad and the union of Zeus with Hera, he speaks mythologically under the inspiration of the muses themselves. Proclus exemplifies the highest category of poet by Demodocus (Od. 8), the second by Phemius (Od. 1.154, 337; 17.263; 22.331), the third by the singer of Clytemnestra (Od. 3.267ff.), and the fourth by Thamyris (Il. 2.594ff.). Thamyris, an illusionist (φανταστικός), too given to a deceptively varying and impressionistic style (πολυτροπωτέραν . . . αἰσθητικωτέραν), abandoned the simpler (ἁπλουστέρας) song most proper to the muses for a more variegated (ποικιλωτέραν) composition. All four types of poetry are present in Homer, but preeminently the inspired and least commonly the eicastic and fantastic forms.[49]

Proclus defends Homer, accordingly, by claiming that Plato actually intended to banish only imitative poetry, particularly the fantastic (in which the drama entirely consists), but approved of the higher categories which Homer principally employed. To support his argument he draws an important distinction between symbolization and imitation (1.198.9–24).

---

[49] However different their context, the ethical overtones of these stylistic terms, ἁπλόος and ποικίλος, go back at least to the passages in the Phaedrus (277BC) and the Republic (404E, 604E–5A) discussed previously in Chap. 7, n. 4. Narrative poems, for instance, should present the imperturbability of the demigods and valorous deeds of the heroes so that the young may be led to imitate the simple integrity (τὸ ἁπλοῦν) rather than the sophisticated variety (ἀντὶ τοῦ ποικίλου) of their character (1.66.10–18). These terms recur often and take on stronger ontological connotations than they had for Plato, since Proclus implicates them securely in his system. See, for example, their use in 1.162.4–9 from which he proceeds immediately to a useful recapitulation of his philosophical terminology (1.162.9–163.8). See as well 1.159.10–20, 1.160.7–10, passim, along with the occurrences cited above from the commentary on Euclid. In addition, the terms used to describe the style of Thamyris are very suggestive for future literary criticism. In fact, the illusionistic versatility (πολυτροπωτέρα) of Thamyris suggests the busy triviality (πολυπραγμοσύνην) of anyone who concerns himself with style at all when there is explication of doctrine to be done (1.164.9–10).

How could one call that kind of poetry "imitation" which interprets divine matters by means of symbols (διὰ συμβόλων) if symbols are not imitations of the realities of which they are symbolic? For opposites (τὰ ἐναντία) can never be imitations of one another (the shameful, that is, cannot be an imitation of the beautiful, nor that which conforms to nature an imitation of what does not conform to nature). But it is the essence of symbolization (συμβολικὴ θεωρία) to indicate the nature of the real (τῶν πραγμάτων) by what is most strongly antithetical to it. If, then, a poet is inspired and reveals by means of symbols the truth of existent things or if, by means of knowledge, he reveals to us the order itself of things, such a poet is neither an imitator nor can he be proved wrong by empirical demonstrations (προκειμένων ἀποδείξεων).[50]

Several things should be observed in this passage. Beginning with its conclusion, it is clear, first, that neither type of poet associated with the two categories of knowledge above the line, *nous* and *episteme*, is mimetic; second, that the symbol as an instrument for representing the truth (ἀλήθειαν) appears to be distinguished from knowledge as an instrument for representing the order (τάξιν) of reality; and third, that

[50] Although this passage is quoted by Crome (p. 187) and twice by Coulter (pp. 50–51, 118), it is important to reemphasize it in the context of Plotinus' two types of likeness and of the development of literary theory as a whole which I have been tracing. Plotinus' double likeness (ἡ ὁμοίωσις διττή . . . , 1.2.2.5) in the context of ethics seems to have generated several literary distinctions in Proclus (see Chap. 8, n. 3). First, as mentioned in Chap. 8, n. 10, Proclus differentiates generally between the ethical representation of human institutions by means of mimetic likenesses (εἰκονικῶς) and the physical representation of the cosmos by means of symbols (συμβολικῶς). This differentiation leads him to distinguish two types of myth (τὸ τῶν μύθων εἶδος εἶναι διττόν, 1.81.12), one appropriate to the educative inculcation of civic virtues, one to the visionary grasp of divine correspondences (1.80.12–81.28, 1.84.24–26). Corresponding to the two types of myth are two types of harmony (ἡ ἁρμονία διττή, 1.84.23) in general—one, again, appropriate to the pedagogic disciplines, the other to the symbolic evocation of the divine. The first is an imitative harmony (ἁρμονίαν . . . μιμητικήν, 1.84.14) which incites young souls to virtue; the second is an inspired harmony which, moving the listener with ecstatic force, is too strong for moderate temperaments. Similarly, Proclus, working with *Crat.* 383A–91C as Festugière points out, distinguishes between two types of existing words (διττῶν δὲ ὄντων ὀνομάτων, 1.170.2). The first type is of human origin (i.e. by convention), the second is of divine origin and expresses the underlying nature of reality. Issuing from the gods, the second type is both more intellective and more harmonious; it exists "par nature (φύσει)," while the first type exists "par institution (θέσει)." A scale is then established of degrees of resemblance between words and the realities they signify which again corresponds to distinctions indicated by the Divided Line (1.169.25–170.26). And, finally, related by extension to Plotinus' two types of likeness is Proclus' psychological distinction between two activities of intellect (διττόν . . . νοῦν, 2.108.5, 8); the second is that of the imaginative intellect (φανταστικὸν νοῦν, 2.107.17) which is necessary for every soul living in the world of becoming. Insofar as it is imaginative, the intellect projects (προβέβληται) the light of its truth outward in the form of mimetic images (κατὰ μίμησιν, 2.107.25); insofar as it is intellective, it reflects its inner light back upon itself in order to reveal itself to itself (αὐτοφανές). As in Proclus' commentary on Euclid, the first activity sets the soul on the road to knowledge through mimetic comparisons; the second on the road back to contemplation through symbolic identities (2.107.15–108.17).

only mimetic representations of things below the line can be demonstrated or challenged by empirical evidence. While mimesis cannot represent what conforms to nature (κατὰ φύσιν) by imitating what is contradictory to it (παρὰ φύσιν)—since "opposites can never be imitations of one another"—it is the very purpose of symbols to indicate the nature of reality by representing what is most antithetical to it.[51] The symbol, that is, tries to suggest how those things which appear to us to be in most extreme opposition, as Plotinus describes them (τὰ ἐναντία, 3.2.16), are, with respect to the universe as a whole, parts of a concordant harmony. As I indicated previously, such a harmony resembles a quantitative 'mean' between extremes rather than a qualitative 'mean' of 'due measure.' Both the conception of the universe as a *discordia concors* and of the symbol as its most appropriate type of representation conform to the quantitative paradigm of geometrical proportions.[52]

Earlier, in language similar to his account of the unfolding of geo-

[51] It is precisely what is paradoxical in fiction, myth, or symbol which prevents us from relaxing in "apparent plausibility" (1.85.21) and forces us to pursue more complex truths (cf. Coulter, p. 57). For further distinctions between the mimetic likeness (εἰκών) and the antithetical symbol, see *Proclus: Théologie Platonicienne* 1.4, ed. H. D. Saffrey and L. G. Westerink (Paris, 1968), pp. 17–23. The editors cite W. Beierwaltes, *Proklos, Grundzüge seiner Metaphysik* (Frankfort am Main, 1965), p. 171, n. 23. See also Crome, *Symbol und Unzulänglichkeit*, pp. 171, 176–79, 192–93. J. Dillon, "Image, Symbol and Analogy: Three Basic Concepts of Neoplatonic Allegorical Exegesis," in *The Significance of Neoplatonism*, ed. R. B. Harris (Norfolk, 1976), pp. 247–62, points out the overlapping looseness of these terms, but he does not deal with those passages in which symbols are most explicitly distinguished from images.

[52] As discussed in nn. 12 and 32 of this chapter, the binding force of Neoplatonic analogy which holds antithetical extremes in balanced proportion—however much its external form can be expressed in ratios such as the Aristotelian "proportional metaphor"—is not a logical relation in the ordinary sense but an "affinity" which all parts of the cosmos share with each other and with the whole. This affinity is based on the concept of "sympathy" (1.84.10–13) which expresses the participation of all individual existents in the One. The relation of this concept to narrative myth is clearly stated by Proclus in a way reminiscent of Plotinus' two types of likeness (1.86.15–24): daimonic myths which express a relation between one order of existence and another do not assume that certain things are copies (εἰκόνες) of certain other things which are models (παραδείγματα) but rather that the first are symbols of the second by virtue of an analogy (ἐξ ἀναλογίας) based on affinity (πρὸς συμπάθειαν). Nearly all scholarly works on Neoplatonism are forced to deal with the nature of this affinity and its implications for "analogy" (see particularly W. Beierwaltes, *Proklos, Grundzüge seiner Metaphysik*, pp. 153–58 (esp. n. 138), 329–38; S. Gersh, ΚΙΝΗΣΙΣ ΑΚΙΝΗΤΟΣ, pp. 83–90; Crome, *Symbol und Unzulänglichkeit*, p. 167). The adaptations of the Platonic Eros to the concept of 'sympathy' suggest, indeed, a 'feeling shared in common' drawing the *disjecta membra* of the cosmos home to unity. Yet, equally, this συμπάθεια is a 'passivity (i.e., receptivity) shared in common.' What is shared by all things is the capacity to receive (or submit to), in varying degrees, the causal force that emanates from the One. Other than the priority of cause to effect, the relation between degrees of receptivity is not so much a matter of 'logic' in the ordinary sense of qualitative relations expressible in language as of mathematical relations expressible in quantities. Herein lies the difference between the Platonic/Aristotelian relation of knowledge and representation and that of the Neoplatonists.

metrical conceptions into the figures of the cosmos and of noetic ideas into the images of the psyche, Proclus characterizes the 'explication' of divine truths into mythological narratives (1.77.13–30).

Indeed, as the fathers of mythology (οἱ τῆς μυθοποιίας πατέρες) have seen that nature, which produces images (εἰκόνας) of immaterial and intelligible forms and which decorates this visible world with varied imitations of these forms, represents the indivisible (ἀμέριστα) by what is divided (μεριστῶς), the eternal by what is in temporal process, the intelligible by the sensible, the immaterial in a material way, the unextended with spatial extension, and existence firm in repose by constant change—these fathers, following nature and the procession of beings in their appearance under visible (φαινομένως) and figurative (εἰδωλικῶς) guise, imitate the surpassing quality of the models by rendering the creations of the divine by means of expressions as antithetical as possible to the divine. Those who go the furthest in this direction reveal by those things which [in us] are contrary to nature (παρὰ φύσιν) the very things which, in the gods, are superior to nature (ὑπὲρ φύσιν), by failures of rational calculation (παραλόγοις) what is more divine than reason itself, and by objects which appear ugly to us what transcends in its simple wholeness the beauty of any individual part [which remains of necessity incomplete]. In this way, these fathers are likely to put us in mind again of the surpassing eminence of the gods.

In accord with the procession of geometrical figures, Proclus describes the narrative 'explication' of intelligible principles by means of myths primarily in terms of increasing proportions of extension and process to unity and changelessness. The expansion of these proportions in geometry and in myths is described quantitatively and resembles the projection of the idea in the understanding as an image on the screen of the imagination. In each case, the extended geometrical figure, psychological image, or narrative event must undergo a 'turning around' (ἐπιστροφή) and a return to unity if the universal order is to be apprehended in its totality. The geometrical figures of particular circles must draw back into a single concept of circularity; the image must shed its spatial and temporal extension and become again the idea of which it was a projection; and the narrative event must seek an ever more condensed symbolic expression which may appear increasingly antithetical to the truth it is supposed to represent.[53]

[53] This process is roughly that described previously (pp. 183–84) in relation to Plotinus (3.5.9). In an important passage translated by Coulter (p. 120), Proclus explicitly offers the procedure as a method of exegesis: "Just as there is a path of ascent from the phenomenal world to the intelligible, so, too, we must return from the circumstantial details which make up the subject of the dialogue to that single purpose and one goal of the whole composition, and we must subordinate to this, as best we can, all that we have previously considered in isolation, i.e. the characters, the time, and the place" (In Parmenidem, ed. V. Cousin, 630.28–36).

However paradoxical it may seem, I should say that it is because the discursive principles of poetry are conceived of largely in terms of geometrical demonstration that its literal meaning often appears to be beyond rational calculation (παράλογος) and its significance to depend upon arbitrary symbols to bring contradictory extremes into juxtaposed relation. In the first place, Proclus' observations on geometry include a great deal which is not amenable to geometrical analysis. In his commentary on Euclid (pp. 42–45), he describes the idea of circularity as a magnitude without magnitude and a figure without shape in the understanding which "unfolds" itself, first, in the imagination as divided and extended "instances" of form, and, then, in sensible things as imprecise shapes 'contaminated' by their opposites—i.e., circularity by straightness. The most accurate geometrical inquiry must, therefore, try to regain its more perfect intellectual insight by emancipating itself, as Odysseus does from Calypso, "from the pictures projected in imagination." While this 'explication' of geometrical ideas into, and their emancipation from, particularized imaginary magnitudes and shapes may be formally outlined in quantitative ratios, the actual transition from one form of existence to another remains as far beyond rational calculation as Ovidian metamorphoses. Once in the imaginary or sensible realm of infinite variation, furthermore, each image becomes especially 'unpredictable' (παράλογος). And, finally, Proclus maintains that it is only by means of this unlimited, and hence irrational, multiplicity of forms, that the geometer seeks to return to his original unitary conceptions much as the exegete, because he must overcome numerous implausibilities, seeks to strip away the fabulous, and hence irrational, events of the myth to reveal its inner truth.[54]

[54] In his commentary on Euclid, Proclus departs from the earlier Hellenistic spirit with respect to mathematics in ways analogous to his departures with respect to language. That certain 'Asian' influences may be present in both cases is suggested by the similarity between literary and mathematical uses of symbolism in the development of algebra. The fact that algebraic symbolism offers a kind of paradigm for literary symbols suggests the increasingly 'quantitative' nature of symbolic representation in literature since the Renaissance. The following observations of J. Klein epitomize, with respect to algebra, some of the essential contributions to literary discourse described in this chapter. "Now what is characteristic of this 'general magnitude' is its indeterminateness of which, as such, a concept can be formed only within the realm of symbolic procedure. But the Euclidian presentation is *not* symbolic. It always intends *determinate* numbers of units of measurement, and it does this *without any detour through a 'general notion' or a concept of a 'general magnitude.'* In *illustrating* each determinate number of units of measurement by measures of distance it does *not* do two things which constitute the heart of the symbolic procedure: It does *not* identify the object represented with the means of its representation, and it does *not* replace the real determinateness of an object with a *possibility* of making it determinate, such as would be expressed by a sign which, instead of *illustrating* a determinate object, would *signify* possible determinacy" (*Greek Mathematical Thought*, p. 123; see n. 40 of this chapter).

In the second place, we may observe that the formal 'explication' of quantitative ratios provides poetry, in the Neoplatonic system, with a paradigm of discursive argumentation which is inappropriate to the analysis of qualitative experience. The analysis of human experience requires a standard of 'due measure' rather than a standard which arrives at a 'mean' of equidistance from two opposing extremes to be reconciled. In terms of the Divided Line, such a quantitative 'mean' lies between intelligible and sensible extremes, extremes which when 'collapsed' together and juxtaposed at their medial point can best be expressed by a symbol. The symbol's perceptible form, like the Egyptian's hieroglyph or animal statue of the god, having little or no external correspondence to what it signifies, need not 'illustrate' its significance. Like Plotinus' second (nonreciprocal) type of likeness, both Proclus' literary and Thespesion's visual symbols, in reducing the discursive analysis of Plato's dialectic in his *Sophist* or of Philostratus' imagination in his *Life of Apollonius* to geometrical demonstration, maintain the mutually exclusive poles of the ancient dilemma.[55]

C. The Neoplatonic Transmission of the Ancient Dilemma

The unified energies emanating from the One and becoming, through extension, the disparate individual things of our experience become apprehensible to us (ἡμῖν) only as parts of a whole which could, itself, best be known with respect to its own nature (ἁπλῶς). The negotiation between our knowledge of things most accessible to our perceptions and our knowledge of things known only with respect to themselves, that is, may be expressed formally as a relation between the parts and the whole. The parts do not make up the whole but arise out of the whole as differentiating forms 'open' outward from the center (5.8.5). If we could, hypothetically, look outward for a moment from the center, we would see a whole dividing itself into parts which participate in it. Looking inward from our own perspective outside the center, however, we perceive only the parts which stand between us and the internal unity. In order to return to that unity we must reintegrate the parts by

---

[55] In his conclusion, Coulter summarizes the proportional relations that the Neoplatonists saw between the microcosm of a literary work (in this case the Platonic dialogue) and the macrocosm of the universe. Since they based their exegetical methods, and hence their conception of literature, on these relations, it is possible to regard his observations as implicit testimony to the predominantly formalistic influence of Neoplatonism on subsequent literary theory.

reassimilating them once again to the One. We must conceive of them, that is, as 'imitating' the whole.[56]

As Plotinus implies, and Proclus states, our apprehension of the One through the representation of its parts must employ symbols whose external form is antithetical to their significance—the One being antithetical to the manifold—rather than employ verisimilar resemblances. For, from such resemblances which are based upon common characteristics shared by composite things perceived in a composite world, we can only derive plausible arguments built upon discursive reasoning (6.5.2). Although such reasoning derives information from the senses and looks "upwards" to the Intellectual-Principle which "exists apart" (5.3.3), our rational understanding (διάνοια) of causes and effects stands, if not opposed to, at least separated from, both perception and intelligence. With respect to differences (τὸ διάφορον)—and hence to similarities—

Sense-perception (αἴσθησις) and intelligence (νοῦς) may be trusted to indicate diversity but not to explain it: explanation is outside the province of sense-perception, whose function is merely to produce a variety of information; while, as for intelligence, it works exclusively with intuitions and never resorts to explanations to justify them in detail (6.3.18).[57]

[56] The processes of moving outward from the center and then returning inward are described by Plutarch in terms of adding spatial and temporal dimensions to unity and then "abstracting" them from phenomena. As one descends (= the Neoplatonic movement outward) in Plato's hierarchy of disciplines from arithmetic to harmonic sciences, each subsequent science deals with greater physicality. On the other hand, "by abstracting sound from the things in motion and motion from the solids and depth from the planes and extension from the quantities we arrive at the intelligible ideas themselves, which do not differ from one another at all when conceived in respect of their singularity and unity" (Plutarch's Moralia 1001F–2A, trans. H. Cherniss, LCL, vol. 13 [London, 1976]). Clement of Alexandria describes this "abstracting" process by the Neoplatonic term "analysis": when all dimensions have been removed, there still remains the point which has position, "from which if we abstract position, there is the conception of unity" (Stromata 5.11.70.2, trans. in The Ante-Nicene Fathers, ed. A. Roberts and J. Donaldson [New York, 1903], 2:461). These passages are interesting in relation to Grabar's comments on Plotinian influences on medieval aesthetics. See esp. Chap. 8, n. 63.

[57] Armstrong's translation and discussion of a tenth-century Arabic paraphrase of Plotinus' essay 4.3.18 is worth citing in full from JHS 93 (1973):17. "Perhaps the best way of conveying some idea of how Plotinus saw human intellect at its highest, when it has rejoined divine intellect, is to give some of the paraphrase which an unknown tenth-century (or earlier) Arab made . . . of iv. 3 [27] 18. It is a paraphrase rather than a translation, loose and inflated, though containing some genuine Plotinian phrases. But it does bring out the peculiarity of his thought with which we are concerned here rather well. The relevant passage is as follows. 'When soul enters bodies . . . she . . . grows weak and takes refuge in thought and reasoning. For thought is the deficiency of the mind, because mind is defective and imperfect when it needs reason and thought. Similarly, in the case of perfect art, the artist does not need thought but does his work without reflection or thought, while in the case of defective art the artist needs thought and reflection, because, if he wishes to do something and is a weak craftsman, he reflects and thinks how he should act. . . . Someone may ask: If souls do not think in their own disembodied

In his *Elements of Theology*, Proclus provides a tighter ontological framework for this separation of the discursive analysis of our composite reality from both aesthetic and intellective apprehension of the "extremes of being" (τὰ ἄκρα τῶν ὄντων). He proposes that the simplicity of the One, dispensing its causative power throughout the entire spectrum of being, ultimately exhausts itself as the simplicity of matter. If this simplicity (τὸ ἁπλοῦν) be of the One, it will be superior in its power to composite things (τῶν συνθέτων), and if it be of matter, it will be inferior to them.

For if the extremes of being be produced by fewer and simpler (ἁπλουστέρων) causes, the intermediate existences by more, the latter will be composite (prop. 58), while of the extreme terms some will be simpler as being higher, others as being lower. But that the extreme terms are produced by fewer causes is plain, since the higher principles both begin to operate before the lower and extend beyond them to things which the lower by remission of power are precluded from reaching (prop. 57). For the last being is, like the first, perfectly simple, for the reason that it proceeds from the first alone; but the one is simple as being above all composition, the other as being beneath it.

What lies above and below the intermediate existences (τὰ μέσα) which constitute the composite world we live in are too simple—or in Plotinus' language, too pure or too diffuse respectively—to be grasped by a discursive reasoning dependent on logical predication.[58]

The relevance of these distinctions, not only for Proclus' application of Plato's Divided Line to the Homeric epics, but for later attitudes toward poetry in general, comes out in an observation which St. Thomas, to be followed by Boccaccio and Tasso among others, is to make in his commentary on Peter Lombard's *Sentences*.

Poetic knowledge concerns those things which cannot be seized by reason because of their lack of truth, and therefore it is necessary that reason be led indirectly as if by a kind of similitude. Theology, in a similar way, concerns those things which are above reason. The symbolic method (*modus symbolicus*), therefore,

---

world, how can they be rational? We reply: They can do without reason there—the reason which exists in potentiality, with thought and reflection. But the intellectual reason, which exists in actuality, never departs from the soul but is with her always, and she does not think.' To represent God as the Architect or Artisan of the universe, carefully thinking it all out with his designs and plans, as fundamentalist Platonists and most Jews and Christians were content to do, would be for Plotinus and his Arab interpreter to represent him as a very poor sort of artisan: and, it would seem, a philosopher who never did anything but 'think,' in the sense in which we normally use the word, would be a very poor sort of philosopher. 'Thought is the deficiency of the mind.' "

[58] *The Elements of Theology*, Prop. 59. Dodds' commentary on Props. 57–59 is extremely helpful. See also Props. 123, 125, and 128–29.

is common to both, since neither might be assimilated to reason (*rationi pro-portionetur*).[59]

This association of poetry with theology on the grounds of their mutual incompatibility with rational discourse about our composite reality of secondary causes suggests the nature and extent of the Neoplatonic transmission of the ancient dilemma of knowledge and representation. For Proclus, fiction per se is confined to the fantastic or lowest category of the Divided Line—to that disparate extreme associated with formless, material sensations. Where Homer speaks truly of the gods, on the other hand, he virtually becomes for Proclus a 'theologian' expressing the extreme of divine unity in symbols whose exterior form is to be veri-similarly antithetical to their inner significance. In between these ex-tremes lie the didactic subjects appropriate to the scientific disciplines functioning just above the line and phenomenal activities appropriate to mimetic representation, dependent on symmetry and verisimilitude, functioning just below it. Proclus is willing to accept Plato's distrust of those scientific accounts or mimetic representations in the *Republic* which either could not be expressed symbolically or whose appearances could not be saved through allegorical interpretation. His adaptation of the Neoplatonic speculation to literature contains, however, a latent paradox, which affects subsequent neoclassical recoveries.

While mimetic representation is confined to things below the line dividing intelligible from sensible objects, and is, therefore, inferior to symbolic representation, Proclus, nevertheless, places great importance on verisimilar accuracy whenever sensible objects are to be described. In addition, that is, to requiring Plotinus' unifying hieroglyphic symbol, the abrupt antithetical juxtaposition of an external empirical realism with a mystical inner meaning might protect, as well, the spatially and temporally extended events of mimetic imitation. For, if out of scepticism or irresolution we despair of penetrating a realm approachable only through symbols, we may despair as well of discovering any prior or more complex principles of order other than those which can be empir-ically verified. In pursuit of such verification, we may find in verisimilar precision and strict application of stylistic rules an attractive security. Content to reproduce the surfaces of things with the liveliest exactitude, we may come to believe, quite as mistakenly as those who express themselves exclusively in private symbols, that we are resolving, rather than intensifying, the ancient dilemma of knowledge and representation. Both ways, either alone or in combination, lead to the more conservative forms of neoclassicism. Taking 'neoclassicism' to refer to any attempt

---

[59] *Comm. in Prim. Lib. Sent. Magist. Petri Lomb.*, *Prol.* Qu. 1, a5, ad 3 m.

to recover or utilize antiquity, regardless of period or motive, the art of the early Christian centuries offers an interesting example of this Neo-platonic paradox.[60]

In 1946 A. Grabar published his suggestive observations on the con-geniality of Plotinian attitudes to medieval aesthetic principles in the plastic arts.[61] I would like to extend his observations to literature as a way of clarifying the origins and consequences of the paradox just men-tioned. He quotes an important passage on optics in which Plotinus is discussing how it comes about that in the distance "objects appear smaller, and things far apart seem to have only a small space between them, but objects which are near appear the size they are and the distance apart which they are." When seen from a distance, colors and magnitudes both undergo similar changes.

> Both have in common the "less than they are": as regards colour the "less" is blurredness, as regards size the "less" is smallness, and, following the colour, the size is lessened proportionately. What happens to them becomes clearer in things of many and varied parts, for instance, hills with many houses on them and a quantity of trees and a great many other things, of which each individual one, if it is seen, enables us to measure the whole from the individual parts which we observe. But if the form does not reach us in individual detail, the possibility of knowing the dimensions of the whole by measuring its basic size according to the forms of individual parts is taken away. For this applies to things near at hand too; when they have many parts, but we only take a quick glance at them as a whole and do not observe all the forms of the parts, they seem smaller in proportion as the individual details evade our observation; but when all the details are seen, we measure the objects accurately (ἀκριβῶς) and know how large they are. (2.8.1)

Grabar comments that what preoccupies Plotinus is the *true* size, the *true* distance separating things, and the *true* shades of color (p. 18). Such truths could become apprehensible only if all the differences of size and gradations of color were to be seen distinctly and simultane-ously. If a painter were to represent the objects seen in this way, he would have to reveal them as if they existed in a single plane, parallel to the surface of the picture, with no foreshortening or visual perspective.

---

[60] Proclus gives an important position to mimetic representation in the ethical or ed-ucative narrative and image and, as a result, emphasizes verisimilar accuracy in representing things below the Divided Line. See, for example, the following passages in his commentary on the *Republic*: 1.15.1–18, 1.45.15–20, 1.53.8–54.2, 1.56.20–58,27, 1.154.3–10, 1.163.1–64.8, 1.171.15–17, 1.190.11–12. In 1.164.1–8 Proclus emphasizes the strong effect of mimesis upon the imagination and the psychagogic energy of both. Compare Plato, *Rep.* 604E–5A, quoted in Chap. 7, n. 4.

[61] A. Grabar, "Plotin et les origines de l'esthétique médiévale," *Cahiers archéologiques* (Paris, 1946):15–34. Page references will be given in the text.

By ignoring all three-dimensionality, the painter could render with minute care all the details of figure, dress, and accessories and replace colors
subtly varying through a receding atmosphere with colors uniformly
close, firm, and bright. In these ways, he could bring out the (ontologically) true magnitude and tone, the true characteristics of the objects
represented, without distortions caused by perceptual or psychological
conditions.

Continuing to quote Plotinus (2.4.5), Grabar points out that for him
the unseen receding "depth," which three-dimensional perspective seeks
ordinarily to suggest, would in fact only suggest the illusion of an
amorphous extension of matter deprived of the forms which could illuminate it. The intelligence, seeing these forms only on the surface of
a single plane, must presume that the depth below is an obscurity hidden
beneath their luminosity and colors. It follows that the artist wishing
to represent such forms will avoid all suggestions of the material opacity
beneath them as well as of any shadows articulated by them—since these
forms would be equally illuminated in all their parts. However precise
the depiction of surface detail, such an exclusion of three-dimensional
proportions could not help but sharply separate the painted image from
the nature it represented (pp. 19–20). In addition, drawing on a number
of other passages, Grabar shows how Plotinus invites us to suppress the
normal spatial extension between the eye which sees and the objects
seen by letting the one be absorbed into the other (p. 23). In the act of
contemplation we become the object itself by passively permitting *it* to
inform *us*, and to accomplish this submission we must lose all self-
consciousness and, in some measure, even our awareness of vision itself.
The art which has the 'wisdom' to represent the fruits of such contemplation must contain the model to be imitated within itself. "Cette
sagesse-là n'est pas faite de théorèmes, mais est totale; c'est une unité,
non qu'elle soit composée de plusieurs termes qu'elle ramène a l'unité,
mais plutôt, partant de cette unité, elle se décompose en pluralité" (5.8.5).[62]

The attempt to conceive of nature as it would truly be seen in itself
if there were no psychological or material conditions to distort our vision
of it is the first step, so to speak, in the act of contemplation.[63] In order

---

[62] Grabar comments (p. 24) that "Les historiens de la philosophie sont d'accord pour
reconnaître que, avec Plotin, 'c'est la valeur même de la connaissance rationnelle qui est
atteinte' (Bréhier), que ce n'est plus, comme chez Platon, chez Aristote, un outil pour la
connaissance ni le point de départ d'une synthèse progressive (Bréhier); que, dans le
système de Plotin, la connaissance s'est transformée en une émotion imprécise, un sentiment vital sans forme, une 'Stimmung' insaisissable (Eucken)."

[63] The following comments by Grabar suggest that it is only after a process of "abstracting" or "analysis," such as that described in Chap. 8, n. 56, that one attains proper
vision: "Or, pour l'expérience de Plotin, au contraire, sera idéale la vision qui sera 'trans-
parente', comme il dit, c'est-à-dire où les objets ne seront ni autonomes ni impénétrables,

that the content of that act be properly represented, the artist must try to see that, first, "la lumière est égale et diffuse; les ombres portées sont absentes, les autres s'estompent et se neutralisent, comme s'il y avait plusieurs foyers de lumière" (p. 25). Second, that he have the "détails de l'objet représenté (coiffures, costume, tissus avec leurs ornements, armes avec leurs decorations) . . . reproduits avec un soin extrême, qui va jusqu'à gêner l'effet de l'ensemble" (p. 26). And third, in the absence of an ordering perspective, that he give naturalistic details coherence by subordinating them to regular geometric and stereotyped schemes. "L'artiste dispose comme il l'entend, des données de la Nature et, à son gré, introduit un ordre, une homogénéité là où . . . il y avait 'mélange' et désordre." He secures a unity where material things offered a plurality, and thus offers an image *formally* more in accord with a vision of the intelligible order (pp. 26–27). Works of art dating from the reign of Augustus through the third century A.D., Grabar concludes,

Emploient déjà l'image ramenée à un plan unique, la figuration à plat des personnages et des objets, sans volume ni poids, les représentations minutieusement exactes des détails de certains objets (coiffures, . . . etc.) opposées au schématisme géométrique des personnages ou du paysage; enfin, les interprétations ornementales et géométriques des objets et des êtres vivants. (pp. 27–28)

Like the Egyptian's realistically portrayed animal symbol—which Philostratus identifies with, but does not make illustrative of, what it signifies—Plotinus' meticulous natural details, held in an abstract geometrical scheme, do not illustrate the relations of these details to one another or to ourselves in nature, but symbolize their hidden significance with respect to the intelligible realm.[64]

In the original passage on optics cited previously, Plotinus continues by pointing out that

Those magnitudes that are of one form and like colour throughout cheat our sight, too, because it is not very well able to measure them part by part, since it slips off them as it measures by parts because it has no firm resting-place

---

où l'espace sera absorbé, la lumière traversera sans encombre les corps solides, et où le spectateur lui-même pourra ne plus discerner les limites qui le séparent de l'objet contemplé" (p. 25).

[64] Grabar observes that Hellenistic conceptions of art as imitation could no longer serve those who, "comme Plotin, demandent à l'oeuvre d'art, non pas une imitation de la Nature matérielle (imitation immédiate ou idéalisée, peu importe), mais un point de départ pour une expérience metaphysique, un moyen pour créer ce contact ineffable avec le Noῦς que cette oeuvre était censée refléter.—Tandis que toute image de tradition grecque, classique ou hellénistique, fixe les résultats d'une analyse rationnelle de l'objet figuré, Plotin reconnaît dans l'art, tel qu'il le conçoit en vue de sa contemplation de l'intelligible, l'expression d'une connaissance immédiate et totale de l'essence des choses, de l'âme universelle" (pp. 24–25).

given it in each individual part by its distinction from others. And things far off appear near because the real extent of the distance between is contracted for the same reason. The near part of the distance appears in its true extent, from the same causes; but the sight cannot go through the far part of the distance and see its forms as they really are, and so it is not able to say how great in magnitude it really is. (2.8.1)

This recognition of the difficulty in estimating magnitudes when all visual distinctions are lost in uniform surfaces and diffused colors corroborates an optical illustration used later by Plotinus to describe the spiritual trauma which arises in attempting to perceive the One. This description occurs in the final treatise of the *Enneads* and might serve as a fitting summary of Grabar's astute discussion.

What then must The Unity be, what nature is left for it? No wonder that to state it is not easy; even Being and Form are not easy, though we have a way, an approach through the Ideas. The soul or mind reaching towards the formless finds itself incompetent to grasp where nothing bounds it or to take impression where the impinging reality is diffuse; in sheer dread of holding to nothingness, it slips away. The state is painful; often it seeks relief by retreating from all this vagueness to the region of sense, there to rest as on solid ground, just as the sight distressed by the minute rests with pleasure on the bold. Soul must see in its own way; this is by coalescence, unification; but in seeking thus to know the Unity it is prevented by that very unification from recognizing that it has found; it cannot distinguish itself from the object of this intuition. None the less, this is our one resource if our philosophy is to give us knowledge of The Unity. (6.9.3)[65]

The passage is a beautiful account of the psychic disturbance produced by the ancient dilemma and anticipates some of the measures later taken to assuage it. As it approaches the condition of unity, the soul, in fear of the indeterminateness (ἀνείδεον) of the One, retreats outward again to the sensory world which has limit just as the eye, exhausted with the minute discrimination of very small things (μικροῖς) falls back with relief upon things with larger forms (μεγάλοις). As the proper challenge to the soul is the boundariless void of the One, the proper challenge to the eye is the labyrinthine mesh of the manifold. Since vision is so often used to illustrate the soul's activity, it is less surprising that the challenges of soul and sight should complement one another. It becomes

---

[65] It is interesting to compare this analysis of grasping the indeterminate unity of the One to that of grasping the indeterminate disparity of matter (esp. in 2.4.10, 12). Plotinus' treatments of matter (in 1.8, 2.4–5, 3.6) are particularly haunting and suggest at times Proclus' account of how the imagination grasps the mathematical concept of "infinity (τὸ ἄπειρον)" in his commentary on Euclid (pp. 222–23). Seneca uses the comparison of the soul's ascent, rather than descent, to the eyes' relaxing in open vistas after having strained themselves over delicate work in poor light (*Ep.* 65.17).

clearer, that is, why the ineffable significance of a dimensionless unity might be expressed arbitrarily in a meticulously delimited visible form without any further articulation of how they are related to one another. In the Neoplatonic transmission of the ancient dilemma, what is known by intellective intuition has continued to be juxtaposed beside what is known by aesthetic intuition. These two types of things known remain unreconciled, and their juxtaposition, A and B, when expressed in a single representation, will appear as an identification of A with B analogous to that presupposed in Plotinus' second, or symbolic, type of likeness. To understand the consequences of this identification, it is helpful to see it again in the intellectual development which I have been tracing in Part Two of this study.

In his *Sophist*, Plato illustrates one of the conditions necessary for the acquisition and discursive use of human knowledge in the arts by a parable urging the negotiation between the intellectively intuitive gods and the empirically intuitive giants. Similarly, Aristotle often differentiates the knowledge appropriate to the realm of the gods logically and epistemologically from that appropriate to the realm of the giants— were he to use Plato's metaphor—by distinguishing two types of intelligibility. He points out that things may be known either with respect to their own nature—that is, absolutely (ἁπλῶς)—or with respect to our own perceptions—that is, relative to us (ἡμῖν). Since neither kind of knowledge can be demonstrated by deduction from prior principles, both must be apprehended intuitively. Those things known ἁπλῶς are grasped by intellective intuition, while those known ἡμῖν are perceived by aesthetic intuition. However different the nature of their objects, both types of intuition are, as St. Thomas observes of theology and poetry, antithetical to discursive reason. As a result, whenever in the history of the literary and visual arts discursive reason is contrasted with intuitive insight, it is wise to ask whether the intuition in question be intellective or aesthetic or, especially after the Renaissance, a rather confusing mixture of both. Particularly in the eighteenth through the twentieth centuries, writers, often out of a distrust or rejection of discursive reason, have tried to represent first principles, physical or metaphysical, by describing their own sensory impressions of their immediate surroundings. When they do this, they identify the object of aesthetic with that of intellective intuition rather than relate them discursively to one another. As in the case of our Egyptian in Philostratus, an inner (and hence distant) significance, glimpsed by a private, ineffable vision, is embodied in a verisimilarly exact external form recognizable by all.[66]

---

[66] On similar tendencies in the descriptive language of Plotinus, see Bréhier, *The Philosophy of Plotinus*, pp. 6–7. Later Bréhier, in comparing the philosophy of Plotinus to

Since the Renaissance, much literary theory, reflecting the Neoplatonic reconstruction of the ancient dilemma in its terminology, has been an inheritance of the attitudes expressed by Thespesion. If one recognizes, for instance, the liberalism of Apollonius in allowing for the flexible operation of the reason and imagination in artistic representation and the conservatism of Thespesion in limiting art to the nondiscursive symbol, Dr. Johnson and Sir Joshua Reynolds become the liberal Longinian spokesmen of the neoclassical world. William Blake, on the other hand, instead of appearing as an innovative liberator, becomes, in his marginalia on Reynolds at least, a mystagogic reactionary: (1) like Longinus' Caecelius, Blake maintains that neither genius nor knowledge of ideal beauty can be acquired by art, because both are innate; (2) he questions the value of seeking to define 'general nature,' of general methodological principles, and of the generalizing mind by means of which a man like Johnson might hope to move discursively back and forth between aesthetic and intellective insights and (3) like Thespesion, he prefers the exactly detailed verisimilar imitation to the simpler 'general form,' advocated by Reynolds, while, at the same time, he sees, with visionary inspiration, an inner significance in the minutely rendered particulars. For Blake, the sublime object will somehow be contained in, and be identified with, the "singular and particular detail" which will have, perhaps, the hierophantic power of the precisely executed animal representing the Egyptian god. The necessary polarity of what is more knowable absolutely (ἁπλῶς) and what is more knowable relative to us (ἡμῖν) is dissolved in symbolic identity.[67]

that of the Upanishads, says that in the latter "the main thesis is that Brahman [the principle of universal being] is identical with Atman [the principle, as it exists in the human soul], that is . . ., the force which creates and preserves the world is identical with what we discover in ourselves as our true self when we disregard all the activities related to definite objects" (ibid., p. 125).

[67] Both poles *and* their separateness are necessary because they must exist individually for there to be reciprocation between them. This reciprocality refers both to the discursive negotiation which the mind makes between the two *archai* of apprehension—aesthetic and intellective—and to *what* we grasp in our experience by means (and at the point) of that negotiation. What we experience of the world at this point and are to represent in the literary and visual arts best defines, I think, what Johnson and Reynolds mean by "general nature" in *A Preface to Shakespeare* and the *Discourses*. This "general nature" can be abstracted neither to empirical detail nor to generic formulation without its being deformed or destroyed. For an exceptionally perceptive analysis of these important issues after the Renaissance, see W. Edinger, *Samuel Johnson and Poetic Style* (Chicago, 1977).

9. Summary and Conclusion

of Part Two

In Part Two of this study, I have tried to describe the ancient dilemma of knowledge and representation and some of its consequences for the history of stylistic decorum. As an illustration of the dilemma, I borrowed an anecdote from Philostratus concerning the proper way to represent the gods to serve as a kind of parable which might draw various issues into a coherent association with one another. As a parable, it has had the freedom to reinvoke this association when necessary after the particular issues themselves have become differentiated into their separate developments, their individual terminologies, and their specialized applications.

The ancient dilemma arises from a distinction between the excellence of an object to be known and represented and the accuracy with which we can know and represent it. This distinction involves two premises which culminate in an antithesis. The first premise states that the value of knowledge may be measured either by the importance of its object or by the completeness and accuracy of its information about its object. The second premise of the distinction between excellence of object and accuracy of knowledge states that these two ways of evaluating knowledge are inversely proportionate to one another. The more excellent the object, that is, the less apprehensible and, therefore, the less exactly it may be represented. The more accurately the object may be known and represented, by contrast, the less removed from our perceptions and hence the less exceptional it is apt to be. The two premises may be stated as a completed antithesis and the opposing terms established: greater nobility of objects (though less exactly known and representable), on the one hand, and greater accuracy of knowledge and representation (though of less exceptional objects) on the other. The classical resolution of the ancient dilemma would lie, therefore, in the discovery of a method of inquiry commensurate in its accuracy with the excellence of its object.

Both Plato and Aristotle analyzed the objects of knowledge into two 'elementary' types. In accord with the metaphor of the Divided Line,

Plato distinguished intelligible from sensible things which were the objects of the noetic / dianoetic faculties and the doxastic / aesthetic faculties respectively. Intelligible objects, such as Equality itself (αὐτὸ τὸ ἴσον), are those 'recollected' from our former lives and are distinct from their reflections, such as apparently equal magnitudes, in our sensory experience (τὰ ἐκ τῶν αἰσθήσεων ἴσα, *Phaedo* 74A–75B). These two types of objects are each known in a different way, and their respective ways correspond to Aristotle's two types of intelligibility. Throughout his treatises, Aristotle distinguishes objects better known with respect to themselves (ἁπλῶς), such as primary elements, from things better known with respect to our own perceptions (ἡμῖν). Equality itself would better be known ἁπλῶς, while apparently equal magnitudes would better be known ἡμῖν.

Representative of Plato's later dialogues, the *Sophist* emphasizes the need for cognitive inquiry and the expression of its results in the arts of language to bring the 'polar' objects of intelligible and sensible intuition into relation with one another by means of the discursive negotiation of dialectic. Plato illustrates this need for integration by the fable of the 'idealist' gods and the 'materialist' giants, who, as long as they remain exclusive defenders of their own territories, will be in continual conflict. As long, that is, as the intuited first principles of intellection and the intuited first principles of perception remain in isolation from one another as separate 'hypostatized' objects of knowledge and representation, the cognitive and the literary analysis of experience will be deformed. And in the shadows of such deformities of the understanding and its language the eristic sophist may securely hide.

In the *Philebus*, Plato expresses this danger of isolation by criticizing those who arbitrarily juxtapose, as extreme cognitive poles, the hypothetical limits of knowledge directly against one another to the exclusion of the intermediate ranges of experience. The early sections of this dialogue (12C–18E) are among the clearest treatments of the relation between the poles of unity, or the one (τὸ ἕν), as a principle of limit, and of the manifold, or the indeterminate, as a principle of the unlimited (τὸ ἄπειρον). Socrates makes his distinctions in order to show that there exists within any given unifying concept, such as 'pleasure' or 'color' or 'sound,' an indefinite number of differentiations or 'kinds,' two of which at least may be absolutely opposed to one another (ἐναντιώτατα ἀλλήλοις, 12E). As white is antithetical to black, and yet both are colors, so good and harmful pleasures may establish a polarity of extremes within a single concept. To define all pleasure as the good, as Philebus tries to do, is to make all these "most absolute opposites identical" (13A). If such an identity is assumed, the analytical powers of dialectic will be able to make no discriminations of essence or value. If either of the polar extremes, that is, is considered in isolation from the other or if both are reduced to one through identification, the analysis of our experiences, and its expression in language, becomes impossible. Such a reduction is likely to come about through one's actually having become afraid (φοβηθείς) to make the differentiation of 'kinds' which dialetical analysis can bring to light (14A).

The effect of the isolation of one polar extreme from another is the same as that of identifying the polar opposites: in each case the differentiated scale of existence or value lying between the extremes disappears from view. The one and the many become the reverse sides of a single coin: we move from the absolute unity of the one to the absolute indeterminateness of the manifold in a single step. Such a step ought not to be taken, however,

Until we have a view of its whole number between infinity and one; then, and not before, we may let each unit of everything pass on unhindered into infinity. The gods, then, as I said, handed down to us this mode of investigating, learning, and teaching one another; but the wise [i.e. superficially clever] men of the present day make the one and the many too quickly or too slowly, in haphazard fashion, and they put infinity immediately after unity; they disregard all that lies between them, and this it is which distinguishes between the dialectic and the disputatious (ἐριστικῶς) methods of discussion. (16E–17A)

Unless dialectic brings out the gradations of being and truth between the infinite and the one (τὸν μεταξὺ τοῦ ἀπείρου τε καὶ τοῦ ἑνός) which illuminate our conscious life, our knowledge and its representation by the literary, visual, and musical arts can offer little but eristically fashionable opinion. It does us no more good, for example, to know that the polar extremes of the infinite and the one exist than it does a musician to know that there is a lowest and a highest sound: all the arts must establish and 'make something of' the intervals in between if harmonious composition is to be achieved (17B–18C).

For if a person begins with some unity or other, he must, as I was saying, not turn immediately to infinity, but to some definite number; now just so, conversely, when he has to take the infinite first, he must not turn immediately to the one, but must think of some number which possesses in each case some plurality, and must end by passing from all to one. (18AB)

In a word, the relation between the one and the many must be reciprocal (πρὸς ἄλληλα, 18D).[1]

---

[1] So, of course, in all matters of knowledge and representation, Aristotelian demonstration (ἀπόδειξις) deals with the intermediate steps between what can be (more or less) immediately grasped and what cannot, be it the general issue of a problem or thesis (*Top.*

The dialectical activity of the consciousness as described here is precisely that exemplified in the *Sophist*. Without intermediate degrees between the unifying Forms of the gods and the diversifying materials of the Titans, between Being and non-Being, and between truth and falsehood, the polar extremes, such as the one and the many, would either become individually hypostatized or identified with one another. In either case the differentiating luminosity provided by their reciprocal negotiation would diminish, and in the resulting twilight the sophist might eristically elude his pursuers indefinitely. Such a negotiation is achieved by dialectic, than which, for Plato, there is no better road (χαλλίων ὁδός, 16B).

For Aristotle, the natural road (ὁδός) for the investigation of the physical world "must lie from what is more immediately cognizable and clear to us (ἡμῖν), to what is clearer and more intimately cognizable in its own nature (ἁπλῶς)." He illustrates what is clearer *to us*—the composite 'whole' immediately presented to our senses—by a general, as yet "unanalyzed (ἀδιορίστως)" name or concept such as "circle" or "father." As Philebus uses the concept 'pleasure' to refer indiscriminately to all pleasures, the child calls every man "father" until he differentiates (διορίζει) the parental 'kind' of relationship from other kinds (*Physics* 1.1). Similarly, in the beginning of the *Nicomachean Ethics* (1.4.5–7), he praises Plato for asking whether the right road (ὁδός) of inquiry starts from or leads up to first principles—since "in a racecourse one may run from the judges to the far end of the track or reversely"—and concludes that it is proper to start from "what is known to us (ἡμῖν)." The point I wish to emphasize here is not so much at

---

105a7–9) or the terms of a proportional metaphor which must be "reciprocally" related (ἀνταποδιδόναι, *Rhet.* 3.4.4). E. Voegelin has discussed the importance of these passages in the *Philebus* in his essay "Reason: The Classic Experience," cited in Chap. 6, n. 19, and in *The Ecumenic Age*, vol. 4 of *Order and History* (Baton Rouge, 1974), pp. 184–85: "In the exegesis of his differentiated experience, then, Plato symbolizes the mystery of being as existence between the poles of the One (*hen*) and the Unlimited (*apeiron*). Where the One changes over into the Many (*polloi*) and the Unlimited into the Limited (*peras*), there arises, between the two poles, the number (*arithmos*) and form (*idea*) of 'things.' This area of form and number is the In-Between (*metaxy*) of the One (*hen*) and the Unlimited (*apeiron*) (16d-e). The *metaxy* is the domain of human knowledge. The proper method of its investigation that remains aware of the In-Between status of things is called 'dialectics'; while the improper hypostasis of In-Between things into the One or the Unlimited is the characteristic defect of the speculative method that is called 'eristics' (17a)." For the appropriateness of the term *metaxy* for that "reality" whose experience I have described in Part Two as properly represented by the discursive arts, see Chap. 3 of *The Ecumenic Age*, esp. pp. 183–201; see also pp. 226–38, 247–49. What I have called the 'point' of negotiation or reciprocation, Voegelin, too, regards as that "point from which the symbols emerge as the exegesis" of the truth of the *metaxy*, symbols which become distorted when forced to stand for either the divine or the human taken independently of the other (p. 56). For further comment on such distortion, see pp. 33–43.

which end of the track the runner starts as the fact that he runs the whole course. To adapt the metaphor to Socrates' argument in the *Philebus* (18AB) quoted previously, even if the runner starts at the pole of diversity (τὸ ἄπειρον), he cannot leap immediately (εὐθύς) to the pole of the one but must pass through a series of intermediate stages each of which is reached by some definite number of steps. Only in this way can the dialectical inquirer move from one epistemological pole to the other.[2]

The endeavor to find a 'road' or method (μέθ + ὁδός) of inquiry and representation commensurate in its accuracy with the excellence of its objects is expressed in the parable of Philostratus by the Greek, Apollonius. Apollonius maintains that we may most appropriately represent what we know of the divinity of Zeus by the human form, because the most divine manifestation of the cosmos (to us) is its rationality and, among living beings, men are the most rational. The human form itself, that is, may express one of the foremost characteristics of the divine. Pheidias' conception and subsequent representation of Zeus, therefore, become more commensurate in their accuracy with the excellence of what they signify than the animal forms preferred by the Egyptian, Thespesion. For the Egyptian, it is the discrepancy itself between the triviality of the animal form, however expertly rendered, and the divinity it signifies which properly expresses the inscrutability of the god and his unnegotiable distance from us. The animal form, embodying part of the manifold materiality of the Titans and of our own perceptions, is arbitrarily juxtaposed against the divine principle of unity and limit. As do the 'wise' men whom Socrates criticizes for juxtaposing the many directly against the one, Thespesion allows for no intermediate stages

---

[2] Boethius' famous description of Lady Philosophy transmits an 'image' of these intellectual attitudes to the modern world. The lady appears as of indeterminate antiquity, of colossal height which extends even into the heavens and is there lost to our view, and on her dress she has θ (θεωρητική) placed at the top and π (πρακτική) at the bottom. The 'theoretical' disciplines will concern things more knowable with respect to themselves (and hence difficult for us to behold); the 'prudential' disciplines will concern what is clearer with respect to our perceptions. The main purport of the 'image,' however, is to indicate the 'way' from θ to π or from π to θ—how, that is, one can negotiate between them—and this is done by a mediating 'ladder': "Betwixt the two letters, in the manner of stairs, there were certain degrees made, by which there was a passage from the lower to the higher letter." It is specifically this garment, with its interconnected poles, which "had been cut by the violence of some, who had taken away such pieces as they could get." Just how the poles and their interconnections had been defaced, Boethius does not say, but it is not implausible that he refers to sects which, among other types of deformations, had tried to hypostatize one of the extremes independently of the other and incorporate it into a philosophical system (cf. 1.3). *Boethius: The Consolation of Philosophy* 1.1, trans. "I.T.," rev. H. F. Stewart, LCL (London, 1962). For an excellent general study of this portrait, see P. Courcelle, *La Consolation de Philosophie dans la tradition littéraire* (Paris, 1967).

between the extremes, stages by which we can come to understand something of the god's significance.

The argument between Apollonius and Thespesion illustrates the central problem of decorum. Like the other arts, literature seeks to represent our understanding of experience at that point where the acquisitions of intellective and aesthetic intuition attain their most discursively articulated negotiation. Any such negotiation is a continuous process of adjustment, not a condition to be achieved, fixed, and maintained; it is an activity, rather than a possession, of the consciousness. A style which is to represent that activity must achieve decorum through the flexible articulation of this cognitive process with respect to a subject, to an audience, and to an occasion. Decorum itself, therefore, cannot consist of (formal) axioms, (philosophical) propositions, or (rhetorical) sanctions to be codified and transmitted by manuals. It consists, rather, in the ethical and literary criteria for the qualitative judgment of those experiences, actions, and artistic products which are unsuited to quantitative measurement. For all the arts, as Plato says (*Statesman* 284E), owe their beauty and excellence to proper proportion (τὸ μέτριον), right occasion (τὸν καιρόν), propriety (τὸ πρέπον), and "all such standards as have removed their abode from the extremes (ἐσχάτων) and are now settled about the mean (τὸ μέσον)." It is precisely in bringing these extremes together, like a coincidence of opposites, that Thespesion still conceives of the problem of decorum. His symbolic images (ξυμβολικά) which express this coincidence restrict their psychagogic effect to awesomeness (σεμνόν) and fearfulness (ἔμφοβον). Such a restriction greatly narrows the ways in which we can conceive, represent, and feel about the divine.

I have used the term 'psychagogia' (in its best sense) to refer to the act of arousing and 'leading' those feelings in a listener (or reader) which are appropriate, or in proportion, to the significance of what the speaker (or writer) says about a given topic on a given occasion to a given audience. Since different styles evoke different kinds and degrees of emotion, only when the speaker speaks appropriately in this general sense can his style be said to achieve decorum (τὸ πρέπον). The kinds and degrees of emotions that he tries to arouse will depend upon how well he understands both the issues involved and the nature of his listeners. His understanding of both, in turn, will depend on the degree of his integration of the intellective and aesthetic acquisitions of knowledge—an integration revealed, for example, by the speaker's insight into the application of general ethical principles to particular circumstances. Certain styles will articulate that integration more completely in matters which are more effectively known with respect to themselves (ἁπλῶς), others in matters which are more effectively known with respect to us (ἡμῖν). The nature of the subjects, that is, will influence the kind of knowledge we can have of them; what and how much we can know of them will influence how we can represent them with the greatest decorum.

Plato treats the adaptation of style to the speaker's knowledge both of his subject and of the souls of his audience in the *Phaedrus* (270B–72B). He summarizes his analysis in the passage quoted earlier in this study (277BC): only when a man has learned the truth about all the particular things of which he speaks or writes, about the varying nature of his listeners' psyches, and about which type of speech will move which type of psyche, only then can he "arrange and adorn his discourse accordingly, offering to the complex soul elaborate and harmonious discourses, and simple talks to the simple soul." Plato's statement about the psychagogic relation of character to style helps to coordinate the epistemological distinction of ἁπλῶς-ἡμῖν with the stylistic distinctions of ἁπλῶς-ποικίλως and ἁπλῶς-ἀκριβῶς.

In the course of the *Phaedrus* Plato argues that dialectic should provide the formal and cognitive foundations of all rhetorical, legal, and poetic discourse. In addition, he argues that the ever-probing, ever-requalifying oral exchange between disputants has the advantage over written discourse in that a statement once written down can no longer respond to the continuing inquiry of the consciousness. Once fixed, it becomes obsolete insofar as it is no longer able to 'keep up' with the phenomenal process of experience, whose emotion we must recognize, accept, and cope with as best we can. Given Plato's emphasis upon the philosophical responsibilites of language, he is likely to have felt more at ease with the simple, unsophisticated soul (ἁπλῆ ψυχή) which is apt to be easily and beneficially 'led' in the process of dialectical inquiry than with the 'cultivated' soul (ποικίλη ψυχή) whose very cleverness may first be in need of 'purification' (cf. *Sophist* 230A–31B).

Despite Plato's hostility to the democratic conditions of deliberative oratory (δημηγορική) as Aristotle describes them in his *Rhetoric*—conditions most antipathetic to the philosophical instruction of the 'simple soul'—there is an analogous simplicity of soul to be addressed and 'led' in a large miscellaneous audience participating in agonistic debate. The members of such an audience, who are the judges as well as the observers of deliberative contests, are themselves, Aristotle says, without special dialectical or judicial training and, in this sense, are 'uncultivated' thinkers (ἁπλοῦς, *Rhet.* 1.2.12–13; 1357a1–14). The best philosophical respondent in Plato's dialectical discussions, psychagogically speaking, that is, will share this simplicity with Aristotle's audience for the most important kind of rhetorical discourse. However variously sophisticated (ποικίλος) individual members of the miscellaneous audience may be, the deliberative speaker must address them as a group in a style appropriate to a hypothetically 'common,' undifferentiated, and therefore 'simple,' listener if he hopes to sway the majority.

The oral style appropriate for this 'common' listener will also be ἁπλοῦς in the sense of being sketched out in rough and forceful strokes, boldly negligent of the polished refinements and details which render the written encomiastic style ποικίλος. Similarly in Plato, the informal, conversational style of dialectic will be ἁπλοῦς in its avoidance of the meticulously elaborated (ποικίλος) epideictic procedures of speeches or poems written to be read silently or recited aloud. Once allowances are made, that is, for the different intentions, occasions, and subjects of deliberative oratory and dialectical inquiry, decorum in both types of discourse reveals an analogous relation of style to both the type of soul addressed and to the objects of inquiry represented. In each case a relatively unelaborated style (ἁπλοῦς) becomes appropriate to the presentation of subjects which are often better known with respect to themselves (ἁπλῶς) before an audience whose souls are sufficiently free of clouded opinions (ἁπλαί) to be emotionally receptive to either the private inquiries of the Academy or to the communal urgencies of the assembly. Similarly, by contrast, a meticulously refined argument and style (ποικίλως), written for private reading or recitation before a cultivated audience (ποικίλος), will be appropriate to the expression of a sophisticated attitude (ποικίλος) toward a topic which originally elicited, but now perhaps has virtually itself become, a number of conflicting opinions and subjective points of view (ἡμῖν).

The epistemological distinction of how we know things (ἁπλῶς - ἡμῖν) and the stylistic distinction of how elaborately or accurately we may represent them (ἁπλῶς - ποικίλως / ἀκριβῶς) are as closely related to one another in literature as they are in philosophy and rhetoric. In accord with the epistemological distinction, we seek a knowledge commensurate in its accuracy with the nature of the subject to be treated; in accord with the stylistic distinction, we seek a style of representation commensurate in its elaboration with that knowledge. In order to evoke the kinds and degrees of emotions psychagogically appropriate to the occasion, the subject, and the audience, a style must achieve and preserve the proper balance between the formal, cognitive, and judicative intentions of literary discourse. The neglect of one of these intentions in favor of one or both of the other two—a neglect which stands at the center of the issue illustrated by Philostratus in his parable about the visual arts—will make the Greek conception of decorum impossible to attain.

While Plato and Aristotle respond to the ancient dilemma of knowledge and representation as Apollonius does in the *Life of Apollonius of Tyana*, the response of Plotinus and Proclus corresponds to that of the Egyptian Thespesion. *With respect to knowledge*, both Neoplatonists subordinate the intermediate ranges of experience to the ontological extremes of reality, the One and the Manifold, as proper and improper objects of knowledge respectively. Both subordinate, accordingly, the discursive negotiation between the intellective and aesthetic activities of the consciousness to either an intuitive intellection (appropriate to the cognition of unity) or an aesthetic intuition (appropriate to the perception of diversity) in isolation from one another. If grasped and kept separate from each other, the objects of either type of intuition must remain, to a large extent, abstractions.

With respect to representation, the separation of aesthetic from intellective objects of knowledge finds its natural counterpart in the separation of the 'external' verbal or visual form from the 'internal' significance which the form expresses. The Neoplatonists would tend, therefore, to prefer symbols (to mimetic representation) which can express more directly either intellective objects—best known with respect to themselves (ἁπλῶς)—or perceptual objects—best known with respect to us (ἡμῖν)—by external forms which stipulate, but need not characterize, the significance which they embody. Such symbols may stipulate what they signify either by conventionally established designations, attributes, or formal *schemata*, which, however stereotyped, have the public advantage, like coins, of clarity and simplicity. Or they may express their significance by an external form so totally antithetical to what they signify that, however much the private selection and original execution of the form may prevent its becoming stereotyped, it cannot avoid becoming enigmatic. Plotinus helps to distinguish these symbolic tendencies from mimetic procedures by differentiating between two types of likeness.

Plotinus' first (reciprocal) type of likeness, based on kinds of similarity, is more congenial to a mimetic representation of the intermediate ranges of our experience. A mimetic narrative, for instance, presents a discursive sequence of events which are recognizably similar in their casual relations to the events of our own lives. In order to render these relations intelligible, the narrator can perceive and present them only as they emerge in the continuous renegotiation between our intuitive cognition of things known ἁπλῶς and our intuitive perception of things known ἡμῖν. Plotinus' second (nonreciprocal) type of likeness, on the other hand, which is based on degrees of disparity, is more congenial to symbolic representation. In denying a reciprocal relation between its terms of com-

parison, A and B, this type of likeness states the disparity of A from B
rather than their mutual similarity to each other. While we measure A
in relation to (its approach to) B, we cannot measure B in relation to
(its approach to) A: we know, that is, the *relation* of A to B only with
respect to our separately intuited knowledge of B. Since we learn nothing
of their relation from A, the two terms, as heuristic instruments, have
been reduced to one.

Similarly, the symbol predicates no explicit relation between what it
signifies (comparable to B) and the external form (comparable to A)
which embodies its significance. Having lost this reciprocal relationship,
such an external form, whether derived from convention or privately
invented, becomes identified with, but expresses little or nothing about,
the nature of what it signifies. Such an identification increases the formal
emphasis upon literary theory. In his analysis of both geometry and
poetry in terms of Plato's Divided Line, Proclus emphasizes this formalism even more by his account of the imagination whose images
proceed from and return to the understanding in what resemble geometrical ratios. He seems in these descriptions to reduce all forms of
discursive argumentation and representation in the arts to the paradigm
of mathematical demonstration.

Plotinus makes his important distinction between two types of likeness
in order to distinguish human (civic) virtues, which can be achieved
through imitation in accord with the first type of likeness, from the
divine excellences, which must be approached through purification in
accord with the second type of likeness. Traditionally, the concern of
the prudential faculty, the civic virtues, of course, were important in
Neoplatonic ethics from the beginning. Yet, with respect to the Plotinian
intellectual construction as a whole, not only do the prudential arbitra-
tions of *praxis* become subservient to the divine assimilation achieved
through catharsis but they also reflect, to some degree, the imperfections
of the political and circumstantial world of extension in which they must
function. Plotinus regards the ethical pressures of this material world
as labyrinthine forces of competitive interests and entanglements, forces
which exert a kind of baffling bewitchment (γοητεία) upon the human
psyche. We fulfill our greatest ethical potentiality, therefore, by escaping
from this bewitchment through purifying our nature of those passions
and ambitions which prudence has traditionally directed and controlled.
The world, that is, of human relationships, activities, and conflicts—
appropriate for mimetic representation—must give way, as the most
excellent subject matter for art, to the human assimilation to, or even
identification with, the divine. Such an identification—appropriate for
symbolic representation—will tend to disregard those middle ranges of

experience which have always provided literature with its principal materials. At best, these middle ranges will permit the mind to pass as
rapidly as possible through their multiplicities toward the One; at worst,
their terrain will impede our passage by obstacles, detours, and digressions.

When a concept of purification becomes the primary objective of prudential wisdom, any theory of literary decorum becomes impoverished
with respect to its cognitive obligations to analyze qualitative experience
and to its judicative obligations to guide the emotions. Neither psychagogia nor the cognition of qualities can hold an important position
in an ethical theory whose ultimate aim is an ontological and psychological 'purity' in the Plotinian sense. On the one hand, for Plotinus,
the powers of persuasion can but weave further magical snares for the
social, political, and economic bewitchment of the individual soul. On
the other hand, qualities or accidents can only evoke the least substantial,
most transitory, impressions of the objects that we seek to know. It is
precisely upon such impressions that rhetoric casts its most dangerous
spells. The more we are entangled in multiplicity, the more lost we are
among qualities; the further we drift outward toward the boundlessness
of matter, the more ghostly these qualities become; the more they
dissolve into phantasmagorias, the more easily rhetoric can manipulate
them. It is this world of quality which the mimetic arts are condemned
to represent, and the psychagogic effects of their representations continue
to be described by the Neoplatonists in the critical terms of the earlier
philosophers.

As ontological realities approach closer to the One, their natures, in
becoming more ἁπλαί in the sense of pure (unmixed), simple, and unified, become as well more knowable with respect to themselves (ἁπλῶς).
As they descend toward the Many, their natures, in becoming more
ποικίλαι in the sense of composite, variegated, and changeable, become
at the same time more knowable with respect to our own perceptions
(παρ' ἡμῖν). Each god, says Proclus (1.111.16ff.), remains one and the
same (ἁπλοῦς) but appears in various forms (ποικίλος) to human beings
who must grasp divine properties according to their individual capacities.
With respect to knowledge, divine realities are best apprehended by
intellection, terrestrial natures by perception. So, with respect to representation, the most unified realities will be presented simply in symbols. The mimetic illusionist (φανταστικός), on the other hand, will
employ a most elusive (πολυτροπωτέραν) and impressionistic (αἰσθητικωτέραν) style, having abandoned the simplest (ἁπλουστέρας) song,
most proper for the Muses, for the most variegated (ποικιλωτέραν) form
of composition. Such a style will strive for meticulous elaboration and

accuracy of detail (ἀκρίβεια, *cultus*) which characterized, for Aristotle (and Isocrates), written, epideictic compositions.

The negative overtones in Plato's use of ποικίλος as a stylistic term to express the varied differentiations of quality (ποιότης) and their psychagogic effects, particularly with reference to mimesis (*Rep.* 604E–5A), have become more rigidly intensified in the Neoplatonists. Their distrust of our ability to apprehend qualities and to lead the emotions of an audience to a proper judgment results in their isolating and over-emphasizing the formal principles of unity and coherence, an isolation which has contributed strongly to the history of 'aestheticism.' If the ancient balance among the formal, cognitive, and judicative energies of literary decorum is to be reestablished, it will be necessary to recover the concept of 'quality' in the investigation and representation of human experience. The various and corresponding functions of *qualitas* in the poetic, ethical, legal, and logical disciplines become most clearly apparent, and recoverable, in the rhetorical transmission of literary theory.

Part Three

The Quality of Fiction:
The Rhetorical Transmission of
Literary Theory

INSOFAR AS literary discourse was able to integrate and realize the intentions of other disciplines, sometimes historically antithetical to one another, it could define more complicated ethical and psychological relations of the human consciousness to the external world. However small the number of texts *primarily* concerned with the nature of literature in many periods, expressions of these relations, like old-fashioned atoms, are less likely to have ceased than to have gone, as it were, 'underground.' Or, rather, they have lain hidden in the concerns and terminologies of other disciplines: of geometry, the natural sciences, music, and the visual arts; of theology, ethics, and psychology; and of oratory, jurisprudence, and education.[1] In the following sections of this study I wish to indicate the latent survival of these expressions in the disciplines associated with rhetoric and, thereby, to emphasize the contribution of the judicative intention to the formal and cognitive intentions of literary works of art.

A principal advantage of having treated stylistic decorum, earlier, in relation to the epistemological objectives of philosophy in Part Two is to be able to concentrate in Part Three directly upon the nonstylistic contributions of rhetoric to the composition of literature. These contributions have not drawn their share of attention largely because of the common tendency to reduce the discipline of rhetoric as a whole to the treatment of style, or *elocutio*, alone. Such a reduction has obscured the importance of both the argumentative structure and the qualitative examination of human actions which rhetoric has kept alive in the transmission of literary theory. In both its prudential emphasis upon the concept of 'quality' and in its discursive emphasis upon procedures of argumentation, the rhetorical tradition has done most, perhaps, to resist the peculiar imbalances with which such philosophical systems as that of Neoplatonism have threatened the literary analysis of experience.

In order to examine the nature of this resistance, I shall first trace the concept of *qualitas* back to four of its principal sources in logic, law, epistemology, and certain natural sciences. Although the exact meanings of the concept in its original sources vary, as we shall see, with the discipline in question, they designate, generally, those things in our experience which cannot be judged by criteria of quantitative measure-

---

[1] The implications for literary theory discoverable in disciplines which originally contributed to its terminology would remain significant even if specific treatises on literature had been written and lost. The situation is analogous to the transmission of aesthetic theory. There, according to M. W. Bundy, the concepts making up the history of the imagination have been "molded by philosophy, and, specifically in the order of their importance, by metaphysics, psychology, and ethics. Definitions in these realms largely determined the nature of the terms which were to become so important in the vocabulary of the aesthetician and the critic" (*The Theory of Imagination in Classical and Mediaeval Thought*, Univ. Ill. Stud. Lang. Lit. 12, 2–3 [1927], p. 270).

ment. Plato describes such things, in the passage just quoted in the conclusion to Part Two (*Statesman* 284E), as those which owe their excellence and beauty to due proportion, right occasion, propriety, and "all such standards as have removed their abode from the extremes and are now settled about the mean." In addition to ethical and artistic criteria, these qualitative standards of measurement include criteria for discriminating among types of logical predication as well as among types of knowledge we derive from our senses about the physical world.

All four of these sources—logic, law, epistemology, physics—provided, and could subsequently transmit through their various disciplines, meanings of 'quality' already available to the earliest philosophical discussions of *poesis*. These disciplines, in their turn, could use fictional 'images' similar to poetic *imagines* to discover and interpret the general principles inherent in all qualitative, especially prudential, issues. Claiming the freedom from 'historical' accuracy which literature had always claimed, such images could illustrate, furthermore, how these general principles—themselves often hidden from immediate perception and hence more knowable with respect to themselves—might be applied to specific problems and circumstances.[2]

[2] For continuing interrelationships between some of these disciplines, particularly with respect to faculty psychology, in the Thomist commentaries on Aristotle, see E. De Bruyne, *Études d'esthétique médiévale*, 3 vols. (Brugge, 1946), 3:324–29. This work, which continues to be of great importance for the transmission of literary theory as presented in this study, will be cited hereafter as De Bruyne.

10. The Concept of Quality

WE MAY BEST introduce our examination of the rhetorical concept of 'quality' by recalling the distinctions, summarized in the second chapter of Part One, both between the rhetorical and philosophical procedures of inquiry and between the definite and indefinite questions of rhetoric. With respect to procedures of inquiry, analysis and synthesis in rhetoric are structurally analogous to those in philosophy. The initially 'given,' and as yet uninterpreted, events which constitute the rhetorical set of circumstances of a legal case (hypothesis = *causa, quaestio definita*) to be judged corresponds to the initial philosophical problem (or thesis) 'given' to be explained (or verified). The initial rhetorical set of circumstances (hypothesis) is analyzed into its more general issues or questions (theses = *quaestiones indefinitae*), which are procedurally prior in the sense that they must be considered before the more particular *quaestio definita* of the given case can be decided. The initial philosophical problem (or thesis), which is logically prior in the sense that the whole must exist before its component parts can be discovered, is analyzed into its constituent elements and causes (its hypotheses or *archai*). Once revealed, the general theses of rhetoric may be used to interpret the original, insufficiently understood, events of the initial hypothesis; once discovered, the hypothetical *archai* of philosophy may be used to resolve the initial problem or to defend the initial thesis. Except for the inversion of the terminology—in that the rhetorical analysis begins with a *hypothesis* and seeks to reveal the *theses* necessary to *judge* it, while the philosophical analysis begins with a *thesis* and seeks to discover the *hypotheses* necessary to *explain* it—their general procedures of inquiry and demonstration are similar. In each case, one begins and ends with what had originally been given to be judged or explained.

With respect to rhetorical questions, the *quaestio definita*, as indicated previously, referred to a particular legal controversy, to its circumstances of persons, places, and times—which constitute its 'material' or 'hypothesis'—and, by extension, to the case (*causa*) itself. The *quaestio indefinita* or 'thesis,' on the other hand, referred to any general issue or issues involved in a given case. The charge of tyrannicide, for instance, contains within it not just the definite question of did this person kill this tyrant but also the general issue of whether it is justifiable to kill a tyrant. To the extent that such an issue might include other 'individual' cases of tyrannicide, it rendered them 'specific,' and by its generic power could, for the moment, free the discussion from argument over what actually, 'historically' happened in the conflicting accounts (*narrationes*) of events. This temporary freedom, gained by admitting larger considerations of equity, enabled the orator to discover the issues most pertinent to an effective presentation of his case. By seeking the generic issues he could more easily connect, within the particular interpretation of events he was constructing, one seemingly isolated, or even contradictory, incident with another. He could locate within the controversy as a whole the particular point (*status*) upon which the case should be legally argued. And by alluding to issues in which each man could participate emotionally, he could more easily control the feelings of his audience. In sum, the thesis offered a principle of order by means of which the *ethical* significance of disparate events could be grasped and understood. *Individual* motives and acts, by virtue of a genus, become *specific*: that is, their ethical relation to each other becomes intelligible. The thesis provided, furthermore, by articulating the generic question within the previously 'unspecified' *materia*, a *formal* structure of plausible relationships between events analogous, like that of dialectic, to geometrical proof.

This 'involution' of the general question in the particular controversy however, was a reflection, *within the limits of rhetoric*, of the proper balance of the most liberal intentions of philosophy and rhetoric themselves as Quintilian restates it in the preface to his first book. The difficulties in achieving the proper relation of the indefinite to the definite question were, furthermore, historically interwoven with those of achieving a working relation between the two disciplines. Although Plato, Aristotle, and Isocrates all had stated the necessity of grasping the general philosophical issue lying within any given rhetorical controversy, the professional rivalries between the disciplines soon tended to subvert such a relationship. In the Hellenistic period, rhetoricians, in order to extend their influence, repeatedly claimed the right to treat general questions, as well as particular *causae*, while philosophers as often reasserted their exclusive possession of them. Such disagreement over the border line between the subject matter of each discipline, by constantly emphasizing the cleavage between them, could not help but perpetuate the more conservative characteristics of both. The fact that the rival schools competed so markedly for the right to handle theses indicates how clearly the rhetorical issues of the first century B.C. reflected their sources in the disciplinary controversies of the preceding centuries.[1]

A. Thesis and *Qualitas*

For Aristotle, it will be recalled, both dialectic and rhetoric were methods of discovering, ordering, and presenting arguments persuasively on a broad range of subjects. They were general disciplines rather than specialized sciences which had their own particular bodies of knowledge to acquire and transmit. Whereas dialectic, however, might deal with an almost endless variety of topics, rhetoric was primarily concerned with definite subjects appropriate to either deliberative, forensic, or epideictic speeches. These subjects, though varying greatly from one another, each consisted individually of specific circumstances and issues. With respect to their materials, that is, while dialectic debated 'universal' questions which were not limited to given persons and events, rhetoric involved given political decisions to be made and given judicial cases to be decided.

Cicero transmits this distinction in his *Topica* (79–80) by dividing all inquiry into general and particular questions: "The particular is what the Greeks call ὑπόθεσις (hypothesis), and we call cause or case [*causa, quaestio definita*]; the general inquiry is what they call θέσις (thesis), and we call proposition [*propositum, quaestio indefinita*]." As it was perhaps Aristotle's primary concern in his *Rhetoric* to relate rhetorical argumentation formally to dialectical argumentation, in his mature treatises it is Cicero's primary intention to establish the formal relation of the specific to the generic question. Such a relation was difficult to define because the term 'question' itself could refer, as an instrument of inquiry, to either the subject matter of the argument or to the methods by which the subject matter was discovered and presented. The development of Cicero's terminology illustrates, I believe, a shift in emphasis from a

[1] Similar controversies persist today. The 'material' contribution (ὕλη) of the rhetorical hypothesis to literature resembles the contribution which M. Cohen has suggested the study of jurisprudence might be able to make to a contemporary philosophy reduced to "a purely formal discipline," that is, "to such formal problems as the relation of mind or thought to reality" ("Jurisprudence as a Philosophical Discipline," *Jour. Phil. Psych. Sci. Meth.* 10 [1913]:226). The "philosophy of law," a phrase combining in itself philosophical and rhetorical discourse, might elude both the empirical bondage to individually discrete cases and the conceptualist bondage to an inflexible application of statutes and precedents to circumstances for which they were not designed (p. 228). Such a concern with equity encourages the least specialized intentions of both law and philosophy to liberalize the more conservative forms of each.

'material' to a 'methodological' distinction between definite and indefinite questions.

In his early treatise, *De inventione*, Cicero criticizes Hermagoras for dividing the material (*materiam*) of the orator into special cases (*causam*) and general questions (*quaestionem*). Hermagoras, Cicero says, defines a special case as a matter (*rem*) "involving a controversy conducted by a speech with the introduction of definite individuals" and a general question as "a matter involving a controversy conducted by a speech without the introduction of definite individuals." Cicero accepts the materials assigned to the special case but claims that they have already been adequately covered by Aristotle's tripartite division of material (*materia tripertita*) into judicial, deliberative, and epideictic kinds of subjects. Since no further classification of subject matter seems necessary for oratory, Cicero rejects the subjects which Hermagoras assigns to rhetoric in the form of such general questions as the following: "Is there any good except honour?" "Can the senses be trusted?" "What is the shape of the world?" and "How large is the sun?" Such questions (*quaestiones*), according to Cicero, would be remote from the business of the orator even if he had the knowledge and skill of the trained philosopher (*De inv.* 1.7–8).[2]

Cicero's rejection here of these questions as subject matter sufficiently distinct to categorize a type of rhetoric does not lie so much in the *topics* themselves broached in the questions—goodness, honor, testimony of the senses, and even the nature of the cosmos—as in the fact that the questions are supposed to constitute a *materia* which *by definition* excludes definite individuals. As a material distinction, this one attributed to Hermagoras does not work simply because all material of rhetoric must involve definite people, things, and situations. While Cicero recognized the fact that the material of Aristotle's tripartite division in-

---

[2] This exclusion may be a reflection of the old controversy of the contemplative vs. the active life. Jaeger observes that Dicaearchus, in opposition to Aristotle and Theophrastus, held the active life to be superior to the contemplative: he "severed the connexions . . . between moral action and the knowledge of the highest questions, and reached the logical conclusion of which we hear the echo in the author of the *Great Ethics*: 'One must wonder what *sophia* has to do with ethics,' since the latter concerns character and action" (*Aristotle*, p. 451). In excluding speculative questions from rhetoric, the young Cicero is arguing for the "active" life of the orator in the most pragmatic sense. Later, he emphasized greatly the role of thesis or philosophical question in oratory, and Jaeger, in citing his *Ep. ad Att.*, 2.16, shows how he has left Dicaearchus, representing the active, pragmatic life, for Theophrastus, representing the contemplative, scholastic life. For the place of thesis and hypothesis in the attempts in the second and first centuries B.C. to establish the sophistic ideal of the philosophical and rhetorical disciplines perfectly combined in the person of the rhetorician, see von Arnim, *Leben und Werke*, pp. 94–114, H. Throm, *Die Thesis: Ein Beitrag zu ihrer Entstehung und Geschichte* (Paderborn, 1932), and D. Matthes, *Lustrum* 3 (1958).

cluded these particular subjects, he did not go on to show how general questions might become instrumental in understanding and interpreting that material. The fact that he did not take this step in the *De inventione* makes the terms of this early, more limited work genuinely different from, but not preclusive of, the terminology which he developed in his later treatises.

This later terminology reflects the additional influence of a second division which follows immediately upon the first one between particular causes and general questions just considered from the *Topica*. Cicero now divides general questions themselves into theoretical and practical inquiries. "Theoretical inquiries (*cognitionis*) are those of which the purpose is knowledge (*scientia*)," while practical inquiries (*actionis*) concern questions such as "Should a philosopher take part in politics?" (*Top.* 81–82). While theoretical questions are cognitive, practical questions are judicative insofar as they concern not only how to choose the most prudent means to a given end but also how to lead people emotionally to accept that choice (86). This second division seems ultimately to derive from Aristotle, who, following his overall differentiation of philosophical subject matter, divided general questions to be discussed dialectically into ethical, logical, and physical theses or propositions or problems (*Top.* 105b20–26). Logical and physical questions became associated with cognition and ethical questions with action, and the division was later simplified to one between theoretical and practical theses as Cicero describes them (*Top.* 79–82, *De part. orat.* 61–62, *De orat.* 1.68–69). The theoretical thesis was to be argued without implication in circumstance, while the practical thesis, although it remained a general consideration of human behavior, and hence was never identical to a legal case, tended, nevertheless, to seek a point of departure, or a particular application, in a given situation.[3] In dealing with moral issues involved in specific deliberative or judicial decisions, therefore, the practical thesis might avoid both the philosophical abstruseness of abstract questions *and* the ethically restricted particularity and technicality of rhetorical *causae*. The second distinction, based on intentions or faculties, that is, might suggest in its practical thesis a middle ground or a relation

---

[3] The terms 'practical' and 'theoretical' thesis and their accompanying functions, *actio* and *cognitio*, gradually replaced the earlier rhetorical terms of hypothesis and thesis. Quintilian: *hi thesin a causa sic distinguunt, ut illa sit spectativae partis, haec activae* (3.5.11). Cicero describes for Atticus (9.4) his practicing θέσεις πολιτικάς, *in utramque partem tum Graece tum Latine*, which perhaps dealt with matters close to his own life. Theon also divides theses into theoretical and practical, and what he calls πραχτικάς, Hermogenes calls πολιτικάς (G. Reichel, *Quaestiones progymnasmaticae* [Lipsiae, 1909], p. 106).

between the disciplines of philosophy and rhetoric which the first division in the *De inventione*, based solely on *materia*, did not permit.

How the second 'psychological' distinction between purposes and methods of acquiring, analyzing, and presenting the results of inquiry might have combined with, and even informed, the first 'material' distinction between the subjects of inquiry becomes apparent in Cicero's later treatment of the problem. In the *De oratore*, Cicero has Antonius at first reiterate the orator's freedom from the same speculative questions about physics as were rejected some thirty years earlier in the *De inventione*.[4] But Antonius then continues by admitting that if the orator does pursue "that indeterminate, unrestricted and far-extending sort of investigation (*partem quaestionum . . . vagam, et liberam, et late patentem*)," he might properly discuss, within reasonable limits, such ethical topics as "good and evil, things to be preferred and things to be shunned, fair repute and infamy, the useful and the unuseful, besides moral perfection, righteousness, self-control, discretion, greatness of soul, generosity, loyalty, friendship, good faith, sense of duty and the rest of the virtues and their corresponding vices" (2.66–67). He might discuss, in other words, qualitative matters characteristic of the practical thesis. In fact, "all things relating to the intercourse of fellow-citizens and the ways of mankind, or concerned with everyday life, the political system, our own corporate society, the common sentiments of humanity, natural inclinations and morals must be mastered by the orator" (2.68). Such topics would enable the orator "to speak of these very things in the same way as the founders of rules of law, statutes and civil communities spoke" (2.68).

Speaking as a man less learned than experienced (*non tam doctus, quam, id quod est maius, expertus*), Antonius claims that greater skill is required to treat definite controversies in the courts than to amplify commonplaces *in vacuo* in a genteel and erudite fashion (2.72). Greek professors of rhetoric are led to make manuals of such amplifications by their arbitrary division of subject matter into particular cases (*rem positam in disceptatione reorum et controversia*) and into abstract, irresolvable questions (*rem positam in infinita dubitatione*). In accord with this division they evolve rules of *genera* and *species* of cases, on the model of civil law, which are too inflexible to apply to the great variety of materials which oratory must treat (2.78–84). They overlook the crucial fact "that any debate whatsoever can be brought under the notion

---

[4] The two questions are identical: "Quae sit mundi forma? Quae sit solis magnitudo?" (*De inventione* 1.8, trans. H. M. Hubbell, LCL [London, 1960]); *Quanta sit solis magnitudo, quae forma terrae* (*De oratore* 2.66, trans. E. W. Sutton and H. Rackham, LCL, 2 vols. [London, 1959]). Future citations of these works will be to these editions.

and quality of the general kind (*ignari omnes controversias ad universi generis vim et naturam referri*)." That, in fact, the principal issue is always an abstract question of a general kind (*de ipso universo genere infinita quaestio*), for no case turns upon the personalities of the parties (*reorum personis*) without being concerned with universal considerations (*generum ipsorum universa dubitatione*).

Indeed, even where the question is one of pure fact, such as "Did Publius Decius take moneys unlawfully?" the evidence for prosecution and defence alike must have reference to general terms and essential qualities: to convict of extravagance you must refer to profusion; of covetousness, to greed; of sedition, to turbulent and wicked members of the community; to prove that the defendant's accusers are many, you must deal with witnesses in the mass: and conversely all the evidence for the defence will have to turn away from the particular occasion and individual to general conceptions of circumstances and kinds. (2.133–36)

By removing the argument to the general question, the endless charges and lines of defense may be brought under a delimited number of common topics. And in cases where there is no question of fact and only the quality of the act (*qualia sint*) to be considered, general questions become even more important: "For occasions and individuals do indeed enter into the inquiry, but it must be understood that the cases do not depend upon these, but upon general questions" (2.139).

Antonius is criticizing the mutual exclusiveness, or conservatism, of the two types of questions. Despite his greater Isocratean practicality, he seems to agree with Crassus, who maintains that, though it surrenders those of logic and physics, rhetoric must share the general ethical theses with philosophy (1.68–69). Where philosophy has laid exclusive claim even to these, the orator must plunder its territory for the right to treat "the subjects of justice and duty and the constitution and the government of states, in short, the entire field of practical philosophy (*de omni vivendi ratione*)" (3.122). The close agreement in thought and phrasing between Cicero's two chief protagonists on the kinds of indefinite questions proper to rhetoric makes clear what he has added to the views expressed in the *De inventione*. In distinguishing practical theses, which presuppose a relationship between definite and indefinite questions, from speculative theses, which ignore it, Cicero has not only continued to reject the mutual exclusiveness of questions with regard to their respective subject matters. He has also provided a method of moving from one type of question to the other within any *single* subject matter, thereby turning a 'material' distinction into a 'methodological' one. This transition from the particular to the general consideration is analogous to that from the least specialized form of rhetoric to the least specialized form of philosophy.

In Part One I argued that the original terms of an incipient literary theory were borrowed primarily from these disciplines to describe this 'area of transition.' I want to show here, how, within rhetoric itself, the increasing emphasis upon qualitative issues and upon the usefulness of fiction for analyzing them might integrate the judicative with the cognitive responsibilities of a work of literature.[5]

B. Fiction and the *Status Qualitatis*

In both philosophy and rhetoric the closest relation of general to (relatively) specific inquiry lies in their mutual consideration of qualitative issues. With respect to *philosophy*, Cicero divides *theoretical* questions or theses into three kinds in his *Topica* (82–86). The first kind asks whether something exists or happened (*sitne*) and is to be answered by inference and conjecture (*coniectura*). The second kind asks what the thing is (*quid sit*) and is to be answered by definition (*definitione*). And the third kind asks what its character is (*quale sit*) and is to be answered by distinctions between right and wrong (*iuris et iniuriae distinctione*). This third, or qualitative, question, such as "Should one seek glory (*expetendane sit gloria*)," involves what to seek and avoid, what is right and wrong, and what is honorable and base (*de expetendo fugiendoque, de aequo et iniquo, de honesto et turpi*). The topics of such qualitative issues gradually shade into the practical theses of philosophy, concerning

---

[5] Whether or not Hermagoras, as von Arnim suggests (*Leben und Werke*, p. 95), while welcoming general philosophical questions, may himself not have admitted general questions of the more specialized sciences, the practical question, demanding a judgment (*actio*), traditionally has been the most important for literature. Else insists (pp. 273–74) that καθόλου in the *Poetics* expresses the "universal" of "practical questions of human living," not of metaphysical generalities on such subjects as the motions of the stars. C. O. Brink likewise observes that Horace's *Socraticae . . . chartae* (*A.P.* 310) refer to "a philosophy which is a guide to life rather than an intellectual discipline" (*Horace on Poetry* [Cambridge, 1963], p. 131). St. Thomas restates the distinction, so familiar in Renaissance humanists like Sidney, for the Middle Ages: *Prudentia magis convenit cum arte quam habitus speculativi, quantum ad subjectum et materiam. Utrumque enim est in opinativa parte animae et circa contingens aliter se habere* (*S.T.*, 1.2. qu.57 art.4 r.2). For Roger Bacon's emphasis upon *praxis* and the moving of the will as the basis of the superiority of ancient literature, see E. Massa, *Ruggero Bacone: etica e poetica nella storia dell' 'Opus Maius'* (Roma, 1955), pp. 144–55. So Dante writes to Can Grande on the *Commedia: Genus vero phylosophie sub quo hic in toto et parte proceditur, est morale negotium, sive ethica; quia non ad speculandum, sed ad opus inventum est totum et pars* (16); see as well *De Monarchia* 1.3 and Ficino's translation (*Dante Alighieri: tutte le opere*, ed. F. Chiapelli [Milano, 1965], pp. 864, 731–32, 791). So Boccaccio, *Comento* Lez. 1. De Bruyne comments on the gradual extension of *civiles quaestiones* to include almost all moral concerns in the early Middle Ages (1:44–46) and, in discussing St. Thomas' theory of art (3:316–46), gives a good account of the psychological function of the prudential faculty in relation to that of the speculative and productive faculties.

ethical action (*actio*), which deal with duty (*officium*) or with arousing, calming, or removing emotions (*ad motum animi vel gignendum vel sedandum planeve tollendum*), as in the exhortation to seek glory. Cicero concludes by saying these kinds of questions, both theoretical and practical, "are used in inquiries of a general nature, and may therefore be transferred to particular cases (*haec cum in propositi quaestionibus genera sint, eadem in causas transferuntur*)." When philosophical theses are transferred to rhetorical *causae* and are articulated by a system of *status*, it is primarily by means of the qualitative considerations that the general issues in any given controversy may be revealed.

With respect to *rhetoric*, Cicero describes in the *Orator* (45–46) how the speaker, like any other inquirer, is to gain command of the topics (*locos*) of argumentation. In any kind of controversy (*controversia*) or debate (*contentione*), he must ask if the discussion turns upon whether or not a given act was committed (*sitne*), or upon the definition of the act once it has been admitted as a fact (*quid sit*), or upon the character or quality of the act (*quale sit*) once it has been both admitted and defined. These three questions correspond to three of those developed by Hermagoras to establish the principal issue or *status* upon which a legal case might best be argued. The first question is answered by evidence (*signis*), the second by definitions (*definitionibus*), and the third by principles of right and wrong (*recti pravique partibus*). We may ask, for example, (1) Did A kill B? (2) Granted that he did, should we call the act an accident or homicide? (3) If we agree to call it homicide, the question of *qualitas* must be asked in order to determine whether the killing was justifiable, as in the case of self-defense, or not, as in the case of murder. Further qualification must, then, be made, if it is indeed murder, to determine the penalty (or reward, as in the case of killing a tyrant): was the killing premeditated or done in a moment of anger or fear? To make the greatest use of these questions the orator "always removes the discussion, if he can, from particular times and persons (*a propriis personis et temporibus*), because the discussion can be made broader about a class (*de genere*) than about an individual (*de parte*), so that whatever is proved about the class (*in universo*) must necessarily be true of the individual (*in parte*). Such an inquiry, removed from particular times and persons to a discussion of a general topic, is called θέσις (*haec igitur quaestio a propriis personis et temporibus ad universi generis orationem traducta appellatur* θέσις)."[6] If we compare this pas-

---

[6] *Brutus* [and] *Orator*, trans. G. L. Hendrickson and H. M. Hubbell [respectively], LCL (London, 1952), to which edition future references will be made. On the breadth of application of theses, see *De orat.* 1.138–41, 2.104ff.; *Orat.* 125–27. The 'qualitative' question, the *status* or *constitutio generalis*, occurs when, the act and its definition now

sage with the one discussed previously from the *Topica*, we can see that rhetoric shares its three kinds of questions with the theoretical thesis of philosophy and its topics with the practical thesis of philosophy. The rhetorical thesis offers, furthermore, a distance and perspective to one interpreting the confusing detail of a particular case much as the theoretical thesis of philosophy offers principles of analysis to one deciding upon a practical course of action.

Quintilian summarizes the various descriptions of indefinite and definite questions, the division of the indefinite question into theoretical (*scientia*) and practical (*actione*) theses, and the possible rapprochement between 'thesis' and 'hypothesis' (3.5.5–18). The definite question, he says, is always derived from the indefinite, and usually even the indefinite, which has nothing to do with particular persons, is given a specific reference (*sed etiam remotae a personis propriis ad aliquid referri solent*).

For instance the question "Ought we to take a share in the government of our country?" is abstract, whereas "Ought we to take part in the government of our country under the sway of a tyrant?" has a specific reference. But in this latter case we may say that a person is tacitly implied (*sed hic quoque subest velut latens persona*). For the mention of a tyrant doubles the question, and there is an implicit admission of time and quality; but all the same you would scarcely be justified in calling it a cause or definite question (*tyrannus enim geminat quaestionem, subestque et temporis et qualitatis tacita vis; nondum tamen hoc proprie dixeris causam*).

When the terms *general* and *specific* are used, "in every special question the general question is implicit (*in omni autem speciali utique inest generalis*)."

And perhaps even in actual causes wherever the notion of quality comes into question, there is a certain intrusion of the abstract (*in causis quoque, quidquid in quaestionem venit qualitatis, generale sit*). "Milo killed Clodius: he was justified in killing one who lay in wait for him." Does not this raise the general question as to whether we have the right to kill a man who lies in wait for us?

---

established, "there is a question nevertheless about how important it is or of what kind, or in general about its quality, *e.g.* was it just or unjust, profitable or unprofitable (*constat et tamen quantum et cuiusmodi et omnino quale sit quaeritur, hoc modo: Iustum an iniustum, utile an inutile*)," *De inv.* 1.10–12; cf. *De part. orat.* 102. Cicero elsewhere illustrates the importance of qualitative considerations with this question: " 'Then does it make no difference . . . whether a man murders his father or a slave?' If you posit those cases without qualification, their real nature cannot easily be judged (*nuda ista si ponas, iudicari qualia sint non facile possunt*)." It is finally the motive (*causa*), not the nature (*natura*), of the crime which counts (*Paradoxa Stoicorum* 24, trans. H. Rackham, LCL [London, 1960]). Quintilian accepts Cicero's view of the three types of inquiry; they have even been prescribed to us by nature (*ipsa nobis etiam natura praescribit*) and apply to both indefinite and definite issues (3.6.80–81).

There are some, he says with an example previously cited, "who hold that even those questions which have reference to persons and particular cases may at times be called *theses*," provided they are put slightly differently. "For instance, if Orestes be accused, we shall have a *cause*: whereas if it is put as question, namely 'Was Orestes rightly acquitted?' it will be a *thesis*." To the same class as this belongs "the question 'Was Cato right in transferring Marcia to Hortensius?' "[7] Quintilian agrees with Cicero's later position, since "although it is not sufficient merely to handle the general question, we cannot arrive at any conclusion on the special point (*ad speciem*) until we have first discussed the general question."

These passages transmit an important principle of literary theory: the more detailed the *quaestio definita*, or plot, the more precisely the *quaestiones indefinitae*, which reveal its significance, may be expressed. For the greater the particularity with which one investigates the circumstances of a case, the more he is implicated in motives, choices, and other ethical questions of *qualitas*. The further one hypothesizes in circumstance, in other words, the greater the involvement in quality, and the more qualitative the issues, the more extensive the 'involution' in the generic thesis.[8] The use of Orestes to illustrate the difference between a *causa* and a *thesis* suggests the familiarity of Quintilian's readers with literature as a recognized means of analyzing the questions of justice.[9]

In a later passage, already mentioned in Chapter 2, Quintilian discusses the excellence of fictional arguments (καθ' ὑπόθεσιν) for the definition of *qualitas* (5.10.95–99). A fictional argument consists of "the proposition of something which, if true, would either solve a problem or

---

[7] Various famous homicides are used to exemplify the question of quality. See Cicero, *De inv.* 1.18, *De part. orat.* 104; M. Cappella, *De arte rhet.* 7 (*Rhetores Latini Minores*, ed. C. Halm [Lipsiae, 1863], p. 455—hereafter cited as Halm).

[8] Iulius Victor suggests this compounding of qualities (*id est iniectione qualitatum, cum quasi inicitur et supervenit qualitas qualitati*) in illustrating the 'pragmatic' (*negotialis*) division of the qualitative issue. The question at issue in his example, Iulius says, could not even have arisen *nisi adumbrata esset influentibus in se quodammodo prioribus qualitatibus* (Halm, pp. 379–80). See Chap. 10, n. 35. In the plastic arts, *adumbrata* connotes the preliminary roughing out of a statue (*Tusc.* 3.3).

[9] The extensive use of the Orestes story in illustrating legal questions is mentioned by Quintilian who analyzes its detail (3.11.4–12), as does Cicero (*De inv.* 1.18f.). The interpretation of the "bloody sword" in the story of Ajax and Ulysses is given by Cicero (*De inv.* 1.11) and by the author of the *Rhet. ad Her.* (1.18) as an example of the conjectural issue: Quintilian claims it came from the tragic stage (4.2.13). Interpretations of circumstantial evidence occur in Seneca's *controversiae* (7.3,5) but predominate in the first nineteen declamations attributed to Quintilian. For an English version of these, see *The Declamations of Quintilian*, trans. J. Warr (London, 1686). Conjectural issues involving circumstantial evidence are illustrated by situations (*De inv.* 2.14), which are analyzed by a series of questions not unlike those that a novelist might ask in working out his plot (2.45–46).

contribute to its solution, and secondly the demonstration of the similarity of our hypothesis to the case under consideration (*nam fingere hoc loco hoc est proponere aliquid, quod, si verum sit, aut solvat quaestionem aut adiuvet; deinde id, de quo quaeritur, facere illi simile*)." The example given is that of a certain man who, contrary to the law, has failed to support his parents and who, nevertheless, objects to going to prison. This man "advances the hypothesis (*utitur fictione*) that he would be exempt from such a penalty if he were a soldier, an infant, or if he were absent from home on the service of the state." Given these exemptions, the implication is the man may find a related one applicable to himself. Quintilian concludes his discussion by saying that such suppositions are exceedingly useful when we argue "against the letter of the law (*contra scriptum*)" or when "we are concerned with the quality of an act (*verum eadem fictio valet et ad qualitates*)." The fiction functions in a very similar way to the fictional *paradeigma* in Plato's *Statesman* (277–78), in Aristotle's *Rhetoric* (2.20), and in the *Institutio Oratoria* itself (5.11.6).

Quintilian returns to the plot of Orestes in considering the "line of defense" (3.11.1–18).

Orestes has killed his mother: the fact is admitted. He pleads that he was justified in so doing: the *basis* (*status*) will be one of quality, the *question*, whether he was justified in his action, the *line of defence* that Clytemnestra killed her husband, Orestes' father. This is called the αἴτιον or *motive*. The point for the decision of the judge is known as the κρινόμενον, and in this case is whether it was right that even a guilty mother should be killed by her son.

Were the case simply a question of fact (*an sit*), the *"decision of the judge"* and the *"main question"* (upon which the *status* is decided) would coincide, since the first question and the final decision would be concerned with the same point (11). The appropriate literary form would be that of a dramatized murder mystery resolved during a trial in a courtroom such as that conducted so often by Perry Mason.

But when it is stated and denied that Orestes was justified in killing his mother, considerations of *quality* are introduced: the *question* is whether he was justified in killing her, but this is not yet the point for the *decision of the judge*. When, then, does it become so? "She killed my father." "Yes, but that did not make it your duty to murder your mother." The *point for the decision of the judge* is whether it was his duty to kill her (*an debuerit, hic iudicatio*).

This flexible working through the problem of what is and is not justifiable, that is of quality, to a point upon which a judgment can be made and be emotionally accepted, resembles the presentation to an audience, who also must judge and acquiesce emotionally, of a drama like *Hamlet*.[10]

In a more detailed treatment of *qualitas* (7.4), Quintilian concludes that the question of quality "makes the highest demands on the resources of oratory, since it affords the utmost scope for a display of talent on either side, while there is no topic in which the emotional appeal is so effective."

For *conjecture* has often to introduce proofs from without and uses arguments drawn from the actual subject matter, whereas the real task of eloquence is to demonstrate *quality*: there lies its kingdom, there its power, and there its unique victory (*nam coniectura extrinsecus quoque adductas frequenter probationes habet et argumenta ex materia sumit; quale quidque videatur eloquentiae est opus; hic regnat, hic imperat, hic sola vincit, 23-24*).

There is a strong suggestion here that the interpretative, if not fictive, powers of the orator are the most important. Quintilian continually emphasizes the imaginative faculty in the presentation of a construction of events in the most sharply visualized detail. His treatise, as well as the *Rhetorica ad Herennium*, the *De inventione*, and the dependent *Rhetores Latini Minores* edited by Halm, draw the overwhelming majority of their illustrations from epic, drama, and the fictional exercises of the *suasoria* and the *controversia*. These sources, of course, are both well known and easily adapted. As important, however, is the very capacity of fiction, as opposed to 'historical' cases and examples, to receive unlimited qualification through the manipulation of circumstances. When Orestes, for instance, is presupposed to have a different motive for killing his mother, the 'decision' for the judge to make is correspondingly different (3.11.6). Quintilian's description of the various systems of *status* (3.6) is in reality a description of the effort of the mind to gain a 'point' from which to see events in perspective, to determine the indeterminate, so that the events might be evaluated sufficiently to justify reward or penalty. The determination of partially given premises in the succeeding events of a fictional plot offers a model for the process of the mind itself in its efforts to delimit and qualify, in accord with given laws and admitted facts, what has as yet remained unspecified.

---

[10] Iulius Victor says one locates the point of issue by "division." One begins with the general issues common to many cases, and "descends" to special issues proper to the case at hand (*a generalibus gradatim descendet ad speciales, id est ad causae proprias*): *Ita sensim defluit generalitas ad speciem, id est ad τὸ κρινόμενον* (Halm, pp. 385–86). The anonymous *excerpta rhetorica* add that the *hypothesis* or *quaestio specialis* will often supply a defense where the *thesis* or *genus causae* will not. One cannot defend matricide in general, but if a specific person, Orestes, comes forward *ex hypothesi*, his defense can be that he was justified in avenging his father (Halm, pp. 585f.). See Chap. 11, n. 17.

The 'constructed' relation between the law (of nature or of statute) and the human actions to be judged is analogous to that between the 'thesis' and the 'hypothesis' and between the activities of cognition and action in indefinite and definite questions. The chief instrument in such a construction is the *quaestio qualitatis*.[11]

C. *Status* and the Apprehension of 'Quality'

The correspondence of the three main questions of the rhetorical *status* system to an earlier division of philosophical theses, as suggested previously by Cicero (*Top.* 82–86), brings to jurisprudence a wide range of ethical and epistemological considerations. The discrimination of *status* is not just that of kinds of arguments about action but of ways of seeing the action itself. It is the means, according to Quintilian (3.6.21), by which Hermagoras claims a situation can be understood and proofs adduced (*Hermagoras statum vocat, per quem subiecta res intelligatur et ad quem probationes etiam partium referantur*). The orator, unlike the legislator, must *see* the action from a point of view favorable to his client: his end, in a sense, is included among the given premises—certain laws and admitted circumstances—of the case. In precisely defining the *status*, he is focusing, as finely as possible, the photographic picture he wishes to expose on the imagination of his audience.

Before Quintilian gives his own (3.6.80–90), he describes alternative classifications of *status*. The diversity indicates the continuing search for a sensitive adjustment between language and the circumstances it interprets, and it is appropriate that often these classifications are derived from Aristotle's categories, his predicables, or a combination of both. The ten categories, the first four of which are substance (οὐσία), quantity (ποσόν), quality (ποιόν), and relation (πρός τι), classify the kinds or 'conditions' of predicates in their uncombined state. The four predicables of the *Topics* (1.4-5)—definition (ὅρος), which indicates the essential character (τὸ τί ἦν εἶναι) of a particular thing, property (ἴδιον), which indicates an accompanying (necessary) characteristic of that thing, genus (γένος), and accident (συμβεβηκός)—all signify the principal ways in which the subject may participate in such 'conditions.' Quintilian (3.6.23) begins by coupling the first four categories (*elementa . . . circa quae versari videatur omnis quaestio*) with the four *status* of a legal controversy. Substance (οὐσία) answers the question whether a thing is, *an sit*; quality (ποιόν), what is its nature, *quale sit*; quantity (ποσόν) deals

---

[11] For further passages on fictional exemplification, see Chap. 2, n. 6.

with magnitude and number, *quam magnum et quam multum sit*; and relation (πρός τι) with 'competence' and 'comparison,' *translatio et comparatio*. The remaining categories are not *status* but topics (*locos argumentorum*). In the course of his review of other classifications, Quintilian (3.6.49) sees Aristotle as remaining relatively close to the first four categories in his *Rhetoric* (1.13, 3.16): "all enquiry turns on the questions *whether a thing is, of what kind it is, how great it is*, and *of how many parts it consists (Aristoteles in rhetoricis, An sit, Quale, Quantum, et Quam multum sit? quaerendum putat)*."

Aristotle's chief treatment of quality (ποιότης) is found in *Categories* viii. A quality is "that in virtue of which men are called such and such." The first kind he takes up consists of habits (ἕξις) and dispositions (διάθεσις). Habits are more lasting and stable, and include virtues (ἀρεταί) and all types of knowledge (ἐπιστῆμαι). Dispositions "are qualities easy to move or to change, such as heat, cold, disease, health and so on." If a disposition were to become inveterate, it would be a habit. The second kind of quality denotes any natural capacity or innate incapacity. The third kind "contains passive qualities and also affections (παθητικαὶ ποιότητες καὶ πάθη)" such as sweetness and bitterness and coldness and warmth. Such qualities elicit sensations. Color may also arise from affections, as when men blush for shame or alarm, and may designate a kind of person. Very transient conditions of this kind, however, are more properly called affections (πάθη) than qualities (ποιότητες). Passive qualities and affections also exist in the soul, such as irascibility and the like, and are, respectively, lasting or brief. The last kind of quality refers to the form (σχῆμα) or figure of things, such as crooked or straight or triangular. Some qualities may admit of degree, for one man can be more just than another, or one thing more white than another. Mathematical qualities, however, do not admit of degree, for a circle cannot, by definition, be any less or more than circular.[12]

In an alternate treatment Aristotle divides the types of 'quality' into general classes in the *Metaphysics* (5.14; 1020a34–b25): first that by which one differentiates among essences of things not in motion or not *qua* in motion; second, among essences of things in motion. Goodness and badness, falling under affections of things in motion, belong to the second:

For that which can function or be moved in such-and-such a way is good, and that which can function in such-and-such a way *and* in the contrary way is bad. Quality (τὸ ποιόν) refers especially to "good" and "bad" in the case of living things, and of these especially in the case of such as possess choice.

---

[12] *The Categories*, trans. H. P. Cook, LCL (London, 1938).

These terms, like those in the *Categories* describing the concept of quality, resemble closely the definition of virtue in the *Nicomachean Ethics* (2.5–6; 1105b20–1107a27). Virtue (ἀρετή) is "a settled disposition (ἕξις) of the mind determining the choice of actions and emotions, consisting essentially in the observance of the mean relative to us, this being determined by principle, that is, as the prudent man (φρόνιμος) would determine it." Such habits (ἕξεις) are "the formed states of character in virtue of which we are well or ill disposed in respect of the emotions (πάθη)."

Among the alternative classifications of *status* in Quintilian, that related more closely to Aristotle's description of predicables in his *Topics* (1.4–5) seems to have provided Hermagoras with his principal terminology. While the discussion of quality (ποιότης) in the *Categories* bears more strongly on ethics, Hermagoras' term for quality, κατὰ συμβεβηκός, emphasizes the degree of *logical* relevance of the individual circumstances of a case with respect to the selection of the principal issue to be decided by the judge. His four divisions of *status*, which Quintilian (reversing the third and fourth) lists as *coniecturam, proprietatem, translationem,* and *qualitatem* (3.6.56), are as follows: (1) στοχασμός, conjecture regarding the perpetration (i.e. existence) of an act; (2) ὅρος, the definition of the act, particularly with respect to the amount of reward or punishment commensurate with it; (3) κατὰ συμβεβηκός (ποιότης), contingent qualities which bear by chance upon the case proper; (4) μετάληψις, the question of the competence of the given legal body to decide upon the issue. Quintilian points out that to ποιότης Hermagoras appends the phrase " 'according to its accidents,' illustrating his meaning by putting a case where it is enquired whether a man *happen* to be good or bad (*per accidentia, id est* κατὰ συμβεβηκός, *vocat, hac interpretatione, an illi accidat viro bono esse, vel malo*)." The phrase, according to D. Matthes, is borrowed from logic. While the term ὅρος (which can also mean a boundary, limit, or standard of measure) refers to a definition of the γένος and ἴδια of the object to be defined, the term συμβεβηκός, on the contrary, refers to an accident of the object which must be excluded from the definition. It can (*Top.* 1.5) either belong or not belong to a particular thing and therefore is equally excluded from genus and property—although it may become temporarily or relatively a property in certain situations.[13]

[13] D. Matthes, "Hermagoras von Temnos 1904–55," *Lustrum* 3 (1958):147–48. This study is the most detailed treatment of the origins and subsequent influence of the Hermagorean *status* system. For a briefer résumé, see R. Nadeau, "Classical Systems of Stases in Greek: Hermagoras to Hermogenes," *Greek, Roman, and Byzantine Studies* 2, 1 (1959):51–71. In ethics an involuntary action is said to be κατὰ συμβεβηκός (*E.N.* 5.8) and hence morally neutral in that it lies outside the "borders" of the will. In the *Poetics* the

Corresponding to the 'accident' in logic is the accidental attribute itself which is transferred to the mind from the realm of nature in the guise of a perception. In the *Theaetetus* (182AB), assuming for the moment the sophistic view of a universe in continual flux, Plato describes this transference as a union of the 'passive' receiver and the 'active' object whereby the object acquires 'quality' (ποιότης) and the receiver becomes percipient. Knowledge, however, is prevented: since, in the paraphrase of John Burnet, "everything not only moves its place, but also alters its state, we cannot ascribe any quality to what moves; for what we call qualities (ποιότητες) are nothing but perceptual processes going on between what acts and what is acted upon, and accordingly, in the very moment of being named, the quality is gone."[14] Plato associates the accident of logic with the accidental attribute of physics in his seventh epistle (342A–45A). Knowledge of things is brought about first by a name (ὄνομα), then by a description (λόγος), and thirdly by an image (εἴδωλον). The objects of knowledge described by Plato are strikingly similar to the subjects given by Aristotle for his qualitative category:

The same is true alike of the straight and of the spherical form, and of colour, and of the good and the fair and the just, and of all bodies whether manufactured or naturally produced (such as fire and water and all such substances), and of all living creatures, and of all moral actions or passions in souls. (342D)

Because of the inadequacy of language, however, names, descriptions, forms (and the resulting concepts) do as little to illustrate accurately the quality (τὸ ποιόν) of the object as to reveal the reality behind it. Names are unstable and easily transferred; so, too, descriptions alter, which are made up of nouns and verbs. Since the essential reality and the quality (τοῦ τε ὄντος καὶ τοῦ ποιοῦ τινός) are always incompatible, the soul which lets its pursuit of reality be diverted by quality (τὸ ποιόν) is constantly perplexed.[15]

---

same phrase is used to describe the error in fact or belief which is "accidental" to mimetic representation (1460b16). By analogy, in law whatever does not lead to the establishment of the central question of the case—prior to a judgment of the moral issues then to be considered—lies outside the case proper. Hence a *legal* narration of the facts, in its narrowest historical sense as a kind of definition of the given circumstances, may exclude explanatory detail and even motives (*De inv.* 1.28; Alcuin, *Rhet.* 22). It is a kind of outline waiting to be "filled in," in the *confirmatio* (*De inv.* 1.34–43), by qualifying *colores*. In this it resembles, not only the bare *thema* of a declamation, but also Aristotle's conception of the dramatic hypothesis (*Poet.* 17), which excludes from its primary *ekthesis* accidents of motive, names, and circumstances (see pp. 50–52 of this study). The accidental qualities will then be brought in to confirm the speaker's or dramatist's interpretation of events on the basis of which he is asking the audience to respond in a certain way.

[14] *Greek Philosophy: Thales to Plato* (London, 1924), p. 245. Diogenes Laertius claims that Plato was the first to employ the term ποιότητα in philosophical discussion (3.24).

[15] *Plato: Epistles*, trans. R. G. Bury, LCL (London, 1952). Later references to *Epistles*

Plato, assuming for the moment that all things are in a continual flux of combining and dissolving elements, is forced to mistrust qualities, both as perceived and as described in words. Such mistrust could only discourage the rhetorician seeking a system of *status* intended to determine the most uncertain of probabilities, the actions of men. It is to the existence of station (στάσις) at various points within motion (κίνησις), postulated by Aristotelian physics, that the mind owes its power to discriminate and categorize physical attributes. At such moments of cessation or change of direction (στάσις), the mind may perceive the state of things, that is, locate a middle (μέσον) between a beginning and an end. The continuum must be 'broken into' to be seen. The term *status* may come to the rhetorical and logical arts from the use of *stasis* in such a context. For in the flux of human action, the intentions of two people 'collide' and are momentarily held still at the point of *controversia*, permitting an analysis of the situation to be made and the nature of the required proofs to be determined. For Hermagoras, these were the two objectives of *status*: to understand the situation (*subiecta res intelligatur*) and to apply appropriate lines of argument (*probationes etiam partium referantur*).[16]

The Hermagorean adaptation of Aristotelian logical terms, perhaps by means of their possible association with physics, to the fluidity of actual cases, may be further clarified, with respect to *qualitas* as 'accidental' (κατὰ συμβεβηκός), by the atomistic view of the perception of matter. As indivisible, irreducible, and indestructible units, according to Epicurus, the atoms do not possess any "qualities (ποιότητα) belonging to perceptible things, except shape, weight, and size" (1.54).[17] With the dissolution of any compound, to which it owes its existence, "every quality (ποιότης) changes," for unlike atoms, "qualities (ποιότητες) do not remain in the changing object" (1.54–55). All qualities that are predicated of body (κατηγορεῖται σώματος) have no existence separate from the body; nor are they material parts of the body. "Rather we should suppose that the whole body in its totality owes its own permanent existence to all these" (1.69). They, in turn, can be perceived and distinguished "provided always that the aggregate body goes along with them and is never wrested from them, but in virtue of its com-

---

will be to this edition. Compare Aristotle's discussion of accident in *Meta.* 1025a14–35, 1026a33–27a28: " 'Accident' is only, as it were, a sort of name. Hence in a way Plato [*Soph.* 254A] was not far wrong in making sophistry deal with what is non-existent; because the sophists discuss the accident (συμβεβηκός) more, perhaps, than any other people" (1026b14–17).

[16] I am much indebted in this paragraph to the analysis of O. A. L. Dieter, "Stasis," *Speech Monographs* 17, 4 (1950):345–69. See Chap. 10, n. 22.

[17] *Epicurus*, trans. C. Bailey (Oxford, 1926), p. 31.

prehension as an aggregate of qualities acquires the predicate of body" (1.69). Epicurus (1.68–73) divides qualities into "properties" (συμβεβη-κότα) and "accidents" (συμπτώματα). The first permanently accompany the body and are necessary to our conception of it; the second are temporary characteristics or "accompaniments." Both have a real existence and inhere in a body which owes its unity or wholeness (καθόλου) to them. Even accidents "are seen to be just what our actual sensation shows their proper character (ἰδιότητα) to be."[18]

In this distinction between the two types of qualities there remain something analogous to the Aristotelian division of the predicables into "property" (ἴδιον) and "accident" (συμβεβηκός) and something analogous to his distinction, within the category of quality itself, between "habit" (ἕξις) and "disposition" (διάθεσις). While the term συμβεβηκός can have the secondary meaning of "property" for Aristotle (Meta. 1025a30), Epicurus sees qualitative attributes primarily as "permanent properties" and accidents as "inferences" we make from them. When Hermagoras designates the qualitative status as κατὰ συμβεβηκός, he perhaps draws upon both the "accident" of Aristotelian logic and the "permanent property," the principal ποιότης of Epicurean physics and psychology. Since we owe our knowledge of each aggregate body "in its totality" to such permanent properties, the qualitative issues in a legal decision might be more reliably grouped and described than the accidental predication of Aristotle's Topics alone would suggest. Even Aristotle's categories, other than that of substance, remain "mere offshoots and concomitants of being," and, though apprehensible in and by virtue of a substance, each quality still "is an abstraction."[19]

Of particular importance for the rhetorical status of quality, in its attempt to define a controversy in greater ethical particularity, is Cicero's discussion of form in relation to matter and our perception of it. In describing Antiochus' view, as representative of the Old Academy, that entities are matter (materia) informed by a force (vis), he apologizes for coining the term qualitas to render ποιότης and identifies it with the entity, or body, itself (quod ex utroque, id iam corpus et quasi qualitatem quandam nominabant). The passive principle of matter receives a given

---

[18] Both terms are relative to each other: a "property" of one thing may be an "accident" of another, as slavery is a property of "slave," but an accident of "man." The principal distinction seems to be that properties "are directly perceived in acts of apprehension, but the συμπτώματα only in relation to such acts: e.g. we see a man in a certain attitude, etc., and thus know that he is writing," Epicurus, pp. 235, 240. Lucretius translates the terms as coniuncta and eventa (1.449–50). See Bailey, Epicurus, pp. 235–44, and his The Greek Atomists and Epicurus (New York, 1964), pp. 300–9, for commentary and general discussion. Diogenes Laertius summarizes Epicurus' position (10.51–73). See Chap. 11, n. 3.

[19] Sir David Ross, Aristotle, p. 165. Also Bailey, The Greek Atomists, p. 301.

'whatness' by means of qualifications (ποιότητας) imposed by the active principle of form; it becomes a particular thing with certain properties.[20] Qualities are either primary, that is, such principles or elements (*initia et elementa*) as air, fire, water, and earth, or secondary, that is, whatever is made up out of them. Matter is formless (*sine ulla specie*) and devoid of either type of quality (*carentem omni illa qualitate*), while out of matter all things are formed and produced (*expressa atque efficta sint*). In the course of his discussion Cicero shifts the meaning of *qualitas* from the individual entity produced by the combination of matter and a force to the qualifying agent itself (*illa vis quam qualitatem esse diximus*). Through this agent matter "is made into the things which they term 'qualified,' out of which in the concrete whole of substance, a continuum united with all its parts, has been produced one world (*illa effici quae appellant qualia, e quibus in omni natura cohaerente et continuata cum omnibus suis partibus unum effectum esse mundum*)." This qualifying and productive agent is called the soul of the world (*quam vim animum esse dicunt mundi*). In the realm of perception, sensory information of the world remained unreliable, and only the mind could perceive what was "eternally simple and uniform and true to its own quality (*simplex et unius modi et tale quale esset*)." What could remain true to its own quality Plato called the *Idea*, Cicero the form (*hanc illi* ἰδέαν, . . . *a Platone ita nominatam, nos recte speciem possumus dicere*). Herein lay, perhaps, Cicero's conception of the quasi-divine nature of the Ideas (*quiddam divinum esse*): the world soul alone, by means of the Ideas, could exert its qualifying force throughout eternity. Only through this force was the power, however limited, of apprehending formal structure extended to the mind.[21]

[20] Cicero's description of a *corpus* as a "qualified thing" bears a certain resemblance to the Epicurean predication of "an aggregate of qualities" as a *body*, which "in its totality owes its own permanent existence" to them (1.69), and to Aristotle's conception of a thing known first as a composite whole (καθόλου) in his *Physics* (1.1). The idea, however, of a body as a combination of Limit and the Unlimited, in the form of "qualified extension or space," goes back to the *Timaeus*. If one might speak of a "negotiation" between the monad and the dyad, which results in the apprehension of the physical world, the metaphor may be applied to the relation between the limit of an abstract principle of law and the unlimited randomness of human actions—a relation which can only be apprehended by a kind of "equity." As limits imposed upon the continuum can only manifest themselves as images with such and such qualities (*Tim.* 49–50), so the imposition of legal statutes upon ever-varying human actions can only manifest its most nearly perfect adjustment in the image of fiction. See Chap. 10, n. 25.

[21] *Academica* 1.24–33, trans. H. Rackham, LCL (London, 1961). The Stoic association of the formal, active cause with the qualifying "force" of the world soul, which seems to be reflected in this passage, holds also for the faculties of the human soul. M. van Straaten comments that "les anciens Stoïciens considéraient ces δυνάμεις comme des ποιότητες, qui reposent dans l'âme comme dans un substrat, de façon que l'âme serait composée de ce substrat et d'un nombre de qualités," *Panétius* (Amsterdam, 1946), p. 122. Compare

As the Ideas lost their independent existence and became conceptions (of greater or lesser ideality) in the mind itself, they were increasingly concerned with giving an ethical order to the perceived qualities of sensible things. All knowledge (ἐπιστήμη = ἐπί + ἴστημι) is the discovery of a ground upon which to stand, or rather of a resting place (στάσις) within the continuum (κίνησις) from which to observe what is continuous.[22] In selecting a *status*, or position, from which to persuade an audience that it has sufficient knowledge to judge certain actions in a certain way, the orator is most free to make up a convincing interpretation of events out of considerations of *qualitas*. For the most compelling impressions on the imagination and emotions of his listeners will be of sensory and circumstantial qualities. When Quintilian says that the qualitative question (*quale sit*) is the kingdom and the power and the glory of the orator (*hic regnat, hic imperat, hic sola vincit*, 7.4.24), he distinguishes it from the question of occurrence (*an sit*) on the ground that *coniectura* must often introduce proofs from outside (*extrinsecus*) or be bound too much to what actually, i.e. 'historically,' happened (*argumenta ex materia sumit*). Whereas Hermagoras regarded 'quality' as accidental (κατὰ συμβεβηκός) with respect to the case itself, in that it lay outside the definitive limits of the controversy, Quintilian regarded it as definitive with respect to the abilities of the orator. The conjectural question, the principal origin of any issue, could, then, appear accidental in the logical sense of being 'extrinsic' to the proper exercise of the orator's faculties. The increasing predominance of *qualitas* in rhetoric over the other questions of *status* is reflected in the inclusiveness of its technical name in the *Rhetorica ad Herennium* (*constitutio iuridicalis*) and *De inventione* (*constitutio generalis*). The emphasis upon the orator's capacity *as artist* to play upon the emotions of the audience, as upon a harp (*Brut.* 199–200), is perhaps the culminating victory of

---

Cornford's discussion of δυνάμεις in connection with the *Sophist* (see above, pp. 109–10. Later, St. Augustine will associate the activity of the Holy Spirit with the *status qualitatis* in its power to instill in men a delight in the preservation of that knowledge of the Father which is conveyed by the Son (*dulcedo in ista cognitione permanendi, Ep.* 11). For the activity of the Holy Spirit with respect to the medieval conception of the poet as theologian, see pp. 357–60 of this study.

[22] The epistemological implications of the *status* system are suggested by Plato's observations on names, which ought to indicate the essence (οὐσίαν) of things which are in flux: "Let us first take up again the word ἐπιστήμη (knowledge) and see how ambiguous it is, seeming to indicate that it makes our soul stand still (ἵστησιν) at things, rather than that it is carried round with them, . . . And ἱστορία (inquiry) means much the same, that it stops (ἵστησι) the flow. And πιστόν (faithful) most certainly means that which stops (ἱστάν) motion. Then again, anyone can see that μνήμη (memory) expresses rest (μονή) in the soul, not motion" (*Crat.* 436E–37B, trans. H. N. Fowler, LCL [London, 1926]). See Chap. 5, n. 5, of this study for Aristotle's account of first principles' "coming to rest" in the soul.

'artificial' over 'inartificial' proofs as Aristotle distinguishes them (*Rhet.* 1.2).

In conclusion, the concept of 'quality' originates in the relative and interrogative pronoun 'what.' The apprehension of the 'whatness' of physical objects—of that which makes a thing the kind of thing it is— is the apprehension of their sensible attributes (*Physics*, 7.2–3). When the things defined are human actions, quality becomes ethical. When actions are judged in a particular controversy (*actio, contentio = hypothesis*), the question of *quale sit* designates a judicial *status* which is particularly concerned with distinctions of right and wrong (*iuris et iniuriae*). In the rhetorical 'hypothesis' of a given controversy awaiting *iudicatio*, it is the question of quality that involves the orator more and more in particular detail. In concerning itself primarily with ethical deliberation, it must utilize, in revealing the generic considerations lying behind the individual case, the hypothetical procedures of the elenchus of moral dialectic, however simply these procedures may be articulated in the pursuit of *loci communes* or *questiones indefinitae*. In persuasively ordering the materials of these disciplines, it will, at the same time, participate in their formal structure of hypothetical argument, which Aristotle (*E.N.* 3.3.9–13) and Quintilian (1.10.37–38) compare to the structure of geometrical analysis. What primarily concerns us in this chapter, however, is the efficiency with which fiction, through utilizing the hypothetical functions of rhetoric, philosophy, and geometry within its own narrative 'hypothesis,' can apprehend and analyze qualities. This efficiency reflects the ancient association of the concerns of poetry with those of equity.

D. Quality, Equity, and Poetry

It is necessary at this point to repeat again the Greek intellectual presupposition that I used earlier to differentiate the attitudes of Plato and Plotinus toward likeness and proportion in the arts. In the *Statesman* (283D–84E), Plato says that "excess and deficiency are measurable not only in relative terms but also in respect of attainment of a norm or due measure." The first type of measurement is quantitative and is "concerned with the relative greatness or smallness of objects." The second type is qualitative and is "concerned with their size in relation to the fixed norm to which they must approximate if they are to exist at all." Like all the arts which owe the effectivenes and beauty of their products to the second, τὸ μέτρον, the art of governing must establish justice in accordance with "due occasion, due time, due performance, and all such standards as have removed their abode from the extremes and are now settled about the mean (τὸ μέσον)."[23] The relation between the two types of measurement in the application of a 'quantitatively' invariable code for (amounts of) rewards and penalties to 'qualitatively' various moral actions constitutes for Plato the principal difficulty in establishing and preserving equitable laws.

Included in the art of kingship is the art of lawmaking (νομοθετική). Law, by its very nature, "can never issue an injunction binding on all which really embodies what is best for each."

The differences of human personality, the variety of men's activities, and the inevitable unsettlement attending all human experience make it impossible for any art whatsoever to issue unqualified (ἁπλοῦν) rules holding good on all questions at all times. (294B)

It is impossible for what is invariable "to deal satisfactorily with what is never uniform and constant (πρὸς τὰ μηδέποτε ἁπλᾶ)." To illustrate this problem Plato gives an example of an athletic trainer who must prescribe a routine of exercises and diet for his entire group of pupils, not for each one individually. So the lawmaker cannot prescribe "every act of a particular individual and sit at his side, so to speak, all through his life" to tell him what to do. In the event that the trainer must go away, he might well write down his prescriptions for his pupils to follow, but if he were to return sooner than he had planned, he would not hesitate to substitute new prescriptions for those he had left in accordance with the new conditions that he found. The ideal legislator, too, would substitute new laws for those which had ceased to be beneficial, even though they had been duly enacted and recorded. He would guide the state, as a captain his ship, not by written codes alone, but by the "practical application of his knowledge." In the absence, however, of an ideal legislator, the citizen is in double jeopardy: first, that a ruler may change the established laws for his own benefit, and second that, if there were to be no changes in the constitution out of fear of such abuse, one could never incorporate new knowledge into the legal system. Since a citizen will suffer more from the tyrannical abuse of the laws than from their rigidity, Plato felt that, for all their limitations, laws, written and unwritten, must remain the basis of any constitution (294–300).

The code of law, however, cannot remain static. When the legislator tests his laws out in practice, he will discover many "lacunae which some successor will have to correct, to ensure that the constitution and system of the society he has founded may steadily improve, not deteriorate." Like a painter who must constantly retouch his canvas in order

---

[23] See pp. 171–73 of this study.

to achieve a figure of great beauty and now, about to die, must assign a successor to preserve and improve on his workmanship, the legislator must train others to be curators of his laws. He has left an outline of the system; they must fill in the details, amending always in the way which promises to make every citizen truly excellent in the virtues of the soul "proper to human character" (*Laws*, 769B–71A). No matter how vigilant the curator, however, "the different cases are countless and their circumstances are widely unlike," so that the problem arises of how much to leave to the discretion of any particular court. Though a statute may provide for most cases, it cannot be applied to all. For this reason, in order to affix a penalty, say, for wounding someone, one must ask who is wounded and where and how and when and by whom. It is in the effort to 'qualify' a quantitative measurement that equity seeks its due proportion. The questions, as Plato develops them in his subsequent discussion, suggest a rudimentary *status* system: occurrence, definition, qualifying circumstances (875Eff.). If the application of legal precept to events demands continuous adjustment, the statute itself will gradually be 'qualified' in order not to leave undue discretionary powers to the court.[24]

The function of equity as a negotiation between quantitative and qualitative measurement in law is suggested by Plato in the most general terms in relation to the establishment of a constitution of laws. It is Aristotle who gives the concept its ethical and legal formulation familiar to us today. In his famous definition of virtue (ἀρετή) as a settled disposition (ἕξις) of the mind achieved by the observance of the 'mean' *relative to each situation*, he extends the terms of Plato's *Statesman* (283D–85B, 294–97) to the evaluation of individual choice and action (*E.N.* 2.6). He too uses the examples of the athletic trainer and of the arts which seek due proportion, but since he is dealing with individual moral choice, which is qualitative, he distinguishes and rejects the concept of an arithmetical mean. Milo, the wrestler, must have the exercise and the diet proper for him in relation to the progress of his training, not an amount precisely halfway between a lot and a little food for people generally. The quantitative measure, whether it decides the amount of penalty for a legal code or of emotional response for an ethical one, must be 'qualified' with regard to the requirements of the individual case. The quantitative measure is abstract, general, inflexible, and impersonal; the qualitative is 'substantial,' particular, applicable, and ca-

---

[24] *Laws*, trans. A. E. Taylor in *The Collected Dialogues of Plato*. Future references will be to *Laws*, trans. R. G. Bury, LCL, 2 vols. (London, 1926). When one argues for the extension of a statute to a given situation not explicitly covered by it, he argues from a written to an unwritten law by "analogy (*rationcinatio*)." See Cicero, *De inv.* 2.148–53.

suistic. As Cicero says, for the later Academic tradition, *qualitas* refers to a thing which is particular by virtue of its combining matter with attributes. With regard to acts, equity deals with particular things which fit neither fixed precept nor random precedent and which, qualitatively speaking, may be unique. Lying between the completely determined and the completely undetermined, it combines what it can of each as form (*vis*) and matter (*materia*) are combined in a 'quality' (*corpus*).[25]

Like virtue, equity too is a settled disposition (ἡ ἕξις αὕτη ἐπι-είκεια). Drawing upon principles as changeless as the universal law of nature, equity may serve as a rectification of civil justice. Such a rectification is necessary for two reasons. First, because the "rules of justice and of law are related to the actions conforming with them as universals (τὰ καθόλου) to particulars (τὰ καθ' ἕκαστα), for the actions done are many, while each rule or law is one" (*E.N.* 5.7; 1135a6–8). Second, because, while a law *must* by definition be made "to speak in general terms (εἰπεῖν καθόλου)," it is not possible for it to do so correctly (ὀρθῶς), for a case may always arise which is an exception to the rule (παρὰ τὸ καθόλου). When such a case arises, the error lies not in the law as a law, or in the lawmaker, but in the given conditions that the "material of conduct (ἡ τῶν πρακτῶν ὕλη)," human behavior itself, is irregular. The necessity, then, of having "to speak in general terms (εἰπεῖν καθόλου)" under such a condition results in a statutory pronouncement which is insufficiently articulated (ἁπλῶς εἰπών) because it must leave something out (παραλείπει). In its logical relation to its subject matter—the particulars to which it applies—the law must 'speak' generally (καθόλου). But, given the added condition of being forced to exclude exceptional instances because of the nature of its material, the written law as promulgated and applied will be too simply roughhewn (ἁπλῶς), too inflexible, too boldly unqualified in its statement. While inferior to absolute justice, equity may still correct this rigid exclusiveness of the statement (διὰ τὸ ἁπλῶς), "of the (written) law, to supply deficiencies consequent upon its universality (διὰ τὸ καθόλου)."[26]

[25] For a more detailed discussion of virtue as a 'disposition,' see pp. 122–23 of this study. It is precisely in terms of the relation between the determinate and the indeterminate that St. Thomas comments upon Aristotle's definition of equity discussed later in this chapter. Law as universal *deficit in particularibus*, since *non omnia possunt determinari secundum legem*; it must be through a *sententia* that the *universale dictum legis applicatur ad particulare negotium*. Because the *materia humanorum operabilium est indeterminata*, the *regula, quae est lex*, must be *indeterminata* and not fixed in itself (*In decem libros Ethicorum Aristotelis ad Nicomachum expositio*, ed. F. M. Spiazzi [Torino, 1964], p. 298). See Chap. 6, n. 27, Chap. 10, n. 27.

[26] The translation in this sentence is by E. M. Cope, *An Introduction to Aristotle's Rhetoric* (London, 1867), p. 191. *Politics* 3.11.6–9 treats the general problems of applying written and unwritten laws. For various meanings of ἁπλῶς, see above, pp. 132–34. With

When a case occurs which the laws do not adequately cover, the equitable judge is to consider what "the lawgiver would himself decide if he were present on the occasion." Such ghostly consultation might not only make the individual law more flexible but also gradually enlarge the legal code itself. "For what is itself indefinite can only be measured by an indefinite standard, like the leaden rule used by Lesbian builders; just as that rule is not rigid but can be bent to the shape of the stone, so a special ordinance is made to fit the circumstances of the case." The qualitative Lesbian ruler, here distinguished from a quantitative measure of penalty, mitigates the inflexibility of general laws. Paradoxically, the generality of a legal code is deficient because it can never be general enough—since, could it have been so, it would have included the exception. If the special ordinance is eventually incorporated into the statutes, the exceptional qualitative instance will have increased the universality of the laws (*E.N.* 5.10; 1137b12–33).[27]

Aristotle relates equity to quality even more closely in his *Rhetoric* (1.13.13–19; 1374a25–74b23). Laws must be legislated as if they covered all instances (καθόλου εἰπεῖν), whereas in fact they only hold good usually (ἐπὶ τὸ πολύ), for it is impossible to cover an endless number of specific circumstances, such as the kinds of weapons used to inflict

---

regard to written laws, ἁπλῶς refers to the inflexible *exclusiveness* and lack of qualification of the statute with respect to its expression, while καθόλου refers to the *inclusiveness* of the statute with respect to the individual instances which fall under it. A law which is inclusive in the range of cases it embraces, once promulgated and applied to a particular case, will appear to exclude, in the absoluteness of its statement, some individual qualities of that case. Drafting laws ἁπλῶς means in such a way that they always apply (*Ath. Constit.* 9.2), and primitive laws tend to be ἁπλοῦς in the rough, uncompromising baldness of their statement (*Pol.* 2.5, 1268b39). For other uses of ἁπλῶς as "without qualification," see *Top.* 2.11, 115b30–35; *Physics* 1.8, 191b15; and *On Coming-to-be and Passing-away* 1.3, passim. For the formula ἁπλῶς εἰπεῖν, see Bonitz, *Index* 77b10–23.

[27] J. Stroux, "Summum ius summa iniuria," *Römische Rechtswissenschaft und Rhetorik* (Potsdam, 1949), pp. 9–66, emphasizes the role of equity as supplement or completion: "Aus den 'Lücken im Gesetz' resultiert ihm das Wesen der Billigkeit als Besserung des Gesetzes durch Ergänzung: ἔστιν αὕτη ἡ φύσις ἡ τοῦ ἐπιεικοῦς ἐπανόρθωμα νόμου ᾗ ἐλλείπει διὰ τὸ καθόλου (Eth. Nic. 1137b25). . . . Auch für Aristoteles ist Billigkeit Notbehelf zur Verwirklichung richtigen Rechts gegenüber der Unvollkommenheit, die dem Gesetz als Menschenwerk anhaftet" (p. 19). For St. Thomas' analogy of the function of equity with the completion of a sketched outline, see Chap. 6, n. 28. His comment on Lesbos is detailed: *In Lesbia enim insula sunt lapides duri qui non possunt de facili ferro praescindi ut dirigantur ad omnimodam rectitudinem; et ideo aedificatores utuntur ibi regula plumbea. Et sicut illa regula complicata adaptatur ad figuras lapidis et non manet in eadem dispositione, ita oportet quod sententia iudicis adaptetur ad res secundum earum convenientiam* (In Decem Libros Ethicorum, p. 298). For the place of equity in Aristotle's ethical thought and its subsequent influence, see M. Hamburger, *Morals and Law: The Growth of Aristotle's Legal Theory* (New York, 1965), esp. pp. 89–110; E. Barker, *The Politics of Aristotle* (Oxford, 1969), pp. lxiii–lxxvi, 146, 362–72; and G. Kisch, *Erasmus und die Jurisprudenz seiner Zeit* (Basel, 1960) and *Melanchthons Rechts und Soziallehre* (Berlin, 1967), esp. pp. 168–84.

wounds, by a single ordinance. Equity rectifies the unavoidable omissions in the law as promulgated (ἀνάγκη ἁπλῶς εἰπεῖν) and is most likely to intervene in situations where leniency is appropriate.

It is equitable to pardon human weaknesses, and to look, not to the law but to the legislator; not to the letter (λόγον) of the law but to the intention (διάνοιαν) of the legislator; not to the action itself, but to the moral purpose; not to the part, but to the whole; not to what (ποιός) a man is now, but to what (ποιός) he has been, always or generally; to remember good rather than ill treatment, and benefits received rather than those conferred; to bear injury with patience; to be willing to appeal to the judgement of reason rather than to violence; to prefer arbitration to the law court, for the arbitrator keeps equity in view, whereas the dicast looks only to the law, and the reason why arbitrators were appointed was that equity might prevail.

The category of quality (τὸ ποιόν) clearly informs this description.[28]

In the context of these considerations, equity may be related to poetry in several ways. First, in the *Poetics* " 'universal' means what kinds of thing (τὰ ποῖα) a certain kind of person (τῷ ποίῳ) will say or do in accordance with probability or necessity" (1451b8–10). The kinds of thing said or done will indicate certain moral qualities of character (τὰ δὲ ἤθη καθ' ἃ ποιούς τινας) which, in turn, confer certain qualities (ποιάς) upon the actions themselves (1450a1–7). Equity gains its freedom from (written) statutes and poetry its freedom from (recorded) history by concentrating upon qualitative issues. Equity seeks the proper relation between the individual controversy to be judged and the body of statutes to be applied to it, while poetry seeks the proper relation of given particular events, historical or imaginary, to a principle by means of which they may gain significance. Both poetry and equity embody

---

[28] *The 'Art' of Rhetoric*, trans. J. H. Freese, LCL (London, 1926). See Chap. 10, nn. 36, 39 and Chap. 14, n. 3. In a later passage in the *Rhetoric* (3.16; 1417a15–22) it is clearly the qualitative issues of moral purpose which distinguish the narrative of oratory from "narratives" of mathematics (i.e. specialized treatises): to give the narrative a moral character we should "make clear our moral purpose; for as is the moral purpose, so is the character, and as is the end, so is the moral purpose (ποιὸν δὲ τὸ ἦθος τῷ ποιὰν ταύτην· ἡ δὲ προαίρεσις ποιὰ τῷ τέλει). For this reason mathematical treatises (μαθηματικοὶ λόγοι) have no moral character (ἤθη), because neither have they moral purpose; for they have no moral end." As in the Socratic dialogues, "accompanying peculiarities of each individual character" become "ethical indications." Hence, characterization will particularize the narrative in quality. In contrast, the process of "demonstration involves neither moral character nor moral purpose" (3.17; 1418a15–16). It is precisely their inflexibility in seeing things morally, legally, and epistemologically as either true or false that leads Cicero to criticize the older Stoics, while reasserting his allegiance to Plato and Aristotle, in his *Pro Murena* (61–65). These Stoics have no means by which to ascertain the balance of equity between the 'quantities' of fact, on the one hand, or of statute on the other (see, pp. 281–84, 287–95 of this study. His criticism of their stringency is in accord with that of jurisconsults who lose sight of equity, the spirit of the law, in grasping only onto the *verba* (*Pro Mur.* 27–29). See Chap. 14, n. 8.

these relations in a particular 'case,' a dramatic plot or a legal decision, which mitigates, through the full articulation of specific attributes, the abstract exclusiveness of fact or decree. Both remain καθόλου in their analysis of as many parts as possible in relation to the whole without becoming ἁπλῶς by trying to express either whole or part in isolation from the other. Second, it is precisely in its 'equitable' function that the fictional example (καθ᾽ ὑπόθεσιν) is useful for Aristotle and Quintilian when considerations of quality enter a case.[29] It is only as a fiction, furthermore, that one might summon the original lawmaker from the dead to interpret his general statute *as if* he could have foreseen or could now see all individual cases and its application to them (cf. Aristotle's *Magna moralia* 2.1). Third, the rhetorical paradox that the more circumstantial the situation, the more generic its issues ultimately become because of the ever-increasing need for qualification is reflected in equity as it is in fiction. For in qualifying the quantitative measure of legal penalties, one is actually rendering the law, if it can incorporate special ordinances as modifications, more independently universal with regard to its application. Less has to be left to the discretion of the court. And, finally, since equity in law is analogous to the 'mean' in ethics, which is not an average but an ideal only to be approximated with respect to each *individual* case, it may express, like fiction, the ethical relation between particular events in history and thus fulfill the rhetorical and moral purpose of an *exemplum* (παράδειγμα).[30]

The 'condition' of equity (ἐπιείκεια), as of the 'mean' (μεσότης), must be maintained from moment to moment in existence by the continual readjustment of static quantities to altering qualities. Conceived as a point on a graph, it moves unceasingly within a reality whose quality it seeks to measure and describe in relation to arbitrarily determined axes. Derived from ἐπιεικής (ἐπί + εἰκός = fitting, appropriate, reasonable), equity in law corresponds to decorum in style (τὸ πρέπον) and,

[29] Since poetry is "universal" without being "absolute" and at the same time is fundamentally "hypothetical," Else's note on the opposition between ἐξ ὑποθέσεως and ἁπλῶς is significant (p. 308, n. 25). He cites *Meta.* 13.1082b32, "in relation to their hypothesis (ὑπόθεσιν) they are right, but absolutely (ὅλως) they are wrong" (trans. H. Tredennick, LCL), and glosses ὅλως as ἁπλῶς, citing Bonitz (*Index* 797a34–57) for many other examples of the opposition. Similarly, in the important passage quoted previously (Chap. 2, n. 48) from the *Rhetoric* (1.2.15), Aristotle juxtaposes arguments based on probability against arguing ἁπλῶς. The connotations of "purely" (as distinct from "compositely"), "exclusively," and "absolutely" all associate ἁπλῶς more with uncompromising historical or preceptive "truth" of fact or statute than with the probable universal of poetry.

[30] For the substitution of "paradeigma" for "hypothesis" as a term for fiction, see Appendix A. The illustrative and heuristic functions of "paradeigma" are clearly related by Plato to each other and to the use of μῦθος to fill in the details of an outlined sketch (περιγραφήν) of an ideal king (*Statesman* 277–78).

in a composition as a whole, to the 'due' treatment of a subject in relation to its ethical importance (τὸν καιρόν). These conceptual activities all 'estimate' a *particular* thing or state in relation to a qualitative norm of 'due' measure, to which it owes its very existence (*Statesman* 283D), by taking into account the circumstances in which it moves or exists. Each estimation must change with the temporal progress of its object toward its given realization or completion. This is particularly true of the concept of καιρός which denotes the precise proportion in which a thing ought to occur in order for it to fulfill its purpose. For the poet, it connotes the principle in accordance with which he should 'lay out' his materials most advantageously with regard to his intention and to their importance.[31] The dynamic and individual nature of the objects of qualitative measurement elucidates further Quintilian's preference for the *status qualitatis* over the *coniecturalis*. The *coniecturalis* asks only whether a thing happened. Its 'material' is static, fixed (or absent) in history, in which the arguments it seeks are bound (*argumenta ex materia sumit*).[32]

Plato expresses great distrust of the static in his discussion of *mimesis*. However confusing the flux of appearances may be, the mind itself must try to keep step with them by means of a continuing dialectic of definition and redefinition. If the efforts of language relax after the establishment of any proposition, that proposition is instantly obsolete—just as qualities (ποιότητες) in the moment of their being named are gone. This is the reason for Plato's reservations about the written language in the *Phaedrus* (274C–78E). What is written down, be it a law, a speech, or a poem, risks immediate obsolescence, for, like a statue, it is incapable of revision through an exchange of language. Out of such a context arises Plato's recurring comparison of writing laws with writing poems. When asked about a pattern (παραδείγματος) for education, the Athe-

---

[31] For this interpretation of καιρός, I am indebted to the commentary of G. Lanata in her edition of *Poetica Pre-Platonica, testimonianze e frammenti* (Firenze, 1963), pp. 93–97, and to E. L. Bundy who first called my attention to its significance in Pindar. See now: J. R. Wilson, "KAIROS as 'Due Measure,'" *Glotta* 58, 3–4 (1980) and "KAIROS as 'Profit,'" *CQ* 31, 2 (1981); W. H. Race, "The Word καιρός in Greek Drama," *TAPA* 111 (1981).

[32] There will be a smaller place for equity in a purely conjectural issue, since, as Plato observes (*Laws* 875E), the occurrence or nonoccurrence of an alleged act must always be decided by the individual jury whatever the penalty fixed by legislation might be. Cicero says the same thing about the thesis (*Orat.* 126). Compare the observations of M. Cohen on the possible contribution of jurisprudence to epistemology: "Consider how much would our controversy over the nature of truth have been enriched if, instead of our easy dichotomous division of propositions into the true and false, we had taken notice of what lawyers call legal fictions. . . . These propositions like the statement of the actor, 'I am thy father's spirit,' are not adequately characterized when we say merely that they are true or that they are false" ("Jurisprudence as a Philosophical Discipline," p. 227).

nian comments that in looking back over the day's discussions "it appeared to me that they were framed exactly like a poem (ποιήσει)" and that a better pattern (παράδειγμα) for educators was not to be found (*Laws*, 811CD). Our polity (πολιτεία), he says later to imaginary traveling players in a passage already quoted in connection with mimetic probability, "is framed as a representation of the fairest and best life (μίμησις τοῦ καλλίστου καὶ ἀρίστου βίου), which is . . . the truest tragedy." As artists and actors, we are rivals of yours, for "we are composers (ποιηταί) . . . of the fairest drama (δράματος), which . . . true law, and it alone, is by nature competent to complete" (817B). Laws are like compositions of poets (ποιητῶν) but take greater moral responsibility (*Laws*, 858C–59B), for of all studies, legal regulations most improve their students and best serve as a measure for other types of literature (957CD).

In the *Statesman* (294A–301B), law at its most inflexible is depicted as a willful, ignorant man who refuses to answer questions (294C), at its best as an imitation (μιμήματα) of the ideal constitution (297C, 300C). The true artist in law will imitate the true original (μιμεῖσθαι τὸ ἀληθές, 300D); ordinary lawmakers will make imitations (μιμῶνται) to accord with their own character (301AB). Imitation by the ideal lawmaker corresponds to that by the ideal dramatist and even the ideal painter (cf. *Rep.* 472BE); in each case the value of the imitation is proportionate to the ideality of the model. That a perfect constitution would be impossible to achieve, except in waxen models or in dreams, however, should not deter the lawmaker from making his pattern (παράδειγμα) for imitation as true and as beautiful as possible. Where a particular detail occurs in it which might ultimately be impracticable, let it be omitted at a future time and approximations of it then be substituted. Only after the best model has been completely set forth should the expediency of its actual legislation be discussed: "for the constructor of even the most trivial object, if he is to be of any merit, must make it in all points consistent with itself" (*Laws*, 746AC).[33]

In the absence of an ideal artist or interpreter, all imitations for Plato were in danger of obsolescence. Since they could not embody (as perfect products might) the permanent qualities of the Ideas, the poem, the law, and the painting all needed to be 'requalified' in the experience of in-

[33] The ideal of consistency is similar here to the coherent probability sought in the dramatic plot. That such consistency can only be realized in wax or dreams is suggestive for the later development of the literary genre of the dream-vision. See also Plato's analogy of the malleability of gold with regard to the depiction of qualities (*Tim.* 49D–50B). It is interesting that Dio Chrysostom, in enumerating the various materials within which artists may depict characteristics of the gods, says that molding in wax "most readily answers the artist's touch and affords the greatest opportunity for change of intention," that is, for the correction of error in the original design (12.44).

dividuals moment by moment to exist at all. If this did not happen, any artistic construction of the surface of events at any given moment might crack, as a death mask freshly molded upon living features, because of the metabolism of the reality beneath it. Through equity the law as an "image of things naturally noble and just (τὸν νόμον εἰκόνα τῶν φύσει καλῶν καὶ δικαίων)," to borrow Aristotle's phrasing (*Top.* 141a21), could be rectified by the curators' responsible application. So poetry and the plastic arts, while not 'rewritten' in themselves by each generation, nevertheless, could provide an 'image' of equity through the flexible extension of their emblematic application. For Plato, they might illustrate certain human potentialities for order, which might otherwise remain unperceived. For Aristotle, the 'equity' of fiction lay in its capacity to analyze qualities of character and action for members of an audience freed momentarily from emotional responses demanded by the actual events of their own lives. Like the leaden rulers of the Lesbian builders, equity and poetry might remain sufficiently supple to measure a continually changing reality by interpreting legal and ethical sanctions fixed and passed on by history from generation to generation. Like the tale of Er, saved with him from the rigor of transmigration and oblivion, these 'images' might now save us if we could be persuaded to trust them (*Rep.* 621B).[34]

E. The Hypothesizing Image and the Problem of Interpretation

The concept of 'quality' is rooted deeply in the Greek logical, physical, and moral sciences. In equity it originates, perhaps, in the ancient dis-

---

[34] Cicero intends to draw his *conception* of the ideal orator as a likeness taken from a face which is perceived only in the mind (*ut ex ore aliquo quasi imago exprimatur*). Though the ideal itself, like Plato's Form, does not 'become' but remains forever, the conception men have of it will fade (see Chap. 10, n. 42). Nevertheless, that conception remains more stable and capable of being transmitted than the particulars which, while partially embodying it, continually cease to be (*Orat.* 7–10, 18–19; cf. *Acad.* 1.30–32). The law as an "image" of natural justice (*Top.* 141a21) resembles the image (εἰκών) that Isocrates wished to give of his thought and life in the interests of equity (see pp. 61–62 of this study). Very similar motivations lie behind the *Lives* of Plutarch. D. A. Russell comments that "thus to describe the *bios* of a great man was to say 'what sort of man he was' (poios tis ēn) and to regard him, in a sense, as one of ourselves" (*Plutarch* [London, 1973], p. 102). Other characteristics of the portraits conform to the objectives of equity (ibid., pp. 101–3). With respect to the Lesbian ruler, an amusing example might be Xenophon's account of an armorer who claimed the proportions of his suits were better than those of other artisans (*Mem.* 3.10.9–12). Socrates asks him how he can make a well-proportioned breastplate for an ill-proportioned man. By making it fit! is the reply. Well-proportioned, Socrates responds, does not mean in relation to absolute proportions, then, but to the wearer.

crimination of a flexible measure of 'due' proportion from one arithmetically determined. Against a written code of penalties must be measured the 'suitability' of any penalty for a particular act here and now.
'Suitability' was closely bound to the concept of time: what was fitting
when the law was written down may not be fitting later. The temporal
consideration, later associated with the term καιρός itself, was conceived
hypothetically as the intention (διάνοια, *sententia, voluntas*) of a lawmaker *were* he to come back to life to reformulate his law for the case
now to be decided. Any such assumption suggests a form of discourse
which is in itself fictional. Like the *dianoia* of 'thought' in dramatic
speeches which 'qualify' the action of characters, the ghostly will of the
lawmaker might be said, in the language of the *Poetics* (1450b5–12), "to
express what is involved in a given situation and is appropriate (τὰ
ἐνόντα καὶ τὰ ἁρμόττοντα)" in its attempt "to prove that something is
so or not so, or express some general view (καθόλου τι)." "Thought,"
indeed, belongs to rhetoric, for it "includes all those effects which have
to be deliberately produced by speech." These effects include "(1) proof
and refutation, and (2) the producing of emotions, such as pity, fear,
anger, and the like [and also exaggeration and depreciations]" (*Poet.*
1456a34–b2). In Roman rhetoric these considerations are nearly all associated with the *status qualitatis*, which Cicero says (*De part. orat.* 66)
will always concern "either honour or utility or equity (*de honestate
aut de utilitate aut de aequitate*)."[35]

---

[35] *De partitione oratoria*, trans. H. Rackham, LCL (London, 1960). The three methods
of inquiry (*coniectura, definitio, consecutio*) associated with the three types of *status* pertain
to either the acquisition of knowledge or to the performance of action. With respect to
knowledge, the qualitative inquiry (*consecutio*) concerns "investigating a particular thing's
consequence" such as "is it occasionally the duty of a good man to tell a lie?" *Consecutio*
has two forms: (1) simple questions concern what things are to be desired or avoided (*de
expetendis fugiendisve rebus*), what things are right and what wrong (*de aequo aut iniquo*),
and what is honourable and what dishonourable (*de honesto aut turpi*); (2) comparative
questions concern whether two things are the same or different and which of two things
is preferable. With respect to *action*, the inquiry either involves duty (*officium*), which
asks what conduct is right and proper and includes the whole range of virtues and vices,
or it is involved in "producing or in allaying or removing some emotion (*aliqua permotione
aut gignenda aut sedanda tollendave*)." This summary by Cicero (*De orat.* 3.111–18) of
the topics of qualitative inquiry embraces the main concerns of literature in preceding and
subsequent centuries, and suggests, in associating quality with the investigation of consequences, the synthesis of fictional representation—see pp. 296–305 of this study and *De
part. orat.* 66, 101–4; *Top.* 89f.; *De inv.* 1.12. In order to adapt these commonplaces to
law, Cicero divides the qualitative issue into legal (*negotialem*) and equitable (*iuridicialem*)
questions. The legal question involves only a dispute over a point of law. The equitable
question deals with the nature (*natura*) of justice and the principle (*ratio*) of reward and
penalty. It is divided, in turn, into absolute (*absoluta*) questions which concern rightness
or wrongness when clearly apparent in the act itself and assumptive (*assumptiva*) questions,
which involve an act which in itself cannot be approved but might be defended on the
grounds of extraneous circumstances (*De inv.* 1.14; 2.62ff.). When Quintilian redefines

It is generally agreed, Cicero maintains (*De inv.* 2.156), that the end of forensic rhetoric is *aequitas*, a division of *honestas*. The honorable, when it is sought for its own sake, is virtue, "a habit of mind in harmony with reason and the order of nature (*animi habitus naturae modo atque rationi consentaneus*)." When it is sought for some accompanying benefit or profit, it is called "advantage" (*utilitas*). As a result, things are to be either sought (*petendarum*) or avoided (*vitandarum*) and these are circumstantially 'qualified' (*attributae*) by "necessity" and "affection" (2.158–59).

"Affection" is a change in the aspect of things due to time, or the result of actions or their management, or to the interests and desires of men, so that it seems that things should not be regarded in the same light as they have been or have generally been regarded. For example, it is an act of baseness to go over to the enemy, but not if done with the purpose (*animo*) which Ulysses had (2.176).

Many matters, therefore, must be understood with reference to time (*tempore*) and intention (*consilio*). In taking occasions and persons into account "one must consider not what is being done but with what spirit anything is done, with what associates, at what time, and how long it has been going on (*considerandum est et non quid, sed quo quidque animo, quicum, quo tempore, quamdiu fiat, attendendum est*)." The term *affectio* reflects here various meanings of ποιότης, and its description corresponds to Aristotle's discussion of equity.[36]

---

negotialis and *iuridicalis* (3.6.57ff.), the distinction between them comes to resemble that between indefinite and definite questions, the former considering questions without particular persons, the latter considering the same questions with respect to them. Iulius Victor treats the distinction in detail (Halm, pp. 378–82). See Chap. 10, n. 8 and Chap. 13, n. 14.

[36] The "relativity" of *affectio* is brought out by contexts in which we would translate the word as *relation* (cf. Lewis and Short, 1). Considerations of equity arise particularly when "quality" is involved ("quale sit id, de quo consideretur"): "For it often happens, owing to exceptional circumstances (*tempore*), that what is accustomed under ordinary circumstances to be considered morally wrong is found not to be morally wrong." The example Cicero gives is the traditional exoneration of murder if the victim happens to be a tyrant (*De officiis* 3.19, trans. W. Miller, LCL [London, 1961]). Elsewhere (*De part. orat.* 42–43) Cicero says that actions done owing to emotional and mental disturbance (*motu animi et perturbatione*) cannot be defended in court but in open debate they can on the basis of qualitative issues (*in quo quale sit quaeritur*). The author of the *Rhet. ad Her.* comments that "according to circumstances (*tempore*) and a person's status (*dignitate*) virtually a new kind of Law (*novum ius*) may well be established" (2.20)—trans. H. Caplan, LCL (London, 1964). This relation to individual circumstances is not only fundamental to Aristotle's definition of the 'mean' but also to his judgment of the morality expressed in plays: "As to the question whether anything that has been said or done is morally good or bad, this must be answered not merely by seeing whether what has actually been done or said is noble or base, but by taking into consideration also the man who did or said it, and seeing to whom he did or said it, and when and for whom and for

When an act is admitted but claimed to have been justified on the grounds of its 'quality,' "the entire theory of right" (*iuris est omnis ratio*), Cicero says, ought to be kept in mind (*De part. orat.* 129–37). Rightness (*ius*) is categorized under nature (*natura*) and law (*lex*), and each of these is subdivided into divine right (*divinum ius*), which concerns religion, and human right (*humanum ius*), which concerns equity (*aequitas*) in the most general sense. Equity may either concern (under *lex*) what is fair and good (*aequi et boni ratione*) or (under *natura*) reciprocation of benefits (repayment or gratitude) or of injury (revenge). Falling only under the equitable category of *lex* is the subdivision of written statutes and of unwritten laws. Written statutes concern either public laws or private contracts. Unwritten laws consist of custom, convention, or the consensus of men. To classify questions of interpretation solely within the category of *lex*, four subsidiary '*status*' (*legales*) were developed: (a) questions involving a conflict between the letter and the spirit of the law (*ex scripto et sententia*, κατὰ ῥητὸν καὶ διάνοιαν); (b) questions involving ambiguity (*ambiguitas*, ἀμφιβολία); (c) questions involving a conflict of statutes (*contrariae leges*, ἀντινομία); (d) questions involving the absence of a law which must be supplied by analogy or precedent (*collectio*, συλλογισμός). Of the primary system (*status rationales*), the definitive and qualitative questions are particularly applicable to these specific types of interpretation described in detail by Cicero in the *De inventione* (2.116–54).

When public morality is no longer held to account by statute (*lege*) or civil law (*iure civili*), Cicero maintains (*De off.* 3.69) that it will still be judged by moral law (*naturae lege*). This is a universal law (*ius gentium*) which unites men in the widest bonds of interest, and ought (*debet*) to be the foundation of civil law. It fails to be so because "we possess no substantial, life-like image of true Law and genuine Justice; a mere outline sketch is all that we enjoy (*veri iuris germanaeque iustitiae solidam et expressam effigiem nullam tenemus, umbra et imaginibus utimur*)." We are not even willing, furthermore, to imitate our rough sketch despite the fact that it is drawn from "excellent models which Nature and Truth afford (*feruntur enim ex optimis naturae et veritatis exemplis*)." This language, so powerfully reminiscent of the Platonic εἰκός and παράδειγμα—themselves 'likenesses' useful in both law and poetry—indicates how the kind of fictional hypothesis that Cicero strongly defends in his *De officiis* (3.39) might be able to sketch the shadowed images of natural law and equity.

what reason; for example, to secure a greater good or to avoid a greater evil" (1461a6–11—trans. W. H. Fyfe, LCL [London, 1953]). His terms are almost identical to Cicero's definition of *affectio*.

Cicero is defending Plato's use of the *fabula* of Gyges' ring against "certain philosophers" who criticized it on the grounds that the story was pure fiction (*fictam et commenticiam*). He responds that they miss the significance of this ring and fail to see what it illustrates (*vis huius anuli et huius exempli*) if they are unwilling to understand the hypothetical nature of the fiction. They refuse to see the meaning of "if possible" (*id si posset*) and the fact that no one ever claimed such a ring could exist. The 'assumption' of its existence serves to bring out clearly whether those willing to entertain it might seek what only favored their self-interest (*quod expediat*) or might flee all that is dishonorable (*omnia turpia per se ipsa fugienda*). This fable, then, might be an imitation of one of the models (*exemplis*) offered by nature and truth, an imaginary "sketch" (*umbra et imaginibus*, as opposed to a completed statue, *expressam effigiem*) that we must work from in the absence of a more complete portrait of justice. The word *vis* denotes not only the formal character of the example but the force of its significance in terms of what should be sought or avoided (*expetendum aut fugiendum*).[37]

Any written legal code is an outline, as Plato says (769B–71A), a sketch to be filled in by experience, which is in part preserved in unwritten laws and customs. Conceived as a building (793BC), the structure of recorded legislation may be held together by the mortar of such traditions (cf. 858B). For Cicero, as well, statute and civil law offer but a rough sketch of the ideal portrait—something with which to start, an ἀρχή. The process of filling in bears a marked analogy to the completion of the dramatic outline (ὑπόθεσις), to a *mimesis* to which Plato himself compared his *Laws* (817B). The bare dramatic 'hypothesis' corresponds to the bare outline of facts and of (apparently) applicable laws available within a written constitution—to the *imago*, as Quintilian calls the initial sketch of a declamation (4.1.4). Assuming names, characters articulate motivation in speeches, action in episode. They 'qualify' the events cited in the 'argument' of the play as the 'mortar' of moral law interprets, through consideration of equity, the established statutes so that they may take hold of the case to be judged. Both outlines offer a place from which to move toward more detailed realizations: the completed play corresponds to the completed litigation, the catastrophe to the final judgment. The development of both the drama and the litigation are 'interpretations' of the 'given': in the play the skeleton of events is given, in anticipation of plausible causation; in the litigation the selection of stat-

---

[37] Cf. Plato, *Prot.* 326CD. In the passages from Aristotle and St. Thomas on the degree of exactitude appropriate for the treatment of ethical qualities, cited above, pp. 125–29 (see esp. Chap. 6, n. 28), the Good itself can only be treated in outline, as in a fable, which, if well laid down, can be filled in gradually by others with the help of time.

utes, in the hope of applying them when the circumstances are understood. The 'hypothesis' or plot as the *arche* of a play corresponds, in other words, to a "basis (ὑπόθεσις) in the law" from which as "a starting-point (ἀρχήν) you can prove anything with comparative ease."[38] This legal use of 'hypothesis' as an *arche* clearly corresponds as well to the definition of 'beginning' which I cited from the *Metaphysics* in Part One with respect to the drama: an *arche* "means the point from which (ὅθεν) a thing (πρᾶγμα) is first comprehensible, . . . e.g. the hypotheses of demonstrations" (*Meta.* 5.1.2; 1013a15–17).

When the interpretation of laws becomes fraudulent (*malitiosa*) or oversubtle (*nimis callida*), Cicero says (*De off.* 1.33) the greater their force the greater their injustice (*summum ius summa iniuria*). This is particularly true in the interpretation of oaths, treaties, and wills, which fall in the category of controversies over public and private contracts involving the *status legales*. Such controversies usually occur "over the letter and the intent (*ex scripto et sententia*)" when "one party follows the exact words that are written, and the other directs his whole pleading to what he says the writer meant" (*De inv.* 2.121). In a sense, Cicero's long discussion of arguments to be used in debating the terms of a will illustrates the problem of interpreting any law whose writer must be imagined to come forward from the dead to explain its application. All such debates, indeed, turn upon whether or not a document is to be taken as a "picture," so to speak, of the writer's true desires (*suae voluntatis quasi imaginem*, 2.128). The picture must remain a kind of *umbra*, a shadowy reflection, of the author's original intention (*voluntas*).[39]

[38] Aristotle, *Rhetoric* 3.17.10, 1418a25, trans. W. R. Roberts; in completing E. M. Cope's commentary, J. E. Sandys renders the sentence: "Besides, in forensic pleadings, the *law* supplies a subject; and when once you have your starting-point, it is easier to find your proof" (3:203). In an unpublished dissertation, "The Influence of Legal Procedure on the Development of Tragic Structure" (Stanford University, 1980), K. H. Eden analyzes the relation between the legal and dramatic representation of experience in the Greek, Roman, and Renaissance periods, with special emphasis upon the coordinating function of the 'image.'

[39] A visual metaphor is also suggested in *leges nobis caras esse non propter litteras, quae tenues et obscurae notae sint voluntatis* (*De inv.* 2.141). What Cicero says of oaths— *semper autem in fide quid senseris, non quid dixeris, cogitandum* (*De off.* 1.40)—applies to any oral or written agreement. The interpretation of wills might fall under *sanctitas*, i.e. the relation of men with departed spirits (*manes*)—as distinct from that with gods (*pietas*) or with men still living (*aequitas*)—as Cicero divides the topics of equity (*lato sensu*) in his *Topica* (89f.). For further treatment of *scriptum* vs. *sententia* in the interpretation of wills or laws, see Aristotle, *Rhet.* 1.15, 1375a25–75b25; *Rhet. ad Alex.* 1421b36–22a4; *Rhet. ad Her.* 1.19, 2.13–14; *De inv.* 1.55f., 1.68ff., 2.138–41; *Topica* 96; *De part. orat.*, 136–37; *De orat.* 2.110; *Inst. orat.* 3.6.43, 5.10.95–99, 7.6.1ff. *Sententia* was interchangeable with *voluntas* for the original intention of the testator (*De part. orat.* 136; *Brut.* 198). In his essay, "*Summum ius summa iniuria*," J. Stroux maintained the thesis that Greek rhetorical theory influenced the formation of Roman jurisprudence particularly through questions of equity such as *scriptum* vs *sententia* (see esp. pp. 33–

In distinguishing his two great models, Cicero remarks (*Brut.* 144) that Marcus Antonius excels "in creating a presumption of probability, in allaying or in provoking a suspicion (*coniectura movenda aut sedanda suspicione aut excitanda*)," while Lucius Crassus is unsurpassed "in interpretation, in definition, in unfolding the implications of equity (*in explicanda aequitate*)." It is, therefore, not surprising that Crassus argued the intention of the testator against a literal interpretation of the document upheld by Quintus Scaevola, the great expert in technical jurisprudence, in the famous testamentary case of Manius Curius. Each pleader upheld the civil law from different points of view in such a way that Crassus appeared the best jurist among orators, Scaevola the best orator among jurists (145). Scaevola tried to prove that Curius, "who had been named as heir in the event that an expected posthumous son should die before said son had reached his majority," could not inherit because, in fact, no posthumous son was born (195). He argued that any leeway given to the strict interpretation would invite further perversions of the text by unscrupulous lawyers (196). Crassus responded that the

38). His thesis has been widely debated. F. Schulz, *History of Roman Legal Science* (Oxford, 1953), stressed the remoteness of such Greek rhetorical *topoi* (and of the legal philosophy which Cicero derived from them) from the actual practice of jurisprudence (pp. 71–75). See also H. F. Jolowicz, *Historical Introduction to the Study of Roman Law* (Cambridge, 1939), pp. 423f. and H. Caplan's notes to his edition of the *Rhetorica ad Herennium* (LCL), pp. 90f., 94. For support of the rhetorical influence, see M. Hamburger, *Morals and Law*, pp. 89–110, esp. pp. 108ff. with bibliography on the controversy. S. F. Bonner reviews the problem in connection with the common division of cases by declaimers into *ius* and *aequitas*. Implying his support of Stroux, he gives Quintilian the last word (7.6.1): *scripti et voluntatis frequentissima inter consultos quaestio est, et pars magna controversi iuris hinc pendet; quo minus id accidere in scholis mirum est, ubi etiam ex industria fingitur* (*Roman Declamation* [Berkeley, 1949], pp. 46–48). See, as well, 7.4.10–12. That treatments of equity in later legal codes may only be fictional interpolations has, in itself, interesting implications for literary theory (see Hamburger, p. 108, n. 3). The problem, finally, of interpreting legal documents is not markedly different from that of interpreting literary texts. We must understand what the author originally intended to say, his *voluntas*, before considering what the text can mean for us today if its integrity is to be preserved, and, by means of its integrity, our own. But the only access we have to the writer's *voluntas* is through his *scripta*, which must be interpreted, like the written law, by an act of the historical imagination and the disciplines at its command. That act starts with the text itself as all investigation starts with the present reality to be understood. We 'analyze' it backward in time until the writer's meaning becomes apparent as a beginning, and then, following the laws of the historical elenchus, we come forward again in synthesis to the present. Only if no contradictions emerge to refute our assumption about its original meaning can we understand it in relation to ourselves—that is, understand how the author might explain his words to us were he living today. (See my "The Practice of Historical Interpretation and Nashe's 'Brightnesse Falls from the Ayre,'" *JEGP* 66 [1967]:501–18; "The Definition and Practice of Literary Studies," *NLH* 2 [1970]:187–92; and Appendix C of this book.) So too with the visual arts. Given the metaphor *imago voluntatis* for the intention of the testator, it is amusing how closely Quintilian's questions concerning the *voluntas* of artists, with respect to the interpretation of their works, resemble those of modern iconographers: *cur armata apud Lacedaemonios Venus* and *quid ita crederetur Cupido puer atque volucer et sagittis ac face armatus* (2.4.26). See Chap. 14, nn. 8, 13.

written will should be the 'will' of the deceased (197–98). He argued the equity of observing the clear intention of the testator (*aequum bonum, testamentorum sententias voluntatesque tutatus est*) and the danger of being trapped in words (*verbis*), in the interpretation of wills or of anything else, when the actual wishes of the writer are ignored (*si neglegerentur voluntates*). Cicero praises both men highly but agrees with the judgment that went in favor of Crassus.

Crassus was the more proficient in the *art* of rhetoric, Scaevola in the *science* of jurisprudence. The two skills were combined most perfectly by Servius Sulpicius, an expert in civil law, a knowledge of which Quintilian so strongly stressed (12.3.1–11), who could treat his knowledge *as an artist* by virtue of his understanding of dialectic, the art of arts (*artem omnium artium maximam*). Through dialectic he could analyze the whole into parts (*rem universam tribuere in partis*), set forth the implicit (*latentem explicare*), clarify the obscure, distinguish the ambiguous (*ambigua primum videre, deinde distinguere*), and measure the true and false by determining the consequences of given premises (*quae quibus propositis essent quaeque non essent consequentia*). In this idealized portrait (*Brut.* 152–53), the liberal intentions of rhetoric and philosophy complement each other. The intrusion of the indefinite question into a particular case occurs with considerations of quality (*Inst. orat.* 3.5.10) or equity: when a victim happens to be a tyrant (*De off.* 3.19), such implicit conditions of time and quality (*subestque et temporis et qualitatis tacita vis*) mitigate the crime of murder (*Inst. orat.* 3.5.9). As dialectic brings out the order of legal science, the general question brings out the ethical significance which lies latent and implicit in the bare words of a document or in the admitted facts of a criminal action.

It is Crassus himself who summarizes this position, which the present and the preceding sections have endeavored to clarify (*De orat.* 3.120). The most desirable speeches

Are those which take the widest range and which turn aside from the particular matter in dispute to engage in an explanation of the meaning of the general issue, so as to enable the audience to base their verdict in regard to the particular parties and charges and actions in question on a knowledge of the nature and character of the matter as a whole (*a singulari conroversia se ad universi generis vim explicandam conferunt et convertunt, ut ei qui audiant natura et genere et universa re cognita de singulis reis et criminibus et litibus statuere possint*).[40]

[40] Among Cicero's contemporaries there was no one *qui dilatare posset atque a propria ac definita disputatione hominis ac temporis ad communem quaestionem universi generis orationem traducere* (*Brut.* 322). Quintilian stresses the importance of equity, quality, and general questions which underlie all particular cases just as strongly (1.pr.16–18, 12.2.15–28). A. Michel observes that arguments for *voluntas* tend toward generic questions, for the *scriptum* toward particular *causae*: "Les premiers sont philosophiques, les seconds dépendent de la philosophie comme toutes les 'hypothèses' qui introduisent la

The philosophical thesis is chiefly responsible here for establishing a basis (*statuere*) from which to understand and judge particular actions. Not only is the generic question fundamental, then, to the *status* system itself, but it is also, perhaps, as a form of dialectic, the bond which Cicero describes in his defense of the poet Archias as relating all the humanistic arts to one another.[41] This relation exists by virtue of a community of letters (*de studiis humanitatis ac litterarum*) in which the ultimate objectives to be pursued by the orator and the poet are the same (3). Unlike statues, which imitate only the body, literature presents an image of the virtues of the mind, completely articulated by the most ingenious men (*virtutum nostrarum effigiem . . . summis ingeniis expressam et politam*, 30). It is these portraits (*imagines*), so finely cut (*expressas*) by Greek and Roman authors in order to be seen and imitated (*ad intuendum . . . ad imitandum*) by all, that Cicero places before himself (*mihi . . . proponens*) in order that his mind and soul will conform to theirs in his care for the Republic (14). Such a portrait is not one of an

---

'thèse' dans la réalité, le droit dans le fait" (*Rhétorique et philosophie chez Cicéron: essai sur les fondements philosophiques de l'art de persuader* [Paris, 1960], p. 463).

[41] *Pro Archia* 2: *Etenim omnes artes, quae ad humanitatem pertinent, habent quoddam commune vinculum et quasi cognatione quadam inter se continentur.* The power of literature (*Latinae litterae*) to preserve the past is symbolized in Cicero's *Laws* by the Marian Oak, which lives forever because it is planted by the poet's imagination (*sata est enim ingenio*). The olive tree of the Acropolis and Ulysses' palm of Delos, also, symbolize men's recognition that things may last beyond nature through recollection. When the individual tree is destroyed, still there will be another to take its place, and it will be both a different tree and yet the same tree. The 'historian' will inquire about the individual tree as he will about whether these or those things in a poem *fictane an vera sint*. He misses the point, however, if he expects the *veritas* to be given in the manner of a witness in court (*a teste*) rather than that of a poet (*a poëta*). For there are indeed *alias in historia leges observandas* than *in poëmata*. The standard of one is factual truth, of the other, delight—albeit that Herodotus and Theopompus mixed in *innumerabiles fabulae* (*De leg.* 1.1–5). This passage is one of Cicero's most nostalgic appeals for the cultural continuity he defines in his *Pro Archia*. His comments on the different kinds of witnesses are repeated by Petronius (*Satyr.* 118). Both writers are foreshadowed by Aristotle when he contrasts recent with ancient witnesses such as the poets (*Rhet.* 1.15). Those recent witnesses who themselves risk something in the trial will be reliable in conjectural testimony about whether an act was or was not committed, but "if it is a question of the quality (ποῖον) of the act, for instance, whether it is just or unjust, expedient or inexpedient, they are not competent witnesses." The passage reveals an important connection between history as empirical knowledge of recent facts and the "novelistic" literary genres, which goes back to the *Odyssey*. Both are distinguished from poetry, not as prose from verse, but as recent from ancient testimony: history and the novel involve the *status conjecturalis*, poetry the *status qualitatis*. The *status conjecturalis* fall under the strictures of "exact" verification; they can be proven to be true or false. The *status qualitatis* claim only the approximate truth of men's continuing ethical experience. The equitable testimony of the poets, their true *voluntas* expressed in the written "testaments" of their poems, may account for much of the feeling and some of the formal structure of the late medieval genre of the *Testament*. In it the poet expresses his *sententia* in the *scriptum* as if he were there, alive, interpreting it for the reader. It is interesting that the distinction between a novel and a poem may ultimately be a legal one.

ideal pattern of nature or true justice to which we have no access (*De off.* 3.69–70), but the *virtutum nostrarum effigiem*, drawn from the 'life' of exceptional men by exceptional artists. Because this model, this *imago*, and this artist all exist in the actual world as we know it, the portrait can be more easily 'filled in,' for the detail is available. With other earthly things, of course, the portrait will fade. But like the equitable interpretation of a legal code, it may survive in the sympathetic hands of later artists who reinterpret it for a continuing present whose duration it is always rash to underestimate.[42]

[42] The desire to find exemplary models in literature and in nature is characteristic also of Cicero's treatment of the state. While Plato described a republic which could not exist and his successors discussed types of constitutions in the abstract (*sine ullo certo exemplari formaque rei publicae*), Scipio seeks to combine both methods in an account of the founding and development of the Roman state (*De republica* 2.21–22, trans. C. W. Keyes, LCL [London, 1948]). Though embodying the same principles as Plato, he will avoid the shadowy image of a commonwealth (*non in umbra et imagine civitatis*, 2.52) and use the actual history of the greatest republic in order to show what *kind* of a state it was that the discussion is trying to make clear (*quale esset id, quod ratio oratioque describeret*, 2.66). Cicero's exemplary practice is very much like that of Isocrates' use of historical "paradeigmata" (*Dem.* 34, *Nic.* 35, *Antid.* 277) and is central to Renaissance literary methods: he takes as his models (*exempla*) distinguished people and ages (*inlustribus in personis temporibusque*) and to these his discussion will conform (*ad quae reliqua oratio dirigatur mea*, 2.55). A similar concern with historical exemplification is apparent in his essays: *De sen.* 3, *De amic.* 18–21, *Parad. Stoic.* 10. Cicero wishes, furthermore, to produce in the mind of his readers a mental image of such men as Crassus, as Plato did of Socrates, which is on an even grander scale than the portrait he actually presents (*De orat.* 3.15). It is interesting that Africanus appears in the younger Scipio's dream "taking that shape which was familiar to me from his bust rather than from his person (*ea forma, quae mihi ex imagine eius quam ex ipso erat notior* [*De rep.* 6.10])." Owing to the equity of ancient customs and to the eminent men who protected their institution, Cicero claims the republic once "was like a beautiful painting (*picturam egregiam*)." Its "colours (*coloribus*), however, were already fading with age," and, as Plato warned must be done (*Laws*, 769BC), the present time "not only has neglected to freshen it by renewing the original colours, but has not even taken the trouble to preserve its configuration and, so to speak, its general outlines (*formam saltem eius et extrema tamquam liniamenta* [5.2])." Such pictorial exemplification is equally responsible for the affective power of history and fiction (*De fin.* 5.61–64). Though questioning the value of Academic probability (*Contra acad.* 3.18), St. Augustine also stresses the hortatory and emotive efficacy of literary imagery (*De doct. christ.* 2.6; *Ep.* 55.11.21; *De trin.* 8.4–6). The capacity of the image, while deriving its existence from sensation, to survive any particular period of the temporal flux perhaps derives from, among other sources, Plato's own late formulation of time itself as a moving image of permanence (*Tim.* 37D–38B). When we speak of motion, as J. Burnet comments, our language is "unscientific and pictorial. It can only convey an 'image' of the truth," but, nevertheless, Plato "had shown already in the *Sophist* that to be an image was not to be nothing" (*Greek Philosophy*, pp. 342, 349). Cf. St. Augustine, *Solil.* 2.10 and *Retract.* 1.1.11. On the capacity of the various arts (and faculties) to express *imagines* of that which cannot be imitated by the senses, see Xenophon, *Mem.* 3.10; Cicero *Orat.* 7–19; Dio Chrysostomus, *Disc.* 12; and Philostratus, *Life of Apollonius* 6.19. I have pointed out some relations of these passages to Plato, Horace, and Longinus in HMP and HASD, cited in n. 1 of Part Two.

11. Rhetoric and the Structure
of Fiction

In Part One of this study, I illustrated the intentions and principles of order of a literary work by describing how the functions of hypothesis, borrowed from geometry, philosophy, and rhetoric, respectively, combined and reinforced one another in a fictional hypothesis or *argumentum*. In Chapter 10 I have tried to show how the subject matters common to the rhetorical and literary analysis of experience are related by their mutual concern with the concept of *qualitas*. In Chapter 11, I wish to show how the formal disposition of these subjects in rhetorical structures presupposes and transmits principles of construction analogous to those of poetic composition.

Both Plato and Aristotle saw that the introduction of a geometrical measurement into the analysis of ultimate ends and of moral action, still expressed in Spinoza's wish "that men's actions and appetites could be discussed as if they were as undoubtedly subject to rational law as lines, planes, and bodies,"[1] could meet with only limited success. For eschatology, the premises of geometry were themselves too arbitrarily derived from sensory experience to give subsequent deductions a greater validity than that of self-consistency. Without valid premises, such consistency would become merely a rigid measuring rod, broken into ar-

---

[1] *Humanas actiones, atque appetitus considerabo perinde, ac si Quaestio de lineis, planis, aut de corporibus esset* (*Ethics*, III, *Opera Posthuma* [1667], p. 94, quoted from A. Arber, *The Mind and the Eye* [Cambridge, 1964], p. 86). Miss Arber, as a biologist, is observing that a "principle of uniformity" in nature can never be *proved* scientifically by induction or deduction. She suggests that such a uniformity "should be treated neither as a datum, nor as a conclusion from an argument, but as an *hypothesis*," for hypotheses "advance merely to higher and higher degrees of probability as they are found to 'work.' " Originating in intuition, they "take their rise through processes including but transcending discursive thought." This is one of many passages on the use of hypotheses in the biological sciences in her book which are suggestive for fictional structures. With regard to a uniformity of nature, Aristotle remarked (*Meta.* 1090b19–20) that "observed facts (ἐκ τῶν φαινομένων) show that nature (φύσις) is not a series of episodes (ἐπεισοδιώδης) like a bad tragedy" (trans. T. B. L. Webster, *Art and Literature in Fourth Century Athens* [London, 1956], p. 54). Compare the Epicurean criticism of a Stoic providential Intelligence who must be brought in to 'save' nature like a *deus ex machina* in a tragedy to save the plot (Cicero, *De nat. deor.* 1.53).

bitrary lengths without beginning or end, to be applied at random to fragments of experience. For ethics and law, a quantitative measurement of rewards and penalties, fixed by a statutory code, could never encompass the infinite variety of individually qualitative acts. Plato replaced the geometrical with the dialectical hypothesis in his eschatology, while Aristotle, following Plato, distinguished the 'mean' of ethics clearly from that of mathematics and developed the theory of equity in law.

Both men, however, utilized the quantitatively consistent paradigms of geometrical demonstration, insofar as possible, to ensure a logical coherence within the artistic productions of nonquantitative disciplines. The principal objective of this 'formal' coherence, in rendering an interpretation of qualitative issues as intelligible as possible, was persuasive plausibility. An intuitive insight into qualitative issues, which could show how certain actions might be measured in relation to an ideal of equity, resembles the mathematician's insight into the relation between premises, which could produce certain desired conclusions. While both kinds of insights, as long as they remained hypotheses, would appeal to the imagination, the *demonstration* of either kind, by emphasizing the plausible or certain internal coherence as grounds for belief, would appeal to the emotions to acquiesce in the truth of the original intuition. The *fictional* demonstration of qualities which defines a subtler application of a given quantitative norm, such as a legal code, to circumstances is comparable to the *logical* demonstration which reveals in its deductive consequences the conclusions latent in the premises of the given problem. The distinguished geometer, K. F. Gauss, is reputed to have remarked: "I have had my results for a long time; but I do not yet know how I am to arrive at them."[2] His results may become 'public' and persuasive only in the demonstration of how they are arrived at. In drama, it is also by the process of the analysis and synthesis of 'qualities' through speeches and episodes that the audience is led to acquiesce emotionally in the conclusion already 'given' in the hypothesis of the play. The mathematician's remark is reminiscent of an old story which Plutarch tells of Menander. Upon the approach of the Dionysian Festival, an intimate friend asked the dramatist whether he had composed his comedy. "Menander answered, 'By heaven I have really composed the comedy: the plot's all in order (ᾠκονόμηται γὰρ ἡ διάθεσις). But I still have to fit the lines to it' " (347EF).[3]

---

[2] Arber, *Mind and the Eye*, p. 47.

[3] "On the Fame of the Athenians," *Plutarch's Moralia*, trans. F. C. Babbitt, LCL (London, 1936). So Acro on Horace *A.P.* 311: *Menander, cum iam fabulam disposuisset, etiam si nondum versibus adornasset, dicebat, se tamen iam conplesse (Acronis et Porphyrionis Commentarii in Q. Horatium Flaccum*, ed. F. Hauthal [Berlin, 1866], 2:628). For the analogy of poetry with mathematics and its contribution to literary formalism,

A. Fiction and the *disputatio in utramque partem*

The method of arguing alternately on both sides of a question (*in utramque partem*), originally practiced by the Peripatetics, was developed by the later Academic schools of philosophy. Recognizing the fallibility of sensory perception, these schools claimed by means of such debate to be able to arrive at a degree of probability (*verisimile*) sufficiently great to permit choice and action. Their conclusions, though never certain, could be verified by experience to some extent and become grounds for deliberations about the future. Such moderately skeptical attitudes offered to forensic and deliberative oratory the confidence and flexibility of an Isocratean pragmaticism. The method of debate necessitated, at the same time, a suspension of belief which was congenial to the justification and practice of a poetic which sought to analyze a fictional situation in the light of what men are *likely* to say and do. It is largely owing to the rhetorical validation of the doctrine of probability that Cicero's depiction of the ideal orator could incorporate and transmit the most important ethical intentions of Aristotle's *Poetics*.

I owe my ability as an orator, Cicero says (*Orat.* 12), not to the schools of the rhetoricians (*ex rhetorum officinis*) but to the grounds of the Academy (*ex Academiae spatiis*), and he advises Brutus that were an orator to adopt his precepts from philosophy, they should come from the Peripatetic or Academic schools (*Brut.* 119–20). More specifically, it is to the Middle Academy that orators must go for their most important skills: division, definition, procedures of argumentation, analysis of premises and consequences, and the perception of the true, the probable, and the false (*De part. orat.* 139–40). Without such training they could not command the topics of good and bad, right and wrong, utility and

---

see pp. 42–45, 187–89, 200–219, 367–69 of this study. Among other passages in S. Buchanan's *Poetry and Mathematics* (New York, 1962), esp. pp. 56 and 108, the following is particularly relevant: "Mathematics deals with relations, and poetry deals with qualities. A sphere results when we can see the *relations* holding between *qualities*. Then the two series can be correlated. Mathematical functions find elementary values in qualities. Qualities find their relations in the functions of mathematics. Whenever this happens, a system is recognized, and it takes on a quasi-independence and reality. Often the effect in the thinker is a conviction. Belief attaches itself only to such systems. The further expansions and the wider assumptions are ignored and there is a resting point for thought in a mathematico-poetic allegory" (pp. 146–47). Within the dramatic situation the hero develops, in terms of mathematics and poetry, "a system of relations, his idea; and the events have supplied a corresponding set of qualities" (p. 148). Buchanan's terms of analysis are unhistorical. While he recognizes the formal intention of mathematics and the cognitive/judicative intentions of philosophy and rhetoric, he does not make clear how the "relations" and "qualities" express themselves as aspects of one another. See Chap. 14, n. 1.

inutility, virtue and vice (*de bonis vero rebus et malis, aequis, iniquis, utilibus, inutilibus, honestis, turpibus*). Unlike the Sceptics, the Academics believe some knowledge is possible and hope "by arguing on both sides to draw out and give shape (*tamquam exprimant*) to some result that may be either true or the nearest possible approximation to the truth" (*Acad.* 2.7). The word *exprimant*, borrowed from sculpture, again suggests a preliminary model in clay which can include, potentially, the finished conception within it.[4] In the same way, either a philosophical or a rhetorical hypothesis may be said to consist of a set of assumptions which contain the conclusion *in potentia* depending on whether one is postulating generic elements or investigating as yet uncoordinated circumstances of a given case. A plot outline may be said, equally, to contain the catastrophe to be realized when names, speeches, and episodes are filled in. It is precisely in the discovery of the probable truth (or model) in any particular situation (*in quaque re veri simile esset inveniri*) that the method of these schools (*Peripateticorum Academiaeque consuetudo*) is the most effective (*Tusc.* 2.9). Cicero himself remarks upon the resemblance of the Academic method of debate (*Academicorum more contra communem opinionem*) to the dialogue of tragedy and comedy (*De nat. deor.* 3.72–73). And Quintilian highly recommends the plays of Menander, as well as those of Euripides, as models for the orator: "so perfect is his representation of actual life (*omnem vitae imaginem*), so rich is his power of invention and his gift of style, so perfectly does he adapt himself to every kind of circumstance, character and emotion" (10.1.69).[5]

[4] For the relation of such a model to *imagines* see pp. 275–84 of this study. Unlike the more exact specialized disciplines, such as geometry, Cicero says, philosophy demands only a mind keen in pursuing the probable answer to every problem (*in quoque verisimile est eliciendum acutis*). If one could speak, like Aristotle, *in utramque sententiam*, or, like Arcesilas and Carneades, argue against any thesis (*contra omne quod propositum sit disserat*), "he would be the one and only true and perfect orator." Those who teach by manuals simply sketch (*depingere*) their juvenile trifles, whereas Cicero intends to unfold (*explicemus*) the total office of an orator (*De orat.* 3.79–81). Of the many other passages treating the close relationship of the Academic and Peripatetic methods of argumentation to oratory, see *Acad.* 1.15–17, 1.46; *De off.* 2.7–8; *De fin.* 2.1–2, 4.1–7; *Tusc.* 1.17, 5.10–11; *De orat.* 3.105–10, 3.122–25, 3.145; *Orat.* 46–49; *De fato* 3; *De div.* 2.150; *Inst. orat.* 10.1.35. In Tacitus' *Dialogus*, Maternus' preference for poetry over oratory is really based upon his agreement with Messalla that the past "general culture," which rhetoric shared with philosophy, is no longer possible. The more contemplative discipline is chosen when the active is no longer feasible in order to preserve the best of the earlier tradition. The importance of the *Dialogus* in the rhetorical transmission of literary theory, particularly in the Renaissance, has not been sufficiently appreciated. See A. Michel, *Le "Dialogue des Orateurs" de Tacite et la philosophie de Cicéron* (Paris, 1962).

[5] Though Quintilian feels the orator need not swear allegiance to any one philosophical code, his description of the Epicurean, Sceptic, Stoic, Academic, and Peripatetic attitudes toward rhetorical training make it clear that the last two would be most useful to the most important topics of rhetoric: *de virtute, de re publica, de providentia, de origine animorum,*

It is hardly surprising that an epistemology dependent upon the analysis and synthesis of the verisimilar should be congenial to literature, a form of discourse so dependent on verisimilitude. Their alliance, however, extends to the mechanics of perception itself. In their efforts to discover the truth by arguing on both sides of any issue, Cicero claims that the Academic philosophers must retain some standard of guidance.

> Our position is not that we hold that nothing is true, but that we assert that all true sensations are associated with false ones (*omnibus veris falsa quaedam adiuncta*) so closely resembling them that they contain no infallible mark to guide our judgement and assent. From this followed the corollary, that many sensations are *probable* (*probabilia*), that is, though not amounting to a full perception they are yet possessed of a certain distinctness and clearness (*visum quendam haberent insignem et inlustrem*), and so can serve to direct the conduct of the wise man. (*De nat. deor.* 1.12)

This position was directly opposed to the view of the Older Stoa that sensory impressions could be distinguished by cataleptic signs as being *either* true or false: it was the wise man's responsibility to assent to the true and to reject the false sensation (*Acad.* 1.40f.). Though Carneades, the most skeptical of the Academic philosophers, held that no sensory "presentation" (*visum*) could result in true perception (*perceptio*), he still claimed many could result in a probability sufficient for action. In fact, for nothing to be probable would be against nature and a subversion of all of life (*etenim contra naturam est probabile nihil esse, et sequitur omnis vitae ea . . . eversio*).[6]

> Thus the wise man will make use of whatever apparently probable presentation (*specie probabile*) he encounters, if nothing presents itself that is contrary to that probability, and his whole plan of life will be charted out in this manner. (*Acad.* 2.99)

The implications for literary theory in these passages are extensive. What is being described is virtually a process of 'elenchus,' not of the reason but of the imagination, not of propositions to be defined but of sensory impressions to be verified. This "logic of the imagination" is formally

---

de amicitia. Such themes, which elevate both the mind and the language, deal with *quae vere bona, quid mitiget metus, coerceat cupiditates, eximat nos opinionibus vulgi animumque caelestem erigat* (12.2.23–29). I treat the following cognitive and epistemological matters here in relation to rhetoric rather than in Part Two in relation to philosophy because I am primarily concerned with their psychological contribution to persuasive argumentation.

  [6] Such a lack of probability could only exist in a fable such as Aesop's, which the *progymnasmata* describe as *naturally* impossible (κατὰ φύσιν). Isidore, too, comments that fabulous things are those which did not happen and could not have happened because they are *contra naturam* (*Etym.* 1.44.5). For the categorization of types of poetry on the basis of degrees of verisimilitude in Boccaccio, see Chap. 12, n. 14.

analogous to the elenchus of moral dialectic which I have discussed in relation to Aristotle's *Poetics*.[7] It is deeply involved in the psychological procedures of mnemonic systems, of the handling of *topoi*, and of placing vivid representations (*visiones*) before the inner eye of the audience. And the fact that its psychological material is a *visum quendam insignem et inlustrem*, whose virtue is probability, relates its processes clearly to the literary functions of *imagines* and *exempla*.[8]

[7] Cf. Chap. 3 and Plato, *Rep.* 523Bff. A representative of the Middle Stoa, Panaetius greatly modified the older Stoic views on psychology in the direction of the Academy. He realized one might have a distinct "impression" of a ghost and yet at the same time, be prevented from "believing" in it by the knowledge that the dead do not return. The impression must be "clarified," as in Cicero's account mentioned previously, by the assurance that no obstacle has presented itself to call the image's truth into question. This assurance of the probability of the image can only be given by the reason through its elenchus of impressions. This experimental rationalism in finding criteria for objective truth, which replaced the more intuitive criteria of the older Stoics, closely resembled the system of Carneades. As M. van Straaten concludes, "ce que Carnéade trouvait nécessaire pour la réalisation de la plus grande probabilité qui soit possible, Panétius estimait indispensable pour une conviction de la vérité" (*Panétius*, pp. 133–35). Such modifications by the Middle Stoa are most important for Cicero's views of the literary *imago* and its power to represent such virtues as he takes up in the *De officiis*. The image could utilize the psychological power of *clarity* (ἐνάργεια, σαφήνεια) of the Stoic φαντασία καταληπτική *within* the academic structure of argumentation *in utramque partem* so necessary for fiction. A selection of the clearest inductive materials from sensory impressions could be accepted as 'given' and cast immediately in a deductive demonstration of persuasive argument. Carneades' view of "probable presentation" or "probable and unhampered presentation" (φαντασία πιθανὴ καὶ ἀπερίσπαστος) is discussed in *Acad.* 2.33–34. The formal beauties of literary construction are placed in the service of the Stoic representation of virtue; their value A. Michel points out: "La vertu, dans un monde sans certitude, ne se suffit plus à elle-même. Elle a besoin de l'art pour paraître belle" (*Rhétorique*, p. 115). Among the tendencies of the Middle Stoa which might be studied in relation to the qualitative concerns with equity are the preoccupation with motive in the analysis of states of mind, as distinct from the act itself (cf. *Panétius*, pp. 147f.); the increasing social responsibility (p. 176); the emphasis upon natural law as a bond between all men as distinct from laws of national or religious communities (pp. 203–11); and the central position of the concept of *humanitas* in its ethical system (pp. 220–22). These attitudes are fundamental to such Renaissance writers as Montaigne and have in part been obscured by an overemphasis upon their more flamboyant skeptical statements.

[8] Cicero comments on how moved we are when hearing or reading about some magnanimous deed like that of Orestes' offer to sacrifice himself. Such noble examples fill both history and legend (*talibus exemplis non fictae solum fabulae verum etiam historiae refertae sunt*) and reveal actions done for the sake of virtue (*De fin.* 5.63–64). The Greek word ἰδέα was used for the literary *imago* perhaps as early as Aristophanes, who may be referring to a visually striking picture, such as that of Socrates in a basket, as a "dramatic idea" in the *Clouds* 547–48 (suggested by R. Harriott, *Poetry and Criticism Before Plato* [London, 1969], p. 136, n. 3). Later, included among the rhetorical "Schemata Dianoeas," edited by Halm, is: "'Ἰδέα est, cum speciem rei futurae velut oculis offerentes moto animo concitamus. Cicero: Videor mihi videre hanc urbem, lucem orbis terrarum atque arcem omnium gentium, subito uno incendio condidentem" (p. 73). Cf. St. Augustine, *De trin.* 8.4–6. The arrangement of images in "places" in an inner perspective of memory (*De orat.* 2.357–59) and their power to move the emotions by evoking prudential *intentiones* through vivid *ideas* continued to offer a psychologial basis for literary and pictorial exemplification. See Chap. 2, nn. 17, 20; Chap. 14, nn. 1, 11; and *JWCI* (1973), 31.

The increasing despair of finding, in the twilight world of the probable, a sufficient intellectual clarity to sustain the emotional balance necessary for ethical action brought with it a growing distrust of the liberal arts and a greater dependence on precept and the will.[9] This despair, on the authority perhaps, among other influences, of the older Stoic analysis of sensory perception, may have influenced the restriction of the Hellenistic distinction of the three types of narration, not properly associated with legal arguments, essentially to two in subsequent literary theory. The first type is *fabula* in which events have neither truth nor verisimilitude (*nec verae nec veri similes res*); the second is *historia*, an account of actual occurrences remote in time (*gesta res, ab aetatis nostrae memoria remota*); the third is *argumentum*, a fictional occurrence which has a likeness to truth (*ficta res, quae tamen fieri potuit*). This clarification by Cicero (*De inv.* 1.27) is also given by the author of the *Rhetorica ad Herennium* (1.12–13) and by Quintilian (2.4.2), who indicates a scale of verisimilitude by placing *argumentum* in the second position. Sextus Empiricus (*Adv. gram.* 1.263) follows Quintilian's order in giving examples of history (ἱστορία), fictional plots (πλάσμα), and myth (μῦθος). The older Stoic unwillingness to consider, between the true and the false, a 'probable' sensory impression sufficiently reliable for action is parallel to the deepening ancient cleavage between fact and fable, which tends to exclude the verisimilar as a distinct *kind* of narrative. The *argumentum* is seen increasingly as a proportion of truth (facts and doctrine) to falsity ('lies' or entertainment) and is judged to be *utile* or *dulce* accordingly. This antithesis denies to fiction the Academic suspension of belief, the use of the sensory *visum* as a 'psychological hypothesis' awaiting verification, and the 'expression,' by means of a discussion *in utramque partem*, of an *imago* as an ethical 'model.'

The desire to be certain, either of the truth or of the falsehood of any

[9] *Tota rerum natura umbra est aut inanis aut fallax*: so Seneca concludes his tragic epistle to an intellectually exhausted world (*Ep.* 88.46). In words similar to Macbeth's disillusioned comparison of life to a shadow and an idiotic tale, he describes the failure of the liberal arts to achieve ethical significance. (Cf. similar Stoic attitudes in Philo Judaeus' *De congressu*, esp. 61–62 for the possible source, via a Latin translation, of Macbeth's lines [5.5.24–28]). Even in the philosophical schools, disputes *in utramque partem* (43) have led only to a Platonic world of appearances behind which no Forms can be perceived. So A. Michel: "Cicéron choisit une attitude platonicienne dans un monde où l'on doute des Idées. . . . L'éloquence est la langue des sages dans un monde qui doute de la sagesse" (*Rhétorique*, p. 99). So St. Augustine will comment, with respect to his *Contra academicos*, how by this time the methods of Academic discussion had led men to a skeptical indifference toward the liberal arts and to a moral "lethargy so profound, that not even by the heavenly trumpet can they be aroused" (*Ep.* 1, trans. J. G. Cunningham, *A Select Library of the Nicene and Post-Nicene Fathers*, ed. P. Schaff [New York, 1892], 1:219). In sharp contrast, see Cicero's depiction of Ulysses as the philosophical explorer in quest of a knowledge of the arts (*De fin.* 5.48–64).

statement, characterized the pedagogical interpretations of literary texts by the grammarians and professors of specialized disciplines. Strabo's concern over the truth of Homer's geographical information is typical, and in his impatience with the Epicurean Eratosthenes he often asserts that poetry is fable grafted upon fact (1.2.19). His terms are Horatian and Stoic. The 'office' of a poet (ποιητικὴν ἐξουσίαν) consists of a combination (συνέστηκεν) of ἱστορίας, διαθέσεως and μύθου. In the scale of verisimilitude, *diathesis* would properly correspond to *plasma*, *hypothesis*, and *argumentum*, as Plutarch uses *diathesis* for the plot outline of Menander's comedies (347EF), but as the middle term in a 'synthesis,' for which the poet strives, it tends to be reduced to a mixture of fact and myth.[10]

Plutarch's strongly didactic attitudes toward poetry led him to a position similar to Strabo's. In fact, the first paragraph of the *Lives* states the relation between history and fiction in geographical terms.

Just as geographers, O Socius Senecio, crowd on to the outer edges of their maps the parts of the earth which elude their knowledge, with explanatory notes that "What lies beyond is sandy desert without water and full of wild beasts," or "blind marsh," or "Scythian cold," or "frozen sea," so in the writing of my Parallel Lives, now that I have traversed those periods of time which are accessible to probable reasoning (εἰκότι λόγῳ) and which afford basis for a history dealing with facts (ἱστορίᾳ πραγμάτων), I might well say of the earlier periods: "What lies beyond is full of marvels and unreality, the land of poets and fabulists (ποιηταὶ καὶ μυθογράφοι), of doubt and obscurity (πίστιν οὐδὲ σαφήνειαν)." . . . May I therefore succeed in purifying Fable, making her submit to reason (ἐκκαθαιρόμενον λόγῳ τὸ μυθῶδες) and take on the semblance of History (ἱστορίας ὄψιν). But where she obstinately disdains to make herself credible, and refuses to admit any element of probability (τὸ εἰκός), I shall pray for kindly readers, and such as receive with indulgence the tales of antiquity.

History is *terra cognita*; fiction *incognita*, which must be rendered probable in order to pass for history. If it, indeed, becomes credible, it becomes "pure" (ἐκκαθαιρόμενον) in the eyes of its readers. The 'cathartic' effect of plausibility bears an interesting relation to the emotional effect of tragedy upon the audience. For Aristotle, the hero's acts are rendered καθαρός in the eyes of the spectators by their being 'made reasonable' through a process of revealing the causal relation between events.[11]

[10] *The Geography of Strabo* 1.2.17, trans. H. L. Jones, LCL (London, 1917). P. De Lacy reaches the same conclusion on *diathesis* in observing the Stoic need to mix truth with falsehood in the poetic elaboration of doctrine ("Stoic Views of Poetry," *AJP* 69 [1948]:267–69). For Strabo's adherence to the Stoic sect (1.2.34, 2.3.8), see Jones' introduction, p. xviii.

[11] *Plutarch's Lives*, trans. B. Perrin, LCL (London, 1914). The connection here between

In the important passage on truth and lying in his essay on "How to Study Poetry" (16), Plutarch observes that fiction provides the pleasure which most people look for in poetry because the truth is austere by comparison (αὐστηροτέραν) and cannot deviate from the most unpleasant subject matter. Neither stylistic devices nor harmonious periods please as much as fictional composition itself (διάθεσις μυθολογίας). Since there can be no poem without fable (ἄμυθον) or falsehood (ἀψευδῆ), 'untruth' has replaced the Aristotelian power of mimesis to bring out the generic significance of our particular experience as the property which most distinguishes poetry from history. Though fabulous events should give the illusion of reality in their own right, there is, as in Strabo, a strong suggestion that plausibility is gained by combining history with fiction. At least Plutarch seems to associate historical with philosophical truth (ἀλήθεια) in distinguishing them from fiction (17DE), and poetry very clearly contains a mixture of philosophic truth within its fables (14EF, 15F, 28EF, 32EF, 36E). The student must learn to separate that truth from fable as Strabo tries to separate geographical fact from myth. Both men have returned to the terms 'truth' and 'untruth' of Plato's early arguments with the Sophists.[12]

When the middle term in the scale of verisimilitude combines the properties of both extremes in varying proportions, it loses its own properties. Moralists, like Plutarch, and specialists, like Strabo, seek to analyze a narrative into its true and false components in order to reveal

ἐκκαθαιρόμενον λόγῳ and catharsis, as discussed by Else (pp. 224–32, 423–50), may appear strained. In relation, however, to Plutarch's comparison of fiction to "color" which gives a desirably illusionistic coherence to fabulous events in poetry as well as biography, it is quite suggestive with regard to the psychological response of the audience (see Chap. 12, pp. 312–17 of this study). The act of the hero, in Else's words, is plausibly presented to the spectator "and his conscience accepts and certifies it to his emotions, issues a license, so to speak, which says: 'You may pity this man, for he is like us, a good man rather than a bad, and he is καθαρός, free of pollution' " (p. 438). The hero's (given) actions in the story must be made credible for the audience of tragedy to believe them 'purified,' as the given events of fable must be made probable for the reader of history to believe them reliable. The rationalistic separation of fact from fable is given an interesting further dimension in Cicero's De divinatione where the miraculous coincidence is clearly distinguished from 'scientific' cause and effect (see Chap. 14, n. 1).

[12] The moral superiority of actual deeds over historical and artistic representations of them—and hence of the prudential over the productive faculty—is argued by Plutarch (345C–51B). See Chap. 12, n. 11. The reaction against "rhetorical history," as well, tended to sharpen the cleavage between truth and falsehood, utility and pleasure. In rejecting panegyric exaggeration, Lucian asserts repeatedly that history aims only at truth (ἀλήθεια) and can admit no lie (ψεῦδος), whereas in poetry the only law is the will (δόξαν) of the poet. History aims solely at being useful (τὸ χρήσιμον); pleasure is purely incidental (Lucian, "How to Write History," 7–9, 38–44, 50–51, trans. K. Kilburn, LCL [London, 1959]).

its pedagogical value as a preparation for philosophical studies.[13] In such a context lie the poet's objectives in Horace's famous passage (*A.P.* 33–44) on benefiting (*prodesse*) or delighting (*delectare*) or doing some of each (*simul et iucunda et idonea*)—terms which go back to Plato (*Gorgias* 474E–75A, 478B; cf. HASD, pp. 57–58). With regard to fictions, those give most pleasure which are nearest to truth (*ficta voluptatis causa sint proxima veris*): the legendary plot (*fabula*) must not strain our credulity. With regard to profit, though no poems can be without it (*expertia frugis*), *poemata* must not be *austera*, and the context implies that this would happen because facts too literally followed, as Plutarch warns, are more austere (αὐστηροτέραν) than fiction. Since he does best who *miscuit utile dulci*, one should, therefore, mingle fact with fable, as Horace insists earlier in his epistle: *atque ita mentitur, sic veris falsa remiscet, / primo ne medium, medio ne discrepet imum* (151–52).[14]

---

[13] The justification of literature—indeed of the liberal arts—as a preparation for later, more mature studies is perhaps the fundamental bequest of the Hellenistic period to literary history. Be they rhetorical, philosophical, or theological, or preparatory for law or for medicine, such studies tended to be specialized, practical, and intolerant. From the beginning, writers such as Strabo (1.2.3) and Plutarch (*Mor.* 14–37) tried to defend literature pedagogically on the specialists' terms rather than to analyze the operations of the mind which literary discourse uniquely combined. Their efforts conform to the Stoic desire, in Michel's words, for a "science certaine du langage correct (ἐπιστήμη τοῦ εὖ λέγειν)" so that each art may be "un système de certitudes pratiques" (*Rhétorique*, pp. 114–16).

[14] In his "An Essay of Dramatic Poesy" Dryden has Lisideius quote these lines and comment that the French poet "so interweaves truth with probable fiction that he puts a pleasing fallacy upon us; mends the intrigues of fate, and dispenses with the severity of history, to reward that virtue which has been rendered to us there unfortunate" (*Criticism: The Major Texts*, ed. W. J. Bate [New York, 1952], p. 141). That imitation avoids the severity of what it imitates, as the *Poetics* states (1448b4–19), is a claim also attributed to Aristippus by Diogenes Laertius (2.90). Though Horace's phrase *veris falsa remiscet* resembles Cicero's *omnibus veris falsa quaedam adiuncta* (see p. 289 of this chapter), its meaning differs. In the *Odyssey*, to which Horace refers here, 'true' manners combined with 'false' incidents (*speciosa miracula*) do not yield the 'probable.' The narrative remains a mixture of two terms, fact and fable. Cicero, on the other hand, is saying that true and false impressions can resemble one another so closely (*tanta similitudine*) that our judgment of any *one* of them can only claim probability and must await later verification. The mixing of fiction with fact has a *structural* motivation in Horace: that the middle follow from the beginning and the end from the middle. As in a syllogism, one must 'invent' the middle terms, since the beginning and the conclusion are 'given' (cf. pp. 47–49 of this study). Artistically speaking, *facta* or *vera* will simply represent the 'given' in any form; the *falsa* or *ficta* are what must be supplied by the mind. The distinction corresponds to that between nature and art, and more specifically in rhetoric, between inartificial and artificial proofs. F. Solmsen has shown the relation of the development of the second kind of proof from the first in rhetoric to the increasing concern with causation and its analysis in dialogue in Greek drama (*Antiphonstudien: Untersuchungen zur Entstehung der Attischen Gerichtsrede* [Berlin, 1931], pp. 53–59). A Horatian mixture of *falsa* with *vera* can also, according to Quintilian, be used by the rhetorician to make a fictional *narratio* plausible (4.2.89). Horace's clear parallel between *miscuit utile dulci* and *veris falsa remiscet*, in which the true is useful and the fictional attractive, is expressed later as *ioca seriis miscere* (traced by E. Curtius, *European Literature and the Latin Middle Ages*,

The Hellenistic analysis of poetry into its true and fabulous components cannot, of course, be attributed primarily to Stoicism, even though I have illustrated it in terms of the older Stoic psychology. At a very early date the allegorical interpreters of ancient poems had tried to segregate factual from fictional incidents, and this practice was continued by Hellenistic antiquarians and later by the grammarians. Neither Epicureanism nor Scepticism could offer a concept of the probable any more congenial to fiction than that of the Stoics.[15] Cicero, on the other hand, in objecting to the more dogmatic elements in the thought of the Academic philosopher Antiochus (*Acad.* 2.132), expected, even in the study of nature, neither more nor less than a probable truth (2.127–28). His own Academic method of disputation *in utramque partem* provided a formal structure, especially adaptable to the fictional analysis of experience, in which belief might remain suspended until the most probable solution could be identified. When Horace cautions that fictions should be *proxima veris* to be pleasing (*causa voluptatis*), he reveals the restricting imposition of rhetorical and historical verisimilitude upon poetic theory. Cicero, in contrast, sees the mind, when it is struck by any likeness to truth, as filled with the deepest pleasure a human being is capable of (*si vero aliquid occurrit quod veri simile videatur, humanissima completur animus voluptate*).

---

trans. W. R. Trask [New York, 1963], pp. 417–35). A variety of passages defending *ioca* in medieval literature are cited by G. Olson, "The Medieval Theory of Literature for Refreshment and its Use in the Fabliau Tradition," *SP* 71 (1974):291–313. In the Carolingian attitudes toward the visual arts the *utile* lay in the commemorative, historical function of the work while the ornamental function provided the *dulce* (see De Bruyne, 1:275–305).

[15] For Epicureanism, see P. De Lacy, "The Epicurean Analysis of Language," *AJP* 60 (1939):85–92 and [with E. A. De Lacy] *Philodemus: On Methods of Inference, Philological Monographs* 10, *APA* (1941); *The Rhetoric of Philodemus*, trans. H. M. Hubbell, *Trans. of the Conn. Acad. of Arts and Sciences* 23 (1920), pp. 243–382; and the material on the terms *poesis, poema,* and *poeta* cited in Appendix A, p. 372. With regard to the probable, Philodemus' is similar to the older Stoic view: "The relation between truth and its opposite is not the same as between two probabilities, one more probable than the other. We must have either truth or falsehood. Would one accept probability in place of truth except in cases where truth is impossible of attainment? A man should examine carefully and search for truth, and not use vain enthymemes" (p. 321). Despite their conviction that *no* truth can be found, the Sceptics placed no more faith in the probable than the Epicureans with respect to the liberal arts. Compare *De fin.* 1.71–72 with the following passages from Sextus Empiricus: "Against the Geometers" (1–17), "Against the Grammarians" (265), "Against the Rhetoricians" (60–71), "Against the Logicians" (1.166–89), and "Outlines of Pyrrhonism" (1.226–31). For similar views of the Epicurean Colotes, who says fictions are inept for instructing us in the *habitum animarum* and *rerum caelestium notionem,* see Macrobius (*Comm.* 1.2.3–4). Despite Macrobius' finding a philosophical use for fiction, the Neoplatonists preferred to express their experience symbolically in terms of truth and/or falsehood than mimetically in terms of probability in the way that Plotinus preferred his second (nonreciprocal) to his first (reciprocal) type of likeness. However different his

B. *Argumentum:* Analysis and Synthesis

Quintilian observes that in addition to the presentation of proofs the word *argumentum* may refer to plots of plays (*fabulae ad actum scenarum compositae*), to themes of speeches, indeed to all written materials, and even to the subjects and designs of artists. With regard to proof, as to analogy in general (1.6.4), all arguments must demonstrate what is uncertain by means of what is certain (*fidem dubiis adferens*). The Greeks called all such arguments πίστεις, which, though literally translated *fidem*, is more properly rendered *probatio* (5.10.8–10). Once these arguments have been discovered, they must be arranged as persuasively as possible, for it is not sufficient simply to make the separate limbs of a statue, one must put them together in proper proportion. Indeed, Nature herself would perish if order did not sustain her in existence (7.pr.2–3). The great importance of *dispositio*, the second faculty of rhetoric, for the formal preservation of all the humanistic disciplines suggests how rhetoric might transmit, along with the emphasis upon the qualitative interpretation of events, the structural requirements of Aristotle's *Poetics*. The structure of rhetorical argumentation exhibits the same contrary 'movements' of analysis and synthesis in the presentation of proofs as I argued—in the case of dramatic plots—were analogous to those of geometrical analysis.

In order to dispose his material in a persuasive arrangement, the orator must 'divide' it into questions which will bring out, in a way favorable to his client, the issues latent in the principal issue to be decided by the judge. Quintilian describes how these questions may be ordered in a series of increasing specificity (7.1.23–28). The order, however, in which one *discovers* the questions in the analysis by division will be "quite different from that which we employ in actual speaking," that is, in the synthesis of presentation. He gives an example of how the issues, once divided, might appear in presentation from a 'theme' of a *controversia*: "Suppose a brave man to choose another man's wife as his reward (*optet enim vir fortis alienam uxorem*)."

The ultimate *species* is found in the question whether he is allowed to choose another man's wife. The *general* question is whether he should be given whatever he chooses. Next come questions such as whether he can choose his reward from the property of private individuals, whether he can choose a bride as his reward, and if so, whether he can choose one who is already married.

---

solutions, St. Augustine's *Contra academicos* uses similar arguments against the verisimilar.

Accepting the theme and its specific question as given, the speaker 'leaps' to the most general question with which to begin and returns 'downward' toward the particularity of the initial problem. Such a synthesis is like the printed photograph of which the latent generic questions, discovered by analysis, appear ghostly in the preliminary negative.[16]

Quintilian then uses the same *controversia* to illustrate the process of analysis, which precedes the presented synthesis, and why its sequence of questions reverses the order of specificity employed "in actual speaking."

For that which as a rule occurs to us first, is just that which ought to come last in our speech: as for instance the conclusion, "You have no right to choose another man's wife." Consequently undue haste will spoil our division of the subject. We must not therefore be content with the thoughts that first offer themselves, but should press our inquiry further (*ultra*) till we reach conclusions such as that he ought not even to choose a widow: a further advance is made when we reach the conclusion that he should choose nothing that is private property, or last of all we may go back to the question next in order to the general question (*ultimum retrorsum, quod idem a capite primum est*), and conclude that he should choose nothing inequitable.

This advancement 'backwards' (*retrorsum*) to more and more generic questions, which are then to become premises of persuasion from which the *presented* (deductive) argument returns 'forward' to the initial specific 'theme,' corresponds to the analysis in dramatic composition. The dramatist must analyze his given dramatic hypothesis into questions capable of yielding a sufficiently detailed and coherent interpretation of the events given in his outline for his completed play. The ultimate unfolding of the entire play, like that of the oration, in its finished form before an audience is his deductive synthesis: the 'demonstration' that the catastrophe is justified by probability or necessity. The question raised in the initial analysis of the outlined plot will reveal the central, if less immediately apparent, general underlying issues to be brought out in the final synthesis.

Quintilian illustrates his deductive synthesis even more simply in a *suasoria*.

---

[16] Quintilian adds the fact that "we should descend from the *common* to the *particular* (*a communibus ad propria*) is much the same, since what is *common* is usually *general* (*communia generalia sunt*). For example, 'He killed a tyrant' is *common*, while 'A tyrant was killed by his son, by a woman or by his wife' are all *particular*" (7.1.28). The procedure resembles that of reaching a definition of a particular object experienced: *a genere perveniendum ad ultimam speciem* (5.10.56). To the same theme of a hero's choosing another's wife as a reward, Fortunatianus adds additional details to illustrate how qualities can be compounded: *cum qualitas qualitati supernascitur* (Halm, p. 95; see also pp. 379–80).

I went back from the ultimate *species* (which generally contains the vital point of the case) to the first general question or descended from the *genus* to the ultimate *species*, applying this method even to deliberative themes.[17] For example, Numa is deliberating whether to accept the crown offered him by the Romans. First he considers the general question, "Ought I to be a king?" Then "Ought I to be king in a foreign state? Ought I to be king at Rome? Are the Romans likely to put up with such a king as myself?"

In order for Numa to organize his argument by these questions (the last being the closest to his given 'theme'), he will have had to 'analyze' the original question. Once its generic elements, which have lain perhaps unnoticed within it, have been revealed, he is able to reach back among them for the first and most general issue and then 'come forward' in the synthesis of his presentation toward the specific theme he is deliberating. Without the analysis he could not have chosen the most generic issue nor have perceived the order of increasing specificity which constitutes his synthesis.[18]

---

[17] *Solebam et hoc facere, ut vel ab ultima specie (nam ea fere est, quae continet causam) retrorsum quaererem usque ad primam generalem quaestionem, vel a genere ad extremam speciem descenderem, etiam in suasoriis.* The *vel . . . vel* would seem to mean here little more than *both . . . and* (= *et . . . et*: Lewis and Short, *vel* I B 2 a). However the division of relevant questions is grasped, their order in oral presentation must conclude with the specific question being examined. Compare Iulius Victor, *De divisione*, partially cited in Chap. 10, n. 10: *in omni statu divisio rectius ordietur a generalibus quaestionibus, quae in unaquaque causa generales esse potuerint, et a generalibus gradatim descendet ad speciales, id est ad causae proprias, . . . Ita sensim defluit generalitas ad speciem, id est ad τὸ κρινόμενον. Eadem ratio est divisionis et in ceteris omnibus statibus. Intuendum tamen est, ne nimis immoremur generalibus quaestionibus, sed praecipuam congressionem ad causae proprias conferamus species. Disputatio enim generalium apud animos iudicum praeparabit tantummodo aditum, ut magis persuadere possis, cum de specialibus disputabis. Ceterum omnis causae firmitas in τῷ κρινομένῳ est, id est specie iudicii propria* (Halm, pp. 385f.). Among certain *excerpta rhetorica* included by Halm (pp. 585–89) is a passage stressing the usefulness of special questions for the defense, thus exemplifying the association of hypothesis with the *iudicatio* of a particular case (cf. Appendix A, pp. 374–78): *Thesis est quaestio generalis, hypothesis specialis. In thesi, id est in generali quaestione, tantummodo de rebus ipsis sine persona quaeritur: adhibitis personis res quoque communiter; nam quos genus causae premit, species saepe defendit. Si enim secundum thesin, id est generalem quaestionem, quaeratur an animadvertendum sit in matricidam, dubium non erit quin debeat animadverti; sed si ex hypothesi persona accesserit, invenit defensionem: ut si quaeratur, animadvertendum sit in Oresten matricidam, dubium non erit, quam debet animadverti; hac enim se Orestes ratione defendit, quod patrem vindicaverit.*

[18] St. Thomas comments that prudential judgment concerns the particular case, which he calls an *extremum: quod dicitur extremum, quia et ab eo incipit nostra cognitio ad universalia procedens, et ad ipsum terminatur in via descensus.* To reach the *universalia*, one takes a *via ascensus* (De Bruyne, 3:323). De Bruyne insists that "allégorisme peut s'élever du sensible au spirituel, il peut aussi descendre du spirituel au sensible." Allegory cannot exist "sans l'union du spirituel et du sensible dans l'*involucrum* symbolique" (2:336ff.). Stated in this way, such an *involucrum* offers a typically medieval form of the negotiation between Aristotle's two types of intelligibility. In a slightly similar manner,

The argument of fiction, as of rhetoric, is *implicitly* inductive—in the mind of the writer—but *explicitly* deductive in the work produced and in its effect upon the audience. In order to appeal most strongly to the emotions, the analysis of the given situation must select its premises beforehand so that the narrative argument may appear *as if* it had required no inductive process to arrive at the premises from which deduction might begin. By not having to deal with historical particulars, a fiction can remain tacit about the selection and acceptance of its premises in order to gain the emotional concentration of a deductive synthesis. In the absence of the logical uncertainties of an inductive argument, it can confirm and qualify the initial premises of the given plot by revealing their consequences in episode, speech, and character. Its 'demonstration' gathers up and intensifies all causal relations, as a lens gathers rays of light, and focuses them upon the catastrophe.[19] As in the case of Plato's laws, the 'mortar' by which the incidents are related to one another consists of questions of quality and equity. The process of analysis of the rhetorical hypothesis into its component theses, described by Quintilian as special into general questions, offers a method of defining quality

---

the portrait involves for St. Bonaventure the "montée du modèle à l'idée que s'en fait l'artiste" and the "descente de l'idée à l'oeuvre qu'il exécute" (3:210f.). However different the arts involved, these examples reflect, in a medieval context, the procedures of analysis and synthesis. The relation of these procedures to the *dialectical* use of hypothesis in the Socratic dialogues, treated in Chap. 2, is exemplified by Xenophon (*Mem.* 4.6.13–15). In search of grounds for a definition Socrates would lead the discussion back to a suitable premise (ἐπὶ τὴν ὑπόθεσιν), clearly underlying other instances easily admitted, and then, bringing out their similarity to the less clear instance in question, would reveal the general issues latent within it. See n. 20 of this chapter.

[19] It is interesting that later, in the development of algebraic analysis and synthesis, a comparable 'suspension' or 'hiding' of analytic procedures occurs. In his *Greek Mathematical Thought* (pp. 166–68 and nn. 235–37) J. Klein describes this process in his treatment of François Viète's *Introduction to the Analytical Art* (1591) of which he appends a translation by J. W. Smith: "But that solution is preferred to others which does not derive the synthetic operation from the equation, but derives the equation from the synthesis, while the synthesis proves itself. Thus the skillful geometer, though a learned analyst, conceals this fact and presents and explicates his problem as a synthetic one, *as if* thinking merely about the demonstration that is to be accomplished" (p. 347, my italics). A further Renaissance analogy between algebra and literary fiction appears if one compares this statement with Sidney's insistence that poetry, unlike other arts and sciences, has no specific subject matter, but that "the Poet onely bringeth his owne stuffe, and dooth not learne a conceite out of a matter, but maketh matter for a conceite" (*An Apology for Poetry*, in *Elizabethan Critical Essays*, ed. G. G. Smith, 1:180). In this case, the mathematical synthesis or formal argument corresponds to Sidney's "conceite" (the organizing conception), the equation or proposition (the specific *material* of mathematics) to his "stuffe" or "matter." This is *the* fundamental cognitive (as opposed to ethical) argument in Sidney's *Apology*: it is Aristotelian and the fact that it underlies the four or five most celebrated passages in his defense of poetry has not been sufficiently recognized. See Chap. 1, pp. 18–19 of this study.

in such a way that it can be conveniently 're-presented' deductively in a work of art.[20]

Cicero, like Quintilian, defines argumentation as an *explicatio argumenti*: "This process is achieved when you have assumed (*sumpseris*) either indubitable or probable premises from which to draw a conclusion that appears in itself either doubtful or less probable" (*De part. orat.* 46). There are, however, two ways of presenting an argument once the questions have been revealed by division. One "aims directly at convincing (*ad fidem*) and the other devotes itself to exciting feeling (*ad motum*)." An argument

Proceeds directly, when it has put forward a proposition (*proposuit aliquid*) to prove, and has chosen (*sumpsit*) the arguments to support its case, and after establishing these, has returned to the proposition and drawn the conclusion (*his confirmatis ad propositum se rettulit atque conclusit*); but the other form of ratiocination proceeds in the opposite way, backward: it first assumes the premises that it wants and establishes these, and then after exciting emotion throws in at the end what ought to have been premised [i.e. proposed] at the start (*illa autem altera argumentatio quasi retro et contra: prius sumit quae vult eaque confirmat, deinde id quod proponendum fuit permotis animis iacit ad extremum*).[21]

---

[20] With respect to logic, the inductive process of establishing middle terms, or rather the relation of a first term to a middle term, occurs within the writer's mind as the analysis of the possible ways to *construct* a story. Then since, as Aristotle says, "the last step in the analysis seems to be the first step in the execution of the design" (*E.N.* 3.3.12), the writer, assuming the middle terms to have been established already, *presents* the conceived construction in the form of the work which the audience actually experiences. The "third term," the catastrophe, appears to be deductively concluded by syllogism. These distinctions are set forth in the *Prior Analytics* (2.23–24). They depend, as does much of my discussion of fiction, on the fact that the human mind seems to proceed from particular to universal whereas its logical processes descend from universal to particular (*Meta.* 7.4; 1029b3–12). This accounts for the paradox of fiction which I described in Chap. 3: the generic issue is implicit in and prior to the specific issue. That is, in practical terms of composition, the more detailed the analysis of particular events, the more precisely articulated the significance of those events can be. The process by which we understand their significance is by going 'backward' in analysis from (given) individual particulars to the *genera* implicit in them by virtue of which, after we have come 'forward' again in synthesis, these same particulars may be considered specific. It should be recalled that in rhetorical terminology, which refers to subject matter, the *genera* are described as *theses*, the particular situations as *hypotheses*. In dialectical terminology, which refers to the formal procedure by which we discover and present that subject matter, the *genera* are described as *hypotheses* (literally that which *underlies* the theses), the particular 'situations' (i.e. the initial propositions to be tested) as *theses*. The rhetorical thesis corresponds to the dialectical hypothesis, and they combine with one another in the paradoxical term *thema*, a 'proposed hypothesis,' of declamation. With respect to Socrates' inductive method of inferring a conclusion on the basis of its similarity to questions to which his opponent has already responded affirmatively, Quintilian says that in an oration, where such questions, ordinarily expressed in a dialogue, cannot be asked, it is usual to *assume* them and their rejoinders and to proceed to a conclusion (5.11.3–5).

[21] Georgio Valla glosses *quasi retro* as an argument *quae non directè proponit, assumit,*

The first method begins with a stated proposition to be proved, establishes premises from which arguments in support of the proposition logically follow, and concludes when the proposition may be restated as a conclusion. The second method, withholding the proposition to be proved, discovers the premises necessary to produce it, confirms them, and finally supplies the proposition (now with the authority of a conclusion by virtue of its premises having been established) which was initially withheld. The first, or direct, method (*ad fidem*) first calls for an inductive analysis of a proposition into its premises and then constructs its deductive demonstration, or synthesis, in the form of a syllogism. The second, or indirect, method (*ad motum*) *appears* to be wholly a deductive synthesis, the demonstration of which appeals most strongly to the emotions. The unstated proposition is reached in such a way that at the time of its first explicit mention, it is already (emotionally) accepted as a conclusion.[22]

& concludit: sed quae vult concludere, sibi primò assumit, deinde confirmat (*De partitione oratoria M. T. Ciceronis Dialogus* [Lugduni, 1545], p. 223). Earlier in the *De part. orat.* Cicero points out that in indefinite questions one aims at conviction but that in definite cases one seeks not only to convince but to excite emotion: *Nam est in proposito finis fides, in causa et fides et motus. Quare cum de causa dixero, in qua est propositum, de utroque dixero* (9). This reassertion that the general question is latent in the specific case associates the power to move with the particular circumstances. Compare Bartholomaeus Latomus' commentary on this passage in the edition cited previously (69): *Natura [definitae quaestionis] enim talis est, quia omnis motus ex opinione boni vel mali nascitur. Nihil autem bonum vel malum nisi cum persona coniunctum. Personam autem sola causa continet, cui deinceps caeterae circumstantiae, res, causa, locus, tempus, modus adiunguntur. Itaque fit, ut sola etiam causa motus sit capax.* This associates the concept of *qualitas* again with increasing specification. A. Michel comments that "la passion, dans une cause, se rattache à l' 'hypothèse.' Elle concerne donc *res et personas*. . . . La 'thèse' des discours veut rester rationelle. La passion subsiste: mais elle est au niveau de l' 'hypothèse.' Elle conduit les esprits vers l'idée générale, elle les pousse à l'admettre dans les circonstances données" (*Rhétorique*, pp. 244, 256).

[22] The withholding of one's own opinion (i.e. the *propositio*) is, of course, necessary for any *argumentum in utramque partem*. Cicero attributes this method to Socrates and claims to imitate him "in trying to conceal my own private opinion, to relieve others from deception and in every discussion to look for the most probable solution (*ut nostram ipsi sententiam tegeremus, errore alios levaremus et in omni disputatione quid esset simillimum veri quaereremus*)"—*Tusculan Disputations* 5.11, trans. J. E. King, LCL (London, 1960). That one may "relieve" others of self-deception is an echo of Plato's description of the "catharsis" of error achieved through a process of elenchus in dialectic (*Soph.* 230BE). The cross-questioning (ἔλεγχον) is the greatest of purifications (καθάρσεων), since by being forced to recognize his self-contradictions, a person gains intellectual humility. I suggested the relation of this form of catharsis to that of the *Poetics* in Chap. 2, n. 57. (For more detailed considerations of the relation, see A. Ničev, *L'énigme de la catharsis tragique dans Aristote* [Sofia, 1970], and my review in *Jour. Hist. Phil.* 14 (1976):101–4.) The passages suggest the close connections between a dramatic argument, the method *in utramque partem*, and the emotional effect, brought about by an elenchus in which the *propositio* is withheld, as it is in Cicero's argument *ad motum*. The representation of Socrates' inductive, conversational analogies reveal a similar effect by withholding the central question until the person he questions admits the analogies, which that person

In the passages cited previously, then, Quintilian describes the division in *controversiae* and *suasoriae* of the rhetorical hypothesis into theses latent within it and its subsequent 'reconstruction' in the presentation of the argument as something 'completed' and acceptable as a conclusion by virtue of the revelation of the general questions which confirm and qualify its specific issue. Cicero describes two ways to present the questions, once a division has been selected, which differ in their psychological effects. One appeals *ad fidem*, that is, to a belief in the logical probability of the argument. The other is organized *ad movendos animos* and withholds or suspends the proposition to be demonstrated until its premises are sufficiently confirmed to state it as a conclusion. The latter method makes most explicit what is implied in the general purpose of division itself: that the material of constructing a persuasive argument is sought by analysis, while the power to move is effected in the demonstrative synthesis. Induction diffuses emotional force, deduction concentrates it.

Whether it be immediately stated or temporarily taken for granted, the initial proposition in both of Cicero's methods corresponds to the declamatory theme and to the dramatic hypothesis. His first method, however, might be regarded as more congenial to the *controversia* and to comedy, the second to the *suasoria* and to tragedy. In both the *controversiae* and comedies the plot is 'made up' of private, and hence less familiar, persons and circumstances. The historical or legendary anonymity of the characters permits them often to become recognizable general types whose interrelationships must be restipulated by the action of each new exercise or play. The particular delightfulness of the plot arises from its plausible resolution of the initially enigmatic stipulations of the given situation. Its tact and grace lie in the variations which can dispose the apparently alogical events to their logical conclusion. Since the persons, being more typical than individually 'known,' are to be characterized primarily through incident, the given circumstances must be clearly 'propounded' if the author's ingenuity is to appear in their analysis and synthesis. He must satisfy our need for logical arrangement by a 'dialectic' of character and incident rather than by arousing emotions strong enough to make us acquiesce in a catastrophe.

The *suasoria* and tragedy, on the other hand, may more often take for granted the audience's familiarity with their speakers and plots. As specific individuals, their characters are exemplary rather than typical; as famous 'situations,' their plots fulfill, rather than surprise, our ex-

---

might not do could he foresee the contradictions into which they were to lead him (*De inv.* 1.51–54). The purification of this spontaneous elenchus may be partially intended in such dramatically presented dialogues as Cicero's *Tusculan Disputations*, which he offers, not as a narrative, but *eisdem fere verbis, ut actum disputatumque est* (2.9).

pectations. Like the proposition of the argument *ad motum*, the premises of the suasorial or tragic argument emerge simultaneously with their demonstration. They contain within them the potential thesis and catastrophe, which the successive stages of the presentation, unfolding as consequences, confirm. This confirmation or proof (*confirmatio*) of the premises brings about an emotional acquiescence in the catastrophe as a jury might acquiesce in an advocate's presentation of a case. The proposition and the response that it demands in each instance are suspended until the end: the hero's death, however undeserved, finally appears to the audience as necessary or probable; the verdict requested by the advocate on the basis of evidence (offered as confirmation of the indictment) finally appears to the jury as probably (*probabiliter*) or necessarily (*necessarie*) justifiable (*De inv.* 1.44). While *controversiae* and comedies seem to exploit the process of argumentation itself (*ad fidem*), *suasoriae* and tragedies seem to rely more on a form of demonstration calculated *ad movendos animos*.[23]

The technical confirmation or proof of an oration follows the proposition (the *expositio* or ἔκθεσις of what is to be proved),[24] the statement of the facts (*narratio*), and the analysis of events into questions (*partitio* or *divisio*). Specifically, confirmation contributes credibility (*fidem*), authority (*auctoritatem*), and support (*firmamentum*) to the argument by describing and interpreting the particular qualities of persons and actions (*De inv.* 1.34–43). Qualities of persons include their manner of life

[23] In the Renaissance Iacobus Strebaeus, commenting on Cicero's distinction, says the argument *ad fidem* looks to the removing of doubts (about gaining a certain verdict) by proof, while the argument *ad motum* looks to moving the listeners to accept the desired verdict. The structure of the first is syllogistic, while that of the second avoids syllogism because *si initio rem proponeret, eamque simpliciter confirmaret, non tam vehementer arderet affectus: ut in argumentatione Dialectica nullae graves excitantur tragoediae, quando rectissimum argumentandi ductum prosequitur* (*De partitione oratoria M. T. Ciceronis Dialogus* [Ludguni, 1545], p. 220). The relation between *ethos*, as proper to comedy, and *pathos*, to tragedy, as Quintilian discusses them (6.2.8–36), bears upon the ways of handling the proofs. That appealing *ad motum* would utilize that force of eloquence which "not merely compels the judge to the conclusion toward which the nature of the facts leads him, but awakens emotions which either do not naturally arise from the case or are stronger than the case would suggest" (24). S. F. Bonner, on the other hand, comments on the similarity of materials in comedy and the *controversiae* (*Roman Declamation*, pp. 37ff.). Quintilian associates the *suasoria* with deliberative oratory (3.8.6) and the treatment of indefinite questions or theses on such subjects as whether marriage is desirable: "Put such discussions into the mouths of specific persons and they become deliberative declamations (*suasoriae*) at once" (2.4.25; cf. 3.5.8).

[24] Similar is the setting forth (ἔκθεσις) of the materials to be treated in the construction of a geometrical diagram and of a dramatic plot (see Chap. 2, pp. 50–58). The *Rhet. ad Her.* says the *propositio est per quam ostendimus summatim quid sit quod probari volumus* (2.28), and the editor glosses *propositio* and *expositio* as πρότασις or λῆμμα—a word corresponding, in its rhetorical meaning, to hypothesis and later to *thema* (Chap. 2, n. 36).

(*victus*), fortune, habit, feelings, interests (*studia*), and achievements. Qualities of actions include a brief summary of what is at issue—murder of a parent, betrayal of one's country—followed by the reasons why and the means by which the act was done, as well as by what preceded and followed the deed. Qualities particularly concerned with the performance of the action include place, time, occasion, and manner (*modus*), the last including the state of mind (*quemadmodum et quo animo*) in which the act was committed. Was it done with intention (*prudentia*) or with lack of intention (*imprudentia*) as a result of ignorance, accident, necessity, or strong emotions such as anger or love? A very similar list of qualitative considerations might help to amplify the premises of a dramatic hypothesis in the persuasive organization of speeches and incidents. In fact, the author of the *Ad Herennium* draws mainly on such considerations when he illustrates the last three (of five) parts in a perfect rhetorical argument—confirmation, embellishment, and summary—with an analysis of the literary proposition "that Ulysses had a motive in killing Ajax" (2.28–30).[25]

As discussed in the second chapter of this study, logical development (*ordo*) is as necessary to the persuasiveness of rhetorical as of geometrical proofs. Each type of proof, Quintilian says, arrives in its own way at conclusions from definite premises and "by arguing from what is certain proves what was previously uncertain" (1.10.37). While the materials of geometry, however, are quantitative and admit of certainty, those of oratory and literature are qualitative and admit only of probability. As Plato says, number may define exact identity and difference, while words and letters which express quality (ποιοῦ) in the form of an image (εἰκόνος) may sketch but the essential character of a thing (*Crat.* 432AE). Or, as Aristotle more briefly puts it, analogy signifies equality among quantities but similarity among qualities (*De gen. et cor.* 2.6; 333a30–31). Herein may be distinguished the basic antithesis between fact and fable (*vera* = identity, *falsa* = difference) on the one hand and the verisimilar *argumentum* on the other. The latter reflects the very nature of literary analogy itself suspended in qualitative probability which must constantly resist the danger of being resolved either into the true or into the false.

[25] Following the analysis of Ulysses' motivation into the five parts of a speech, comes a description of how the argument in each part may be defective (2.31ff.). The defects of the *ratio* lie primarily in insufficient causality (2.35ff.), while those of the *rationis confirmatio* lie chiefly in arguing from assumptions which are themselves open to question (2.38ff.). In the *confirmatio* lies the strongest support of the total argument, and most of its illustrations come from the drama. The names of the five parts of a speech in the *Rhet. ad Her.* might be compared to Cicero's terms for the five steps in deductive proof (*De inv.* 1.67).

Pascal's father is reputed to have hidden his own books on geometry so that his son might not be seduced from his literary studies by his desire for a certainty only mathematics could provide. Pascal discovered the books, and his philology suffered accordingly: the verisimilar could not compete with the true. Yet for Aristotle, Cicero, and Quintilian, as for Plato himself, the verisimilar might risk drawing *formally* upon the structures of true demonstration and appropriate their emotional power of conviction for poetry and rhetoric. The ways in which forensic and deliberative rhetoric preserved for literature its 'dialectic of qualities' can be examined in the construction of the legal-literary exercises of declamation. The declamatory procedures often included, and were often transmitted by, the elementary exercises of the *progymnasmata*, which, in turn, formed the elementary basis of literary education for the Middle Ages and the Renaissance.

12. DECLAMATION AND THE EARLY
EXERCISES

I HAVE TRIED to describe the conditions most congenial to the rhetorical transmission of the principles of literary discourse. Both rhetoric and poetry were chiefly concerned with questions of *qualitas* and *aequitas* in the interpretation of real or imaginary events. Both drew upon similar structures of argumentation to present their interpretations as persuasively as possible. The ethical materials and formal procedures of rhetoric, furthermore, did not simply remain analogous in theory to those of literary fictions but became virtually indistinguishable from them in the practice of the schools of declamation. As described by the elder Seneca, the *controversiae* and *suasoriae*, drawing on philosophical as well as rhetorical sources, realized the intentions of literary discourse in a type of fictional construction which even the elementary rhetorical exercises of Roman education could pass on to succeeding centuries.[1]

---

[1] Of the extensive literature on the schools of declamation, the most useful studies for our purposes are H. Bornecque, *Les déclamations et les déclamateurs d'après Sénèque le Père* (Lille, 1902); H. Bardon, *Le vocabulaire de la critique littéraire chez Sénèque le Rhéteur* (Paris, 1940); and S. F. Bonner, *Roman Declamation in the Late Republic and Early Empire* (Berkeley, 1949)—with their bibliographies. References to Bonner and Bardon will be given in the text. The edition of Seneca used is that of H. Bornecque, *Sénèque le Rhéteur: controverses et suasoires*, 2 vols. (Paris, 1932). My paraphrases from the Latin are indebted to his translation. In his concise and detailed account of the origins and development of declamation, Bonner indicates its extensive debt to both philosophy and rhetoric by two of his main headings: 1. *"Philosophical 'theses' and their relation to 'controversiae' and 'suasoriae'"* (pp. 2–11): 2. *"Greek rhetorical studies as a background to 'suasoriae' and 'controversiae'"* (pp. 11–16). He describes, as well, the relation of declamatory procedures to the *status rationales*, to the *status legales*, and to the illustration of *status* by fictional examples in rhetorical treatises (pp. 12–16). His first four chapters are an excellent general background. In addition, E. P. Parks, *The Roman Rhetorical Schools as a Preparation for the Courts under the Early Empire (Johns Hopkins University Studies in Historical and Political Science* 63, 2 [Baltimore, 1945], pp. 9–122), is particularly useful with regard to the prominent place given to equity in the exercises (pp. 78–85). He cites Latro's words (*Controv.* 9.4.9) *in lege . . . nihil excipitur; sed multa, quamvis non excipiantur, intelleguntur et scriptum legis angustum, interpretatio diffusa est* as the keynote of the spirit of the schools and emphasizes the various applications of natural law with illustrations from the declamations (p. 84). I have dealt with the characteristics of 'scholastic' style in the articles cited as MHP and HASD in the first note of Part Two.

A. Declamation

In the beginning of his work (1.pr.12), Seneca defines the *controversia* in relation to traditional terminology. Before Cicero, he says, the subjects declaimed were called "theses." Later, Cicero practiced privately before friends what were called "causes," while now the exercises of the schools are called "controversies" (*controversias nos dicimus: Cicero causas vocabat*). While Seneca may well be describing three stages of development, as S. F. Bonner suggests (p. 2), he is also indicating the sources of particular elements of the *controversia* itself. The term "thesis" (*propositio*), with its origins in philosophical discourse, refers to the general topic 'proposed' for discussion from one or more points of view without the delimitation of particular persons or circumstances. The term *causa* (*hypothesis*), with its origins in rhetorical discourse, refers to the particular controversy which is *given* by circumstances, rather than 'proposed,' to a deliberating body for adjudication. The *controversia* combines the functions of the 'thesis' with that of the 'hypothesis': it 'proposes' for discussion a set of particular circumstances for adjudication by a 'deliberating' audience. The paradoxical combination of a 'proposed hypothesis' was to be realized most easily in a fiction and, indeed, corresponds closely to the fictional *argumentum* of a dramatic plot. This concept of a 'fictional proposition' required a new term, and the declamatory schools settled on 'theme.' The *thema*, whose root verb, as that of 'thesis,' is τίθημι, suggested the act of 'setting out for discussion,' while the problem set forth was made up of given circumstances to be interpreted in the light of one or more fixed statutes.

Each fictional case, which was debated again and again, consisted of a title, one or more legal prescriptions, and a set of circumstances of varying degrees of complexity. For example, the fourth of Seneca's first book is entitled "The proven soldier who has lost his hands" (*vir fortis sine manibus*). Two 'laws' follow the title: (1) whoever catches a couple in the act of adultery will not be prosecuted if he kills them, and (2) one is permitted to punish one's mother and one's son for adultery. The

---

These characteristics lend themselves, and further precision, to the terms of analysis developed in Chaps. 5–8 of this study. Generally speaking, the schools cultivated idiosyncratic preciosity in style and an ever more varied (ποικίλος) and refined (ἀκριβής) ingenuity. See Chap. 12, n. 5. For the influences of the schools of declamation on Renaissance drama, see E. Waith, "John Fletcher and the Art of Declamation," *PMLA* 66 (1951):226–34, and "*Controversia* in the English Drama: Medwall and Massinger," *PMLA* 68 (1953):286–303; J. B. Altman, *The Tudor Play of Mind* (Berkeley, 1978); and K. H. Eden, "The Influence of Legal Procedure on the Development of Tragic Structure" (Ph.D. diss., Stanford, 1980).

'situation' is given after these prescriptions: "a proven soldier has lost his hands in the war. He surprises his wife in the act of adultery, and, being helpless himself, orders their adolescent son to kill his mother and her lover. The son refuses, and the lover escapes. The father disowns the son." The declamation, which then takes place, consists of arguments first in behalf of the father, then in behalf of the son. The situation of the fifth exercise of the first book, "The man who has seduced two women" (*raptor duarum*), which turns upon the legal prescription that "the woman who is seduced can choose whether her seducer should be executed or should marry her without dowry," is equally brief: "a man rapes two women in one night; one chooses his death, the other to marry him." Obviously, both cannot have their way, and the debate follows over whose choice is to prevail. Other 'plots' are considerably more involved, such as "The priestess bound over to prostitution" (*sacerdos prostituta*), which is argued in relation to the prescription that "a priestess must be chaste and pure and born of chaste and pure parents."

A virgin, captured by pirates and put up for sale, is bought by a prostitutor and put to work. She asks those who wish her favors, however, to pay her fee (which she has to pass on to the prostitutor) without making her earn it. A soldier who refuses to agree to this arrangement tries to rape her, and she kills him. She is charged with murder, acquitted, and returned to her native country, where she applies for the priesthood. (*Controv.* 1.2)

The sufficiency of her purity for such a sacred calling is then debated.

The brief setting forth of the fictional circumstances and the legal conditions corresponds closely to the initial dramatic hypothesis such as that given in the *Poetics* (17). The law, added to the outline of declamatory incidents, serves the same function as the sacrificial custom stipulated in Aristotle's 'argument' of the *Iphigenia*. "A certain girl" has come to a country "in which it is the custom to sacrifice all foreigners to the goddess" and is made a priestess. Unknown to her, her brother arrives; he is captured, and, about to be sacrificed, is recognized and saved. After setting up this broad outline, one may assign "various names and expand [it] with episodes" (1455b1–16). The outlines of declamation and of drama, though firmly fixed like premises themselves, are capable of producing a wide variety of finished constructions. They contain within them, like the block of marble which holds latent within itself all possible configurations, the potentiality for almost infinite qualification. Both the rhetor and the dramatist gradually 'reveal' this qualification by defining motive and choice more and more specifically in speeches and episodes.

In his edition of Seneca, whose collection is called *Oratorum et rhe-*

torum sententiae divisiones colores, Bornecque says once the subject has
been posed

Ceux qui le traitent commencent par exposer les arguments qui, étant donné
les textes de lois invoqués, prouvent la culpabilité ou l'innocence de l'accusé; ils
les présentent isolément, sans qu'on leur demande de se préoccuper de les en-
chaîner; ce sont les avis, les *sententiae.* Puis on s'efforce de grouper, en un plan
simple et logique, les arguments précédemment fournis: c'est la *divisio.* Gé-
néralement elle se compose de deux parties, qui ont rapport, l'une au droit,
l'autre à l'équité: l'accusé pouvait-il, devait-il, agir de cette façon? Après les
sententiae et la *divisio,* l'on trouve les couleurs (*colores*): ce sont les motifs,
indépendants de la loi, allégués pour expliquer, pour excuser, pour colorer, en
quelque sorte, les paroles ou les actes qui sont à la charge de l'inculpé. (p. ix)

The "opinions, divisions, and colors" do not indicate the sequential parts
of the *controversia,* which seem to have been adapted from oratory
(*prooemium, narratio, argumenta, epilogus*), but refer to methods of
persuasive presentation. *Sententiae* might be used in any section of the
exercise, while *divisiones* would occur directly after the *narratio* and
colores in the *argumenta.*[2] The order in which Seneca usually takes up
these methods of persuasion, however, indicates a scale of increasing
hypothesization and a pattern of analysis and synthesis which is analogous to the construction of a dramatic plot.

The 'problem' as proposed in the 'theme' and awaiting 'resolution'
consists of *given* particular circumstances to be presented to an audience
for judgment in the light of one or more *given* general 'laws.' The events
plus the laws are fixed, like the dramatic hypothesis to be 'filled in' or
the geometrical diagram to be analyzed, and can be 'resolved' only by
an increasingly particularized interpretation of motive, circumstance, and
intention (*voluntas*) of the law. The declaimer prepares the audience for
his analysis by giving one or more opinions about the case in the light
of which he will then proceed to analyze the events or the law itself.
The analysis proper consists of a division of the given thematic question
into more categorical questions from among which those may be selected
which will yield the conclusion he hopes to reach. And finally these
questions are 'synthesized' into a still more highly particularized hypothetical 'construction' of the events or of the law on the basis of which
the declaimer can argue for conviction or acquittal. Such a construction
was called a *color.* Since the *controversia* was a debate *in utramque
partem,* each declaimer, once he had offered an interpretation of the

[2] See Bonner, pp. 54–57. The *sententiae,* in the broader sense of 'considered opinions,'
tended to be expressed more and more as *sententiae* in the narrower stylistic sense of
brief, wittily balanced antitheses or 'points' (*traits*). The same tendency can be observed
in the literary debates of courtly love, in the conversational courtesy books, and the *novelle.*

'theme' from one side of the question, might be obliged to offer one from the other.

The way in which declamatory presentations gain their vitality can illustrate certain underlying principles of all fictional narrative more clearly, perhaps, than finished literary works. Within the declamation there is a steady tension between the absolutely fixed limitations of the theme and the unlimited freedom of interpretation within the theme.

Once the subject (*thema* or *materia*) was clearly announced, it would be the duty of each declaimer to abide strictly by the set of circumstances (*positio*) envisaged; he would be at liberty to use the utmost ingenuity in alleging motive, in relating one act to another within the theme, in explaining away an awkward situation, provided he did not alter the facts of the case; this would be to upset the theme (*thema evertere*) and defeat the object of the declamation. (Bonner, p. 51)

It was in the interest of more flexible interpretation that the given conditions of the themes remained brief and generalized. The more 'abstract' they were, the more fully they could be 'determined' by the speaker himself.[3] Insofar as the main incidents and law(s) are *given*, they represent an inflexible measurement of 'history' or 'statute' against which the qualitative issues of equity must be evaluated in the development of the case being presented. In the *divisiones* and *colores* of these exercises one can see laid out, as on an anatomical chart, the argumentative structures which organize the ethical materials of both rhetoric and fiction.

The *divisio*, Bonner notes (pp. 56–57), "was the skeleton plan of the whole argument—its function was 'ostendere ossa et nervos controversiae.' "

The main division of argument, which is closely observed in the Senecan exercises and recurs in those attributed to Quintilian, is into (i) *ius* and (ii) *aequitas*. The first consideration is given to the strictly legal position: is the defendant empowered by law to act as he did (*an liceat, an possit*)? Secondly, even supposing his actions to have been legally correct, was he morally justified in acting as he did? (*an debeat, an oportuerit*). Each of these main sections would involve a number of questions, one dependent on another, for the issue was not often a simple one; these questions, if of strict law, were entitled *iuris quaestiones*, if

---

[3] For the same reason, Bornecque comments, that "les personnages sont toujours de simples abstractions, père, fils, riche, pauvre, pirate, sans la moindre caractéristique; à l'élève de mettre les *couleurs*" (*Les déclamations*, p. 86). Quintilian says that in the schools as distinct from the forum "the facts of the case are definite (*certa*) and limited in number (*pauca*) and are moreover set out before we begin to declaim: the Greeks call them *themes*, which Cicero [*Top.* 21] translates by *propositions*" (7.1.4).

of equity, *tractationes* (though occasionally Seneca uses *quaestiones* loosely of both).

This analysis of the 'problem,' stated in the *thema* for debate, into questions dealing both with what is or is not permitted by law and with what pertains to matters of equity recalls the orator's inquiry into the principal *status* of his case. The conjectural *status* (*an sit*) is eliminated in most declamations, since the acts are accepted as 'given' by the theme. The definitive (*quid sit*) and qualitative (*quale sit*) *status*, therefore, provide the major division of the declamatory questions. The question of *quid sit* principally concerns the definition of the act in relation to a legal code which stipulates how much (*quam multum*) penalty is demanded for each category of crime. The qualitative *status*, on the other hand, concerns all matters of *aequitas* which might qualify the act in the eyes of the judging audience by taking into account individual motives, psychological states, and other special circumstances. Whether an act is permissible (*licet*) or possible (*possit*) with regard to an externally applied statutory measure is one question; whether it properly, according to 'due' measure (*debere*), ought (*oportet*) to be so regarded once it is fully understood, that is, 'qualified,' is quite another.

These two kinds of measurement, which I have designated as quantitative and qualitative in earlier sections of this study, will be present in any artistic account of human actions. As I have argued, the leaden ruler of the Lesbian builders in Aristotle's description of equity can be most subtly applied in a fiction. Such an application may be seen in Bardon's analysis (pp. 68–77) of the *divisio* of questions in three of Seneca's *controversiae* (1.1; 1.2; 1.4), the themes of the last two of which I recounted previously. In the theme of "The proven soldier who has lost his hands," the *divisio maior* is, as is customary, between law (*ius*) and equity (*aequitas*). The *quaestio* of law is subdivided into two *quaestiones minores*: (a) is a son permitted (by law) to avenge an act of adultery when the (abused) husband is not present, and (b) would he be permitted to do so if the husband were on the spot but were as helpless as if he were not there? In the major division, the topic of equity is called not a *quaestio* but a 'development' (*tractatio*), and it is divided into three *tractationes minores*: (a) ought a son, even if his father does not order him to do so, kill the adulterous wife of a proven soldier; (b) ought he to do so at the command of his father even if his father were able to avenge himself; and (c) ought he to do so when his father is both unable to do it himself *and* orders him to do it? Bardon concludes that "*ius* et *aequitas* désignent deux ordres de développements différents, ayant l'un et l'autre leur vocabulaire. *Ius* commande *quaestio*, *posse*,

licet; aequitas commande *tractatio, debere, oportet"* (p. 76).[4] It is the
'developments,' of course, which allow the greatest freedom in the considerations of circumstances and motives and give the most subtle final
configurations to the unified construction of events as it is presented to
the audience. The sequence of these developments, question by question,
as if in pursuit of the proper *status*, offers a structure of responses to
actions stipulated by the plot which the dramatic or narrative poet might
easily follow. As Quintilian says of the orator, the rhetor finds his
greatest challenge and power in the treatment of such a qualitative issue,
and it is here that the 'colors' have their greatest effect. In fact, the
success of the *divisio* itself might, to a great extent, be measured by the
persuasiveness of the *color* which it permits to be drawn.

As fragmentarily recalled by Seneca, the *colores* of the rhetors are
often brief and expressed with sententious wit. Since, however, the
'color' was chiefly concerned with motive, which permitted the broadest
latitude of interpretation, it is reasonable to assume that in the complete
controversia they exploited these 'constructions of events' in much more
detail. As Bonner observes (p. 55), the term *color*, corresponding to
χρῶμα, before Seneca's day "applied only as a general word for 'cast' or
'tone' of style."

But in Seneca it takes on the quite different meaning of "twist of argument,"
"plea," "excuse"; and it is very interesting to note, in view of the legal associations of the *controversiae*, that the term "color insaniae" survives in the
Digest, meaning a "plea of insanity," in connection with the *querela inofficiosi
testamenti*. The *colores*, though often so expressed that they were themselves
sententiae, would mainly occur in the section devoted to *argumenta*, though
they would be foreshadowed in the *narratio* (*Contr.* IV, 3,3, cf. VII, 1,20).

The 'colors' were 'glosses' upon the events stipulated in the theme which
offered particular interpretations of the actions of the defendant.

By a slight shift of argument, by an added insinuation, or a guileless plea, they
tone down the guilt or represent it in even more glaring colours. The *colores*
are the Persian carpet of the declaimer; look at it from one angle and the colours
are bright and clear, the pattern simple, but observe it from another angle, and

---

[4] Bardon points out that the terminology was by no means consistent. Yet, when
concerned with equity, the *quaestio* still "fût réservé au développement moral se limitant
à un cas précis, tandis que *tractatio* se rapporterait au développement de portée générale"
(p. 71). Though occasionally *tractatio* could treat equity "sous ses deux formes, générale
et particulière," the term is never found in the treatment of *ius* (p. 74). The concern with
divisio in the Oresteian issues of the *vir fortis sine manibus* goes back to Aristotle: "The
example of the fallacy of division (ἐκ διαιρέσεως) in the *Orestes* of Theodectes: 'It is just
that a woman who has killed her husband' should be put to death, and that the son should
avenge the father; and this in fact is what has been done. But if they are combined,
perhaps the act ceases to be just" (*Rhet.* 2.24.3).

the shade deepens, the pattern changes, and the whole appears in a different light. (p. 56)[5]

It is easy to see how important the 'colors' would be for the 'developments (*tractationes*)' of equity.

In behalf of the girl, for instance, who wishes to be a priestess (whose trials were previously described) the rhetor Fuscus could give this *color*.

The immortal gods have wished, with regard to this young girl, to show all their power and to make it perfectly clear that no human force can resist their majesty: they thought that it would be a miracle [and therefore an indication of the support of the applicant], if one should find liberty in a captive, modesty in one prostituted, innocence in a woman accused of murder. (*Controv.* 1.2.17)

Some *colores*, such as that of Albucious (1.2.18), present small dramatic scenes with dialogue to reveal the defendant's intentions. Others exploit melodramatic descriptions, recommended by Cicero (*Brut.* 42f.) and Quintilian (4.2.123f.), as in the following excuse by the son for not killing his adulterous mother in the *vir fortis sine manibus*.

All of a sudden my mother rushed toward me, and, holding me in her embrace, bound my hands. I am grateful to my confusion that I saw nothing in that bedroom but my mother and father. My father demanded that I kill her, my mother that I spare her life; my father that I not permit a guilty person to go

---

[5] The general meaning of *figura* which Quintilian gives (9.2.75) is very close to *color* (see Chap. 12, n. 11), and both resemble terms used to discuss such figurative devices as allegory in the Renaissance. Galileo, in criticizing Tasso's narrative incoherence, compares his allegory to a carefully determined oblique point of observation necessary for bringing certain types of illusionistic paintings (called 'anamorphoses') into focus. This oblique perspective turns such a painting, when seen normally from in front, into a confusion of lines and colors. So allegory compels the "narrative, originally plainly visible and viewed directly" to "adapt itself to an allegorical meaning seen obliquely, and implied" (trans. E. Panofsky, *Galileo as a Critic of the Arts* [The Hague, 1954], p. 13). The obliquity is reminiscent of Lactantius' view, discussed in this chapter, that a *poeticus color* is a real incident *obliqua figuratione obscuratum* (*Div. Inst.* 1.11.30); see also Isidore, *Etym.* 8.7.10. Galileo also compares the fragmentary nature of Tasso's stanzas to a tarsia picture made up of a composite of little varicolored pieces of wood (*Galileo as a Critic*, p. 17). Both passages suggest the notorious incoherence of declamatory structures and points of view as a series of verbal *lumina* and interpretive *colores*. Galileo further compares the *Gerusalemme Liberata* to a "study of some little man with a taste for curios"—bric-a-brac like dried insects, little antique figures, and sketches by Bandinelli or Parmigianino: the "jumbled *Kunst- und Wunderkammern* so typical of the Mannerist age." In contrast, he praises the *Orlando Furioso* by comparing it to "a regal gallery adorned with a hundred classical statues" and "countless complete historical pictures" (*Galileo as a Critic*, pp. 18–19). Mannerist *curiositas*, as declamatory *lumina* and *colores*, is associated with the enclosed proximity of the cabinet, in contrast to the more open and extensive gallery, which perfectly realizes the Horatian distinction between the painting to be viewed from close up and that to be seen from a distance (see MHP and HASD). Galileo includes the intricate allegory which strains the reader's glossatorial powers among the other Hellenistic forms of figurative ingenuity.

unpunished, my mother that I do not make myself guilty; my father recited the law against adulterers, my mother that against parricides. (*Controv.* 1.4.9)

Had Agamemnon appeared as a ghost, Orestes, like Hamlet, might have been made to weigh such pleas of a betrayed father in the bedroom of a suppliant mother.

Though expressed in the opening *sententiae* against the philandering young man in *raptor duarum*, his alleged intentions are cited again for development among the *colores* after the analysis of *divisio*: "he was on his way to attack a third young lady, had the night not given out!" So, too, the circumstances of the 'morning after,' included under *sententiae*, might have been drawn out as a *color* to set the scene of a play.[6]

The next day one heard in the house the tears of one young lady and the lamentations of her mother who sobbed with broken hopes. At the same instant, from another house arose other cries, other tumults. People gathered as if threatened by a public calamity. It would scarcely be believed that there were only two seducers, and yet now this single enemy of public chastity is led away who had not found it sufficient in a single night to satisfy himself with just one girl. (*Controv.* 1.5.1)

A more favorable 'construction' could also be put upon the young man's activities: "The day after, when one tells him of his mistake about the night before (since he believed he had raped only one girl), the young lady before whom he first begs on his knees for pity wishes to marry him, while the other young lady, irritated by a feeling of being second best, demands that he die." The degree of ingenious flippancy depended greatly upon the material of the theme.[7]

As Quintilian points out in detail (4.2.88–124), the very way that one presents the facts and describes the circumstances in the *narratio* can constitute a 'gloss.' In fact, if it is taken metaphorically to include all events and issues, the *color* might be considered the completed presentation of the case itself. And the same thing might be said of any argument which arises over the interpretation of events, whether real or imaginary. It is interesting to see how the declamatory usage of 'color'

[6] For other examples of *sententiae* which also serve as *colores*, see Bornecque, *Les déclamations*, p. 53.

[7] Fortunatianus uses this theme to illustrate one form of *iniectio qualitatum* which occurs *cum qualitas qualitati supernascitur. Rapta raptoris mortem aut indotatas nuptias optet. Rapuit et profugit: dedit eam pater marito alii, reversum raptorem vult pater producere ad magistratum: ille contra dicit. Quo modo hic supernascitur qualitas qualitati? quoniam, quae antea rapta erat, hodie iam nupta est* (Halm, p. 95). This theme with variations is mentioned by Philostratus (*Lives* 569), is commonly treated in collections of declamations, and occurs in the *gesta Romanorum*. The process of increasing qualification is fundamental to the building of narrative incident. See Chap. 10, n. 8.

clarifies the term's meaning in analogies between the literary and plastic arts.

In stressing the priority of the sequence of actions over 'character' and 'thought' in dramatic composition, Aristotle draws an analogy with painting.

Further, if a writer strings together speeches expressive of character and well-turned expressions and arguments (ῥήσεις ἠθικὰς καὶ λέξεις καὶ διανοίας), he will not be accomplishing what we said was the function of tragedy; it will be accomplished much more by the tragedy which makes a less full and satisfactory use of these elements, but which has a plot, a structure of events (μῦθον καὶ σύστασιν πραγμάτων). It is very much like the case in painting: if someone should smear (ἐναλείψειε) the picture with the most beautiful colors, but at random (καλλίστοις φαρμάκοις χύδην), he would not please us as much as if he gave us a simple outline on a white ground. (*Poet.* 6.14–15; 1450a30–b3)[8]

[8] For the complicated textual history of this passage see Else (pp. 251–63). The metaphorical importance of χύδην for Aristotle's analogy with painting is perhaps greater than his recent commentators have suggested. Derived from χέειν (= to flow) and usually rendered 'at random,' 'confusedly,' 'without order,' the word also has a technical literary meaning of prose composition as distinct from measured verse (μέτρα), as in Aristotle's *Rhetoric* (1409b7), which corresponds to *oratio soluta* as opposed to *oratio numerosa* or *metrica*. (With regard to Aristotelian usage, N. A. Greenberg comments that "if meter is impressed upon a *logos*, the *logos* will become *poiema*," "The Use of *Poiema* and *Poiesis*," *HSCP* 65 [1961]:268). In addition, there is a strong connotation, among the usages of χύδην, of a whole whose parts are as yet unstructured but which are, nevertheless, capable of σύνοψις (cf. Plato, *Rep.* 537C, *Laws* 858B). This is the basic meaning of Socrates' use of χύδην in criticizing the arrangement of the parts of Lysias' speech in the *Phaedrus* (264BE). It is not that they "are thrown out helter-skelter," as H. N. Fowler renders the phrasing (LCL), that is, that Lysias has used *no* art, but rather that he has used poor art. There is no rhetorical necessity (ἀνάγκην λογογραφικήν) for the order of his topics; he has arranged them as they have occurred to him. The parts of a discourse, on the contrary, should be as clearly organized as those of a living being (ζῷον). Plato, furthermore, distinguishes the freely flowing prose of dialogue in his *Laws* from poetic composition (ἐν ποιήμασιν) by the word χύδην (*Laws* 811DE). Such passages strongly suggest a specific literary meaning for the term which brings out precisely Aristotle's distinction in the *Poetics*. However essential the arguments, verbal expressions, and characterizing speeches may be, considered by themselves they are only potential dramatic materials awaiting realization in the coherent shaping of the incidents. In this sense, they resemble the 'bricks' which must be collected one by one (χύδην) in constructing the edifice of Plato's laws (858B). If laws are simply heaped up indiscriminately, for which Aristotle also uses χύδην (1324b5), no direction will be apparent in the legislation. Once outlined, the plot may 'receive' the other dramatic materials as the design on white may receive the 'flow' of colors. In this sense, the common term of the analogy between poetry and painting may be χύδην itself which has a distinct meaning for each of the arts. Free flowing speech (prose) in contrast to measured speech (poetry), the informal association of topics in dialogue in contrast to logically ordered discourse: both contrasts illustrate a distinction between the disparate materials of drama and their principle of coherence. So, also the materials of painting, the colors, will flow in an unsatisfying profusion if there is no cohering principle of outline. The verb upon which χύδην depends is ἐναλείφω, to anoint or dye. In an Aristotelian passage on the growth of embryos (*De gen. an.* 2.6; 743b20–25), cited as a gloss on the verb as early as the sixteenth century (*Petri Victorii Comm.*

The plot is compared to a line drawing on a white background, while arguments, phrasing, and speeches expressive of character are compared to colored dyes applied at random in flowing profusion. Several centuries later Plutarch modifies the analogy by comparing the illusion of reality to color added to the outline of historical events. When poets tell intentional lies, it is to give pleasure, since they feel the truth is too austere in comparison with fiction.

For the truth, because it is what actually happens, does not deviate from its course, even though the end be unpleasant; whereas fiction, being a verbal fabrication, very readily follows a roundabout route, and turns aside from the painful to what is more pleasant. For not metre nor figure of speech nor loftiness of diction nor aptness of metaphor nor unity of composition has so much allurement and charm, as a clever interweaving of fabulous narrative (διάθεσις μυθολογίας). But, just as in pictures, colour (χρῶμα) is more stimulating than line-drawing because it is life-like, and creates an illusion, so in poetry falsehood combined with plausibility (πιθανότητι ψεῦδος) is more striking, and gives more satisfaction, than the work which is elaborate in metre and diction, but devoid of myth and fiction (ἀμύθου καὶ ἀπλάστου).[9]

Plutarch not only prefers color to outline but has changed the meaning of the terms of the analogy. He contrasts the severity of an historical or scientific account, which he compares with the outlined design of a

---

in prim. lib. Arist. de arte poet. [Flor., 1560], p. 71 and *V. Madii et B. Lombardi in Arist. lib. de poet. communes explanationes* [Venet., 1550], p. 114), it seems to mean 'to paint within lines': "All the parts are first marked out in their outlines and acquire later on their colour and softness or hardness, exactly as if Nature were a painter producing a work of art, for painters, too, first sketch in the animal with lines and only after that put in the colours" (trans. A. Pratt, *The Works of Aristotle* [Oxford, 1912]). I. Vahlen viewed the analogy in the *Poetics* as two stages in a process such as that described previously. Bywater, paraphrasing Vahlen in his own commentary, says that the process is "(1) λευκογραφεῖν εἰκόνα, and (2) ἐναλείφειν φαρμάκοις, and serves to illustrate the order of procedure in Tragedy, where the μῦθος is said to come first, as the ἀρχὴ τῆς τραγῳδίας, and the ἤθη second" (*Aristotle On the Art of Poetry* [Oxford, 1909], p. 171). Though Bywater feels his analysis is unnecessarily subtle, Vahlen's account corresponds exactly to the general process of composition I have been describing. Though he does not point out the technical literary meaning of the word, he comments on the *vis vocabuli* χύδην, *quae consilium et necessitatem excludit*, and cites the *Phaedrus* (264B) and *De gen. an.* (743b23)—*Aristotelis de arte poetica liber* (Lipsiae, 1885), p. 123. Vettori, as well as Maggi, presumably also saw the two stages in Nature's 'painting' an embryo as applicable to two stages in 'painting' a play: *id est animantem illam, quam prius lineis tantum ductis descripserint, postea coloribus illinunt* (*Comm. . . . de arte poet.*, p. 71).

[9] "How to Study Poetry," *Moralia* 16. This distinction may be indebted to Aristotle's earlier discussion of mimesis (1447b9–23) in which he excludes Empedocles as Plutarch himself does in this passage. The relation of Plutarch's distinctions to the dichotomy of the true and the fabulous narrative is discussed on p. 293 of this study. Petronius likewise contrasts the poet free to go *per ambages* of mythical allusion and exalted prophecy to the historian bound to give a scrupulous account of things that really happened as if on oath before witnesses (*Satyr.* 118). See Chap. 10, n. 41.

painting, to the attractiveness of fictional composition, which he compares with its colors. As colors give the picture a lifelike, illusionistic quality, fictional elaboration if plausibly handled gives life, illusionistically, to history regardless of whether or not the historian has employed meter and poetic diction. Plutarch has substituted the charm of imaginary episodes, 'colored' to make them seem real, for Aristotle's mimetic freedom of generalization as the principal power of poetry. The greater their naturalistic illusion, the more easily such episodes may either pass for history itself or mingle with it, as Horace advises that the poet *veris falsa remiscet* (*A.P.* 151). Color is what *deceives* the eye. In this sense, it corresponds to the *color* of declamation which puts a certain 'complexion' on the events to be judged which, otherwise, in their austere and probably incompletely recorded historical reality, might not elude the strictures of the declamatory laws.

Once one allows for the difference in the comparisons with painting, there is a correspondence between the analogies of Aristotle and Plutarch with regard to literary structure. The word χρῶμα has a basic meaning of 'skin' and its color or 'complexion,' much as the noun χρώς (= skin, flesh, complexion), with the associated verbs χρώζω and χρώννυμι meaning to 'tinge,' 'stain,' or 'paint.' These words refer to qualities of the outermost surface of things in the way that Plato complains that poets and painters, in their imitations, attend only to the outward forms and colors of their models (ἐκ τῶν χρωμάτων δὲ καὶ σχημάτων θεωροῦσιν, 601A). Such forms and colors are the material of our 'aesthetic' experience; they make up the appearance which presents itself to us first and which, therefore, is better known with respect to our own perceptions (ἡμῖν) than with respect to itself (ἁπλῶς). It is, in other words, what we start with when we ask how this or that thing comes to be as it *is*, here, before us. It lies like skin or flesh over a skeletal structure to which we must penetrate by analysis if we are to answer the 'problem' it poses of *what* it is. In terms of actions, it is the situation as we might know it in its visible configurations. If, on the other hand, we start with a skeletal outline of events, the *argumentum* of the play or declamation, the 'color' will be as yet unspecified, awaiting determination in the construction of the completed work.

The direct sensory experience of something's 'qualities,' of how it appears or is heard, is suggested in the musical designation of a 'chromatic scale,' which, in the Middle Ages, was referred to technically as *musica ficta*.[10] This 'colored' scale modifies the basic division of notes in order

---

[10] See E. E. Lowinsky, "The Musical Avant-garde of the Renaissance or: The Peril and Profit of Foresight" in *Art, Science, and History in the Renaissance*, ed. C. S. Singleton (Baltimore, 1967), pp. 113–16.

to offer a subtler configuration to the ear. In order to understand how it is able to perceive this 'appearance,' however, the ear might be said to move 'back' in analysis to the underlying structure of the original *divisio* of sounds, and then, with these 'in mind,' to move 'forward' again in synthesis to the chromatic reality with which it started. This musical relation of color to division indicates how the literary admonitions about 'color' correspond to each other in the *Poetics*, in the *Controversiae*, and in Plutarch's *How to Study Poetry*. Aristotle said the poet must not content himself with writing ethical speeches and arguments for his characters, even though these are actually what we will be hearing on the stage. The poet must first concentrate on the underlying structure of events, on the 'line' itself of the drawing. In declamation, also, although they may be insinuated throughout the exercise, *colores* will be most effectively contrived after the structure of the *quaestiones* and *tractationes* supporting them has been made clear by the *divisio*. And Plutarch, too, compares 'color' to an imaginary gloss of plausible incidents which may interpret an already existing outline of events by giving them the deceptive appearance, the illusion, of actuality. Since an historical account is an image of our real world and a fiction an image of history, 'color' lies at two removes from actual events (348AB).[11] Once the 'color' has served its purpose, it must be recognized and removed so that the truth, moral and historical, may once again be revealed. The process, thus expressed, resembles Plutarch's pedagogical defense of reading poetry as an inducement to studying philosophy.

The extension of Seneca's use of *color* as a pretext (*praetextum*) to poetic fictions generally is clearly established for future centuries by Lactantius in his influential defense of poetry. Lactantius was a teacher in the rhetorical schools before his conversion, and he gives credit to that exercise in fictitious cases (*exercitatio illa fictarum litium*) for his later oral facility (*facultas dicendi*) in pleading (*peroremus*) the 'cause' of truth (*causam veritatis*). As great orators have sometimes turned to

---

[11] "A myth (μῦθος) aims at being a false tale, resembling a true one (λόγος ψευδὴς ἐοικὼς ἀληθινῷ); wherefore it is far removed from actual events, if a tale is but a picture and an image of actuality, and a myth is but a picture and image of a tale (λόγος μὲν ἔργου, καὶ λόγου δὲ μῦθος εἰκὼν καὶ εἴδωλόν ἐστι). And thus those who write of imaginative exploits lag as far behind historians as persons who tell of deeds come short of those that do them" (*Moralia* 348AB). The concept of *color* resembles that of *figura* in Quintilian which implies a different meaning from the one expressed and occurs frequently in *figuratae controversiae* (9.1.14, 9.2.65). *Figurae* may serve as a psychological counterpart of the use Quintilian assigns to hypothesis (5.10.96): "Some things, again, which cannot be proved, may, on the other hand, be suggested by the employment of some *figure*. For at times such hidden shafts will stick, and the fact that they are not noticed will prevent their being drawn out, whereas if the same point were stated openly, it would be denied by our opponents and would have to be proved" (9.2.75). See Chap. 12, n. 5.

philosophy in their later years, he will compose his *disputatio* about divine things in accord with the formulations of civil law (*institutiones civilis iuris*) and call them his *divinas institutiones* (*Div. Inst.* 1.1.10). The importance of this legal terminology in the rhetorical transmission of literary theory to the Middle Ages cannot be overemphasized.[12]

In his euhemeristic account of pagan mythology Lactantius' use of *color* might well conform to Plutarch's educational program. The stories of Jovial rapes are simply commemorative elaborations of actual events whose historical truth has been obscured by time and the human imagination. Such an elaboration of history is a *poeticus color* (1.11.19). For poets do not make up the events themselves, which, if they did, would be most foolish, but rather they put a certain 'color' upon their subjects' actions—add it, as it were, to the facts (*non ergo res ipsas gestas finxerunt poetae, quod si facerent, essent vanissimi, sed rebus gestis addiderunt quendam colorem*, 1.11.23). It is their *poeticae licentiae modus* which permits them to proceed by feigning, since their *officium* is to represent those things which have truly happened as decorously converted into other forms by means of indirect figurations (*ut ea quae vere gesta sunt in alias species obliquis figurationibus cum decore aliquo conversa traducat*, 1.11.24). If they feigned everything, however, they would not be poets but liars, for some germ of historical truth must lie beneath their *figuris versicoloribus* lest they be called *mendaces et sacrilegos* (1.11.24, 30,34–36).[13]

---

[12] *L. Caeli Firmiani Lactanti Opera Omnia*, ed. S. Brandt and G. Laubmann, *CSEL* 19 (Vindobonae, 1890–1897), pp. 3–4. For a brief account of literary studies and the early Christian writers, see E. Curtius, *European Literature*, pp. 446–67, esp. pp. 454–55 on Lactantius and his influence. One cannot more fittingly stress the importance of these passages and those immediately to follow than by recalling that they include the principal theoretical citations of Petrarch's coronal oration (trans. E. H. Wilkins, *Studies in the Life and Works of Petrarch* [Cambridge, Mass., 1955], pp. 300–313) as well as the fact that Boccaccio relies heavily on the *Institutes* in his *Genealogie deorum gentilium*. (For the relation of Petrarch's *Privilegium* to his oration, their sources, and the precedents for, and circumstances of, the ceremony itself, see Wilkins' admirable "The Coronation of Petrarch," *Speculum* 18 [1943]:155–97.) The alternative phrasing in Lactantius' epitome of his *Institutes* (pp. 11–12) is worth consulting as a gloss on *color* and *figura* in Quintilian's sense.

[13] Lactantius' euhemeristic view of mythology and his conception of 'poetic license' as the right to elaborate upon historical events are closely anticipated in the Augustan period by Strabo. In discussing Homer's factual accuracy in the *Odyssey*, he says (1.2.11) that one should "assume that Homer was convinced that those regions were the scene of the wanderings of Odysseus, and that, taking this hypothesis (ὑπόθεσιν) as fact, he elaborated the story in poetic fashion (ποιητικῶς)." He took, that is, "the foundations of his stories from history" (1.2.9). More interesting, however, is Strabo's account of 'poetic license' (ποιητικὴν ἐξουσίαν) itself, which consists of the right to compound "history, rhetorical composition (διαθέσεως), and myth" (1.2.17). The aim of history is truth, of "rhetorical composition" vividness (ἐνέργειαν), and of myth pleasure (ἡδονήν) and amazement (ἔκπληξιν). These aims must be combined, for "to invent a story outright is neither plausible

This euhemeristic view of fiction, then, continues to regard poetry as a mixture of fact and fable—for without *vera* there could be no *colores*. It contributes greatly, as well, not only to the respectability of poetry by making it appear to share some of the truth of history, but to the categorization of types of poetry on the basis of degrees of verisimilitude.[14] Not only for Lactantius is *color* synonymous with *velamen*, *figura*, *figmentum*, and *figuratio*, but in Scriptural exegesis it is metaphorically associated with the literal meaning of a text—be that historical or figurative—as distinct from its allegorical meanings. Through such comparisons as St. Gregory's of a text with a painting where the literal meaning corresponds to the superficial colors and the allegorical truth to the 'things' themselves which are drawn, the ancient usage of *color* is passed on to widely varied literary contexts in the Middle Ages and Renaissance.[15]

---

nor like Homer; for everybody agrees that the poetry of Homer is a philosophic production." Lactantius' *poeticae licentiae modus* and *poeticus color*, then, correspond closely to Strabo's ποιητικὴν ἐξουσίαν and διαθέσεως + μύθου.

[14] Compare Macrobius' account of the type of *fabulae* properly used by philosophers: *argumentum quidem fundatur veri soliditate sed haec ipsa veritas per quaedam composita et ficta profertur, et hoc iam vocatur narratio fabulosa, non fabula, ut sunt cerimoniarum sacra, ut Hesiodi et Orphei quae de deorum progenie actuve narrantur, ut mystica Pythagoreorum sensa referuntur* (*Commentarii in somnium Scipionis* 1.1–2, ed. I. Willis [Lipsiae, 1963], pp. 5–6). Boccaccio clearly categorizes the types of *fabulae* on the basis of their narrative similarity to factual truth. The first type superficially lacks all verisimilitude; the second *in superficie non nunquam veritati fabulosa conmiscet*; the third *potius hystorie quam fabule similis est*; and the fourth is an old wives' tale which *nil penitus in superficie nec in abscondito veritatis habet* (*Genealogie deorum gentilium libri*, ea. V. Romano [Bari, 1951], pp. 706–7). The justification of poetry by associating it with history becomes more pronounced in Christian defenses of fiction. (In the final *Seniles*, for example, Petrarch tries to give Boccaccio's *fabellae* greater respectability by treating them as *historiae*—cf. V. Branca, *Boccaccio Medievale* [Firenze, 1964], pp. 102–4, 121–22, nn. 3–6.) The contribution of the Christian euhemeristic, humanistic, and even exegetical traditions to an already strong Hellenistic emphasis upon history in rhetorical and poetic theory, is most important for the origins and later developments of neoclassicism. As Quintilian proclaims, *tanto robustior quanto verior* (2.4.2). In the context of law, to judge an action one must know what actually happened; history, *res verae gestae*, becomes the handmaiden of justice; *res fictae*—in the guise of a false testimony (*mendacium*)—of injustice. The rhetorical influence of Horace's attitudes toward poetry upon Renaissance neoclassicism may best be seen in the opening chapters of B. Weinberg's *A History of Literary Criticism in the Italian Renaissance* (Chicago, 1961). For the possible legal influence on the concept of the poet as liar, see Appendix B.

[15] See St. Gregory's *prooemium* to his *Super cantica canticorum expositio* (Migne, *PL* 79.473): *Sic est enim Scriptura sacra in verbis et sensibus, sicut pictura in coloribus et rebus; et nimis stultus est qui sic picturae coloribus inhaeret, ut res quae pictae sunt ignoret. Nos enim, si verba quae exterius dicuntur amplectimur, et sensus ignoramus, quasi ignorantes res quae depictae sunt, solos colores tenemus. Littera occidit, sicut scriptum est, spiritus autem vivificat* (II Cor. iii. 6); *sic enim littera cooperit spiritum, sicut palea tegit frumentum; sed jumentorum est, paleis vesci; hominum, frumentis.* This passage, with the rest of the *prooemium*, is later borrowed word for word by Richard of St. Victor (*PL* 196.406A). The exegetical use of the comparison of Scripture with painting

B. The Early Exercises

In his introductory remarks on declamatory theory, Quintilian says that declamation "includes practically all the exercises" which he has been describing in his first two books (2.10.2). Among these exercises, those which specifically concern the *primordia dicendi* (1.9.1) were called *progymnasmata* or *praeexercitamina*. They were used, in various combinations, first by the grammarian and then by the rhetorician in their program of general education, the ἐγκύκλιος παιδεία (1.10.1), which ultimately prepared the student for the active life in the forum or in the imperial administration. I want to draw attention to the importance of several of these exercises for the transmission of the forms of rhetorical argumentation before illustrating, with reference to Boccaccio, how these forms are implicit in all fictional narratives. Because the exercises corresponded to constituent parts of declamation, which could easily be utilized by other literary genres, they passed on the habits of Roman education more pervasively and for a longer period than even the *suasoriae* and *controversiae* themselves.[16]

The order of the exercises in the extant *progymnasmata* seems to have been based upon a scale of increasing difficulty, though the reasons why certain ones should be considered more difficult than others are not always clear. The treatise of Aphthonius, which I shall use as illustrative of the collections despite considerable variation among them, is organized as follows: (1) fable (μῦθος), (2) narrative tale (διήγημα),

---

influences the medieval scholia, as well as Renaissance commentaries, on Horace's analogy of *ut pictura poesis* (*A.P.* 361–65). See H. J. Botschuyver's *Scholia in Horatium* (Amstelodami, 1935), 1:447, where *superficies verborum* and empty *sonoros versus* are compared to what by this time was considered the inferior picture to be viewed from a distance and the serious *sensus et materies* to the picture considered to be superior and to be scrutinized from nearby.

[16] For the early exercises see G. Reichel, *Quaestiones progymnasmaticae* (Lipsiae, 1909); H. I. Marrou, *Histoire de l'éducation dans l'antiquité* (Paris, 1960), pp. 238ff., passim; T. J. Haarhoff, *Schools of Gaul* (Johannesburg, 1958), pp. 68–78; for their broader context of legal debate, see D. Matthes, "Hermagoras von Temnos 1904–55," *Lustrum* 3 (1958):58–214 and S. F. Bonner, pp. 1–26; for the transmission of the exercises in the Middle Ages and Renaissance, see D. L. Clark, "The Rise and Fall of Progymnasmata in Sixteenth and Seventeenth Century Grammar Schools," *Speech Monographs* 19 (1952):259–63 and C. S. Baldwin, *Medieval Rhetoric and Poetic* (New York, 1928) with an English translation of Hermogenes (pp. 23–38); for Priscian's Latin version of Hermogenes, see Halm, pp. 551–60, and for Salutati's MS of Priscian's exercises with other minor rhetorical manuals, see B. L. Ullman, *The Humanism of Coluccio Salutati* (Padua, 1963), p. 154; and for the textual transmission of Theon's exercises, see I. Lana, *I progimnasmi di Elio Teone* (Torino, 1959). For Aphthonius, I have used *Rhetores Graeci*, ed. L. Spengel (Lipsiae, 1854), 2:21–56 and "The Progymnasmata of Aphthonius," trans. R. Nadeau, *Speech Monographs* 19 (1952):264–85.

(3) chria (χρεία), (4) proverb (γνώμη), (5) refutation (ἀνασκευή), (6) confirmation (κατασκευή), (7) commonplace (κοινὸς τόπος), (8) encomium (ἐγκώμιον), (9) vituperation (ψόγος), (10) comparison (σύγκρισις), (11) characterization (ἠθοποιΐα), (12) description (ἔκφρασις), (13) thesis (θέσις) [and hypothesis (ὑπόθεσις)], (14) legislation (εἰσφορά). The pedagogical motivations are immediately observable in the division of the traditional categories of narration in the first two exercises. Quintilian distinguishes three forms of literary narration, *fabula, argumentum, historia*, from the *narratio* of legal suits (2.4.2). As an exercise for very young students, however, he had earlier recommended the *Aesopi fabellas* as the next step above fairy tales (*fabulis nutricularum*) in sophistication (1.9.2). Limiting the term in this way, Aphthonius explicitly adopts *fabula* for the tale with a moral in his first and most elementary exercise, and then lists the three types of narration in his second exercise as "dramatic (δραματικόν)," "historical (ἱστορικόν)," and "civil (πολιτικόν)." The dramatic corresponds to Quintilian's *argumentum*, the historical to his *historia*, and the civil to his *narratio* used in legal suits (*in causis*), since Aphthonius defines πολιτικόν as that which "public orators use in their cases (παρὰ τοὺς ἀγῶνας οἱ ῥήτορες κέχρηνται)." Whereas Quintilian distinguishes three forms of literary narrative from the legal *narratio*, the *progymnasmata* distinguish three kinds of narrative, of which one is the legal *narratio*, from the didactic fable. To compensate, perhaps, for narrowing Quintilian's category of *fabula* to a tale like Aesop's in the first exercise, Aphthonius subsequently permits *argumentum* and *historia* to have more freedom than usual in their use of fabulous materials. The "dramatic" narrative may deal with fiction generally (πεπλασμένον) and the "historical" may simply repeat "tales of old (παλαιὰν ἀφήγησιν)."[17]

The exercises of refutation and confirmation, which Quintilian sees as specifically combined with narrative (2.4.18), are primarily concerned with a questioning or defense of the truth of the *narratio*. Aphthonius

---

[17] Though Suetonius is not chronologically explicit, he describes exercises preceding the development of the *controversiae* and *suasoriae* which are similar to the *progymnasmata*. Besides explaining *figuras, casus*, and *apologos* (i.e. Aesopian tales—Quintilian 5.11.20) in speeches, teachers would compose (as models) *narrationes* (briefly or at length), encomia or vituperations, moral essays on the expedient or inexpedient, questionings or defenses of "the credibility (*fidem*) of myths (*fabulis*), an exercise which the Greeks call 'destructive' and 'constructive' criticism." These exercises are succeeded by debates upon historical narratives (perhaps representing, like *suasoriae*, famous persons in well-known situations) or upon actual events of recent time (more similar to *controversiae*). He gives two examples, easily adaptable to *novelle*, which he implies might illustrate either fictitious or legal materials ("fictas aut iudiciales")—*Suetonius, Rhet.* 1, trans. J. C. Rolfe, LCL, 2 vols. (London, 1959). When the rhetoricians took up debates, the earlier exercises seem to have fallen to the grammarians and to have remained with them.

gives, as an example of a narrative to be refuted and then confirmed, the tale of Apollo and Daphne, which is to be considered on the grounds, or "topics," of obscurity (ἀσαφεῖ), implausibility (ἀπιθάνῳ), impossibility (ἀδυνάτῳ), inconsistency (ἀνακολούθῳ), lack of decorum (ἀπρεπεῖ), and irrationality (ἀσύμφορον). The refutation resembles Plato's questioning of the ancient sophistic view that poetry could teach a body of specialized information. The confirmation of the tale, on the other hand, offers an elementary defense of fiction which transmits to succeeding centuries at least one essential presupposition of both rhetoric and poetry.

A confirmation is a showing of proof for any thing set forth. However, one must prove neither those things clearly manifest (λίαν σαφῆ) nor those utterly impossible (ἀδύνατα), but those which have the middle position (μέσην τάξιν) [between the extremes]. (p. 270)[18]

This exercise, which "encompasses all the power of the art," here transmits the Academic justification of the verisimilar in conformity to which the orator may argue persuasively *in utramque partem* and the *imago* may establish its psychological territory between the true and the false impression. This insistence upon a "middle position" in the exercise of confirmation is significant in that it resists the tendency in poetry as well as rhetoric to dissolve the verisimilar *argumentum* into a mixture of true and false events. Priscian makes this perfectly clear: indeed those things which are most clearly either false or true, such as the fables of Aesop or indisputable historical accounts, are neither to be refuted nor confirmed; for refutations and confirmations must necessarily be made of those things which admit of judgments on both sides of the question (*quae vero planissime sunt falsa vel vera, nec refutanda sunt nec confirmanda, quales sunt fabulae Aesopiae vel historiae indubitabiles; oportet enim refutationes et confirmationes de illis rebus fieri quae ancipitem adhibent opinionem* [Halm, p. 554]).

The Academic belief that the verisimilar, balanced between the true and the false, can provide sufficient grounds for choice is particularly congenial to literary theory. Neither an extreme Pythagorean separation of a 'true' intelligible world from a 'false' world of appearances nor the early Stoic division of 'true' sensory impressions from 'false' ones allows for the "middle position" required by fiction. Posited between fact and

---

[18] Aristotle also observes that "we ought not to discuss subjects the demonstration of which is too ready to hand (σύνεγγυς) or too remote (λίαν πόρρω); for the former raise no difficulty, while the latter involve difficulties which are outside the scope of dialectical training (κατὰ γυμναστικήν)." This passage from the *Topics* (105a7–9) is quoted by John of Salisbury, along with the Elder Seneca (*Controv.* 1.pr.21), in his criticism of overly loquacious logicians (*Metal.* 2.8).

fable, the *argumentum* offers sufficient grounds of belief for the audience to acquiesce temporarily in the probability of an action. Similarly, as Plato analyzes it in the *Sophist*, the 'image' possesses sufficient reality to *be* largely false and, thereby, by representing degrees of truth, to indicate human potentialities for privation or fulfillment. What is accepted as psychologically, doctrinally, or historically final and true, on the other hand, gives little scope to either fiction or the Academic method of debate. One must withhold his assent if he is to proceed into greater and greater qualification.

This psychological balance in the apprehension of probability is accompanied in these exercises by that judicial balance between the speculative thesis and the circumstantial hypothesis which earlier I compared to the 'area' of fiction in the discovery of *status*.[19] In his thirteenth exercise Aphthonius restricts the hypothesis (*causa*) to questions involved in circumstances: "person, act, cause, and so on." Regarding the theses, he distinguishes the political (πολιτικαί), practical or active, theses from the speculative (θεωρητικαί) theses. The political thesis concerns metropolitan affairs, such as marriage, sailing, and fortifications, while the speculative considers intellectual questions, which "do not originate within the experience of man," such as whether or not there are many worlds. While the speculative thesis lies at the opposite pole to the experiential particularity of the rhetorical hypothesis, the practical thesis, lying between the extremes, implicates theoretical principles of behavior in real human actions and gives both significance.

The literary forms of the speculative and practical theses are implicitly distinguished in the two earlier exercises of the proverb and the chria. The speculative thesis will always tend to culminate in the proverb (γνώμη), "promoting something, or opposing" something "universally (ἀπροσώπως) proclaimed," as it is prescribed in the fourth exercise. The practical thesis as it approaches a hypothesis, on the other hand, will naturally strive to arrive at a judgment (*iudicatio*), at some "advice bearing appropriately on some person," as required by the third exercise (χρεία). The intermediate ground of the chria between the proverb and the unpredicated event remains the no-man's land between the indefinite and definite questions whose exploration had always demanded the greatest imagination and experience.[20] It is more, perhaps, by virtue of the

---

[19] See pp. 32–34 of this study, esp. Chap. 2, nn. 7–10, and pp. 252–58.

[20] See Chap. 1, n. 5. Isidore describes the distinction between *sententia* and *chria* in precisely the same terms as earlier writers and as he himself distinguishes *thesis* from *hypothesis* (2.15): *De Sententia. Sententia est dictum inpersonale, ut* (Ter. *Andr.* 68): *Obsequium amicos, veritas odium parit. Huic si persona fuerit adiecta, chria erit, ita:* "*offendit Achilles Agamemnonem vera dicendo*," "*Metrophanes promeruit gratiam Mithridatis obsequendo.*" *Nam inter chrian et sententiam hoc interest, quod sententia sine*

exploration of this twilight territory in the final and most difficult of these exercises than by virtue of their treatment of fable and narrative that literary theory owes its transmission to the rhetorical tradition.

The fourteenth exercise concerns the proposal of a law (εἰσφορὰ νό-μου). The working out of a legal code had been compared in some detail by Plato to the composition of a poem. Their similarity lay to a great extent in the achievement of an equitable relation between an inflexible statutory system and an inexhaustible variety of human behavior on the one hand and between a finished, and therefore fixed, written composition and a human nature in need of constant redefinition on the other. Aphthonius says

Some have considered the proposal of the law to be an exercise, for it is a more or less complete hypothesis, but it does not meet all the requirements of the hypothesis. For a person is introduced in it, but not one well-known to all; in this respect, it is more than a thesis but less than a hypothesis. In the ways in which it generally brings in the appearance of a person, it goes beyond the thesis; in the same ways, it does not clearly (σαφῆ) present the circumstances and, therefore, falls short of a hypothesis. (p. 283)[21]

The proposal of a law (or the opposition to it) will be worked out under the same topics as a "deliberation on action (πραγματικήν): the lawful, the just, the useful, and the possible." The example which Aphthonius gives might well have figured in a *controversia* similar to the *vir fortis sine manibus* or the *raptor duarum*: "An Opposition to the Law Which Requires that an Adulterer Be Put to Death on the Spot." The objection to the law is basically that all crimes, including adultery, should be examined by a court for the protection of all concerned. As in the preceding exercise of the thesis, "counter-theses" or opinions (*sententiae*) are interspersed which serve to guide the defense of the right to a trial. The counter-theses are either emotional ejaculations ("Nay . . . but over-great are the wrongs of adulterers") or banal opinions about the nature of just retribution ("What will be the difference in executing

---

persona profertur, chria sine persona numquam dicitur. Vnde si sententiae persona adiciatur, fit chria; si detrahatur, fit sententia (Etym. 2.11, ed. W. M. Lindsay [Oxford, 1962]).

[21] See Reichel, pp. 36–37, 107–8, and Quintilian 3.5.8–9. The necessity for the hypothesis to introduce not just a particular person but one who is well known to all is an important characteristic of the *exemplum* in its development from the hypothesis which I have traced in Appendix A—to whose bibliography should be added the citations to V. Branca and S. Battaglia in Chap. 13, n. 12. Exemplary power is gained from the 'historically' recognizable. No statement of this principle is clearer than the one that Dante places in the mouth of Cacciaguida (3.17.136–42). The confinement of the rhetorical hypothesis within the limits of history, however, had often to be relaxed in law as in literature by the use of *personae fictae* in the interests of a greater power of generalization. See Chap. 2, n. 8, Chap. 12, n. 22, and Chap. 14, n. 12.

an adulterer or in handing him over to the judges, if from both he will sustain the same death?'') This exploration *in utramque partem* brings out, as in a dialogue, the qualitative issues of the case.

This middle territory, the *tertium quid* of Quintilian (3.5.8–9), in which a person is posited, and even circumstances implied, though neither are specified as to name, act, or motive—and so fall short of a *legal* hypothesis—corresponds to the *dramatic* hypothesis of fiction. This fictional *argumentum*, awaiting realization in speeches and episodes, contains its shadowy figures—to recall a metaphor used earlier—as if in a photographic negative: the figures seem similar to the people photographed but their features must be brought out by development. Although, psychologically, they resemble the deceptive sensory impressions of Stoic dreams and hallucinations, within the Academic traditions of rhetorical argumentation the verisimilar world of fiction may draw upon the 'legitimacy of the probable.' It may offer, as Quintilian claims for declamation, a *iudiciorum consiliorumque imago* (2.10.12).[22]

The 'psychological' middle ground of the probable lying between the true and the false and the 'judicial' middle ground lying between the general principle or law and the disparate particularity of human actions became increasingly interdependent. Although referring originally to kinds of subject matter, the terms 'thesis' and 'hypothesis' came more and more to refer to kinds of activity—the first signifying the intellectual examination of a question (*inspectio, perspectio*), the second the judgment of particular actions (*iudicatio, actio*). These activities not only suggest two distinct operations of the mind but coincide with the cognitive and iudicative intentions of literature which literary theory is obligated to define and protect. The first activity is the contemplation of any thing or action about which we can pose the 'problem' of how it

---

[22] It is interesting how the medieval arguments over the real existence of universals crossed and recrossed this middle area. John of Salisbury comments that terms which are considered universal cannot be defined by logic or analyzed by grammar too strictly. Relative pronouns themselves which are used to qualify universals grammatically are suspended between the generic and the specific much as an indefinite agent is postulated in the proposal of a law: "In the saying: 'Wise and happy is the man who has recognized goodness, and has faithfully conformed his actions to this,' the relative words 'who' and 'this,' even though they do not designate the specific person [and act], are nevertheless in a way limited, and freed of their indefiniteness, by specification as to how they are to be recognized" (*The Metalogicon of John of Salisbury* 2.20, trans. D. D. McGarry [Berkeley, 1962], pp. 124f.). Such pronouns, as well as more definite figurative expressions like "A tree both bore the cause of our death, and that of our life," do not descend to the particular thing but retain their generic freedom. Cf. Chap. 14, n. 12. It is just when such a statement as "a good man will be one who . . . " becomes a premise in an enthymeme, as Michel observes of Aristotle and Cicero (*Rhétorique*, pp. 205–6), that the thesis enters the rhetorical argument. Compare B. Snell's remarks on the philosophical importance of the Greek definite article in *The Discovery of the Mind*, Chap. 10: "The Origins of Scientific Thought."

came to be as it is; the answer will come with the discovery of principles of order and causation. The second activity is the coordination and application of such principles to those composite realities of particular experience whose significance for the observer can thereby be more completely understood and evaluated. The first activity demands the reservation of judgment necessary to any scientific analysis; the second the qualitative flexibility of any casuistic measurement: verification in either case may draw effectively upon the verisimilar demonstration of Academic probability.

In dealing with ordinary experience, these activities, of course, never exist separately but rather strive for a finer and finer adjustment to one another in a single act of discernment. In human actions the proper relation between them, which could reveal the general principle underlying the particular circumstances completely enough to render them significant, had always been located in the concept of equity. As I tried to show earlier, equity may be determined by examining the qualitative issues in the making and application of laws. Such issues recur through much of the *progymnasmata* as through the *controversiae* and may be clearly illustrated in the seventh exercise of the commonplace (κοινὸς τόπος) against a tyrant. The terms recall the Platonic and Aristotelian discussions of justice as well as the Roman considerations of *aequitas*. The speaker against the tyrant will appeal to the intentions of the founding fathers who tried to devise "norms of conduct from which they worked out one standard of judgment for all" in order to balance "the vagaries of fortune (τύχης) against the uniformity of laws (νόμων)." The tyrant is most likely to alter these laws for his own benefit, and in this case his intentions (γνώμην) can neither be concealed nor excused. Whereas others when on trial for present acts may be absolved, in the interests of equity, on the basis of their former integrity, the tyrant will be condemned for both his present and his past life. When his total character is taken into account, as Aristotle says of both poetry and equity, we will be able to judge him for what he actually is. It is in order to explore the grounds for such a judgment that the narrative forms of literature, in verse and prose, may claim their greatest formal license to invent or reconstruct events. This license to invent, in the rhetorical as well as the poetic sense of *inventio*, is clearly claimed, as we shall now see, in the development of the novella.

13. Capellanus and Boccaccio: From *Questione* to *Novella*

Before turning to Boccaccio, it is useful to look at the *De amore* of Andreas Capellanus. Andreas has taken the subject matter and its principal divisions from Ovid's *Ars amatoria* and *Remedia amoris* and 'disposed' them in a structure of scholastic debate. His structure, however, is as scholastic in Seneca's sense of the *controversiae* and *suasoriae* as the terms of his argument are scholastic in the sense of medieval 'school disputation.' The cases of the earlier rhetorical schools enjoyed a more pronounced immunity from the ethical consequences of the issues debated than the *quaestiones disputatae* or *quodlibetales* of the later theological schools. In this sense, they might correspond more to the conditions under which younger students in the Middle Ages practiced the *praeexercitamina* as John of Salisbury describes them in the curriculum of Bernard of Chartres (*Metal.* 1.24). So long as the Senecan exercises were merely preparatory for the actual encounters of the forum, they could remain in the cool and shaded protection of the declamatory halls and gardens. The young *declamator* might enjoy there the leisure (σχολή) of the *umbrosi loci* (cf. *Controv.* 3.pr.12–15 and 9.pr.1–5) until, as an *orator*, he must face the dust, heat, and noise in the full sun before a real judge instead of an appreciative audience. The part that the *locus amoenus* plays in the discursive activities of the Muses, whether in the *Phaedrus*, the *De oratore*, or the *Decamerone*, is not primarily as a setting for physical comfort as opposed to discomfort but for the contemplative as opposed to the active life.[1]

---

[1] E. T. Donaldson rightly sees Andreas' scholastic argument on both sides of the Ovidian question as diversion for clerical, as well as courtly, ingenuity ("The Myth of Courtly Love," *Ventures: Magazine of the Yale Graduate School* [1965], pp. 16–23). The form of the *De amore*, however, should be placed in the still broader declamatory tradition which had already contributed so much to the medieval literature of *débat* (see H. Walther, *Das Streitgedicht in der lateinischen Literatur des Mittelalters* [Munchen, 1920], esp. pp. 17–27, 126–35, and E. Curtius, pp. 154f. for the continuing influence of the *declamationes* attributed to Quintilian). For the early influence of declamatory presentation upon the literary habits of Augustan society, see my articles MHP and HASD previously cited. Horace's analogy, in distinguishing a presentation before a friendly audience from one

The engagement in a fictional debate, where umbratical *quaestiones* offer their shaded amenities to the excursions of wit, corresponds to an entrance into a walled garden or a dream-vision, or even to the departure on a quest or pilgrimage. All offer a period of artistic immunity before demanding a return to the moral realities of the listener's world. This moral suspension is the most characteristic license of medieval fictions, *its* freedom from historical and philosophical prescriptions as Sidney was later to describe them. The awareness of the necessity to return, however, may linger subtly over the journey, the debate, and the garden—even over the dream—and morally qualify the words and actions of the protagonists for one another and for the reader. In the debate, this qualification extends equally to both sides of the question and beyond them to a total context represented not by the didactic *content* of either one, or of their combination, but by their *form* which expresses the writer's relation with his audience. In such a relation the author need not reject overtly, with satire or irony, one side while didactically emphasizing the other. As will be seen in the following account, Andreas need not 'lecture' his young friend Walter or his readers. All need only to be reminded that the *private* perspective of the artist *qua* artist is distinct from the *communal* perspective of the artist *qua* human being. The first requires a delimitation which gives a temporary sanctuary from initial and final causes; the second a community in which each man sees himself in relation to those causes and to all other men. At most, Andreas must remind Walter of the 'artistic conditions' of their debate by casting his last three paragraphs as an admonition which shares certain characteristics with the ancient palinode. This admonitory convention might best be regarded as the author's public recognition that his immunity, as artist, has expired.[2]

---

before an impersonal and perhaps hostile one (see below), has distant implications for all scholastic debates. For Andreas, I have used the Latin text of E. Trojel as it is reprinted by S. Battaglia (*Trattato d'Amore* [Roma, 1947]) and the translation of J. J. Parry (*The Art of Courtly Love* [New York, 1941]). For dating and biographical information, see P. Rajna, "Tre studi per la storia del Libro di Andrea Cappellano," *Studi di filologia romanza* 5 (1891):193–272.

[2] This view of the moral efficacy of fiction, independent of its preceptorial or allegorical intentions, I have sketched in greater detail in Appendix B. Nearly all subsequent uses of the Stesichorean palinode appear to derive from the *Phaedrus* (Cf. Plato, *Ep.* 3.319E; Philostratus, *Life of Apollonius* 6.11). As a prayer for the withdrawal of what had been granted to a previous prayer imprudently made, the 'palinode' occurs in the second *Alcibiades* (148B). The likelihood of such imprudence is recognized in the Pythagorean prohibition, reported by Diogenes Laertius (8.9), against our ever praying for ourselves on the grounds that we cannot predict what will turn out well for us. A similar difficulty faces the maker of laws (*Theat.* 179A), and with respect to their hymns, poets must be carefully censored lest, in hope of gaining a blessing, they inadvertently, like Midas, ask for a curse (*Laws* 801). St. Augustine introduces his *Retractationes* with an echo of this

In the *Praefatio*, Andreas represents Walter as already in love and as asking both how love can be maintained between lovers and how those who are not loved (*qui non amantur*) in return may cure their own passion.[3] In the following very brief *accessus ad amoris tractatum*, An-

---

ancient legal censorship: "*ut opuscula mea sive in libris sive in epistulis sive in tractatibus cum quadam iudiciaria severitate recenseam et, quod me offendit, velut censorio stilo denotem*" (ed. P. Kröll, *CSEL* 36 [Vindobonae, 1902], p. 7). For uses of παλινῳδία by Christian writers for the "Stesichorean recantation," for "repentance" or simply for "changing one's mind" (*palinodiam canere*), see G. W. H. Lampe's *Patristic Greek Lexicon*. Although there is little chance that much detail of the *Phaedrus* could have been known to Andreas, Plato's dialogue bears a striking resemblance to the *De amore* in theme and structure. Both works concern the arts of love and of discourse. The relation between Socrates and Phaedrus is close to that between Andreas and Walter: Andreas gives in to Walter and writes an *ars amoris* of which he claims to disapprove. Socrates gives in to Phaedrus and rewrites Lysias' praise of the nonlover's superiority in the art of love whose thesis he later reverses in his palinode. Lysias' pragmatic emphasis upon the nonlover's ability to manipulate the beloved expediently reflects the intention behind Andreas' Ovidian *ars amoris*. Socrates' recasting of the speech, though it *purports* to take the same side, functions, in effect, as Ovid's *remedia amoris* in that its undisguised banality clearly exposes the cynical assumptions which Lysias' poor composition had obscured. Similarly, the banality of the antifeminist argument in Andreas' *reprobatio*, some of which is no less secular in its terms than his preceding Ovidian arguments, might equally emphasize for Walter as a young courtier the triviality of the assumption behind such arguments. As Socrates' palinode in praise of the Platonic Eros offers an escape from the secular context in totally new terms, so Andreas' palinodial conclusion urges Walter to accept the broader Christian perspective of divine love. Although for Socrates the contemplative garden of the Muses is turned inside out (since the active life of the 'outside world' is *within* the enclosed city, 227–30), both speakers, having reaffirmed that all *artists* must one day be judged as *men*, lead their young listeners back out of the scholastic *locus amoenus*. Much closer in time to Andreas' relation to Walter is St. Augustine's to his student Licentius in their 'retreat' at Cassiciacum: see Chap. 13, n. 3.

[3] As Andreas finds Walter already in love and agrees to teach him its art so that he may proceed more cautiously in the future (*Praef.*), so St. Augustine finds Licentius so in love with poetry (*fingendis versibus vacavit, quorum amore ita peculsus est*) that he feels responsible to persuade him to give philosophy the larger share of his affection (*Contra acad.* 3.1). The interesting parallel between the two texts lies in the *way* Andreas and St. Augustine go about discouraging their students. They both wish them to learn to practice their respective *artes, amatoria* and *poetica*, with the greatest skill, although neither teacher approves of the arts themselves. Andreas teaches the *plenamque amoris doctrinam*, not so that Walter should become a lover, but that *eius doctrina refectus et mulierum edoctus*, he become better able to resist the temptation (p. 362). Not to have written the treatise would be to have given in to *inertia* (p. 416). St. Augustine, likewise, finding Licentius eagerly composing verses, tells him: *Opto quidem . . . tibi ut istam poeticam quam concupisti, complectaris aliquando: non quod me nimis delectet ista perfectio; sed quod video te tantum exarsisse, ut nisi fastidio evadere ab hoc amore non possis; quod evenire post perfectionem facile solet* (*Answer to Skeptics*, trans. D. J. Kavanagh [New York, 1943], pp. 128, 140). Only through perfecting an art will one either grow weary of it or become impatient with it through being difficult to please. In this context, a teacher may, with complete sincerity, give the best possible instruction in an activity of which he disapproves. With regard to the word *fastidium* it is interesting that the first reason given why Boccaccio's *brigata* should return to Florence is "*acciò che per troppa lunga consuetudine alcuna cosa che in fastidio si convertisse nascer non ne potesse*" (10. *Concl.* 6). Storytelling, as other arts, if continued too long (so, perhaps, as to be no longer a challenge), may become irksome, and to avoid its becoming so, one returns to

dreas lays out the topics to be treated under Walter's first request. These topics constitute the material of Books I and II.i–vi. Book III introduces the topics concerned with Walter's second request. Chapters vii and viii which conclude Book II, however, appear to illustrate the structural components of a *questione d'amore* in digressive isolation from the rest of the treatise. Chapter vii, *de variis iudiciis amoris*, gives twenty-one briefly outlined situations with a single *iudicium* or *sententia* pronounced by one of the court ladies. Chapter viii gives a list of thirty-one rules for lovers (*regulae amantibus*), in accord with which, presumably, such *iudicia* might be arrived at. If taken together, the two chapters provide the exact ingredients of the declamatory *excerpta* from the collections of Seneca and Calpurnius Flaccus. The *regulae* correspond to the *leges*, the circumstantial *quaestio definita* about which a *iudicatio* is sought to the brief statement of the given facts in the *controversia*, and the *sententia* of the judiciary lady to the opinion (*sententia*) by the rhetor. She, too, may organize arguments by division of questions—often philosophical—and cast a certain color upon events.[4]

The *tema*, then, of a *questione d'amore*, as of a declamation, is a 'proposed hypothesis' consisting of a brief outline of events and of one or more general rules or 'laws' in the light of which the given actions may be interpreted. In both cases the events, like those of the dramatic hypothesis, are given without names, speeches, or episodes, and hence are susceptible to various constructions. We start with the relatively

---

the active life of the city. This perhaps is the same *fastidium* that Augustine hopes will return Licentius' attention to philosophy.

[4] It is interesting to see in how many of the 221 stories, whether among the fifteen derived from the *controversiae* or not, this structure is apparent in the *gesta Romanorum* as printed by W. Dick in *Erlanger Beiträge zur englischen Philologie* 7 (Leipzig, 1890), 2:1–273. A law, a proclamation, or a contract is initially given which the subsequent incidents violate in such a way that its application is ambiguous and some equitable adjudication is required. The structure is syllogistic in that the law forms the major premise while the act falling under it forms the minor premise. The brief adaptation of the *raptor duarum* (3) opens with a formula repeated twenty-four times in various stories: such and such a king *regnavit, qui statuit pro lege, quod.* . . . The legal *thesis* once established, the theme is completed by the circumstances to be judged, the *hypothesis*, which are introduced by some variation of *accidit casus, quod.* . . . As Bornecque observes (*Les déclamations*, pp. 84–86), the tales arrive at a 'conclusion' whereas the *controversiae* remain 'undetermined.' In the case of the *raptor duarum*, the judgment in the tale is that offered by Seneca's lenient rhetor who argues that *inter pares sententias mitior vincat* (1.5.3). The rhetorical origins and transmission of this structure in medieval narratives, including that used in the setting up of such questions as those debated in the *De amore* and the *Filocolo*, are revealed in the school illustration of a dispute, transcribed from Cicero (*De inv.* 2.153–54), in a Carolingian treatise. *Nam scripti controversia est ea, quae ex scripta lege nascitur, hoc modo: Lex: qui in adversa tempestate navem reliquerint, omnia amittant, et eorum sint onera et navis qui remanserint in ea.* A narrated incident then follows which is not quite covered by the law and must be adjudicated (*The Rhetoric of Alcuin & Charlemagne* 9, trans. W. S. Howell [Princeton, 1941], p. 76).

'definite question' proposed in the given circumstances and, working 'backward,' we analyze it in order to arrive at that principal thesis (or theses) latent within the events which permits us to evaluate them. The given facts might be these: x chooses to marry a for his rank and wealth rather than b for his intelligence and honesty. The latent theses to be revealed and examined might be: should one marry at all; is intelligence preferable to wealth, honesty to rank; if the answer is yes in each case, will it be correct in all situations without exception? When we have found the proper thesis to argue, as we might find the proper *status* in a *causa*, we may present our answer by moving 'forward' again to the given situation with which we started. The thesis should permit us to relate details, which before seemed disparate, to one another in a coherent whole.[5]

The most important section of Andreas' treatise is that concerned with how to persuade the girl who has been selected—as Ovid describes his second office: *labor est placitam exorare puellam* (*Ars amat.* 37). Love is acquired, Andreas says, principally by three means: beauty, honest behavior (*morum probitate*), and fluency of speech (*copiosa sermonis facundia*). The last he illustrates by eight dialogues, since refined eloquence (*ornatum eloquium*) has often the power to compel the hearts of the unloving to love. In each dialogue a man from the middle, the lesser titled, or the higher titled class tries to persuade a lady from one or the other of these classes to love him. Throughout the speeches rules of love (*regulae, praecepta, leges,* or *normae amoris*) are presupposed and invoked to confirm or refute an opinion wherever they seem applicable. Twelve of the laws are summarized in the fifth dialogue. Though their formulation is not debated (as in Aphthonius' proposal of a law) but given (as in the *controversiae*), the dialogues share an important characteristic of the final progymnasmatic exercise with the declamations. They introduce speakers with some circumstantial delimitation, and so exceed a thesis, but, since these persons remain not only unknown but unnamed and the circumstances barely sketched, the questions fall short of being hypotheses. All the other exercises of the *progymnasmata* might be illustrated to some degree by the dialogues.

As the dialogues proceed, they include more brief hypothetical situations, such as the *iudicia* in II.vii, by which one speaker may elicit or

---

[5] The structure of the *questione d'amore* is foreshadowed in Plutarch's *Amatorius*. The participants retreat from the noisy town of Thespiae to the 'garden' of Mount Helicon, where a series of general questions about love arise from a narrative incident involving a wealthy young widow's pursuit of a handsome but poor adolescent. One such general thesis asserts that "To choose a woman for her wealth rather than for her character or birth would be ignoble and base; but if character and good breeding are added, it would be ridiculous to shun her" (*Moralia* 754A, trans. W. C. Helmbold, LCL [London, 1961]).

clarify either the other's opinion or his own. It is these in relation to the given *regulae*, perhaps, that most reveal the structural origins which the dialogues share with the declamatory exercises of late antiquity. If one allows for the greater sexual violence of the *controversiae*, the issues of their proposed hypotheses often resemble those of the *De amore*.[6] Variations, for instance, on the following situation posed in the eighth dialogue recur in the declamations.

The noble lover of a certain woman set out with the royal expedition, and while he was gone false rumors were spread everywhere that he had died; after the woman had heard them and had carefully inquired into the matter, she observed the customary and reasonable period of mourning which she thought was due to dead lovers; then she took another lover. But after a short space of time had elapsed, the first lover came back and asked to be given the usual embraces; but the second lover forbade her to give them to him, for he said that the second love had been perfected and reciprocated. (pp. 138–39)[7]

Predictable complications arise whose resolution the speaker introduces by invoking the legal language of equity: the solution of the question (*enodatio quaestionis*) hangs more upon the lady's judgment or inclination (*arbitrio vel voluntate*) than on either the understanding of a preceptive rule (*regularis intellectu praecepti*) or on a special mandate

[6] The greater luridness may simply result from the fact that the declamations deal with criminal, rather than social, *quaestiones*. It is, however, very difficult to gauge the attitudes of any earlier age toward matters we may regard as sensational. When Boccaccio, for instance, comments at length upon Dante's reference to "Seneca morale" (1.4.141), he lists as praiseworthy books the most famous of the moral essays, and continues: "Ma sopra tutti fu quello *delle Pistole a Lucillo*, nel quale senza alcun dubbio, ciò che scriver si può a persuadere di virtuosamente vivere, in quel si contiene: e quello ancora che si chiama *le Declamazioni*" (*Il Comento di Giovanni Boccaccio sopra La Commedia* Lez. 16, ed. G. Milanesi, 2 vols. [Firenze, 1863], 1:397f.). Subsequent references will be to this edition and cited in the text. The declamations, along with the *Epistulae morales*, are recommended especially for their moral instruction in contrast to the *Apocolocyntosis Divi Claudii*, which is "molto più poetico che morale." However more delicate we may consider Andreas' courtly refinements than the *mores* of the *controversiae*, he, nevertheless, suggests that force is not out of place with country girls (1.11).

[7] As in Seneca (cf. *Controv.* 2.7) traveling spouses often return home to similar complications in the declamations. Among the shorter exercises attributed to Quintilian occurs the following (no. 347): *Adulterum cum adultera liceat occidere. Uxor peregrinantis mariti mortem rumore cognovit. Heres inventa, nupsit adolescenti cuidam, & domum in dotem dedit. Supervenit maritus nocte: utrumque occidit. Reus est caedis.* Variations upon the "spouse surprised" or the "double seduction" occur again and again, often qualified by having a rich man in competition with a poor man. In fact, the conflict of interests between rich and poor pervades the *controversiae* almost as much as the considerations of social rank dominate the dialogues of the *De amore*. Among those attributed to Quintilian involving distinctions of wealth or sexual questions or both, with occasional travel, see nos. 247, 251, 252, 257, 259, 262, 270, 276, 280, 286, 301, 335, 343, 344, 347, 363, 379, as well as a number assigned to Calpurnius Flaccus (*M. Fabii Quintiliani . . . Declamationes XIX majores et . . . CXLV minores . . . curante Petro Burmanno* [Ludg. Bat., 1720]).

of love (*amoris speciali mandato*, p. 250). Similarly, the verbal wit characteristic of the rhetorical schools and of their student, Ovid, occurs in the enigmatic choice given by the lady to two equally ardent suitors (p. 135).

"Let one of you choose the upper half (*pars superior*) of me, and let the other suitor have the lower half (*pars inferior*)." Without a moment's delay each of them chose his part (*propriam sibi partem*), and each insisted that he had chosen the better part (*potiorem se partem elegisse*), and argued that he was more worthy of her love than the other man was because he had chosen the worthier part (*pro dignioris partis electione*).

In the subsequent debate *in utramque partem*, one lover takes one side (*pars quaestionis*), one the other (*altera pars*), and each thinks he has the *pars dignior* of both the lady and the argument.

The urbanity of Andreas' advice as a whole lies in the 'scholastic' detachment which enables him to debate Ovidian material in the terminology of Christian ethics. He may remain a *scholasticus* in Seneca's sense of a school rhetorician without needing to fear, for the moment at least, any real *iudicatio* from the outside world. He may explore Ovid's three main divisions of the art of love (11. 35–38)—choosing the girl, persuading her, and making their friendship last—with the same security with which he is then able to present 'the other side of the question,' the *reprobatio amoris*, using Ovid's *Remedia amoris* and other antifeminist materials. This hyperbolic repudiation is, equally, a scholastic *tour de force*. Since all must eventually return from the school of debate to the world of action, however, Andreas can, without violating his literary form, point out to Walter that continence will indeed one day be weighed by a balance in the real Court of Heaven.[8]

Andreas brings the Ovidian material, the declamatory argumentation *in utramque partem*, and the temporary scholastic freedom from the exigencies of the practical moral life to bear upon the topical interest in

---

[8] If one allows for the arbitrary inclusion of nearly all valuable activities in his concept of "play" and the exclusion of clearly pejorative uses of the word, Huizinga's general description of the "rules of the game" in Chap. 1 and the materials in Chaps. 6 and 9 are useful for showing how the division of the artistic and prudential faculties manifests itself in various forms of discourse (*Homo Ludens* [Boston, 1967]). C. S. Singleton mentions the applicability of Huizinga's study, which itself refers to the amatory debates as a form of "play" (p. 125), to a definition of courtly love ("Dante: Within Courtly Love and Beyond" in *The Meaning of Courtly Love*, ed. F. X. Newman [Albany, 1968], pp. 47–48). Abbé Norbert De Paepe, "*Amor* und *verus amor* bei Andreas Capellanus. Versuch einer Lösung des *reprobatio*-Problems," *Mélanges offerts à René Crozet* (Poitiers, 1966), pp. 921–27, sees the courtly conversations also as a kind of play (*Spiel*). The impossibility, he feels, of this more refined love's existing in the real world outside of the fictional debates forces Andreas, when the fiction can no longer be sustained, to accept physical love as the only possibility, to judge it, and to reject it in the *reprobatio*.

courtly love. Lest anyone misunderstand his intentions, however, he explains in his final paragraphs why his little book seems to present two different attitudes toward love (*duplicem sententiam propinabat*). In the first part, he says he has given in to Walter's "simple and youthful request" to have the *artem amatoriam* explained. If he reads this part well, it will show (*demonstrabit*) him how to gain all the physical pleasures of love. If he follows its *regulas*, however, he will lose the grace of God and the fellowship of good men. In the second part, therefore, Andreas has written something useful, even though Walter had not requested it. If his student can understand the treatise as a whole and carefully put its advice into practice (*eiusdem doctrinam operis executione complere*), he will not trust in the youth of his body but, always prepared to receive the Bridegroom Himself, will earn God's favor in this life and the next. To understand the work as a whole, however, is to recognize the principles of its literary form. Andreas may enjoy his scholastic immunity and at the same time be perfectly sincere in his palinodial reminder to Walter that the immunity concludes with his conclusion. Given the legal terminology of each, his admonition against indulgence in courtly love, in the face of Divine Justice, shows a witty correspondence to Seneca's warnings against the leisurely subtleties of scholastic display in the face of an actual judge. The exercise of the halls is to the pleading of the forum what the *quaestio amoris* of the royal court is to the *quaestio caritatis* of the Eternal Court.[9]

---

[9] Since Boccaccio (*Comento* Lez. 16) and Petrarch in his many references to the *controversiae* in his *Epistolae familiares* do not distinguish the works of the younger from the elder Seneca, and similarly since such MSS as that of Salutati (cf. B. L. Ullman, *Humanism of Coluccio Salutati*, p. 171), as indeed many complete Renaissance editions, contain work of both men without distinguishing between them, it is difficult to know how widely the father's declamations were known in the earlier Middle Ages. Fifteen of the 'controversial' plots are represented in the *gesta Romanorum*; E. Norden refers to verse paraphrases of the declamations of Seneca and Quintilian (*Die antike Kunstprosa* [Leipzig, 1898], pp. 897–98); B. L. Ullman points out that the declamations attributed to Quintilian, at least, were represented in the *florilegia* which probably originated in northern France in the twelfth century (*CP* 27 [1932]:35–37); to the references to Quintilian in Chap. 13, n. 1 may be added St. Jerome's citation from *Decl.* 13.2 quoted in the *Historia Calamitatum* of Abelard (trans. J. T. Muckle [Toronto, 1954], p. 52). Gilbert de la Porrée refers directly to Seneca's declamations (*PL* 64.1255BC), and John of Salisbury, in his criticism of trivial subtleties of school logicians (*Metal.* 2.8) quotes Seneca's comment on the excessive subtlety of the rhetors (*Controv.* 1.pr.21) and later reminds Becket (*Metal.* 4.prol.) of Seneca's words on the pleasures of reminiscence (*Controv.* 1.pr.1). John also compares the mock battle of military training (*militie imaginarie*) with the early education of a logician (*Metal.* 3.10) in a manner reminiscent of Seneca's contrast of the training in both the gladiatorial and rhetorical schools to the actual combat in the arena and forum. *Digladiari* is an early metaphor for verbal disputes (Cic. *Acad.* 1. frag. 1, LCL, p. 457) and is retained in humanistic criticism of scholastic debate. As in Andreas' second dialogue, the *miles amoris* of Ovid's *amores* is compared to the real soldier with the connotations, similar to Seneca's, of leisure (*otium*) and escape as opposed to trial and responsibility (cf.

The *questioni d'amore* in Book IV of Boccaccio's *Il Filocolo* stand midway between the *iudicia amoris* of Andreas and the *novelle* of the *Decamerone*. With regard to setting, the shaded leisure of scholastic gardens is mentioned only in passing by Andreas in a letter composed in the seventh dialogue to the Countess of Champagne asking for her *iudicium*.[10] After having supported each position with reasonable arguments (*suam partem videretur rationabili sententia roborare*), the speakers submit the matter to their absent arbitrator, and the setting is forgotten. The hero of the *Filocolo*, on the other hand, is specifically asked to join a group making holiday by entering a lovely garden. Since he had been about to continue his search for his beloved, Biancofiore, his entering itself constitutes a minor truancy in that the quest of his 'active life,' his *pellegrinaggio*, is postponed.[11] To order their festivities most satisfactorily, the group decides to spend the hottest hours sitting by a shaded fountain, discussing *questioni d'amore*. Each member of the group proposes (*proporre*) a more or less circumstantial question. Fiammetta, who has been chosen queen, gives her *riposto* (i.e. *responsum, sententia*) concerning the central issue (or issues) which lies latent in the situation and must be brought out before a judgment can be reached. Most of the issues would fall within Aphthonius' general definition of a thesis, "a reasoned examination of any thing under consideration," and, were the legal terminology to be completely expressed, under the *status qualitatis*. As in the *progymnasmata* (or the declamations) a counter-thesis (or *altera pars*) about the question under consideration is directed to the queen by the original proposer of the question. The queen then confirms her initial *guidicio* and gives her reasons in a rebuttal against the alternative interpretation.

Two of the questions in the fourth book of the *Filocolo* (4, 13) are recast as the fifth and fourth tales, respectively, in the last book of the *Decamerone*. The thirteenth *questione*, in which men and women act *senza nome 'e senza paese*, as V. Branca rightly points out, ceases to be

D. W. Robertson Jr., *A Preface to Chaucer* [Princeton, 1969], pp. 408–10). Given the relationship between their patrons, and John's frequent embassies, Andreas might easily have known the *Metalogicon* (1159) with its direct reference to the *primo declamationum* of Seneca, and may even have met John himself. For the manuscript tradition of the elder Seneca, see H.D.L. Vervliet, "Les manuscrits médiévaux de Sénèque le Rhéteur," *L'antiquité classique* 33 (1964):431-41.

[10] The shaded leisure necessary for having disputations about love is clearly described: *Quadam ergo die, dum sub mirae altitudinis et extensae nimis latitudinis umbra pini sederemus et amoris essemus penitus otio mancipati eiusque suavi et acerrimo disputationis conflictu studeremus investigare mandata . . .* (p. 176).

[11] "Io mi sono un povero pellegrino d'amore, il quale vo cercando una mia donna a me con sottile inganno levata da' miei parenti; e questi gentili uomini i quali con meco vedete, per loro cortesia nel mio pellegrinaggio me fanno compagnia" (*Il Filocolo*, ed. S. Battaglia [Bari, 1938], p. 297). Subsequent references will be to this edition and cited in the text.

a *caso astratto*, an *esercitazione oratoria*, in the fourth novella and acquires a *determinazione e concretezza* by implicating its events in recognizable times, places, and personages.[12] This 'determination' of the *casistica amorosa* in a fictional narrative, however, is best understood as an illustration of the literary development which I have been tracing. In the novella, the persons, acts, and motivations (αἰτία), by which Aphthonius distinguishes an hypothesis from a thesis, offer a more complete interpretation of the given question, especially when they reveal what *kind* of an action or person is involved (*quale sit*), than the abstract casuistic treatment of the problem.

More striking is the proposal of the fourth *questione d'amore* of the *Filocolo*, in which Quintilian's observation on the usefulness of fiction for qualitative issues (*fictio valet et ad qualitates*, 5.10.99) finds precise exemplification. Menedon tells the queen that it is now his turn to propose a question but excuses himself for the way in which he must do it.

And now, if I am too lengthy in my presentation, I ask you and those present here to pardon me, for it would be impossible to attempt to give in sufficient detail (*interamente*) what I intend to propose, if a story, which perhaps will not be brief, did not precede it.[13]

[12] Branca, *Boccaccio Medievale* (Firenze, 1964), p. 109. See Chap. 13, n. 4. Branca's study, especially Chap. 4 "Le nuove dimensioni narrative" (originally presented at the University of Padua in 1954), is particularly helpful for the exemplary structure of the *novelle*. See as well, S. Battaglia, "Dall' esempio alla novella" (*Filologia romanza* 7 [1960]:21–84) and "Carattere paradigmatico e qualità realistiche dell' esempio medievale," both included in *Giovanni Boccaccio e la riforma della narrativa* (Napoli, 1969), pp. 1–81. Important for the origins of Boccaccio's questions, several of which are treated also by Andreas, is P. Rajna, "L'episodio della questioni d'amore nel *Filocolo* del Boccaccio" (*Romania* 31 [1902]:28–81). It is interesting how the method of speaking *in utramque partem* is reflected in the names for divisions of poems in some of the source material in the sense of taking turns: *partimen, joc partit, jeu parti, partito, giuochi partiti* (pp. 52f.). Rajna comments on the close relation between the *questioni* and the *novelle*: "nel *Filocolo* questioni d'amore che prendono volentieri aspetto e possono aver anche contenuto di novelle, nel *Decamerón* novelle che possono dar materia a questioni" (p. 34). Questions 10 and 12, for instance, contain narrative possibilities ingenious enough to yield *novelle*. The eighth question, to look back on the preceding stage of development, is identical to those of Capellanus: "quale di due donne deggia più tosto da un giovane essere amata, piacendo egualmente a lui amendue, o quella di loro che è di nobile sangue, e di parenti possente, e copiosa d'avere molto più che il giovane, o l'altra la quale non è nobile né ricca, né di parenti abbondevole quanto il giovane" (p. 343).

[13] "E da ora, s'io nel mio parlare troppo mi distendessi, a voi e appresso agli altri circustanti dimando perdono, però che quello ch'io intendo di proporre interamente dare non si potrebbe a intendere, se a quello una novella, che non fia forse brieve, non precedesse" (p. 311). This general process corresponds to the rhetorical revelation of general truths within the particular circumstances of a case. When to a universal denunciation of vice, Quintilian says, one adds a name, it becomes an accusation. No general truth is so universal, however, that it can fit any case without some link to the specific controversy, lest it appear tacked on. Moral commonplaces must seem to arise from the very nature

The famous analogue to Chaucer's *Franklyn's Tale* follows in which the lady and her husband remain unnamed, the wooer of the lady is called Tarolfo, and the magician, Tebano. The lady promises to give herself to Tarolfo, if he can bring a January garden into bloom as if it were May; Tebano enables him to do this. The lady confesses her indiscreet promise to her husband, which he says she must fulfill in order to preserve her honor. When Tarolfo learns of his generosity, he reciprocates by releasing the lady from her pledge, and Tebano, in turn, refuses to accept the payment he has justly earned from Tarolfo. The question is then asked which man has shown the greatest *liberalitá*. The queen responds "Bellissima è la novella e la dimanda" and proceeds to 'analyze' the question by designating the possession which must be given up by the kind of liberality shown by each person. The husband gives up his honor, the wooer the consummation of his love, the magician his prospective riches. This division once made, it remains to consider *quale di queste tre cose sia piú cara*. Honor is to be cherished, concupiscence to be shunned (*è da fuggire*), and money should be regarded as undesirable, since it often diverts one from the virtuous life. Since honor alone of the three is to be sought, the husband is judged to be most liberal, for he gives up the most valuable possession.[14]

Menedon then offers the counter-thesis that the husband had no alternative but to abide by his wife's pledge, and, where there is no choice, it is impossible to be liberal. He then explores a commonplace on the miseries of poverty, and, on the basis of the detail made possible by the narrative, he is able, through comparison, to illustrate the thesis that Tebano faced the greatest loss and should therefore gain the judgment. The queen responds that she will show (*dimostrare*) where Menedon is in error. A wife, she argues, should be regarded as a limb of her husband's body, and, therefore, the promise of her body could not have been valid in the first place without the consent of her husband. The

---

of the circumstances and persons involved (2.4.22–32). On the other hand, remove those persons and the definite question returns to a general disquisition (*De part. orat.* 106).

[14] The question of what should be sought and avoided, so fundamental to the *questioni d'amore* and to the *novelle*, almost inevitably involves the comparison of what is more (or less) *honestum, aequum*, or *utile* and the means to attain (or avoid) it. *Comparatio*, characteristic of the practical thesis, was regarded in the rhetorical treatises primarily as a complication of the qualitative issue (*De part. orat.* 66; *De orat.* 3.111–17). See Chap. 10, n. 35. Plutarch's 'comparisons,' appended to certain of the *Lives*, based on the actions just narrated, resemble the *iudicia* of the love debates whose questions demand a 'fiction' of detail. D. A. Russell calls them "model answers for a rhetorical exercise: you have heard the two stories, what points of similarity and difference can you see?" He cites Quintilian on encomium and invective and on comparison (2.4.21): " 'Which is the better man and which the worse?' This gives double the amount of material to handle and deals not only with the nature of virtues and vices but with the degree (*modus*) in which they are present. Plutarch's *sunkriseis* are specimens of this kind of work" (*Plutarch*, p. 110).

promise being void, Tarolfo is only giving up an illicit sensual satisfaction, which reason would command him to do anyway (*per ogni ragione siamo tenuti d'abbandonare i vizi e di seguire le virtú*). Regarding Tebano, the queen proceeds to put a *color* upon the motivations for his actions worthy of the best of Seneca's rhetors. She suggests that he imagines suddenly how riches will bring him cares, how Tarolfo will plan to kill him to recover his castles, how his subjects will plot against him, and how thieves will rob him. Unable to rest, he then thinks of the peace he enjoyed when poor and for this reason firmly refuses to accept the payment due him. Given these motives he cannot be called *liberale, ma savio*. The queen in this manner refutes the counter-thesis and confirms her own *giudicio* in favor of the husband.

The important point should now be clear: the novella is necessary to define the question in sufficient detail to permit the qualitative issues to be explored *interamente*. The articulation in hypothetical circumstances reveals the equitable relation between the insufficiently determined incidents of the proposed theme and the ethical principles by which they might be evaluated. As Aristotle said with regard to both equity and poetry, the qualitative question should not be treated in relation to an isolated act confined to fragmentary *quaestiones*, but in relation to what *kinds* of people, as revealed by their lives as a whole, are performing the action. From ingenious debate *about* the question in the *De amore*, the emphasis has shifted to the detailed presentation and definition *of* the question by means of fiction in the *Filocolo*.

When the same *questione* is recast as a novella to illustrate the general topic of actions performed *liberalmente ovvero magnificamente* in the tenth day of the *Decamerone*, significant changes take place.[15] The names Dianora and Gilberto are added for the lady and her husband. The narrative is shortened by omitting the long search for the magician, and the wooer, Ansoldo, appears more clearly as the initiator of the action. Quite reasonably the narrator, Emilia, considers him to be the chief exemplification of *liberalitá* in the story (10.5.26) whereas in the *Filocolo* the husband and the magician had been proposed. The debate which completes the structure of the *questione d'amore* is barely suggested and, then, only at the beginning of the following tale. The novella is introduced by a brief outline of events, the 'proposed hypothesis,' which lies like a *thema* somewhere between a *quaestio indefinita* and a *quaestio definita*. After a few words about the preceding story, the outline is followed by the further 'hypothesization' in episodes and speeches of the novella itself. Except for the inclusion of proper names, the prelim-

---

[15] All references will be to *Decameron*, ed. V. Branca, 2 vols. (Firenze, 1960) and will be cited in the text.

inary *argumentum* closely resembles those of declamation and of Andreas' *iudicia amoris*. There are, however, no separate *leges* or *regulae*
given explicitly as part of the material of the individual tales.

The development of the *novelle* in relation to the types of rhetorical
questions I have been examining suggests a possible process of composition. The author first analyzes the 'given' events of the outline in
order to decide what latent theses (or significance) should be revealed
as principles of moral coherence in the construction of the novella. This
part of the process, of course, takes place in his mind, but it corresponds
to other analytical procedures such as those in the declamatory *divisiones*, the courtly *ragionamenti*, or even the analysis of a geometric
diagram. He then presents his 'determination' of incidents deductively
in a synthesis (the story itself as written out), in which he need not
mention how he arrived at his interpretation of events at all. The fact
that the premises of fiction must be assumed by the reader as 'given'
permits the writer to withhold the inductive procedures by which he
arrives at, and analyzes, his preliminary configuration of incidents. The
elimination of the inductive process, as we have seen in the case of
oratorical composition, then permits him to draw upon the emotional
power of concentrated deductive demonstration.[16]

Boccaccio opens the tale which follows (10.6) by saying it would take
too long to relate *i vari ragionamenti* of the ladies about which character
had shown the greatest *liberalitá*.[17] The king, after allowing some time
for *disputare*, asks that the next narrator, Fiammetta, draw the company
away from the dispute by telling a story (*che novellando traesse lor di
quistione*). She responds that indeed a group such as theirs should speak
so *largamente* that no obscurity (*strettezza della intenzion*) might provide further grounds for debate (*materia di disputare*). *Largamente
ragionare* suggests openness, candor, and copiousness, while *strettezza*
implies restriction, sophistry, and brevity: the open hand of rhetoric as
opposed to the clenched fist of dialectic. That Fiammetta, as her namesake
earlier in the *Filocolo*, quickly consents to bring their pastime back from
disputative questions of philosophical discourse to the 'middle ground'

[16] See Chap. 11, pp. 299–302. As I suggested in Chap. 4, n. 3, fiction is a form of logical
presentation which can avoid the paradox of an infinite regress.

[17] The definition of a question to be discussed *in utramque partem*, which underlies
Boccaccio's story 10.5 and to some degree controls its structure, seems equally to be the
objective of Chaucer's Franklin who concludes his analogous tale by saying: "Lordynges,
this question, thanne, wolde I aske now, / Which was the mooste fre, as thynketh yow?
/ Now telleth me, er that ye ferther wende. / I kan namoore; my tale is at an ende" (*The
Complete Works of Geoffrey Chaucer*, ed. F. N. Robinson [Cambridge, Mass., 1933], p.
174). Robinson cites other instances of rhetorical questions asked at the end of stories or
episodes, but the most pertinent one he cites from the *Canterbury Tales* (1.1347ff.) solicits
no discussion from the pilgrims themselves (pp. 774, 831).

of rhetorical *themata*, so congenial to fictional development, is not surprising. Not only was a debate about degrees of *liberalitá* among the characters an implicit organizational principle within the preceding tale, but the disputative structure had imposed its order explicitly upon the relation between the tales themselves in the first half of the tenth day. The first five stories are clearly told as competitive illustrations of the theme which had been set (10.4.47–48; 10.5.3, 26). The tenth day itself was in danger of subordinating the fictional presentation of questions *interamente* once again to the subtleties of controversial *sententiae* or courtly *iudicia* in an attempt to cover, *in utrasque partes*, each isolated consideration.[18]

[18] On several occasions Boccaccio reasserts the poet's immunity from doctrinal criticism and from the logical severity of disputation by distinguishing the schoolroom from the garden—*both* of which are secure from the practical exigencies of the forum: *Phylosophorum insuper est in ginnasiis disputare; poetarum in solitudinibus canere* (*Gen. deor. gent.* 14.17; cf. 14.4, 14.5, 14.7, 14.11 and Osgood's n. 1, 14.19). Defending the length of the *Decameron*, he says he has written for those at leisure, for "le cose brievi si convengon molto meglio agli studianti, li quali non per passare ma per utilmente adoperare il tempo faticano. . . . E oltre a questo, per ciò che né ad Atene né a Bologna o a Parigi alcuna di voi non va a studiare, più distesamente parlar vi si conviene che a quegli che hanno negli studi gl'ingegni assottigliati" (*Concl.* 21). And so, also, the "strettezza della intenzion," which threatened the tales of the tenth day, "molto più si conviene nelle scuole tra gli studianti che tra noi" (10.6.3). Similarly, although the variety of errors and of (unspecified) works, clearly including doctrinal matters, permits no certainty, the phrasing of the "condemnation of 1277," which includes Andreas' *De amore*, allows for the possibility that certain objections may have been raised primarily because the students' questions were indecorous when debated in the schools where they were out of place: *nonnulli Parisius studentes in artibus proprie facultatis limites excedentes quosdam manifestos et execrabiles errores . . . quasi dubitabiles in scolis tractare et disputare presumunt* (*Chartularium Universitatis Parisiensis*, ed. H. Denifle [Paris, 1899; repr. Bruxelles, 1964], 1:543). The generic context of these distinctions goes back at least to Plato's comparison of the philosopher with the rhetorician (*Theaet.* 172C–75), which is reflected in Boccaccio's comparison of the poet with the lawyer (*Gen. deor. gent.* 14.4). Being free from the timekeeper of the forum, the philosopher may converse in peace at his leisure, pausing and continuing his argument, or leaving it for a new topic or illustration at will, not caring how long or short his discourse is so long as he fully presents the truth (172DE). Plato compares this type of leisure explicitly to that appropriate to telling stories (*Rep.* 376D). As Orlando says, "there's no clock in the forest" (*As You Like It* 3.2.303). The specific context pertains to a distinction between types of philosophical discourse itself once one enjoys the shaded leisure of contemplative activities. Opposed to the specialization of eristic disputation proper to the schools is the liberal philosophical discussion about the general nature of virtues and vices proper to their novelistic illustration in the garden. The more liberal the philosophical intention, the closer to the poet's. An exact parallel, furthermore, exists between *types* of rhetorical discourse. Long speeches on questions of justice and injustice belong to the liberal intentions of deliberative oratory, while disputation among private persons over contracts is broken up into bits of questions and responses (*Soph.* 225AC). The most detailed discussion of these types of rhetorical discourse is in Aristotle's *Rhetoric* (3.12). By Horace's time Aristotle's distinctions have been applied to poetry and underlie his famous analogy of poetry with painting. As in philosophy, the most liberal intention of rhetoric is nearest the poet's. The most liberal terms of both disciplines, regarding technique as well as intention, merge and become almost indistin-

In conclusion, there are several interesting correspondences between the structures of the *controversiae* and of the *Decamerone* as a whole. Except for the first and the ninth day, the storytellers must accommodate their material to the topic assigned the day before—to *la data proposta*. Filomena first suggests that they restrict their stories within certain limits (*ristrignere dentro ad alcun termine*) so that each person might have time to recall beforehand an appropriate tale (1.concl.10). Dioneo, however, wishes to be exempt from this restriction when he has something to tell about which pleases him more; in return, he agrees to speak last on each day. His petition is granted provided he end the day with something diverting, especially if the group happens to be tired of *ragionare*, that is, of discussing *il tema proposto*. Dioneo has, in the language of declamation, reserved the right "to overturn the theme" (*evertere thema*). Similarly, when Emilia is appointed queen of the ninth day, she says, on the afternoon before, that since they had spoken so many days in accord with a fixed 'law' (*sotto certa legge ristretti*), she intended to release everybody from a given subject. As a result, all would return refreshed and submit confidently to the stipulated topic of the final day (*nelle usate leggi ristrignere*).

The daily topics are indefinite with regard to person but delimited with regard to the kinds of circumstances which might be exemplified in the *novelle*. These *leggi* which delimit the selection of materials for the stories correspond to the declamatory *leges* (or courtly *regulae amoris*) which restrict, indirectly, the kinds of incidents to be included in the situations of the *controversiae* (or *questioni d'amore*). The outline, which each tale wears on its forehead (*nella fronte*) to warn the incautious reader (*Concl.* 19), corresponds to the circumstantial incidents, which, together with the *leges*, make up the *thema*, or 'proposed hypothesis' to be debated. The *novelle* themselves, tacitly including, and resolving into one another, the functions of *divisiones*, *sententiae*, and especially *colores*, correspond to the final constructions which the rhetors present to their audience. As the storyteller *largamente* 'determines' his brief *argumentum*, with due regard for his *legge*, by an increasing particularity of qualifying episodes and speeches, so the rhetor, with careful

---

guishable in literary theory. In writing brief moral essays (*genus exercitationum*) Cicero says he transposes materials treated in the schools disputatiously (*in scholis* θετικῶς) to his own rhetorical style of discourse (*ad nostrum hoc oratorium transfero dicendi genus*). If questions such as "What then *is* good?" are discussed too dispassionately (*lentius*), they will be tiresome: they need to be "illuminated (*illustranda*)" by the life and actions of eminent men, for "wordy discussion of them seems to be excessive subtlety" (*Parad. Stoic.* 5, 10). Quintilian, too, often distinguishes the style of the philosophical schools from that of rhetoric, but see esp. 5.14.27–32. These distinctions apply to the views of narrative which Boccaccio expresses here. See Chap. 14, n. 2.

respect for the 'given' laws, works out at leisure his argument from its 'given' premises to its realization in plausible detail.[19]

Nowhere does Boccaccio assert the logical structure of fiction more clearly than in his characterization of 'old wives tales' which exhibit the antithesis of poetic composition (*Gen. deor. gent.* 14.9).

I care little that critics condemn the fourth type of tale, since it seems neither to proceed from a sufficiently consistent beginning (*a nullo satis congruo videatur principio moveri*), nor to be strengthened by any support of art, nor to be conducted to an end required by any principle of order (*in finem ordine deduci debitum*). Such stories have nothing in common with the fictions of poets (*cum fabulis poetarum*), albeit that the detractors of poets think that their fictions differ in no way from those.

This powerful deductive movement of fiction from sufficient premises to probable or necessary conclusions by means of artistic consistency has been transmitted from Platonic and Aristotelian sources to the Middle Ages principally by the rhetorical tradition. This deductive movement became implicated in the qualitative materials of fiction through the early fluctuating functions of thesis in relation to those of hypothesis. The analysis and synthesis of these materials have continued to be formulated in questions with distinct functions which remain visible in the rhetorical exercises but which attain a 'fictional resolution' and 'disappear' in more sophisticated literary works.[20] I have tried to examine these functions while they are still *explicit* in the exercises in order to

---

[19] Analogous to the determination by the *leggi* of what materials, or arguments, were to be included in the *novelle* of a particular day, Quintilian remarks (7.1.14) that even "in scholastic themes . . . the laws are sometimes stated merely with a view to connecting the arguments of the case (*in scholasticis ponuntur ad coniungendam modo actae rei seriem*)." With respect to the leisure shared by the literary artist and the rhetor of the schools in their truant retreat from the active life of the forum, two anecdotes stand out in the long tradition, already fully suggested in Plato (*Phaedrus* 278E), which culminates, for antiquity at least, in the *Dialogus* of Tacitus. In explaining why he fails as a declaimer though he excels in the forum, Cassius Severus comments that he is used to addressing a judge, not an audience seeking entertainment; to responding to an adversary in debate, not to himself; and to avoiding superfluous words as much as those which would prejudice his case (*Controv.* 3.pr.12). In the same spirit Quintilian relates how the poet Accius, when asked why—given his great skill in repartee in his tragedies—he did not become a lawyer, "replied that in his plays the characters said what he himself wanted them to say" (5.13.43). The artistic construction of *colores* could not be made "against the clock." As in the declamations and Lactantius' *Divine Institutes*, the verb *colorare*, meaning a construction (often deceitful) put upon motives or actions, continues to be used by Andreas (1.9) and Boccaccio (*Decam.* 1.3.7; 8.7.10; 9.1.7).

[20] When, for instance, specific *leges* or *regulae* are 'unexpressed,' the 'natural laws,' expressing the universal intentions of justice which the writer shares with his readers, must take their place. Fiction, released from the prescriptions of law or preceptive philosophy as well as from the stipulations of history, operates upon the same principles as equity. See Chap. 10, nn. 36, 39.

show something of their *implicit* activity in fiction and in the structures it shares with other humanistic disciplines. The relation of indefinite to definite questions remains for all such disciplines the pivotal point about which any qualitative issue may freely turn and indicate a principle of coherence among otherwise irreconcilable emotions and seemingly unrelated incidents.

14. Summary and Conclusion of Part Three: The *Commune Vinculum* of Quality

As a concluding summary of Part Three, I shall briefly recapitulate the literary implications of the concept of *qualitas* and the principal steps of its transmission through the rhetorical tradition with illustrations of its permanent importance for fiction from several works of Boccaccio. The function of 'quality' in literature corresponds closely to its function in ethics, rhetoric, law, and Scriptural exegesis. This correspondence may suggest for us the basis for a unified theory of the humanistic disciplines such as Cicero mentions in his defense of the poet Archias (*Pro Archia* 2): "for all the arts which pertain to men as human beings have a certain common bond and, as if by a certain natural kinship, are held in relation to one another (*etenim omnes artes, quae ad humanitatem pertinent, habent quoddam commune vinculum et quasi cognatione quadam inter se continentur*)."

In his *Apologie for Poetrie* Sir Philip Sidney recalled from Plato and Aristotle, Horace and Plutarch, the Church Fathers, and from their mutual beneficiaries, the central principles of Ciceronian humanism upon which to base his defense of literary studies. In demonstrating the capacity of fiction for ethical analysis and persuasion, among his reasons for preferring poetry to history is that the example presented by the historian "onlie informes a coniectured likelihood," whereas the poet may "frame his example to that which is most reasonable." The historian, confined "in his bare *Was*," must often "tell euents whereof he can yeelde no cause: or, if hee doe, it must be poeticall."[1] As mentioned

---

[1] *Elizabethan Critical Essays*, 1:168f. Certain topics discussed by N. W. Fisher and S. Unguru in "Experimental Science and Mathematics in Roger Bacon's Thought" (*Traditio* 27 [1971]:353–78) might be mentioned here. Bacon's attempt to describe quality in quantitative terms (*major vero pars praedicamenti qualitatis continet passiones et proprietates quantitatum*, p. 373, n. 90) is brought back into a balanced relation of quantitative to qualitative measurement congenial to fiction by a strongly qualitative strain in his conception of quantity itself. First, quantity and mathematical demonstration are closely

earlier (Chap. 2, n. 47), we might observe today that history records disparate events, random effects, and its literary structure reflects random progressions. Insofar as the historian 'interprets' these effects and puts them together so that a pattern of possible causation emerges, he is indeed 'constructing,' not 'recording,' but his construction is never *certain*, *final*, or *true*. It must be constantly revised in accordance with new data, new effects: its allegiance is always to the events, never to any given construction of events. Now, fiction is the reverse. Events do not occur at random; they are chosen and causes are presupposed for effects: the relation between cause and effect *is* certain, final, and true.

---

associated with sensory perception (*sed quantitas est maxime sensibilis*, p. 373, n. 89) and with visual exemplification which renders the demonstration apprehensible and persuasive (*exemplum sensibile, et experientiam sensibilem figurando et numerando, ut omnia ad sensum manifestentur: propter quod non potest esse dubitatio in ea*, p. 360, n. 32). Such insistence on visual exemplification offers a counterpart in the physical sciences to St. Thomas' emphasis upon the value of sensory images in Scripture (*S.T.* I I, qu. 1, ar. 9) and to St. Augustine's upon the power of emblematic figures to move the emotions (*Ep.* 55.11.21). All these views reflect the rhetorician's faith in *enargeia* to move an audience. Second, the proper observer does not record isolated phenomena at random but is directed by a prior intuition about which questions will reveal causes for which effects. Bare facts alone, like Sidney's "bare *Was*" which yields "no cause" unless it be "poeticall," will, for Bacon, produce only the bare truth without the cause (*nudam veritatem sine causa*, p. 365, n. 53). So, in law, Cicero says (*Parad. Stoic.* 24), if you simply give the bare facts, their qualitative "reality" necessary for judgment is apt to be lost (*nuda ista si ponas, iudicari qualia sint non facile possunt*). Bacon's psychological emphasis upon persuasive demonstration and upon the observer's seeing individual experiments in the light of his total experience gives the measurement of quantities a qualitative shading. Analogously for law, Quintilian could see the quantitative *status definitivus* ultimately reduced to qualitative considerations (7.4.15–16). The similarity, furthermore, of Bacon's terms to Cicero's distinction between divination and science is striking. Divination is based on random coincidence and, never moving beyond pure conjecture, can never establish causes for effects (*De div.* 1.12–16, 24f., 35, 86, 127; 2.146f.). It is pure empiricism and can only be thought of as an art at all *sub specie aeternitatis*—when enough time shall have elapsed for sufficient recurrence to be observable. Among the three nonlegal types of narrative, *fabula* would correspond to divination, *res gestae* to history. In the humanistic defenses of literature, such as Boccaccio's and Sidney's, it is plausibly presented causation which most distinguishes poetry, in subject matter and structure, from old wives' tales, a phrase which St. Augustine himself had used for ancient divinations (*C.D.* 4.30). Ben Jonson continues this tradition when he remarks to Drummond of Hawthornden that John Owen's epigrams were "bare narrations" and Sir John Harrington's were simply "Narrations and not Epigrames" (*Ben Jonson*, ed. C. H. Herford and P. Simpson [Oxford, 1925–1952], 1:138, 133). Admittedly tangential, the increasing efforts of medieval science to find quantitative methods to measure qualitative experience, nevertheless, will have a bearing on artistic representation. The reader should consult with particular care the detailed studies of Anneliese Maier; see also C. Wilson, *William Heytesbury* (Madison, 1956) and A. C. Crombie, *Robert Grosseteste and the Origins of Experimental Science, 1100–1700* (Oxford, 1953); and for a particularly remarkable expression of the quantification of qualities by graphic means, see *Nicole Oresme and the Medieval Geometry of Qualities and Motions*, trans. M. Clagett (Madison, 1968). For the possible contributions of Oresme to the development of analytic geometry, esp. in Descartes, see J. Klein, *Greek Mathematical Thought*, pp. 300–306 (n. 323).

We do not revise *Hamlet* as we learn more about the psychic phenomena of apparitions.

As a finished construction whose 'demonstration' is deductive, whose formal principle is consistency, and whose qualitative material is articulated by causation in event and by motivation in character, fiction, released from the particularities of history, gains the generalizing freedom of exemplification. In his *Genealogie deorum gentilium* (p. 706) Boccaccio defines a *fabula* as an exemplary or demonstrative discourse under the guise of a fiction whose narrator's intention is revealed once the external covering is removed (*fabula est exemplaris seu demonstrativa sub figmento locutio, cuius amoto cortice, patet intentio fabulantis*). That the nature of Boccaccio's exemplification owes more to the illustrative and hortatory *exemplum* of rhetoric than to the heuristic and eschatological *exemplar* of philosophy and theology is clear from his *Proemio* to the *Decamerone*. He says his *novelle* reveal pleasant or unhappy love affairs (*casi d'amore*) and other happenings subject to chance, in recent as well as in ancient times. These will not only bring *diletto* but *utile consiglio* insofar as his listeners can learn what should be shunned and what should be pursued (*in quanto potranno cognoscere quello che sia da fuggire e che sia similmente da seguitare*). Such understanding cannot occur, however, unless their minds are released simultaneously from care by what is delightful in the stories (*le quali cose senza passamento di noia non credo che possano intervenire*). This relief for the moment of the ladies' *malincolia*, corresponding to the temporary 'scholastic' immunity of the garden from a pestiferous world, is a necessary psychological condition for the beneficial effect of art. If the *novelle* offer a temporary release from the exigencies of the active life, or Andreas' casuistry from that of a real court, it is for the purpose of sharpening the moral sense. The members of the *briggata*, having left a city where *la reverenda autorità delle leggi* (*Intro.* 23) has collapsed, return to it better prepared to deal with the situation after the *licenzia* of the country. So Walter, once he has considered Andreas' two points of view in the leisure of courtly argumentation, may judge more securely between the *regulae amoris* and the *lex caritatis*.[2]

---

[2] The need for relaxation and the value of entertainment, proclaimed by Plato (*Laws* 653C–58A) and Cicero (*De orat.* 2.19–24), is stressed as well by moralists and theologians in the Middle Ages. The terms of their arguments retain something of the ancient defense of the schools of declamation despite the ambivalence of later ancient attitudes toward the rhetor's, or the poet's, retreat from the active life of the forum in Quintilian (10.3. 22–27) and Tacitus (*Dial.* 9, 12–13). Quintilian, for instance, comments that although the schools present but a false semblance of forensic practice (*in falsa rerum imagine*) and that a young man should not remain too long in their shade (*umbra*) lest he later fear real dangers (*vera discrimina*) as he might the full sun (*velut quendam solem*), declamatory exercises may indeed nourish eloquence with a refreshing variety and relief from the

Boccaccio does not confine this formulation of the ethical effects of literature to his *novelle* but extends it to poetry in general. In his *Vita di Dante* (22) he says that poets, once allowances are made for their different subject matter, work in the same way as the writers of Scripture in that they reveal the causes of things, the effects of virtues and vices and what we are to shun and to pursue (*le cagioni delle cose, gli effetti delle virtú e de'vizi, e che fuggire dobbiamo e che seguire*). In a similar way the queen in the *Filocolo* had argued that reason binds us all *d'abbandonare i vizi e di seguire le virtú* in her analysis of the fourth *questione d'amore*. Indeed, again and again the topic *de expetendo fugiendoque*, originating in discussions of moral philosophy and underlying all questions of the *status qualitatis*, of equity, and of *voluntas* as opposed to *scriptum*, provides Boccaccio with his principle of exemplification. The principle is not limited to the Horatian dichotomy between *dulce* and *utile* or to the involution of a hidden *sensus* in an external *figmentum*. It embraces, on the contrary, the entire rhetorical analysis of definite and indefinite *quaestiones* and of practical and speculative *theses*, whose subtlety in the representation of motives, actions, and judgments had been explored at least since Homeric times. When qualitative issues enter any case through *quaestiones indefinitae*, as Quintilian observes, fiction can be most useful. So, reciprocally, a fictional *argumentum* can particularize the general questions and, by giving them a specific significance which can be repeatedly experienced, make them part of the 'history' of the consciousness.[3]

---

contentionum asperitate fatigata. For if one only treats the *cotidiana pugna* of legal actions, his mind will become dull and stiff (10.5.14–18). I have discussed the antithesis between the "shade" of the rhetorical schools and the "sun" of the forum in MHP and have added many comments—including this one—by Quintilian, and others, in HASD. St. Augustine seems to have associated the etymology of the word *academia* itself with the idea of retired seclusion: *sed ab hoc jam litigioso tribunali secedamus in aliquem locum, ubi nobis nulla turba molesta sit; atque utinam in ipsam scholam Platonis, quae nomen ex eo dicitur accepisse, quod a populo sit secreta* (*Contra acad.* 3.9.18). His editor, D. J. Kavanagh, suggests that he regarded the word as "composed of ἕκας = afar off, and δῆμος = the populace," and points out that Suidas thought of the original Greek form as Ἑκαδημία (pp. 255–56). For the value of relaxation, especially as urged by medical writers, see G. Olson, *Literature as Recreation in the Later Middle Ages* (Ithaca, 1982).

[3] All references to the *Vita* are cited from *Vita di Dante e difesa della poesia*, ed. C. Muscetta (Roma, 1963), pp. 33–39. For the relation of the illustrative and hortatory *exemplum* of rhetoric to the heuristic and eschatologial *exemplar* of philosophy and theology, see Chap. 14, n. 12, of this study and Appendix A. In addition to the bibliography there, see the essays of V. Branca and S. Battaglia cited previously. Battaglia particularly stresses the ethical neutrality of the *exemplum* as an illustration for either good or bad actions. He cites Festus' *exemplum est quod sequamur aut vitemus* and Forcellini's definition of an example as something proposed for imitation *tum in bonam, tum in malam partem* (p. 10, n. 1). The Academic treatment *in utramque partem* of the ancient topics of moral philosophy could be easily adapted to exemplary narrative by casting them in the form of what to seek and what to avoid. Aristotle associates the form with deliberative

A. The Death of Paolo and Francesca

The subtlety with which a fictional construct may reveal ethical causes for historical effects may be seen by comparing Dante's treatment of the death of Paolo and Francesca with Boccaccio's account of it in his *Comento sopra la Commedia*. In giving her brief biography, Francesca tells Dante nothing of how she and her lover died beyond the fact that she is still afflicted by the thought of it and that she considers the villainy of its perpetrator to be equal to Cain's. Nor does Dante ask about it. Rather, he is concerned about an entirely different matter: at the time, he asks, when you both were sweetly sighing, at what point and in what way did Love bring it about that you became aware of one another's undeclared desires.

> Ma dimmi: al tempo de' dolci sospiri,
> a che e come concedette amore
> che conosceste i dubbiosi disiri?[4]

Francesca responds with her famous account of their reading the romance of Lancelot in the garden, and of how Paolo kissed her when they read of the kiss that the courtly hero gave to Guinever. Galeotto, the Arthurian go-between, is compared not only to the book itself, in bringing Paolo and Francesca together, but also to the author of their own romance, since they were to live the story from then on.

Boccaccio, assuming the responsibility of an historian in commenting upon the episode, gives the following account of Francesca's biography. She was the daughter of Guido Vecchio da Polenta. This gentleman of Ravenna hoped to confirm a long-awaited peace between himself and the Malatesta family of Rimini by marrying Francesca to Gianni, the

---

rhetoric (1358b22–29), whose principal virtue is prudence through which happiness (εὐδαι-μονίαν) may be attained (1366b20–22). The attainment of happiness governs what things are to be pursued or avoided in oratory (1360b2–14) as it does the selection of actions in the drama, since men are happy with respect to their actions (1450a20). A passage in the *Rhetoric* discussed earlier in relation to equity (Chap. 10, n. 28) shows how the rhetorical tradition might transmit this form of representing ethical choice for literary purposes (1417a16–35). Here (as later in 1418b1–3) Aristotle insists that the orator draw attention to his own prudence and virtue rather than to his skill in argumentation. If an expression revealing prudence seems unprepared for, he should add a reason (αἰτίαν) for it as Sophocles does in *Antigone*. The same thing would hold true for adding motivations through episodes to any dramatic hypothesis (cf. pp. 50–52). Of the endless considerations of what to pursue or avoid, the following is a representative selection: *Tim.* 87B; *Top.* 104b1ff.; *Rhet. ad Her.* 3.4; *De inv.* 2.158–59; *Top.* 84; *De orat.* 2.67; *De off.* 1.153; *Hor. Serm.* 1.1; *Juv. Sat.* 10; *Per. Sat.* 4; *Sen. De tran.* 9, *Ep.* 22, 31, 32, 60, 95; *Inst. orat.* 3.6.56; Diog. Laer. (Epicurus) 10.30, 117, 132; Isidore *Etym.* 2.4.3.

[4] *La Divina Commedia* 1.5.118–20, ed. G. Vandelli (Milano, 1949).

son of Signor Malatesta. Guido was advised, however, that if Francesca, being a headstrong young girl, were ever to get a good look at Gianni before the ceremony, she would flatly refuse to have him. So, in order to avoid any such breakdown in negotiations, Guido agreed to a ruse whereby Gianni's brother Paolo would come, marry Francesca by secret proxy, and bring her back the same day to Rimini. Paolo was *bello*, *piacevole*, and *costumato molto*, and when he came to Ravenna, Francesca, having had him pointed out to her through a peephole as her husband-to-be, placed all her expectation and affection on him. Everything went according to plan, and she was unaware of any deception until she saw Gianni get up beside her on the morning after the day of the marriage. She was not only quite put out at this but, continuing in the love she originally conceived for Paolo, met with him as often as Gianni was off on neighborhood business. It came about, however, that Gianni, having been informed of their affair, returned unexpectedly one day in time to see them enter a room and lock themselves in. When he pounded on the door, Paolo opened a trapdoor in the floor of the room and, about to go down through it, told Francesca to let Gianni in, which she immediately did. In the act of jumping, however, Paolo caught his coat on a nail and stuck halfway down through the opening into the room below. Gianni rushed at him with a dagger, and Francesca, having thrown herself between them, was accidentially stabbed through the chest. Very *turbato*, Gianni pulled the dagger out, and having struck Paolo on the head, killing him, left the lovers both dead and returned to his business affairs. On the following morning the two lovers were buried in the same tomb with many tears.

I have omitted one comment by Boccaccio which occurs after his noting Francesca's rude awakening to find Gianni beside her and her continued desire for Paolo. Boccaccio says "How (*come*) she managed to get together with Paolo, one never hears tell, unless it really was as Dante writes which it is possible for it to have been. But I believe rather that it was a fiction (*fizione*) constructed in accord with what might possibly have happened, for I don't believe the author knew that it happened in this way."[5] Boccaccio's question of 'how,' his *come*, whose historical details have never come to light, is different in kind, not in degree, from Dante's question of 'how' (*come*), which is concerned not with what happened but with an awareness of change in states of feeling. Boccaccio's *come* is historical, external, and quantitative; Dante's is ethical, internal, and qualitative. It is precisely in its ability to define 'quality' that the

---

[5] *Il Comento* Lez. 20: "Col quale come ella poi si giungesse, mai non udii dire, se non quello che l'autore ne scrive, il che possibile è che così fosse. Ma io credo quello essere piuttosto fizione formata sopra quello che era possibile ad essere avvenuto, chè io non credo che l'autore sapesse che cosi fosse" (1:477–79).

fiction of reading Lancelot, and by extension the act of fictionalizing itself, finds its effectiveness. A fiction has a greater power than history to define a state, or 'disposition,' of an individual's emotions and to reveal *how* that disposition is related to an external order—in this case, of the rewards and penalties in the afterlife. It negotiates between the shifting psychological world of accidental qualities and the fixed, statutory world of Divine Law, between that best known to us (ἡμῖν) and that best known in itself (ἁπλῶς). Even if Boccaccio had known the details about *how* Francesca came, historically, to an understanding with Paolo, the details would not have answered Dante's question *a che e come*, which, three years after Boccaccio's *Comento*, Benvenuto da Imola glosses, scholastically, as *ad quid et qualiter*.[6] Fiction 'fills in' the causal relations between historical events which are immutably 'given' by the past to the present but which can never be sufficiently complete to provide their own qualification. Dante's particular *fizione* illustrates this power of connection in the literal sense in that the romance of Lancelot provides the 'qualification' by means of which Paolo and Francesca interpret their own historical circumstances. But in the wider perspective of Dante's reader, their interpretation is itself interpreted more specifically by further qualification gained from moving further from the immediate events to more and more universal considerations. This intellectual process of arriving at greater causal specification by means of greater generalization of enquiry entered, as we have seen, very early into defenses of literature.

Aristotle observes as a general principle that it is through repeated experiences that we become aware of the universal, which is precious (τίμιον) because it reveals the cause (*Post. an.* 88a5–6). It is precisely this general principle which distinguishes the relative importance of history and poetry for Aristotle in the *Poetics*: history "tells what has happened," poetry "the kinds of things that can happen. And in fact that is why the writing of poetry is a more philosophical activity, and one to be taken more seriously, than the writing of history; for poetry tells us rather the universals (τὰ καθόλου), history the particulars. 'Universal' means what kinds of thing a certain kind of person (τῷ ποίῳ τὰ ποῖα) will say or do in accordance with probability or necessity." If, indeed, the universal is precious because it reveals the cause, and if, in tragedy, the universal means what kind of thing a certain kind of person

---

[6] *Comentum super Dantis Aligherij Comoediam*, ed. G. W. Vernon and J. P. Lacaita (Florentiae, 1887), 1:213: "Dicit ergo: *ma dimme a che e come*, idest ad quid et qualiter *amor concedette*, idest permisit tibi, *che conoscessi i dubiosi desiri*, quasi dicat: quomodo potuisti cognoscere quod Paulus amaret te concupiscenter, quod erat dubium propter vinculum affinitatis!" For Cicero, although the treatment of *how* (*quemadmodum*) something came about might enrich the *narratio* (*De orat.* 2.328), it lent its greatest support to the *confirmatio*, especially when one asked about the *modus* of an action, that is *quemadmodum et quo animo factum sit* (*De inv.* 1.41).

will do or say, then the qualities of speech and action of the characters may be seen as revealing causal relations between events. Despite the fact that tragedy is not primarily an imitation of "men as such but of an action" whose end is "a certain action, not a quality (τὸ τέλος πρᾶξίς τίς ἐστιν, οὐ ποιότης)," actions are performed by certain people and these "must necessarily have certain qualities of thought and character (ποιούς τινας εἶναι κατά τε τὸ ἦθος καὶ τὴν διάνοιαν) for it is thanks to these elements that we speak of their actions too as having a certain quality (ποιάς τινας)." The " 'characters' are those indications by virtue of which we say that the persons performing the action have certain moral qualities (ἤθη καθ' ἃ ποιούς τινας), and 'thought' the passages in which by means of speech they try to prove some argument or else state a general view." These famous passages define a relationship between the arrangement of incidents (σύνθεσιν τῶν πραγμάτων) and the combination of character with thought that introduces quality (ποιότης) into events which otherwise would remain ethically unpredicated.

If poetry, then, owes its superiority over history to its illustration of the universal, and the universal indicates "what kinds of thing a certain kind of person will say or do," the efficacy of fiction lies in its ability to qualify the actions which are 'given' in the plot. But, to a great extent, the actions 'given' in the plot to be qualified by the dramatist for his audience correspond to any set of events 'given' by the past to the present. For, in either case, as in any act of comprehension, an *individual* particular must become a *specific* particular in order to be understood: that is, it must gain the elucidating shelter of a *genus*, a type of construction, a *poesis* of the consciousness, by which the mind itself realizes its potentiality.[7]

B. The Spirit and the Letter

Having traveled 'backward' by means of an historical analysis of 'quality' in fiction, we may select from an earlier section of this study a

---

[7] In the medieval considerations of optics, a similar ratiocinative power is accorded to the senses. Alhazen, Witelo, and Roger Bacon distinguish simple perception from apperception, the latter becoming a kind of *argumentum*—a syllogistic process so rapid that we are unaware that it is taking place (cf. De Bruyne, 2:244ff.). In the process from perception to apperception the individual particular becomes specific. St. Thomas, also, accounts for our sensory enjoyment of proportion by granting a rational potentiality to the senses: *sensus ratio quaedam est et omnis virtus cognoscitiva* (*S.T.* 1.1 qu. 5, art. 4, ad. 1). Cf. Sir David Ross as cited earlier: "The passage from particulars to universals . . . is made possible by the fact that perception itself has an element of the universal; we perceive a particular thing, it is true, but what we perceive in it is characters which it shares with other things" (*Aristotle* [London, 1966], p. 55).

premise sufficiently general for our recapitulation and, using it as a beginning, an ἀρχή, we may come 'forward' again in a synthesis of corresponding functions of 'quality' in other humanistic disciplines. The Greek postulate that "excess and deficiency are measurable not only in relative terms but also in respect of attainment of a norm or due measure," is stated by Plato in the *Statesman* (283D–5B) and applied directly by Aristotle to the evaluation of individual choice and action (*E.N.* 2.6). Virtue (ἀρετή) is defined as a settled disposition of the emotions (ἕξις) in which the mind seeks a *qualitative* 'mean' appropriate to the particular situation as distinct from an arithmetically *quantitative* midpoint applicable to *all* situations. Later in the *Nicomachean Ethics* (5.10) he further extends Plato's terms to equity in law, which, like virtue, he calls a settled disposition (ἕξις). This *habitus*, or ethical condition, constitutes an adjustment of a 'quantitatively' inflexible legal statute, handed down from the past, to present 'qualitatively' various moral actions. In contrast to the rigid measuring rod of a statutory code, he compares equity to the leaden ruler of the Lesbian builders, for, as it "can be bent to the shape of the stone, so a special ordinance is made to fit the circumstances of the case." The Lesbian rule, here distinguished from a fixed measure of reward or penalty, rectifies the statute in such a way as to express how "the lawgiver would himself decide if he were present on the occasion."

For the historian who, in Sidney's words, has "in his bare *Was* . . . many times that which wee call fortune to ouer-rule the best wisedome," the past event itself can impose a 'quantitative' inflexibility comparable to the letter of the law, were a judge to enforce it in situations where the statute no longer applied. Poetry brings out the significance of past events as equity brings out the intention (*voluntas*) of the lawmaker. As the concept of 'quality' informed Aristotle's discussion of the universal in the *Poetics*, so his discussion of equity in the *Rhetoric* turns upon the same consideration. It is equitable, he writes, "to pardon human weaknesses, and to look, not to the law but to the legislator; not to the letter (λόγον) of the law but to the intention (διάνοιαν) of the legislator; not to the action itself, but to the moral purpose; not to the part, but to the whole; not to what (ποιός) a man is now, but to what (ποιός) he has been, always or generally." Ποιός, as in the *Poetics*, refers to what *kind* of man we are dealing with, for it is only by asking this qualitative question that we can understand his actions which are presented to us for judgment. The legislator has replaced the dramatist. The judge sits instead of the audience. The 'letter of the law' (λόγος) makes its rigorous demands from the past instead of the 'bare' incidents of the 'given' plot outline (μῦθος). Like the *dianoia* of 'thought' in dramatic speeches which 'qualify' the action of characters, the ghostly will of the lawmaker, his *dianoia* (*voluntas* or *sententia*) may be invoked, in the very words of the *Poetics* (1450b5–12), "to express what is involved in a given situation and is appropriate" in its attempt "to prove that something is so or not so, or express some general view (καθόλου τι)." This close association between legal and poetic terminologies is expressed in Plato's frequent comparisons of the lawmaker with the poet. The making of laws, as of poems, is a *mimesis,* and both imitations suffer, in his eyes, from a static obsolescence once they are written down, because they can no longer keep pace with the shifting phenomena with which they must deal. Aristotle's contribution to the fluidity and precision of definition and predication, in coping with the variable world of sensation, was fundamental to his defense of all intellectual disciplines primarily dependent on the arts of language.

Adumbrated in Plato's works and provided with a terminology and logical context by Aristotle's *Topics* and *Categories,* three central organizing principles begin to inform nearly all inquiry during the Hellenistic period. These principles were stated as three basic questions: (1) *an sit,* does something exist, or did something happen; (2) *quid sit,* if it exists or did happen, what is it; (3) *quale sit,* given its existence and definition, what *kind* of a thing or act is it—that is, *how* did it come to be as it is or to have happened as it did. These questions had the greatest influence upon forensic rhetoric and, adapted to law in the second century B.C. by Hermagoras, offered a method of arriving at the particular point at issue—the *constitutio* or *status* upon which a case was to be argued. The first question, *an sit,* is answered by conjecture about evidence and is called *conjecturalis.* The second question, *quid sit,* is answered by definition and is called *definitivus.* The third question, *quale sit,* is answered by considerations of right or wrong, honor or dishonor, justice or injustice, and of what should be sought or avoided; and it is called *generalis.*

The term *generalis* reflects the major division of all inquiry into indefinite, or general, questions and definite, or particular, questions. The generic considerations latent in every controversy no matter how circumstantial, when brought out by indefinite questions, will always tend to shift the *status* of a case to quality, because, as Quintilian says, qualifications usually involve "a certain intrusion of the abstract." The question of whether Orestes killed his mother leads to a definite issue, a *causa* or *hypothesis,* but the question whether he was justified in killing her will lead to a *thesis.* Such a justification must analyze motives and circumstances in order to reveal in the total situation the most universal considerations of equity. It is such an analysis of causation which had made poetry, for Aristotle, more universal than history. It is not surprising, then, to find Quintilian recommending fictional propositions for the examination of the qualities of an action (*fictio valet et ad qualitates*).

Quintilian associates the three questions of *status* explicitly with the first three of Aristotle's *Categories* (3.6.23). The category of substance (οὐσία) answers the question of whether a thing is, *an sit*. The category of quantity (ποσόν), dealing with magnitude and number, *quam magnum et quam multum sit*, answers the definitive question, *quid sit*, because the definition of the act is made in order to determine *how much* reward or penalty is called for by the statutes. And the category of quality, which Aristotle says is "that in virtue of which men are called such and such," particularly with respect to the choice of a good or bad means to a given end, answers the question about the nature of a thing, *quale sit*. The significance for humanistic studies of the correspondence between the *categories* and the three questions of *status* lies in the persistence of the two measurements, the quantitative and qualitative, as described by Plato. Once we accept the existence of a thing, οὐσία or *an sit*, the mind defines it *both* quantitatively, *quid sit*, and qualitatively, *quale sit*. In law, the *quid sit* corresponds to the 'letter of the statute,' which is 'given' by the past to the present; and the *quale sit* invokes the considerations of equity by which the original intention (*dianoia*) of the lawmaker may be realized in terms of the present. In literature, the *quid sit* corresponds to the particular set of events of his plot, often 'given' by tradition, which the poet may qualify but not violate; and the answer to the question of *quale sit* expresses through episode, characters, and *their* 'thought' (*dianoia*) the present significance of incidents which we have found already outlined in the past. In this sense, the record of history offers a 'quantitative rule' by the very fact that it is given and unalterable; it is the arithmetic 'mean' of events. The equitable *constitutio qualitatis* of poetry and, by extension, of other humanistic studies, on the other hand, offers the leaden rule of the Lesbian builders—the adaptation of the rigid testimony of time to the irregular masonry of immediate experience.

Stated in this way, these considerations apply equally well to Scriptural exegesis. The New Testament, the New Will, receives the 'letter of the law' from the Old Testament, but only by an interpretation of its Spirit, can the Will of the Lawmaker be understood and applied, here and now, to the present. What equity is in Roman testamentary law, charity is in Scriptural testamentary law: in each, the letter, the *scriptum*, must be put aside to reveal the *voluntas* of the writer of the will. It is precisely in this sense that we may say with St. Paul that charity is the *fulfilling* of the law (Rom. 13.10).[8] When relieved of his responsibilities as historian and commentator, Boccaccio grasped this exegetical function of fiction with great astuteness. He compares poems with the prefigurative books of the Old Testament: "For in the absence of historical verification, neither one is concerned with the plausibility of the literal meaning, and what the poet calls fable or fiction our theologians have named figure (*nam, ubi absit hystoria, neuter de possibilitate superficiali curat, et quod poeta fabulam aut fictionem nuncupat, figuram nostri theologi vocavere*)."[9] It was precisely the 'history' of how, of *come*, Paolo got

[8] The influence of Roman legal terminology upon St. Paul's vocabulary and, through his epistles, upon the language of Scriptural exegesis, and, through exegetical interpretation of both sacred and secular texts, upon the transmission of literary theory from antiquity would be a fruitful subject for a separate study. As background: A. N. Sherwin-White, *Roman Society and Roman Law in the New Testament* (Oxford, 1963); D. Daube, *Studies in Biblical Law* (Cambridge, 1947) and *Aspects of Roman Law* (Edinburgh, 1969). Certain correspondences, furthermore, between the four 'rational' *status* and the four 'levels' of exegesis and between the subsidiary 'legal' *status* and the semantic challenges to the exegete are suggestive. For example: one must arrive at a 'position' to 'see' the meaning of the case and of the text; there may be several *status* in a single case as there may be several 'points of observations' for a single text; and in neither the case nor the text need all the *status* nor all the meanings be involved or brought out. In the Middle Ages, the invocation of the author's intention (*intentio, sententia*)—corresponding to the lawmaker's intention (*voluntas, sententia*)—in the face of possible misinterpretation at a later date of the literal meaning of the fiction (*figmentum*)—corresponding to the written law (*scriptum*)—may often refer to a legal analogy instead of an allegorical *involutum*. Juan Ruiz's defense of his work is a case in point: " 'Lo primero, que quiera bien entender a bien juzgar la mi entención por que lo fiz', e la sentencia de lo que y dize, e non al son feo de las palabras; e segund derecho, las palabras sirven a la intención, e non la intención a las palabras" (*Libro de Buen Amor*, ed. R. S. Willis [Princeton, 1972], p. 11). In objecting to lawyers as critics of poetry, Boccaccio points out, as Cicero says of the jurisconsults (*Pro Mur.* 27–29), that they offer only a strict interpretation of the law without understanding its intentions (*sola scriptorum valent memoria non ex ingenio, sed ex literis legum latorum iura reddentes*). They limit themselves to particular trivialities, such as *nunquid ardens femina solvi posset a frigido viro*, taking no note of important—though remote—manifestations of nature (*circa excelsa aut semota nature*). To become totally involved in statutes that vary relative to place and time is to ignore the *stabilis* and *fixa scientia, eternis fundata atque solidata principiis*, of the laws of nature which concern the poet (*Gen. deor. gent.* 14.4). See the notes to this chapter in C. G. Osgood's edition, particularly n. 12, which locate literary terminology firmly in ethics and the most liberal concerns of legal science (*Boccaccio on Poetry* [New York, 1956], pp. 148–53). In a certain sense, the entire philological enterprise behind the *Genealogie* is 'exegetical': a reconstruing of the old Law, the *scriptum* of the pagan past, in terms of the new Law, the *voluntas* of the Christian present. This is possible in literature because fiction, having no one way *per figmentum vera referendi* (Macrob. *Comm.* 1.2.10), can be seen through like a *velamentum* so that the poets may appear as the *eruditos viros* they really were. Having perished from not being understood (*falsa opinione perisse*), they are now *redivivi* and restored as *reipublice insignes*, through whom *ad altiores sensus etiam ingenia legentium excitantur* (15.1). This hermeneutic spirit combines easily with Cicero's expression of literary culture in the *Pro Archia* which concludes Boccaccio's fourteenth book. See Chap. 10, n. 39, Chap. 14, n. 13, and Appendix C.

[9] *Gen. deor. gent.* 14.9. The passage is strikingly similar to Plutarch's didactic observation: "Philosophers, . . . for admonition and instruction, use examples (παραδείγμασι)

together with Francesca that was lacking and that Boccaccio claimed Dante supplied by the *fizione* of the romance of Lancelot. Dante's fiction reveals, as do the interpretive 'prefigurings' in the Old Testament, the qualitative realities of present experience as they might be filled in against a background of the quantitative and unalterable imposition of rewards and penalties by Divine Justice. We as readers, here and now, may see *how* these people came to be where Dante finds them, because their emotional condition, or disposition (ἕξις), their *constitutio qualitatis*, is revealed to us. Without the generic context, the *individual* particular could never become· *specific*.

In his eleventh letter (to Nebridius), St. Augustine applies the three questions of *status* to the modes of existence of the Trinity. The first, *an sit*, concerns the original cause of all existence, and hence refers to the Father; the second, *quid sit*, asserts that existing things are *this* or *that*, and refers to the Son as the Logos; the third, *quale sit*, concerns the power of a thing to remain in its own generic form, and refers to the Holy Spirit. The Son conveys to men a knowledge of the Father as the first principle of the knowledge of all existent things; the Holy Spirit instills in men "a certain inward and ineffable charm and sweetness of remaining in that knowledge (*quaedam interior et ineffabilis suavitas atque dulcedo, in ista cognitione permanendi*)."[10] This ghostly power of 'quality' to preserve the generic nature of a thing is the primary intention, not only of exegesis, but of literature and of all humanistic studies. In the legal and ethical sciences it is done by continual adjustment of fixed measures, such as that of statutory laws, to present circumstances in an effort to bring the *voluntas* of the 'legislator' back to life. According to Quintilian (5.10.98), legal fictions were particularly effective in such appeals to the spirit, as opposed to the letter, of the law. In literary fiction it is done by a continual construction of events in order to bring about, through the memory and the imagination, their completion, their fulfillment, in the consciousness. When, after listening to Virgil *nomar le donne antich e' cavalieri*, Dante says that compassion overcame him so that he was *quasi smarrito*, Boccaccio offers the following explanation:

In these words the author intends to teach us that we should not simply observe the pains of the damned; but by examining and knowing them, and knowing

---

taken from known facts; but the poets accomplish the same result by inventing actions of their own imagination, and by recounting mythical tales" (*Mor.* 20C). Boccaccio twice states that what the syllogism is to philosophy, fiction is to poetry (ibid., 14.9, 14.17). The second passage clearly implies the syllogistic coherence of the poet's invention.

[10] *Letters of St. Augustine*, trans. J. G. Cunningham, *A Select Library of the Nicene and Post-Nicene Fathers of the Christian Church*, ed. P. Schaff (New York, 1892), 2:230; Latin is cited from *PL* 33.77.

we are worthy of the same punishment for our sins, we should have compassion
not for them, who are punished by Divine Justice, but for ourselves. . . . [And
to emphasize this] the author has the habit of showing that he feels passion,
sometimes more, sometimes less, in each location: as if, there, some sin were
being punished in which he recognized himself as the sinner.[11]

The fiction, and Dante's fictional reaction to it, throws a generic illumination upon the most specific of all particularities, the individual
consciousness. Dante's response is an 'affection,' whose 'cause' is presented to us in the 'quality-giving' fiction. Through it we understand
that the *kind* of thing which *was* true, *individually*, in the past for others
is true, *specifically*, in the present for ourselves. That *genus* is logically
prior to *species*, as cause is to effect, is the paradox of all fiction: it is
only through additional generic qualifications that we may proceed to
greater and greater specification.[12]

---

[11] *Il Comento* Lez. 19: "In queste parole intende l'autore d'ammaestratci, che noi non
dobbiamo con la meditazione semplicemente visitar le pene de' damnati; ma visitandole
e conoscendole, e conoscendo noi di quelle medesime per le nostre colpe esser degni, non
di loro, che dalla giustizia son puniti, ma di noi medesimi dobbiamo aver pietà, . . . E usa
l'autore di monstrare di sentire alcuna passione, quando maggiore, e quando minore in
ciascun luogo: e quasi dove alcun peccato si punisce del quale esso conosca se medesimo
peccatore" (I: 474). Such emotional effects Plato had recognized and distrusted in mimetic
representation, for few "are capable of reflecting that to enter into another's feelings must
have an effect on our own: the emotions of pity our sympathy has strengthened will not
be easy to restrain when we are suffering ourselves" (*Rep.* 606B, trans. F. M. Cornford).
Diogenes Laertius comments (3.80) that Plato often intermingles myths "with his works
in order to deter men from wickedness, by reminding them how little they know of what
awaits them after death (*Lives of Eminent Philosophers*, trans. R. D. Hicks, LCL, 2 vols.
[London, 1925]). See Chap. 2, n. 51. Quintilian sees the power to enlist the feelings of
a judge as the *spiritus* and *animus* of oratory (6.2.5–7). He describes the force of visual
images to arouse the emotions in a passage (6.2.24–36) which forms the basis and source
of Hamlet's reflections on his being moved as "in a fiction, in a dream of passion" by the
players. This power to move the listener by vividly describing or presenting either one's
own emotions or those of others is a rhetorical commonplace of which Dante, as indeed
Boccaccio (cf. *Decam.* 5.8), takes full advantage. Walter Map, in a passage rarely cited by
literary historians, brings out the ethical psychology underlying the medieval justification
of secular narrative. He distinguishes, furthermore, the emotions of this world, under the
power of the artist, from those of the next. To turn from the first to the second constitutes
a kind of palinode. "For history, which is based on truth, and fable, which weaveth a
tissue of fancy, both bless the good with a happy end so that virtue may be loved, and
damn the bad with a foul ending, wishing to render wickedness hateful. In narratives
adversity succeedeth in turn to prosperity and *vice versa*, with frequent change of fortune,
in order that, both being always kept before our eyes, no forgetfulness of either may arise
on account of the other, but that each may be kept in due bounds by proper infusion of
its opposite. Thus exaltation or destruction will never pass the mean; that is to say, by
the contemplation of things to come, meditation will neither be empty of hope nor free
from fear—I mean, of temporal things to come, because that 'perfect charity' which is
heavenly 'casteth out fear.' " *De Nugis Curialium* 1.31, trans. F. Tupper and M. B. Ogle
(London, 1924), pp. 78–79.
[12] On this paradox see Chap. 3. A chapter of John of Salisbury's *Metalogicon* on the
nature of universals (2.20) bears equally upon the rhetorical distinctions in relation to

In view of these considerations, Boccaccio's demonstration that poetry may be regarded as a form of theology in his *Vita di Dante* (21–22) may be seen as more closely related to the rhetorical, than to the Neoplatonic, tradition. As if against the detractors who could not distinguish poetry

---

fictions. Aristotelian universals, expressed in such concepts as "genericness" (*genus*) and "specificness" (*species*), are for John simply *notiones* (ἐννοίας) or *phantasiae* (εἰκονό-φανας), *imagines*, and *umbrae* of things which actually exist. Take away the existent particular objects and such *monstra* will vanish like dreams or like the images of the objects reflected in the pure mirror of the mind (*tanquam in speculo, native puritatis ipsius anime*). John calls these mental forms *exemplaria* and the real objects of which they are the images (*imagines*) *exempla*. Herein lies the early association of *exemplar* with the *imago*, giving the image the value of universality, and the *exemplum* with the rhetorical illustration, giving the example the value of particular demonstration. These associations foreshadow Sidney's attribution of universality to the poetic image and an illustrative validity to the historical example. That both the generic significance and the exemplification (*significatio* and *illustratio*) come, in general practice, to be expressed in the single term *exemplum* shows the increasing imposition of rhetoric and history upon poetic theory for their didactic value. John points out, however, that *universalia*, though without existence in themselves, may be considered "substantial" (*substantialia*), that is, necessary prerequisites and hence "causes," with respect to our *knowledge* of particular things (*ad causam cognitionis*). Things may be prior to concepts (i.e. mental representations of them) *existentially* but concepts are prior to things *cognitively*. Starting with given things or deeds, we proceed *inductively* from individuals to species to genera and, then, "confirm" our knowledge by returning *deductively* (with genus and species now functioning as prior conditions, or causes, of individuals) to the initial things and deeds, which may now be regarded as "interpreted." As in the qualitative *status* of a legal case, John maintains that generic terms denote not "what" but "what kind of what" (*quale quid*) a thing or act is. Such denotation is perforce general, and John, as an Academic, will not demand the degree of accuracy expected of exact sciences which leads others into contentious debate. In his Creation God distinguished things by the general categories of number, weight, and measure (*Sap.* 11.21). *Numerus* differentiates things, *pondus* gives them generic value (*ad generis dignitatem*), and *mensura* provides quantitative delimitation. Quoting St. Augustine (*De gen. ad lit.* 4.3–5), who describes weight as *omnem rem ad stabilitatem trahens*, John associates *pondus* with the qualitative *status*, which Augustine himself placed under the protection of the Holy Spirit. (The identification of *pondus* with love is metaphorically stated in the *City of God* [11.28] and in the *Confessions* [13.9]—and developed by Dante [3.1.136–41]—and of *pondus* with *voluntas* as a unifying power negotiating between sensory images in the mind and the magnitudes memory assigns them [*De trin.* 11.10–11].) Universals, on the other hand, are *figuralia: genera et species non omnino quid sunt sed quale quid quodammodo concipiuntur: et quasi quedam sunt figmenta rationis seipsam in rerum inquisitione et doctrina subtilius exercentis*. Fictions, now in the guise of universals, are accorded validity, once again, in the investigation of quality. Civil law, in turn, will have, John says, its own kind of fictions (*ius ciuile sua figmenta nouit*), as indeed will all branches of learning (cf. Chap. 2, n. 8, Chap. 12, n. 21, and Appendix A, n. 10). The conclusion is that *genera* and *species*, which are exemplars of particular things (*exemplaria singulorum*), as instruments of learning, may be regarded as a *monstruosa . . . figmentorum speculatio* which may dispense with the consideration of individual things (*usque ad uentilationem singularium*). It is only through the abstracting power of fictions, John suggests, that one may free oneself from the unique properties of a particular substance. This freedom of the 'universal' is similar to that of poetry from the particularities of history and that of rhetoric from the particular circumstances of a legal controversy. *Joannis Saresberiensis Episcopi Carnotensis Metalogicon*, ed. C.C.I. Webb (Oxonii, 1929), pp. 99–113.

from 'old wives' tales,' he directs his argument against those who regard it as only *un fabuloso parlare*. To these he says that if we examine the matter *con ragione*, we can see that the ancient poets imitate the footprints of the Holy Spirit (*le vestigie dello Spirito santo*). As Scripture expresses *sotto velame* the deepest secrets which in due time will be openly demonstrated in fact (*a debito tempo per opera, senza alcuno velo, intendeva di dimostrare*), so the poets *sotto coperta d'alcune fizioni* treat what is past, what might be present in their time, or what they presume or desire might happen in the future. Though the ends of the two 'scriptures' are different, their method of presentation (*modo del trattare*) is the same. What St. Gregory says of Sacred Scripture is true as well of the writings of the poets: in each, in a single narrative discourse are revealed the text and the mystery which lies beneath it (*in un medesimo sermone, narrando, apre il testo e il misterio a quel sottoposto*). As the poets reveal in their inventions the causes of things, the effects of virtue and vice, and what we ought to avoid and to pursue, so the Holy Spirit sets forth, either under the figure of some history (*configura d'alcuna istoria*) or by the *senso* of a vision or in the *intendimento* of a lamentation or by some other means, how the acts of Christ's life may indicate to us the way to our own salvation. As the proper fiction of a poet, as distinct from that of a prattler, must be worked out to a conclusion required by logic (*in finem ordine deduci debitum*), so the hidden prefigurations recorded by the Holy Spirit will, at the required time (*a debito tempo*), be realized according to the equitable logic of *caritas* in 'works.' Both the fictions of poetry and prefigurations of Scripture give final answers to the *quaestio qualitatis*, and we may think of that question, perhaps, as the *commune vinculum* which Cicero says binds all the liberal arts together.[13]

We must emphasize, in conclusion, that the reason for St. Augustine's

---

[13] The importance of the relation between Scripture and secular poetry for the Humanists generally may be seen in C. Trinkaus, *In Our Image and Likeness* (London, 1970), pp. 555–774, esp. in his treatment of *theologica poetica* (pp. 683–721). See also E. Curtius, *op. cit.*, pp. 214–27, and C. S. Singleton, *Dante Studies* I (Cambridge, Mass., 1954), pp. 84–98. The technical analogies between Scriptural allegory and secular exemplification are satisfactorily brought out by De Bruyne, 2:302–70. When Boccaccio movingly laments that the difficulties of composing the *Genealogie* will be *non aliter quam si per vastum litus ingentis naufragii fragmenta colligerem* (1.pr.), he says that it is only by revealing the hidden significance of these disparate tales that a principle of order will emerge by which to arrange them (*porro, princeps eximie, uti componendo membra deveniam, sic sensus absconditos sub duro cortice enucleando procedam*). Functioning as a thesis, such an interpretation will reveal not only the *voluntas* of the ancient authors but offers a principle of formal coherence long obscured beneath the misunderstood *litterae*. So in the human community, beyond the private world of humanistic letters, the equity of natural law will supply the mortar for the fragmentary laws of society. See Chap. 10, n. 39, Chap. 14, n. 8, and Appendix C.

comparison of the three Greek questions of *status* to the three manifestations of the Trinity is to illustrate the fact that no one of them can
exist except as an aspect of the other two. Plato and Aristotle would
have agreed. The empirical quantitative measure of the *historiae na-
turalium* and the evaluative qualitative measure of the *studia humanitatis* exist only in terms of each other and by virtue of there being
something there to measure in the first place. We begin, always, with
the *an sit*. The humanistic disciplines must not remain, however, to
return to Sidney's phrase, with the "coniectured likelihood" of the *individual* example of history. They must proceed through the *status
conjecturalis* and *definitivus* to the *status generalis*, that is, to the *specific*
example of poetry, for the historian "is so tyed, not to what shoulde
bee but to what is, to the particuler truth of things and not to the general
reason of things, that hys example draweth no necessary consequence"
(p. 164). Quintilian, similarly, observed of oratory that since the *status
conjecturalis* must often find "proofs from without and uses arguments
drawn from the actual subject matter," the demonstration of *qualitas*,
subsuming as well the *status definitivus* (7.4.15–24), remains the kingdom, the power, and the glory of eloquence (*hic regnat, hic imperat,
hic sola vincit*). So also for Sidney, the poet, epitomizing the ideals of
the humanistic disciplines in the power and freedom of fiction, "dooth
not learne a conceite out of a matter, but maketh matter for a conceite"
(p. 180). If the sciences learn their knowledge out of a matter, the
humanities understand a matter in terms of a conception of its continuing
human significance. If the scientist lays greater claim to a knowledge of
the Son, the humanist preserves the *suavitas* of the Holy Spirit.

Synopsis

I HAVE CONCLUDED each of the three preceding Parts with a separate chapter recapitulating the central topics developed in it (Chapters 4, 9, 14). The reader who wishes a summary of the materials and arguments of this study as a whole, therefore, may best review these chapters in the order of their appearance. Here I want to relate the intellectual distinctions, which have provided the principal terms of analysis in the individual Parts, briefly to one another.

Part One describes the formal, cognitive, and judicative intentions (or 'offices') of literary discourse and relates these intentions to their corresponding (1) faculties (productive, speculative, prudential), (2) kinds of discipline (mathematical, philosophical, rhetorical), and (3) contributions to the Good (beauty, truth, justice), as these correspondences are outlined in the Preface. Part One deals primarily with the formal intention of mathematics which performs two functions. It permits an 'assumption of existence,' which the fictional premises of literature share with the *archai* of geometrical demonstration, and, at the same time, provides the principles of order by means of which all such demonstration attains external proportion and internal coherence. The first function is ontological and establishes the conditions necessary for production; the second is logical and accounts for the utility and/or beauty of the product. Through these functions, the mathematical intention, as a common denominator, permits the originally antithetical objectives of philosophy and rhetoric to combine with one another in the analysis of a hypothetical situation and, thereby, brings the three principal intentions of literary discourse into balance. Just how the coordinating principle of mathematics actually combines (by combining with) the objectives of philosophy and rhetoric and gives literary expression to these objectives by extending its formal structure to fiction appears most clearly in the interrelated functions of 'thesis' and 'hypothesis' in these disciplines. When these functions cooperate most closely with each other, the procedures of analysis and synthesis in philosophy and rhetoric achieve their least specialized forms and, thereby, approach one another. The more similar these procedures become, the more the 'liberal' activities of their respective disciplines contribute to the literary analysis of experience.

Part Two deals with the cognitive intention of a work of literature. Before one can evaluate and represent his experience, he must understand it, and the nature of this knowledge will depend upon the nature of the experience to be understood. The kind and degree of cognitive accuracy permitted by the nature of this experience will, in turn, determine how a knowledge of it may be appropriately represented. With respect to the cognitive obligations of literary theory, therefore, the relation between the knowledge appropriate to the subject and the representation appropriate to our knowledge of it will, to a large extent, determine the conditions of stylistic decorum.

As stated earlier, the term 'decorum' refers to the criteria to be observed in judging those things in our experience whose excellence lends itself more appropriately to qualitative than to quantitative measure. Like all other things, those falling under qualitative measurement may be more accurately known either with respect to their own nature (ἁπλῶς) or with respect to our perceptions, that is, 'to us' (ἡμῖν). A knowledge of things more intelligible in themselves will appear to derive from our intellective intuition as a first principle, a knowledge of things more intelligible to us from our perceptual intuition as a first principle. In reality, however, all knowledge is derived, not from one kind of intelligibility in isolation from the other, but from a negotiation between the two. In this reciprocation we experience the highest degree of consciousness, and it is the knowledge derived from this experience which literature and the visual arts strive to represent.

The finest 'point' of cognitive adjustment negotiated between intellective and perceptual intuition corresponds not only to the adjustment between the disciplines themselves which contribute their energies to literary discourse, but to the kinds of adjustment to be negotiated between the functions of their respective forms of thesis and hypothesis as I have described them in Part One. In rhetoric the thesis, as a prior and more generic principle, is remote from the senses, and hence more intelligible in itself; the hypothesis, consisting of immediately apprehensible circumstances, is more easily grasped by our perceptions. In philosophy, on the other hand, the thesis to be demonstrated or problem to be resolved or object to be explained is presented 'to us' as a whole to be analyzed into its underlying hypotheses—its elements, principles, or causes—which are remote from our senses and must ultimately be grasped 'in themselves.' But, in both rhetoric and philosophy, analysis and synthesis—and their instruments, thesis and hypothesis—must negotiate reciprocally if they are to bring the content of the consciousness to light.

The problem of this negotiation, with regard to knowledge, recurs, with regard to representation, in the guise of two distinct kinds of comparison. One type of likeness is between two things which are essentially different in kind and thus cannot be based on qualities held in common; the other is between two things of the same kind and rests, therefore, on a common denominator of shared characteristics. The first type is nonreciprocal and tends to be stated in terms of identity: a man may become more (or less) like God, but God cannot become more like man. The second type is reciprocal and is stated in terms of kinds and degrees of similarity: two portraits of the same person may resemble each other to the degree and in the ways that each resembles the model.

The nonreciprocal likeness is characteristic of symbolic representation. The external form of the symbol, which we grasp perceptually (ἡμῖν), need not express anything about the character of what it signifies, which must, then, be known primarily with respect to its own nature (ἁπλῶς) by some other means. The greater the discrepancy, in fact, between its form and its signification, the more excellent the symbolic representation might appear to be. The symbol, therefore, will keep the kinds of things characterized by the two types of intelligibility separate, and in isolating them from one another, is in danger of hypostatizing each, in turn, as a separate object of knowledge. In such separateness all negotiation between the two poles is lost, and the mind is left to grasp the one empirically in sensation as 'factual truth' and the other in visionary conjecture as 'doctrinal truth.' The reciprocal likeness, on the other hand, is characteristic of mimetic representation. The external form will not simply stand in place of, but will try to describe the nature of, what it represents. What is more known to our perceptions remains in negotiation with what is more known in itself. The more verisimilar the representation of properly selected details, the more accurately and completely they may express the meaning of the work of art.

While identity and equality, which characteristically express quantities, furthermore, are relations associated with symbolic representation, similarity, associated with mimetic likenesses, reveals and describes qualities. Similarity between qualities forms the basis not only of comparative analogies such as metaphor and simile, but of all verbal, as opposed to arithmetical, discourse. While the symbol may claim the certainty of an exact equivalence, of an arbitrarily asserted identity, between its external form and what it signifies, it expresses no relation between them. The image, on the other hand, expresses a relation between them but only on the probable grounds of verisimilarity. When a philosophical system, such as Neoplatonism, contributes to this opposition between quantitative precision, formal or cognitive, and the qualitative nature of experience subject to literary analysis and of language itself, its influence becomes conservative. Mathematical form, expressed efficiently in symbols, becomes the exclusive model for all artistic form—even for arts like literature whose structure is essentially discursive rather than symbolic. In such conservatism similarity yields to identity, probability to certainty: as the word vanishes in the number, so the image in the symbol. With respect to both knowledge and representation, it was the rhetorical transmission of literary theory which did most to restore the judicative analysis of 'quality' to its proper place in the readjusting balance of decorum.

While Parts One and Two deal with the formal and cognitive intentions of literature respectively, Part Three describes the judicative intention by examining both the materials and the argumentative methods of rhetoric. While the object of philosophy is the understanding of what is *true* or *false* about a thing, the object of rhetoric is the persuasive interpretation of given circumstances for the purpose of judging a particular action to be *right* or *wrong*. 'Truth' is involved, not for itself, but for its power to elicit *fides*—a 'trust' sufficiently strong to cause a jury to 'act' upon its verdict. Since one should not 'judge' something before 'understanding' it, a discussion of the judicative may reasonably follow that of the cognitive obligations of literary discourse.

The relation of rhetoric to the balanced intentions of literature itself as described in Part One appears most dramatically in the three governing questions of *status* which mirrors them. The first, or existential, question, "Did something happen?" (*an sit* = was someone killed?), provides the 'assumption of existence,' which will, like the *archai* of any inquiry, contain and hence initiate certain formal conditions of procedure. The second, or definitive, question, "Granted something did happen, what was it?" (*quid sit* = granted someone was killed, was it an accident or murder?), corresponds to the cognitive intention of literary discourse, since it includes the general definition of the act in accordance with a knowledge of the circumstances. The third, or qualitative, question, "Granted both that something happened and that it was such and such a thing, what 'kind' of such and such a thing was it?" (*quale sit* = granted that it was murder, what 'degree' of murder was it?), corresponds to the judicative intention of a literary work. To persuade a jury to accept and 'act upon' the verdict proposed, the orator must bring to light all prejudicial or extenuating circumstances of his case, as a dramatist might bring out the motivations of his characters through speeches and episodes.

It is the reciprocation between the definitive and qualitative *status*, however, that establishes equity, and it is the obligation of equity that most reveals the close relation of law to *poesis*. Equity depends upon the application of a fixed statute—whose *amounts* of penalty or reward for given acts are 'quantitatively defined'—to the infinitely variable circumstances of individual cases. Since the statute remains 'unqualified' by the circumstances as they might become apprehensible 'to us' (ἡμῖν), it can only measure individual situations 'absolutely (ἁπλῶς).' Equity offers a correction of this inflexibility in the form of a negotiation, comparable to that between the two types of intelligibility, between discrete instances and a general principle by which to understand and judge them. As literature requires the integration of formal, cognitive, and judicative principles of order to achieve this negotiation, law requires that all three questions of *status* bear upon one another—like, as St. Augustine suggests, the three separate manifestations of the Trinity. The 'existential' *status* (*an sit*) corresponds to the Father, whose frequent representation as a geometer combines his ontological and formal principles; the 'definitive' *status* (*quid sit*) corresponds to the Son as the Logos through which we have knowledge of the Father; and the 'qualitative' *status* (*quale sit*) corresponds to the Holy Spirit which joins them together and maintains them in unity. In this way the members of the Trinity—like the Muses of mathematical, philosophical, and rhetorical discourse respectively—may be said to act as if they were 'of one mind.'

In the transmission of literary theory resistance against imbalance among the three principal objectives of literature has been threatened in the two ways defined most fully in Part Two. These ways both result from the hypostatization, as an object of knowledge, of either those things better known with respect to our perceptions or those things better known in themselves. If either is taken separately, it becomes an abstraction, and the knowledge of reality, which must be achieved through a negotiation between the two, becomes fragmented. Such a separation bears an analogy to that between the ancient antithetical intentions of rhetorical and philosophical discourse. Insofar as the object hypostatized is better known with respect to ourselves it resembles the material, or hypothesis, of rhetoric—the circumstances immediately presented to our senses to be interpreted. Insofar as the object hypostatized is better known with respect to itself it resembles the first principles, elements, or causes—the hypotheses of philosophy—to be discovered in order to resolve a problem or demonstrate a thesis. As our knowledge is derived from a negotiation between our experience of things known ἡμῖν and that of things known ἁπλῶς, so the rhetorician must seek a similar negotiation between the given incidents of his particular case and those ethical and legal principles of order which enable him to judge it and to present that judgment persuasively. The less reciprocation there is between the intentions of rhetoric and philosophy, the more literary discourse, in assimilating their functions, will inherit that form of conservatism peculiar to whichever intention the writer emphasizes at the expense of the other.

When literary theory overemphasizes its rhetorical intention, literature is apt to become too concerned with the isolated representation of things better known to our perceptions: that is, with historical 'truth.' In striving to give an accurate factual account, a literary fiction may become inappropriately committed to verisimilarly exact representation. The character on the stage, that is, should resemble his counterpart in actual life as much as possible. This verisimilitude, so characteristically the object of neoclassical rules, leads, at its most conservative, to a 'mimetic' formalism of uniformity: a 'quantitatively' measureable proportion of similarity (*simile*) to truth (*verum*) in the rhetorical quest for persuasive probability (*verisimile*).

Contrariwise, when literary theory overemphasizes its philosophical intention, literature is in danger of becoming too concerned with the isolated representation of things better known with respect to their own nature: that is, with some form of doctrinal 'truth.' To escape from historical change or the distortion of individual interpretation, such truths may seek shelter in symbols. Their symbolic expression, however, can assert little more than a principle of unity, simplicity, or purity, so dear to eighteenth- and nineteenth-century 'aestheticism,' and leads, at its most conservative, to a 'symbolic' formalism of uniqueness: a 'quantitatively' stipulated identity.

Whether an imbalance in literary theory be in favor of rhetoric or philosophy, therefore, their respective mimetic and symbolic procedures of representation will both contribute to literary formalism. Yet, of the two disciplines, it seems that philosophy has had the more conservative influence upon discussions of literature and to have rendered formalist tendencies, whatever the strain cultivated in any given period, more contagious. The emphasis upon formal and cognitive, at the expense of judicative, intentions in the Neoplatonic reconstruction of ancient literary theory, for instance, has steadily increased until it virtually dominates contemporary methodologies in the study of literature. Whether it be the 'neoclassical' formalism of *uniformity* or the 'aesthetic' formalism of *uniqueness*, the shadow of the Neoplatonic One has fallen, with Hegelian definition, upon both mimetic and symbolic representation. At their most intransigent, the neoclassicist and the aestheticist may each reflect the Neoplatonic tendency to separate completely, or arbitrarily to identify, the objects more appropriate to one type of intelligibility and those more appropriate to the other. They, too, since both separation and identity preclude negotiation, may have failed to find, like the Egyptian, Thespesion, in the parable of Philostratus, an effable relation between the verisimilar likeness and what it signifies. These later permutations of the ancient dilemma of knowledge and representation, however, must be left to further studies in the literary analysis of human experience and its continuity.

APPENDIX A. *HYPOTHESIS* AND *EXEMPLUM*

IN THE PRECEDING STUDY I have tried to suggest how the following observation by Richard McKeon on the scientific method might be applicable, at a much earlier date, to literary theory: "The controversy concerning thesis and hypothesis merged with Plato's dialectical use of hypothesis and Aristotle's differentiation of thesis, hypothesis, and definition and contributed unsuspected commitments and implications in modern discussions of scientific method."[1] The commitments and implications, arising from these particular terms among others, helped to formulate the literary analysis of experience as a balanced combination of formal, cognitive, and judicative intentions. While bringing out the presence and meaning of these commitments in early discussions of literature, I have stressed as well the contribution which these terms have made to the continuity of literary theory. This continuity, however, sometimes becomes obscure when an important term, through being drawn into antithetical relations with other terms, becomes too specialized and must yield its more general meaning to another word. This, I believe, happened when 'hypothesis' yielded to 'exemplum.' The reasons for this change illustrate the philological processes which I described in my Preface.

Throughout this study the 'hypothesis' of literary discourse has referred to the initial outline of narrative materials. The literary 'hypothesis,' therefore, never refers to literary discourse itself—that is, to the finished work—since it all but disappears within the author's development of his thesis through characters, speeches, and episodes. A literary hypothesis remains an instrument of literary discourse as the hypotheses of geometry, philosophy, and rhetoric are instruments of their respective disciplines. The hypothetical outline is a logical step in the construction of the completed poem.

In the later Hellenistic period the word 'hypothesis' in its technical

---

[1] "Rhetoric in the Middle Ages" in *Critics and Criticism, Ancient and Modern* (Chicago, 1952), p. 295.

literary sense of a fictional outline appears to have become increasingly restricted in two ways: first, by becoming a synonym for 'subject matter' in general, and, second, by having to respond, as a result, to changes in attitude toward poetic subject matter itself. The first restriction becomes apparent when the word 'hypothesis' is drawn into antithetical distinctions with other terms, like 'verbal expression' (λέξις), in such controversies as that over the terms *poesis, poema,* and *poeta.* In the third century B.C., for instance, Neoptolemus associates the word 'hypothesis' with *poesis* and λέξις with *poema,* thereby suggesting that the chief meaning of 'hypothesis' lay in 'subject matter' *as distinct from* how that material might be expressed. Later, the satirist Lucilius stressed the completeness of the poetic subject by identifying *poesis* with an *opus totum* such as a complete *Iliad* (*tota Ilias una*) or the unified material of Ennius (*una ut* θέσις *annales Enni*). Varro, similarly, called *poesis* a continuous argument (*perpetuum argumentum*) as in Homer's *Iliad* or the *Annales* of Ennius.[2] For both men, on the other hand, the term *poema* represented a short poem or a section of a longer poem, and seemed primarily concerned with verbal expression. With its emphasis upon complete and unified subject matter, as distinct from elaborated passages contained in longer (or isolated in shorter) poems, 'hypothesis' nearly becomes synonymous with 'thesis.' It loses, that is, its connotations of something temporarily to be assumed for the sake of arriving at something else and of the particular circumstances of a case to be judged.[3]

Having become a synonym for subject matter, 'hypothesis' suffers its second restriction by becoming a term for only one of the three Hellenistic types of narrative subject based on their respective kinds of material. Of these three types, the first (*fabula,* μῦθος) narrates things neither true nor like the truth; the second type (*argumentum,* ὑπόθεσις, πλάσμα) presents fictional occurrences which might have happened; and the third type (*historia,* ἱστορία) represents things that actually did happen. Sextus and others restrict 'hypothesis' to the second type, es-

---

[2] These examples are given by A. Ardizzoni, ΠΟΙΗΜΑ, *ricerche sulla teoria del linguagio poetico nell' antichità* (Bari, 1953), p. 26. For further treatment of these terms, see N. A. Greenberg, "The Use of Poiema and Poiesis," *HSCP* 65 (1961):263–89; A. Rostagni, *Arte Poetica di Orazio* (Torino, 1930); and C. O. Brink, *Horace on Poetry* (Cambridge, 1963).

[3] Lucilius' use of θέσις seems to have absorbed the Neoptolemian 'hypothesis'—unless 'thesis' is to distinguish the historical subject of the Ennian epic—and to foreshadow the later term *thema.* Perhaps this use of 'thesis' also suggests what Matthes (citing Cicero, *Orat.* 126) describes in rhetoric as the tendency to equate θέσις with τὸ κρινόμενον, or 'central issue to be judged' (*Lustrum* 3 [1958]:129–32), with interesting implications for the drama. In *Orat.* 126 Cicero calls a general question, usually associated with a thesis, a *perpetua quaestio,* which may have a relation to Varro's *perpetuum argumentum.*

pecially to comic plots, and, as a result, the 'argument' in other genres tends to lose the distinctive character of all literary discourse and to become a grayish mixture of the first and the third types of subject—a mixture of fable and history,.of the completely false and the completely true (see Chap. 11, pp. 291–95). Since no mixture of *falsa* and *vera* can, in the strict sense, produce the probable (*verisimile*), the term 'hypothesis' loses its precision as a general term for fiction.

In addition, the Hellenistic separation of the three types of material tended to identify the *cognitive* distinction between *false* and *true* with the *judicative* distinction between *wrong* and *right*. This is apparent when Horace and Plutarch recommend mixing true things (*facta*), associated with what is useful (*utile*), with false things (*ficta*), associated with what is pleasurable (*dulce*). While fact and fiction refer to existence and concern knowledge, profit and delight refer to ethics and concern judgment. The involvement of these two different kinds of criteria with one another, which increases from the Augustan period on, again tends to bring the first and third types of narration more abruptly into immediate juxtaposition. The second hypothetical or verisimilar type, if it does not shade off into either of the other types, tends to retain, both cognitively and judicatively, a very ambivalent status between them.

Lastly, the Hellenistic restriction of 'hypothesis' to the verisimilar type of subject matter, even if that type were to become and remain dominant, in the genetic sense, would tend to exclude from the concept of fiction the cognitive function of myth and the judicative function of history. Myth, as Aristotle comments, arouses the mind with wonder to the investigation of truth and may, therefore, become a philosophical instrument. History records the judgments of men in the form of their actions and thus may express the judicative authority of time over all individual decisions and events. The more the word 'hypothesis' excludes these narrative concerns from literature, the less able, again, it becomes to express a general conception of fiction capable of coordinating speculative and practical inquiries into human experience. The gradual emergence of another term to express such coordination appears most clearly in the history of two distinctions which Aristotle made concerning the term 'thesis.'

In the first distinction described previously in Chapter 10, Aristotle divided theses to be discussed into ethical, logical, and physical topics (*Top.* 105b20). The first became associated with action, the second and third with cognition, and the distinction was later simplified to one between practical and theoretical theses as Cicero describes them (*De part. orat.* 62; *Top.* 79–82). The theoretical thesis could be considered without extension in circumstance, while the practical thesis tended to seek a point of departure or a specific application in a circumstantial controversy. The more the practical thesis dealt with ethical questions implied in specific decisions about actions, the more it moved away from a specific legal controversy toward deliberative rhetoric. The closer it remained bound to a given set of circumstances, the more closely it resembled a *causa* or 'hypothesis,' which demanded a specific judgment. R. Robinson comments that from the beginning "hypothesizing is positing with a view to future action" and sometimes specifically as a proposal: "Thus the physician lays down (ὑποθέσθαι) prescriptions for the treatment of the sick."[4] It is not surprising, therefore, that Cicero defined the objective of the practical thesis as *actio* and later rhetoricians defined the end of hypothesis as *actio, iudicatio,* or *contentio.*

Aristotle's second distinction indicates the way in which the theoretical thesis became more easily identified with the cognitive intention of philosophy and the practical thesis with the judicative intention of rhetoric. He divides the thesis into a definition which states what a thing is, on the one hand, and a hypothesis which asserts whether or not something exists, on the other (72a19–25). We may argue about definition without reference to existing circumstances, but any question of controversy must 'assert' the existence of its circumstances.[5] While 'definition' corresponds, that is, to the theoretical thesis, 'hypothesis,' in asserting existence, is a necessary condition of the practical thesis. In fact, the practical thesis appears to combine the assumption of existence, characteristic of geometrical hypotheses, with the particular events which demand judgment and action, characteristic of rhetorical hypotheses. When definition is added to the mathematical and rhetorical hypotheses, the thesis as a whole offers a combination of three activities which form a dialectical analogue to the formal, cognitive (i.e. definitive), and judicative intentions of literature.

Cicero devoted much of the *De oratore* to redefining the relation between thesis and hypothesis. Originally, in Hermagoras, the relation resembled that between the materials of theoretical and practical theses— that is, one between different types of subject matter. Cicero changed the distinction between subject matters to one between methods, objectives, or even faculties in analyzing the *same* subject matter. He sees theses as implicit in hypotheses as genus is implicit in species. Such a transformation enabled him to embody in his theory of oratory not only

---

[4] *Plato's Earlier Dialectic* (Ithaca, 1941), p. 102.

[5] See Chap. 3, n. 3 of this study. So St. Augustine considers what constitutes a hypothesis: it is nothing other than the circumstances, which Hermagoras calls the *peristasin*, without which there cannot be any kind of controversy (*est igitur circumstantia rerum, quam* περίστασιν *Hermagoras vocat, sine qua ulla omnino controversia non potest esse*). *Rhetores Latini Minores*, ed. C. Halm (Lipsiae, 1863), p. 141.

the best Greek formulations of the relation between philosophy and rhetoric, but to preserve and transmit the particular intentions of literary discourse. The specific finds significance (definition) in the generic and the generic realizes its potentiality for assertion in the specifically existing controversy (hypothesis). Aristotle's two types of thesis are joined, and Cicero summarizes their union: "a discussion is a division of a cause and a dispute, for what is limited contains an element that is unlimited, and all matters contained in the former have a reference nevertheless to the latter (*est consultatio* [i.e., *propositum* = θέσις] *quasi pars causae quaedam et controversiae: inest enim infinitum in definito, et ad illud tamen referuntur omnia*)."[6]

Following the Ciceronian tradition, Quintilian and the later rhetoricians hesitated to consider a general issue completely separately from one dealing with detailed circumstances. Perhaps under the influence of the practical thesis, they sought the 'middle ground' which Cicero had described. The description by Sulpitius Victor is perhaps most detailed and most relevant for fictional constructs, one of which he mentions below as it might be used in the *controversiae*. It is usually claimed, he says, that a thesis is a topic for rational discussion which excludes definite persons and that a hypothesis is such a topic which includes them. But each of these definitions is wrong, for a thesis can concern circumstances involving definite persons if the question is posed in this way: "Should Socrates marry?" If the topic for disputation is stated differently, however, as "Socrates considers the question of whether he should get married," it would not be a thesis but a deliberative hypothesis (*causa*). In sum, when we dispute whether he ought to do this, it can be a thesis even though he is a specific person. A hypothesis, in its turn, can exist without a specific person, as in the following example. A certain man is discovered by himself, and since he holds a bloody sword and is burying the corpse of a man just slain, he is accused of murder. This 'question' sets up a given circumstantial case to be judged even though no specific individuals are mentioned. It is better, then, Sulpitius concludes, to regard a thesis as a question whose aim is cognitive (*inspectio*) and a hypothesis as a question whose aim is judicative (*actio et iudicatio*).[7]

---

[6] *De Partitione Oratoria*, 61, trans. H. Rackham, LCL (London, 1960). On the thesis in general, see G. Reichel, *Quaestiones Progymnasmaticae* (Lipsiae, 1909), pp. 97–108; H. Throm, *Die Thesis: Ein Beitrag zu ihrer Enstehung und Geschichte* (Paderborn, 1932), passim; and B. Riposti, "Quid Cicero de thesi et hypothesi in *Topicis* senserit," *Aevum* 18 (1944):61–71.

[7] The entire passage should be given.

Thesis est, ut quidam volunt, res rationalem disputationem recipiens sine definitarum personarum circumstantia: hypothesis res rationalem disputationem recipiens cum definitarum personarum circumstantia. Verum reprehentitur utraque haec definitio, ideo quod utraque invertitur contra. Nam et thesis potest habere definitae personae

St. Augustine makes a similar discrimination concerning the two types of questions. In a thesis, he says, there should be an investigation (*perspectio*) into what kind of a thing something is; in a hypothesis, there should be a controversy over an issue (*contentio*). The difference between a thesis and a hypothesis is simply the difference between cognition and judgment. In a thesis, therefore, one asks what all men ought to do; in a hypothesis, what one man or another or several men—certainly in any case what a definite type (*modus*) of man—ought to do. The main difference, then, is this: in a thesis, we seek, as if we were ignorant, what it is best to do; in a hypothesis, we defend, as if we were informed, a given action as best.[8] These statements are very suggestive about the effort of rhetoric to achieve the balance between intellectual perception and judgment of particular situations, as well as about how this balance might protect that of literature. For Aristotle, the universalizing function of poetry could reveal what a definite kind of man might do; for Isocrates, a fiction could best represent the kind of man he wished to appear to be. In each case, the cognitive thesis enters to qualify the particular circumstances of the case to be judged. So equity will seek to define what kind of a man a person generally or habitually is. If one starts with what a certain type of man (*definitum hominum modum*) does and proceeds to a perception of what all men should do (*quid omnes oporteat facere*), the moral intention would resemble, as well, the later peripatetic tradition of Neoptolemus and Horace.

Similarly, when Boethius uses the terms to distinguish the material of dialectic from that of rhetoric, he suggests a middle ground by qual-

---

circumstantiam, si ita ponamus: "an Ciceroni post consulatum eundum in provinciam fuerit": vel, quod exemplum positum est apud Graecos: "an Socrati uxor ducenda fuerit." Neque enim esset thesis, si illo modo poneretur: "deliberat Cicero, an post consulatum eat in provinciam," aut "deliberat Socrates, an ducat uxorem": quae sunt causae deliberativae. Sed quoniam nos hoc disputamus, debueritne ille facere, est thesis, quamvis sit definita persona. E diverso: "quidam in solitudine inventus est, cum gladium cruentum teneret et recens cadaver occisi hominis sepulturae daret: reus fit caedis." Haec quidem certa causa est; potest enim ille, quicumque repertus est, reus fieri, etsi definitae personae circumstantiam non habet. Melius ergo et thesis et hypothesis definiri videntur hoc modo: Thesis est res rationalem disputationem recipiens, cuius finis inspectio, hypothesis res rationalem disputationem recipiens, cuius finis actio et iudicatio; sic enim videtur ad certam definitionem utrumque esse perductum. . . . Thesis est "an uxor ducenda": quod si rei fiant de moribus iuvenes, quod iuraverint ne uxores ducerent, erit hypothesis. (Halm, p. 314)

[8] "Dein illo etiam distare haec duo genera quaestionum, quod in thesi perspectio sit alicuius rei qualis sit, in hypothesi contentio: et quantum interest inter perspectionem et contentionem, tantum inter thesin et hypothesin esse discriminis. Deinde in thesi quaeri quid omnes oporteat facere, in hypothesi quid unum aut alterum aut paulo plures, certe definitum hominum modum. Etiam illa differentia accedit, quod in thesi quasi ignorantes quaerimus quid sit optimum factu, in hypothesi quasi scientes defendimus" (Halm, p. 140).

ification. Dialectic must, he says, assume certain circumstances concerning persons or actions in its disputations, even though it transfers its principal emphasis from them to the thesis which it is discussing. Likewise, rhetoric can assume a thesis, although it draws everything finally to its particular controversy (*hypothesim*). Each discipline treats its own material but assumes that of the other in order that it might gain support from (utilize to the fullest?) the faculty more appropriate to its own subject matter.[9] The function of the thesis easily becomes associated with that of a general observation, or commonplace, about experience in any type of discourse. As late as 1600 John Hoskyns, in an informal treatise on style, could describe how a *sententia*, used specifically to characterize a character in Sidney's *Arcadia*, might bring a generic significance to a particular fictional event. "*Evarchus* making his life the example of his lawes, his accōns arising out of his deedes, which all may be taken for rule, & comonplaces, by putting the generall name for the speciall (as they say) drawing it [i.e. the general name] *a Thesi ad Hipothesin*; from a position to a supposicōn." The process is one of transferring a "general name" (noun) from its (natural) place in a thesis to its (adopted) place in a hypothesis—thus "putting [= substituting] the generall name for the speciall."[10]

The rhetorical application of thesis and hypothesis to methods and activities rather than to subject matters did, indeed, facilitate the adaptation of these rhetorical terms to literary analysis. The cognitive acts of *perspectio* and *inspectio* and the judicative acts of *contentio* and *actio et iudicatio* ideally might complement one another, as knowledge and judgment, in any single work. *Perspectio* would consider the significance of the controversial events 'laid out' in the *contentio*. The problem

---

[9] "Rursus dialectica quidem si quando circumstantias, veluti personam factumve aliquod ad disputationem sumit, non principaliter, sed omnem ejus vim thesim de qua disserit transfert. Rhetorica vero si thesim assumpserit, ad hypothesim trahit, et utraque suam quidem materiam tractat, sed alterius assumit, ut proniore in sua materia facultate nitatur" (*De diff. top.*, IV; PL 64:1205–6).

[10] *The Life, Letters and Writings of John Hoskyns*, ed. L. B. Osborn (New Haven, 1937), p. 154. In the *Topica* (86), Cicero states that all types of general questions may "be transferred to particular cases (*in causas transferuntur*)" and, contrariwise, in *De part. orat.* (106), he observes that particular controversies are 'recalled to' unlimited questions again once the definite persons and occasions are removed. For a suggestive parallel in the development of Cartesian mathematical analysis, see J. Klein, *Greek Mathematical Thought*, pp. 209–10: "From this we easily conclude that there will be no little profit in transferring that *which the intellect allows us to say about magnitudes in general* (*in genere*) to that specific form of magnitude (*ad illam magnitudinis speciem*) which is depicted most easily and distinctly of all in our imagination." Compare Aristotle's comments on geometry and the imagination (Chap. 2, pp. 39–41). Insofar as Hoskyns' use of *ad hypothesin* (with respect to *thesis*) would be rendered *ad speciem* (with respect to *genus*), it is interesting to note the legal associations of the term *species* even when applied to algebraic letters for indefinite magnitudes (see Chap. 2, n. 8 and Chap. 14, n. 12).

remained, however, that there were still two terms, two intentions, and these continued to reflect the ancient antagonism between philosophy and rhetoric. Instead of the significance remaining immanent in the events, as genus in species, the cognitive thesis tended to separate from the hypothetical narrative, to float digressively within it or to attach itself, like the moral of Aesop's fables, to its conclusion. Since, on the other hand, genus is apprehended by thought and species by the senses, the specific function of narrative could come naturally to be that of illustrating or exemplifying a generic proposition. From this process of exemplification the term *exemplum* not only became easily associated with all types of narration, but from the beginning it included more than the particular instances of rhetorical argument. It combined in a single word the functions of both thesis and hypothesis and, as a result, became the more useful term for fiction, while 'hypothesis' was reserved for its more specialized uses not only in literature, but in mathematics, philosophy, and rhetoric. This came about for several reasons.

The relation that hypothesis later developed to thesis in rhetoric, that of species to genus, was already implicit in Aristotle's discussion of example. "When two statements are of the same order (γένος), but one is more familiar than the other, the former is an 'example' (παρά-δειγμα)." To establish the probability of a particular proposition, more familiar instances, which fall under the same "universal" (τὸ καθόλου), are cited (*Rhet.* 1357b29–37). The example, however, could be fictional as well as historical (1393a25–94a19) and later was to take its place beside other types of fictional arguments, which Quintilian called καθ᾽ ὑπόθεσιν (5.10.95–99) and whose function Iulius Victor was still later to describe in Quintilian's own words: a fiction is a "proposition of something which, if true, would either solve a problem or contribute to its solution, and secondly the demonstration of the similarity of our hypothesis to the case under consideration (*Fictio autem est proponere aliquid, quod, si verum est, aut solvat quaestionem aut adiuvet: deinde id, de quo quaeritur, facere illi simile*)."[11] Whether the example be historical or fictional, when it is the more familiar of two propositions, it renders the other proposition intelligible or probable by virtue of the genus it establishes to include them both. Its functions are first to establish this genus and then to assume it as a point of departure for supporting the second proposition, thus performing certain dialectical functions of hypothesis.

There is a more important reason, however, for the greater adaptability of *exemplum* to fiction, which bears directly upon the intentions of literary discourse I have been describing. The Greek word for *exemplum*,

[11] Iulius' Latin is cited from Halm, p. 403; the English is cited from Butler's translation of Quintilian (5.10.96) in LCL.

παράδειγμα, combined in a single term for fiction a cognitive function of definition with an exhortative function of illustration. Aristotle not only uses the word in the rhetorical sense of the more familiar of two instances but in the sense of an ethical model defined for the sake of comparison with something else. In the *Poetics* (25.17; 1461b9–14) he says that one way to justify the improbable is with reference to a greater excellence than, admittedly, can be found in reality. Although such a man as Zeuxis painted may not exist, still his character might be understood as a definition of human potentiality, as a παράδειγμα. Plato had used the same term for his verbal depiction of his Republic considered without reference to its actual existence (*Rep.* 472DE). Later, Cicero refers to such a description as an exemplar (*De rep.* 2.22). Today we might associate a purely cognitive definition with the word *exemplar* and an illustration contributing to rhetorical probability with *exemplum*. When, however, the moral example cited is a person, as when Cicero says (ibid., 1.1) that when we study Cato *quasi exemplari ad industriam virtutemque ducimur* or Horace says that *utile proposuit nobis exemplar Ulixen* (*Ep.* 1.2.18), the verbal definition (making no claim to existence) is combined with the illustration of a particular (existent) man. In the Renaissance, therefore, Thomas Cooper could regard the words as virtually synonymous.[12] The same may be said for the concept of *imago*, which, along with *exemplum* and *parabola*, formed one of the three types of comparison. The combined function of definition and illustration in a single word has created much of the uncertainty about the 'Platonic' and/or 'Aristotelian' origins of 'example' and 'image' in Renaissance writers like Sidney and Spenser. The point to be stressed here is that the concept of *exemplum* could combine the philosophical and rhetorical intentions in a way congenial to literary discourse, while the specialized literary use of 'hypothesis' could not.

Plato relates the illustrative and cognitive functions of παράδειγμα to one another in connection with fiction in the *Statesman* (277A–78B). In order to fill in the details of an outlined sketch (περιγραφήν) of a perfect king, he uses a fiction (μῦθος) as an illustration. It is difficult, he says, to define a complex idea without using examples, because we learn principally by comparison, as children come to recognize new syllables by identifying letters they know from familiar words. These familiar words become παραδείγματα, and, when rightly compared with the unfamiliar syllables, the two together form one true idea. Plato then extends this analogy to the understanding of all natural phenomena

---

[12] *Thesaurus Linguae Romanae & Britannicae* (London, 1578), v. *exemplar: Exemplar, pro exemplo positum legitur, ita vt parum inter se differant Exemplum & Exemplar. Cic. Quintil.*

through exemplification and, finally, applies this figurative method to the achievement of scientific knowledge of the most important matters such as statesmanship. The method is illustrative, but its purpose is heuristic. As the example gains clarity, the idea becomes apprehensible.

The heuristic function of an *exemplum*, in the sense of a pattern to be followed or a model to be imitated, bears a relation to Plato's Ideas analogous to that of the geometer's diagram to the truths he wishes to demonstrate. On the one hand, neither pattern claims to 'picture' the qualities or dimensions of something actually existing. But, on the other, each hypothesizes, like fiction, an existent illustration, in letters or lines, of a more familiar, nearer, more apprehensible instance analogous to what is to be grasped. Not only is the *Republic* an exemplary paradigm (παράδειγμα) existing in words (ἐν λόγοις), like a definition, which might or might not come into being (*Rep.* 592AB), but its later form described in the *Laws* is also an actual drama, like an illustration, "framed as a representation of the fairest and best life, which is in reality, as we assert, the truest tragedy" (*Laws* 817B; cf. *Rep.* 398AB). Plato himself says that the movements of the stars should be considered "as patterns (παραδείγμασι) to aid in the study of those [ultimate] realities, just as one would do who chanced upon diagrams (διαγράμμασιν) drawn . . . by Daedalus or some other craftsman or painter" (*Rep.* 529E). Such usages suggest the association of *paradeigma* with *diagramma* in Aristotle's comparisons of mental images to geometric diagrams (*De mem.* 449b32–50a6 and *De an.* 431b5–20) and of the process of deliberative choice to the analysis of such a diagrammatic construction (*E.N.* 3.3.9–13).[13]

In all these instances, the cognitive and illustrative combine their philosophical and rhetorical energies in a paradigmatic *exemplum* or *imago* which could serve as a literary term for fiction. The principal function of the *paradeigma* becomes the discovery of a genus by means of which a more important and elusive concept, falling under the same genus, might be understood.[14] To regard a fictional narrative, then, as

[13] Proclus' treatment of geometrical figures increases the mathematical connotations of the combined illustrative and heuristic functions of Plato's paradigmatic diagram. The geometrical image (εἰκών), he says, serves at the same time both as a likeness of the suprasensory reality which it is to signify *and* as an exemplary representation (παράδειγμα) of that reality, which it renders sufficiently apprehensible to the senses to be emulated. See p. 205 of this study.

[14] Compare Plato's definition in the *Statesman* (278C): "An example is formed when that which is the same in some second unconnected thing is rightly conceived and compared with the first, so that the two together form one true idea." On the *paradeigma* in general see the following: K. Alewell, *Über das rhetorische* ΠΑΡΑΔΕΙΓΜΑ (Leipzig, 1913); R. Robinson, *Plato's Earlier Dialectic* (Ithaca, 1944), pp. 214–34; V. Goldschmidt, *Le paradigme dans la dialectique platonicienne* (Paris, 1947); P.–M. Schuhl, *Études sur la*

a *paradeigma* is to see a set of specific events in pursuit of a generic significance by means of which a comparable, though less readily comprehensible, set of specific events—perhaps in one's own experience—might be seen more clearly. The resulting increased awareness constitutes the 'moral' effect of literature. That the *exemplum* itself was often employed as a purely didactic method for practical ends does not lessen its original intention to embody in a single structure the philosophical and rhetorical hypotheses of literary discourse.[15]

---

fabulation platonicienne (Paris, 1947); P. Grenet, *Les origines de l'analogie philosophique dans les dialogues de Platon* (Rouen, 1948); T. B. L. Webster, *Greek Art and Literature 700–530 B.C.* (London, 1959), esp. pp. 90–99.

[15] A passage in the *Problemata* attributed to Aristotle relates a number of connections previously emphasized in this study closely to one another (18.3): "Why is it that men prefer examples (παραδείγμασι) in speeches and tales (λόγοις) rather than enthymemes? Is it because they enjoy learning (τῷ τε μανθάνειν χαίρουσι) and learning quickly? And they learn more easily by examples and tales; for what they learn in this way is an individual fact, but enthymemes are a demonstration based on generalities (ἐκ τῶν καθόλου), which are less familiar than individual facts (τὰ μέρη). Moreover, we are more ready to believe in facts for which many bear witness, and examples and tales resemble evidence (μαρτυρίαις); also proofs supported by evidence are easy to obtain. Again men gladly learn of similarities, and examples and tales display similarities (ἔτι τὸ ὅμοιον μανθάνουσιν ἡδέως, τὸ δὲ παράδειγμα καὶ οἱ μῦθοι τὸ ὅμοιον δεικνύουσιν)." Here learning and the perception of resemblances are associated as sources of pleasure, and *exempla* teach well because (1) being identified with particular narrative accounts and tales (μῦθοι) which are based on similarity, they bring pleasure, and (2) bearing witness to facts, their evidence is more convincing than general propositions organized in enthymemes. *Aristotle Problems*, trans. W. S. Hett, LCL, 2 vols. (London, 1970).

APPENDIX B. ART AND PRUDENCE,
THE *DUPLEX PECCATUM POESIS*, AND THE
MORALITY OF FICTION IN THE
MIDDLE AGES

NOT ALL DISCIPLINES, Aristotle says, admit of the same degree of exactitude (*E.N.* 1.3). Scientific disciplines, employing the theoretical faculty of the mind, deal, primarily, like mathematics, with the invariable and may achieve highly accurate results. The disciplines employing the prudential and productive faculties, on the other hand, deal with the variable and therefore are capable of only approximate results. Not only are the productive and prudential faculties both distinct from the theoretical faculty with respect to accuracy, but they themselves perform different activities which are judged by different criteria. When these different activities are performed by a single individual, such as an artist, he may be judged both with respect to the quality of what he *makes* (that is, *qua* artist) and with respect to the quality of what he *does* as a member of his community (that is, *qua* human being). Problems may arise when these two criteria come into conflict.[1]

The distinction between the judgment of an artist with respect to the quality of his product and the judgment of him with respect to his actions as a moral agent goes back at least to Plato (*Prot.* 318B–23B). It received its most influential formulation from Aristotle (*E.N.* 6.5) and, adopted by St. Thomas (*S.T.* 1.2. qu. 21 art. 2 and qu. 57 art. 3 and 5), led to the separation of art, as an activity of the productive faculty, from morality, as an activity of the prudential faculty. While the resulting amorality of the arts did much to render them suspect, it also could provide them, to some extent, with a doctrinal immunity.

Aristotle indicates the way in which such an immunity might be

---

[1] I would like to express my indebtedness to the lectures of Professor C. S. Singleton for enabling me to see an ever-widening application of the distinction between the prudential and productive faculties to the arts of the Middle Ages and the Renaissance.

conceived by distinguishing between artistic and ethical responsibility for error with respect to intention. "In Art," he says, "voluntary error is not so bad as involuntary, whereas in the sphere of Prudence it is worse, as it is in the sphere of the virtues" (E.N. 6.5.7). Since prudence (φρόνησις) is the chief virtue which separates the 'political' from artistic activities which are primarily productive, this passage connects Aristotle's discussion of art in E.N. with an important distinction in his defense of poetry. In the *Poetics* (25.3–4; 1460b13–22) he distinguishes the productive (ποιητικῆς) from the prudential (πολιτικῆς) arts with regard to their standards of correctness (ὀρθότης). Faults in the poetic arts may either be accidental or essential. If the poet has a (factual or doctrinal) misconception about what he is imitating but represents that misconception accurately in the way that he wishes to, his mistake is accidental to his art. The error, therefore, is *voluntary* insofar as he succeeds in doing what he intends to do. The mistake, however, becomes essential to his art if he fails to represent his intended conception, be it true or false in itself, in an artistic manner. Insofar as he fails to do what he tries to do, the error is *involuntary*. In art, therefore, a voluntary error (in fact or belief) may be accidental (and hence excusable)—while an involuntary error may be essential (and hence reprehensible)—with respect to a product. In ethics, on the other hand, it is the reverse: a voluntary error is essential (since one is responsible for what he chooses)—while an involuntary error is accidental (since one is not morally responsible for what he cannot help)—with respect to an action. Indeed, Plutarch, referring to successful poetic deception as an accidental and therefore voluntary error in this special sense, later cautions the reader twice about the opinion, attributed to Gorgias, that the poet who deceives is more honest than one who does not "because he has done what he promised to do" (*Mor.* 348C; cf. 15D).[2]

Aristotle uses the phrase κατὰ συμβεβηκός for both the 'accidental' (voluntary) error of poetry (*Poet.* 1460b16) and the 'accidental' (involuntary) error of ethics (E.N. 5.8), the legal condition of which Cicero later designates as *imprudentia* (*De inv.* 1.41). The accidental error may be compensated for in a productive art by artistic means (the prudential or factual considerations being temporarily suspended), while the essential error cannot be because it is an error of the artist *qua* artist. The double criterion of truth for the productive and prudential faculties in

[2] Plato discusses the relative merits of voluntary and involuntary action in ethical, athletic, and artistic activities at length in the *Lesser Hippias* (271E–76C). The whole discussion, which smacks of a sophistic exercise, suggests that the question may have been a commonplace of rhetorical debate. Seneca repeats the Aristotelian formulation of the question in *Ep.* 95.8–9.

E.N. provides the grounds for the 'double fault,' the *duplex peccatum* (διττὴ ἁμαρτία), of artistic representation in the *Poetics*. It is necessary, of course, to distinguish this abstract separation of art from prudence, based on the artist's ability or inability to fulfill his intention, from the poem itself which is a prudential statement as well as a 'product.' The restriction of ποίησις to mean ποιητική in the sense of the technical powers of the productive faculty, or of the faculty itself, leads directly to the doctrine of art for its own sake.

In an earlier passage in the *Poetics* (1448b4–19), Aristotle remarks that the object or action which is imitated may be unpleasing or ignoble in itself but that its representation will delight us, nevertheless, by either its verisimilar fidelity or its artistic execution. Both passages from the *Poetics* seem to be turned by Plutarch into a strongly moralistic identification of factual (i.e. historical) with moral truth (the prudential criterion) in opposition to fictional representation (the artistic criterion) in "How to Study Poetry" (*Mor.* 17–18). What pleases us is not whether the object imitated is beautiful or ugly in itself but the likeness the artist achieves technically. In the case of dramatic actions, as well, the reader distinguishes the morality of the content (πρᾶξιν) from the art (τέχνην) with which it is imitated; one may condemn the first while he admires, at his own risk, the second (18AD).

This double criterion of value, reflecting the earlier distinctions of the subject matter (prudentially evaluated) from technical skill (productively evaluated), had from the beginning tended to shift the ethical responsibility from the teacher to the practicer of an art and from the producer to the user of an object. As in the case of laws, the products of the other disciplines might be used for good or for harmful ends. What Plato has Gorgias argue in defense of rhetoric (*Gorg.* 456D–57C; cf. *Rep.* 332–34), Aristotle reasserts: one cannot reject the art of rhetoric just because in the wrong hands it can be misused, since there is practically no human accomplishment which could escape a similar charge (*Rhet.* 1.1). Any art considered abstractly as a knowledgeable skill in *how* to do something may be used on either side of a question (*in utramque partem*) with respect to moral issues, and hence to the moral condition of anyone who practices it, without being considered immoral in itself. The artist *as artist* loses all his immunity from prudential criteria only when his potentially harmful product can be used in *no possible* beneficial way.[3]

---

[3] A clear example of such an artist would be the biblical maker of images (Wisdom 13.5). Yet, even in religious art, many of the writers whom De Bruyne cites show, with no consciousness of blasphemy, a remarkable ingenuity in isolating, and thus protecting, aesthetic from doctrinal criteria in justifying the enjoyment of the visual arts (cf. *Études d'esthétique médiévale*, 3 vols. [Brugge, 1946], 1:261–305, 364–70; 2:100–106; 3:210–

St. Augustine himself comments that there are rules of eloquence which, adaptable to true as well as to false principles, cannot be blamed if they are perversely employed. There are other similar principles, used in true *or* false causes, which are good insofar as they can make things known or believed or can move men to seek or avoid particular things (*De doct. christ.* 2.36). Presumably, teaching or putting such rules into practice is not reprehensible. Indeed, even a teacher of the art of courtly love might claim an artistic license as Peter the Chantor, head of the school of moral philosophy at Paris at the end of the twelfth century, testifies. When asked about the art of love "He replied that 'the art itself is good but its use is evil.' The next question was then 'does not he who teaches the amatory art use it and sin mortally?' To which it was replied that the teacher 'does not use it but transmits it. He who corrupts women by its means uses it. Nevertheless, the teacher transmits it, not for use but as a warning.' "[4]

In the *De amore* Andreas Capellanus, indeed, 'warns' Walter but in a literary context similar to that in which Boccaccio later warns his readers: "Each thing is good in itself with respect to some other thing, but when put to a bad use it can be injurious to many things, and I say the same thing about my stories." If the listener puts them to bad use, it is his sin, not theirs, for they could never injure a mind *ben disposta* (*Concl.* 8–14). Boccaccio retains his artistic freedom by placing the moral responsibility for his *novelle* upon those who use them in acquiring (or losing) the ultimate *humana bona* (cf. St. Thomas' commentary on *E.N.* 6.5.7 and *S.T.* 1.2. qu. 57 art. 4, r. 2). Similarly, once Walter has learned the art of love which Andreas teaches, its use will be his responsibility. He can, in fact, having acquired the art, gain more credit for not using it, since to God one is more pleasing who does not take advantage of an opportunity to sin which he has been granted than one to whom the power to sin has not been given (*qui opportunitate non utitur concessa peccandi quam cui delinquendi non est attributa potestas*, p. 362). In this spirit Andreas adds the *reprobatio amoris* for Walter's *utilitati* (p. 416) as the second part of his *duplicem sententiam*.

The meaning of *duplicem sententiam* bears strongly upon the relation of the structure of the *De amore* to its interpretation as a whole. I think that the Academic discussion of a question *in utramque sententiam*

14, 290–344). Plato frequently makes the general distinction between the producer and user of something made (i.e. *Rep.* 601C, *Crat.* 390BD), and Aristotle suggests how the moral responsibility might easily be shifted from the maker of something to the person for whom he makes it (*Physics* 2.2).

    [4] Quoted by J. F. Benton, "Clio and Venus: an Historical View of Medieval Love," in *The Meaning of Courtly Love*, p. 31. This view of the use of the product conforms with *S.T.* 2.2 qu. 169 art. 2 ad. 4.

accounts for Andreas' *duplicem sententiam* more simply with regard to *form* than the Averroistic "double truth" can do with regard to *content* as discussed by A. J. Denomy. To translate the phrase—rendered as two "points of view" by Denomy (p. 125) and J. J. Parry—as a "double lesson" or "a lesson with two sides" as D. W. Robertson, Jr., does, is to place the emphasis again on doctrinal content.[5] Though "lesson" is a perfectly valid meaning for *sententia*, it has, perhaps, an unnecessarily pedagogic connotation for its context. The metaphorical language in the *De amore* as a whole is legal: a *court* in which a *judgment* is given on a *question* of love. Throughout the treatise *sententia* is used as a "considered opinion," a judgment in favor of one side or the other—a *iudicatio* or *responsum*. It must be through a *sententia*, St. Thomas says, that the universal statute of the law is applied to a particular case (*universale dictum legis applicatur ad particulare negotium*).[6] That there are close correspondences with the terminology of exegetical interpretation, of the syncretic endeavor of *sic et non* in canon law, and of the literary form of the *quaestiones disputatae* as well as of the *Summa*, cannot be denied.[7] Yet opinions about scriptural or canonical *texts* are not under consideration here but rather fictional situations or *causae*, which brings the debates of courtly love much nearer to scholastic rhetoric than to scholastic philosophy. Debates of this kind developed early even in the ancient philosophical schools. Cicero reports that such ethical decisions, discussed *in utramque partem*, were made with regard to fictional *quaestiones* by Hecaton, the pupil of Panaetius. The examples Cicero gives (*De off.* 3.89–92) would not be out of place in the Senecan declamations; in fact, he says, their issues "are like so many points of the law disputed among the Stoics (*quasi controversa iura Stoicorum*)."

Andreas has furnished (*propinabat*) two 'opinions' on this Academic question presented to Walter, and the audience, for judgment. The most plausible referent for *duplicem sententiam* would continue to be, I should think, the two sides of a question argued in the manner of Aristotle on any subject from two or more points of view (*Aristotelio more de omnibus rebus in utramque sententiam*, *De orat.* 3.80) or the two-sided disputation in which a general question could be copiously discussed from each side (*ancipites disputationes, in quibus de universo genere in*

---

[5] A. J. Denomy, "The *De Amore* of Andreas Capellanus and the Condemnation of 1277," *Mediaeval Studies* 8 (1946):107–49, esp. 148–49; J. J. Parry, *The Art of Courtly Love* (New York, 1964), p. 211; D. W. Robertson, Jr., *A Preface to Chaucer* (Princeton, 1969), p. 395.

[6] See Chap. 10, nn. 25 and 27. In this sense, the *sententia* is related to the rhetorical meaning of 'hypothesis' as a *contentio* or *iudicatio*.

[7] For a discussion of some of these meanings, see G. Paré, A. Brunet, P. Tremblay, *La Renaissance du XIIe siècle: les écoles et l'enseignement* (Ottawa, 1933), pp. 267–74.

utramque partem disseri copiose licet, 3.107). So Cicero defends the debater's right to defend a view he may not believe (*De fin.* 2.2). So Quintilian illustrates his argument that a good man must occasionally defend the guilty (12.1.33–45) by pointing out that "the Academicians, although they will argue on either side of a question, do not thereby commit themselves to taking one of these two views as their guide in life to the exclusion of the other" (35). In fact, "justice becomes yet more manifest from the contemplation of injustice," and many are the "things that are proved by their contraries (*aequitas fit ex iniqui contemplatione manifestior, et plurima contrariis probantur*)." So earlier (2.17.36) he says that the orator will not always maintain what is true: "There are occasions when the public interest demands that he defend what is untrue (*non semper autem ei, etiamsi frequentissime, tuenda veritas erit; sed aliquando exigit communis utilitas, ut etiam falsa defendat*)." Priscian converted the debate over an *ancipitem opinionem* into an elementary literary exercise for the Middle Ages (Halm, p. 554). Robertson's opinion that "the discouragement to the pursuit of love is thus something that runs through the whole work, not something confined to the last book," in overly restricting the argument to one side of the question, perhaps takes insufficient account of the literary form. As a result, the reader might interpret nearly all the arguments on the *other* side of the question in a figurative or ironic sense unintended by the author.[8] The argument of literary discourse would thus be sacrificing its form in order to render a moral judgment more definitively explicit— the same judgment, be it said, that the literary context makes perfectly clear in its own way.

In his "retracciouns" Chaucer wishes to retain only those works "writen for oure doctrine" (cf. 2 Tim. 3.16). They have an explicit prudential value for the man who—like himself from then on—is simply to be a member of the community he has been addressing, while works such as *Troilus and Criseyde* and the *Canterbury Tales* appear to take no overt ethical responsibility for their audience.[9] Yet, even within the

---

[8] *Preface to Chaucer*, p. 395. This danger is loosely analogous to one that St. Augustine shrewdly points out with respect to scriptural exegesis: "It often happens that a person who is, or thinks he is, in a higher grade of spiritual life thinks that those things which are taught for those in lower grades are figurative. For example, if he embraces the celibate life and has made himself a eunuch for the Kingdom of Heaven, he thinks it necessary to take anything the sacred books admonish concerning the love and rule of a wife as figurative rather than literal," *On Christian Doctrine* 3.17, trans. D. W. Robertson, Jr. (New York, 1958), p. 94.

[9] The importance of this distinction was recognized by W. A. Maddon, "Chaucer's Retraction and the Mediaeval Canons of Seemliness," *Med. Stud.* 9 (1947):173–84. All citations of Chaucer are from *The Complete Works of Geoffrey Chaucer*, ed. F. N. Robinson (Cambridge, Mass., 1933).

rejected works, Chaucer, like Boccaccio, can advise some readers to skip such tales as the Miller's and state, as general advice, that "men shal nat maken ernest of game." The principle is that one should not confuse 'prudential' with 'productive' activities. The more complicated feeling in the confessional prologues arises from the manipulation of the distinction within the fictional structure itself. The Pardoner may, with sudden candor, give his *prudential* warning to the pilgrims that they receive Christ's pardon "For that is best; I wol yow nat deceyve," and then immediately step back into his *artistic* role: "But, sires, o word forgat I in my tale." Too slow to follow him, Harry Bailey responds to his mock solicitation as if it were still in "ernest" and castigates him. The Pardoner is furious both about the insults and about having his "immunity" ignored before it had expired. Similarly, Chaucer directly admonishes "yonge, fresshe folkes" at the end of the *Troilus* (5.1835–55) to love Christ who "nyl falsen no wight" and, since He is "best to love," asks them "What nedeth feynede loves for to seke?" In each case the period of artistic immunity is delimited (since the writer and his audience—or the Pardoner and the pilgrims—must function soon again in a communal world), and this delimitation itself, provided that its provisional nature is recognized, gives even the rejected works a prudential dimension. For it is precisely through his release from ethical and historical circumstances that the artist can establish a temporary order of events and of emotions which has the power to increase the listener's understanding of the communal world after he has returned to it. Boccaccio explicitly makes this release through the enjoyment of his stories a necessary condition for their exemplary utility (*Proemio* 14). In a similar manner Suger of St. Denis states that it was the beauty of the visual arts which called him away from outward cares (*ab extrinsecis me curis devocaret*) and permitted him to concentrate upon the virtues of which it was the emblem (De Bruyne, 2:142–43).

The "forme of olde clerkis speche / In poetrie" and the pagan culture it expresses in *Troilus and Criseyde* are to be set aside with other "feynede loves." These, it is implied, will "falsen" those who place their faith in them. They will 'lie,' that is, in the sense of bearing false witness with intent to deceive, as St. Augustine analyzes misrepresentation in his *De mendacio* (cf. *Solil.* 2.9–10). The argument over the value of fiction, judged by prudential criteria, therefore, often turned upon the definition of 'lying' which had the strong legal connotation of giving 'false testimony.' In fact, when Boccaccio defends the pagan poets against charges of false doctrines about the gods, he makes a legal distinction based upon intention. Their error is in *ignorantia facti* rather than in *ignorantia iuris*. That is, their ignorance of the New Testament should be regarded in the same way as that of a law made without their knowledge as opposed to a promulgated law which it would have been their duty to know and to obey (*Gen. deor. gent.* 14.13; *Il Comento* Lez 17, 1:417–26). Their ignorance is 'involuntary' and hence 'prudentially' an *accidental* error, or in the legal terms of the *modus* of a crime—that is, how and in what state of mind was the act committed (*quemadmodum et quo animo factum sit*)—an error committed with *imprudentia* (*De inv.* 1.41). So, too, as long as the ancient poets represent their misconceptions 'intentionally,' they incur only an accidental 'artistic' error as well. Once, however, that misconception is recognized and repeated by a Christian author before a Christian audience who can no longer plead *ignorantia facti*, the response of that audience to the work must be judged on the grounds of *prudentia*. And it is in the face of such a judgment that the protection of artistic immunity may be invoked. The poems, once completed, however, can no longer be regarded by the author under the protection of his office *as artist* (since his period of immunity has expired) but must be regarded by him solely *as moral agent* who now must see them as products to be used. If they have misrepresented the truth, their error, when their reader is misled, becomes voluntary and hence 'prudentially' *essential* and should be so designated. Nevertheless, whatever historical and preceptive value their explicit 'retraction' denies to the poems, it protects, in another sense, the increased awareness of the prudential present (which the artistic experience made possible) by the very fact that the audience is now released from all obligation to reconcile their 'doctrine' with its own ethical convictions.

If one regards the return to the prudential world as 'palinodial,' it reflects a combination of various uses of the word given in Chap. 13, n. 2. Even the strict Stesichorean recantation—which Chaucer himself agrees to make for the Queen of Love (*PLGW* 479ff.)—finds a parallel in *Troilus and Criseyde* in that Troilus' initial prayer to the God of Love (1.421–34) was, indeed, granted, and now, having shown how the benefits turned out badly, Chaucer asks his young readers to withdraw any allegiance they may have had, or requests they may have made, to the god and redirect them to Christ. Even the retraction at the end of the *Canterbury Tales* may be considered as the withdrawal of a 'prayer,' which Chaucer had addressed to his readers themselves, that they accept what he, as an artist, has truthfully 'reported' from his sources—be it fictionally either what he has overheard or what he has found in a book. That the author represent himself simply as a 'recorder' of what he finds was one of the most convenient medieval claims for immunity. Even Dante refers to himself as a *scriba* (*Par.* 10.27). The possibility of a counter-prayer is established by the very necessity of making the original request. This necessity arises from the fact that to speak as an artist is a special activity outside the province of the ordinary citizen implicated in the moral and historical contingencies of his daily life. The retraction of such a request may now be saying to the reader: 'no longer give heed to certain works which I have recorded for you and asked that you accept on the grounds that they were true reports. My artistic function is completed, and henceforth I shall accompany you in my capacity as an ordinary member of your community.'[10]

[10] St. Thomas' formulation of the Aristotelian distinction in the *E.N.* between the prudential and productive faculties may have been influenced by the description of the 'double error' in the *Poetics*. Despite the fact that William of Moerbeke's translation of the *Poetics* is (controversially) assigned to 1278, and in that case could not have been used by Thomas, his phrasing *poetice duplex peccatum* resembles Thomas' *in actu artis contigit dupliciter esse peccatum* (*S.T.* 1.2. qu. 21 art. 2 r. 2). It is possible that 1278 might refer to something other than the date of the translation itself, such as to when the translation was copied by the scribe. Or, more likely perhaps, is the probability that William may simply have mentioned the passage to Thomas at the time he was writing about the arts in his *Summa*, since the *Poetics* illustrates in more detail than Aristotle's other works the relation of art to morality. Although it has been shown that Thomas also drew upon Hermannus Alemannus' translation of Averroes' *Middle Commentary on the Poetics* (1256), Hermannus makes no mention of the 'double error' (cf. W. F. Boggess, "Aristotle's *Poetics* in the Fourteenth Century," *SP* 67 [1970]:284). For a recent treatment of the medieval interpretations of the *Poetics*, see H. A. Kelly, "Aristotle-Averroes-Alemannus on Tragedy: The Influence of the 'Poetics' on the Latin Middle Ages," *Viator* 10 (1979):161–209. (Professor Kelly has written to me privately that he is "inclined to think the similarity of wording and concept coincidental" between Moerbeke and Thomas, because the Scholastics so often speak of various 'twofold sins.' The examples he sent convince me that more specific evidence would be necessary to establish a direct connection. I retain the conjecture here, nevertheless, in hopes that someone may come upon such evidence.)

Appendix C. Presuppositions of Literary Studies

In this study I have taken as granted the following presuppositions, which I here append to the analogy between the interpretation of legal and literary texts suggested in Chap. 10, n. 39. These presuppositions are not subject to logical demonstration. They belong, rather, to the preliminary articles of faith necessary for all intellectual inquiry. Specifically, they constitute an essential part of the *fides quaerens intellectum* of literary studies.

1. That the meaning of written texts, like other subjects of inquiry, can be understood more accurately or less accurately.
2. That understanding is preferable to misunderstanding and the consequent acquisition of knowledge is desirable.
3. That any method of inquiry is subservient (in importance) to what it can discover about the subjects which it has been or will be employed to investigate.
4. That the value of any method will depend upon its success in such discovery and, therefore, may be judged in relation to other methods.
5. That, in the absence of the author himself, no given interpretation of a text can achieve more than probability and hence must remain subject to revision.
6. That the probability of any given interpretation will depend on existent historical evidence and its analysis.
7. That the validity of evidence and its analysis will be subject to the trial of rational examination and discussion.
8. That the end of the *studia humanitatis*, as of all intellectual activities, is not philodoxic—the gathering of as many opinions as possible—but judicative: the identification and selection of those opinions which have the greatest probability (with respect to evidence and analysis) and the rejection of others.
9. That, since the end of this inquiry is the understanding and preservation of written texts, the method of selecting and analyzing evidence in the demonstration of the probability of any given interpretation will be philological in the broadest meaning of that word.

Index

Proper Names and Titles

Topics

(A note which continues to discuss any *topics* already indexed
for the text on its page will not be listed separately.)

to philosophy in, 164-65

Neoplatonic conception of: 'Apollo, 182; art and artist, 189-92; beauty, 185-87; civic virtues, 167-68, 171, 173n, 209-210, 238-40; correspondence, 195-96; decorum, 193-200; dialectic, 179-80; *discordia concors*, 197-98; discourse, 183-93; discursive reason, 181-83, 189-91, 220-21, 227-28; *gnosis* vs. *praxis*, 189, 193-200, 209-210, 238-40; imagination, 183n, 204-209, 217; imitation, 192-93, 197, 212-19, 225n; matter, 176-77, 226n; narrative myth, 183-84; nature and art, 190n, 191n; *nous*, 179n, 202n, 204; the One, 176-83; optics, 223-27; power, 193-200; *praxis* as bewitchment, 198-99, 238-40; process as extension, 180-83, 217; procession and return, 177, 217; proportion, 168, 171, 186-89, 193-96; purification, 168, 186-89, 238; quality, 196-200; simplicity, 175-76; soul, 177-83, 204n; understanding (διάνοια), 177-83, 201-221

nous (νοῦς), *noesis* (νόησις): its function, 88n; as intuitive apprehension, 45-47; Neoplatonic conception of, 202-219; and prudence (φρόνησις), 123n, 124; rel. to divided line, 37-38, 42; and wisdom (σοφία), 118. *See also* analysis and/or synthesis, intuition, knowledge, universal, wisdom

novella, 328-44; declamatory structure in, 339-44; exemplary structure of, 337n; qualitative issues in, 337-41; rel. to *questione d'amore*, 336-41; suspension of inductive method in, 340; uniting definite and indefinite questions, 339-44. *See also* declamation, fiction, *poesis*

obscurity: ontological, 113-16; perceptual, 113-16; stylistic, 137n, 162-63. *See also* darkness, optics, skiagraphia

opinion (δόξα): as opp. to knowledge, 15n; in divided line, 37-38, 42, 61n, 229-30. *See also* conjecture

optics: due distance in, 113; illusionistic foreshortening, 111-14, 223-25; Neoplatonic view of, 222-24; skenographic, 114. *See also* darkness, illusion, obscurity, skiagraphia

oratory, 22-24, 245-52; deliberative, 6, 100-101, 133-36, 142-44, 150, 235; forensic, 6, 133-35; epideictic, 6, 100-101, 133-35, 142. *See also* rhetoric, psychagogia, style

outline (περιγραφή), 125-29, 152, 270n, 272n, 278-79, 315n, 316n, 379; to be filled in (ἀναγράψαι), 125; of maps, 153n. *See also* diagram; style, skiagraphic

paideia, 4, 10, 12, 14

palinode (παλινῳδία), 329, 330n, 335, 358n, 389-90

paradeigma (παράδειγμα): as *exemplum*, 284n, 356n, 378-81; fictional, 127n, 256, 272; in geometry, 204; mimetic, 273-75, 278; the *Replublic* as, 60-61. *See also* exemplar, *exemplum*, idea

paragone (comparison) between: ear and eye, 131-32, 155, 159-60; Homer and Pheidias, 155-60; painting and sculpture, 157-58

particular, rel. to universal (*see* universal): an abstraction when isolated, 96, 162-63; not an object of imitation, 96. *See also* ἡμῖν, perception

pathos, *see* ethos and pathos

perception (αἴσθησις), 16n, 346n; as ineffable impression, 163; in reaching first principles, 91-92; and *in utramque partem argumentatio*, 289-95; involves universals, 91, 122, 352n; Neoplatonic conception of, 178-80, 220; Stoic conception of, 289-95. *See also* intelligibility, two types of; ἡμῖν

peripeteia, 26

philological interpretation, xiv-xvii, 103n, 356n; analysis and synthesis in, 281n; *fides quaerens intellectum* in, 391; presuppositions of, 391; similar to that of laws, 281n, 356n. *See also* exegesis

philosophy, 3, 6; conservative influence of, 83; and jurisprudence, 247n, 273n; Lady Philosophy, 233n; liberalization of, 7-8, 10n, 17; rel. to rhetoric, xii, 20n. *See also* discourse, philosophical; literary discourse, intentions of, cognitive

Library of Congress Cataloging in Publication Data
Trimpi, Wesley.
Muses of one mind.
Includes index.
1. Literature—Philosophy. I. Title.
PN47.T7 1983   808'.00141   82-61389
ISBN 0-691-06568-3